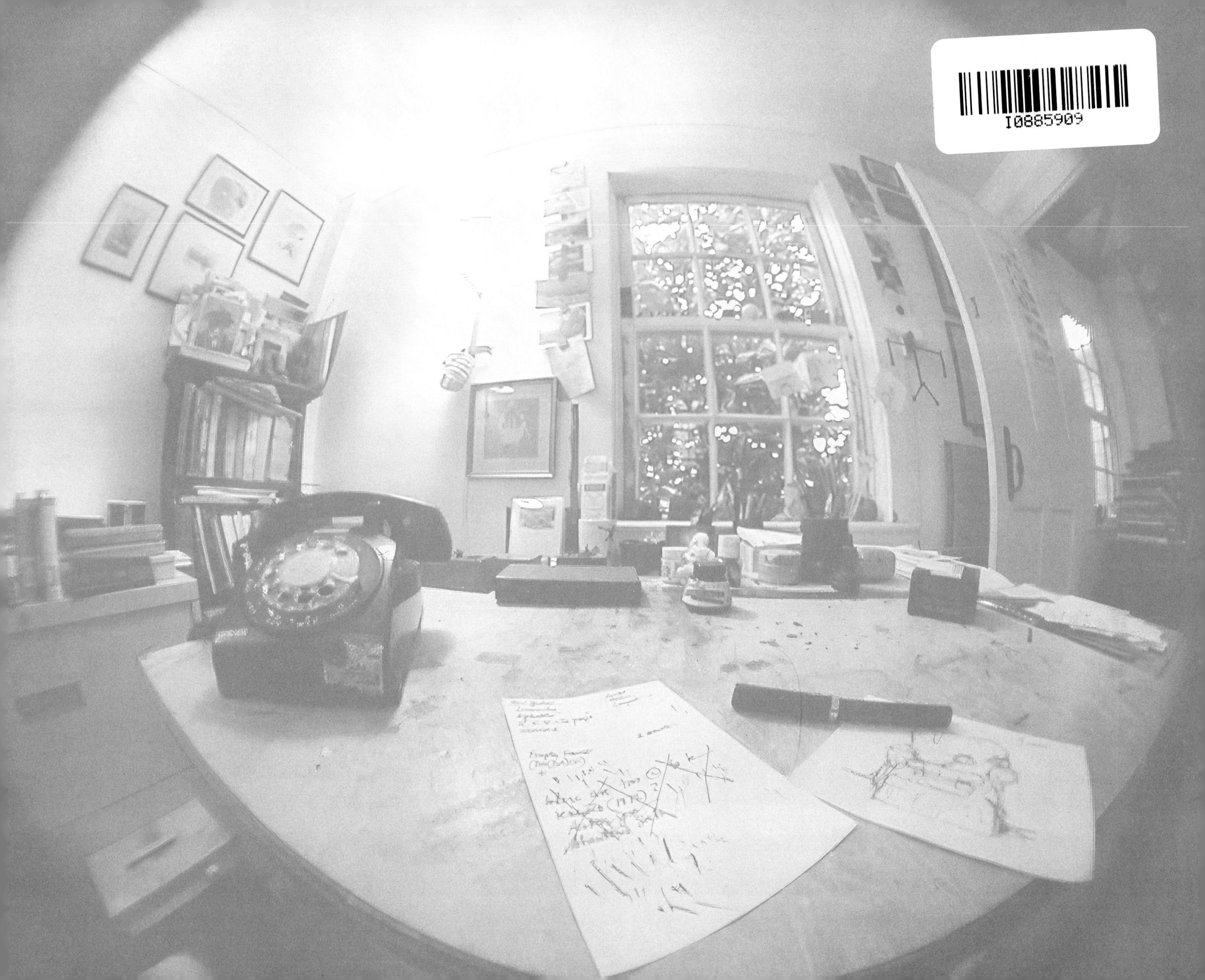

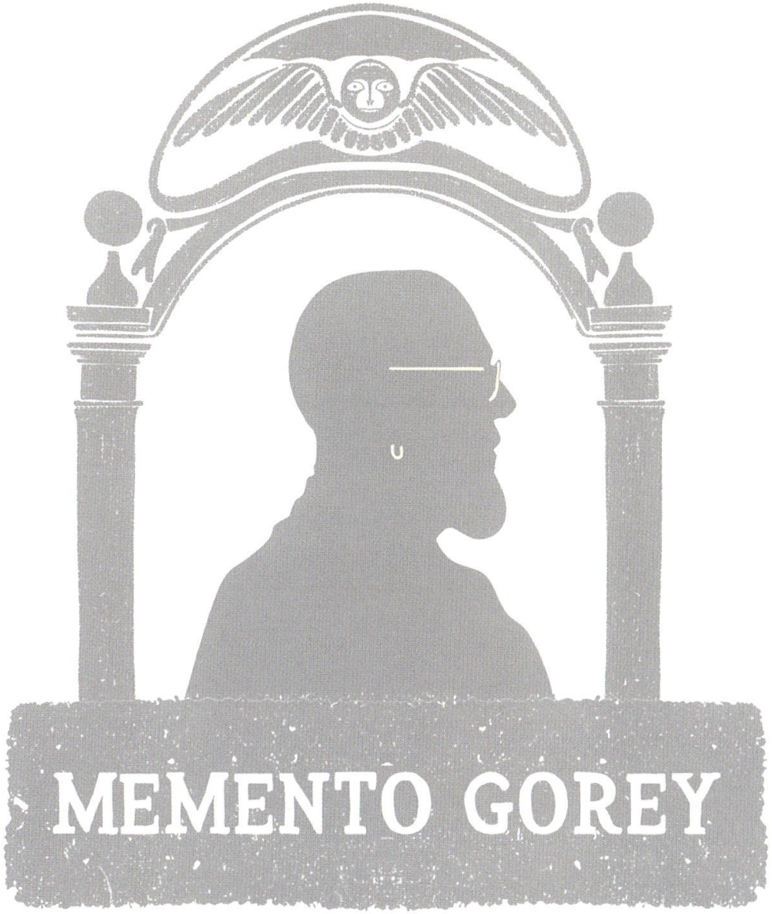

THE LAST INTERVIEWS
with Edward Gorey

Christopher Seufert
Foreword by PAUL THEROUX

SCHIFFER PUBLISHING
4880 Lower Valley Road • Atglen, PA 19310

Other Schiffer Books by the Author:

Cape Cod and the Islands: A Drone's Eye View, ISBN 978-0-7643-5506-6

The Cape Cod National Seashore: A Photographic Adventure & Guide, ISBN 978-0-7643-3995-0

Cape Cod & the Islands Reflections, ISBN 978-0-7643-3405-4

Other Schiffer Books on Related Subjects:

Abandoned NYC, Will Ellis, ISBN 978-0-7643-4761-0

Broadway Poster Art: 1945–1969, Nicholas van Hoogstraten, ISBN 978-0-7643-6751-9

The Cats of Cuba, Emmy Park, ISBN 978-0-7643-5802-9

Transcript of interview with Christopher Lydon, WGBH, is printed with permission of WGBH-TV.
Transcript of interview with Joyce Kenney is printed with permission of Joyce Kenney.
Photo of Julie Harris © Nancy Barr

Library of Congress Control Number: 2025946080

Designed by Beth Oberholtzer
Front cover design by Danielle D. Farmer
Type set in Gorey / Quinn Text

ISBN: 978-0-7643-7127-1
ePub: 978-1-5073-0736-6

Printed in India

10 9 8 7 6 5 4 3 2 1

MIX
Paper | Supporting responsible forestry
FSC™ C016779

Published by Schiffer Publishing, Ltd.
4880 Lower Valley Road
Atglen, PA 19310
Phone: (610) 593-1777; Fax: (610) 593-2002
Email: info@schifferbooks.com
Web: www.schifferbooks.com

For our complete selection of fine books on this and related subjects, please visit our website at www.schifferbooks.com. You may also write for a free catalog.

Schiffer Publishing's titles are available at special discounts for bulk purchases for sales promotions or premiums. Special editions, including personalized covers, corporate imprints, and excerpts, can be created in large quantities for special needs. For more information, contact the publisher.

For Colin Gillis (1968–2023),
a true friend

and for George Koury, CEO,
Last Gasp Enterprises

Contents

Foreword

by Paul Theroux

There's a nice British idiom, often accompanied by a poke in the ribs, "Who is he when he's at home?" In other words, who's the real person and what's the deal? Regarding the enigmatic Edward Gorey, Christopher Seufert's *Memento Gorey* helps answer that offbeat question. Readers have rejoiced in Gorey's work, but the man himself was a tangle of contradictions, and "Nothing personal" seems to have been his motto. If you happened to query him, he would distract you with a witty and unexpected aside. His biographer Mark Dery reports in *Born to Be Posthumous* how when asked to describe his favorite journey, Gorey replied, "Looking out the window."

I read him with pleasure and admiration and knew him as a friend and neighbor on Cape Cod, someone who lived near enough to pop over for a meal at short notice. I was introduced to him by my brother Alexander, who was a close friend of his, saw him more often than I did, and has written a fine portrait of him in *The Strange Case of Edward Gorey*.

Gorey's ripostes were memorable and always amused me, but even as I laughed I felt sure that they were too good to be true. He seemed to be speaking for effect, since—habitually unforthcoming—his mode of being was deflection. When he disparaged a classic movie, then gushed about the TV soap opera *Dallas* ("Barbara Bel Geddes—isn't she to die for?"), I wondered: Does he really believe that? He was an omnivorous reader but might elaborate about a masterpiece such as Conrad's Victory (he designed the paperback cover), then interrupt himself with praise for an Edwardian novel about naughty schoolgirls, such as Angela Brazil's *The Fortunes of Philippa*. And where did his dated and actressy lingo come from? "Not on your tin-type!" he might cry as an admonishment, or on a winter night settling on a sofa in my house: "It's toasty warm here!"

Seufert captures his wayward fluency in these dialogues and interviews, and reading it I was reminded of my bafflement. Whenever I was with him, I made a point of listening and not challenging, thinking: Some things in life don't bear looking into. In Gorey's case it was his raccoon coat, his large collection of castoff women's mink coats, his ratty sneakers, his encumbering his fingers with heavy rings that resembled knuckledusters, his assortment of human skulls, and much else. He sometimes seemed deliberately to embody and flaunt the weirdness of one of his own fictional characters, presenting himself as Ogdred Weary, village eccentric, living among cats and elderly aunts, languidly gesticulating in Yarmouth Port, Cape Cod. And it worked.

Yet, people exploiting their peculiarities often fail to notice they are—even as they over-egg the oddity—a great deal more peculiar than they realize. To Gorey's credit, he didn't care what anyone thought, and might go a bit further in a flourish to disarm any disparager of his clothes or his work, enthusiastically agreeing, "You're probably right, dear!"

I often thought of him in connection with Edward Lear and Henry James. Lear's art work is comparable, not the small watercolors or big oil paintings but the illustrations for *The Book of Nonsense*, and his humorous and sometimes strangely sad poems. Very early in his career, Gorey illustrated Lear's poem "The Dong with the Luminous Nose" and, toward the end of his life, "The Jumblies." I feel sure Gorey related not only to the work but to the man, with whom he had much in common: hardworking, imaginative, sexually unforthcoming, lonely, with episodes of depression Lear called "the Morbids."

Seufert's photographs tell a tale, the collections of items—objets trouvés, knickknacks, random unreadable sticks and stones. In this connection, consider the heartbreaking poem

"The Toys" by the English writer Coventry Patmore, about visiting his tearful young son, whom he'd regretfully scolded and sent to bed:

> For, on a table drawn beside his head,
> He had put, within his reach,
> A box of counters and a red-vein'd stone,
> A piece of glass abraded by the beach
> And six or seven shells,
> A bottle with bluebells
> And two French copper coins, ranged there
> with careful art,
> To comfort his sad heart.

I see that in Gorey's accumulation of homely paraphernalia, because the careful arrangement is more important than the seemingly insignificant objects. "I do the same things over and over," he told Seufert. "I tend to go to pieces if my routine is broken."

Take away the rings, the furs, the sneakers, the skulls, but keep the beard and the wit, and you have a Henry James character—aloof, sexually unforthcoming, lonely. James was an inveterate dinner guest—one social season he attended 107 meals, but despite his apparent sociability, he was deeply lonely and depressive. He spoke about "the essential loneliness of my life" in a letter to a friend. "This loneliness, what is it still but the deepest thing about one? Deeper about me, at any rate, than anything else: deeper than my 'genius,' deeper than my 'discipline,' deeper than my pride, deeper, above all, than the deep countermining of art."

In response to what I take to be his private melancholy, and his horror of intimacy, Gorey was vitalized by his work, his owlish prose, his iconic figures, outfitted in curious clothes, that live in an indeterminate world of mansions and shadows, bicycles and bangers, beset by fatal accidents, challenging you to decode them. He wrote and sketched with intensity, to gratify his taste for fantasy and to cheer himself.

But he could be a social animal too, and if he trusted the listener or photographer—as he obviously trusted Seufert—he was hospitable and a great talker. Everyone who knew Gorey personally was well aware that he was capable of being a good companion. As a consequence, this book of extensive conversations and revealing photographs is especially valuable to anyone who loves Gorey's work and wishes to know more of the man.

Paul Theroux
Sandwich, Massachusetts

Preface

This book, like its companion documentary, has been twenty-five years in the making. I take some solace in the fact that the number is not thirty. I also deliver this book with the comforting knowledge that Gorey himself sometimes had thirty years or more between a project's first scribbling and its printing. This was true not only for his self-published projects, which were many (under his Fantod Press), and his projects for-hire.

Over the course of the documentary, with Edward at his house, the phone would ring, and he would disappear into his studio and return, claiming good-naturedly, "A publisher; I told them not to call back."

I owe great thanks to my mom and dad, Marilyn and Gary Seufert, who have been there throughout the process of conceiving, shooting, editing, and editing again the various galleys of this book. My dad in particular came through as an initial editor over late-night emails. My daughter, Stella, was my in-house photo editor.

Thanks to my friend Richard Koury and his dad (also my great friend) for listening, urging, and listening again. Thanks to Colin Gillis for giving me the final of many kicks in the pants before his too-soon passing in April 2023. Thanks to my son, Ethan, and my daughter, Stella, for growing up with and reciting back with me the many phrases uttered by Gorey in his footage and interviews. "Oh, Jane dear" and "Their birthdays go unnoticed, the poor dears" are given now to our own cats, Winston and Piano. Thanks to Carol Verburg and to the late Andreas Brown for their enthusiasm in the continued shooting of these photographs even after Edward's death, resulting in a four-days-straight documentation of the way Edward left his house in April 2000. I nod to Kevin McDermott, with whom I shot alongside that week, while he produced his classic *Elephant House*. This is proof positive that two photographers shooting the same subject can have two distinctly different yet valid approaches. Shortly after Edward's death, the contents of Edward's house were sold for the benefit of his estate, so we captured a moment in time.

Thanks to Rick Jones and Gregory Hischak for their generous door openings at the Gorey Museum for me to confirm various objects and rooms that have been since recovered, so close to their original state. Thanks to my publisher, Pete Schiffer, and my editor, Sandra Korinchak, for believing in the project. Thanks to Adelyn Lee, Kelly Brennan, Deborah Lopes, and Jessica Ferguson for their transcriptions of these interviews. Thanks also to John LaFleur, Ken Morton, Doug Lloyd, Helen Chough, Jenn Pitman, Maureen Barden, Sandra Forman, Amanda Palmer, Mark Dery, Laurie Sullivan, Richard Robbins, Kimberly Robbins, Jenn Pitman, George Khalil, Brigid Krug, Paul Borde, and Dennis Jones. Thanks finally to all those for whom this space is too small for acknowledgment, and for my various coworkers and photo assistants over the years—you know who you are. If we haven't spoken for years, the time we spent together on this project meant the world to me.

One final note, to the reader. This book just scratches the surface of the images I have of Edward's house, something I'm convinced tells us all as much about Edward as the art he created. There're so many more of the images, and I hope to expand upon this edition. There are also more interviews, snippets, and multimedia treats than this one initial volume can contain.

The interviews are transcribed and edited for meaning and content. This two-step process polishes the spoken, conversational audio into a readable and accurate written document. We have striven to remove unnecessary speech, such as filler words and repetitions, while preserving the original intent and integrity of the speaker. We have kept as light a touch as possible in order to keep the original interview as a primary research source and as a public record without making the subject appear inarticulate due to natural speech patterns.

Thanks to Edward who welcomed my first interview with him with, "Do we have to?"

Christopher Seufert
Chatham, Cape Cod, Massachusetts

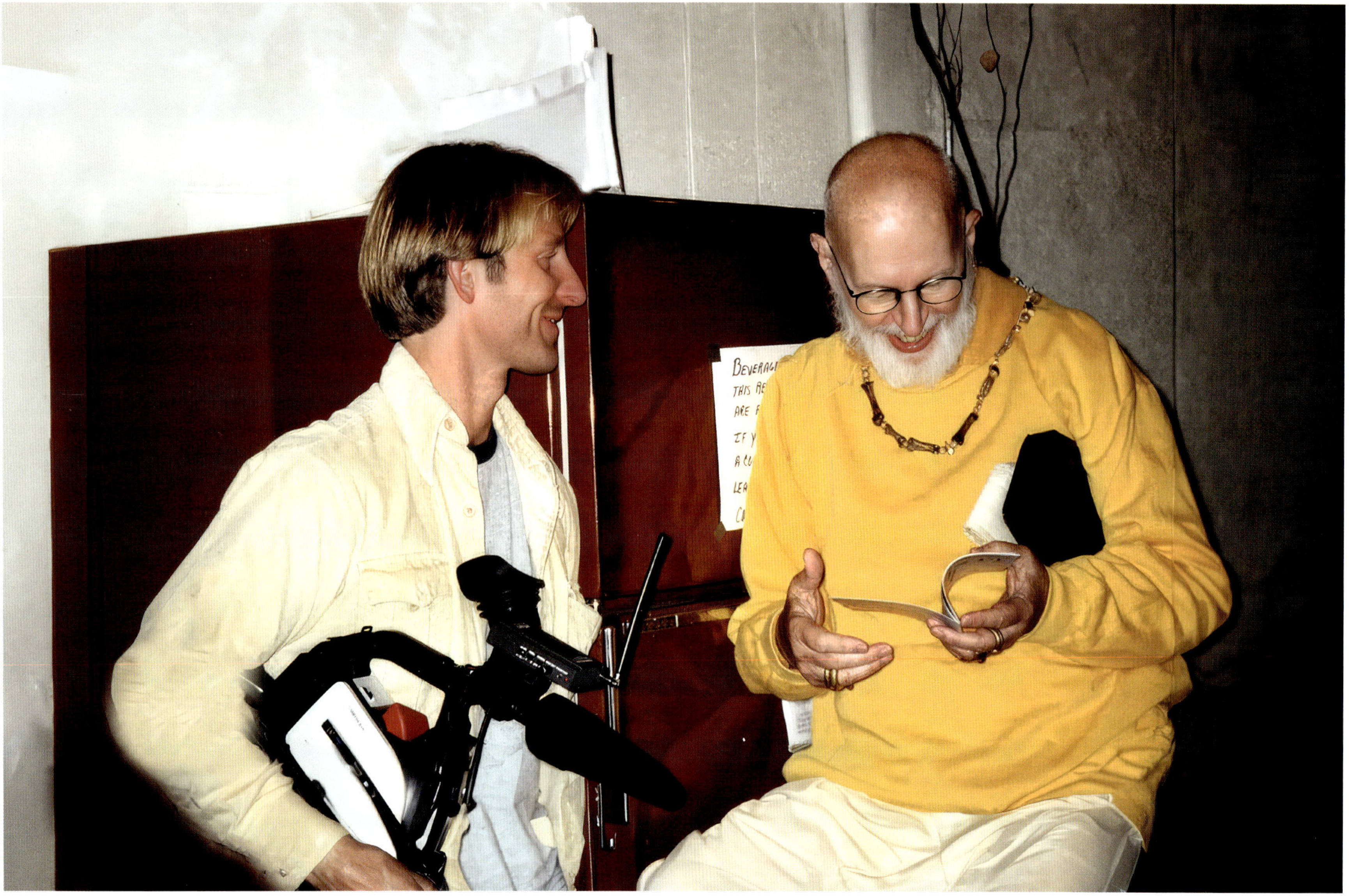

The author (*left*) with Edward Gorey at a rehearsal for Gorey's productions *Hsst!* and *Drat!* at the Cape Rep Theater in Brewster, Massachusetts. October 1999. Photo by Kimberly Robbins

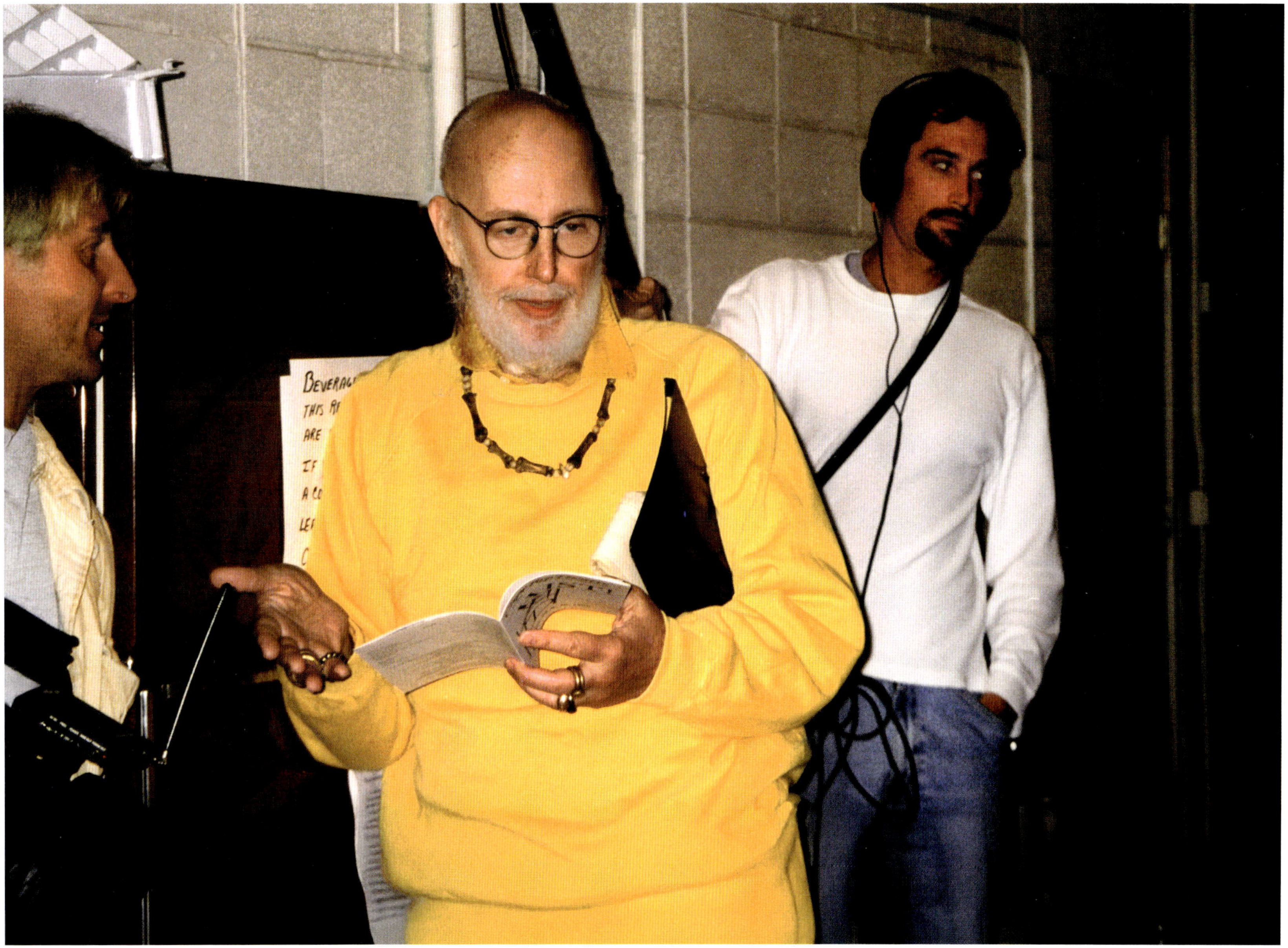

The author (*left*) and sound recordist Richard Robbins with Edward Gorey at a rehearsal for Gorey's productions *Hsst!* and *Drat!* at the Cape Rep Theater in Brewster, Massachusetts. October 1999. Photo by Kimberly Robbins

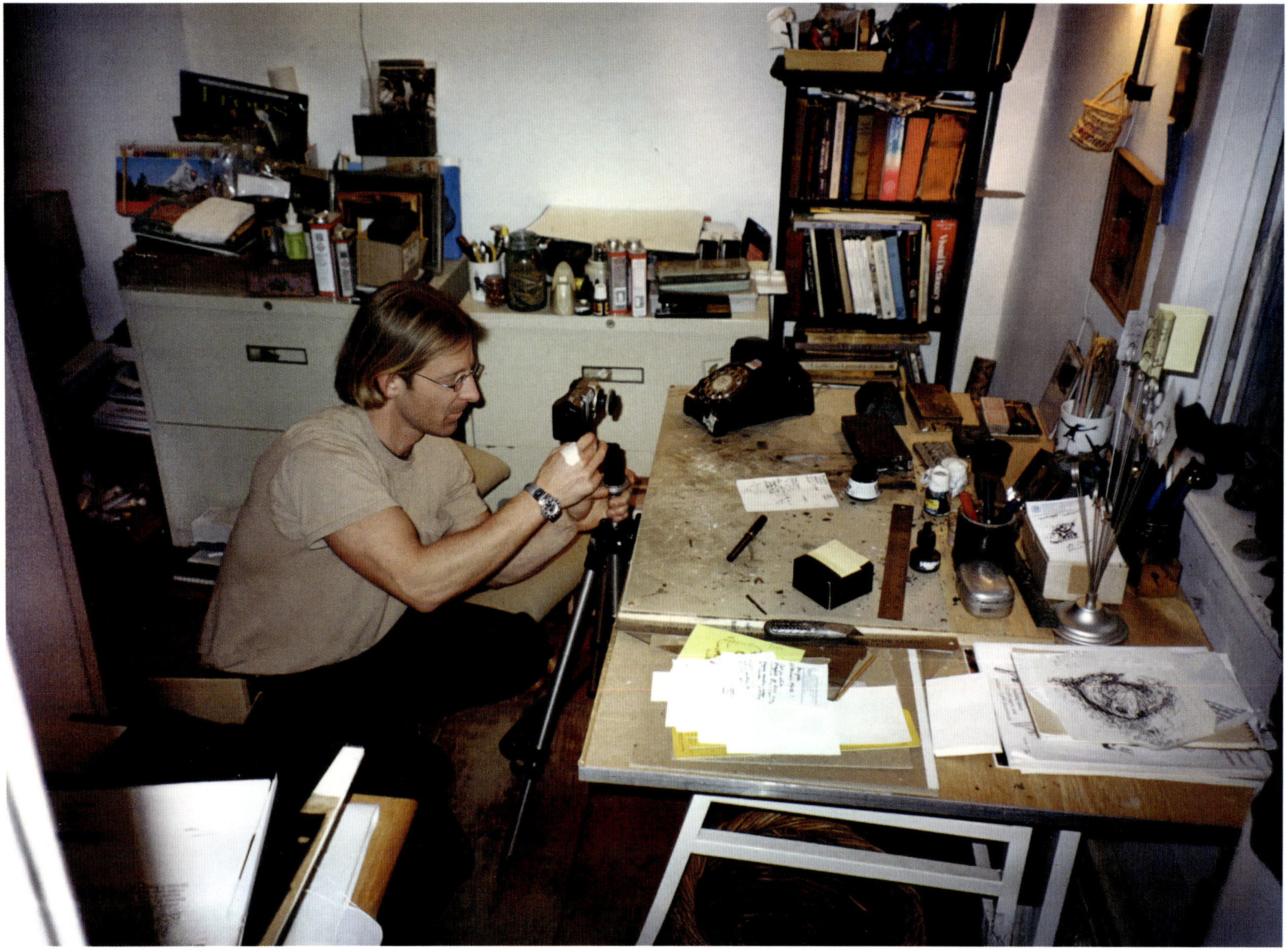

The author shooting Edward's desk with an iPix fish-eye lens the way he left it when he passed away on April 15, 2000. Seufert spent four days that week documenting Edward's house by shooting photos, video, and multimedia hemispheres. Photo: Richard Robbins

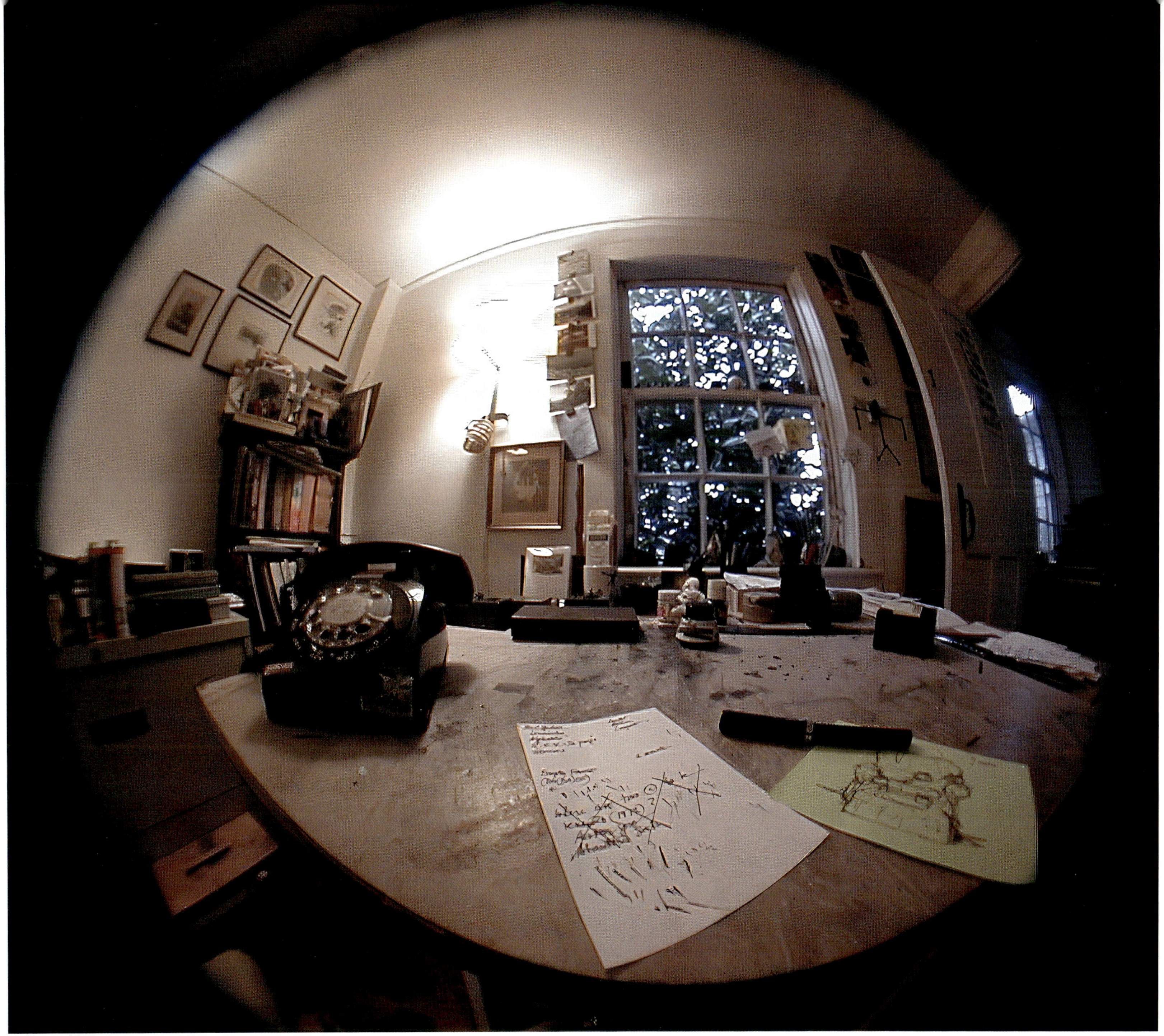

Edward's final to-do list, including a meeting with the band the Tiger Lillies and a phone call with executives at RealMedia about an online project

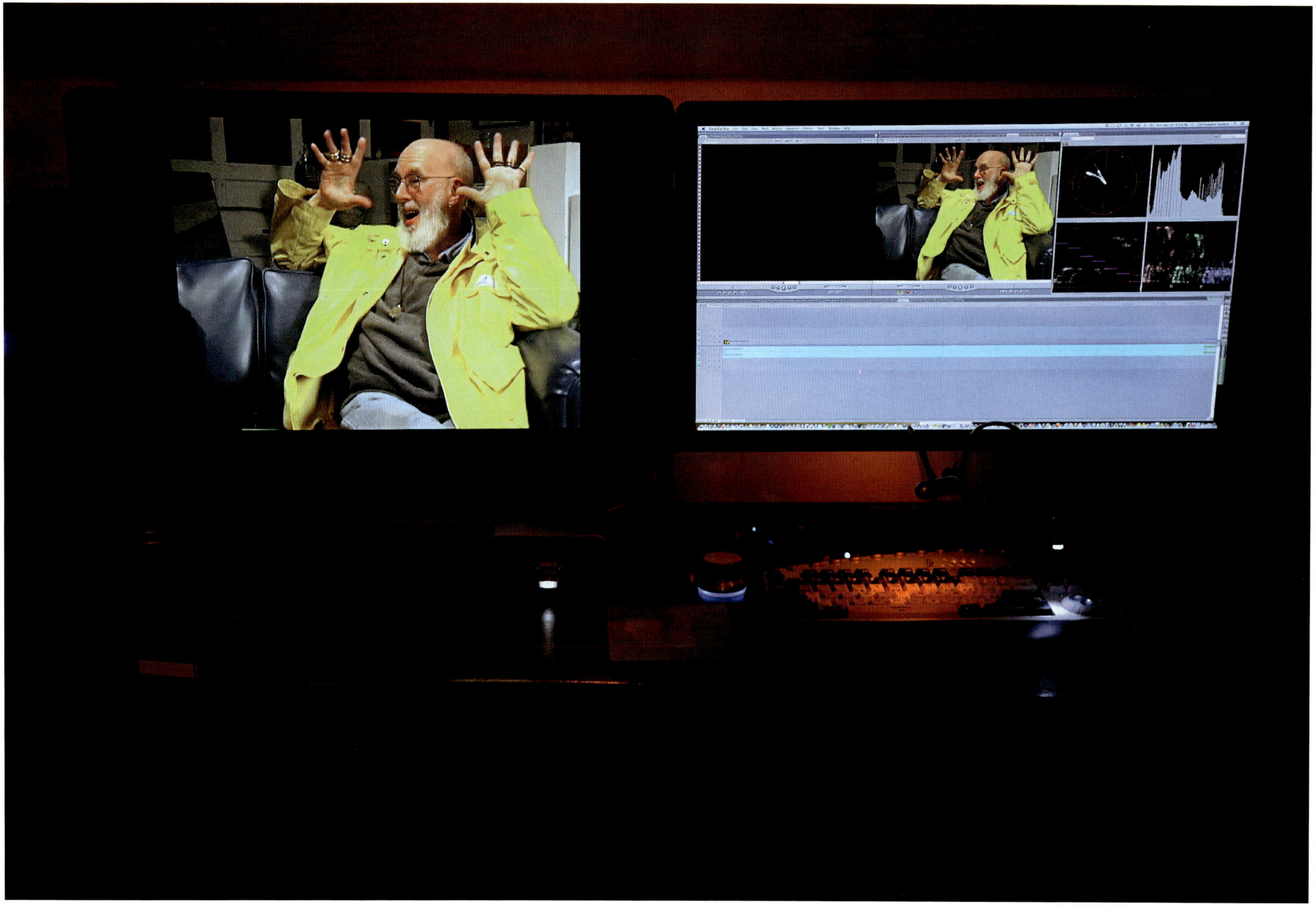

The documentary in production

Interview with Edward Gorey: Cotuit Center for the Arts

OCTOBER 26, 1996

This interview was shot at the Cotuit Center for the Arts (since burned down) in October 1996. The crew and I shot an early rehearsal for *Cautionary Tales for Children* that night, then stayed after with Edward and producer Carol Verburg for an interview about how the play was going. Edward draped himself along the beat-up couch with a bright-yellow rain jacket, jeans, and white Sperry sneakers, and a heavy African necklace hat periodically made a sound on the microphone.

Christopher Seufert: Why don't you sit over here, Carol, to get a better angle. We won't try to address the camera directly, but why don't you sit directly across from him, do sort of a Bill Moyers angle . . .

Carol Verburg: I'll just sit over here and . . .

Edward Gorey: Yeah, right, and I'll make faces right back at you and everyone will wonder . . .

[*Rain drums heavily on the roof . . .*]

CV: What I wanted to know for the press release [of his upcoming play *Cautionary Tales for Children* by Hilaire Belloc].

EG: Yes?

CV: Born in Paris, married an American . . .

EG: Oh, did he?

CV: Yes! He had the most checkered national background . . .

EG: Oh . . .

CV: He went to public school in England, served in the French army, then married an American.

EG: Who was she, does any one know?

CV: Elodie Hogan

EG: Ew, do we know anything about her?

CV: She sounds implausible to me.

EG: Oh . . . [*resignedly*]

CV: He became a British national subject and then served in the British Parliament.

EG: Oh, now that I didn't know either.

CV: What business had he doing all these things?

EG: Well he was a naturalized American . . . uh, English citizen wasn't he?

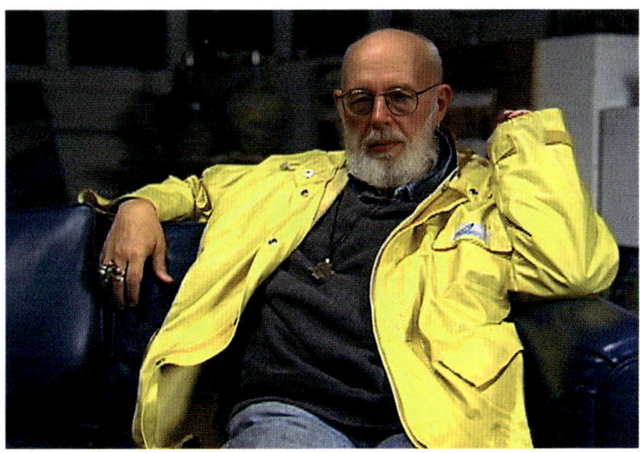

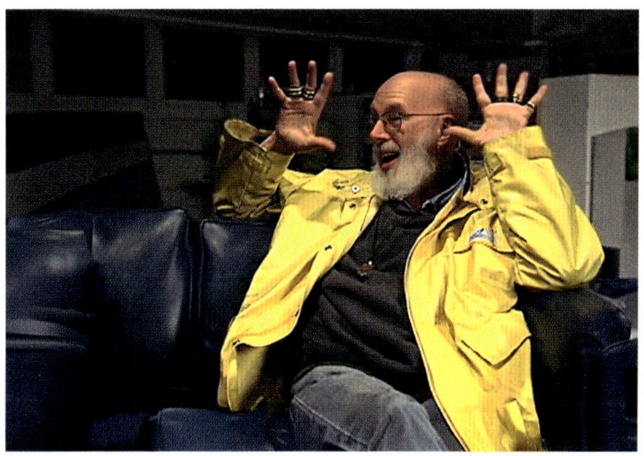

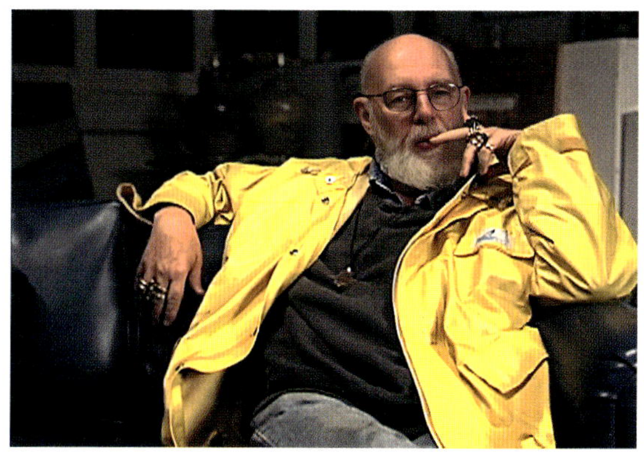

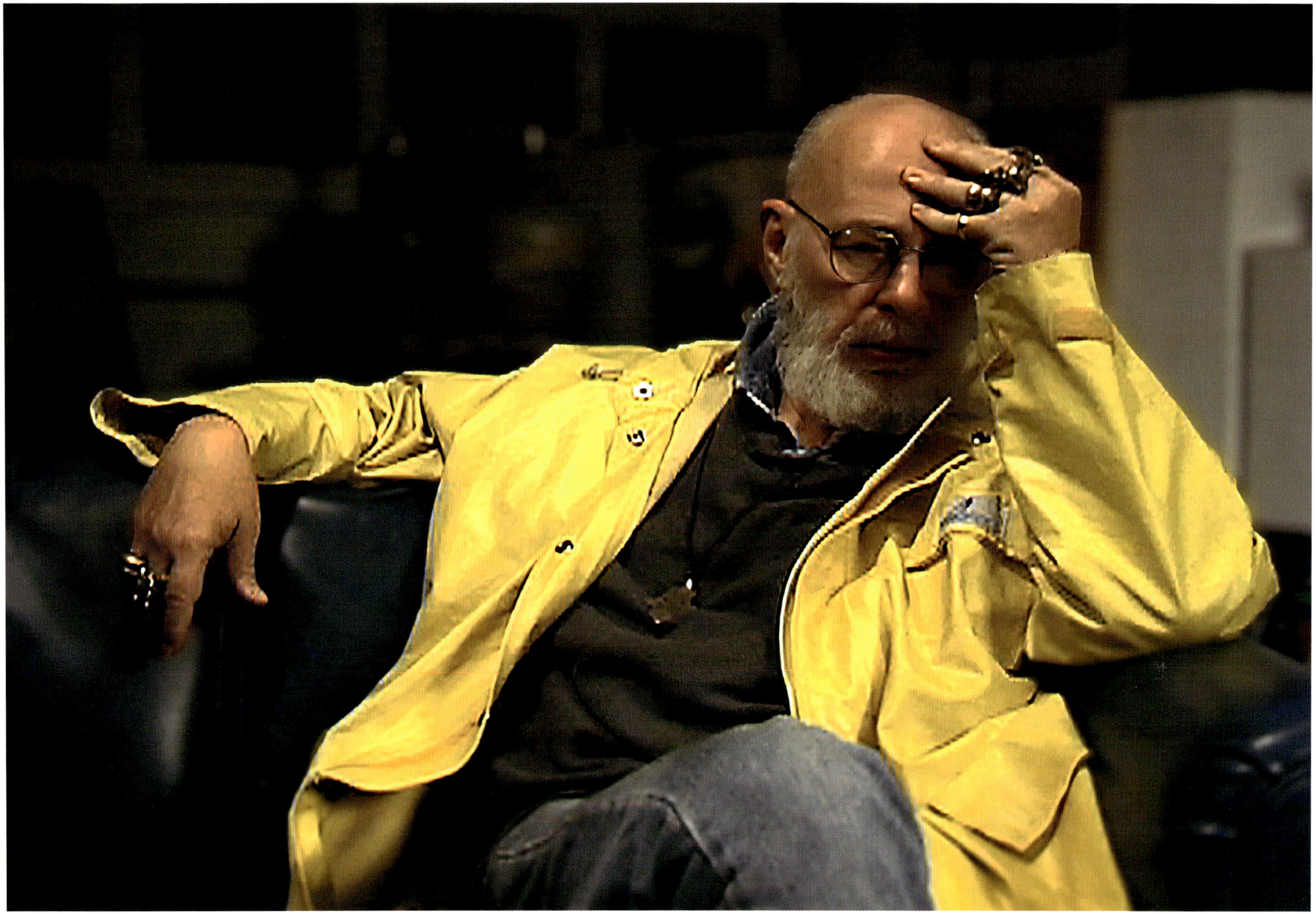

Edward Gorey at his first interview with Seufert on the couch at the Cotuit Center for the Arts (since burned down) in October 1996

CV: Which presumably is how he stopped being Hilaire Belloc [*with French accent*] and . . .

EG: Well, I don't know, I looked it up and all I could really find was "Hilair BELL-oc" or "Hilair Bell-OC," it didn't say which . . .

CV: So did you grow up with his stories? How did you come across *The Cautionary Tales*?

EG: I don't know, I uh . . . [*long pause with rain*] I don't think I knew them as a child . . . but it's one of those . . . Oh, I don't know. No, I don't think I did. I don't think I was really aware of it until maybe college, if then. Somewhere I have an anthology with the *Bad Child's Book of Beasts* and *More Bad* . . . or *Worse Beasts for Worster* . . . or *More Bad Beasts for Worst Children*, or whatever it's called. And then *Cautionary Tales for Children*.

And for the last twelve years I've been illustrating *Cautionary Tales* [*for Children*]. Not, I hasten to add, nonstop [*laughs*]. Years go by! Uh, now I'm hoping to finish it this fall. [1996. It was published posthumously in 2002.]

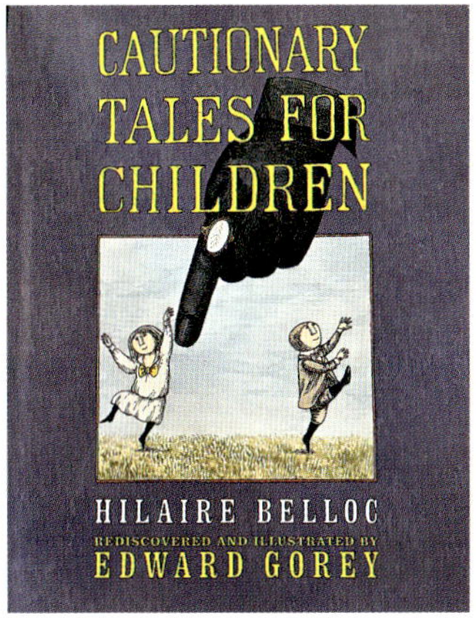

CV: And who's going to publish it? Is that Andy [Andreas Brown of the Gotham Book Mart]?

EG: No it's um . . . oh! Holiday House. They promised not to call me yet again and ask where it was. [*Laughs*]

CV: And they're in San Francisco . . .

EG: No. No, they're in New York.

CV: It's Chronicle that's in San Francisco.

EG: It's Chronicle that's in San Francisco.

CV: They're publishers of . . .

EG: Oh right, yes. God that rain is really . . .

CV: How many Cautionary Tales are there?

EG: Gee, I think there are about twelve maybe. It's funny, because I think all of these that we're doing are practically at the beginning. There's one very, very long one, which is all about Parliament and stuff, that's full of all of these kind of in-jokes about English politics. There's one very unfortunate one that's anti-Semitic about Rebecca Offendort, who slammed doors. The original illustrations I think were by his brother-in-law, or something of the sort. The initials are BTB.

Anyway, they're not very good, but they have a certain verve and whatnot.

CV: Did you want to do this book? Is this your own idea?

EG: I absolutely can't remember. It might have been that Holiday House maybe asked me to do it, because it came after I did at least one of those *Treehorn* books [*The Shrinking of Treehorn*].

CV: What are those?

EG: The *Treehorn* books by Florence Perry Heide.

CV: Oh right. Do you sort of feel like there's more of an affinity with . . .

EG: Oh yeah, I sort of have an affinity for this kind of thing and they're rather more raucous. Harry Graham's *Ruthless Rhymes for Heartless Homes* . . . and there are all those Little Willy quatrains. I don't know whether people still make them up or not.

CV: Oh? Oh yeah.

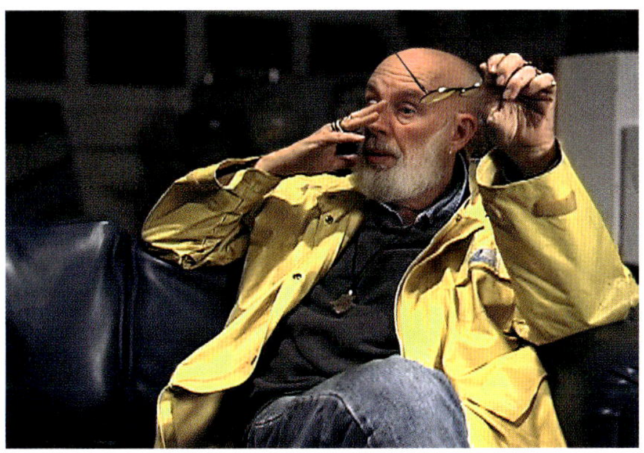

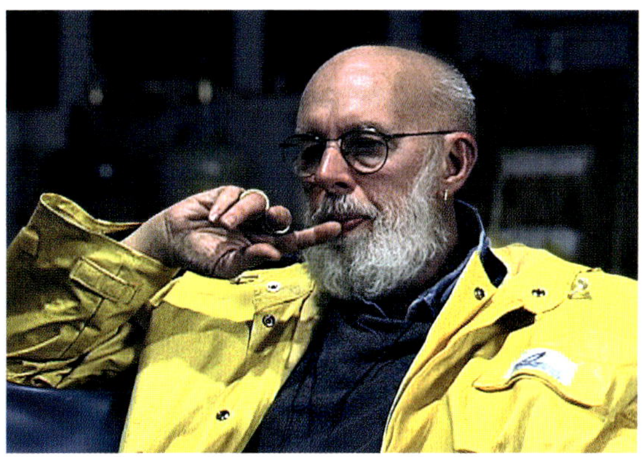

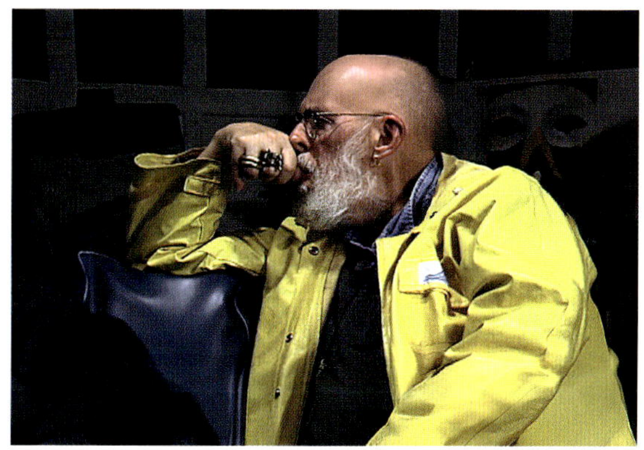

EG: He was the one that invented those. Well, there's Willy and the best of sashes, fell in the fire and was burnt to ashes. By the by, the room grew chilly, but no one wanted to poke Willy, or stir up Willy, or whatever.

CV: I always thought of those things as . . .

EG: Well, when I was a kid in one of the Chicago newspapers there was some column where people used to make up stuff and send them in.

And they had a running column. I think they had a little Willy at least once a week, and maybe every day or something. So people made them up, but I think that was the first.

I think that was the one that started it off. Yeah, they just went on and on and on. And I'm trying to remember . . . there were some others that were fairly famous, and I'm trying to remember what they are, but they're like the Belloc but shorter. They're usually only maybe ten or twelve lines at the most but there are these terrible things that are happening to people.

CV: So did you pick these particular ones out to do the play because they suggested puppets to you?

EG: Well no, really because they're the only ones that translate. I mean the other ones, as I say, there's this great long double one that's about English politics that, you know, is hopeless, and somehow I think he sort of, I would suspect that he got divinely inspired by the first four or five and then it sort of, was more of . . . [*long pause with rain sound and then trailing off*]

CS: I was really surprised that someone else had written something whose style was very similar to yours.

EG: Ah, well, I think I've been influenced a lot by things like, well you know, Lewis Carroll and Edward Lear and the whole tradition of English nonsense verse and stuff.

CV: So that was really a genre that people worked in consciously?

EG: Oh, I think so yeah. Well, and there's, oh God, well not exactly, but there are a couple of people from the late nineteenth century who sort of do much-longer poems, but in very clever rhyme schemes, and you know, sort of narrative things.

Well, of course I suppose it goes back to Thomas Hood, who wrote some very strange and, you know, some really quite violent stuff, not necessarily for children. I'm not sure if they first appeared in *Punch* or not, but I think it was a whole thing back then. I don't know if you can find that actual first person who did nonsense, but I suspect it goes back even further than we think.

CV: How long ago was it, did Edward Lear and Lewis Carroll know each other? Was it a . . .

EG: No, I don't think they did. I have no idea.

Whew, these would have been . . . let's see, Lear was born in . . . I don't know when.

In fact I think Lear was before because Belloc was born in the 1880s or something. Yeah, because he didn't die until 1953 or something so . . .

CV: So, I love the idea of people sitting around in pubs and throwing, and tossing these things off. [*Laughing*]

EG: You know, not necessarily pubs either, because . . .

I mean like Lear you know was a great friend of Tennyson or something, and in fact some of his stuff sounds like Tennyson got slightly askew [*laughing*], and of course some of Tennyson sounds like Tennyson gone slightly askew but whatever, anyway.

CV: So, nobody did this really in the United States?

EG: Ooh gosh . . . There is some stuff but I can't . . . later on there is someone named Oliver Hereford who did stuff like it. I was trying to think if there was anything that became that well known. I don't think anything was quite as popular as Belloc and Lear and Carroll and stuff. I can't think of anybody American.

CV: And nobody illustrated their own, did they?

EG: Harry Graham illustrated his own. He has a funny monogram that looks like it's GH. I tried to track it down and then I, of course, discovered that the GH was really HG and he'd done them himself, I guess.

CV: Hmm.

EG: Then again, they're not artistically very good but they have a kind of awful, vulgar charm to them.

CV: I've got to see these. He was English?

EG: He was English too, yeah. There are a whole bunch of people who, you know, sometimes they wrote verse, sometimes they wrote short, humorous pieces, you know. And all those people I suppose, that you know, contributed to *Punch*. I think a lot of these people were . . . well *Punch* goes back to about 1850 anyway, it may be even older, I'm not sure . . .

CV: Hmm. [*Rain*] Are you ever thinking it'll be something that you'll be using?

EG: Um, as I say, I can't find my copy of the rest of Belloc and I can't really remember the animal ones but I think they were just sort of kind of Ogden Nash's things about animals.

CV: I remember some of them that I learned years ago.

EG: Yeah, I can't really remember any of them.

CV: I think that they are republishing them. I haven't heard them since I was a kid, but I don't get the impression that kids nowadays generally know about them.

EG: No, I think a lot of this stuff kids don't really know about. Though *Matilda*, I know, has been illustrated, you know, three or four times in recent years.

CV: Oh?

EG: Just as a single book.

CV: Huh.

EG: But.

EG: There's a kind of scheme that I had to sort of follow so I'm not tempted; I can't really change the drawings around very much.

CV: And you're doing all of them?

EG: Yeah, all of the *Cautionary Tales* . . . [*long stretch of rain sounds*]. Oh . . . could we stop? [*Laughs*] This is all so . . .

CS: If you could just talk a little bit generally about what this play was about . . .

EG: No. No, it was just, you know . . .

CV: There's always something at the beginning, with the illustrations; was there something where you thought, "Oh Vincent [one of his actors] will go wild with this."

EG: Oh, no. No, because I've been working on it for so long. No, I was just looking for something that

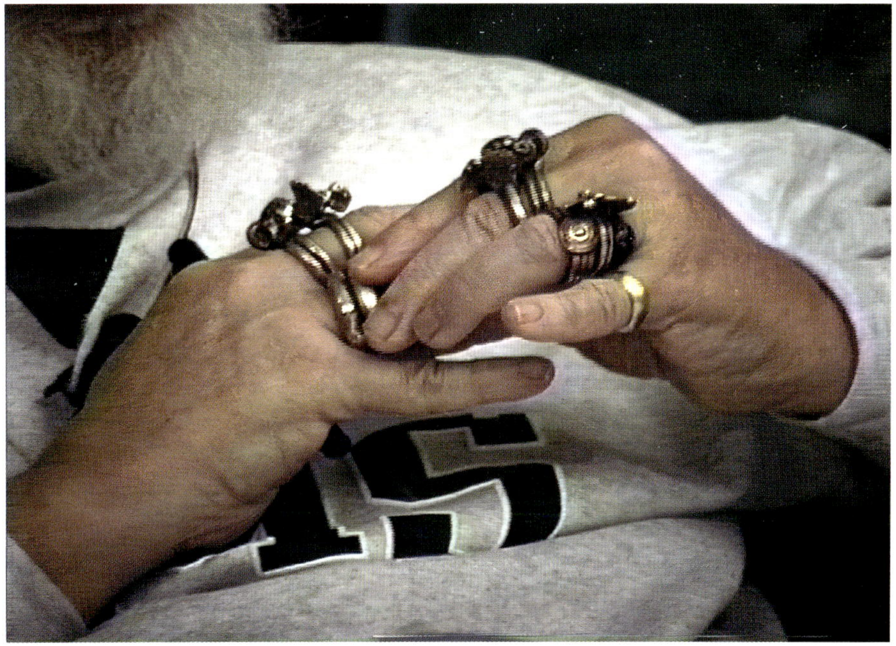

Gorey wore many heavy and, perhaps, impractical rings on his fingers. Not all of them were jewelry but were antiques like napkin or curtain rings.

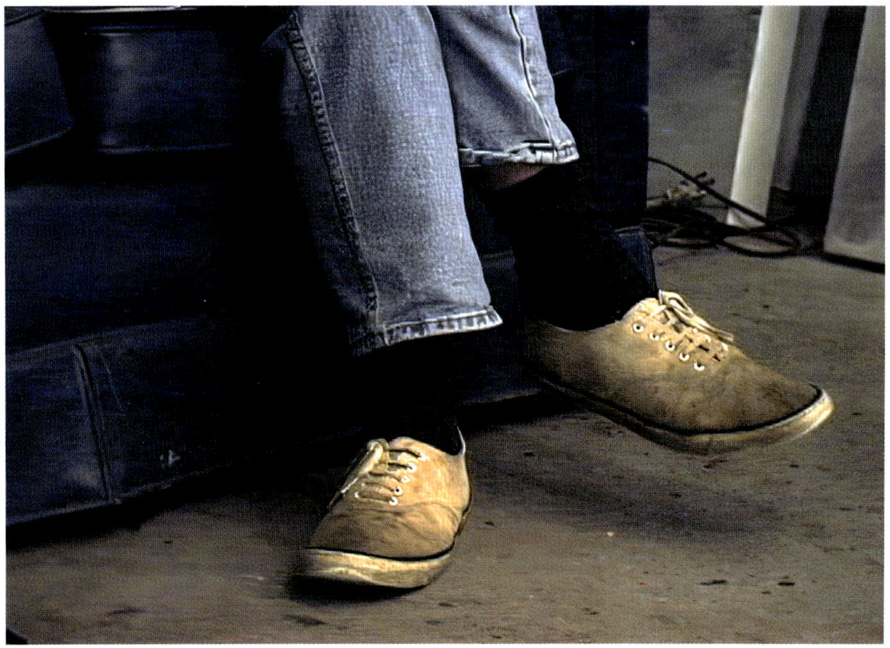

At some point, Gorey's white Converses gave way to Sperry Striper CVOs, which were their traditionally known Top Sider shoes.

we could do so I wouldn't have to write something. I thought these would be sort of neat.

CV: And they happened to be on your desk.

EG: And they happened to be on my desk. Yes, just *staring* at me.

CV: Do you feel that doing them with the puppets is changing the drawings at all?

EG: No. No, because I've done so much, I just have a few drawings left. Well, you'd have to see the drawings but, because of the format the proportions of the drawings are different than I've done before. It's hard to explain.

CV: Hmm.

EG: There's a kind of scheme that I had to sort of follow so I'm not tempted; I can't really change the drawings around very much.

CV: You had said the other day, when we were talking about the show at CTV [Cape Cod Community Television], that you might possibly put . . .

EG: Well, I was just trying to figure out, I'd have to look at them, because . . .

CV: You don't do preliminary sketches, is that right?

EG: No, not really. No, not for this. There's some really rough layouts and everything but . . .

CV: So everything that you've done for it is presumably already laid out.

EG: Yeah, I don't know, we'll have to figure it out [*losing patience*]. [*Long sigh*]

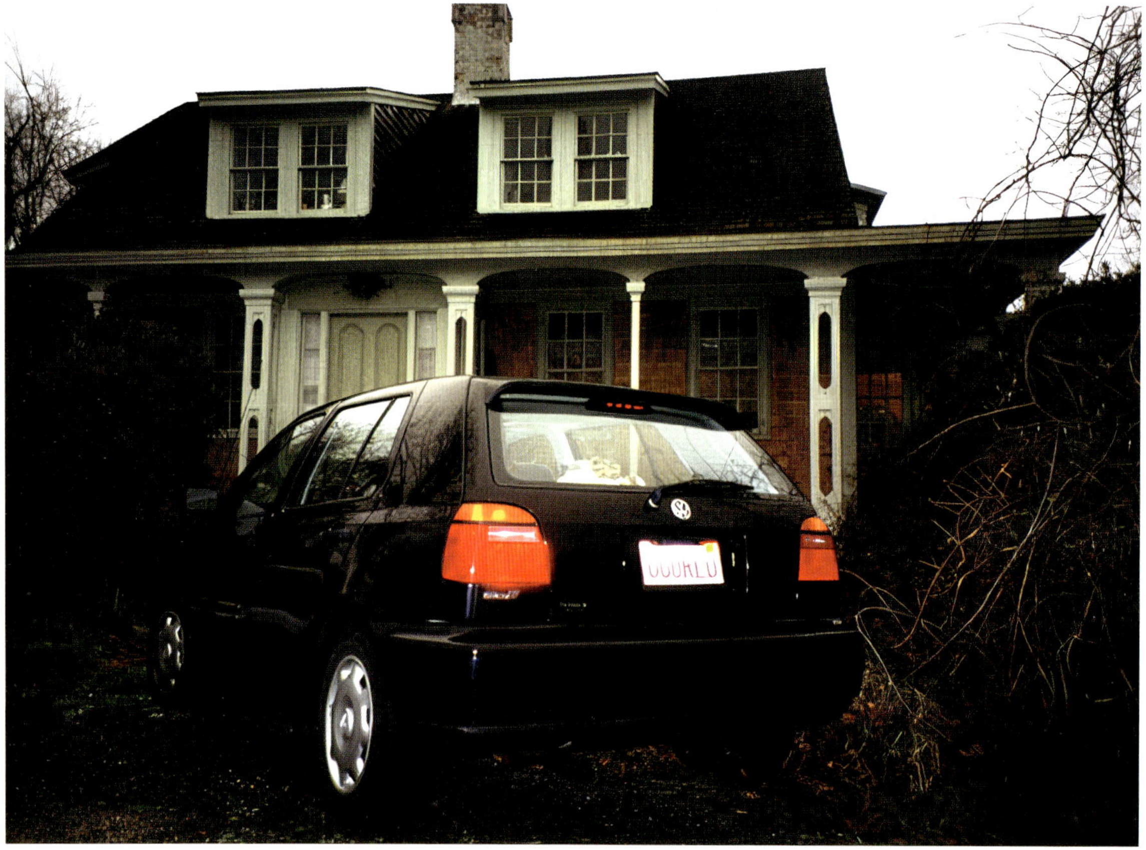

Gorey's car and signature license plate in driveway

CV: Thank you.

EG: [*Laughs daintily, sarcastically*] Are we going around the corner for a beer? [to The Kettle Ho]

CV: I think we'd better.

EG: Yes! [*Grunts dramatically as he stands up and out of frame*]

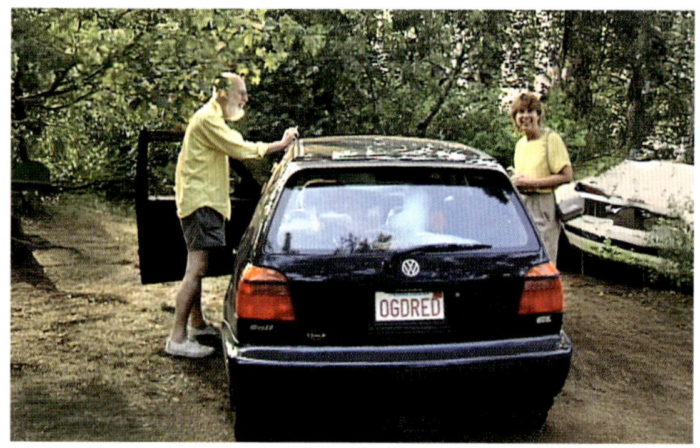

Edward with Carol Verburg getting lunch in Orleans, Massachusetts, October 1999

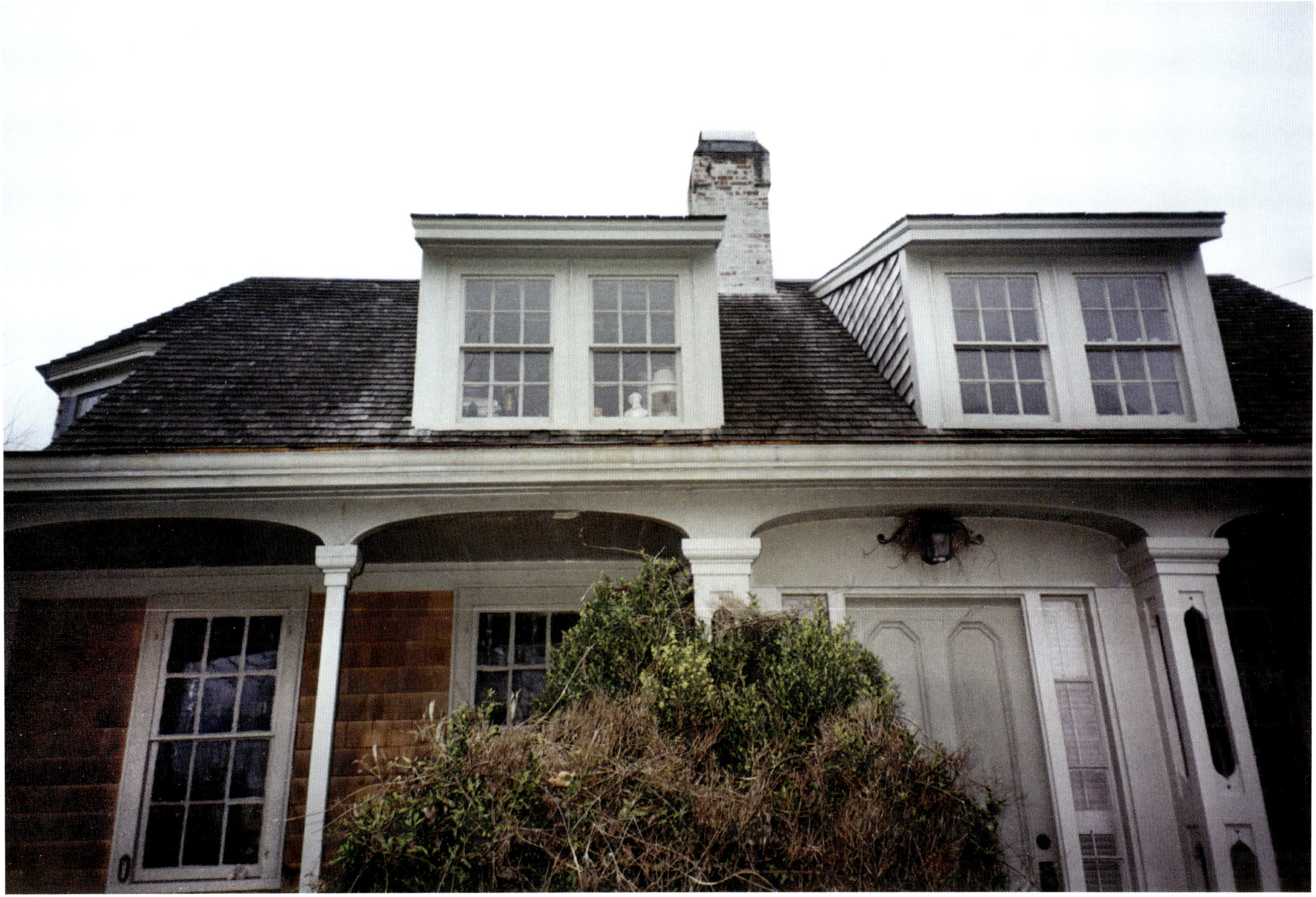

Gorey's house front and the unused front door

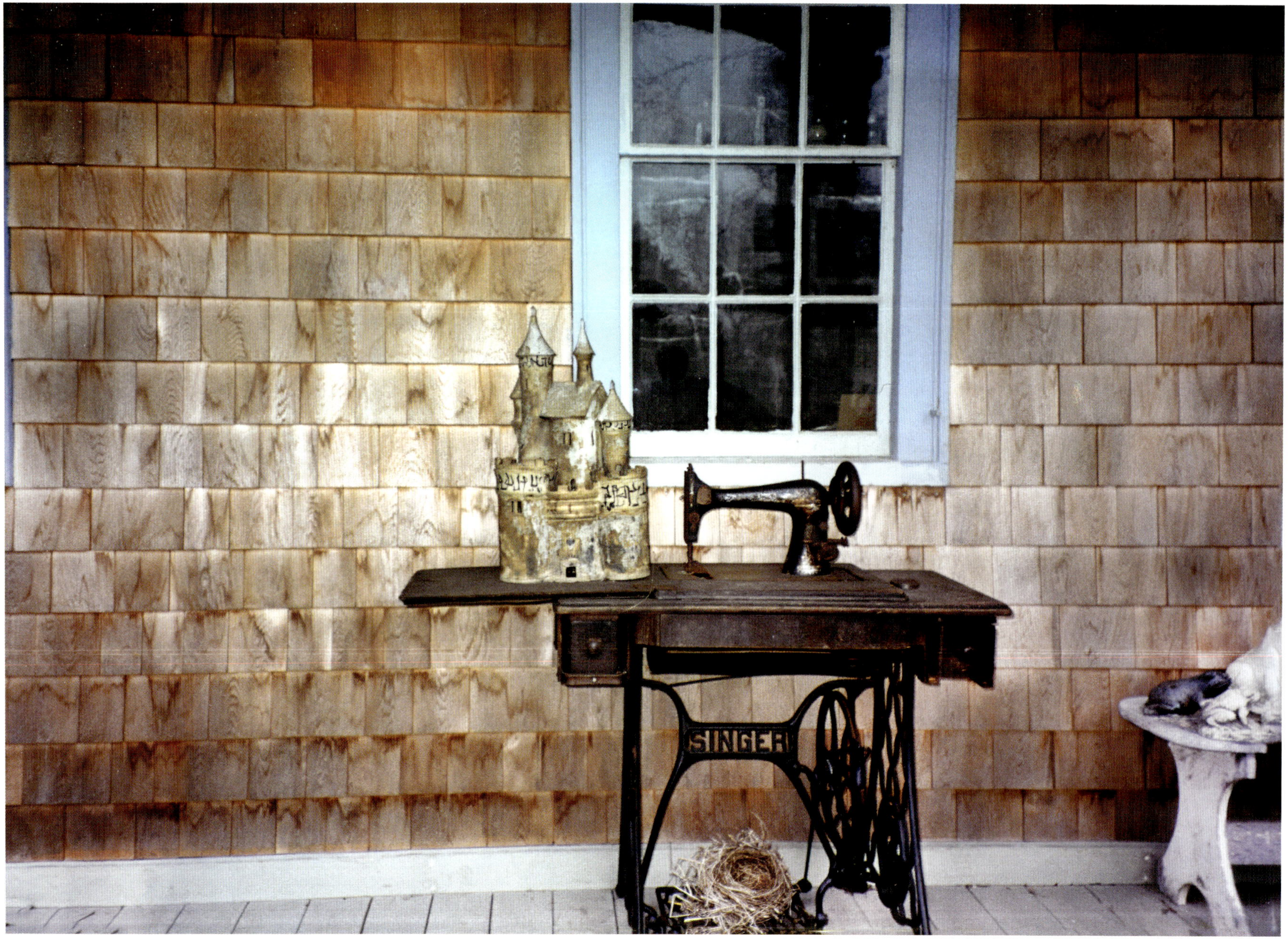

Gorey's exterior exhibits on his deck: sewing machine with sand castle and bird nest

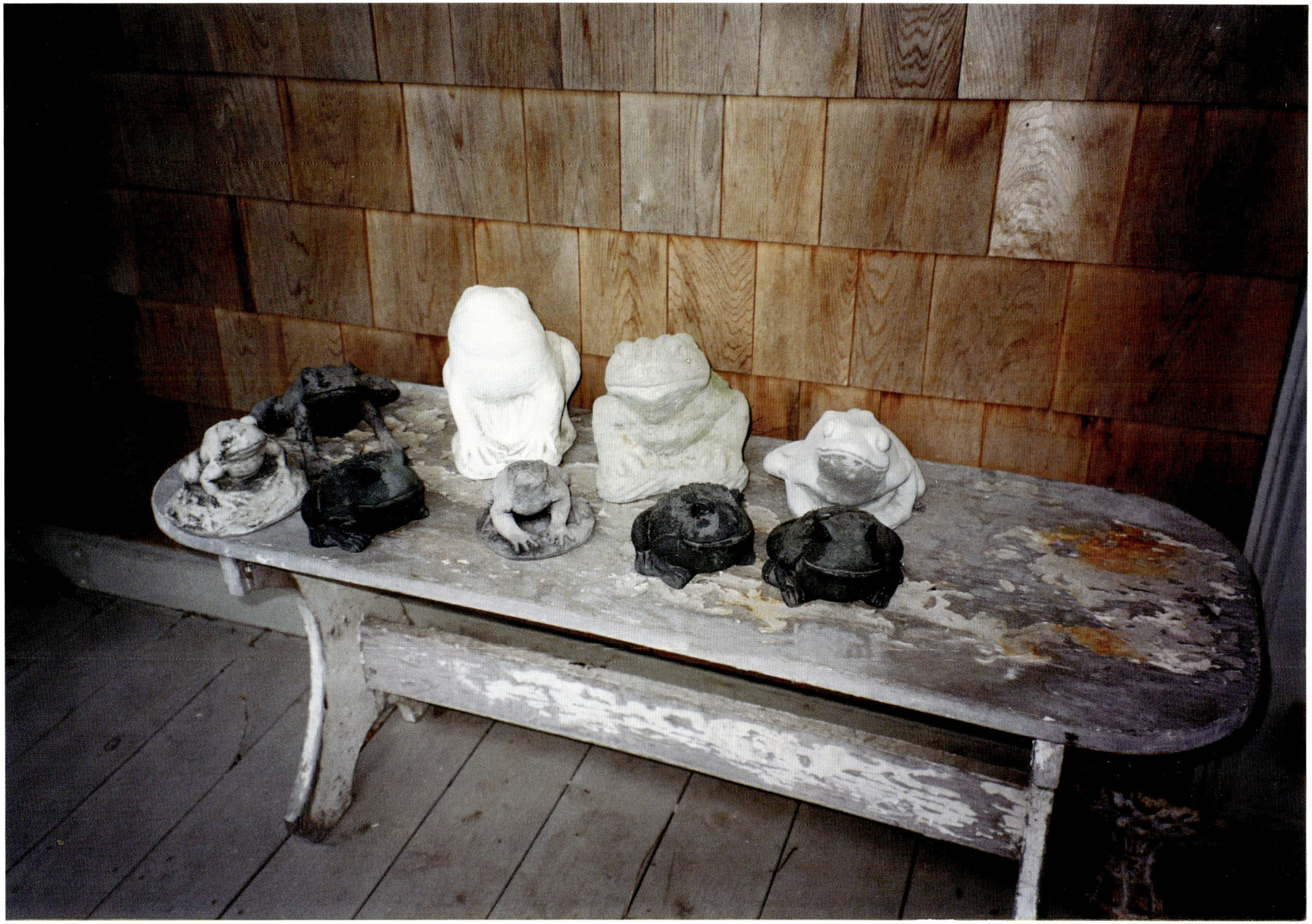

Frog sculpture collection

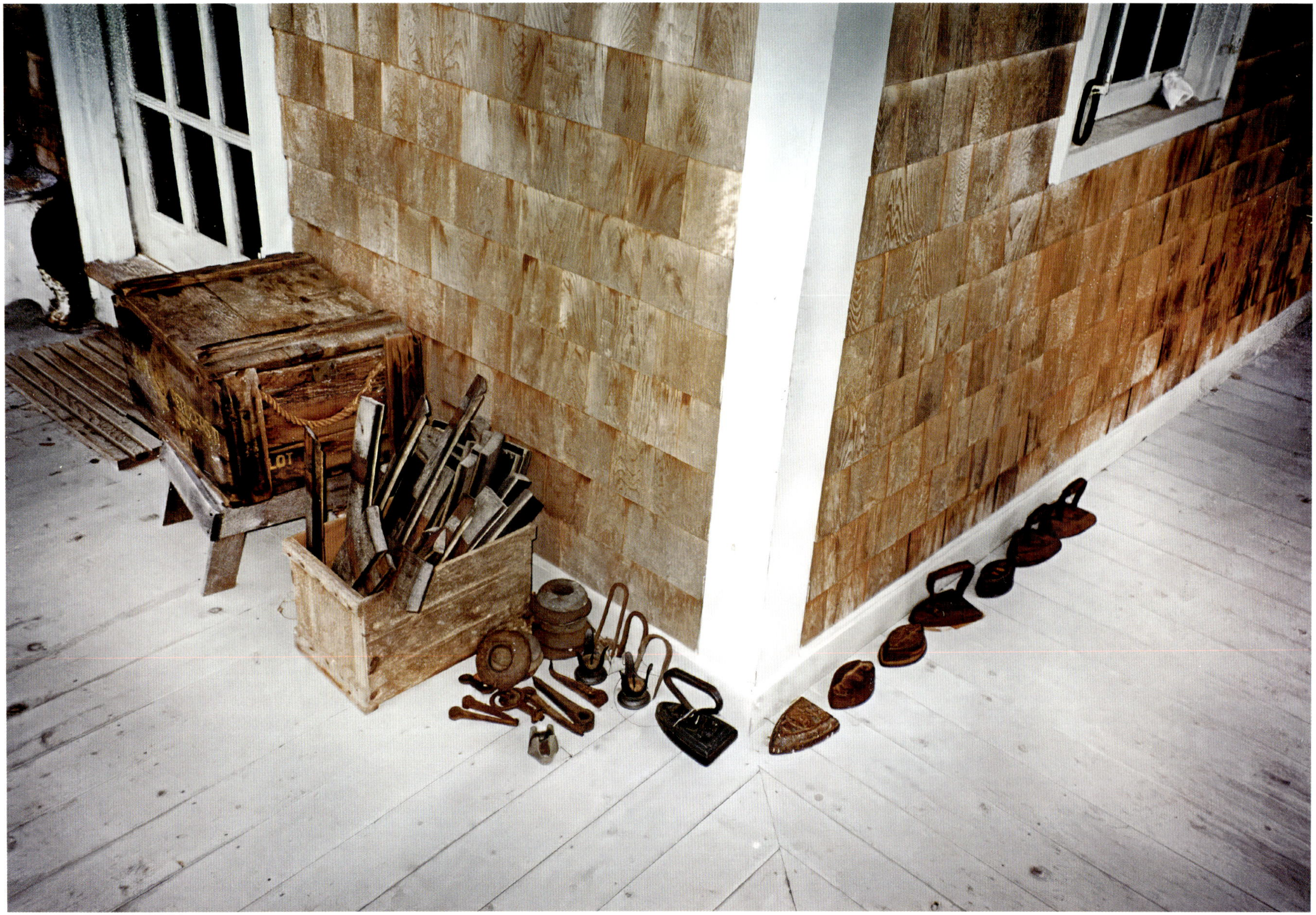

Antique irons and tools

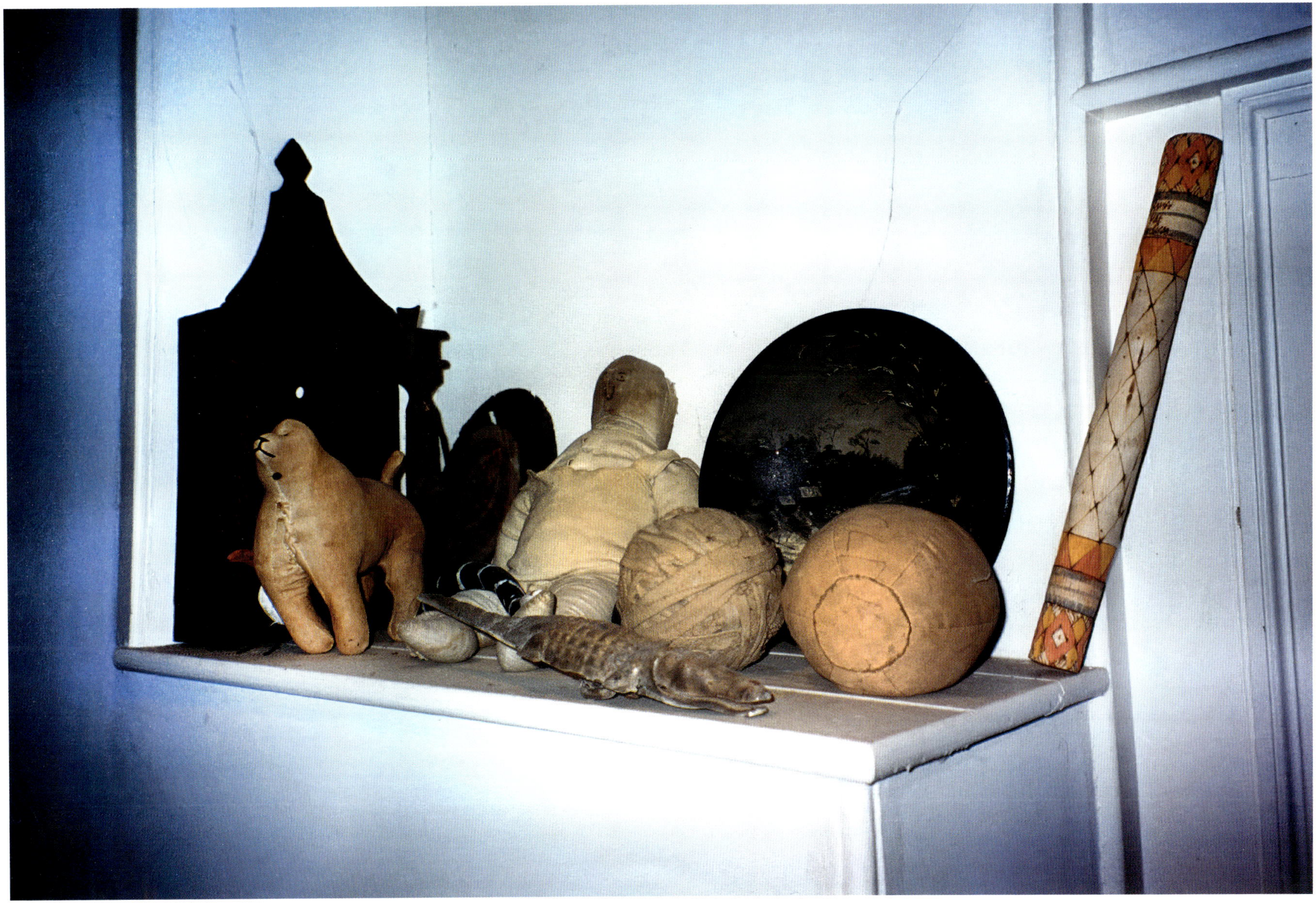

Vintage stuffed animals and alligator

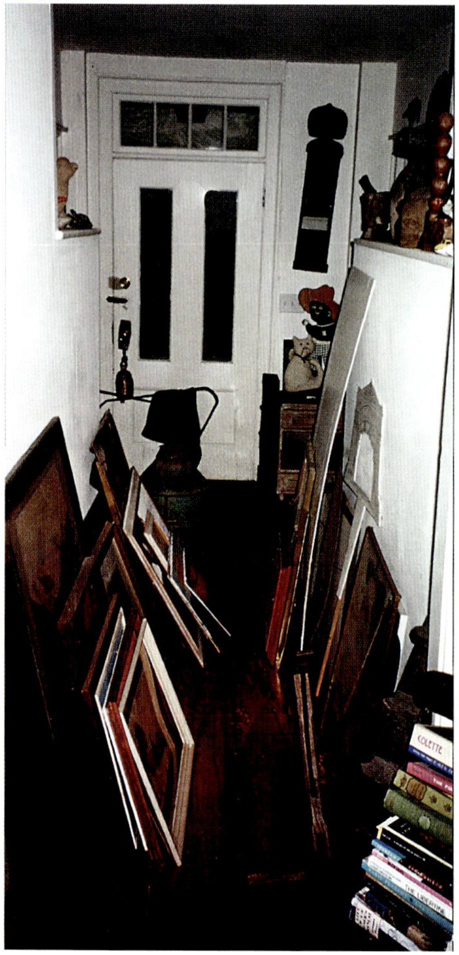

Hallway with artwork waiting to be hung

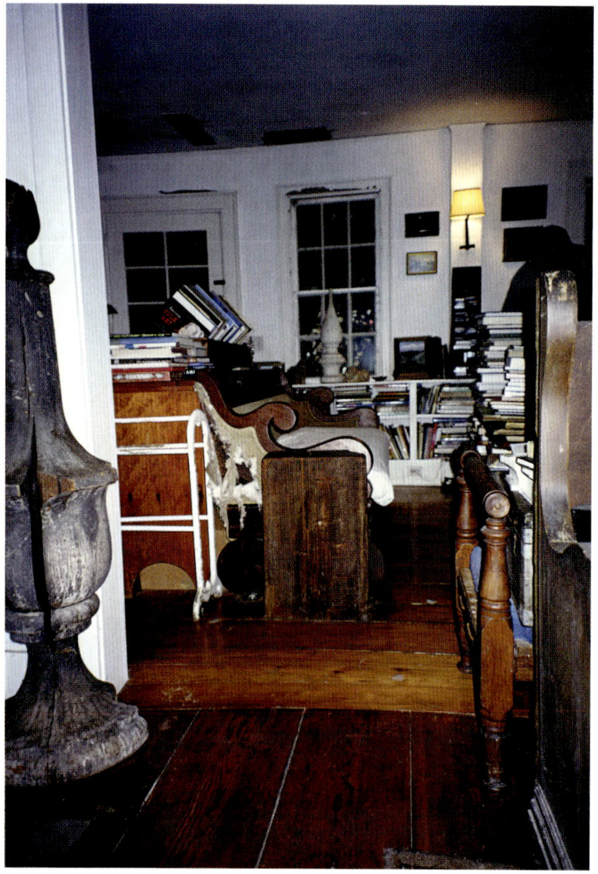

One of many finials crowding the hallways

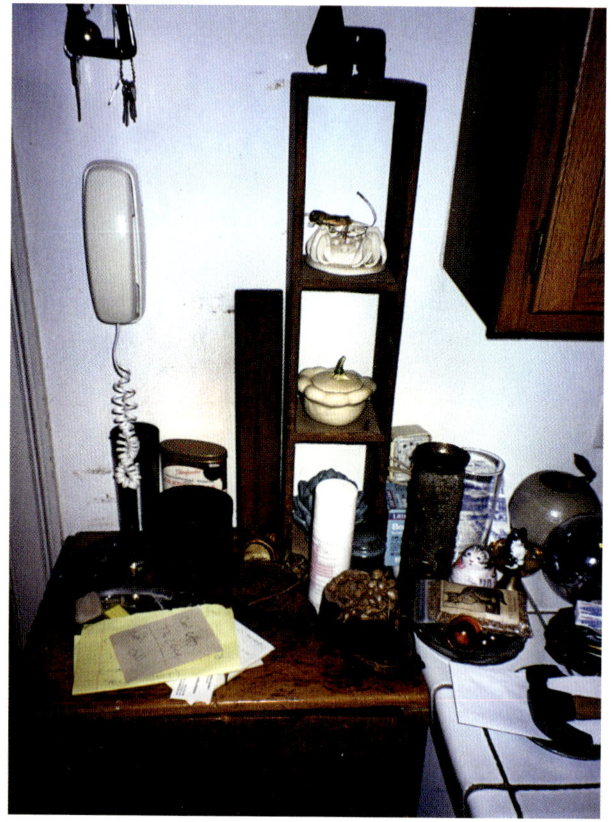

Gorey's main telephone and answering machine in the kitchen. The message announced straightforwardly, "You've reached Edward Gorey's answering machine, wait for the beep." The crew and I went out of our way to record these types of small details from Edward's life, and I'm glad we did, as we found that years later, neither the estate nor the museum had such things. We were then able to get things like a CD with his answering-machine message back to the museum to play once again in his house for visitors.

Interview with Edward Gorey: Jack's Outback

AUGUST 22, 1998

The crew and I met Edward and his producer Carol Verburg at his everyday breakfast-and-lunch place to document one of their working meetings and to warm things up for a shoot at Edward's house, afterward. He wore his white Sperrys, khaki shorts, and denim shirt, along with the ubiquitous rings and necklaces that clanked occasionally into the wireless lavalier microphone. By this time, I had Edward pretty well trained to put that on as soon as we met.

The owner, Jack Braginton-Smith, one of Edward's best friends, swung by occasionally for banter and hamming it up for the camera. Summertime tourists mixed in with the locals and occasionally gawked from nearby booths. Edward and Carol begin by discussing the upcoming production of their play *English Soup* in Los Angeles.

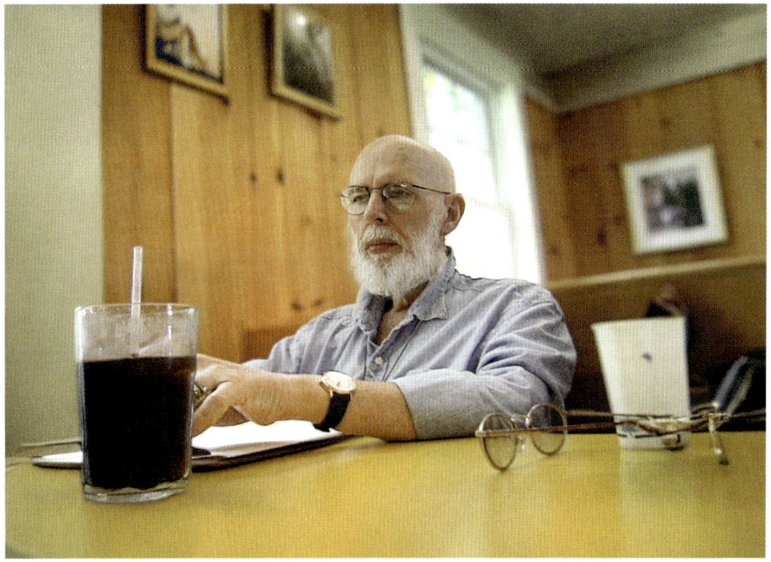

Edward often conducted business and meetings for breakfast and lunch at Jack's Outback, a diner around the corner from his house, often accompanied by several iced coffees.

Carol Verburg: Do you have more of those posters from Jeannie?

Edward Gorey: No, now those, well . . . No, now those, well, now wait a second. Those all went to Andy [Andreas Brown at Gotham Book Mart].

CV: Because those strike me as fodder.

EG: And he said, "Why is one printed in two shades of green and black?," and I said, "I don't knoooww. They just are. I didn't even realize until he pointed it out. It wasn't just one shade of green, it was two shades of green. Talk about *bravura*! [*Leans head down and sips iced coffee from a straw for emphasis*]

CV: You gave me two of them, and my feeling about them is that I love the drawing but I really don't like how they made the poster.

EG: No, I don't love the poster.

CV: I would be inclined . . . I assume you wouldn't be offended if I shipped those two posters off to Dawn [in Los Angeles]?

EG: Oh well, no, she shouldn't . . . well that . . . um . . . well I wish I could figure out [*buries head in hands dramatically*]. I think I had about . . . [*trails off*]. Yes, dear? [*Noticing Carol's expression*]

CV: Would it be conceivable that the etchings would constitute a show in themselves, and then Andy wouldn't have to deal with it at all?

EG: Well, no, probably not. Well of course, Dawn hasn't seen the show has she?

CV: No, what she said is that she wants twenty to thirty pieces for exhibit, with eight to ten minimum for sale, and if you have twenty-five to thirty . . .

EG: Well, I suppose . . .

CV: They have constant shows in there, it's just like the museum.

EG: Well, that's true. Of course Andy may have misunderstood, but anyway, if under the circumstances she really is going to show for only two weeks, I think Andy really will insist on it getting back to him November 15th. He isn't about to let his Christmas show go kerplunk [at Gotham Book Mart].

CV: Right, which is only fair, but as I understand it . . .

EG: But, if you tell her if she isn't going to have anything for sale or put it up before the show opens, then certainly she can have as many etchings and calligraphs as she wants. You can fill the Metropolitan Museum of Art with them, well, if you use multiple copies. But anyway, Emily [the designer] is probably going to get to work on them fairly shortly.

CV: Are they any particular size?

EG: Oh, they're all about . . . one or two of the calligraphs is about this big [*holds his hands to indicate roughly 8 by 10 inches*], but those are the ones that are a little iffy and will be scarce because there won't be that many. As soon as I can locate my list I can say, hopefully, how many of them actually exist.

CV: And the etchings?

EG: And the etchings. No, the etchings are about like this mostly [*holds his hands at about 4 by 6 inches*]. There are Figbash etchings, there are elephant etchings, there are some thumbs . . . [*picks nails*] but most of the thumbs I think are calligraphs. And then there are some random etchings that I did years ago. I mean these all, of course, were done years and years ago, but you know, an etching is an etching. *Timeless*. Just look at Rembrandt! [*Rolls his eyes*]

CV: Absolutely.

[*Camera stops, restarts, and then conversation continues*]

EG: I don't want to go to that concert tonight but I suppose we're going to have to. [*Slouches and grimaces*]

CV: We don't have to do anything.

EG: No, we don't have to do anything, but I feel . . . oh, what's at the movies! Has anybody checked?!

[*Camera again stops and continues*]

CV: [Carol describes her flower, a night-blooming cereus]

EG: And is it still open?

CV: No, it was closed by morning, so I just sat up with it for about half an hour.

EG: Now, will it open again tonight?

CV: No.

EG: Oh, that's it?!

CV: No, it just opens one night out of the whole year. This is why it's called a night-blooming cereus. It's wonderful, magical.

EG: Well, surely, I would think a night-blooming serious [sic] would be open every night for at least a week!

CV: It's not "serious," it's "cereus."

EG: Yes, but I love that it could be serious.

CV: It's a night-blooming cereus. It looks like a cactus that's been flattened, with sort of scallopy branches, a very strange-looking plant. And every once in a blue moon it makes a flower and it comes out looking like one of those light covers that they have for sports lights, or like a work light that you hang for your car when you're working on it. It's this ball in a casing of pink.

EG: Does it belong . . .

CV: It gets bigger and bigger and it gets to be maybe this big and then suddenly it turns into a flower. It's white and inside is this wonderful circle of white petals . . .

[*Camera stops and continues*]

Christopher Seufert: I never knew what the word "city block" meant, growing up in Chatham; it never meant anything to me.

CV: Oh, my gosh!

CS: But now I do know what that means. [Has been living in New York City]

EG: Well, I grew up in Chicago.

CS: People in Boston know . . .

EG: Yes, Boston has blocks.

CS: San Francisco doesn't really have blocks.

CV: It doesn't?

CS: Not really.

CV: It does where I live. [Carol lives in North Beach]

CS: But no one ever uses the term.

EG: Of course New York is very confusing because the crosstown blocks are like ten times more than the uptown blocks.

CV: Yeah.

EG: Chicago has relatively the same size [of] blocks throughout, I think, *square*!

Jack Braginton-Smith: [*Delivering food*] Well, here we are!

CS: What's in the file? [*Noticing Edward's folder*]

CV: This is Friday stuff that we both hate dealing with.

CS: Do you two have lunch as a way of getting theater business done, as a way to touch base during the day?

EG: Yes.

CS: Or is it more of a social thing?

CV: I come here for lunch because without Edward's company there's not much point in being on Cape Cod!

EG: Oh, Carol, you're just saying that. And when you go I'm committing suicide! [*Laughs*] Oooh . . . [*groans*] I don't like to think about it.

CV: This is what I'm here for really, because I have plenty of food in my own house.

EG: I think I'd better go get some more iced coffee.

CV: And I need some more water.

EG: [*Wanders into kitchen, puts ice cubes in his glass, and pours iced coffee from a blue pitcher. He returns to table and groans as he slides again into the booth.*]

CV: Well, we don't have to go.

EG: Yes, we can say, "Oh, we had a rehearsal at the last moment. And we had it in a movie theater!" Something must have opened today. What's this, August 24th?

CV: No, the 21st.

EG: The 21st. Well, I'm sure something opened today,

I'm just sure something opened today.

CV: I just read a lot of movie reviews today in the *San Francisco Chronicle*, but they were all bad.

EG: Oh well, did you read them?

CV: No, I just sort of skimmed the top.

EG: Oh well, that doesn't work . . . bad, bad, bad. Do you remember what any of them were?

CV: Umm . . . *Friends Like Us*, *The Best Man* . . . name some other movies.

EG: I don't think I know those. They don't sound especially lurid to me.

CV: Oh, Wesley Snipes. Did you see that already?

EG: No, what's that one?

CV: The one where he's not a vampire? Stephen Dorff is the vampire. *Blade*.

EG: Oh well, that sounds promising.

CV: It's the one where Wesley is said to be out-Schwarzeneggering Arnold Schwarzenegger, in effect?

EG: [*Delighted*] Oh, well that sounds . . .

CV: You've seen the trailer many times where's he's wearing breastplates and so forth . . .

EG: Yeah, I've seen the trailer, right. Oh right. That's sounds possible, even plausible. [*Demurely*]

CV: Yeah. [*Edward leans his head down to the straw of the iced coffee.*] Yeah, that sounds like the kind of movie we ought to go to in a theater that's right next to somewhere that has large drinks served in coconut shells.

EG: [*Laughs theatrically*] I don't think . . .

CV: And we could have one of those drinks. If we went to the Airport Cinema, Edward, we could go to the Tiki Port and have a scorpion bowl this big [*holds hands out wide*].

EG: The Tiki Port [*whines*], I'd rather die! I'd rather die! Oooh!

CV: It'd be perfect for this particular movie.

EG: Ew!

CV: Well, take your choice Edward. It's either that or the Strauss recital.

EG: Well, it's not the Strauss so much, as, the folk songs that scare me. There were going to be folk songs by her accompanist.

CV: Uh oh.

EG: Oooh, I don't know. It sounded like it would start out at a mildly high level and then slowly sink down to encores like Brahms's *Lullaby* or something.

CV: And we know the seating is not comfortable.

EG: That's true.

EG: Ooooh. [*Interested now*]

CS: Phoebe alarm clock?

CV: My cat. She has a particular note that she strikes when she wants something, that is penetrating in the extreme. Do yours do that, Edward?

EG: No, I haven't had a cat for a hundred years that got up early! Usually they just look at me as if to say, "What are you doing up?!" By the time I've come out of the shower and so forth, and so on, some of them want to go downstairs and get some food, and others couldn't care less. It's very strange.

CV: Well, I was so enthralled with the flower last night that I forgot to fill up Phoebe's bowl.

EG: Poor Phoebe, starving in the small hours, she thought, "How long do I have to wait?" [*Theatrically*]

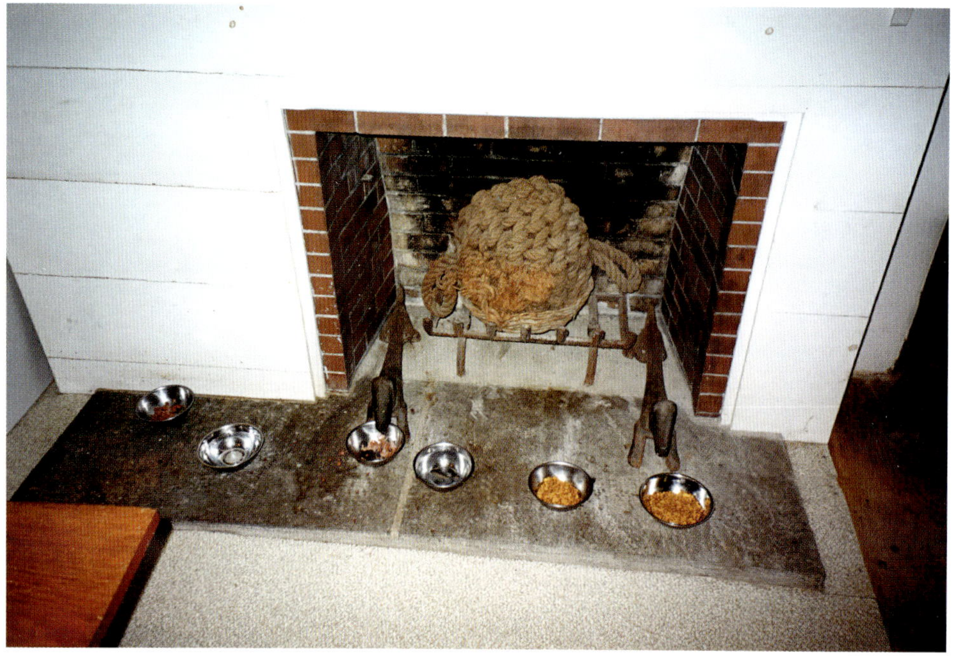

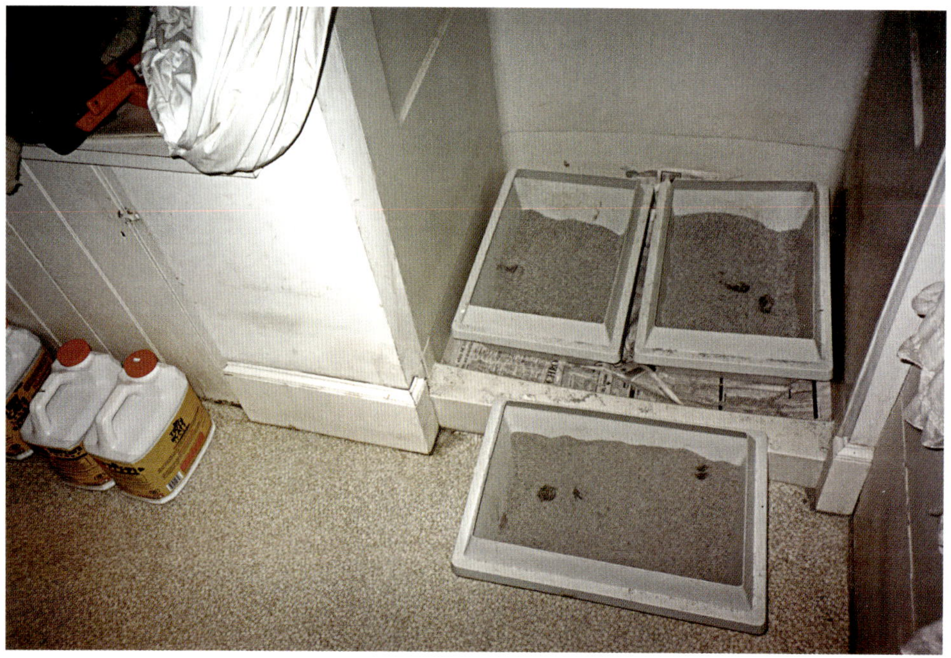

Edward was a cat lover in every sense. He maintained five or so, all rescues, with new ones appearing when there was a feral or orphaned cat brought in. Once in, they were permanent house cats, so the more dysfunctional ones hid expertly in the many hiding spots throughout the house. His downstairs bathroom was set aside as litter box central, and each of the cats had their dish set by the fireplace in the kitchen.

According to Edward, not only did they have their everyday names like Jane, Weedon, George, Thomas, and Alice, but they each had an alternate Japanese name. He kept a log where their dates of entry and then their passings were recorded. When it came to birthdays, he didn't know them, so "their birthdays passed unnoticed, the poor dears."

CV: I think she was just jealous that I was paying so much attention to something other than her.

EG: It's a wonder she didn't go over and knock the petals right off. [*Sticks tongue out*]

CV: I notice Pebble's been eating my peas out of the window box on the deck. [Her other cat]

EG: Oh, really?

CV: Just munching the entire plant.

EG: Oh, well. [*Shrugs shoulders and sips iced coffee*]

CS: So your play, the *English Soup* play for Los Angeles, your last rehearsal is October 1st, is that right?

CV: Yup, if it opens October 2nd, our last rehearsal will be October 1st.

CS: First in Cotuit?

EG: In Cotuit, yes.

CS: So that's sort of your dry run?

CV: Dress rehearsal is what we call it, yes.

CS: Dress rehearsal, but it's really a real performance? You're putting it on and there will be a paying audience there?

CV: Oh yeah, it's going to run for four weeks. The following show in LA is strictly incidental.

EG: [*Edward lets out a long sigh and groan thinking about it.*]

CV: It just requires a lot more planning because we haven't done it before.

EG: Oh, and it also requires God-knows-what after you leave Carol on September whatever it is. The whole thing may just drop. "Hello, Carol? We all went down the tubes!"

CS: So, how is that going to work, Edward, if they go to LA without you and you're normally there for the Cotuit plays directing?

EG: Oh yes, that's right.

CS: How are they going to do it?

EG: They'll run totally amok, they'll take advantage. Except Carol will be there to say, "You don't do it that way now do you?" [*In a sinister voice*]

CV: I'm going to crack the whip. I'm going to come back here right before we go out to LA and watch and make sure they don't try anything.

EG: Oh, I see, yes. [*Loving the idea of it*]

CS: Like order vast amounts of room service?

CV: Oh, they'll do whatever they want to.

CS: Hire limos at all hours of the night . . . [*To Edward*] So are you definitely not making an appearance at all out there in LA?

EG: [*Sipping iced coffee and shaking his head*] No, because for one thing I've got another show, which I'm not directing but it's going to be in Brewster on Halloween weekend.

CS: Is that with Bobby Rosser? [*Hsst!*]

EG: Yeah, her son is directing it, and he wants to take it to New York, so . . . [*Raises his eyebrows several times and winking at the prospect of it*]

CV: Oh, I know what I meant to tell you. I spoke to Wes yesterday . . .

EG: To whom?

CV: Wes?

EG: Wes, oh yes.

CV: And he's achieved a positive attitude about doing the shows in the winter, in the auditorium, so that's definitely a viable thing at this point. [Cape Rep Theatre]

EG: Oh, okay, because I tentatively told Peter Butterfield we could do a show in February at the Museum of Fine Arts in Boston, so we could do a completely new show.

CV: Would this possibly have to do with *Cautionary Tales* [*for Children*]?

EG: Oh, the *Cautionary Tales* thing. [Talking about the dog dances from *Cautionary Tales for Children*] I decided that some had to be more than just one act, to be longer than just little twiddly bits inserted.

CV: I've been wondering if the solution to everything isn't just to dispense with live actors and only have puppets, do you think that makes sense?

EG: Oh, like somebody said, "It's such a relief to have actors you can put away in a box at the end of a performance and not hear them babbling away about this, that, and the other thing, quarreling, and being jealous."

CS: There's that whole thing happening now with virtual studios, virtual actors, have you read about that?

EG: Oh, I've seen bits.

CS: It's actually becoming something of a reality; they create virtual personalities.

EG: [*Shakes his head and makes a face*] I know. I think the whole thing is creepy. Creepy, creepy, creepy!

CV: I know. Oh, speaking of creepy, I read in the *San Francisco Chronicle* that Gwyneth Paltrow has mortally offended Michael Douglas by commenting that since she's twenty-five and he's fifty-four, that if she really had to be married to him in real life it would be kind of creepy.

EG: That girl, I don't think is quite right . . .

Jack Braginton-Smith: [*Again interrupts on purpose*] Here we are . . . two hamburgers. Oh, or have I come to the wrong table?!

CV: Jack would like to be on camera please. [*Points to camera woman*]

EG: [*Ignoring him obviously*] What were they in together?

CV: They were in some movie that hasn't come out yet.

EG: Certainly Clint Eastwood was far too old in *Bridges of Madison County*.

CV: Yes, utterly desiccated, even for Meryl Streep.

EG: And there was something else we saw recently where I thought, "He is just too old for that part, folks. He should not be doing romantic.

CS: Although that was a lot more common a hundred years ago than today.

CV: When all this was happening for money, and the man would have a lot of money by age fifty or so.

EG: Well, as long as . . . I mean, Cary Grant looked great until he died.

CV: And Paul Newman I would marry tomorrow.

EG: Well, he was looking pretty desiccated in, oh, what was that movie? I can't even remember if I saw it or not, but in the trailers I thought, "He really does look too old for this as a romantic lead." [*Nobody's Fool*, 1994]

CV: I think it was the flannel shirt. I remember the trailer where I though that, but I think it was the costume department.

EG: No, I think I'm thinking of something else, but I can't think of what it is now.

[*Camera stops and then begins*]

EG: Oh, the Museum of Fine Arts was thrilled to know that I have other "product" besides myself. [*Laughs*]

CS: Product? Do they call it that really?

CV: Oh yes.

EG: Well I don't but other people do. "Do you have any product?" [*In an upper-class voice*]

CS: Besides yourself.

EG: Yes, besides yourself. So I said we had T-shirts, which I must remember to get back from the museum.

CV: What are you doing for the show, do you know yet?

EG: Oh well, we'll have the usual, a button, a postcard, a poster, T-shirts.

CS: Stuffed anythings?

EG: Well, we always have stuffed anythings if I have anything.

CV: Are you making a poster that's separate from the lithograph?

EG: Oh, yes, yeah, that will be the only thing just like that. The button will just have a Figbash with a soup tureen.

CV: And will there be a mug, do you think?

EG: Well, I might do a mug. I should consult with Andy because mugs do go well, and I don't think we have any left of anything.

CV: The ampersand [mug] never really emerged, did it?

EG: Well, I'm very baffled about that because . . . did we sell them anyplace?

CV: I never have gotten one.

EG: You've never gotten one? Well, I have six left, which I kept on purpose.

CV: Oh, where did they go then?

EG: Well twelve of them went to the museum, but we must've sold them somewhere. I don't know whether I ever sent any to Andy. Anyway, they were sitting in a carton in the room just off the front door, and I discovered them sitting there. A couple of them had gotten chipped and various people . . . well, anyway, I have six left, so you can have one of them.

We might do another bash of mugs because they do sell well, I think.

CS: What else is out there, what other kinds of things do you sell?

EG: Well there are buttons and posters from the plays and T-shirts, though usually only from whatever is current.

CV: Do you have any of these things that we can ship to LA?

CS: You should do a line of Gorey bicycles. A special Gorey edition of Schwinn or something. [*The Epiplectic Bicycle*]

EG: Oh, well, right.

CV: There is a mug with unicycles on it.

EG: Oh. I suppose we should just send out a lot of T-shirts, a lot of mugs, if we do one.

Whatever we have and then she can . . .

CV: She would be ecstatic.

EG: I mean all of this we print if necessary.

CS: Why do you handle all of this yourself? I would think that someone like Andy would coordinate it.

EG: Well, he has a lot of this stuff in New York and I have licensing and stuff, but what we've always done here is—we sell the buttons, we sell the T-shirts, we sell the posters, we sell everything for the benefit of the theaters, whichever one we were working in. Now we do it for ourselves, more or less, the actors . . .

Well, we did take all of the money from Theater on the Bay that last time.

CV: We gave all of the money to the actors.

EG: I gave it all to the actors, and I will probably give it all to them this time.

CV: That would make their lives a lot easier.

EG: Although they did offer to pay us $500 for the puppet show in Boston so . . . blame other people.

CV: Oh good. That'll cover any expenses anyhow.

EG: Well, yeah, and give the actors some anyhow.

CV: Let them have dinner and let them stay overnight if needed.

CS: So, Vincent [Myett] was originally signed on for *English Soup*, right?

EG: Has *anybody* talked to him? Oh, you talked to him, Carol?

CV: Yes, he seems to think that since you were so gracious about it [quitting the show] that you really didn't mind.

EG: Well, I don't, but does he think that he's going to be asked again?

CV: I didn't bring that up.

EG: What did he say? [*Makes embarrassed face*] Did you call him or he call you?

CV: He never said, "I'm sorry." He said, "What I've learned from this is that I really should think things through before I make commitments."

EG: Well, how many months does he need to think it through. He had about six didn't he?

CV: It was really strange.

EG: Of course, I'm so this way myself I really can't blame other people.

CV: The other thing is that he seems to be the only one who thinks it's possible and desirable to do *Macbeth* in February in the Cotuit Center for the Arts.

Phil had said, "No way am I doing that in that building in February." And Petra said, "How can you do *Macbeth* in that space?" And Eric said, "I don't like *Macbeth*." [*Laughs*]

EG: And what did Nicole say?

CV: Well, she's apparently up for it.

EG: Well she's up for anything, yeah.

CV: She's at that wonderful phase, you really like to catch an actor at that phase . . .

EG: Yeah.

CV: . . . when they're still willing to take on anything.

EG: [*Laughing*] Before she realizes it isn't doing her a great deal of good, in a career way. [*In a woman's voice*] "I'm doing tiny productions on Cape Cod. I've had a show on Broadway. I've had several shows off-Broadway." It doesn't work, kiddo, unless you're *very* lucky! [*Pointing finger*]

CV: And unless you're willing to go to New York and go to all the parties.

EG: Well, right and then . . . [*Finishes iced coffee with a flourishing slurp of the straw*]

CV: Well, one must draw the line somewhere.

EG: Well, one must . . . I'm not sure it would've done me much good anyway. Not that I care, but still . . . So Vinnie still thinks that *MacBeth* is going to take place or what?

CV: I guess so. Who knows what lurks in the brain.

EG: Well, it might very well take place. I would say offhand that it's fatal for an actor to have an idea of themselves . . .

CS: You mean to be attached to some idea . . . ?

EG: Well, or something. I mean you know . . .

"Oh well, I don't do this kind of thing." Or "This is beneath me." I mean I can see, "This show isn't right for me." But not as a blanket thing or anything that was even very obvious, necessarily. I mean one kind of, two shows that seem very much alike, one might be good for you and one might not.

Well, it's like illustrating a book. Some books I can illustrate and some I can't and only I know for sure.

CS: A project-by-project basis?

EG: Yeah. Not that I haven't illustrated a lot of books I was no good for but only I realized it. At least as far as I know.

CS: What would those be?

EG: Oh, I can think of . . . Oh, I've done more awful work than you'd believe humanly possible. I don't like to think about it! [*In a sing-songy voice and holding his fingers up*] I like to take the positive attitude and open up my little portfolio. [*Turning invisible pages*]

"Oh, isn't that nice!" [*Blows tongue and rolls eyes*] Anywho.

CV: You should see his show at the Cartoon Museum, Chris.

CS: The what museum?

CV: In between shows, Edward has been creating absolutely gorgeous things. And I see them on the walls and I think, "How did that happen? How did I not even know about this?"

CS: Like what?

CV: The current WGBH catalog, for example . . .

EG: Well, yeah.

CV: The lithographs are like this big and they're just beautiful.

EG: Well, actually I'm always coming across things like that. I came across something the other day and thought, "What in the name of God was this for?" It was terribly complicated. And I thought, "I haven't a clue." It must've appeared in a magazine.

Actually, when it turns out that there was no text, it means that it was a drawing for a magazine or something but then I've forgotten what the magazine was or anything, you know.

CS: Didn't I see a Figbash doll? I think it was a photograph from the fifties with you and a large doll of some sort.

EG: Oh, *The Doubtful Guest*.

CS: Yes, *The Doubtful Guest*. Wouldn't something like that really sell?

EG: Well, somebody did once make a limited-edition *Doubtful Guest* [*holds hands about a foot tall*] by hand, which were about this height. I've got one somewhere. They're probably as scarce as hen's teeth now because I think there were only fifty of them and I think they sold for, I don't know, they were very expensive. And they were very beautifully done.

That one you saw with me in the photograph was one, in fact there were two, that I've seen.

[*Jack Braginton-Smith brings two hamburgers over again; he's clearly been using them as props.*]

JB-S: Excuse me, am I at the wrong table?

EG: Thank you, Jack. [*Not looking at him*] Don't freeze your fingers on those cold hamburgers, which you keep resurrecting.

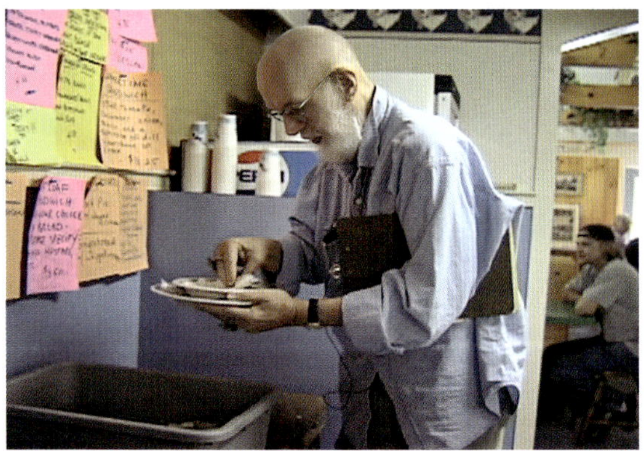

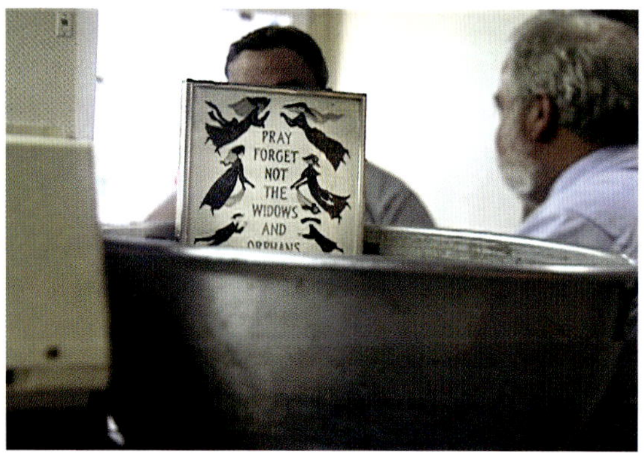

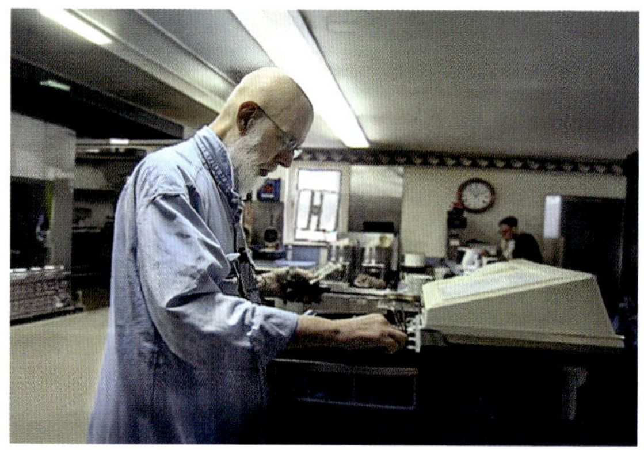

CS: Are they real hamburgers?

CV: Jack's trademark Thumb Burgers. [*Pointing to Jack's thumbprints on top of the buns*]

CS: So, the Doubtful Guest dolls . . .

EG: [*Getting back to the topic*] Well, there were two Doubtful Guests, one was good and one was not so good.

The one in the photograph was not so good, and I don't know what became of it.

CV: Oh, that reminds me, what do you want to do about the scarf?

EG: Oh, hopefully we can find a long striped scarf someplace.

CV: Colleges.

EG: [*With a look of pain*] They don't do them so much anymore. In the old days you used to be able to buy an 8- or 9-foot one, and I haven't seen one that was 6 feet long for years and years and years. They're usually about like this. [*Holds hands 3 feet apart*]

CS: Yeah, they make them really small now, they hardly wrap around your neck.

EG: I know, and they don't do the big wooly ones anymore.

CV: We could always knit one. I used to know how. Scarves were the limit of my ability.

EG: Yeah, I suppose we might find someone who knits.

Camera person Jennifer Pitman: I saw one last week at J.Crew. They have a big sale with really long scarves.

EG: They do? Oh, where was that J.Crew sale, is it all over now?

JP: Yeah, it was at the Sheraton Tara.

EG: Yeah, I picked up a flyer and you couldn't tell where it was the way it was printed.

JP: They had really long scarves there, really long.

EG: Oh really? Well, maybe the new J.Crew catalog will have one in it. I'll look. I used to have dozens of them [scarves] but the moths got them, you know, this, that, and the other thing. But that's a thought.

CV: Maybe the Harvard Catalog.

CS: And how about a *Doubtful Guest* board game?

CV: Have you ever done a board game, Edward?

EG: No. Actually I wanted to do a board game once and I haven't thought about it in years. It had one of the conventional board game gimmicks obviously, but . . . heavens. [*Bites lip in frustration*] Oh . . .

CV: This is worth resurrecting.

EG: Carol, you don't know what resurrection around my house is like! [*Laughs*] It's like digging up bodies. It's like trying to rescue someone from a mine that's been down there for years!

[*Noticing the clock*] Oh dear, yes, well, should we get out of this hellhole? What store are you going to now, Carol?

CV: I'm going to several. Let me just check my list, I'm going to Super Stop & Shop.

EG: [*Leafing through flea market info in a newspaper and reading aloud*] Oodles of beads!

CV: [*Now looking at the paper too*] And a hair tassel workshop for kids!

[*They get up and carry their dishes to the bins.*]

[*Jack Braginton-Smith appears with the two hamburgers again.*]

JB-S: Oh, hi. Are these yours?

EG: Oh yes, those are ours. Would you take them to the yellow booth? [*Motions behind him. They're all yellow. He then walks behind the counter and starts ringing his order at the register, squinting at the keys.*]

Customer: I didn't think they paid you enough to work the cash register, Mr. Gorey. [*As she exits*]

[*Edward puts money into the register and flags down Jack.*]

EG: Excuse me, sir, we never got our two hamburgers, so I didn't bother to pay for them.

JB-S: You didn't? [*Feigns anger*]

EG: No, I didn't bother to pay for them.

JB-S: Oh. [*Starts to walk away, as if to snub him*]

EG: It's all right, I'll still come back some time. Maybe not tomorrow, but sometime.

JB-S: Well, it's been wonderful. [*Sarcastically*]

EG: Oh thank you . . . [*Long groan as he examines a musical concert flyer at the door*]

CV: Let's count the frogs [in the frog pond outside the door].

EG: [*As he exits*] Oh, right!

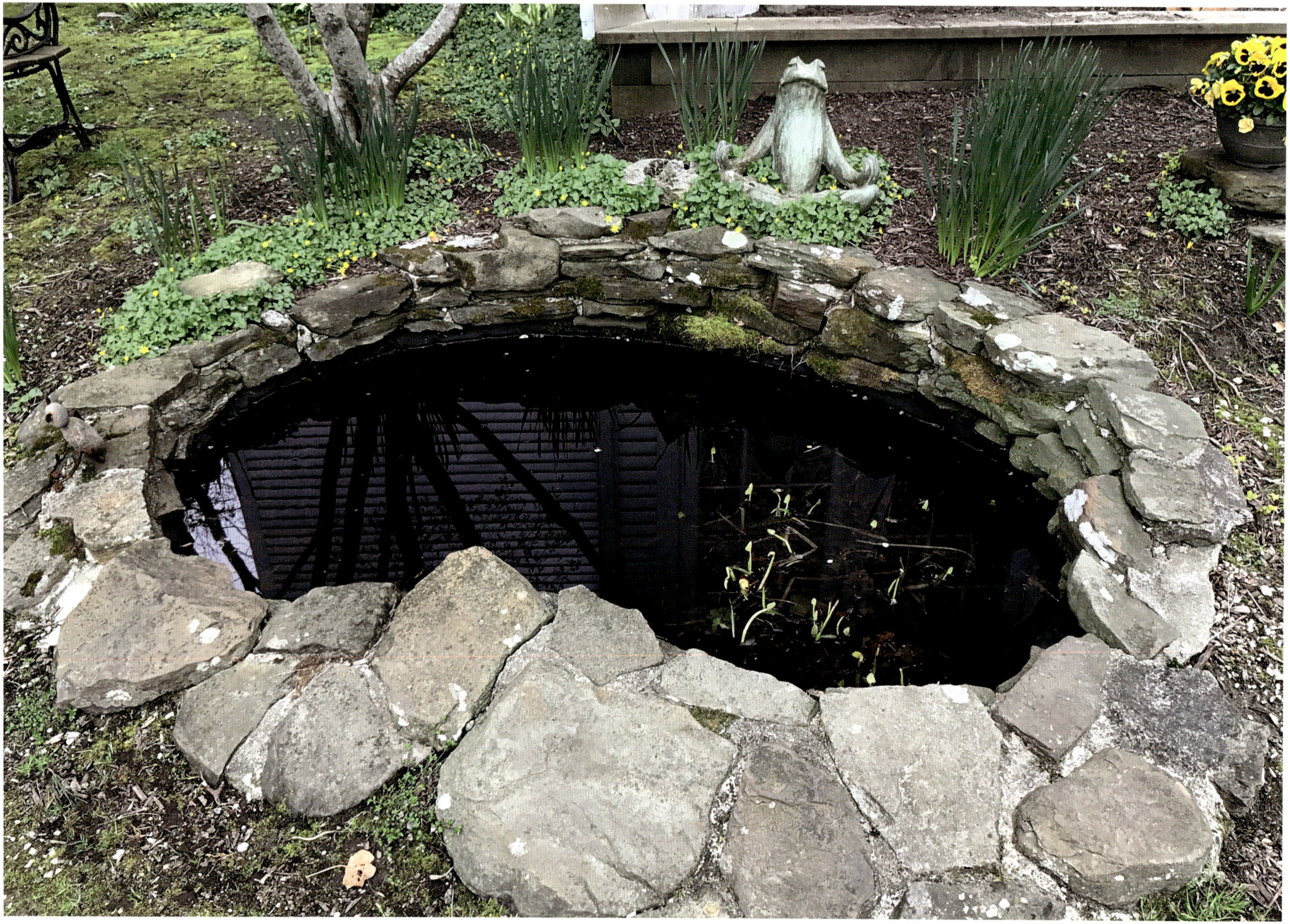

Upon leaving Jack's, Edward would often count the frogs hiding in the lily pads of the koi pond. A five-frog day meant good luck.

CV: There's two. [*Pointing*]

EG: There's two on the ledge, three on the ledge. [*Scanning*]

CV: There's a green one and that's a brown one.

EG: Well, yes.

CV: And on the lily pad.

EG: Oh, I see, that's four.

CV: Oh, I think that's all we have today, that's good. A four-frog day?

EG: There's that pink goldfish.

CV: Oh, here's five!

EG: Oh yes. Heavens! A five-frog day! Keep up the good work, frogs. Wow.

[*We get into his Volkswagen.*]

EG: Are we ready? [*Classical music starts; he is driving me to his house for an interview while the crew follows in a separate car.*]

CS: How do you like your new car? [It's a 1996 VW Golf]

EG: I like it very much, it's about two years old now. Yeah, I like it very much.

CS: The Golfs have an unbelievable service record, from what I hear.

EG: I'm leasing it, so whenever something goes wrong I just bring it in and say, "Fix it! You owe me!" [*Humming to the music*]

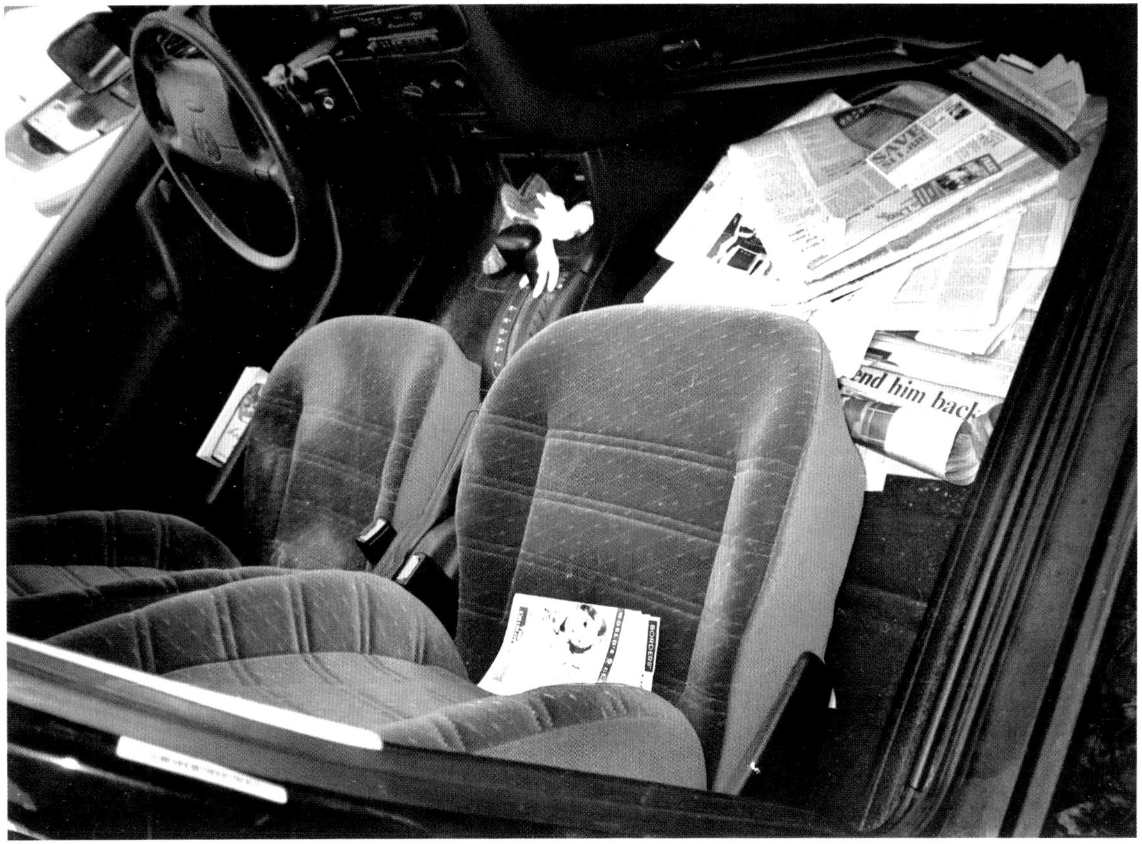

Edward's car always held a current book [*The Life of the Bronte Sisters* here] to read and assorted stuffed animals and Figbashes. Sometimes a theater review.

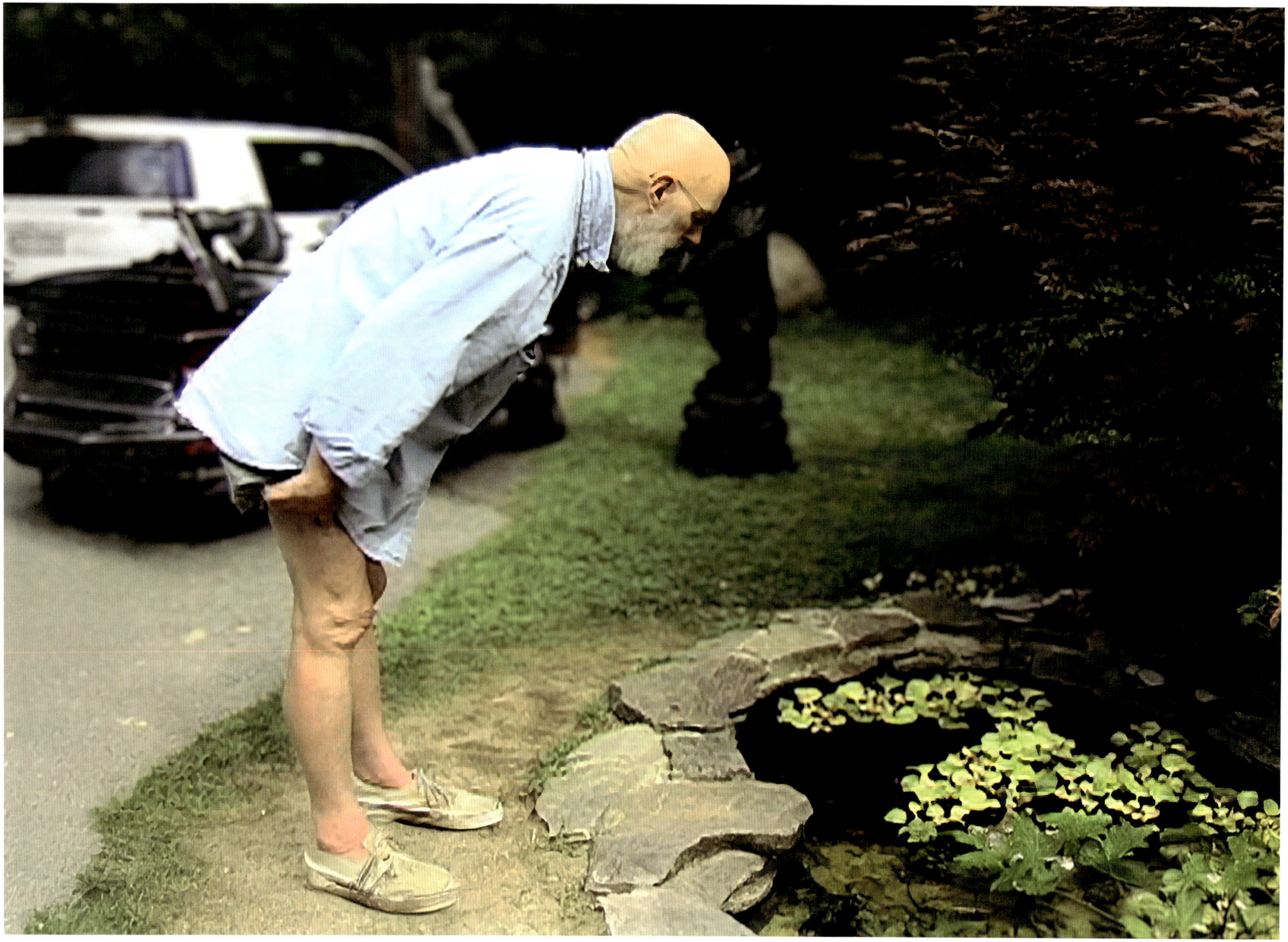

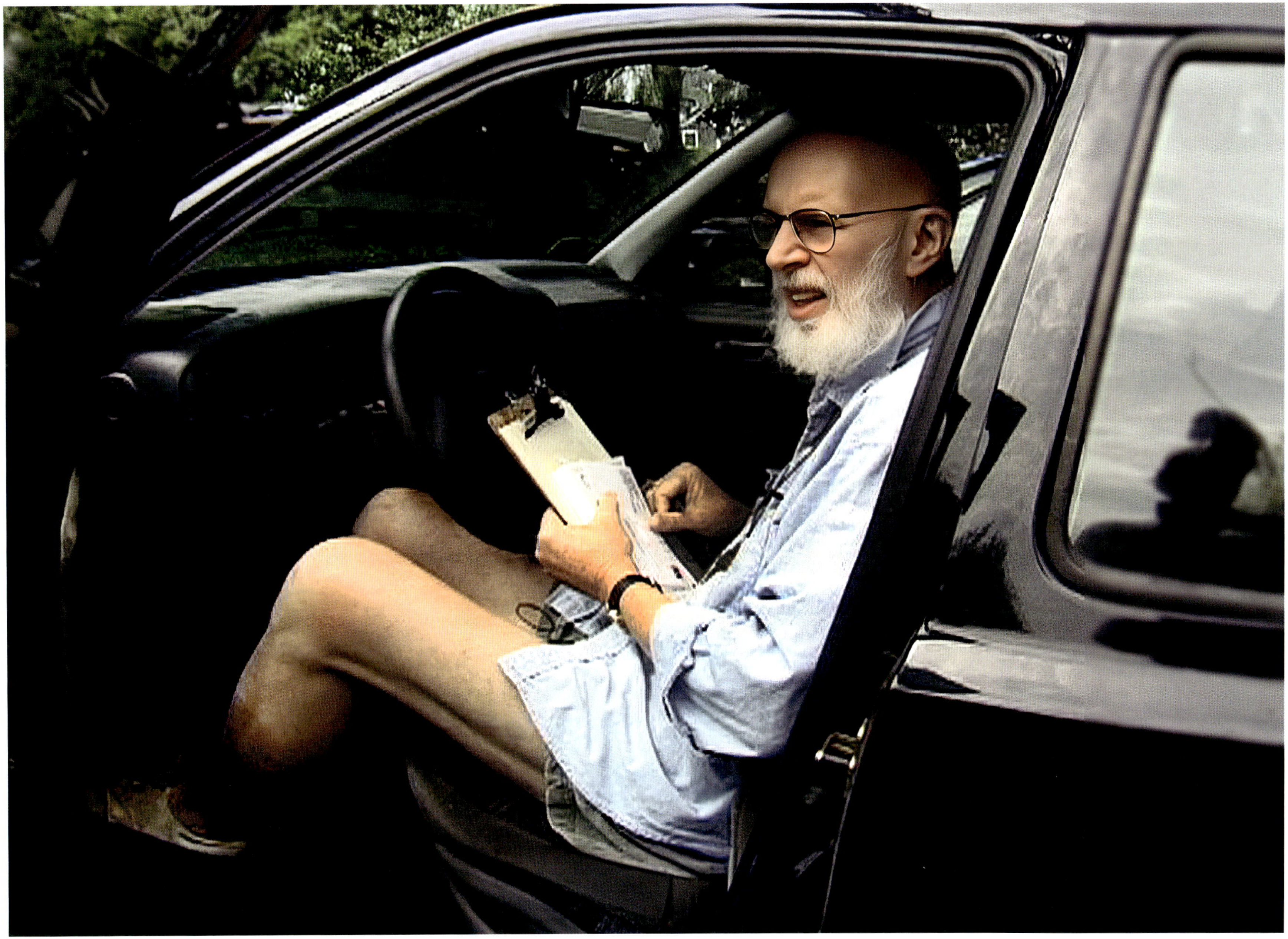

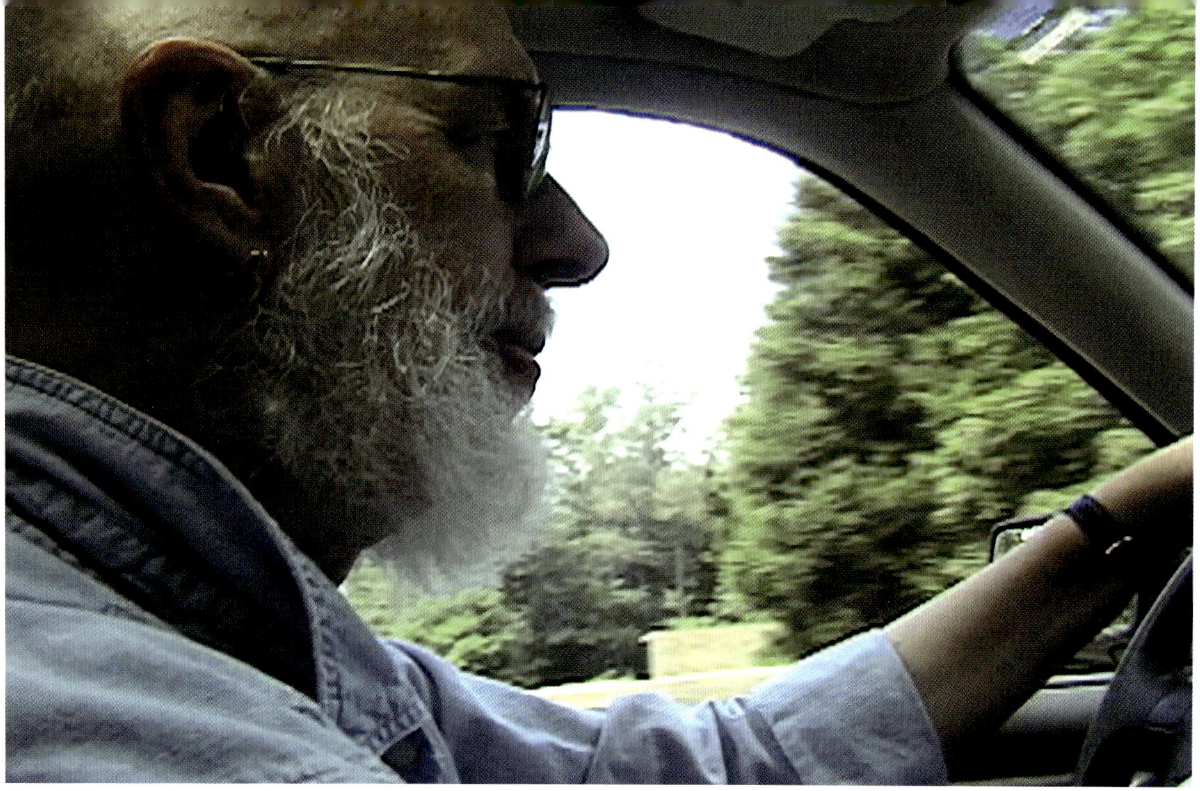

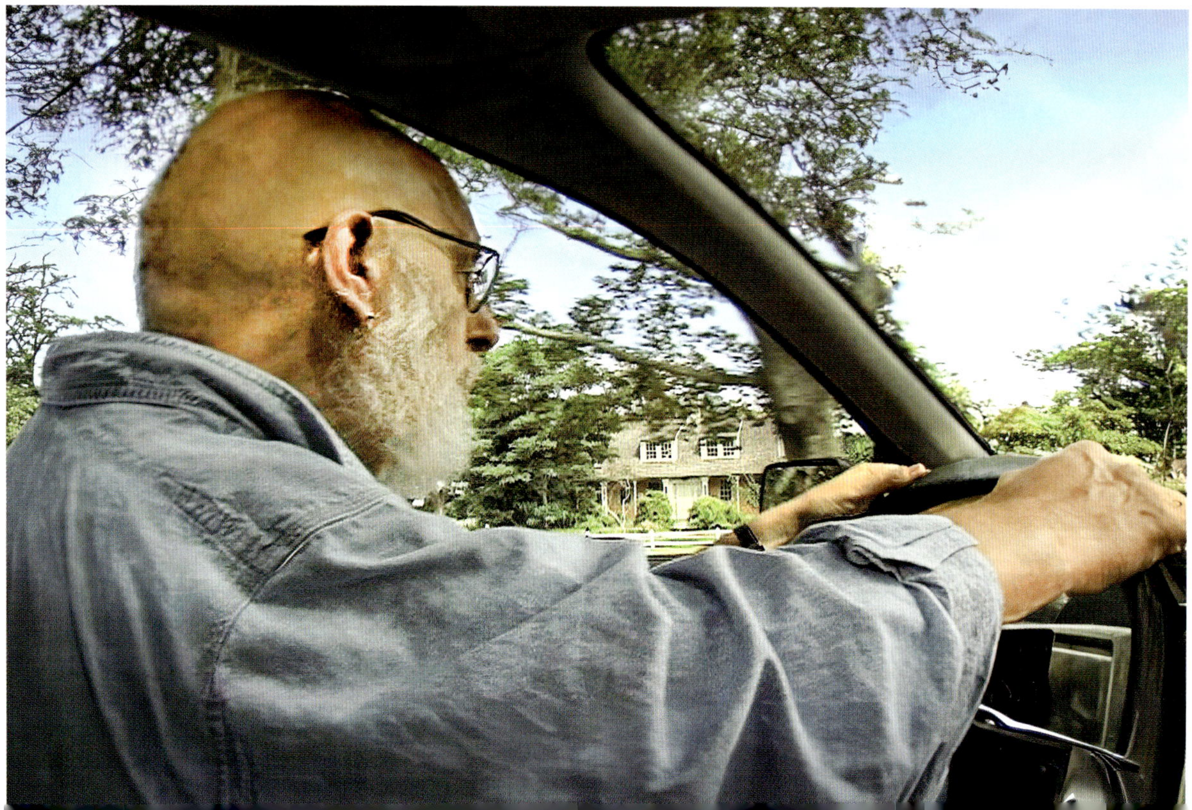

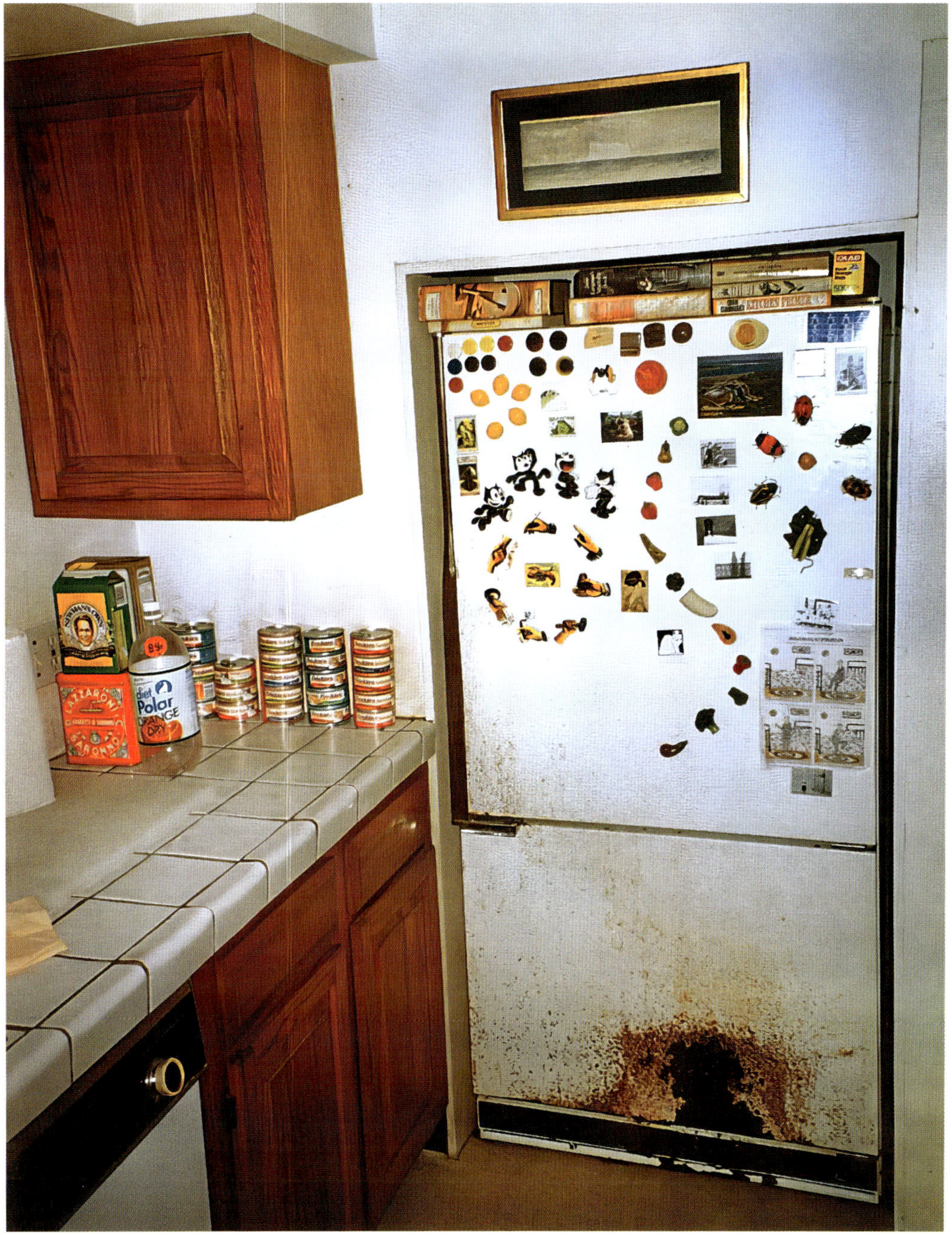

Part of Edward's ongoing art exhibit in his house was an ever changing design of refrigerator magnets. He paid the cat pee degrading the refrigerator door no mind, just as he ignored the hole in his wall created by the raccoons. Like a true New Englander he enjoyed Polar Orange Dry.

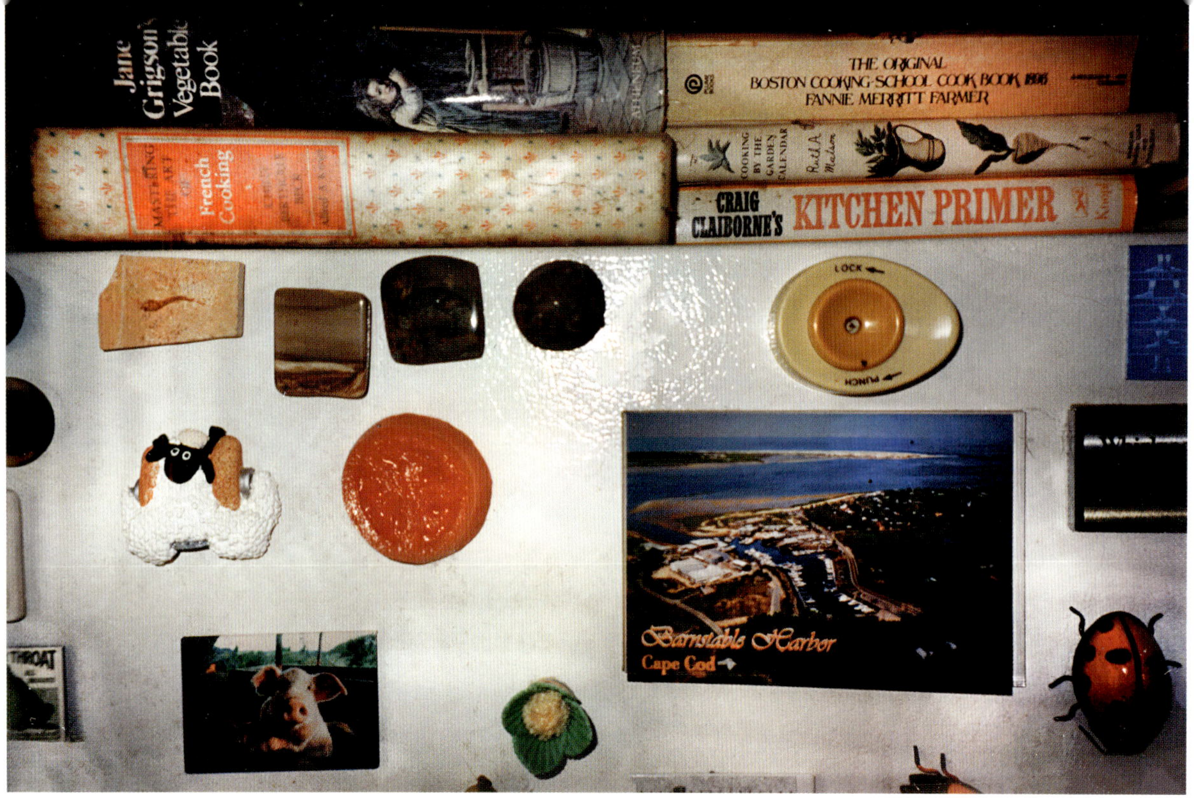
Jane Grigson's Vegetable Book
THE ORIGINAL
BOSTON COOKING-SCHOOL COOK BOOK 1896
FANNIE MERRITT FARMER
French Cooking
CRAIG CLAIBORNE'S KITCHEN PRIMER
LOCK
PUNCH
Barnstable Harbor
Cape Cod

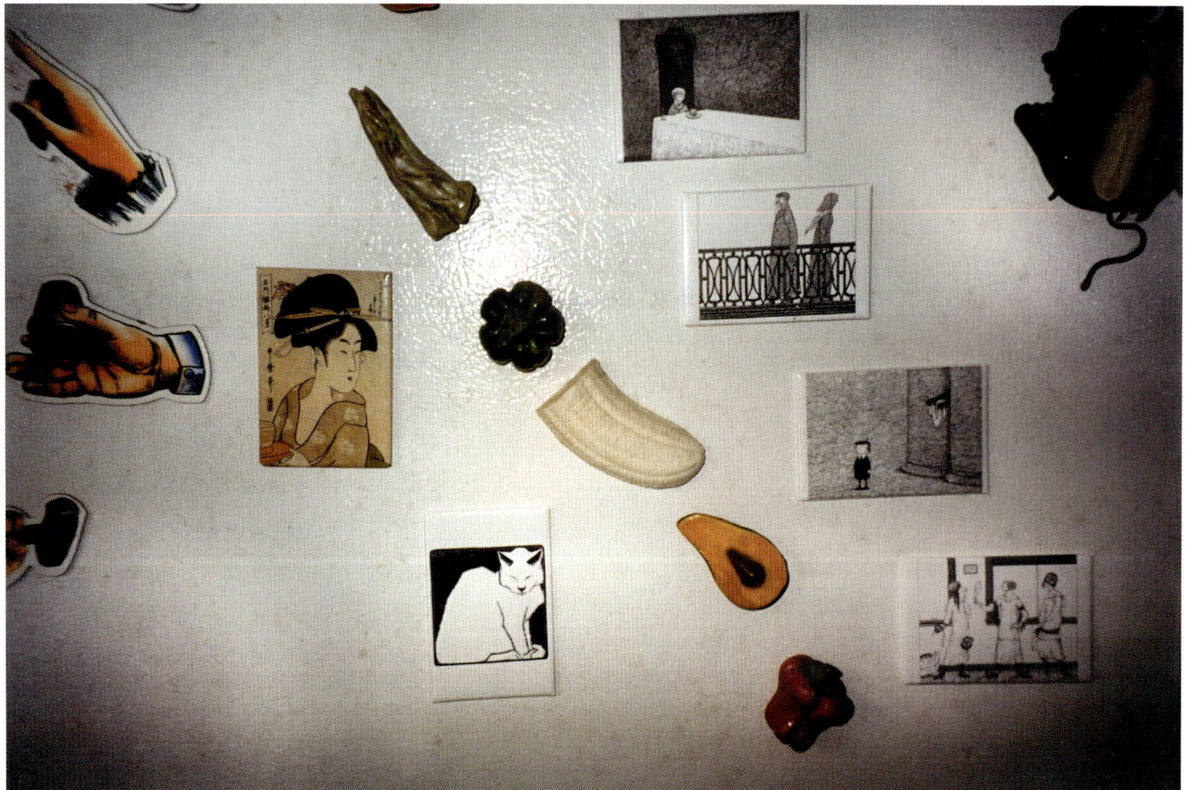

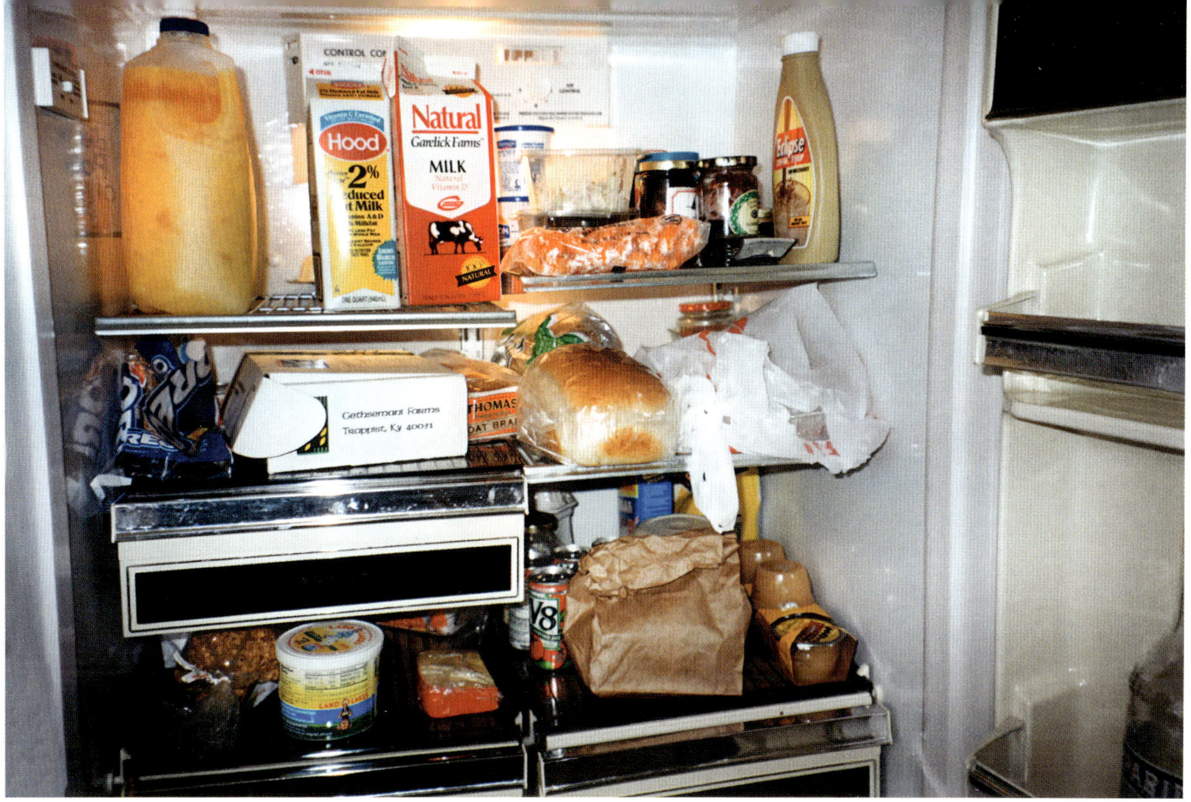
Hood
2%
Natural
Garelick Farms
MILK
Gethsemani Farms
Trappist, Ky 40051
THOMAS

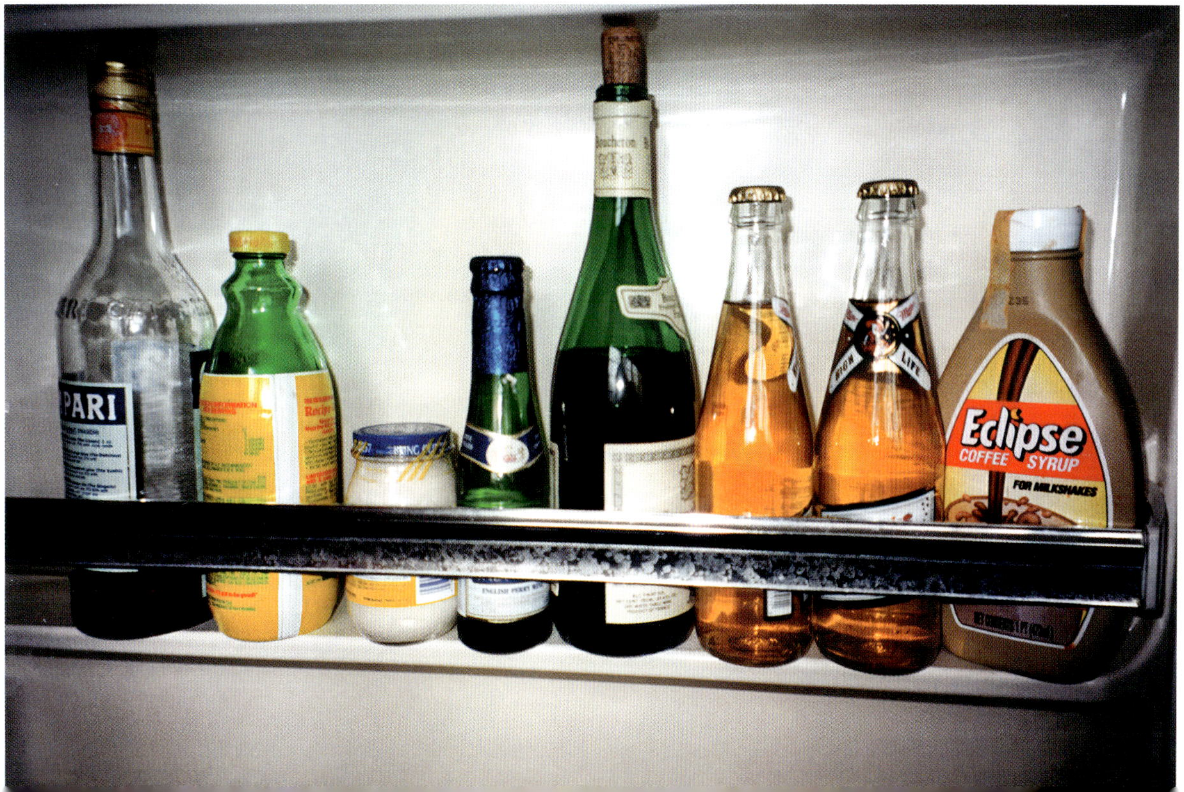
Eclipse
COFFEE SYRUP
FOR MILKSHAKES

Gorey's freezer. He was quite a good cook, occasionally hosting dinners for family and friends. He was a light drinker but enjoyed a great variety of beer, wine, and cocktails, including frozen strawberry daiquiris.

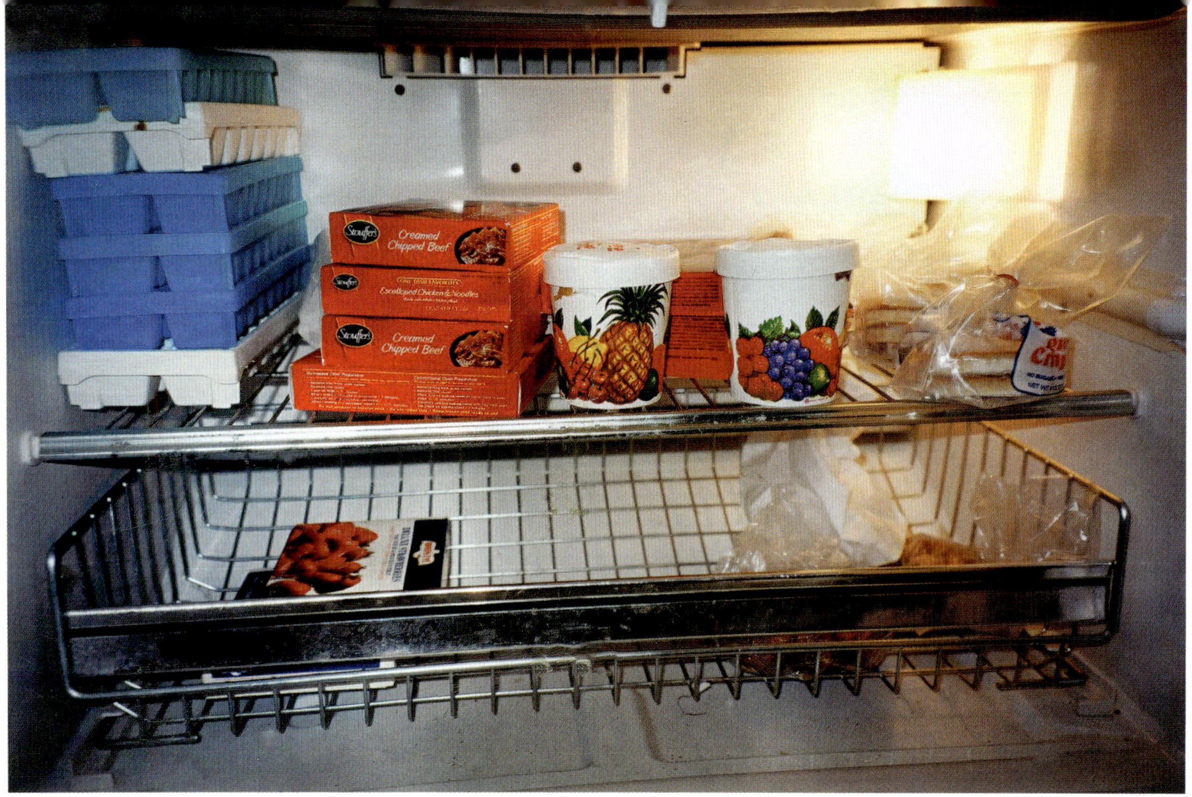

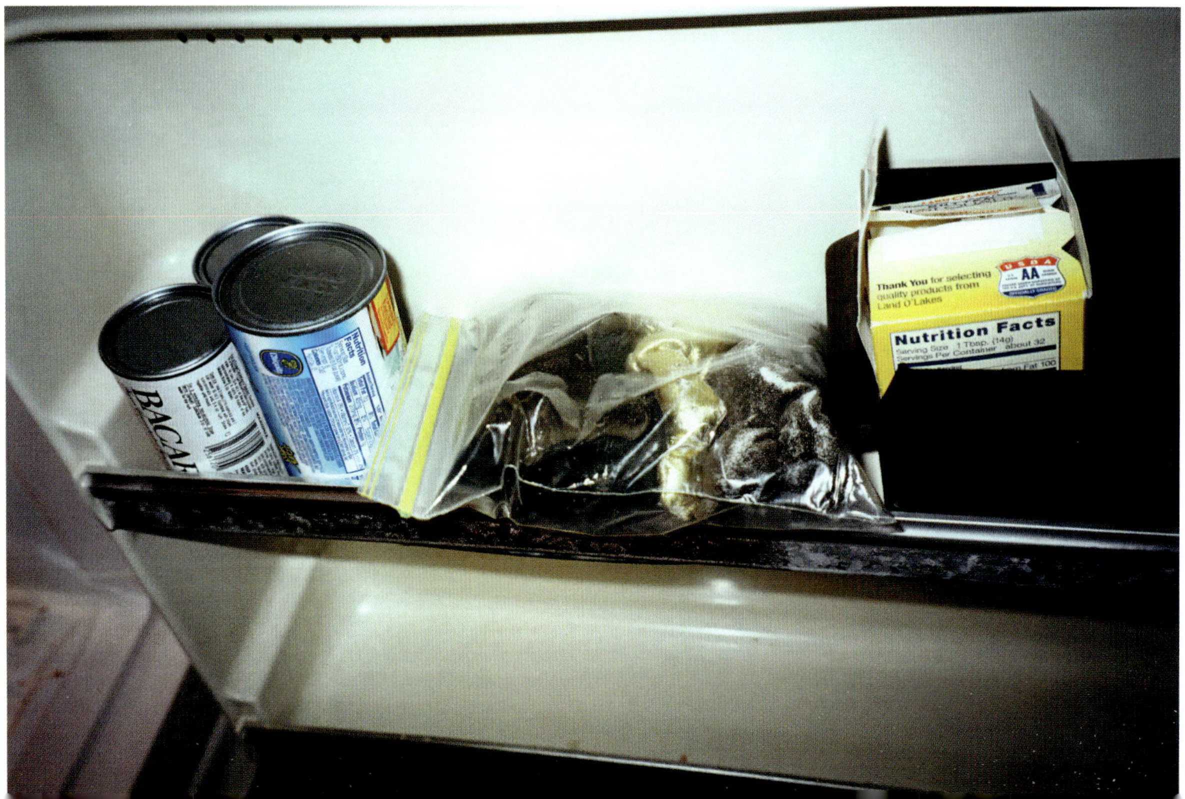

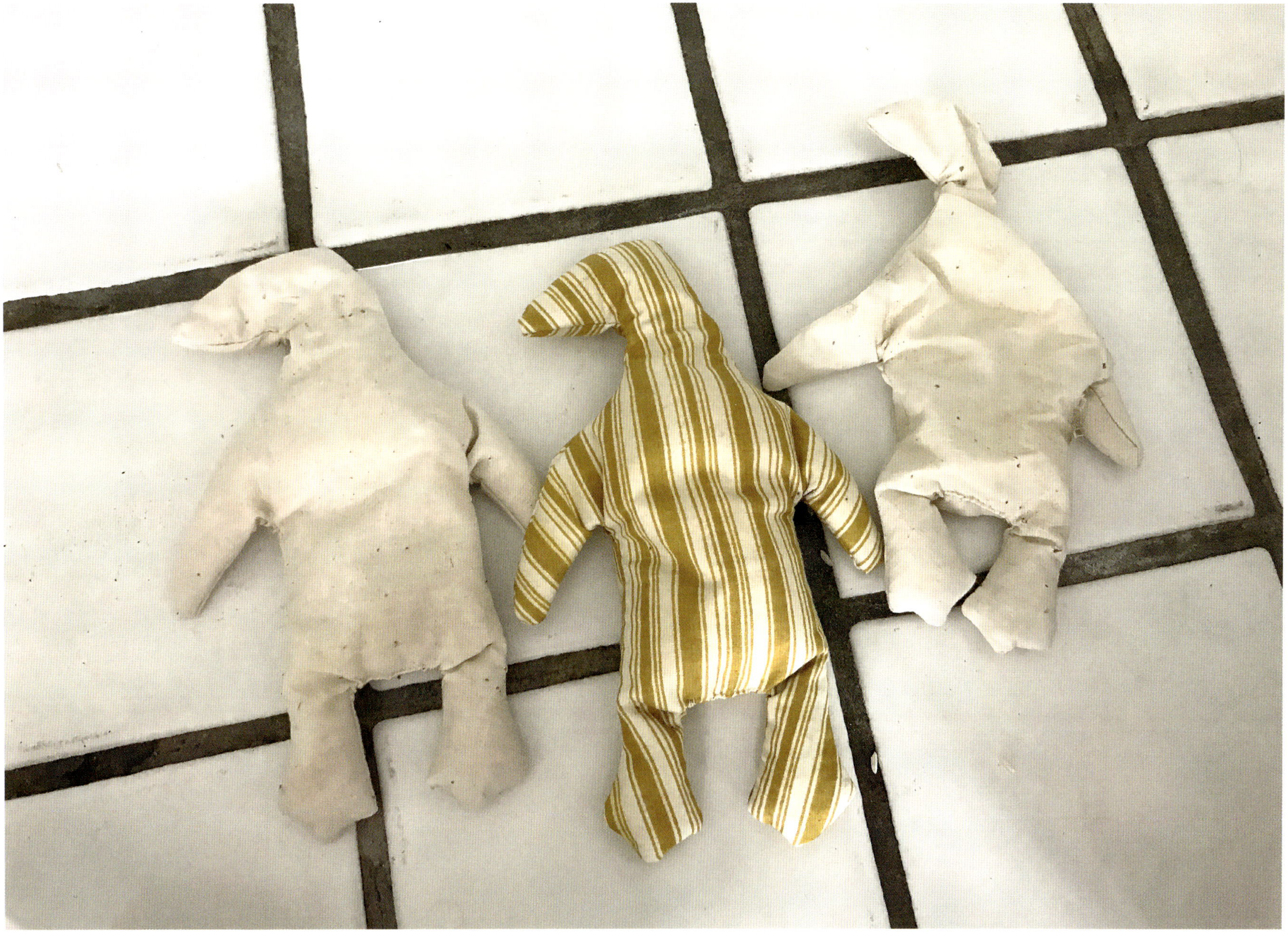

Several stuffed Figbashes that were in his freezer door.

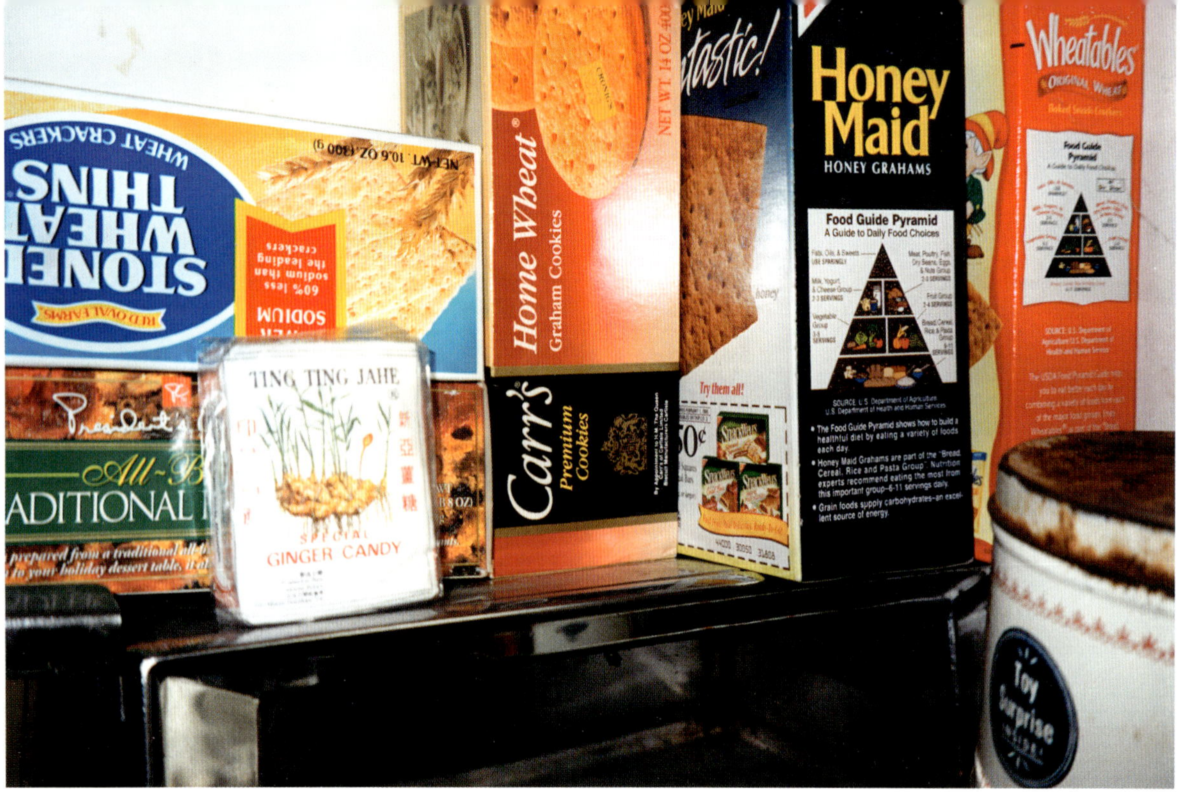
STONED WHEAT THINS
WHEAT CRACKERS
Home Wheat
Graham Cookies
Carr's
Premium Cookies
Honey Maid
HONEY GRAHAMS
Food Guide Pyramid
A Guide to Daily Food Choices
Wheatables
TING TING JAHE
SPECIAL
GINGER CANDY
Toy Surprise

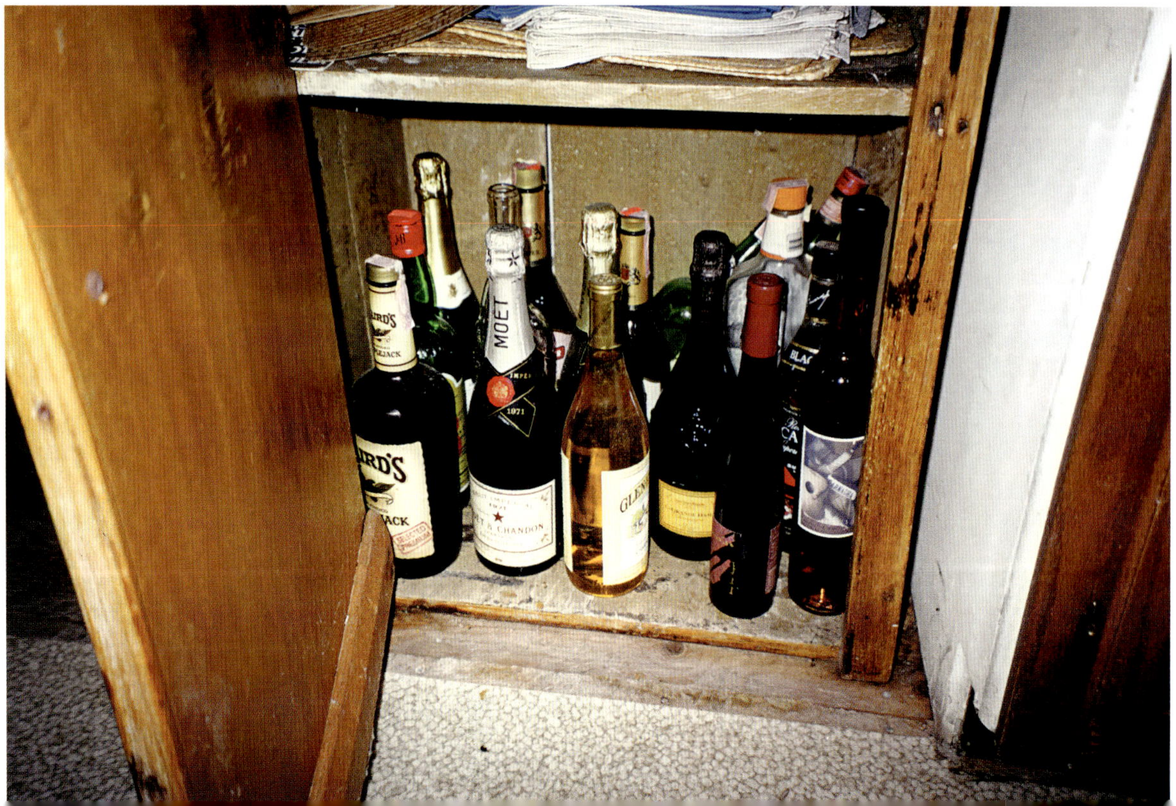
MOET

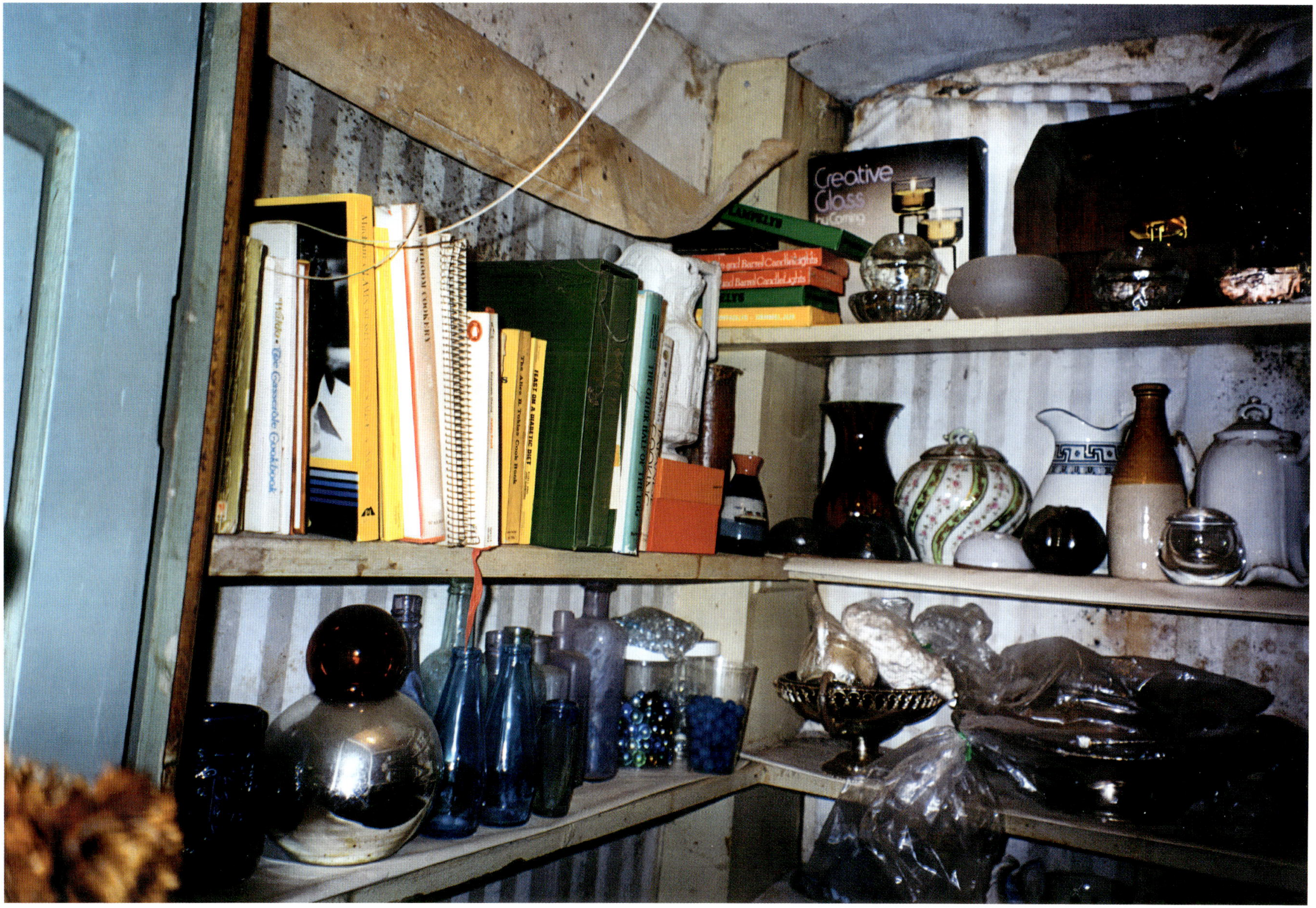
Creative Glass

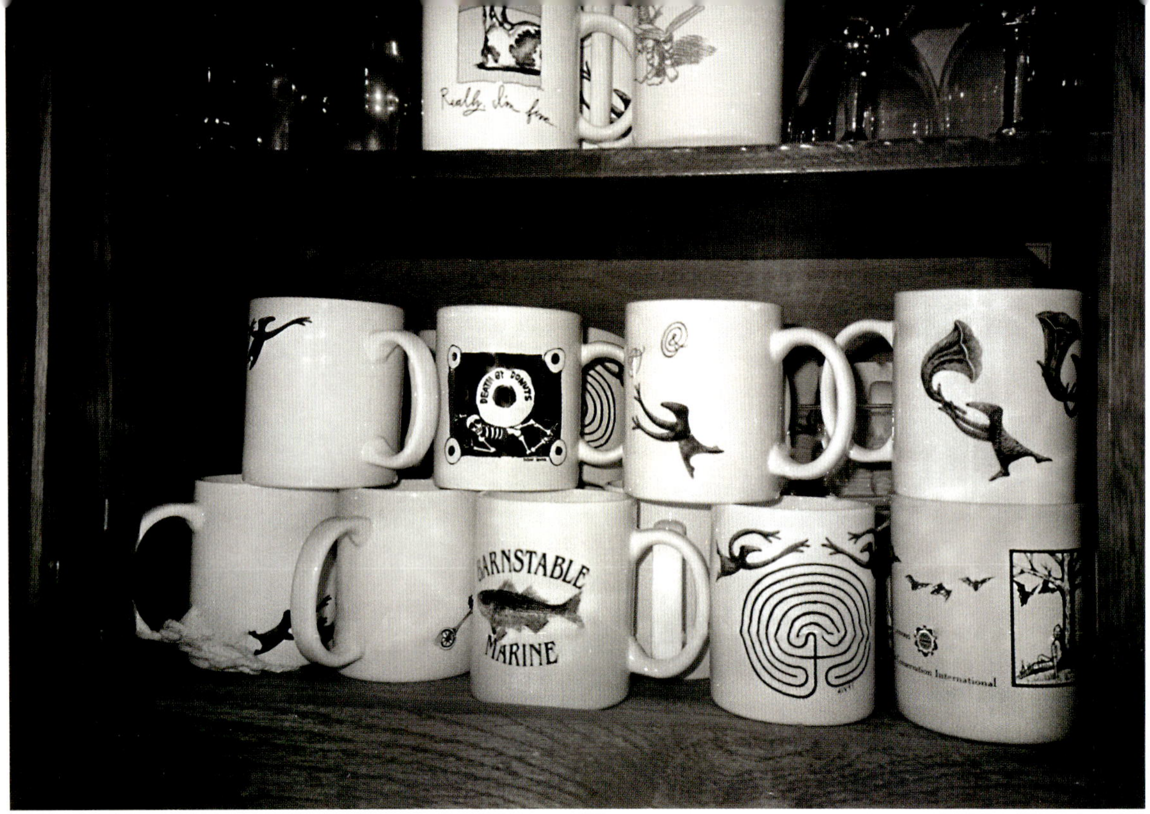
BARNSTABLE
MARINE

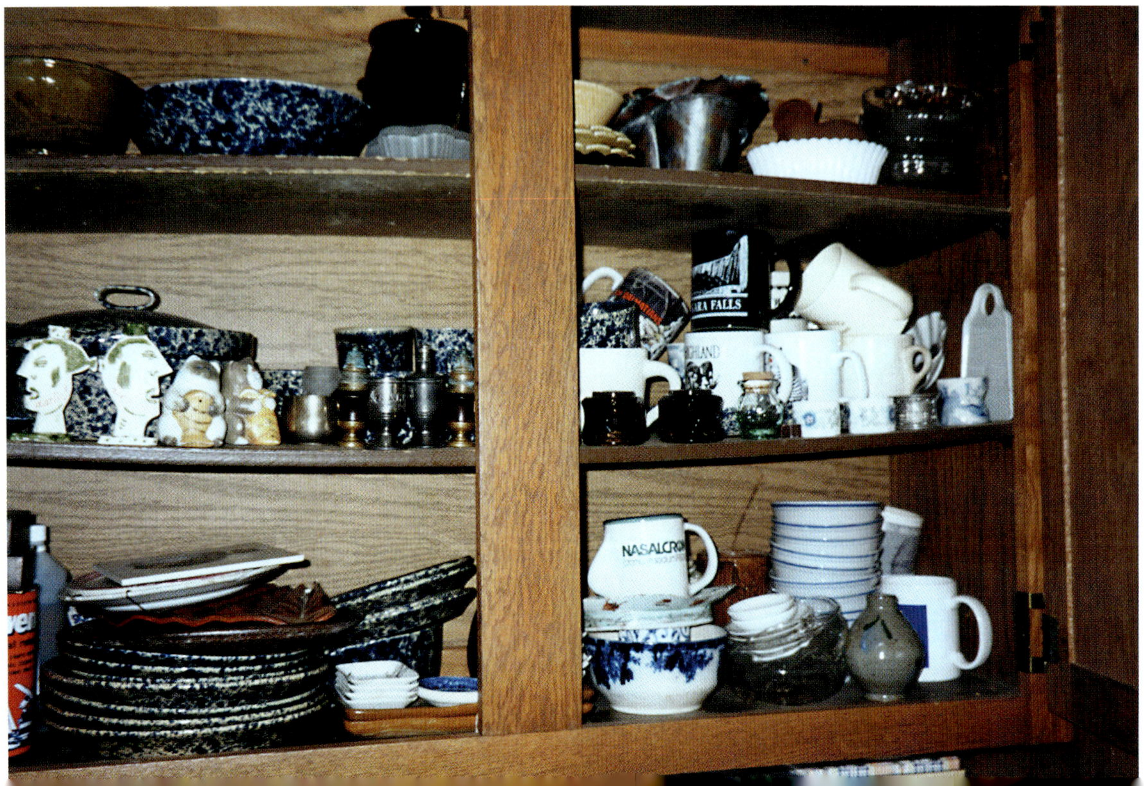
NASALCROM

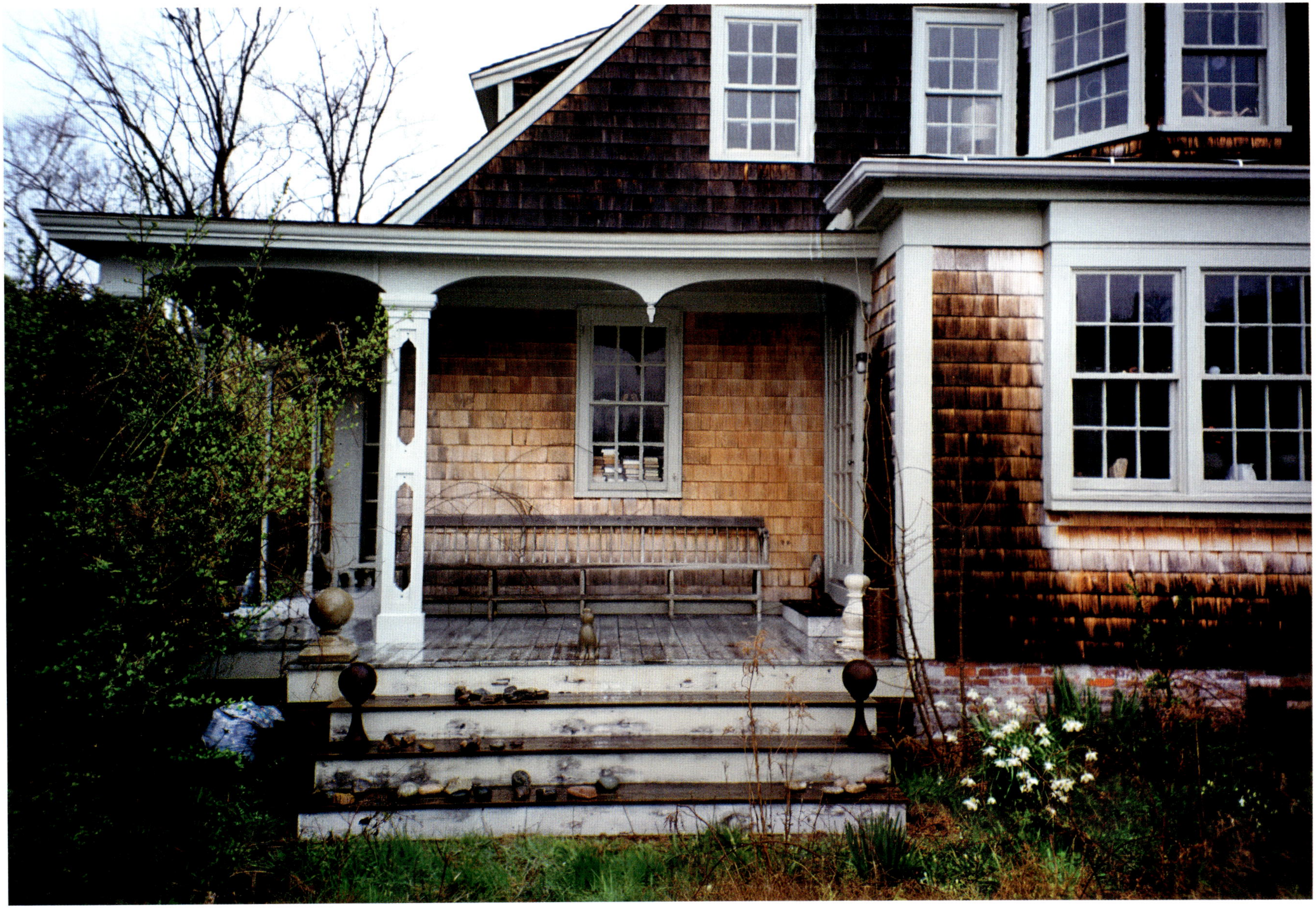

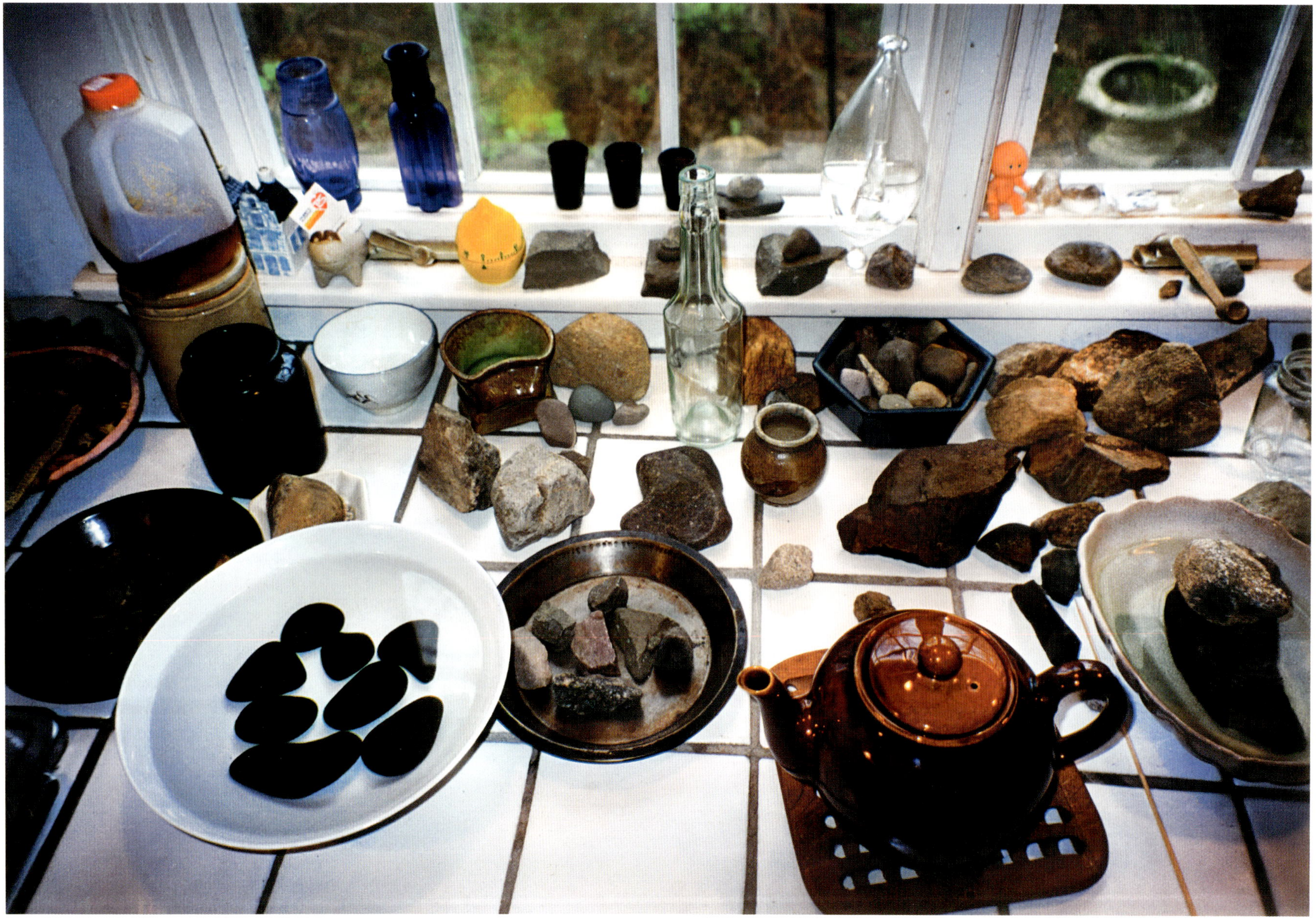

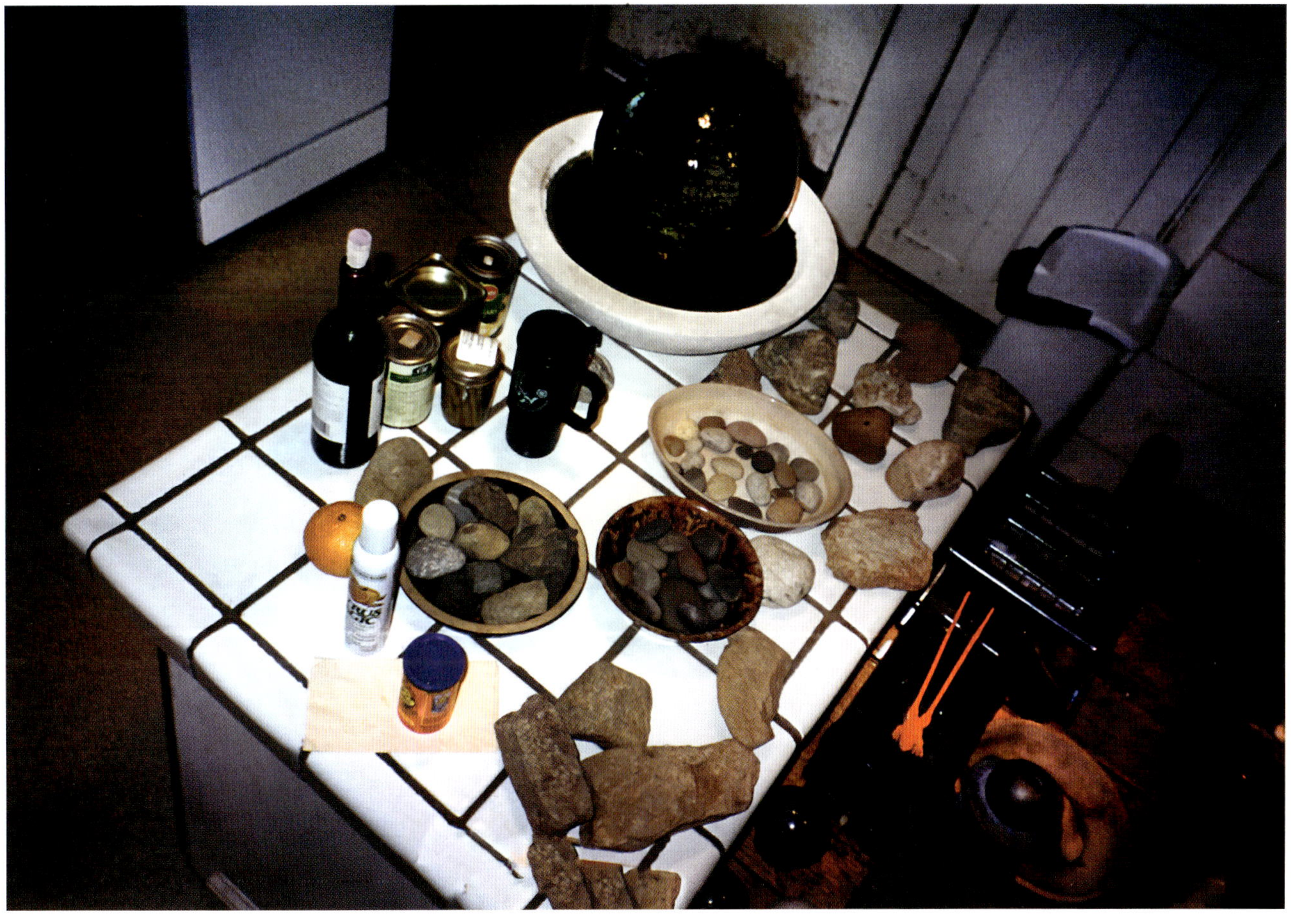

It's fair to say that Edward did not cultivate much open countertop or shelf space. He was actively creating the ongoing museum of objects that surrounded him. He loved rocks of all kinds of material and shape. It wasn't always clear why he picked a certain one to bring home; usually they looked like faces or animals. I believe he also found them grounding in some way. He preserved the aesthetic quality that he admired by keeping them in dishes of water, to retain their original aesthetic, which was paramount. On one of my visits he had just received a box containing a very heavy fountain that he had ordered from the Signals catalog at PBS. He said, "It may have to live in that box for eternity" when I inquired about assembling it. Some time after, it appeared on the kitchen island with water in it (*center top*), but without the motor gurgling. It was an outdoor fountain meant for the garden.

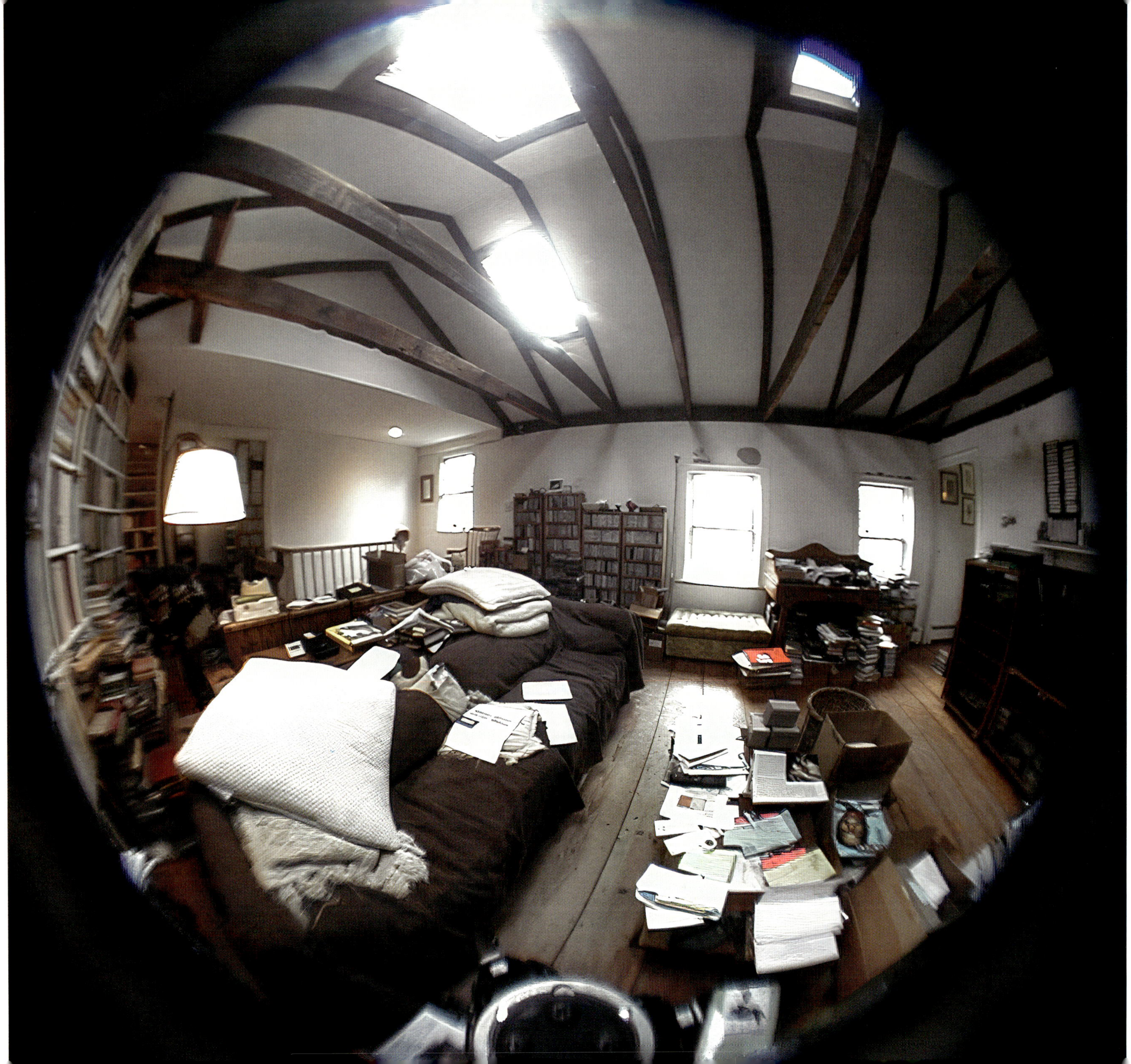

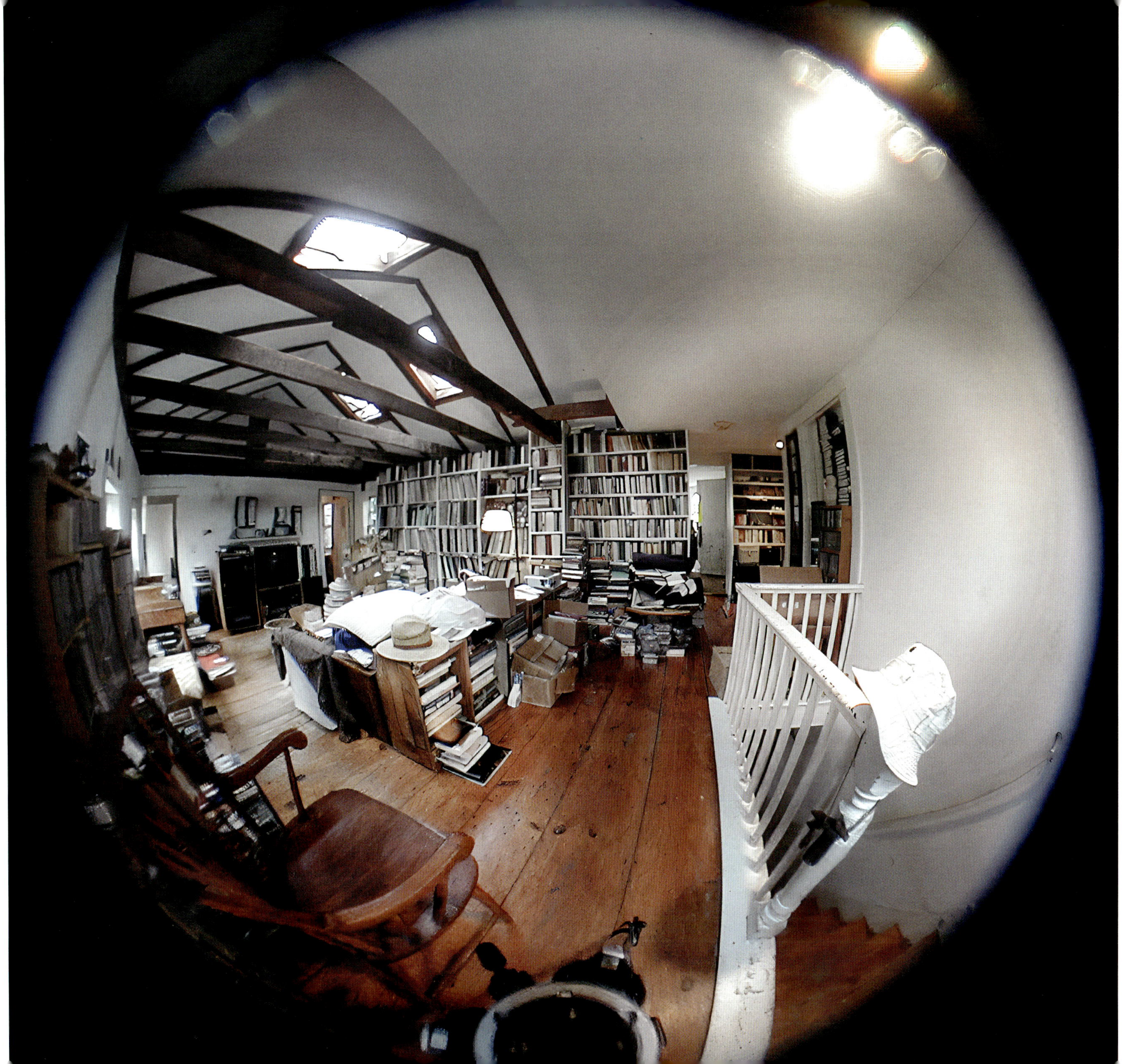

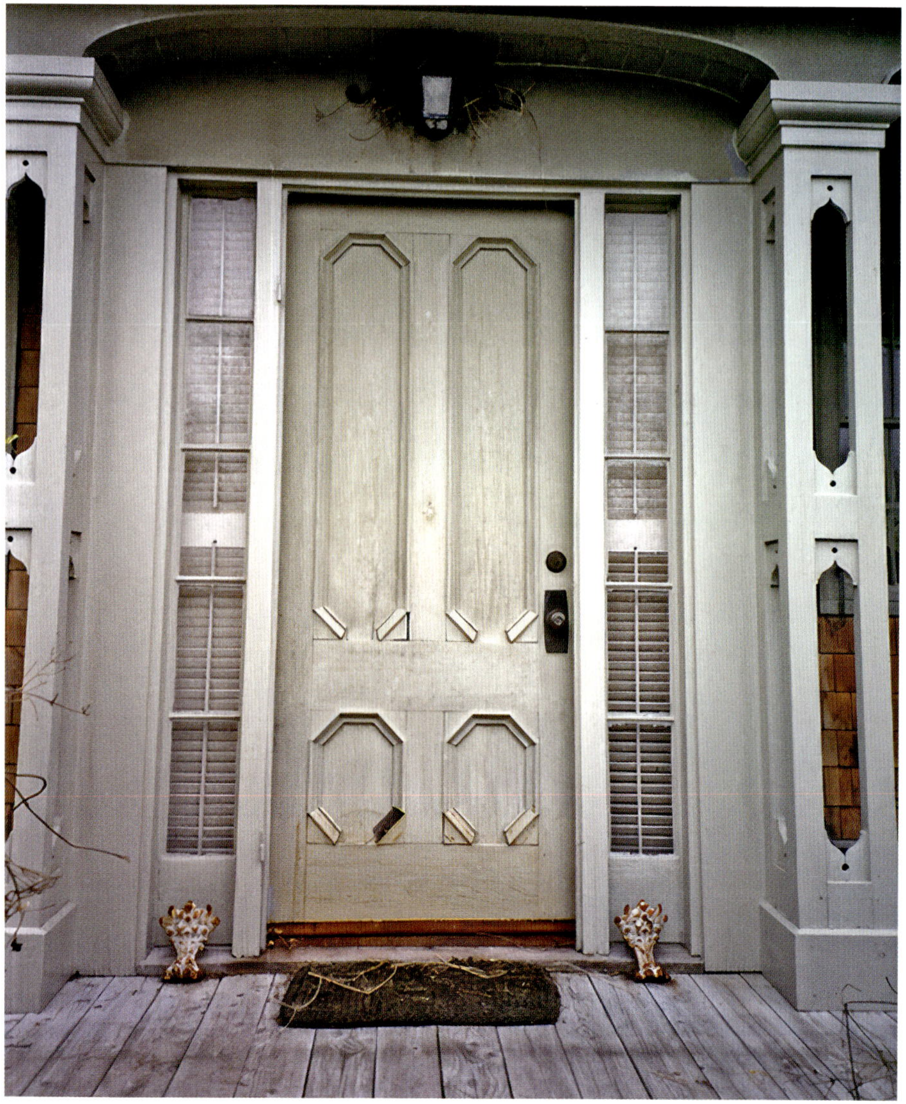

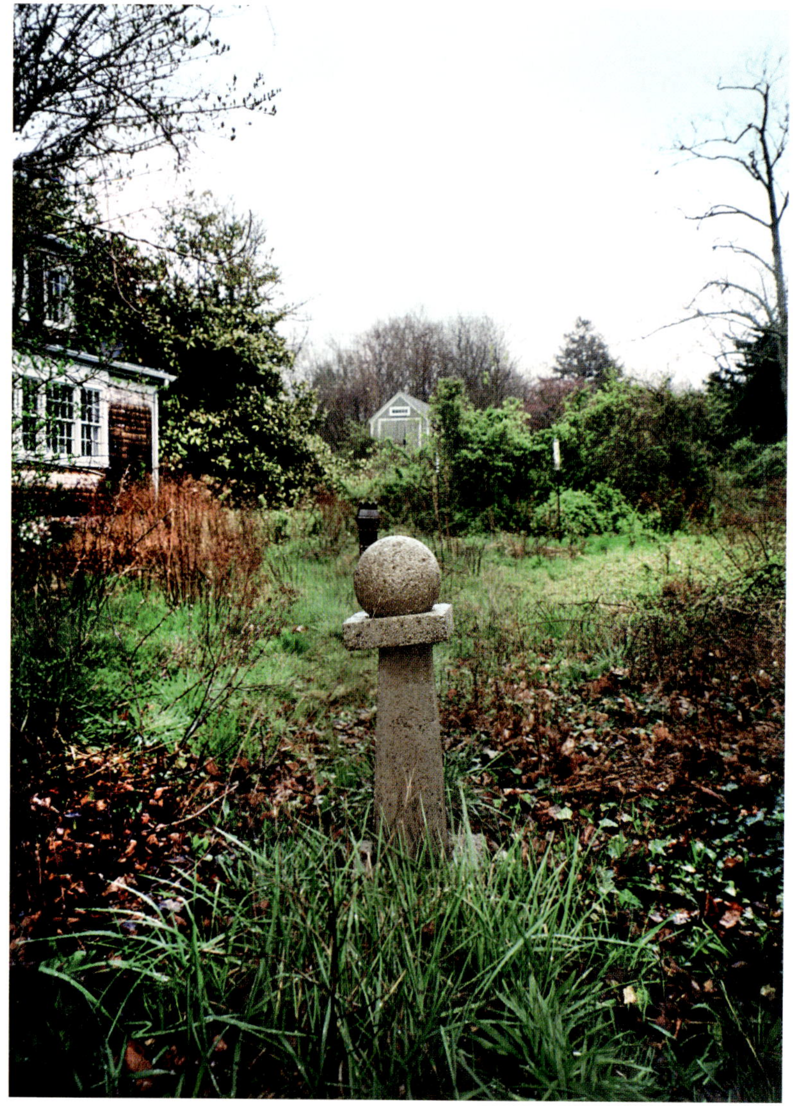

Interview with Edward Gorey: Edward's Kitchen

AUGUST 22, 1998

After the lunch interview on this day, camerawoman Jennifer Pitman and I went back with Edward to his home to shoot him illustrating at his desk. He sat at his kitchen table and went through mail while having a casual conversation with Jenn while I shot around the two floors of his house. Once we convened again as a group, he informed us that he really didn't feel like working and would prefer to just sit and talk. In this way, we would lean more into the types of footage Edward wanted to do, and kept the pressure minimal on him to *perform* for the camera.

CS: [*Pulling up to Gorey's house and noticing objects on Edward's porch*] Do you ever worry about your public stuff here getting stolen by fanatical Gorey fans?

EG: No, I don't really think that is much of a problem. I may talk out of the other side of my face later on, of course.

CS: I was just thinking that someone recognizing your OGDRED license plate may . . .

EG: That's true.

CS: I mean that would be really insidious to steal from someone that you like so much.

EG: [*Whistles happily to music as he parks in the driveway*] Oh, here we are. I'd pull up if I were you. [*Motioning to camerawoman in the car behind him*] People drive down here like maniacs, let's put it that way.

[*Sirens travel by*] Oh please, we weren't going that fast!

[*Opens front door with a kick of his foot; sighs.*] We don't want the cats rushing out.

[*Whistles a tune as he walks through the cluttered foyer*]

Oh, hi, Jane! All right, Jane. Out of the way [*in a baby voice*]. Out of the way, Jane.

Yes, it is you, Jane, who should be out of the way. [*Whistles as he enters the kitchen and thumbs through his mail at the table*]

CS: Why do you call her Jane?

EG: Aahhh well, I had to call her something and . . . actually she has a Japanese name but I can't remember it. [*Laughs*] And so she's, ahh . . . There's Weedon. Oh, hi, Weedon. That's the last you'll see of him, I assure you. [*Opens door for Jennifer Pitman*]

CS: [*In warning*] There are a lot of cats in here, Jen.

EG: There are a lot of cats, so just come in and I'll close the door.

CS: You can just leave the equipment there.

EG: [*Talking to himself and going through a pile of clothes by the door*] Could I have?

No, I couldn't have. What in the hell is all that? What in the name of heaven is this?!

EG: These are all the wrong posters, very strange, very strange.

CS: So this is the one cat you were telling me.

EG: Yes, this is the one cat. [*Flopping tiredly down at the kitchen table*]

CS: How old is she?

EG: Oh, somewhere between six and eight, I'm not really sure. She's becoming middle-aged, well, sort of middle-aged, let's put it that way.

CS: I've got a cat that I got at a baseball game in high school in '85, and he's thirteen now and still looks incredible, he really hasn't aged.

EG: Well, cats don't as a rule, I think, until they get very old. The oldest cat I had lived to be twenty-one. I did know one cat who was twenty-five, I think, and may have lived a couple of years even after that.

CS: Wow!

EG: It was a Persian, long hair, and they used to take it out in New York City with them.

CS: The apartments were perpendicular to the street, and there was a kind of grassy area, and they would take her out there. She didn't run around exactly, she didn't look rickety or anything, but of course they don't turn gray the way dogs do.

CS: That's amazing. Did you bring some cats with you from New York?

EG: None of my cats now have been in New York. The last, well now, let's see . . .

CS: Because they do have a tendency to want to walk back to where they came from, even for many miles.

EG: Well, I haven't had a cat go out for, you know, a hundred years. A lot of people, of course, abandon their pets at the end of the summer. My two oldest ones, they're thirteen I guess, now. I looked out the window one day and there were two kittens sitting on a tree stump out there, and their mother turned up shortly thereafter. I got her in early, but the kittens were quite skittish and one of them I couldn't get in until he was seven or eight months old, and I had to trap him and everything.

CS: They were almost feral, huh? [*Pointing to one peeking out from under the furniture*]

EG: Well, he is just a complete and total idiot. [*Laughs*] Up until about a year ago if he saw me during the day, he would run and hide. If he saw me at night, occasionally he would get up on the bed for about two minutes and then go and disappear again, but this last year he actually got friendly and he now comes upstairs when he wants me to comb him.

CS: Yeah?

EG: And his brother was almost as bad, you know. I got him a little earlier though. The black one, Weedon, will come out when my cleaning ladies are here and everything. But if they start to pet him, he doesn't run away or anything, he just hisses. He really doesn't mean anything by it, it's really sort of a reflex action. But Jane is the only one who comes out, really.

I did have two other ginger cats. Her brother is a ginger cat and he's a sweet cat, but he won't come out for anybody, and then her sister won't come out for anybody, either.

CS: What's a ginger cat?

EG: All yellow, well, I mean all orange. They are only males if they're ginger all over.

CS: Yup, I've had two of those and they were both males, but I never knew that about them.

EG: I did know somebody who claimed they'd seen a female, but I was never quite sure, because it's something like one in a million. And calico cats . . . there are male calico cats but I've certainly never known one. [*To Jane, the cat*] Dear, will you get out of there. Dear! Jane. Hello?

[*Jane is eating dry food that is spilling out from a torn bag in an open cupboard.*]

EG: Oh dear, I really should tidy up in there because they've torn open the dry food.

CS: Is that the dry food?

EG: It's dry food and I left it out overnight. When I bought it I left it out on the porch overnight, and somebody came and nibbled at the corners, and so now they're getting it obviously from there instead of their bowls.

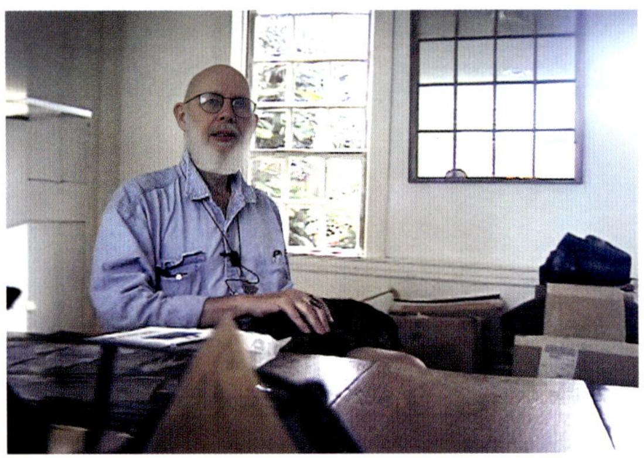

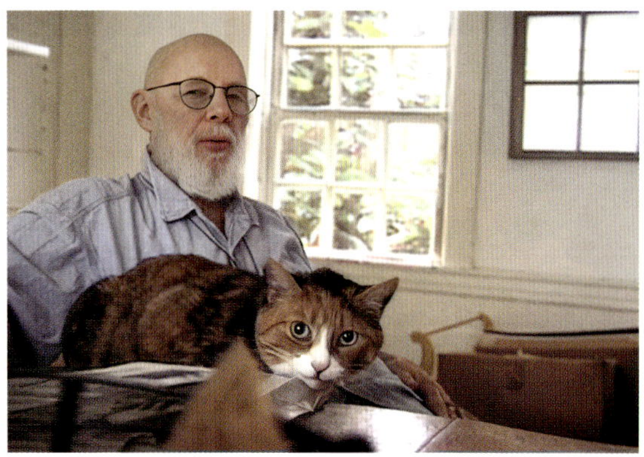

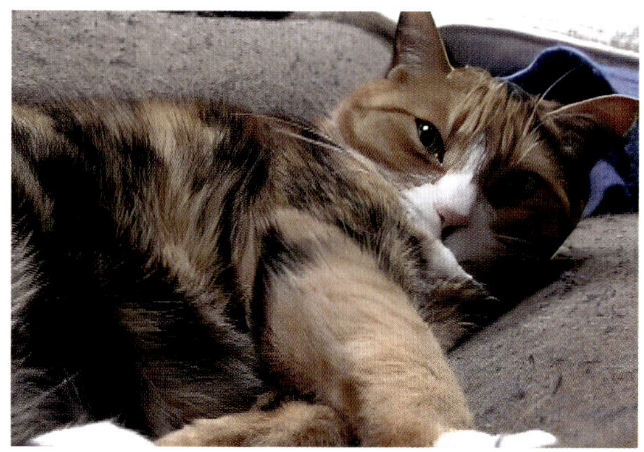

CS: It's serve yourself.

EG: Serve yourself, yes. Well, thank you, Jane. If you do it that way it's even tidier . . .

[*Camera stops and restarts on a tripod.*]

CS: It's nice in here.

EG: Well, if it were cleared out it would be. If it were cleared out and so forth and so on.

Would you mind, I need to see what's in these boxes. [*He turns around to boxes on a child's yellow bed frame that is used as a table.*]

CS: Yeah, you can feel free to do what you need. You don't have to entertain us or anything.

EG: Oh, well, I'm not doing anything, believe me.

What the hell is this? God! [*As he opens a book*]

This is all very mysterious. It doesn't seem to be anything even remotely recognizable. Well, that's recognizable but that's about all. [*As he moves a box off the top and shuffles through the pile*]

Oh . . . [*As he opens a box labeled "Chinese"*]

Chinese books, that's interesting. Yes, all right, what's in here now?

This is God-knows-what. Oh, forget about all of that. Yes, yes, Jane, forget about all of that. [*As he sits down and pets the cat*]

CS: I didn't realize Jack [Braginton-Smith] with his gruff exterior was such a ham in front of the camera.

EG: Oh yes, the very thought sends his heart racing. Oh Jane, Jane, Jane, Jane, Jane. [*He strokes her tail*]

[*Camera stops and restarts as Chris goes to shoot in other rooms around the house.*]

Jennifer Pitman: So, how long have you lived in this house?

EG: Well, I bought it back in about 1979, and I didn't move into it until I think 1985, maybe.

JP: It's beautiful.

EG: [*Sighs*] Well, it would be if it were less cluttered up with junk. How long have you been working with Chris?

JP: Well, I've just been doing an internship and I'm leaving on Wednesday, actually, for Santa Barbara. I'm in my last year at school.

EG: Oh, how do you like it out there?

JP: It's beautiful. Have you ever been there?

EG: No, I've just passed through. What college is it?

JP: It's the College of Santa Fe.

EG: Oh.

JP: Everything's funded there by Greer Garson. [English actress Greer Garson (1904–1996) was a patron of the school.]

EG: Oh! Oh yeah, oh yes, I love Greer. Oh, I didn't realize she did that. Oh well, that's nice.

JP: She and her husband.

EG: He was a big oil something . . .

JP: I'm in film production, movies.

EG: Film production. Do you do all sorts of film production? I mean, do you learn shooting, editing, and all aspects?

JP: Yup, this year I'm learning nonlinear editing. Everything's on computer now, so it's real exciting.

EG: Oh, I'll bet, yeah.

CS: [*Reentering with another camera*] Wow, you have some incredible books up there. There was also another cat up there, a black-and-white one.

EG: That's George, he's so fat he can hardly move. He looks like a coffee table. I feel he should go on a diet, but short of tying up his mouth I really don't know how to stop it. Putting a muzzle on him every night I don't think would exactly be a good idea.

CS: This is different than the last time I was in here shooting. Has the layout changed at all? Maybe it's because I was mainly upstairs with you then, working on the cable TV box with the satellite remote.

EG: Well, no, the layout certainly hasn't changed . . . OUCH! [*Has pain in right hand due to something unseen*] . . . at all. [*Continues to rub right hand*] It may be cluttered up in a slightly different way, but basically it's the same old whatever.

CS: Are these some of the nails from the original house? [*Picking up some square-head nails on the counter*]

EG: No, no. A friend of mine [Consuelo Joerns, a schoolmate from Chicago] gave me those. I don't know where she got them, probably from someplace like here, you know, because they're obviously really old nails. They probably came from the Vineyard because she's lived over there for twenty-five years or so now. Though I may have had them for even longer than that, I don't know. Anyway.

JP: They look like miniature railroad spikes.

EG: Oh right, yeah.

JP: They almost look like bones. [referring to the group of nails]

EG: Yeah, well, I always think of it as sort of a fish skeleton. [*Cat jumps on lap*] Oh, Jane, Jane, Jane, what are you doing, dear? [*Exasperated*] What, what, what, what, what, what what, *what*, *what*, what?

[*Looking at Jenn*] How did you happen to get interested in film, or did you just get interested in film?

JP: I've actually been wanting to do it since I was fifteen and I'm twenty-seven.

EG: Oh, well good.

JP: I'm finally going to finish in May.

EG: Oh, well, great. Would you like to be in Hollywood or somewhere else?

[*Camera stops and restarts*]

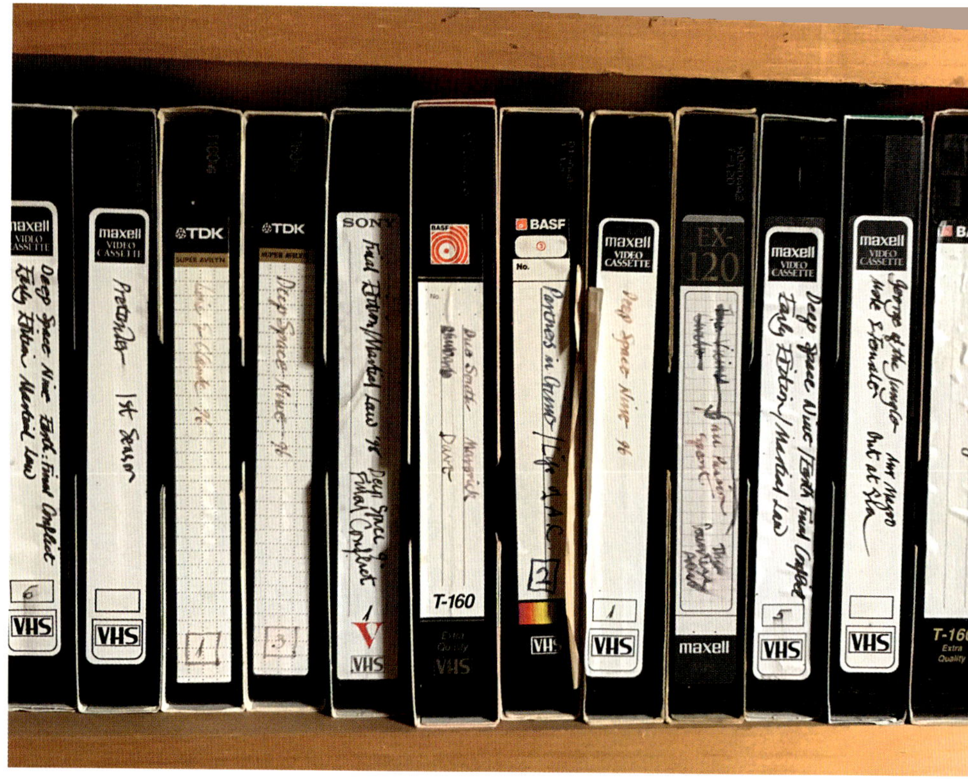

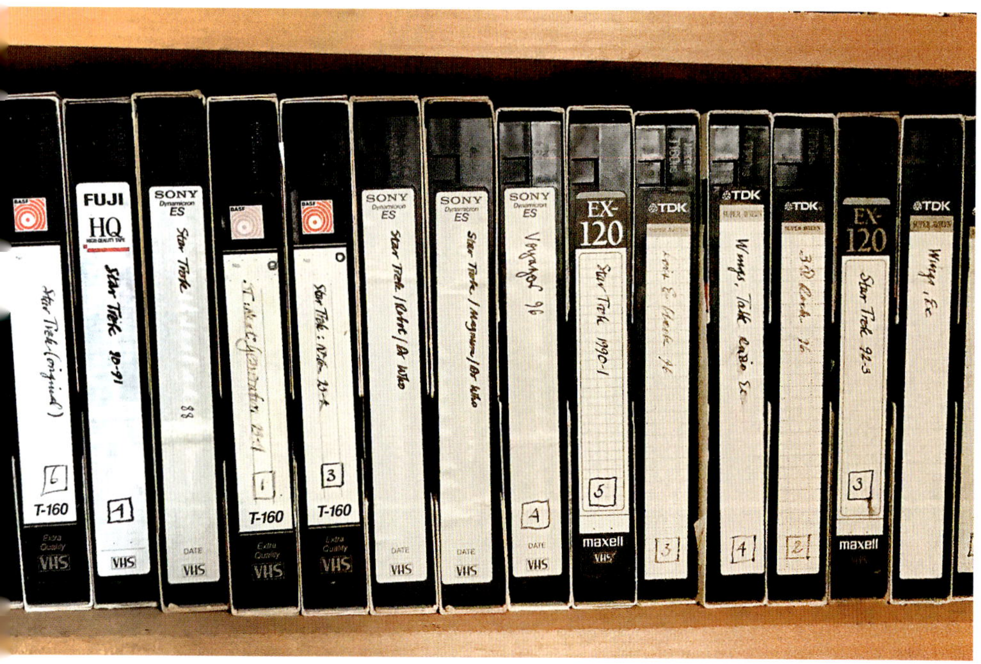

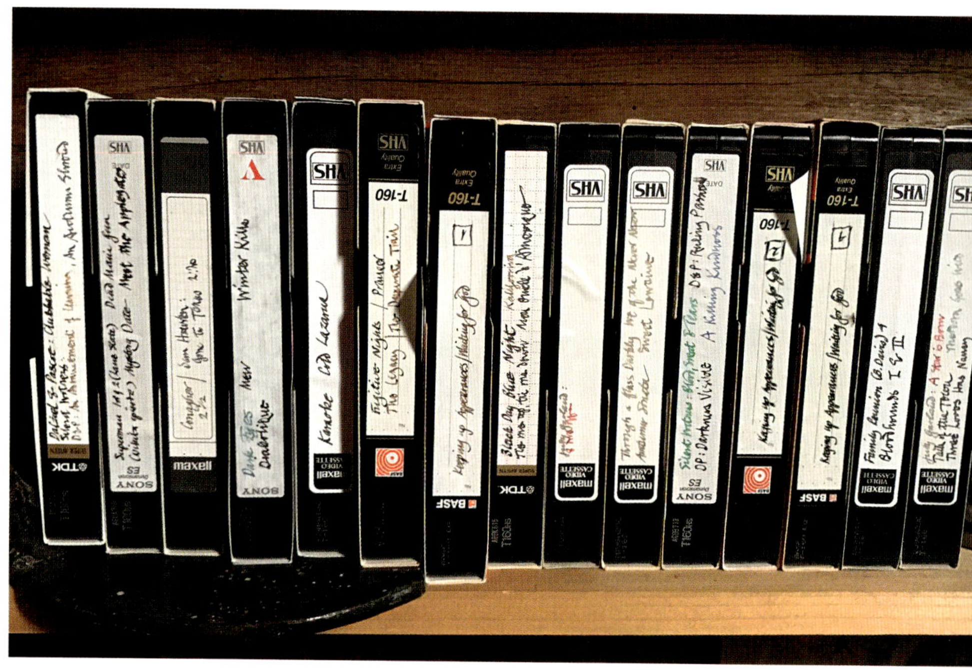

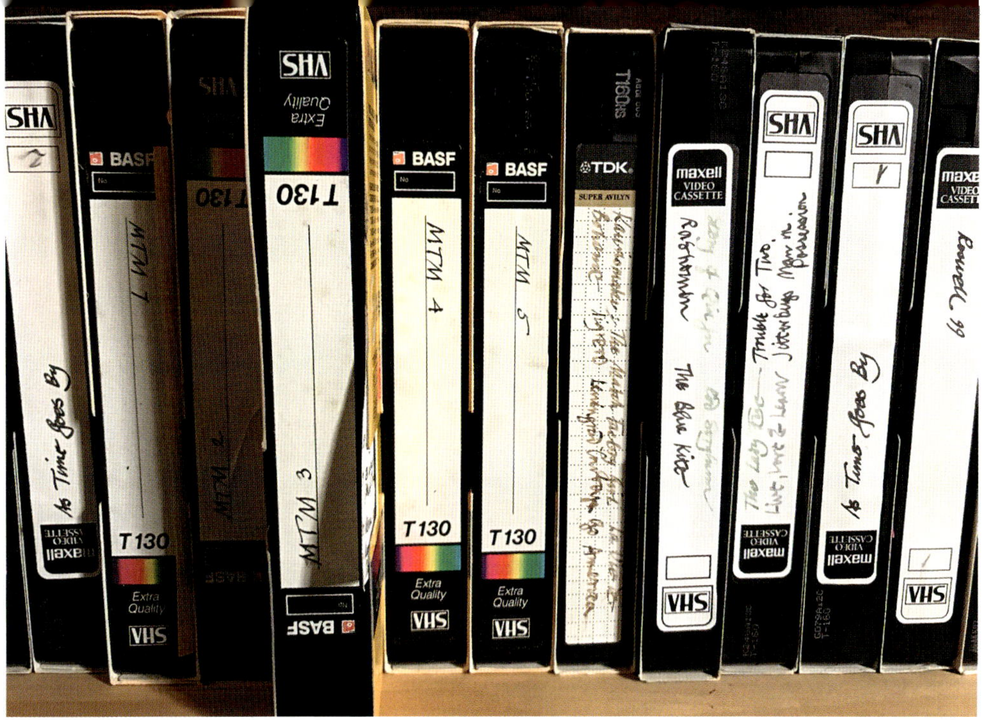

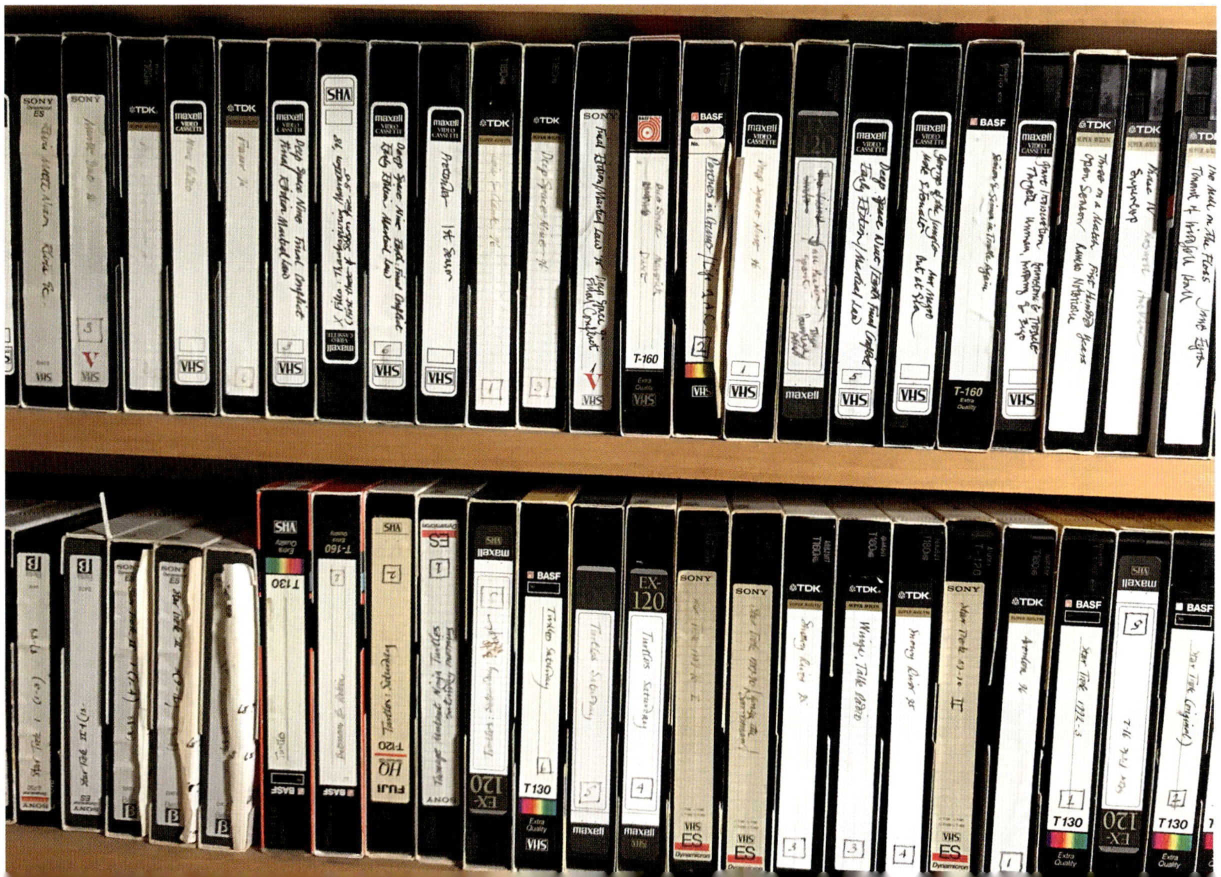

EG: I did a couple of shows in Woods Hole once years ago and it was a nightmare, you know, the parking, the whole thing was just such a nightmare trying to go back and forth. I mean, loved working over there, we did two shows in that, I never remember what they call it, but it's that public building right next to the bridge.

JP: The fire station?

EG: Just to the east of the fire station, and we did a couple of shows in there. I always loved it. It's a lovely building but, both times I think, we managed to get about three rehearsals in the actual performance space. We'd either have to rehearse upstairs or downstairs at the fire station. I don't know what people do when they go over there. There aren't even any public parking spaces. There aren't even any spaces where you can pay to park, you know, and as it was we used to . . . I think finally, I used to pay to park as part of the Woods Hole Laboratory parking. After five or six o'clock you could park in it, finally.

JP: How many shows did you do in that building?

EG: Two. We did one in the summer of '87 and one in the summer of 1990, and I loved doing things over there and stuff, but as I say, it was, of course, trying to get over there for a rehearsal. I think now, getting over there for a rehearsal every night would be like, forget it!

JP: Is it all from the ferry do you think? [*Referring to the traffic congestion*]

EG: Well, well, that too of course is a big thing now because of course, in the old days, you know, there was that one parking lot right by the ferry that got bigger and bigger and bigger, and further back into the side of the mountain or whatever. Then they just began opening parking lots all over the place. And now every time I go over there, I discover a new parking lot and I think, "What is this? This is a parking lot for the ferry? We're miles from there!"

[*Drumming his fingers on the table*] I suppose they send buses and stuff, but even so, I never did quite understand what would happen if you managed . . . well, for one thing, if you came from the other way, you'd find yourself completely at sea for where you would park your car if you were going over to the islands. And of course it's getting harder and harder to get your car off Martha's Vineyard to come back. My friend who lives over there says you often can't even do standby anymore, except certain times.

And she's a resident of Martha's Vineyard, but everyone is making their reservations like around Christmas for the next summer. They just make them for every single weekend and stuff.

JP: That's crazy.

EG: Absolutely loopy! And of course, with the Clintons over there now, she said it's been unbearable for years, but this time around it's just absolutely worse than ever.

JP: I wouldn't want to be over there.

EG: I wouldn't want to be over there either, you know.

JP: Not if you paid me.

[*Camera stops and restarts*]

EG: I have it all written down somewhere, but I haven't had occasion to check for some time so, knock wood [*knocks on wood*].

JP: And how about the cats' birthdays?

EG: Their birthdays pass unnoticed, the poor dears. [*Laughs*]

CS: Do you actually know all of their birthdays?

EG: Well, I know when I got them. I write down when I get them and then when something happens to the poor dears. I have a little notebook dating back to . . . oh, I don't know . . . oh gosh! Probably about 1950.

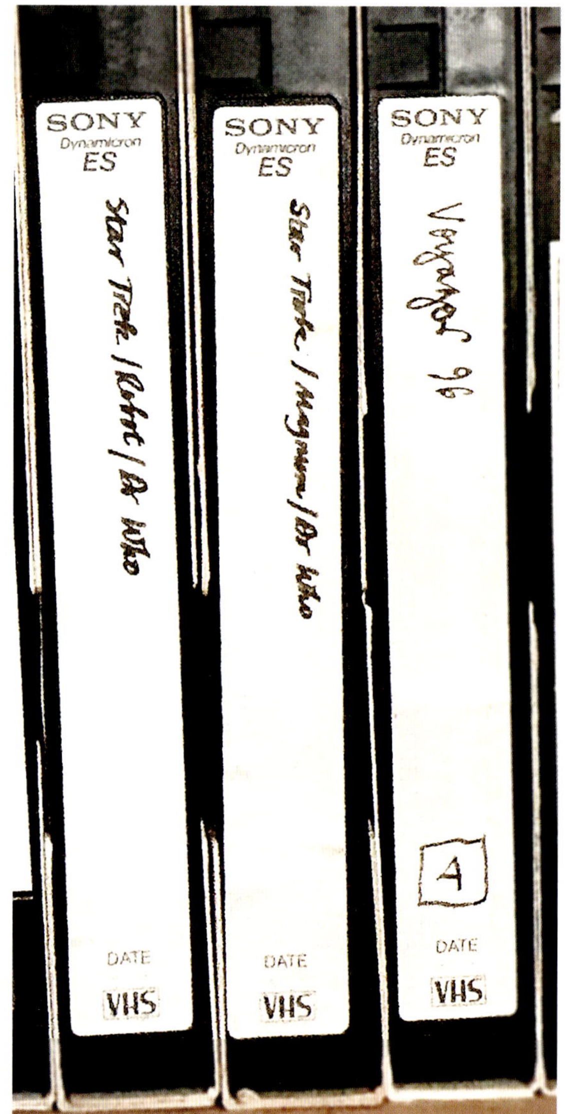

Let's see, I graduated from Harvard in 1950 and I didn't have a cat for a year after that. I think I got my first cat in 1952, and I hadn't had one since I got out of high school, so between '42 and '52 there were ten years that I didn't have a cat, but otherwise I've had cats for well over sixty years.

JP: What do you do when you go away?

EG: I haven't been away for ages and ages.

When I still had an apartment in New York, I could leave them for a weekend perfectly easily with food and water with them not going out or anything. But I haven't been back to New York for about thirteen years. I think that's correct. Well, I was back once for about three hours. I mean I was in New York City for three hours. It took me longer of course to drive there and longer to get back and stuff. I don't miss it, I must say.

JP: It's changed a lot.

EG: I'm sure it has because, even when I was living there. . . . Let's see, I moved there in '53. It changed so much all the time that, you know, I'd think, "What used to be here, this wasn't here two months ago?" And I'd never be able to remember. And I guess now with things like 42nd Street with all the movies being refurbished and the theaters and Disney all over the place and everything. I'm sure I wouldn't recognize it.

JP: It's a mob scene.

EG: What is?

JP: 42nd Street. I was just there a few months ago, just crazy.

EG: And Time Square was really geared up for vast change about the time that I was leaving, and of course all of the cineplexes were opening up, you know, twenty-two movies where one had been before. And so forth and so on. And some times I'd go back almost every weekend or a couple of times a month, and I wouldn't notice so much, but when I got going there less and less I'd notice how creepy it was getting. You know, each time I went down there'd be a noticeable "Ugh!" And then I'd think, "Why am I here?"

[*Acting it out and looking around fearfully*] [*Laughs*]

Which I'd never thought before, you know. I'd never paid the slightest bit of attention, you know. People'd be mugged, murdered, blah, blah, blah, blah, blah, but I never was so . . . But you know, there never was anyplace where something might not happen to you, so why worry?

CS: Yeah.

EG: You know, I knew people who had terrible things happen to them, more or less, you know, in Central Park, any place really, no matter how elegant the address and whatnot, so I just figured, "Well, if something's going to happen to you it's going to happen to you." Because you could very easily find yourself being afraid to go out after dark or even in daylight for that matter, and you think, "Well, that's not worth it."

But, I don't know, there are all sorts of things. If I were in New York, of course, there would be a lot more things I'd be doing there than I am here, but I don't miss doing them. And all the time that I lived down there I didn't really stay there. I was up here more than half the time, practically the whole time.

So, I never really thought of New York unless I was about to go down there or something. And I really didn't like the place all that much. [*Pets Jane, who's now on the table*]

CS: I get very anxious in New York. There's so much going on.

EG: Well, I was beginning to the last time I was there. Though all the time I was in New York, I think I figured I was never home one night. I was always out at something, you know, and I never got home until it was time to go to bed, so to speak, and stuff. But there were times I'd think, "What am I going to do tonight?" And I'd pick up the New York Times and I've seen every movie, there isn't a play I want to see, there's not a concert, not an opera, not a ballet, not a this, that, or the other thing . . . I thought, I'm bored, bored, bored! Oh, where can I go? [*Laughs*]

So, it's all in your mind. Yes, it is. Its all in your mind. I just assume I'm going to be bored out of my wits on Cape Cod.

CS: One thing I really miss being here are places like the coffee shops in San Francisco. I really miss being able to go do work somewhere outside of my house.

And now on the Cape there aren't a whole lot of places to go.

EG: No, there aren't really places to go, that's true.

CS: Not necessarily to be around people, you know.

EG: Well, I mean, have you been to Contrast at all?

CS: Well, that lunch you and I had.

EG: Yeah, that lunch. That was fun, but it's too noisy, and they're getting very la-di-da. Carol and I stopped off there at, I don't know, 5:30 the other night, because we were going to an early movie at the Playhouse or something. And we just sort of sat down and they said, "Oh, would you go and check with someone or other and they'll seat you?" and I thought, "Oh, for Heaven's sake!" You know, the table might be reserved! Oh, come on folks! You know, it's not a New York bistro.

Well, they're trying hard, you know. But as you say, there are no places. Either they're not open at the time that you want to be doing that sort of thing . . . And somehow sitting in Chock Full O' Nuts isn't quite . . . I don't mean Chock Full O' Nuts. I mean Dunkin' Donuts. It isn't quite the same thing.

CS: Yeah, Prodigal Son isn't bad.

EG: Oh, I keep hearing about that, that's that one past the traffic light on Ocean Street in Hyannis?

CS: Ocean Street, yeah. They have weird hours, they're closed on Tuesdays.

EG: And they have poetry readings too, don't they? Someone's always trying to convince me to go to a poetry reading. I think, "Oh, I really must get over there." And then I think, "Poetry reading, I don't want to hear a poetry reading."

CS: The interesting thing about the Prodigal Son is that there are a lot of young creative types up there, and you don't see too many young people in their twenties here on the Cape.

EG: No, that's true.

CS: And they're out there doing things. I don't go there much myself, but I know a lot of people that either write poetry or are into music that do.

EG: Well, the Cape is really not a great place to be young, if you ask me. Yes, exactly. Because there really is not that much to do here. Well, you've been busy doing all of your films.

CS: You have to keep busy, otherwise [*Finger across the neck*].

EG: You have to keep busy or else. And I imagine it would be even worse with my friend on the Vineyard who says sometimes she's going to lose her mind before it's even time for lunch!

Now, the Cape is some kind of funny suburb. People come and go. There isn't a real feeling of, at least I don't get a real feeling of, villages here. You know, I don't care how much they gas on about historical societies and everyone's sort of sitting around Jack's [Outback], but there really isn't what I would consider real village life.

It's too, sort of, fragmented. Obviously there are a lot of people down here who have had interesting lives, but somehow I never hear about them very much, or something or other, I don't know.

CS: I do like the way Chatham has a cohesive center, even though it's mostly there for the tourists. But I do like the way things are concentrated there.

EG: Well, of course the trouble with Chatham, the last time I was down there was June or July, and I thought, "Oh my god!" You can hardly get in or out. But I do agree, Chatham is that kind of place, like Provincetown, which I think would drive me crazy. I did three shows in Provincetown in the summers. And you know, it was sort of goofy and loopy and I thought, "If I had to live here year-round I'd go mad." Finally driving up and down from there was just too much. But there was a kind of a feel.

CS: There's nowhere to park without paying.

EG: Oh well, right, yes. But places like . . . I mean all the towns along here at least seem to me to be quite different. You go into some place [pulls out blue bandana and sneezes dramatically into it] in Dennis and the people you see are completely different from the people you see in Yarmouth Port. And in Yarmouth Port they're completely different from the people you see in Barnstable. And if you go to Brewster, you know, on it goes, and nobody really does go anyplace else as far as you can tell.

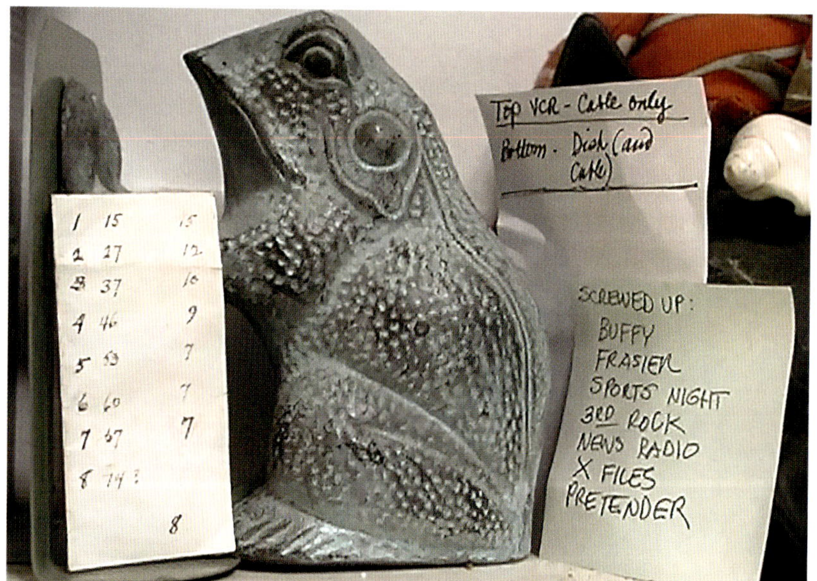

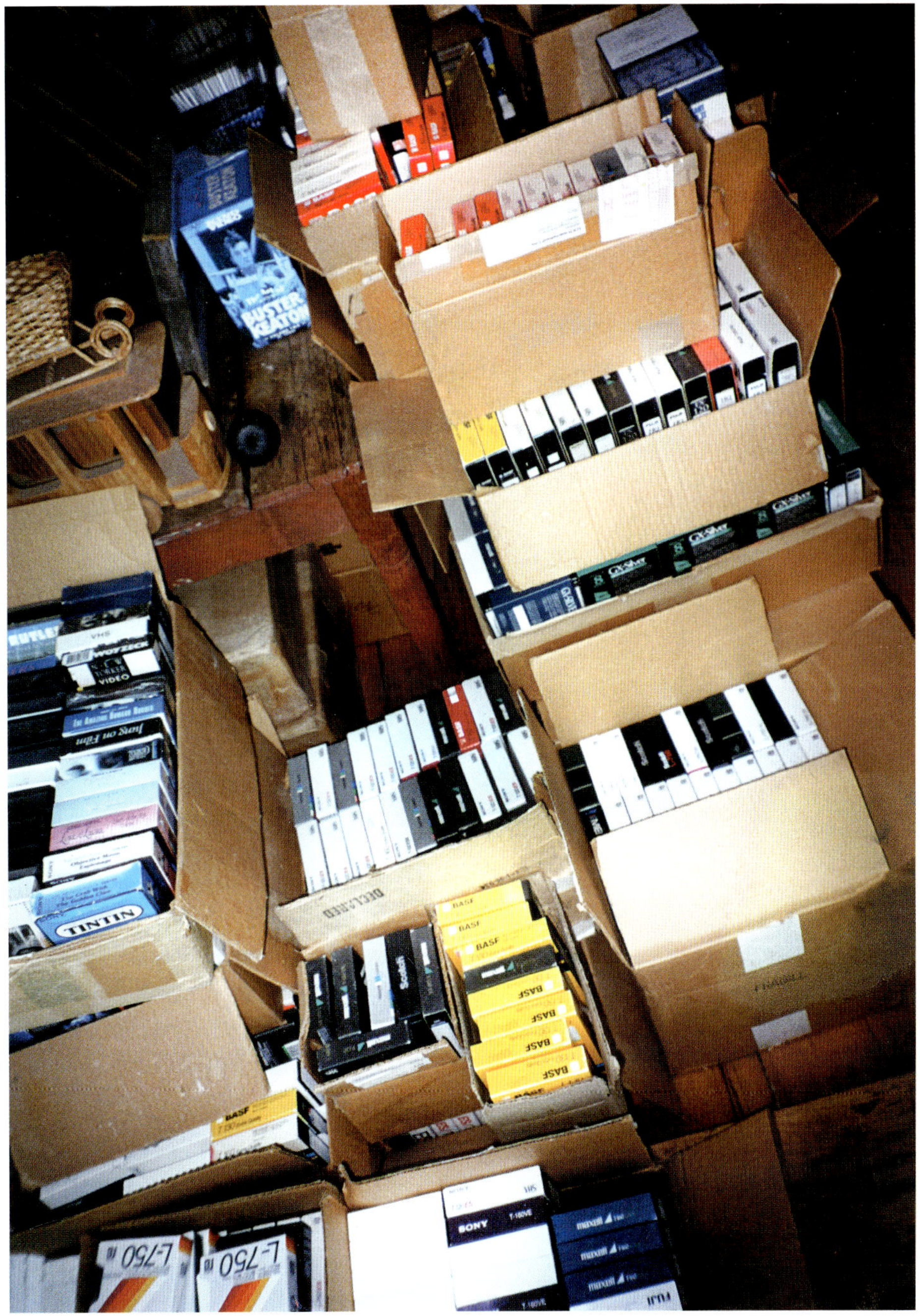
BUSTER KEATON
TINTIN
BASF
L-750
SONY

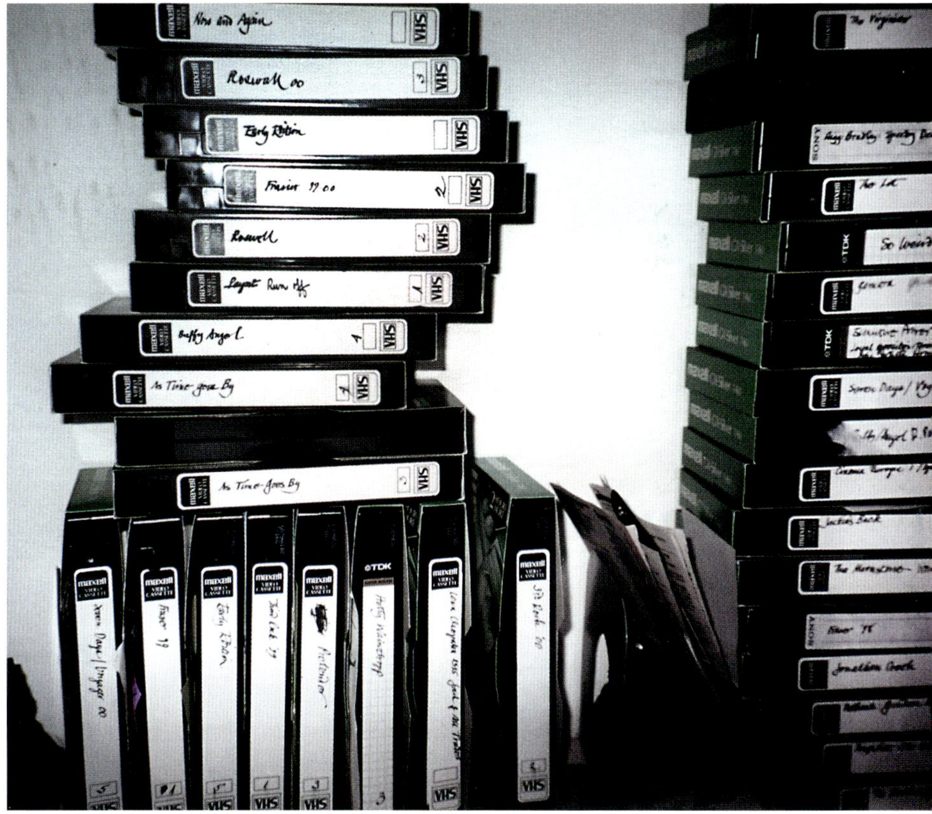
VHS
maxell
TDK
SONY

CS: I think people do that first summer where hey check everything out and then . . .

EG: Yeah, when we were first coming down here, my uncle and aunt had a house over in Barnstable, quite a small one. And there were my two cousins who were in high school and I was a bit older, somewhat older. Then my aunt had a lot of relatives here who were still alive, you know, contemporaries of hers and then older people and stuff. She had an uncle and his large, extended family and everything. And since we had such a small house and everything, we used to drive around all the time, from one end of the Cape to another. We knew every back road, you know?

And it was really kind of fun. It was impossible to stay in the house when it rained because we all went crazy. There just wasn't enough room, and for years it was like that. Then we got a bigger house and it became more and more of a problem to get around.

You know, so gradually you just stop going. You know, "Oh let's go up to Truro!" and then "Oh, do we really have to?" kind of thing. [The story *The Deranged Cousins* is based on their adventures.]

CS: The traffic's definitely inhibiting.

EG: The traffic is just awful. And you know, there are more and more people.

CS: Especially on a cloudy day like today.

EG: Especially because it's now clouded up and everyone who has left the beach is now roaring around. I liked when Borders first opened. I've been loyal to Barnes & Noble for a while, you know I much prefer Barnes & Noble, but they do not have as many books and they do not have the café, and they do not have CDs, and I find myself hanging out there.

Well, not really hanging out there, but I'll think, "Oh, there are a couple of books I want." So, I'll go over to Borders and I'll look around, and I come away with a *lot* more than I intended to buy and everything, and then I'll go and have an iced coffee and a pastry or something and sit there and read one of the books for half an hour or an hour or so, and I know a couple of people who work there, but you know it's not really that anyone is hanging out and meeting their friends there.

But, at least it's "These are the people reading books." And you sort of see everybody mousing around and it's sort of . . .

JCS: I'd like to check that out. Do they sell videos?

CS: When I first started doing films I went around, you know, with a bag under my arm and found a lot of them just don't support locals. They have their buyer in Minnesota.

EG: Yeah, right, nothing local. Borders has a section of Cape authors, and that really is as far as it will go, which is too bad. The thing I'm afraid of, obviously if Barnes & Noble doesn't do something drastic, there's been a rumor now for two years that they were going to buy up the Airport Cinema building and put a second floor on it, and it would have everything but a bed-and-breakfast there.

So far I haven't heard anything more about that, but Borders is obviously doing so well that on weekends you can't even find a parking space. Even so, it's kind of a goofy location because you can turn in one way from Route 132 but not the other way.

People are always saying those places only have the bestsellers and whatnot, which really is not true. I'm always finding obscure things in both Barnes & Noble and Borders. You know, I'll browse a section and come across three or four books that I didn't even know existed. And I'm reasonably well read after all of these years, God knows, I ought to be.

[*Camera shuts off and restarts*]

EG: Carol has sort of quietly assumed that I'm going to write this play for Christmas, which means that would have to be done, sort of, by the first of October.

CS: From scratch?

EG: Not quite from scratch, but mostly from scratch. Well, actually, I don't know.

[*Camera restarts*]

EG: Favorite illustrators. I'm trying to think who's still alive, most of my favorite illustrators have died. Or I think have died, if they haven't died they're a hundred and five. Actually there's a man called Graham Oakley, who's English, who does a series of books about mice in a church. And a cat, whose name I can't remember at the moment. Which are quite lovely. They're very elaborate and very detailed. Very elaborate watercolors and I like those a lot. [The Church Mice series]

JP: I like your etching over there.

JEG: Oh, thanks. I used to keep up much more with what was going on somehow. I don't so much anymore. Well, I mean there used to be couple of good children's bookstores in New York that I used to go to a lot. Or children's book sections.

[*Camera shuts off and restarts*]

EG: With the cable here, half the time you can't see a thing. I mean it's really thoroughly annoying, but we get all sorts of strange little movies that you just have to hit upon or something, because

I get the TV Guide that goes with the Dish, which is impossible to read. I mean if you think *TV Guide* is difficult, this is worse. And then there's something called TV Complete or something that tells you all the thing that you can do on the Dish and whatnot, and you can spend the day going, "Do I want to see this? When is it on? Do I want to see this? When is it on?" Blah, blah, blah.

But occasionally you discover something really kind of marvelous. Marvelous little movies that you've *never* heard of. And you've never heard of the people involved, and you think, "I wonder what became of them?"

And so there's a wonderful movie that I recommend . . . have you ever seen *Suture*? Well, it appeared at Sundance, I think, in 1994. It was made by two "men's names." I presume they were young, and I've never heard a word about them since. And anyway, it's absolutely the most deadpan movie I've ever seen. One of the actors was Mel Harris from *Thirtysomething*.

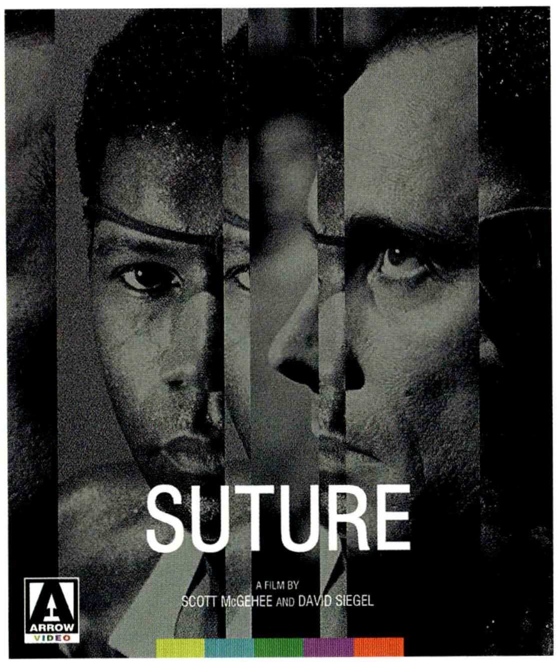

It starts out with a man driving to the airport in someplace like Salt Lake City or something or other. And he picks up his brother at the airport, and you discover he hasn't seen his brother in a number of years, but he's asked his brother to come and testify because he's being sued by somebody, or something or other.

They go back to his house, which is very obviously a car dealership building. It is surrounded by concrete parking lot, and the building itself is kind of Western Modern. The living room is this huge open floor, obviously where the cars were displayed, and then there's this kind of stairway going up the side, and that's where the bedrooms are and everything. And anyway, as the two brothers are driving back from the airport they're talking about their past and "Remember how nobody could tell us apart," "Remember that trick we played on so-and-so." And so one of them is black and one is white. This is never mentioned in the movie. Never. And all through the movie, people confuse them. [*Laughs*] And at the very end the white brother's girlfriend goes off with the black brother . . .

CS: By accident?

EG: Well, it is never, never . . . obviously they were sitting around one night and said, "Wouldn't it be great to do a movie about"; I'm not sure that they're referred to as twins, but they practically are. I mean they must be identical twins or people wouldn't be mistaking them all the time, obviously. And they thought, "This is a great idea for a movie." And they went ahead and did it. And it's got quite a good plot. One or two people you've seen before, but everyone else you never have at all, and I sat after it was over and I thought, "I've never seen a movie like this, it's really great."

JP: And it's *Suture*?

EG: The name is *Suture*.

CS: Did you see it on satellite?

EG: Yeah, it was on Sundance, I believe, and it just said "Rather strange movie about two brothers," or something. It didn't even say what the gimmick was.

CS: Do they have commercials on the Sundance Channel?

EG: I'm not sure. I haven't watched Sundance recently, because all they're doing is showing things that they've had before. They have endless commercials for themselves until you could scream. Earnest young filmmakers talking about "How I did this" and "How I did that" and "We don't care, dear, just put the film on please" kind of thing.

But then there was somebody else who made a couple of movies, I guess he was Canadian.

There was a completely weird one. It starts out in a terribly small town in Canada, and this young man is a barber. And obviously it makes anyplace on the Cape seem like the big city. So anyway, he goes out in his backyard one day and discovers a corpse in a bathtub. The bathtub has been there, but there's a corpse in the bathtub now. And he sort of looks at it, or something or other, and presently a girl arrives and says something to the effect, "Oh there he is, he's my brother. Would you drive me to New Orleans so he can be buried?"

So the barber thinks for a moment, and obviously life is stupefying wherever this is in Canada, so they start driving to New Orleans with the

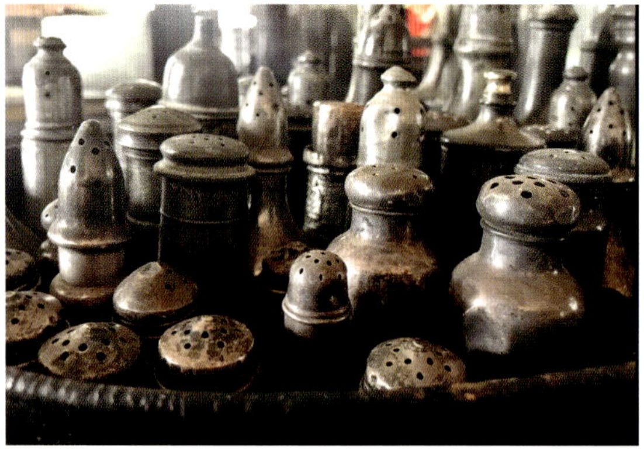

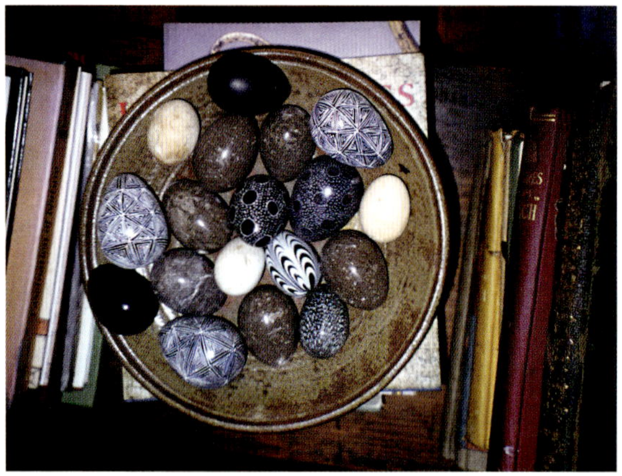

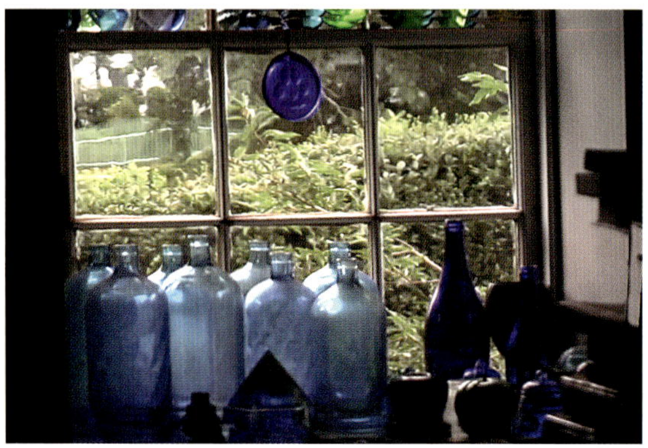

corpse of the brother in the station wagon. You realize quite early on that it's not her brother. It is stuffed with dope, and he's now delivering it to somebody in New Orleans.

In the meantime we crosscut; it's one of these road movies where they keep meeting lots of different people and so forth and so on, and it's quite funny. But in the meantime we keep cross-cutting with a born-again evangelist of some sort who may or may not literally be the devil. And this all comes together at the end somewhere or other, and you never do find out if this other man is the devil or not. You're left completely up in the air as to whether half of this movie is supernatural, whether it's just goofy, or both.

And then I saw another movie which this guy made, that I can't remember at all, and I've never heard of these people and I keep thinking, Where are they when we need them to keep making these wonderful, goofy movies, that obviously barely got released.

JP: Did they go to Sundance?

EG: Well, these two I don't know. I can't even remember on what channel I saw them. More and more the movies go directly to TV, you know, to cable. And I think they get more of a play now if they do go to cable. You know, Linda Fiorentino was going to get nominated for an Academy Award and it turned out her movie had shown on HBO once. I happen to have seen it on HBO the one time it was shown, and I thought, "Why is this movie up for an Academy Award? I saw this on HBO about six months ago." And then they discovered that it had shown on HBO six months ago, so she couldn't get a nomination for the Academy Award, and it was a great little movie. I've seen a couple of others from that director and they're really great little movies, but I guess they'd given up on the thing and it had gone to HBO and someone said, "Oh, let's release this in the theaters," but it was too late. Well, I mean they did release it in theaters but . . .

There are a lot of movies that I have on tape that went to cable, and they'd show maybe once or twice a month at three or four in the morning and that would be it. There had to be some little blurb that made me think, "Oh, I'll tape this and see what it was like," and I have a whole slew of movies like that. I can't remember their names. Of course there are a lot of people who spend their whole careers going directly to cable.

CS: Do you find that you're able to do a lot of your work while watching TV?

CS: [*Trying to bring the interview back to Gorey's work habits*] I find I'm actually kind of the opposite. I'll sit down and I'll say, "Okay, I'm going to do some work while I watch this." Probably a rationalization. And then I'll start working and I'll get completely sucked into the movie.

EG: Oh.

CS: Sitting there sort of mouth agape.

EG: Well, one of my oldest friends, who has a house down here and is here most weekends . . . Alex [Melvin and Alex Schierman] will always rent a movie and I'll say, "What are we going to have to sit through after dinner?," and she'll name them and I'll think [*in a voice*] "Oh dear, why did you rent this?" And quite often when it's all over, I'll say, "Why did you rent this?," and she'll say, "I don't know, it sounded good." [*Laughs to himself*]

CS: I saw *Gattaca* recently.

EG: Oh, I sort of liked parts of that. Now that was Uma Thurman, wasn't it, at her most peculiar. I find her very mysterious. Sometimes I think she's quite beautiful and other times I think, "How did this girl ever get into the movies?" Did you see *Jennifer 8* by any chance?

CS: Yeah, I really liked it.

EG: That I liked a lot. Yeah, that is one of the creepiest movies ever made.

CS: Yeah.

EG: That ghastly apartment building, wherever it was.

All that snow with little tiny flakes all the time, and obviously the heat was never on. The whole thing I thought was scary beyond anything. It really unnerved me. On the other hand . . .

CS: Andy Garcia?

EG: Yeah, Andy Garcia. I thought that was really great.

CS: It was on TV like six times over Christmas, for some reason they were playing it over and over.

EG: Yeah, I just saw bits of it again last week, though I have it on tape. But on the other hand, have you seen *The Avengers*?

CS: No.

EG: [*Cuts throat with finger*] Pff. Cut your throat.

CS: Is that a new movie?

EG: Yeah, at least if you haven't seen the old *Avengers*.

CS: No, I haven't.

EG: Oh, well, the old *Avengers* is one of those great series from, I guess it was the sixties, and it reran on cable here a lot. I think it was on Arts & Entertainment, I've forgotten.

Anyway it was one of those things where the people that saw it originally, it was one of their favorite shows. It was Patrick MacNee. In its heyday it was Patrick MacNee and Diana Rigg and all sorts of wonderful people. It was a kind of spy thriller kind of thing, and they remade it with Ralph Fiennes and Uma Thurman and Sean Connery, poor man, who was completely wrecked by the whole movie. And it's got a couple of good special effects in it, actually, but the rest of it was just ho-hum.

You just think, "Oh dear, why did they think they could make something that was very sophisticated and kind of cool, and not very many special effects back in the sixties. Why do you think you can just pour money into a new one and get the same thing." And the dialogue is all perfectly awful.

CS: [*Again trying to pull the interview back to Edward's work*] Do you ever actually watch the *Mystery!* series on PBS? Because you did the opening.

EG: I watch *Mystery!* occasionally. Most of them I don't watch. There's been a series recently which wasn't on *Mystery!*, which they played after *Mystery!*, called *Jonathan Creek*. I don't know if they're going to play anymore. They played six of them. They were hour shows. The first one was an hour and a half and the other six were an hour, sort of under an hour, which was quite a funny show about a man who worked out magic tricks for magicians. And so that all the plots are based on seeming impossibilities like somebody being on both sides of the Atlantic at once or people in locked rooms was one of the gimmicks. You know, "How do you murder somebody in a locked room?," you know, and all that kind of thing.

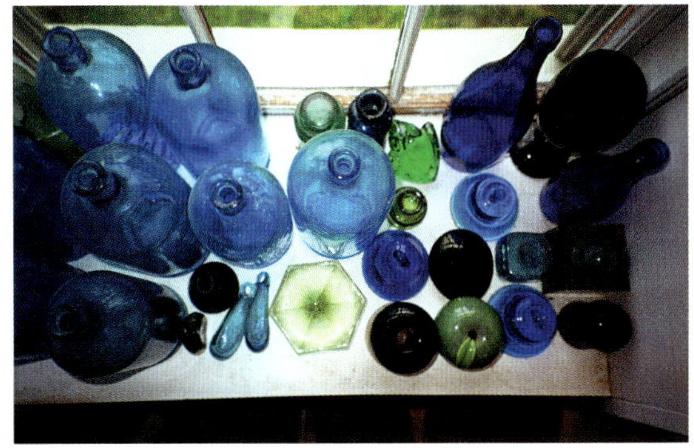

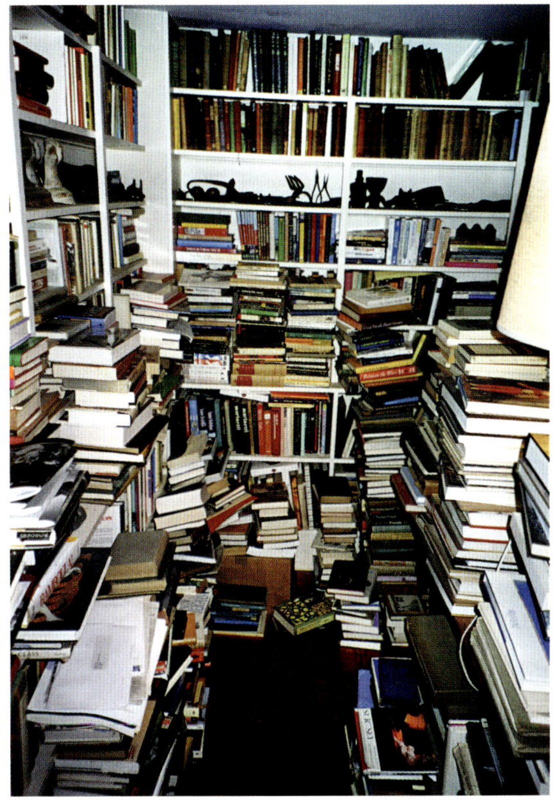

[Pulling the interview away from his work once more]

CS: Did you do the animations out of it [*Mystery!*]? I mean did you do the drawings for the animations, each one?

EG: No, oh, hell no. He did. Derek Lamb did. He and his little cohorts did all the animations. I did some of the original drawings in some cases and then they filled them in and stuff, but I could do no more.

CS: Do you ever have any desire to do something like that, as far as a full-length movie?

EG: Oh well, I would love to. I would love to do full-length movies, but nobody's ever asked me, so what the heck, you know?

CS: Do you think you would need to work with another animator?

EG: Oh yeah. I'd have to work with an animator, God knows. And I don't know . . . Animation, now, I'm not terribly fond of what's current. You know, there's all this terribly angular stuff. I've watched a couple of those. There's a new one on one of the networks, an English one called something, something Eric. Nervous Eric.

CS: Yeah. Yeah. *Stressed Eric.*

EG: *Stressed Eric*, which I thought, you know, was okay. It's very obvious and it's, you know, kind of fun and stuff. I really do not like this very kind of angular style of animation.

CS: So when you said maybe you'd be interested in a full-length movie, it probably wouldn't be animated, it would be real people?

EG: Well, no, either one. I mean there are things. I do have a script. Actually what it started out as was the animation for WGBH, but they said it would last too long. I said, "Not if you make it go fast enough. If you just zip right along it would probably take two minutes." "But no, it would take hours." I thought, "Oh, for heaven's sake." I could probably push it out to over an hour, but . . . You know even the Disney things I thought . . . What was the last Disney? Well, I tried to watch *Pocahontas* and just gave up. *The Lion King* I just loathed, loathed, loathed, loathed! The last one I really liked was *The Little Mermaid*.

CS: Are you talking about the content or the actual animation?

EG: Oh, everything. I thought *The Little Mermaid* was really quite stylish animation.

By the time they got around to *Beauty and the Beast*, and *The Lion King*, and *Pocahontas*, all the computerized stuff I thought was dim to say the least. Was there just another Disney one? I swear I saw one, I've seen something and I thought, "Oh, this really isn't up to snuff."

CS: There was a new Disney thing that's coming out. You're right, what is it?

EG: I thought I saw a completed trailer. What the hell was it? I do know that I turned off *Pocahontas*. Has there been something since? I sort of liked *Aladdin*, oh, and I sort of liked *Hercules*, against my better judgment. But I thought having the muse as being the Supremes was pretty nifty, and I thought there were some funny lines. And all that garish color I thought was so outrageous, you know. But I can't remember now. There was something, but I don't know what it was. The hell with it.

CS: Have you seen, you know any of those documentaries, that are sort of, sort of like the one I'm working on with you, profiling a certain person like R. Crumb or something cinema verité style? Have you ever watched any of those?

EG: I tried to watch *Crumb*, and I got so depressed I had to turn it off. I mean, I just thought, really don't want to know any more about this dysfunctional family that I've already read about, thank you very much. And, let's see . . . I can't think of too many.

Actually I've seen a couple of those biographies on Biography lately. I thought the one on the Nelsons was quite fascinating. And then there was something else. Oh there was . . . damn!

There was another biography on Arts & Entertainment recently, which I thought was quite . . . Some actress . . . who the hell was it?

They had all sorts of things that I didn't really know about her. What the hell was it now?

Someone who's now gone. Oh, who the hell was it? It was like Bette Davis but it wasn't Bette Davis. It was somebody not quite as well known, but anyway I found it quite fascinating.

There were things I didn't know about her. Actually I think the things they do on Biography and Arts & Entertainment are usually pretty good.

CS: I like them. You feel kind of removed watching them though. A lot of times they're already dead. It's formulaic.

EG: Well, yeah, for somebody your age.

Remember, I go back to practically the year one as far as the movies are concerned and so, [*in a voice*] "Oh yes, she was in the first movie I ever saw" or something like that.

CS: I don't really mean removed in the sense that I don't know what they're talking about, but more in the sense of the style of the footage, very stock.

EG: Well, people like that are all completely different, the kinds of movies they appeared in and all the rest of it. For instance, I couldn't care less about Barbra Streisand, so I don't really want to know about her career between then and now. But that's simply because I never liked her very much, but also she came along long after I was impressionable, so to speak.

CS: [*Realizing that they're talking about two different things*] Do you ever find, since you have such a comprehensive knowledge of movies . . .

EG: Been there, done that!

CS: . . . a movie that you don't like or hated when you saw it, that it comes out in some way in your work, even though you actually hated it?

EG: Oh, oh, that's possible. I don't know if I can think of anything offhand, but there are things I hate that I sort of use anyway. I mean, you know, if you really hate something I feel you've got some connection with it. You don't hate something that doesn't ring some sort of bell with you. I mean it's the stuff that you come out of and think, "What was that movie I just saw?" that obviously isn't going to affect you very much.

I think it's more, there are books I hate that have affected me more. I can't think.

Because I don't really hate movies, I just get irritated at them. I think, "Oh, why are you doing this?" Or "What did you think you were doing there?" "Do you really think you can act, Vanessa Redgrave? Forget it! And forget it, Meryl Streep."

There are actors and actresses that I hate and won't go to their movies anymore.

CS: I'm interested in that connection. You have such a huge body of work. The thing that I'm struck by is the sheer amount of work that you've actually brought onto the paper.

EG: Oh gee, really? I sort of look back and think, "Where did it all, where did it all go?" But with movies and things particularly, well I don't read as much contemporary stuff as I used to, though I've always read a lot of different things. But I don't keep up with contemporary things nearly as much as I used to, except for movies. Partly because there aren't that many movies to go to, you know, really. So I end up seeing a lot of things that I wouldn't have seen otherwise.

But I think, why do I hate Meryl Streep so much? She's no worse than a lot of people, though I don't really believe that. I think it's got something to do with, you know, what I've seen before and what is the sort of parameters now of what's good acting. And, you know, I mean there are all those people that really just drive me absolutely crazy, which nobody ever did in the old days. There were people I probably didn't like as much, but I mean I never get quite as incensed as people in the old days as I do at Meryl Streep, and Glenn Close, and Vanessa Redgrave, and Helena Bonham Carter, and gee, let's see who else? Shirley Knight. And they're all acting apparently in the same way, or at least something that really grates on me. I think, "Oh, shut up, stop that, get off the screen, go away!"

CS: You mean they're taking themselves too seriously?

EG: No. God knows people like Joan Crawford . . . I was watching an old Joan Crawford movie the other night, and God knows she was taking herself seriously enough, though she was doing slapstick comedy at the time. No, I can remember when I was younger, when I was a kid, I used to think people like Bette Davis and Kathryn Hepburn and some of the others were overacting wildly. So that's not it.

But the older I got, I thought, "Gee, they really know what they're doing. They may be overacting but they're overdoing it in the right way." But then I think movies made more sense in those days too, sometimes.

CS: I notice that you have a really hands-off approach with the actors in your own plays.

EG: Oh yes, the reason I do it really is so they'll tell me what it is that I've written. Sometimes of course it's a long time before they get around to being able to get to it. I think, I know this is about something. When are they going to tell me what it is? As they maunder along.

CS: What do you mean exactly?

EG: Both Carol and I said when we watched the plays you filmed, you know, my God, in *Wallpaper* they were talking more slowly than you would believe humanly possible! Which I didn't notice at the time. Of course I was in that myself, so I was very nervous. I thought, "Are they ever going to finish this line? Hello? Hello?" [*Yelling in a high-pitched voice*]

And it wasn't apparent to me at all when I was rehearsing. But then just last night, I said, "Let's just go a little faster because we have this terrible tendency to just drag it out longer." They somehow feel, "Oh, well, I want to express this and that and it will take me a while." And so they just go on and on. I don't know . . .

CS: What did you think of the black and white I used in the video? [Referring to a black-and-white video version edited of the play *Wallpaper*]

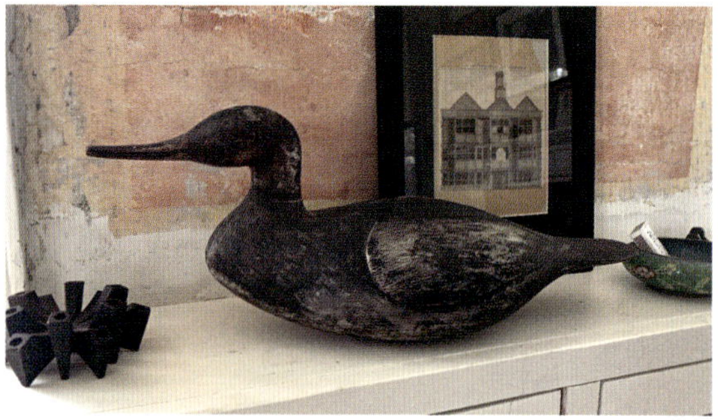

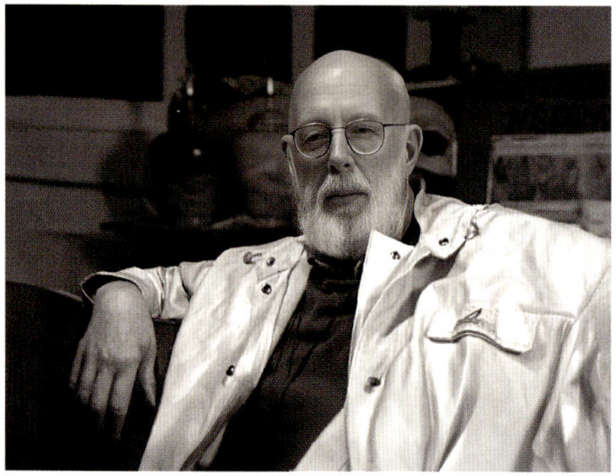

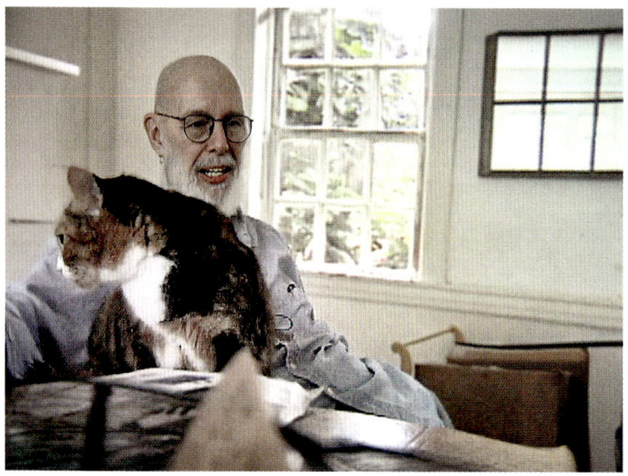

EG: I was very surprised. Everything looked much creepier to me than I remembered it in real life. I thought, "The puppets, my God!"

This looks like it had been smuggled out of Germany in about 1920. You know, this was probably in German originally or something and somebody put a soundtrack on it. It was very strange, so I don't know. I thought it was rather interesting because I hadn't noticed it before when I was watching the puppets that you had filmed in black and white, but anyhow.

CS: I guess the way we got onto that topic was that you seem to have a specific thing that you like about actors and actresses, and, you know, it's surprising that you're so hands off.

EG: Yeah, well I am. Sooner or later it more or less comes out that way for me. And if it doesn't come out that way, there's nothing I can do about it. I mean, because I've, you know, not screamed at, but I've said over and over and over to them, "Would you do this faster, would you do it faster?" And you know, they do it for a minute or two that way, and then, you know, at the next rehearsal they go right back to whatever it was they were planning to do in the first place. There's nothing you can do about it. I guess if you're completely hands-on and they realize that up front, then they will do it. Because quite often I've run into actors asking, "How am I supposed to be doing it?" say, "I don't know, dear, just do it and we'll figure it out later." Or "If I don't like it, I'll tell you I don't like it, but otherwise, you know, go ahead and feel free." So anyway.

CS: Do you feel that you tend to attract a certain type of actor? You have a pretty tight core of people that you work with.

EG: Well, I have now because it's so hard to get people. I haven't auditioned anybody for ages.

And whenever we have auditioned people, somebody will turn up for one production or something and then vanish to jail or, you know, reform school or something or other, [*laughing*] or go back to college or I don't know what. So I haven't really been auditioning. As long as I've got enough people to put on something, I would rather work with people I've worked with before.

CS: So you don't think they all have something in common?

EG: Oh, I think they all have something in common, but I think they also have gotten more in common through the process, because some of them have been doing things with me for twelve years now. So, this is the twelfth season for some of them.

CS: I was surprised at the rehearsal. We were talking to your new actress, Nicole, last night and she said, "I'd never heard of the name Edward Gorey before eight months ago."

EG: Well! [*Feigning outrage*] Well, stupid twit! Stupid twit Nicole! But she does take direction very well. I think she'll be a real asset if she doesn't start carrying on too much. Well, it doesn't matter really because I've noticed in Carol's other play, she tends to be a very actressy actress, which is fine, but she tends to get more actressy over time rather, you know.

The trick is that she slips a little thing in the first five minutes, and it's the first time I see it. By the tenth time around that she's been doing it, she's now managed to get it throughout the entire performance past me. But that's all right.

You know, what the heck. I've had actressy people before. It's just a quality of deadpan I'm actually after.

I'd like them not to try and convince the audience of anything and just let them, you know, make of it what they will. If the actors want to act for their own amusement, okay.

But don't try and get, you know, "This is what I'm trying to tell you." Don't try and tell them anything. Just do it. So . . . [*Looks down at the floor and trails off*]

[*Long silence and looking at floor*] [This is Edward's way of saying he's done.]

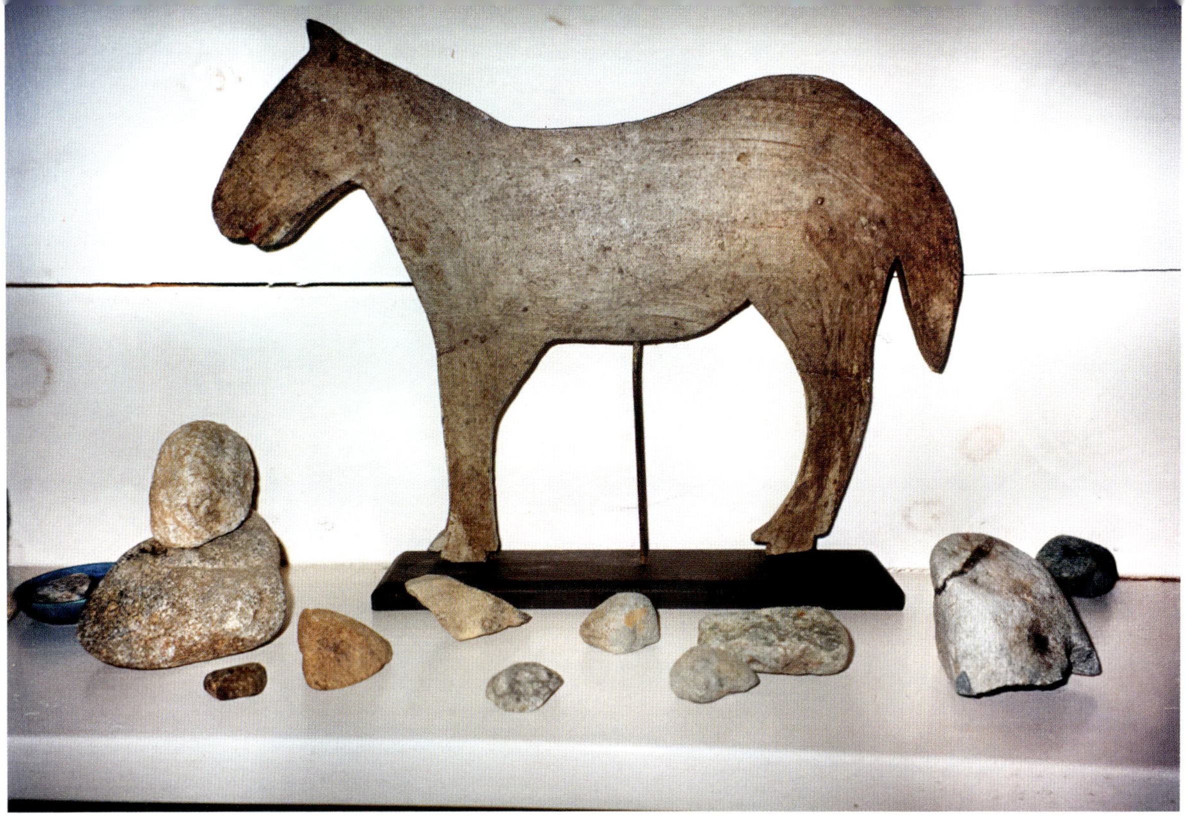

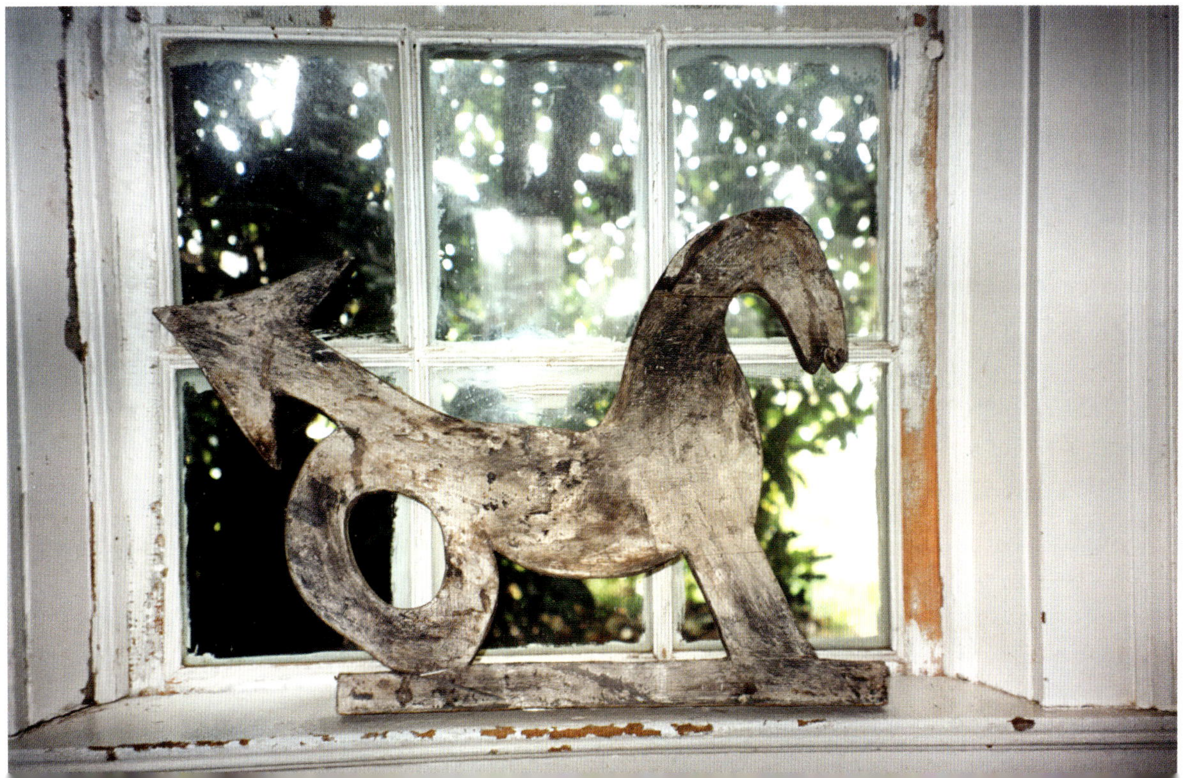

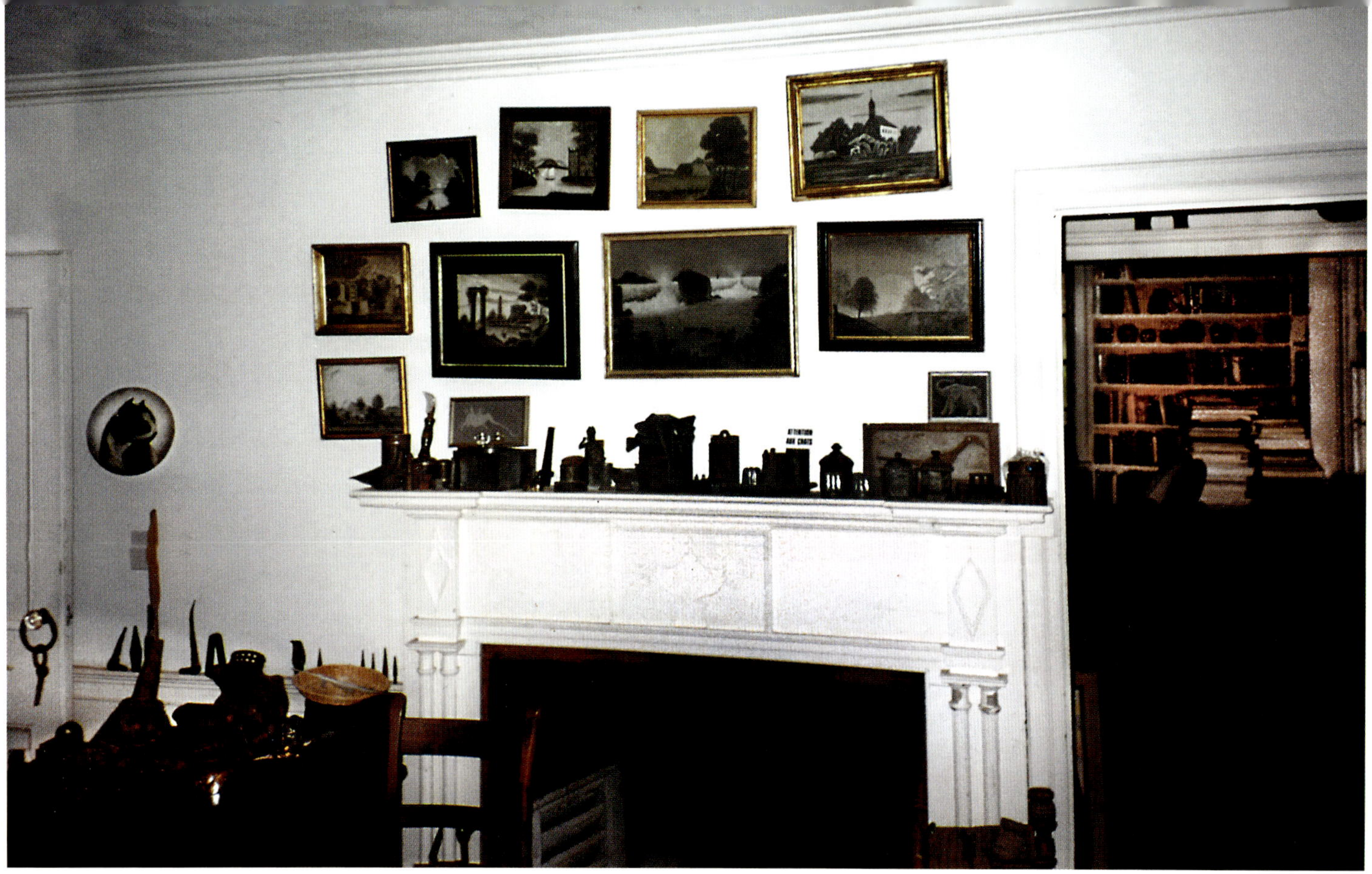

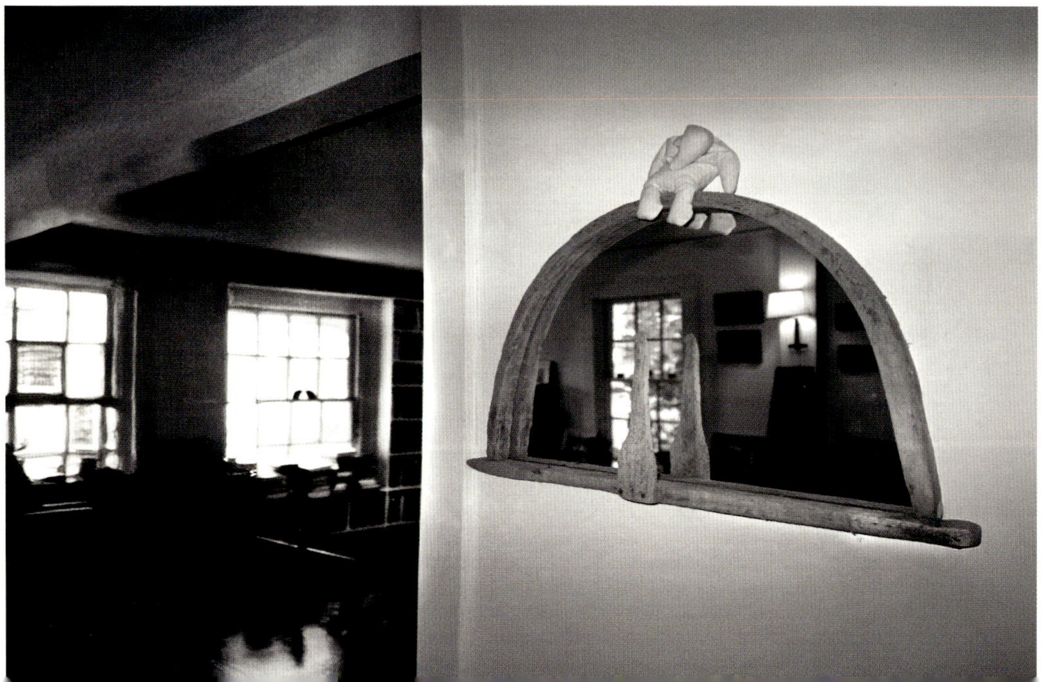

The framed prints on the wall were noticeably set high for the benefit of someone of his stature, at 6 feet, 3 inches, not down at general eye level. This photo shows the black sand paintings that greeted those who entered his house, set high enough that they were even above the height of the doorway into the living room.

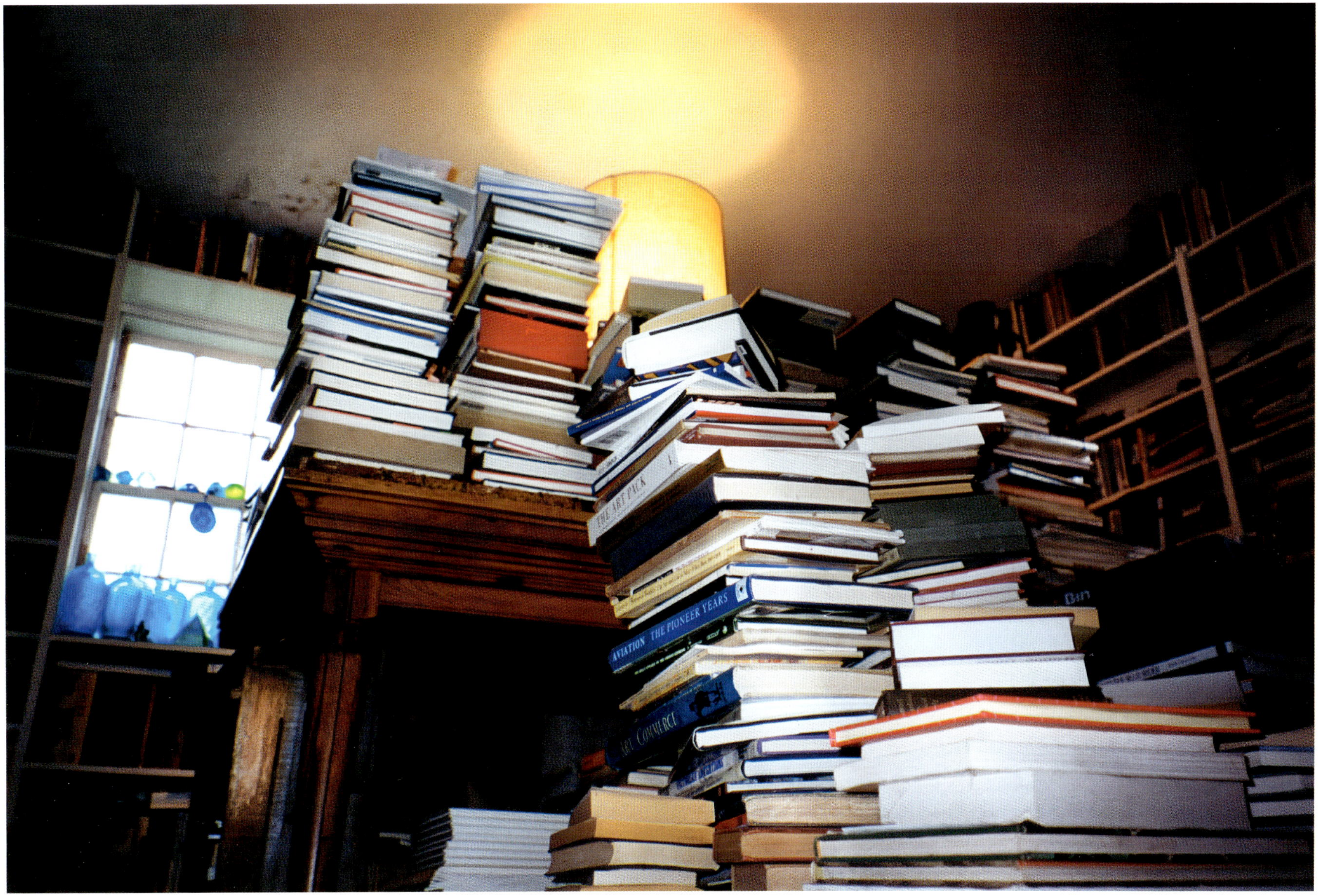
THE ART PACK
AVIATION THE PIONEER YEARS

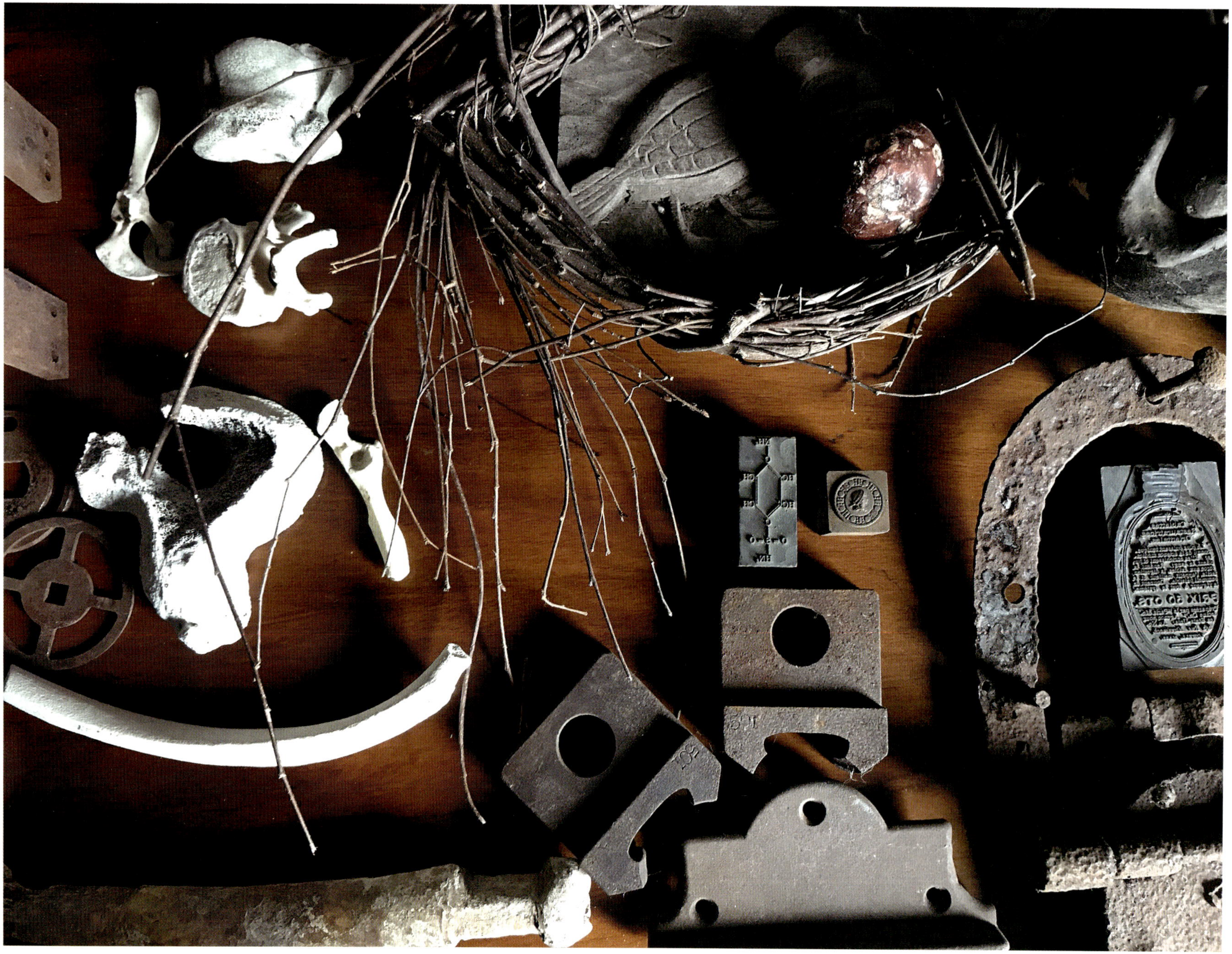

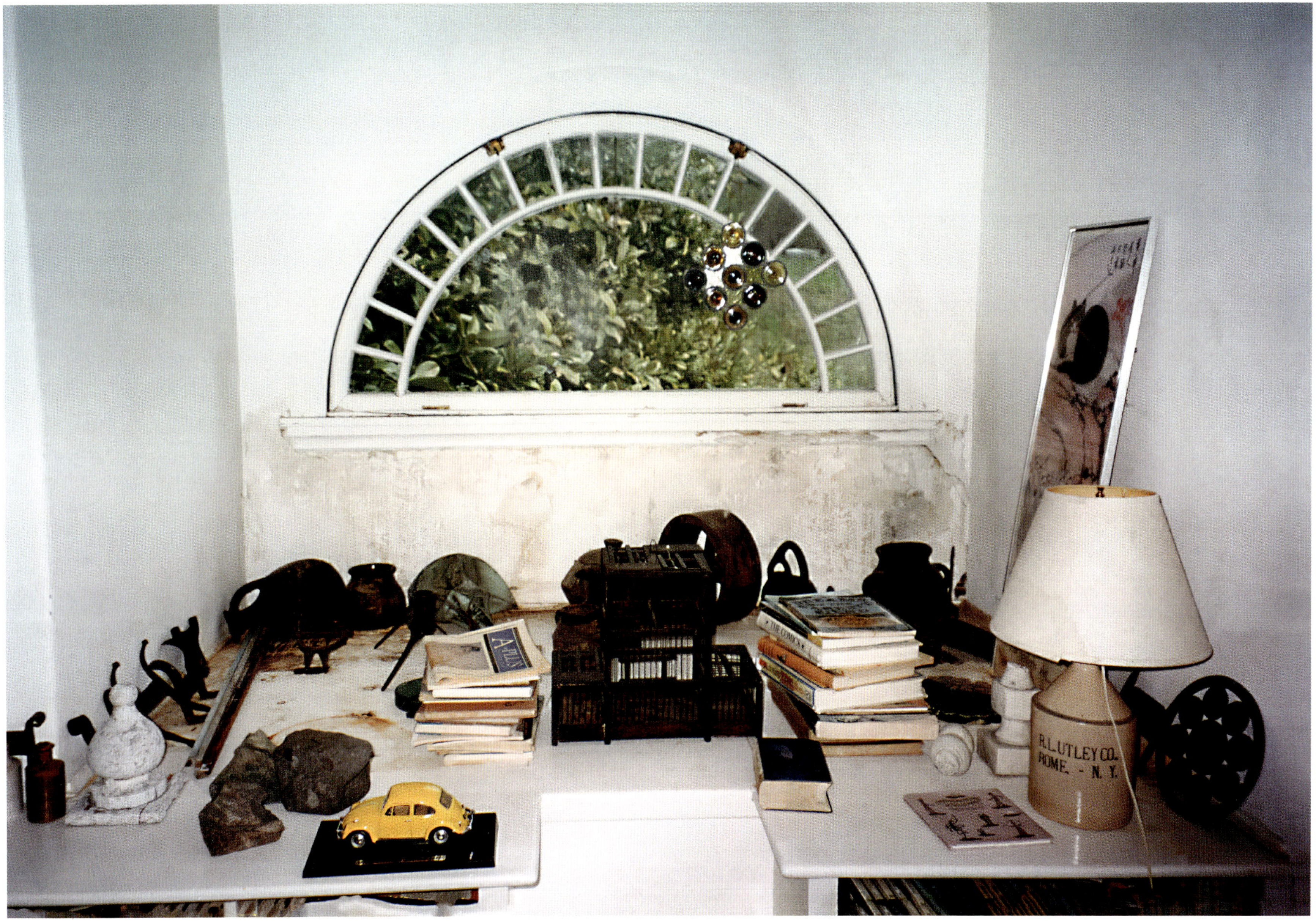
R.L.UTLEY CO.
ROME. - N.Y.

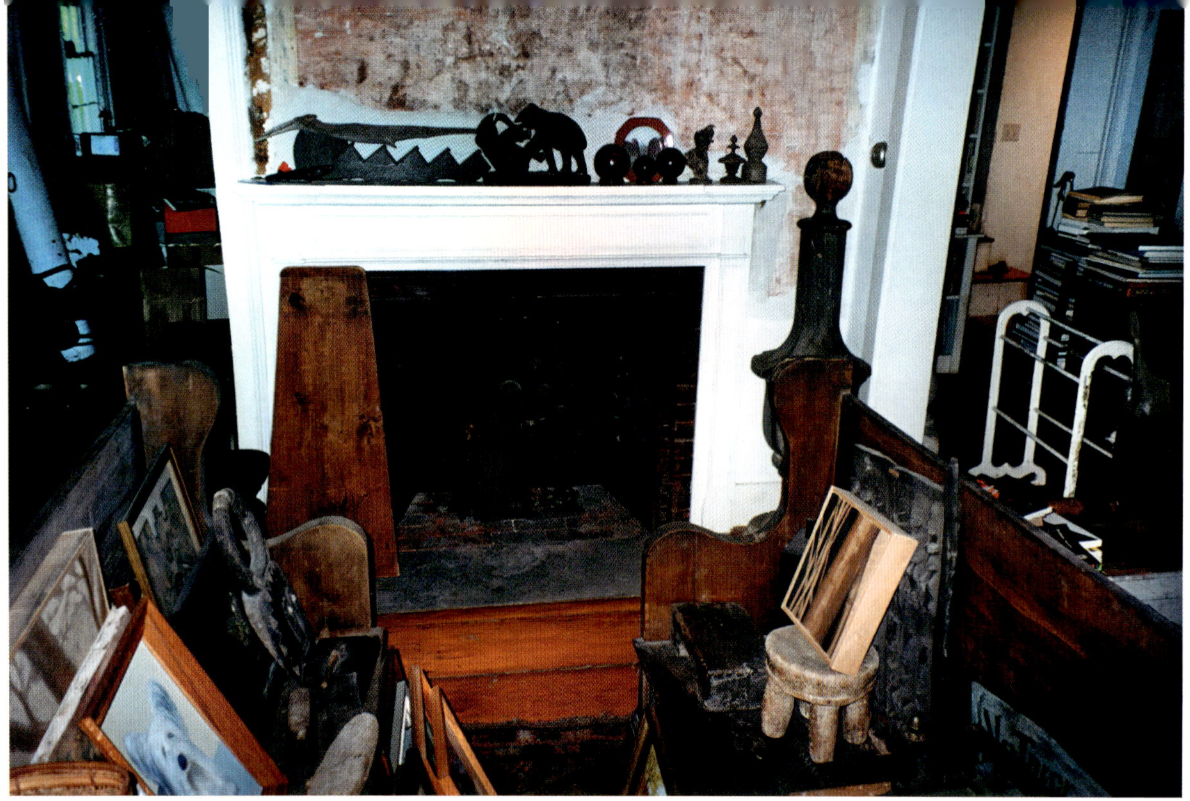

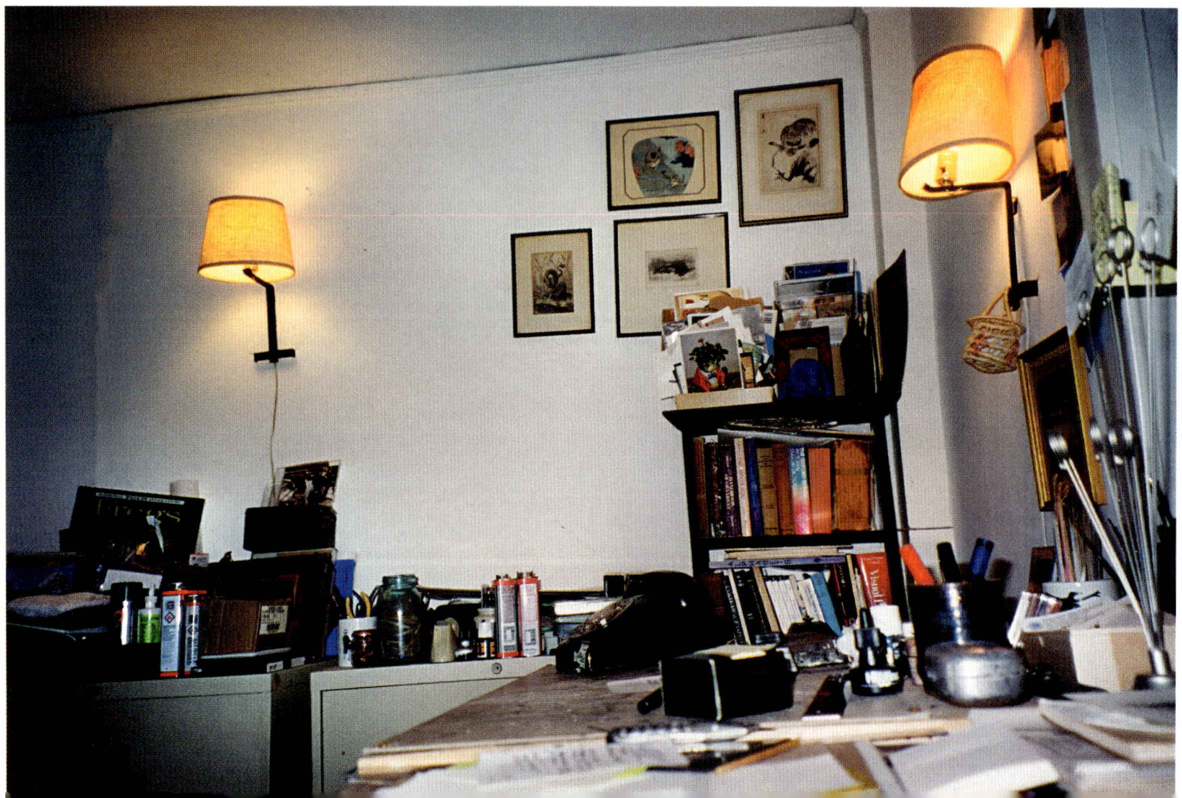

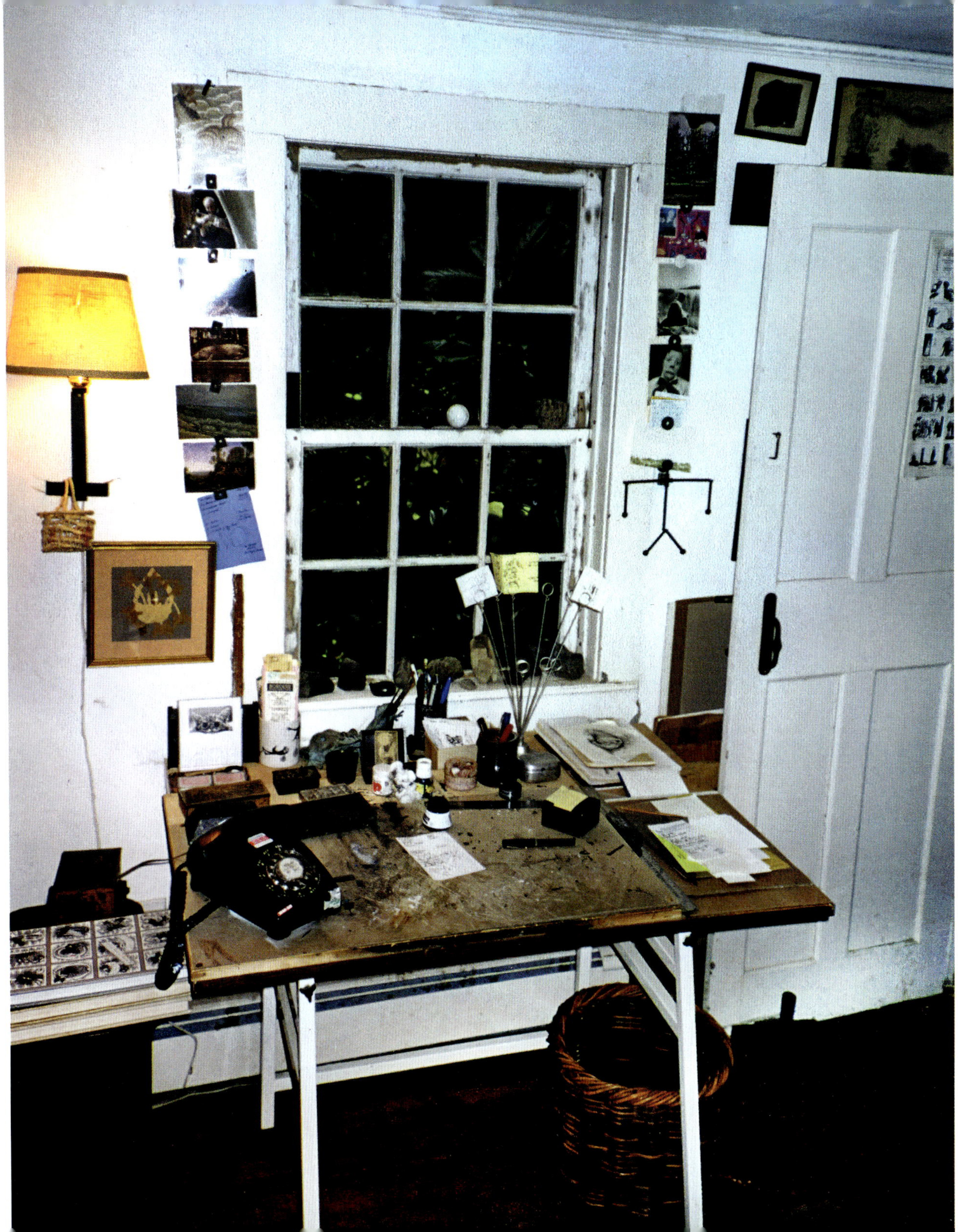

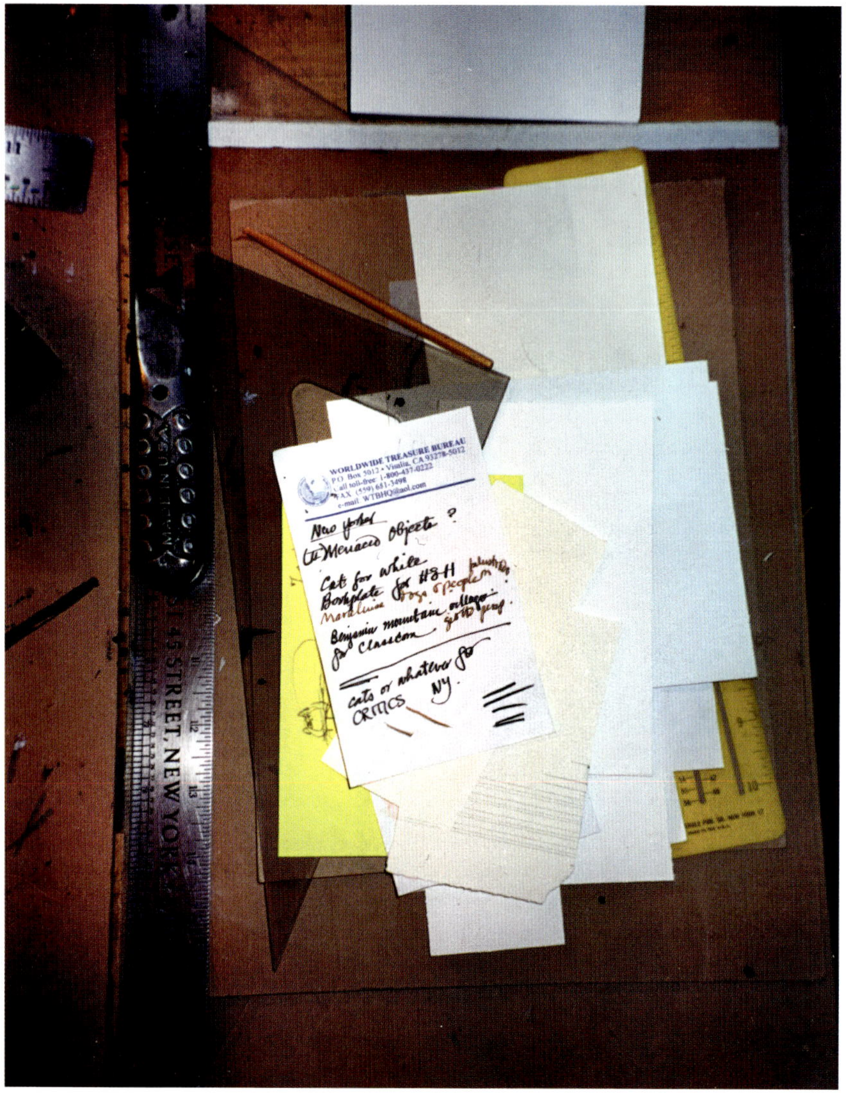
WORLDWIDE TREASURE BUREAU
New Yorker
Menaced Objects?
cats or whatever for
CRITICS NY

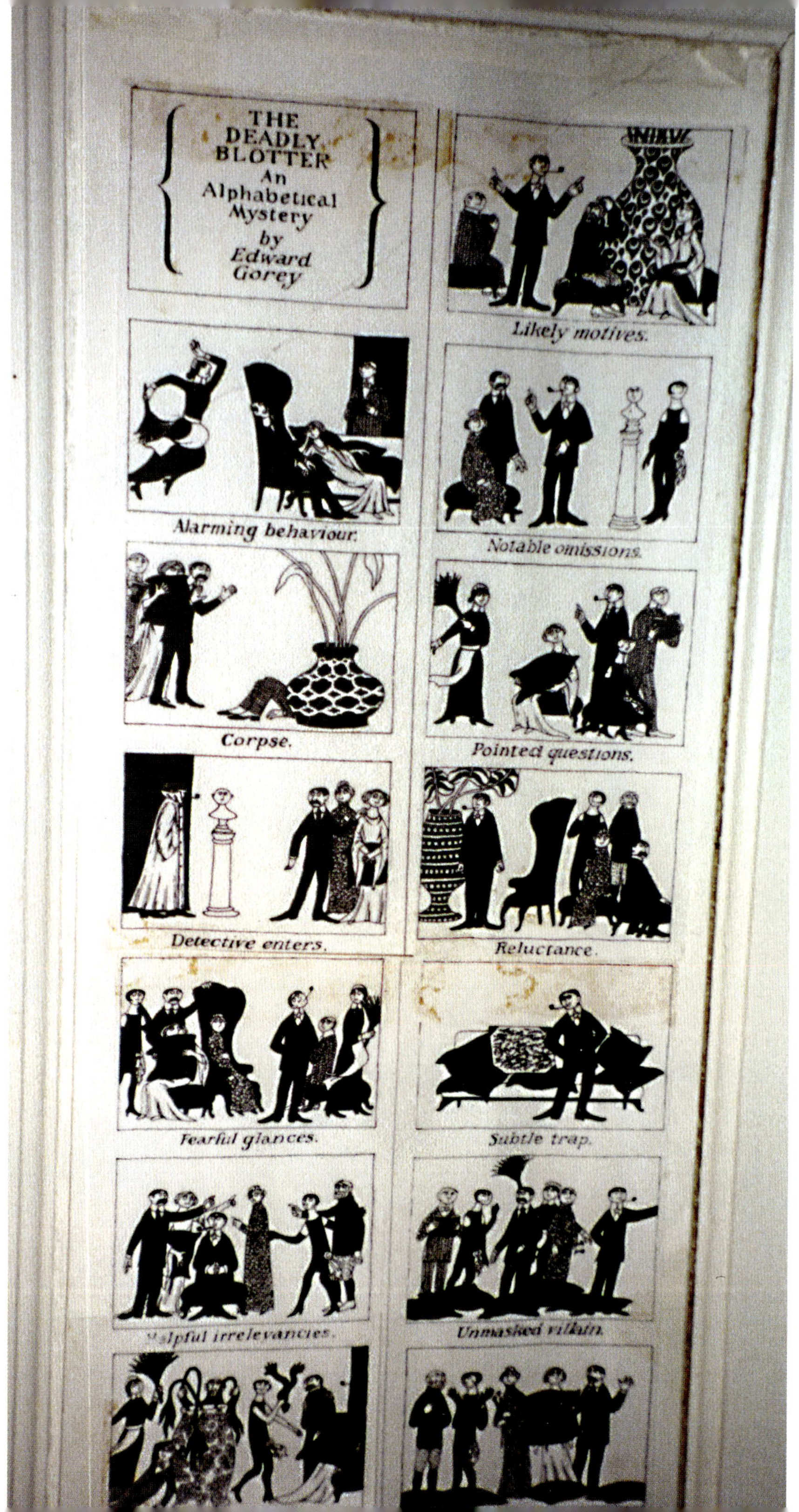
THE DEADLY BLOTTER
An Alphabetical Mystery
by Edward Gorey
Likely motives.
Alarming behaviour.
Notable omissions.
Corpse.
Pointed questions.
Detective enters.
Reluctance.
Fearful glances.
Subtle trap.
Unmasked villain.

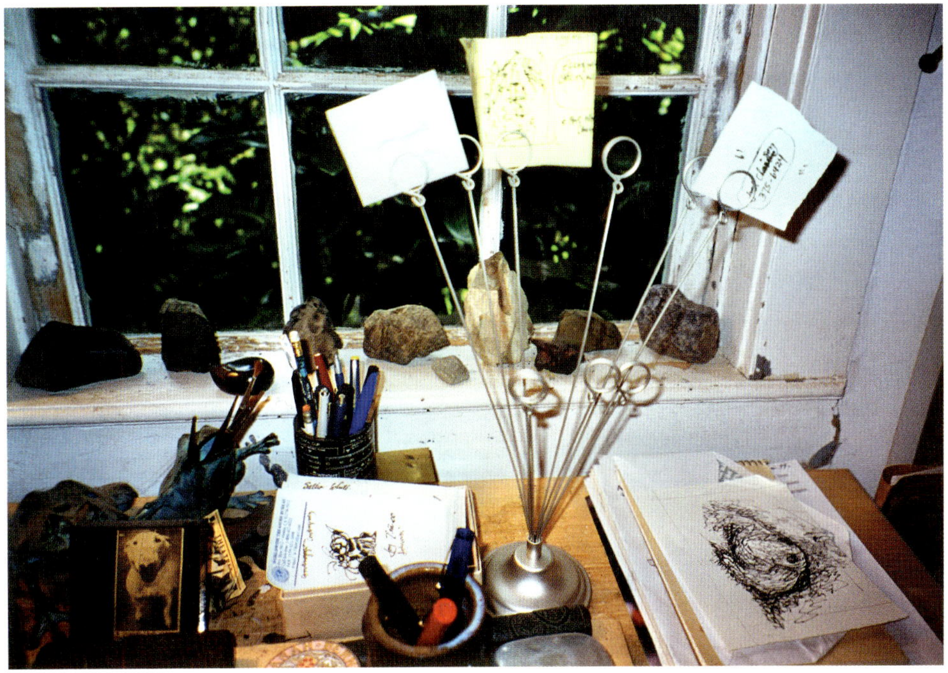

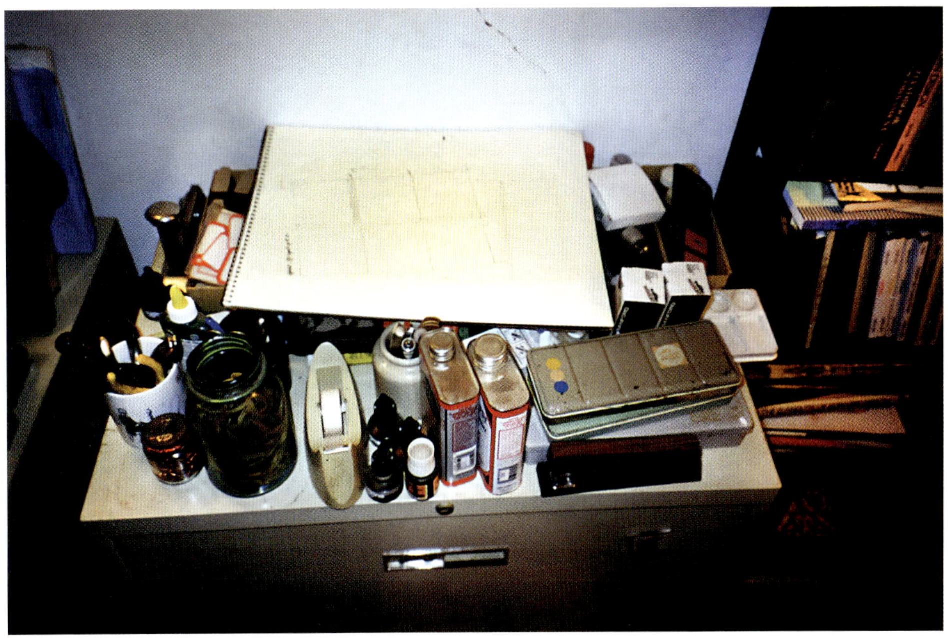

Edward Gorey House curator Greg Hischak stands next to an ink stain near the studio window, caused by a disastrous spill by one of Edward's cats, who were welcome on his desk. His drawing was ruined, forcing him to start over.

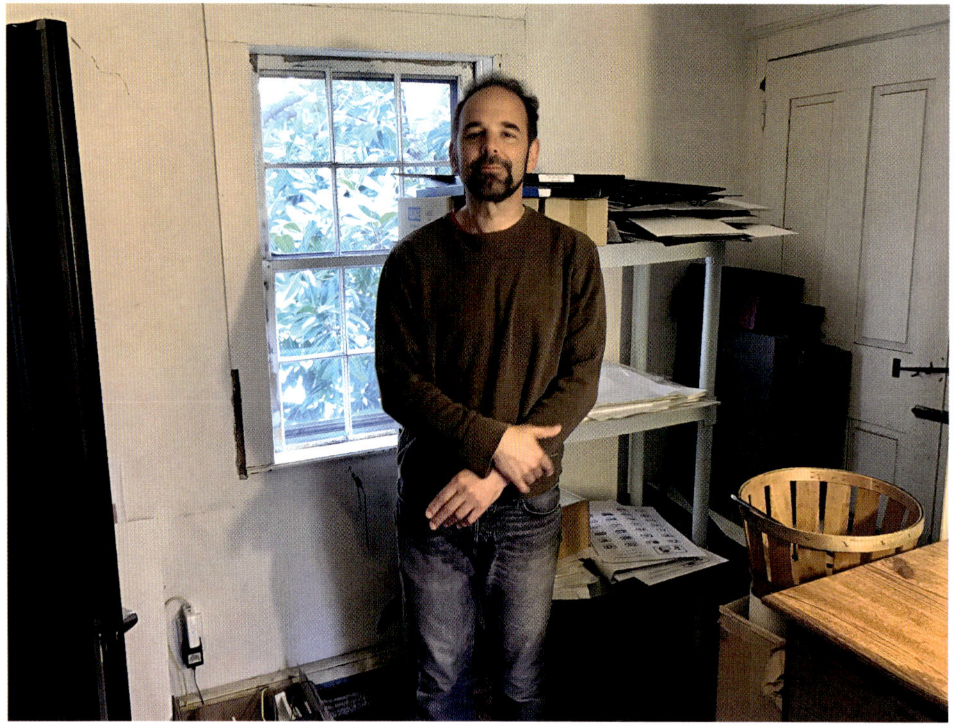

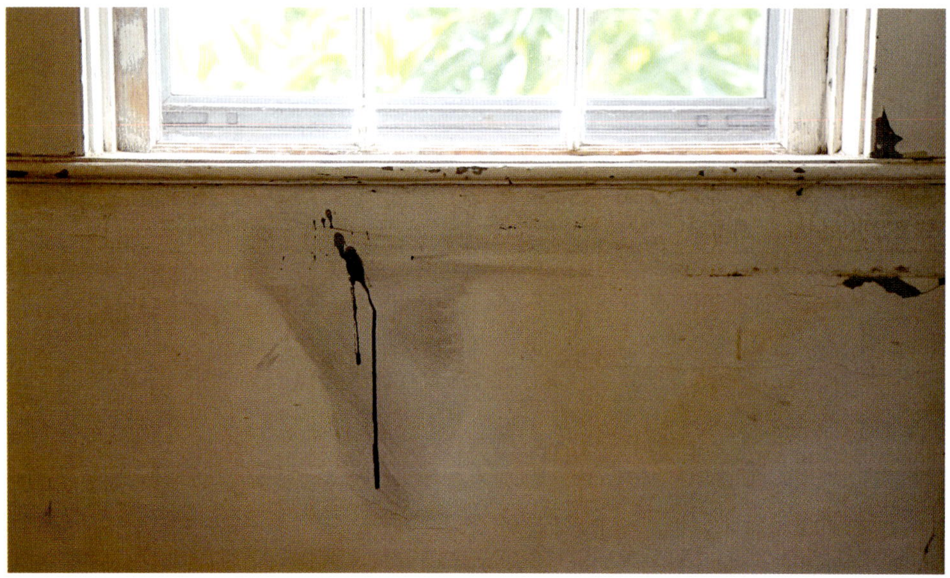

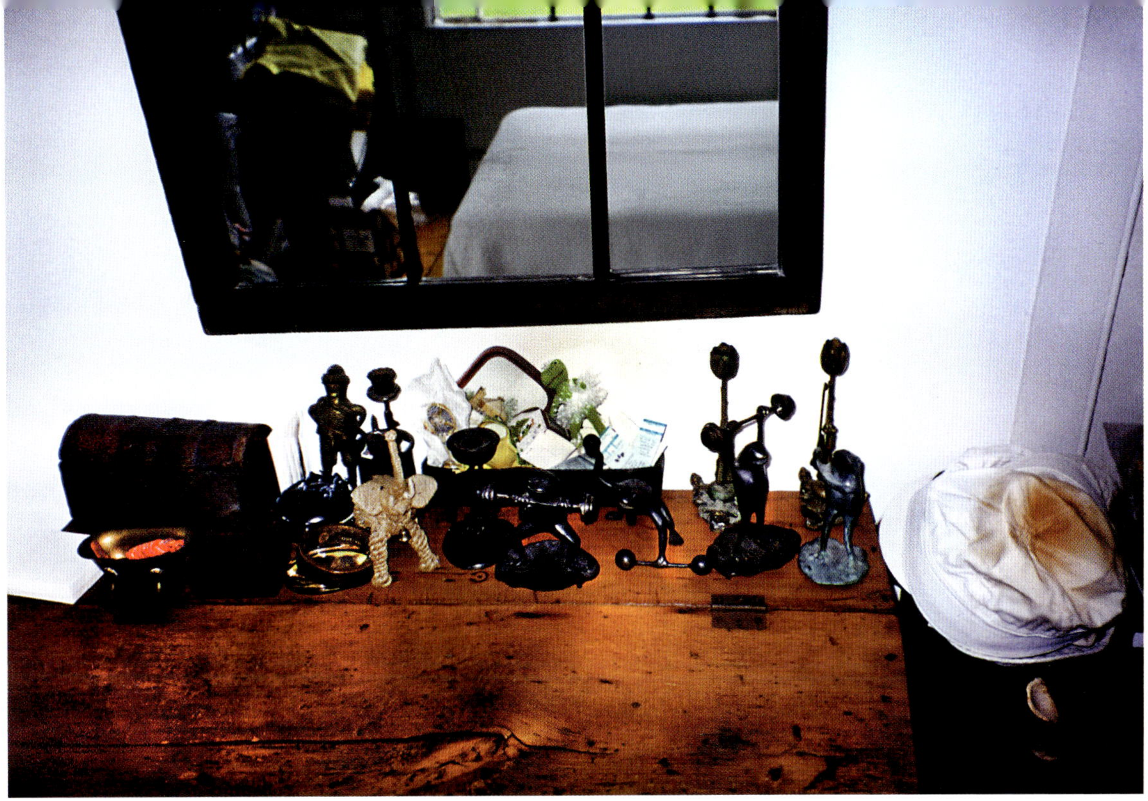

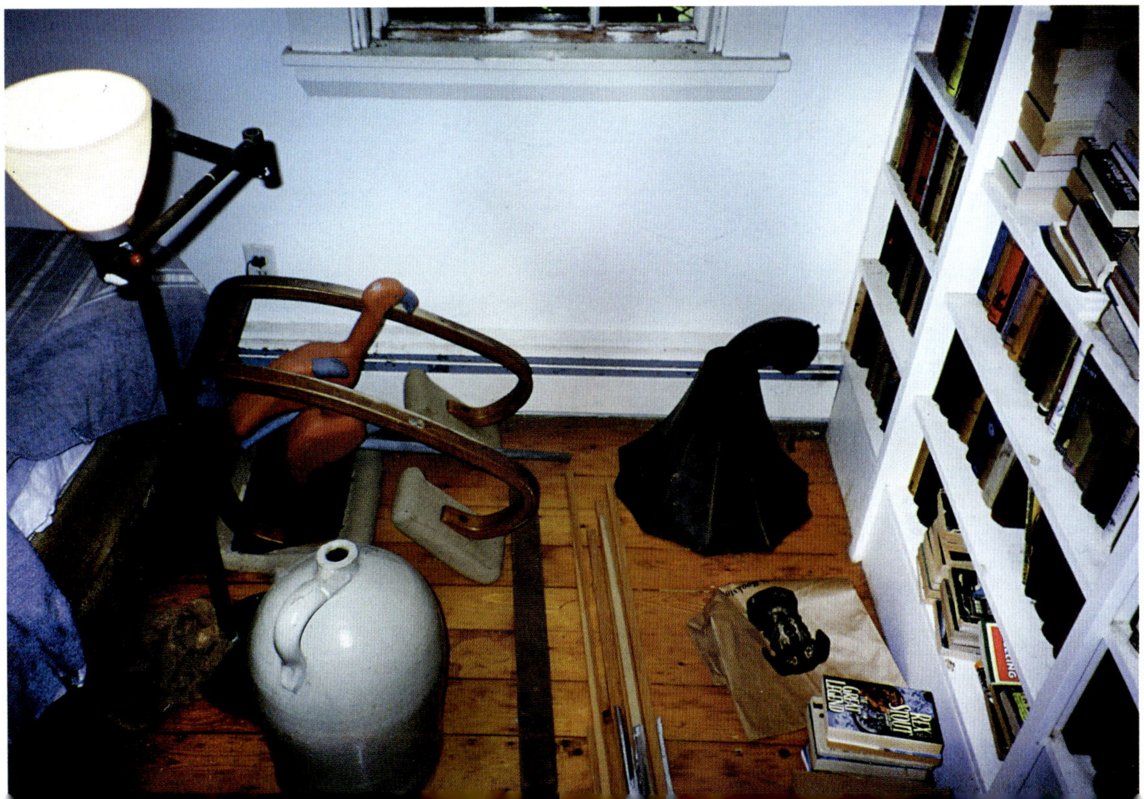

Edward not only surrounded himself with his own work but collected items that inspired him for many of his images as well. Frogs and alligators on the previous page populated the side table in his bedroom, and this gramophone speaker lay on the floor in his entryway.

Interview with Edward Gorey by Christopher Lydon, WGBH

1992

Radio personality Christopher Lydon interviewed Gorey for his show *The Connection* and also shot one of his plays in preparation for WGBH television program about Gorey's theater work on Cape Cod. That program never was put together, but portions of the interview did air on the radio. I met with Lydon at the Nantucket Book Festival in 2013 to discuss both publishing the interview and interviewing Lydon himself about his experience with Gorey. He declined the interview but agreed to let us publish the transcript of his raw conversation with Gorey. On the show he prefaced the interview this way:

Christopher Lydon: Edward Gorey the American genius eccentric. His books are obscure, often morbid and funny at the same time. His stories range from the silly to the surreal to the macabre. An epileptic bicycle ride, a series of pictures of useful urns, a horrid life and death of a hapless child. They're often told in rhyme, giving even the most grisly happening a strangely childlike innocence. Edward Gorey wrote and drew his characters with meticulous fine-point care. He did bland-face humans and other odder things; human figures with prunes for heads or stranger indistinctly drawn characters with still-stranger names.

Sometimes it's what's not pictured, a monster always hovering outside the frame about to descend. Like the vague dread that descends on us as we read. So if we're uneasy, why are we laughing? Edward Gorey in spooky spidery words and pictures is this hour on *The Connection*.

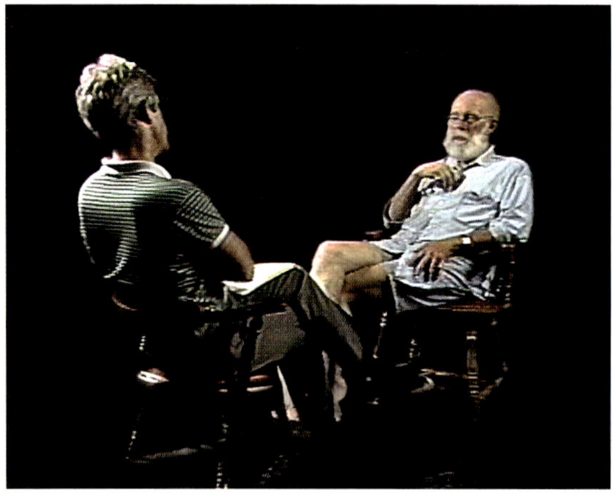

Christopher Lydon interviews Edward in Boston for his radio show *The Connection*. Courtesy of WGBH-TV

PART 1

Christopher Lydon: Do you find yourself putting stories onstage, or do the stories come out of theatrical emotions?

Edward Gorey: Oh, I don't know. I mean up until this show, the other ones I've done have almost entirely been adapted from either books that have already been published or books that haven't been published because the drawings haven't been done for them. And in this show there were a couple of pieces, which were not written directly as stage pieces, but they were somewhere in a limbo between book and stage, and the minute I'd done them, I thought, oh well, I'll put them in the show this time, so I'm beginning to think more I'm gradually adding a little more dialogue to things instead of straight narration. Since this is the third one I've done in two years and the fifth one I've done in the last six, you know I'm beginning to sort of think more in terms of theater when I'm thinking of things.

CL: Is there more of this stuff in the future?

EG: Well, I hope so. I enjoy doing it very much. I enjoy putting it together and I enjoy directing a great deal, which I had never done before. It's very satisfying in a way that doing a book isn't. No matter how many times you do this, no matter how many performances you see of it, it's sort of different every time. With a book, you know it's a book, and there it is sitting on the shelf, and it may strike you differently, you know, at one time or another, but it doesn't have the kind of wonderful open thing that the theater does.

CL: Who is the puppeteer in Edward Gorey?

EG: Well, I don't know. I'd always been sort of interested in puppets, not so much, you know, the ordinary kind of thing, but I mean reading about, you know, well, oriental puppets especially. I have seen some of the Japanese puppets in New York over the years, you know, and was absolutely stunned by them, you know. Those things, which are of course quite different from anything, you know, that you're ever going to see here.

CL: Different from anything I've ever seen. Tell me about it.

EG: Well, you know, I remember it only very vaguely, though I've read a lot about it. The typical Japanese puppet is operated by three people. There's one—the main operator, who is in very gaudy ceremonial costume, and here you're operating a puppet, which I guess is about four feet high. I believe the chief puppeteer operates the head and one arm, and then there are two other people dressed entirely in black. Somebody else operates the other arm, and I guess somebody kind of moves the body around and everything. So you have these three, one obvious person and two kind of shadow people, operating somebody who's about four feet high.

It sounds, you know, so completely unreal, but once you're watching it, I can still remember once back in city center, where somebody is trying to climb the outside of a castle, so this puppet keeps continually climbing up and falling back. I mean, it was just absolutely the most, the greatest pieces of suspense I've ever seen. You knew perfectly well he was going to get to the top eventually. It was wonderful. It's this kind of this, you know, combination of kind of minute reality in a sense; I mean, now those Japanese puppets, they can roll their eyes, and, you know, it's in an aura of complete and total, you know, disbelief in a sense.

That's what I sort of like about puppets. I'm amazed because, well, this is the fifth show, I guess, that I've been doing puppets [that] had usually three puppet pieces in. The people I worked with, in no case was anybody a professional puppeteer, and in fact a lot of people had never operated them before at all. I've never operated them myself at all, and yet, quite often, people would come back and say, "Well, we loved the show, but who were those wonderful people doing the puppets?" and I say, "Well, that was us folks." You know, they can't believe it. You know, it's extraordinary what effects you can get with these.

CL: At the far end from Japanese puppets, there's also something of *Kukla, Fran and Ollie* here, isn't there?

EG: Ah, I suppose so. I've only seen *Kukla, Fran and Ollie* a few times, because I wasn't watching TV in their heyday. Actually, I have not really seen it. Well, there's not really that much puppet stuff to see. I guess there are a couple of those, at least there's I think one troupe that still does the conventional Sicilian puppets some place in Connecticut. I've been through the studio there but I never saw one of their shows. Occasionally you see a documentary, say, on the Chinese puppets, which are the little tiny hand puppets, which are kind of marvelous. I've seen some of those occasionally. And I've occasionally seen, you know, some sort of vaguely avant garde kind of stuff in New York. Usually stupefying boring if I may say so. Marionettes don't somehow don't interest me nearly as much.

CL: Are you a Muppet man?

EG: Ah, I haven't really seen all that much of them. And you know, I adore Kermit and Miss Piggy, but I never really watched them. And I think they suffer slightly, of course, from being very cute. Which you know, I mean, obviously, if you're going to have great success, you have to have the Disney thing. I mean, obviously, you know, the greatest puppets were an ordinary thing. I still, I mean, well, of course, the movies, you know, I mean God knows how much, I mean, you know, you can obviously do special effects that you can't do with regular puppets. TV obviously too; I mean there must be a whole lot going on. The Muppets, just aside from being rods and things and so forth.

CL: What's the opposite of cute? What's the other end of cute?

EG: I suppose the other end of cute is gruesome and sinister and whatnot. Certainly Disney. I worry about cute sometimes. I have a terrible tendency to get cute if I'm not doing something else and stopping myself. As I do fairly cute things. I've sort of wondered where it began. Well, there [is] some pre-Columbian art that I think tends to be cute. I feel somebody thought, somebody who was down there amongst the Incas or whatever. Really, some things are inescapably cute, and I don't think it's just because they happen to coincide with what we think is cute; I think they were cute to begin with.

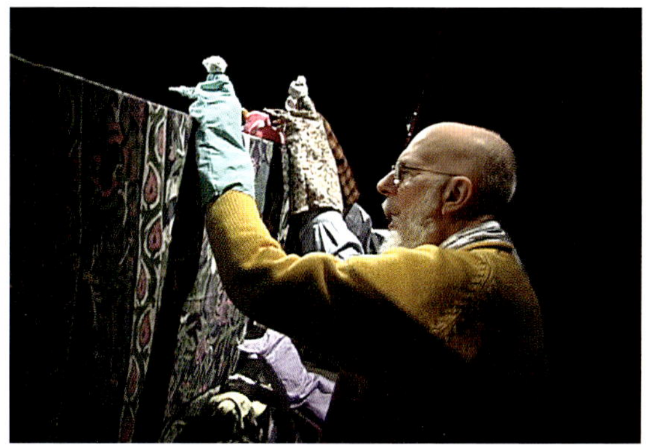

Edward with puppets for *Cautionary Tales for Children*, 1996

CL: Define cute and anti-cute.

EG: Well, cute is Snow White and the Seven Dwarfs and all those darling little animals. And, you know, the opposite, of course, is the wicked queen and Snow White, which surely anybody my age must have never gotten over. I mean kitsch comes into it sort of, but not . . . I think one of the clearest examples of cute overtaking everything is when you look at the original teddy bears and look at the teddy bears we have now and the progression. I mean, the original teddy bears are kind of long and lanky and have kind of long noses and, you know, well, they're not as cuddly because of course, I guess they were, you know, made out of stuffed with horsehair, you know, whatever. But as the years have gone by, I mean, I collect teddy bears in a desperatory sort of way, and they just get cuter and cuter and more and more roly-poly and more and more round. And whoever invented those ghastly plastic eyes that, you know, the eyes move and everything. Terminal had begun to set in there.

CL: Who is the dramatist in Edward Gorey? I take it that goes back [to] at least the college days.

EG: It goes back even before, I think. Actually because the first things that I wrote seriously, for some unknown reason, were plays. I'm hoping, I think I may have copies of them. There was one full-length play and about six or seven one-act plays. I'm hoping that no one else has copies. But I wrote those while I was in the army in World War II. I don't know why I decided to write, but I mean I suppose there must have been some strong dramatic urge at the time. I never tried to get them put on or anything.

CL: What were they about?

EG: Oh, I think they were all very, very exotic and filled with . . . They were pretentious in a way. In another way, I don't think they were as pretentious as they might have been, let's put it that way. I mean, I didn't go in for endless, dopey, poetic monologues for people. They moved right along, they were rather bizarre, I think, and were rather overwritten in way. I can't even remember what they were about now, if anything.

CL: What was the college career in drama?

EG: Oh, none. Well, except the Poet's Theatre actually, in Cambridge, which I was, well, it wasn't my idea. I was one of the founding members of it back in '47 or '48. And it was, well, I think in a way it was sort of unique because it was a bunch of people; it ranged from undergraduates to faculty members at Harvard and Radcliffe and people from Cambridge, Boston. And we wrote, directed, produced, designed, you know, everything ourselves. And it [was] always one of those things that was precarious. I think actually the first production took place in some settlement house in Boston. We used to, we did a couple times, I remember, in Christ Church in Cambridge. I remember we did quite an elaborate double production; I mean there were two nights of different things in the lobby of the Fogg Museum. We sometimes did, you know, kind of readings and things in people's houses. Eventually, well, I left Cambridge at the end of 1952, and I think shortly thereafter the Poet's Theatre sort of got a permanent more or less location in some place on that little street behind where the Harvard Coop bookstore is, I can't remember. But anyway I remember coming back occasionally to Cambridge to see Poet's Theatre productions.

CL: Is the Poet's Theatre important to you in memory anyway?

EG: Oh yeah, in memory I think it was kind of the ideal theatrical experience. Well, sort of working up here and around the Cape has been very much like it because, you know, nobody was paid, and it was all very much you do, doing what you wanted to do, and if the audience wanted to come and, you know, I feel the same way about the group of people I've worked with on the Cape. We have a lot of fun, I hope. And, you know, I think it's . . . well, you know, you're not stuck in the sort of . . . I mean, one of the things about . . . I mean, after all, Cape Cod is not that far from Boston, Providence, or

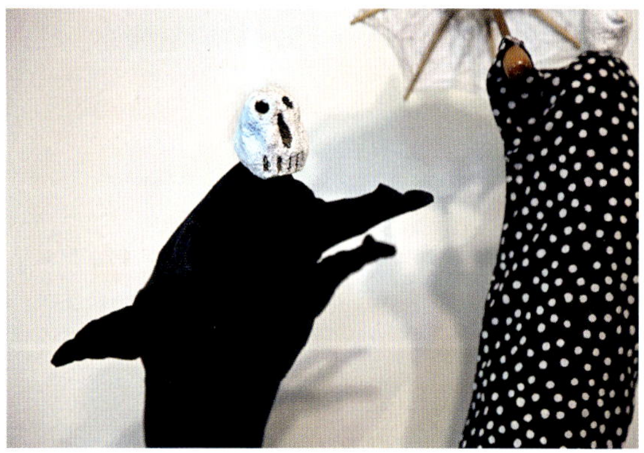

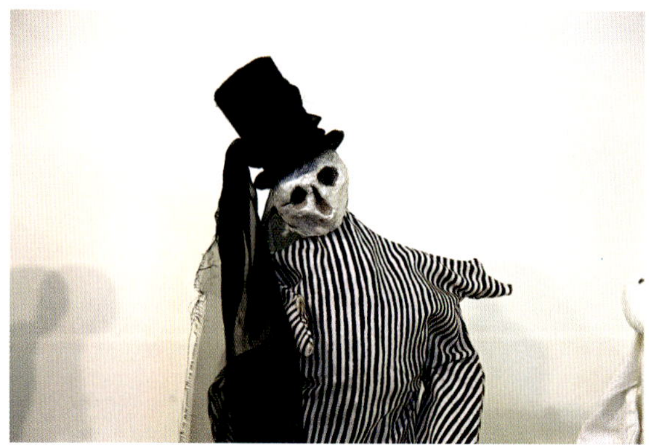

New York, and I don't really see much point in, you know, doing Neil Simon or even Ibsen or something. I mean, obviously not enough stuff is done anywhere, but as long as you're off here, you might as well do your own things and have a good time doing something that nobody's going to see anyplace else.

CL: Were you pleased to be pressed into service as an actor?

EG: Not at the beginning I wasn't. I was horrified. I thought I know I'm going to forget every single line or I'm going have a heart attack or I'm going to suddenly run screaming from the stage, saying I can't face this or something. Actually, it turned out, I think, as a defense the first couple of performances I did I just thought, Will this thing ever end?" I would come off from some bit and I would look to see how many more numbers and would say, "We still have six to do in the first act, we're going to be here forever." My final, my third, performance, which I really began to feel confident, a little bit of confidence in everything and I was making up things as I went along and having a fun time. That made it quite different, but for me I'd rather be up watching everybody. I can't, I

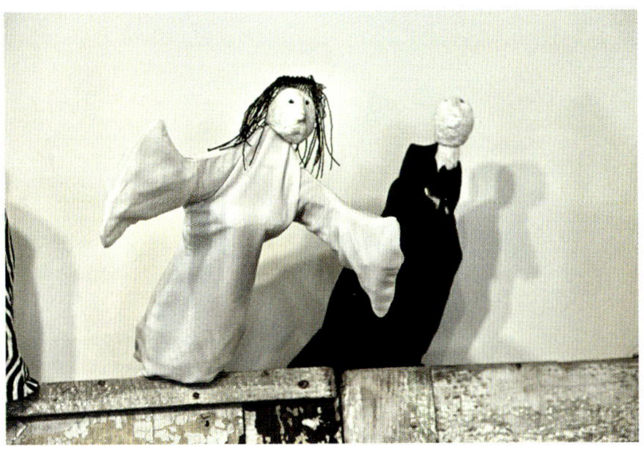

mean, obviously, having acted, you know, a couple of rehearsals and three performances, I really have absolutely no clear feeling of what I'm doing at all, which I find very disturbing, as if you didn't have any physical entity or something. Being a great ballet fan and everything, I know a lot about ballet. I've never danced or anything, but I mean I can at least see how a dancer endlessly, you know, practicing in front of a mirror or in the studios begins to have a real sense of what they're . . . I mean, not only from how they feel through their bodies, but also how it looks to somebody outside. Acting, I mean, I just can't, I have absolutely . . . I'd look in the mirror and think, "Who?"

CL: Who are the drama gods in your reading and your life?

EG: Well actually, I know this is going to sound truly bizarre, but the reason I starting thinking about doing puppets was I got interested in doing Seneca's plays. There's a famous collection of Elizabethan translations, which are absolutely quite wonderful. I mean, his plays are virtually nonexistent, but I kept thinking, "Oh, wouldn't this be fun to do Seneca with puppets." So that's when . . . I started making puppets because somebody introduced me to this sinister, well, not sinister, really quite wonderful substance called celluclay, which is, I guess, is actually made out of newspapers. But I never learned how to make papier mâché in school, I think I skipped that grade or something, so that I'd never known about papier mâché or making maps out of flour and water and stuff. And I have no sculptural, I mean, my sculptural abilities are about yay big and everything. But I was introduced to the celluclay, which you just mix with water, and you can immediately make a puppet head in about thirty seconds and put it in the oven and then it's baked and then you paint it with acrylic and there you are, you have this minimal puppet head. And so at that time, I sort of thought . . . I'm seriously considering doing something with Seneca sometime.

CL: Any other theatrical gods in your head?

EG: Oh, gee. Well, anything that emanates from Japan. Kabuki, anything of that sort. I'm trying to think . . . I'll occasionally see something. My theatrical interests really tend to be ballet, opera, anything that's highly stylized. I don't think realistic theater interests me very much, except for, I mean, old-time musical, but I haven't seen a musical that I've loved for many years. Unless it was a revival of Leave It to Jane, which is my idea of the best musical ever written.

CL: That's good. That's fine. That's perfect. Any other questions? Stop the bandleader; here, come on.

Member of film crew: The embarrassing personal stuff? We know all that.

EG: They know all that. They have photographs.

CL: That's perfect.

EG: Good, Good. [*Unhooks microphone*]

PART 2

[*Crew shoots b-roll while CL and EG speak off-camera casually.*]

EG: You know, the theater opens and you come in and of course nobody has curtain anymore, so you look at the set. And, you know, people would come in and, you know, you usually hold the curtain about eight minutes. I guess seven or eight minutes is the standard thing. And also here, which we used to do here, which we don't do anymore, was just before the lights go down for the play to start, was somebody comes in and makes a little speech about, you know, there's no smoking and the exits are out there and everything and the actor's box because the actors aren't paid and everything.

So I thought, well, why just not do this thing, that doesn't really have a plot, and that you could watch or not watch and it doesn't matter whether you see at all or not anyway. And just have this done with the house lights on and the dim light onstage, and then when it's over, the music for it will stop and then we'll have the little speech and then we'll go on with the regular show.

CL: I see.

EG: Actually, as it turned out, one of our reviewers got nasty about the actor's speech at the beginning, you know, saying everybody was begging for money and whatnot, which we all thought . . . cut his throat. [*Makes motion on throat with finger*]

But anyway, the powers that be sort of decided, well, we wouldn't have the speech. So we now just went from that prologue into the thing, which really wasn't my intention. I thought people would be kind of coming in and talking. I think it's kind of, it's how it makes the play seem to develop a life of its own, I think you just have to let it . . . I can't imagine directing saying, you know, "Tone this down and do this and do that." I just . . . but then again I'm not doing regular drama, you know.

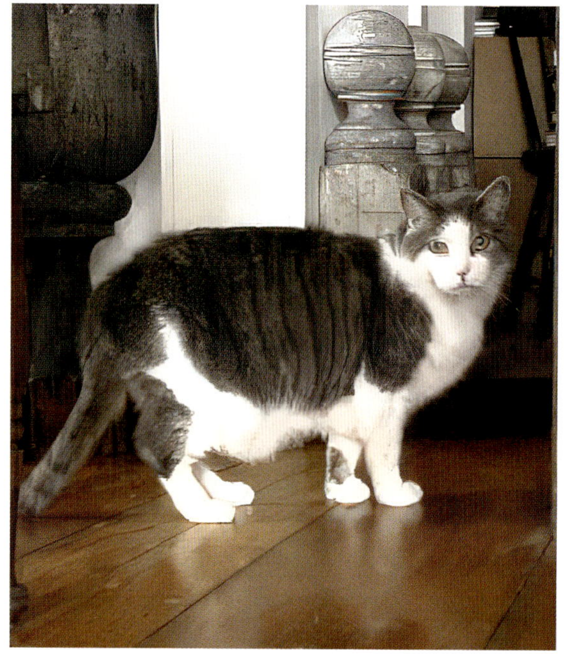

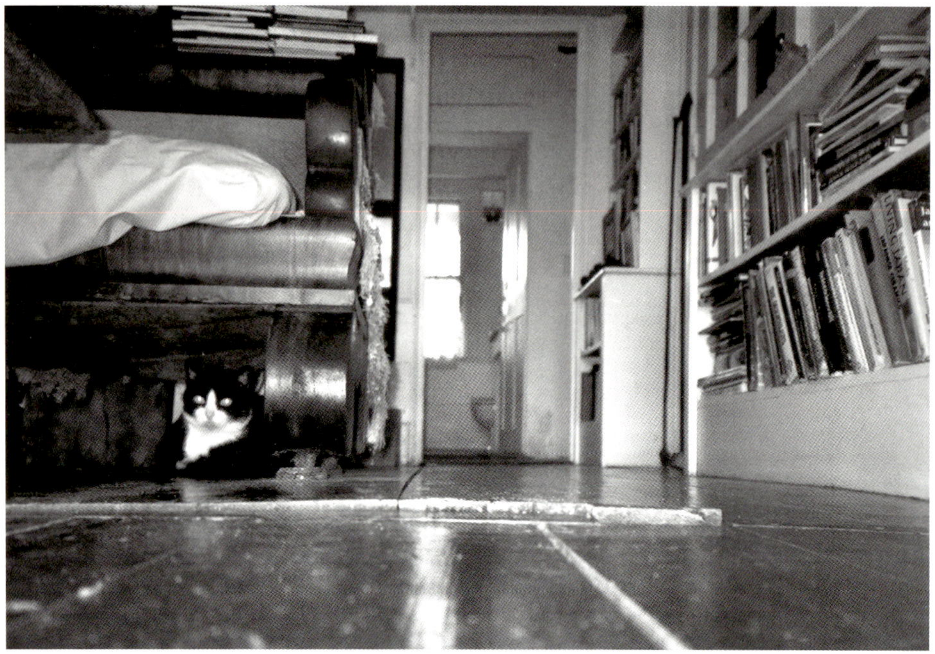

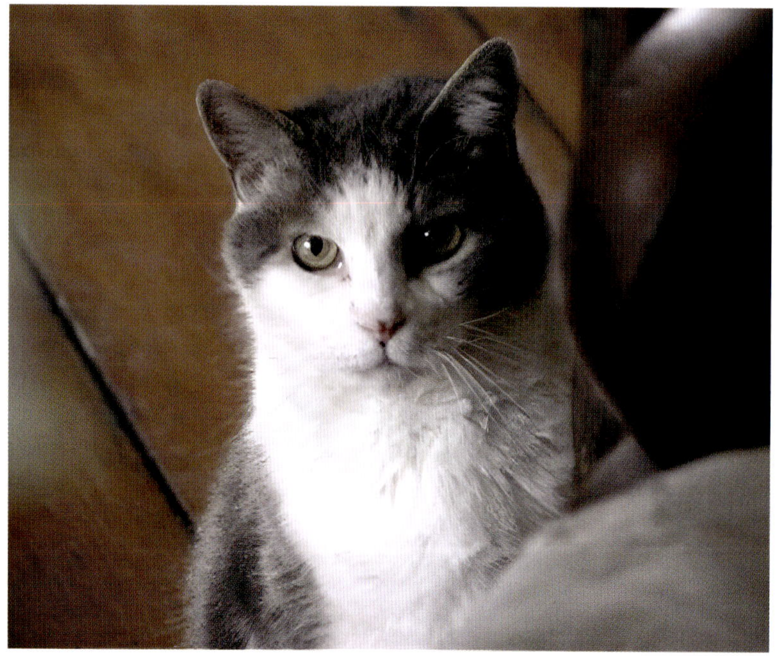

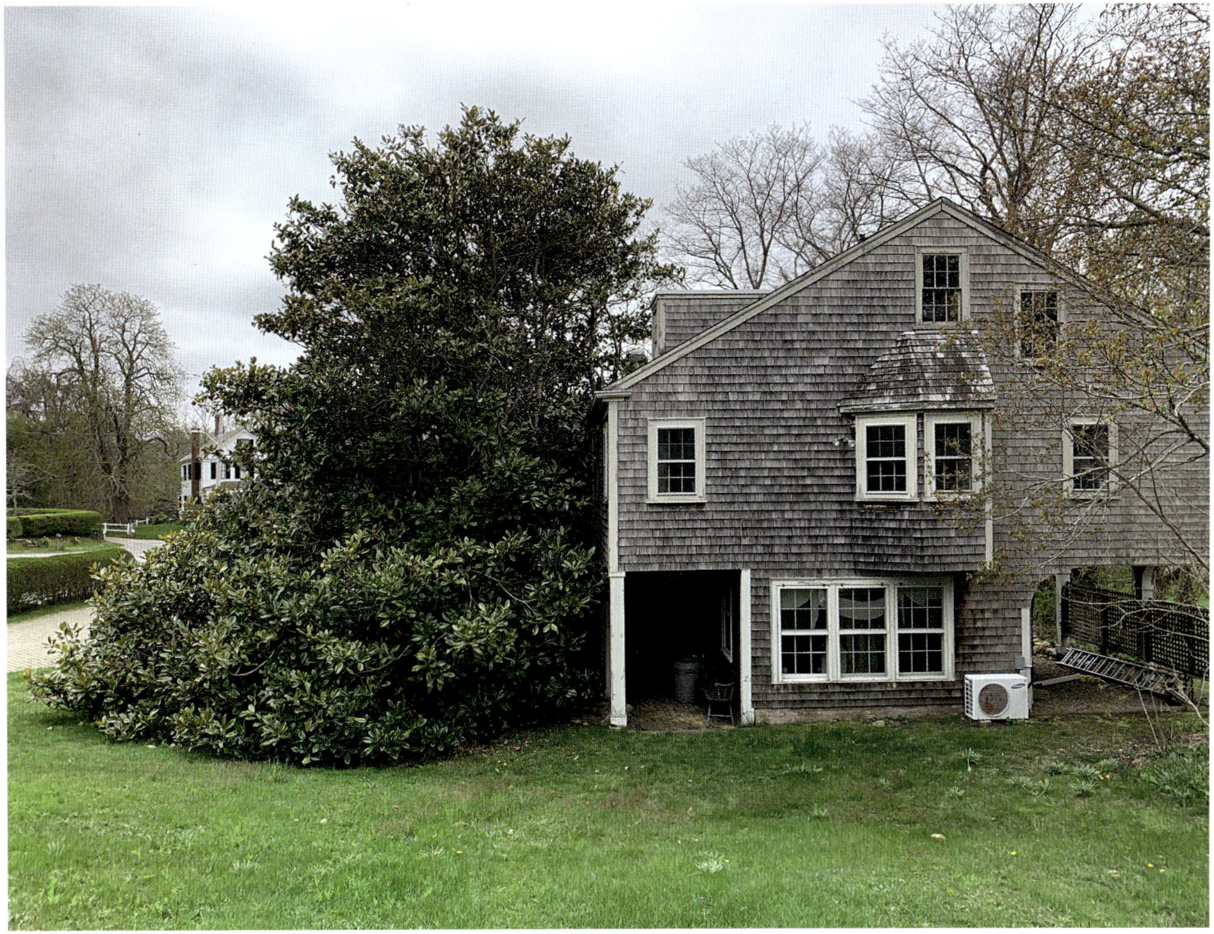

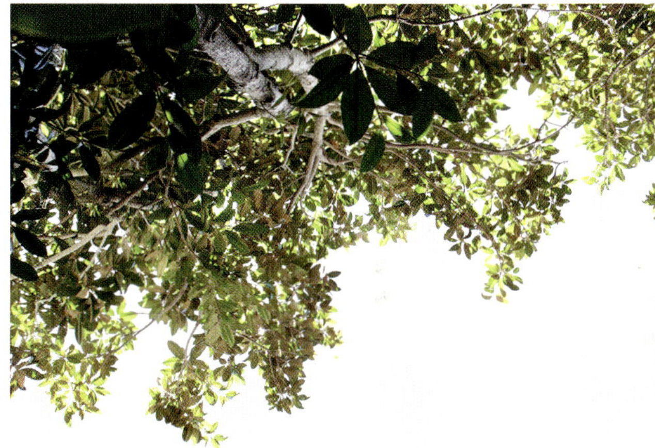

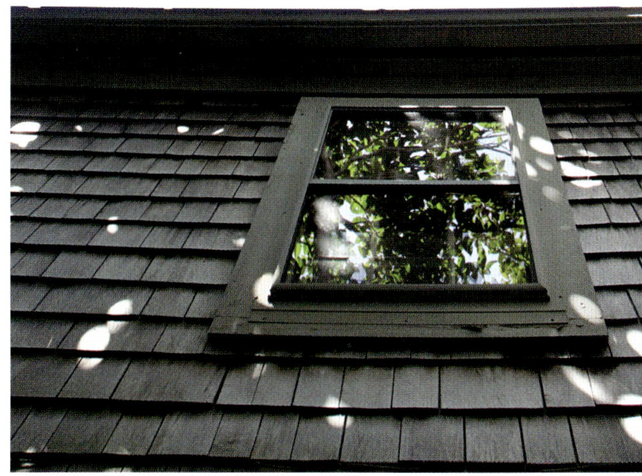

Edward would illustrate with the sound of the southern magnolia tree blowing in the breeze outside his studio window. It was brought back from Mount Vernon in a small pot by the sisters who once resided in the house, Louise and Olive Simpkins.

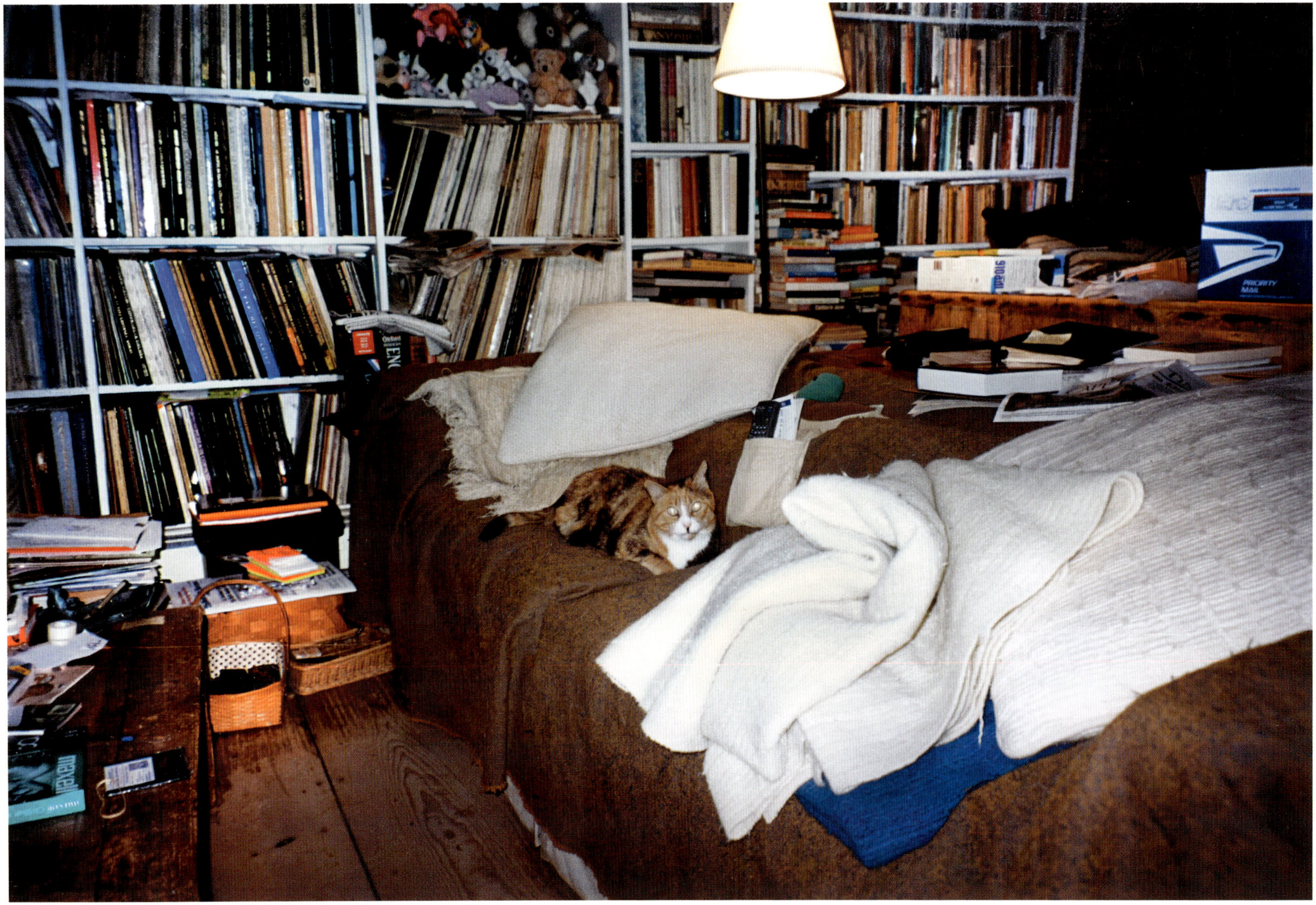

When Edward wasn't out or working, he was here on the couch with cats and a basket of remotes. I occasionally played tech support and helped him reprogram them when his satellite dish, TV, and many VCRs got scrambled. His taste in television programs ranged from *Buffy the Vampire Slayer* to *The Mary Tyler Moore Show* to *The Golden Girls*.

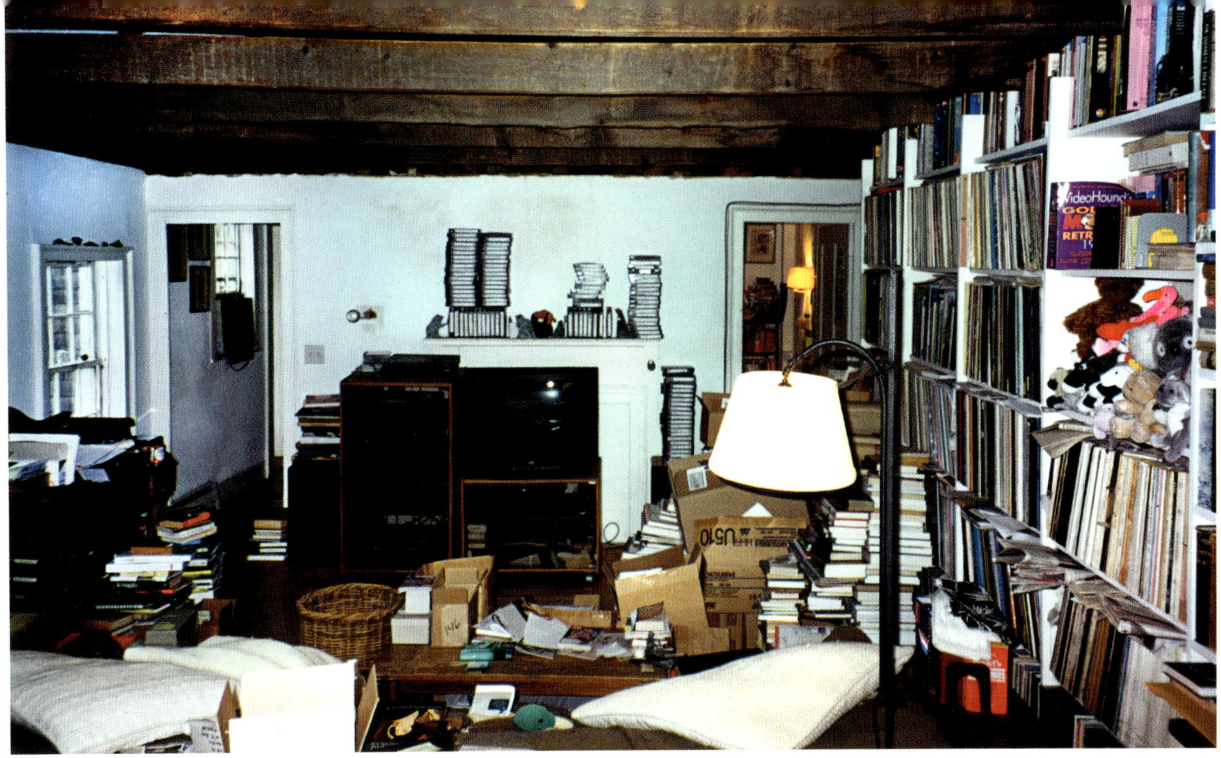

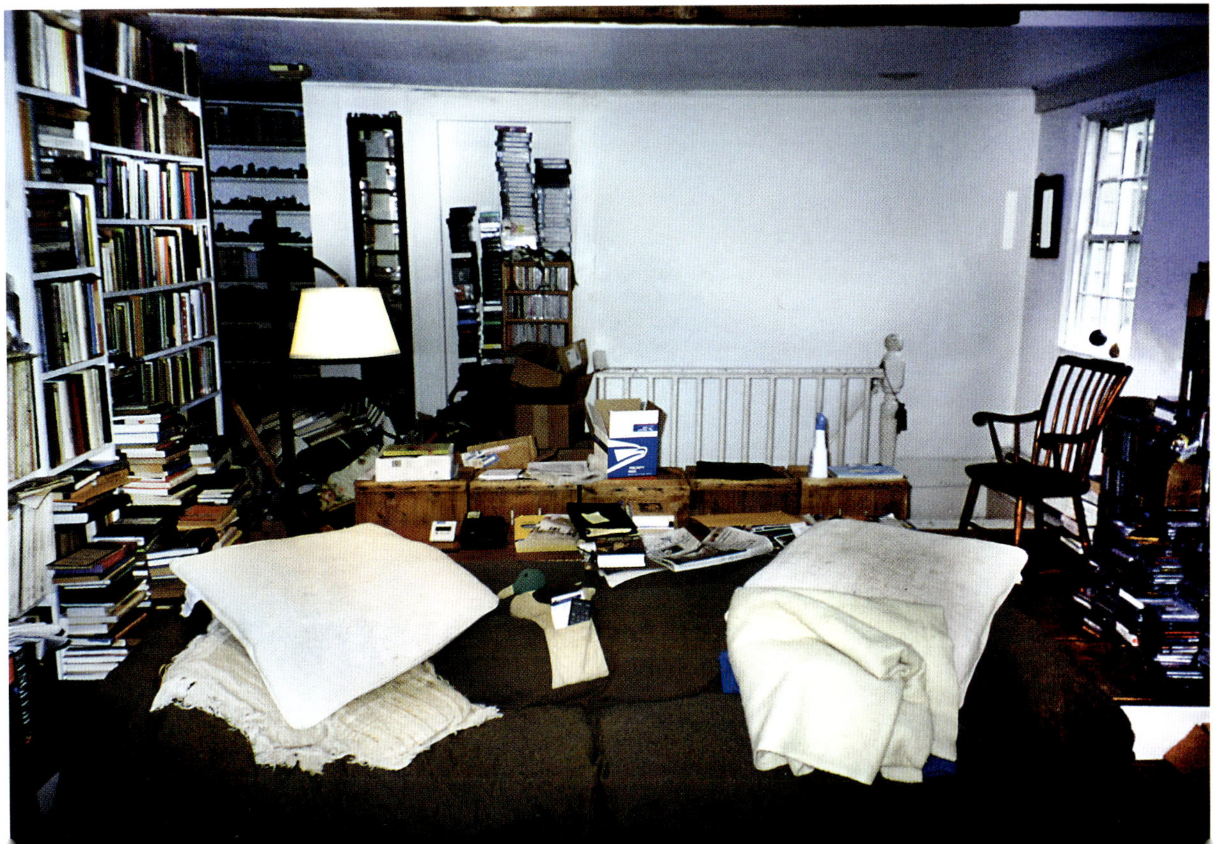

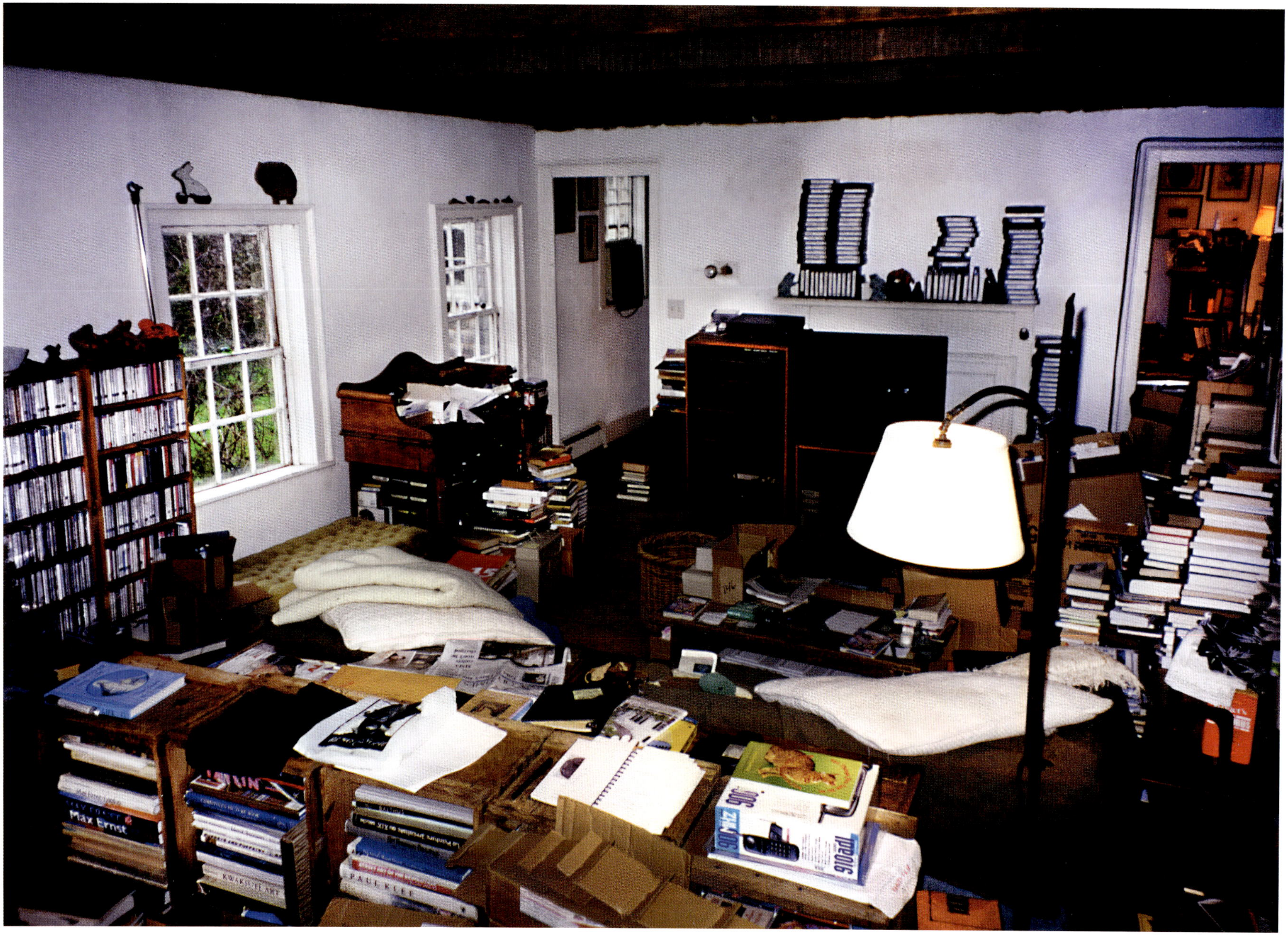
Max Ernst
PAUL KLEE

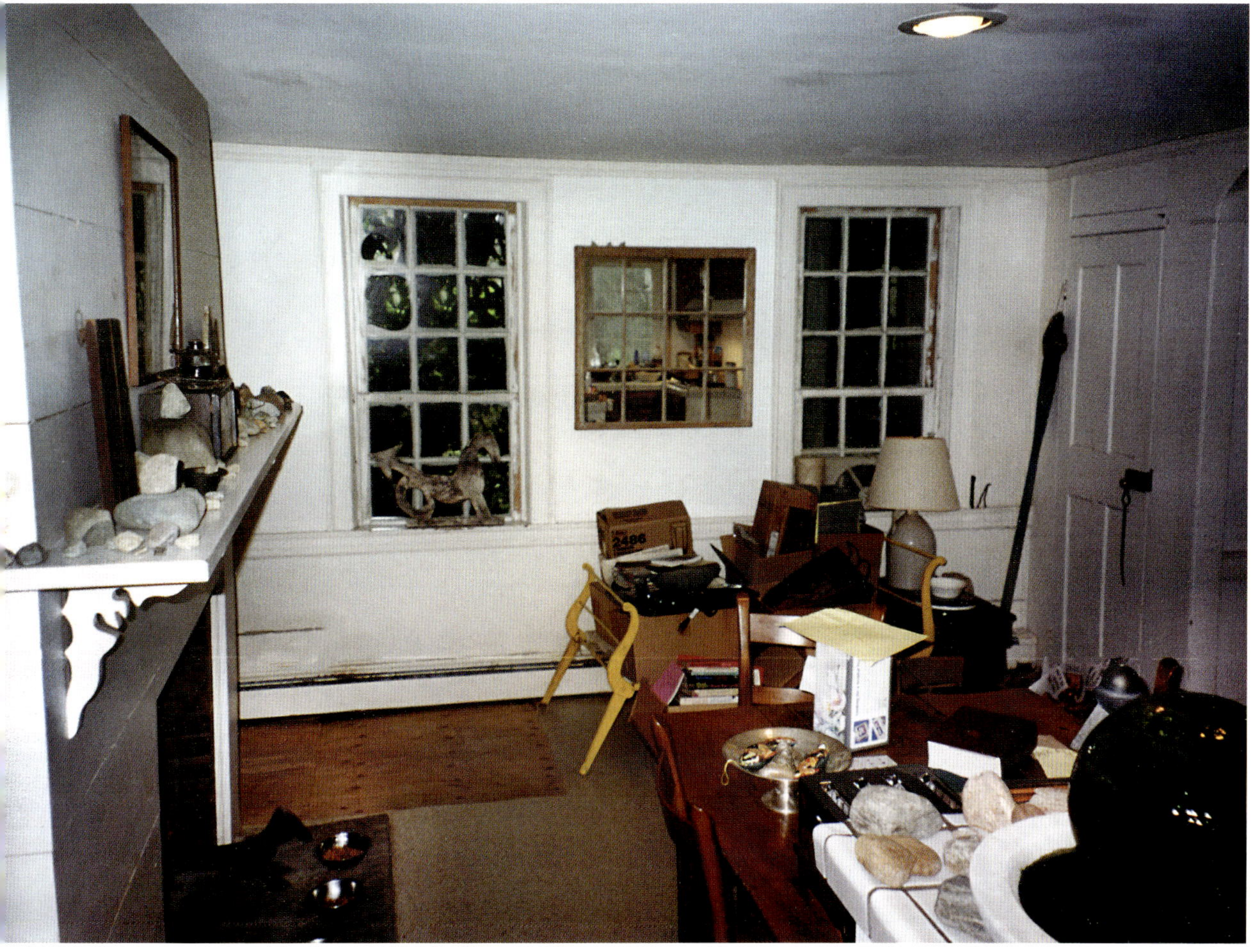

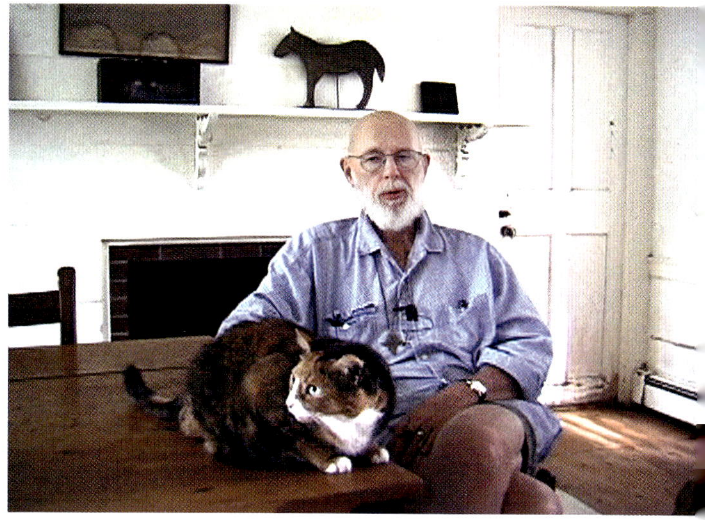

Edward's house could have been seen as a hoarder's den by some, with its scent of cat urine and stacks of boxes, and books blocking passageways, and even doorways throughout the house. It was much more a ground zero for a serious collector, with multiple copies of the same CDs, VHS tapes, and books all competing for space. The house was in every sense his own library; the artwork was set up as his own private gallery, more for his enjoyment than for that of his visitors. Artwork and displays would be set one way when visited in a certain week and then moved around and presented differently the next week.

His yellow metal kitchen couch frame stood as shipping and receiving. His mail was stacked there, and he would often go through the stacks there during our visits and interviews. He wondered in disbelief how celebrities like Carol Burnett reported responding to every piece of fan mail by hand. "Get a life!" he said. He did occasionally send a postcard response like this one: "You've written me to no avail, because I never read my mail."

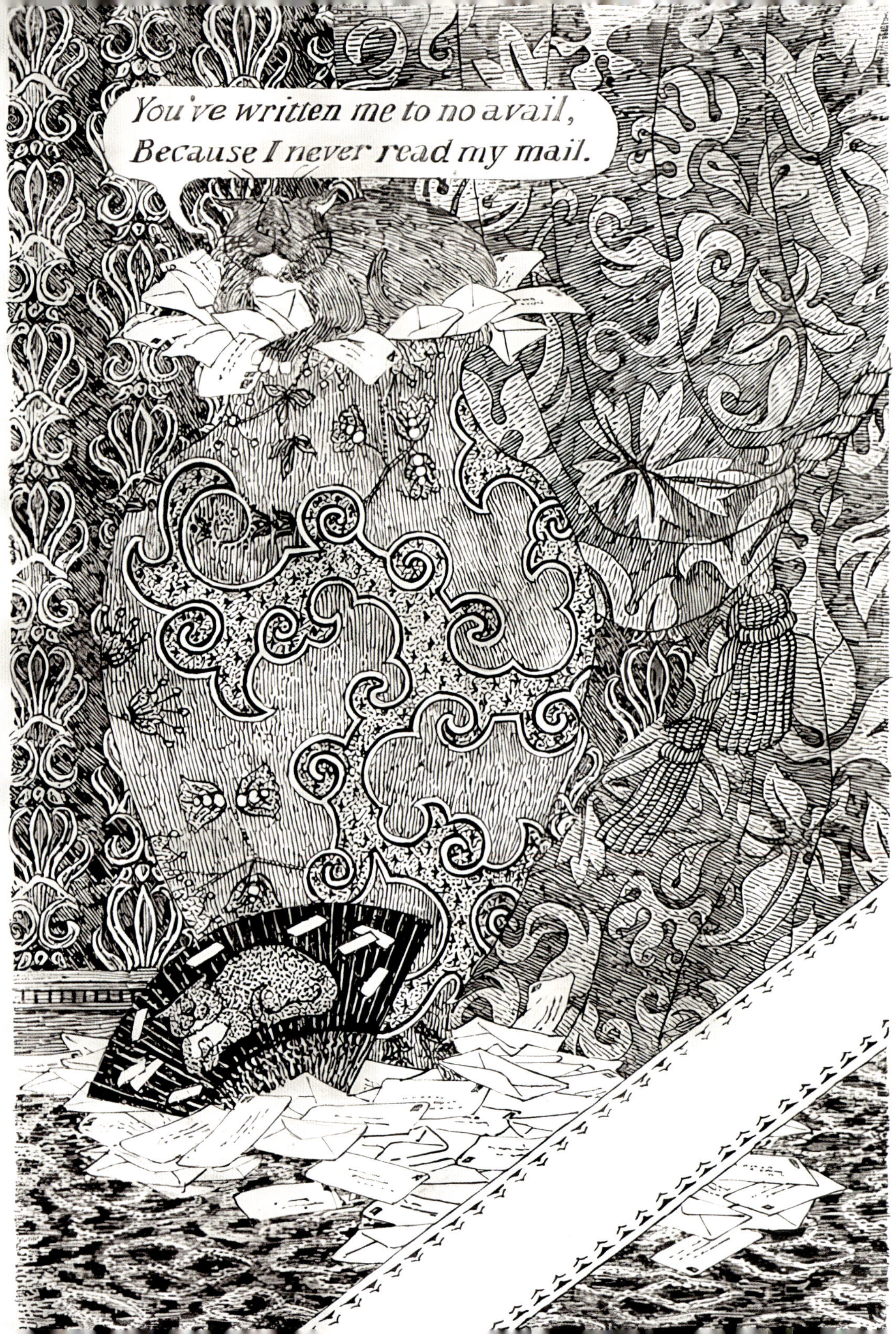

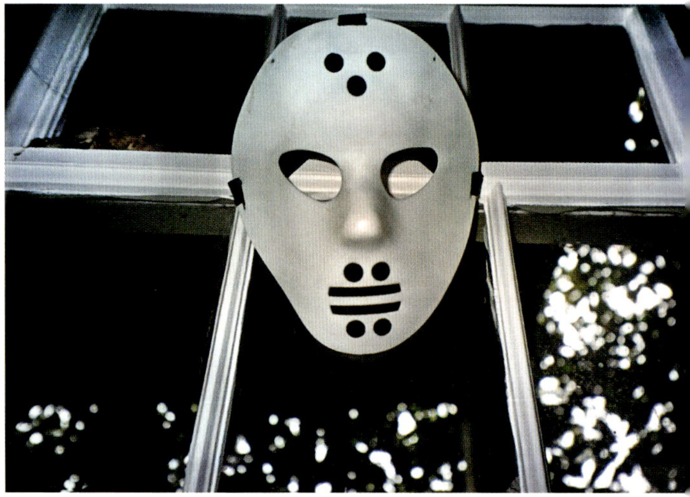

He was always on the hunt for material to use in his plays as well. One afternoon I bumped into Edward, who was coming out of the Borders bookstore in Hyannis. In his arms was a sizable bag filled with a variety of media, books and CDs. He didn't just shop there but frequently lingered, drinking an iced coffee and having a pastry, while reading. He said he was looking for Beethoven bagatelles, "something chirpy," as a soundtrack for one of the plays. We talked about the next shoot, and he then went next door into Pier One home furnishings.

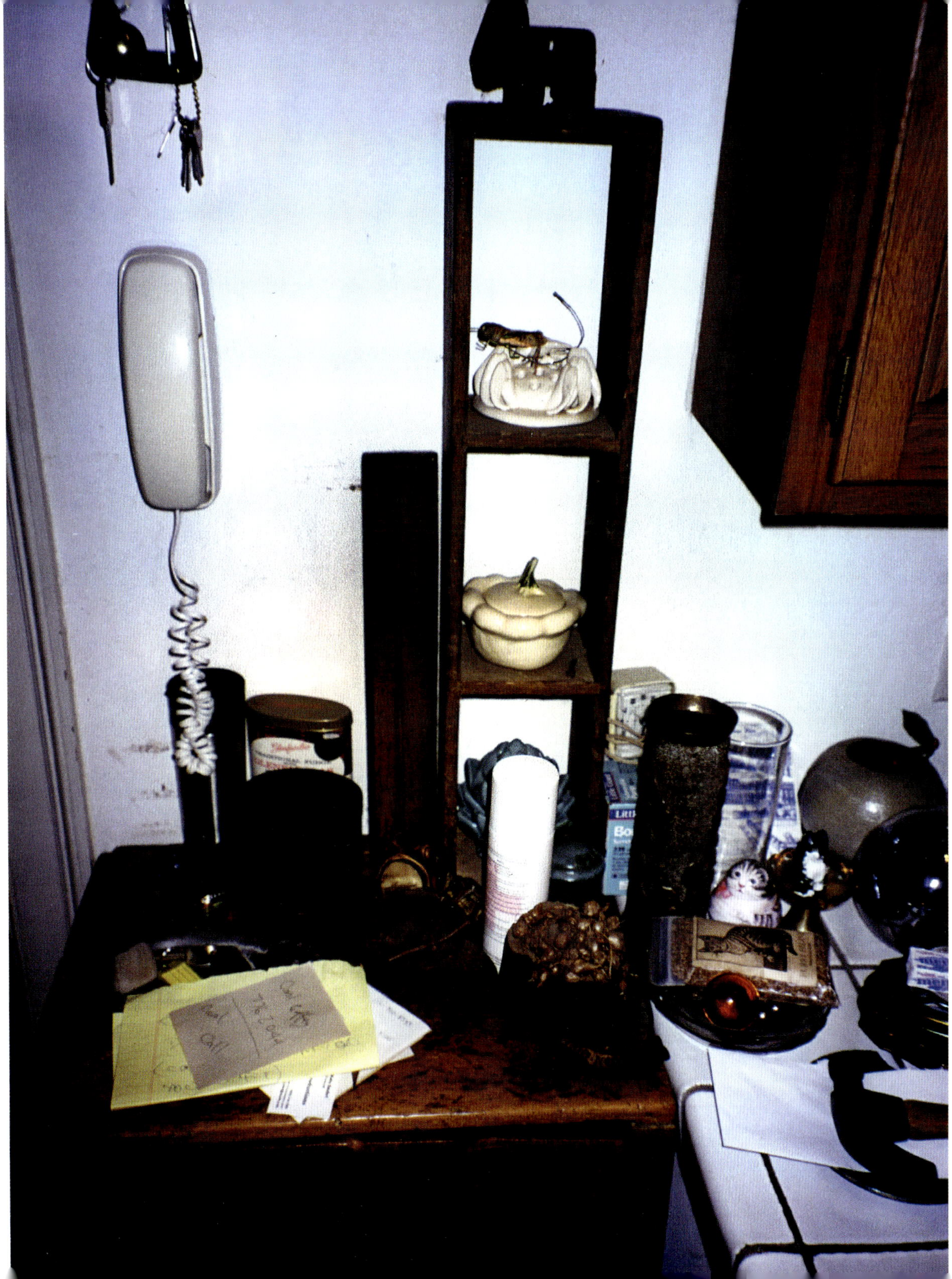

This was Edward's main telephone and message center. His machine had no more than a functional greeting in his typical style. "You've reached Edward Gorey's answering machine, wait for the beep."

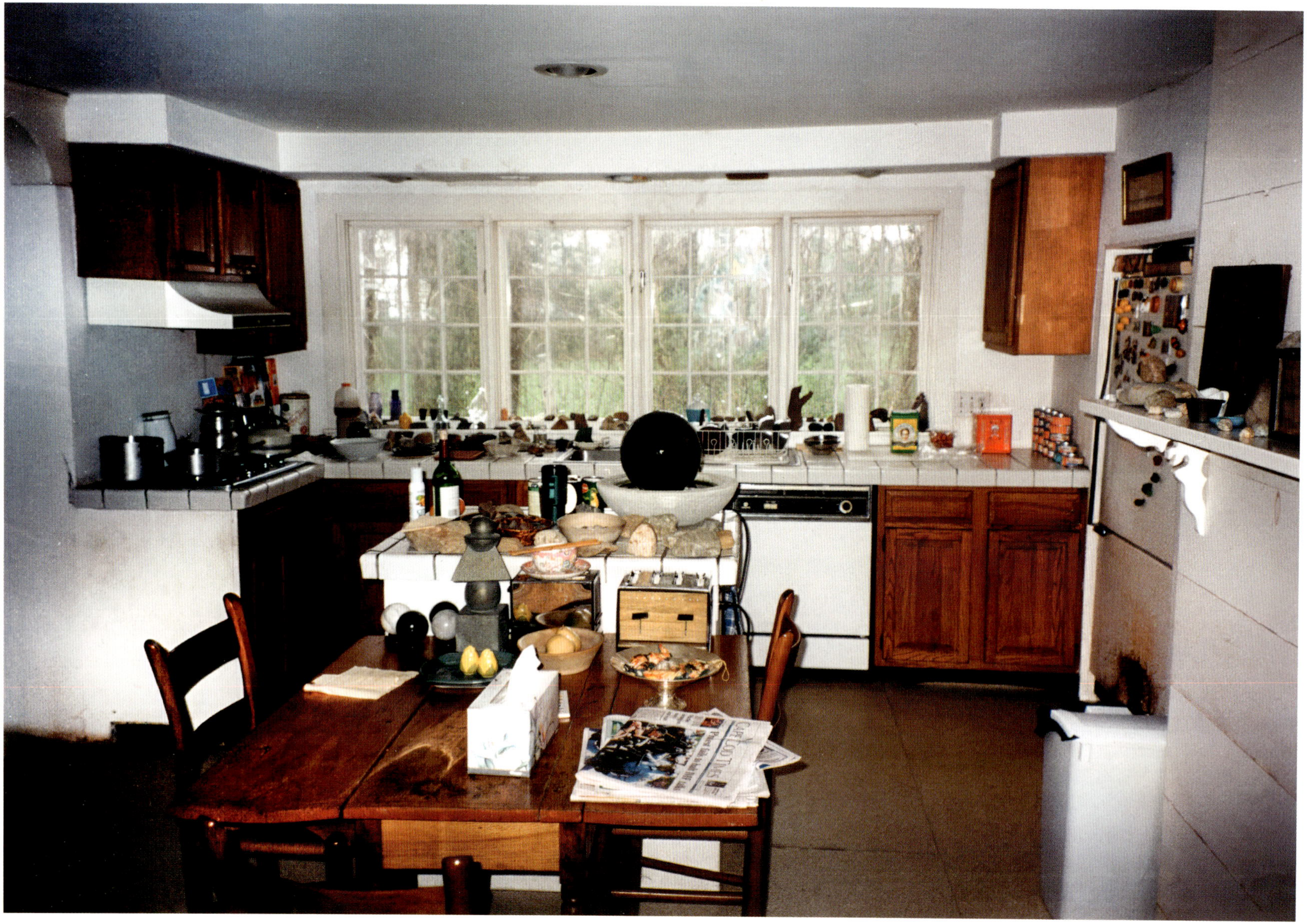

On one shoot, Edward had received a series of heavy boxes from the WGBH Signals catalog. He was setting up the concrete base (*center of photograph*) and working on inserting the water pump. I asked him if I could help him carry it outside, and he said, "Oh, this is for inside. I wouldn't see or hear it out there." He had several outdoor fountains set up inside.

Interview with Edward Gorey by Joyce Kenney, Cape Cod Community Television

1992

I worked at Cape Cod Community Television on staff from 1995 to 1998, and during that time I began independently shooting the documentary with Gorey. I met Joyce Kenney, who was a community producer there who had shot and broadcast a short interview with him as part of a production class they had taken together. Gorey was quite involved at the station, designing illustrations for the on-air community bulletin board and also as a volunteer in master control, cueing programs for broadcast.

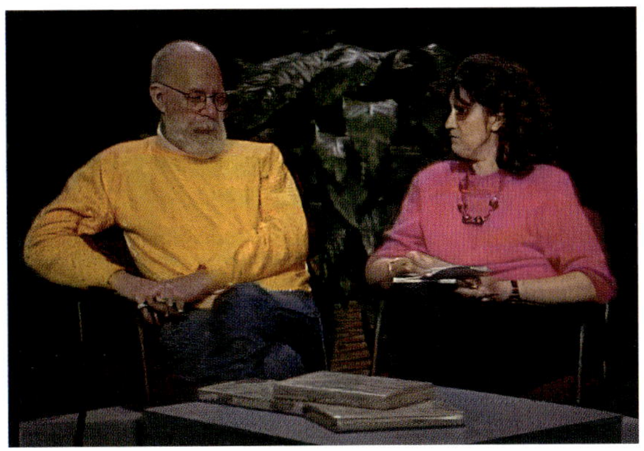

Edward with Joyce Kenney

Joyce Kenney: Hello, this is Joyce Kenney. Welcome to a tribute to Edward Gorey. Edward has kindly consented to be with us today to talk about his works and his many awards. Hi, Ed.

Edward Gorey: Hi, Joyce.

JK: Thanks for being here.

EG: Well, it's a pleasure.

JK: I wanted to start right out and ask you about your Tony Award that you won for Dracula on Broadway.

EG: Well, I don't really remember.

JK: That was for the costumes, wasn't it?

EG: That was for the costumes. I was nominated for both sets and costumes. And it was one of those things I really feel I should not have gotten either one, and the thing was that that year, there's a very huge elaborate set for—on the twentieth century, I guess it was called, which—where it was absolutely marvelous. So, obviously, the sets should've gone, the Tony should've gone in the set for that, which they did, but then everybody [who] wanted to felt sort of guilty, I guess, so they gave me the Tony for the costumes instead.

JK: Not all.

EG: Of which there were all of eight, I think, so I felt that was a little bit silly.

JK: Oh, we have a few photos and posters that we're going to be showing. Also, you're well known for your *Mystery Theater* title sequence in the beginning, and then some of those designs taken from your—

EG: Most of them actually were taken from the books. The first, they're now using after ten years of not doing them; they did a second animation for the mystery titles. But the ones that I did originally ten years ago, some of it was original drawings for the things that a lot of it was taken from my drawings by Derek Lamb, the animator.

And this time around a year ago, when we start working on the other one, actually, the scenarios are pretty much put together by Derek rather than me, and so it's just a question of kind of adapting my stuff for it.

JK: So you watched *Mystery Theater* yourself?

EG: Not all that often.

JK: Not all that often. But they've had some really great ones on. When did you first start to write for yourself, your own work?

EG: Oh, gosh, probably about fifty years ago, I guess.

JK: So, then you were quite young then, practically a baby.

EG: Not really, I'm sixty-six. I wrote in high school, but I was generally more interested in artwork in those days. Then, I was in the army during World War II for three years, and I started to write there more seriously. When I got out, I started doing both drawing and writing. My first book wasn't published until 1953, but I'd started thinking along the lines of very short texts.

JK: So, 1953, was that the one about the baby?

EG: You're thinking of *The Beastly Baby* [1962], but the first one was called *The Unstrung Harp* [1953]. Then the second book, *The Listing Attic* [1954], was limericks, most of which I'd written many years before that. T*he Beastly Baby*, I finally published myself because nobody else would. I had written it quite early along the line, and nobody would publish it, and I finally got tired of peddling it around and so I did it myself.

Self-publishing was how I got started doing the really small books that I do.

JK: So, the writing comes first.

EG: Writing comes first if I—I have tried starting to do the drawings before I finish the text to the book, but I did that once and I never finished the rest. I never finished it. So, after that, I have to have the complete text before I start drawing the drawings.

JK: One of my favorites is *The Loathsome Couple*. Was that based on an actual . . .

EG: That was based on the actual—

JK: . . . couple from England?

EG: It was usually referred to as "the Moors Murders." Emlyn Williams wrote a book about it, and there's another one by Pamela Hansford Johnson. Anyway, it got a lot of publicity in its day and I was "inspired," if that's the word for it. Naturally that sat around for a long time because I hadn't done the drawings for it, but various people saw the text and were rather horrified. Then when it was finally published, we got some flack on the subject. People thought it was just too awful.

JK: Too shocking.

EG: Too shocking, I don't know.

JK: So you reacted emotionally and it was something that bothered you?

EG: I've been reading true-crime books all my life. It's one of my hobbies. That one really got to me in a way which most of them don't, and even after I'd written it, I thought, "Oh dear, how am I ever going to deal with this?" because it really affected me.

JK: You had to do something.

EG: I felt I had to, and then eventually somebody saw the text and said, "Oh, would you do the drawings for it?" It was published originally serially, and then, when my publisher said, "You know, I understand you've been publishing something in the weekly news," I said, "Yes, but I don't think you want it." And he said, "Oh sure we do." And I don't think they ever looked at any of it before it was published. I've always maintained that they just published whatever I turned [in] to them.

JK: Do you think Cape Cod is ready for it; shall I include that part and maybe give them a little curiosity to go out and buy it?

EG: Well, I think it's out of print now probably.

JK: Well, it's in one of your collections. These are the three collections of his books. Do you think you'll ever get to an autobiography? I would love to read that.

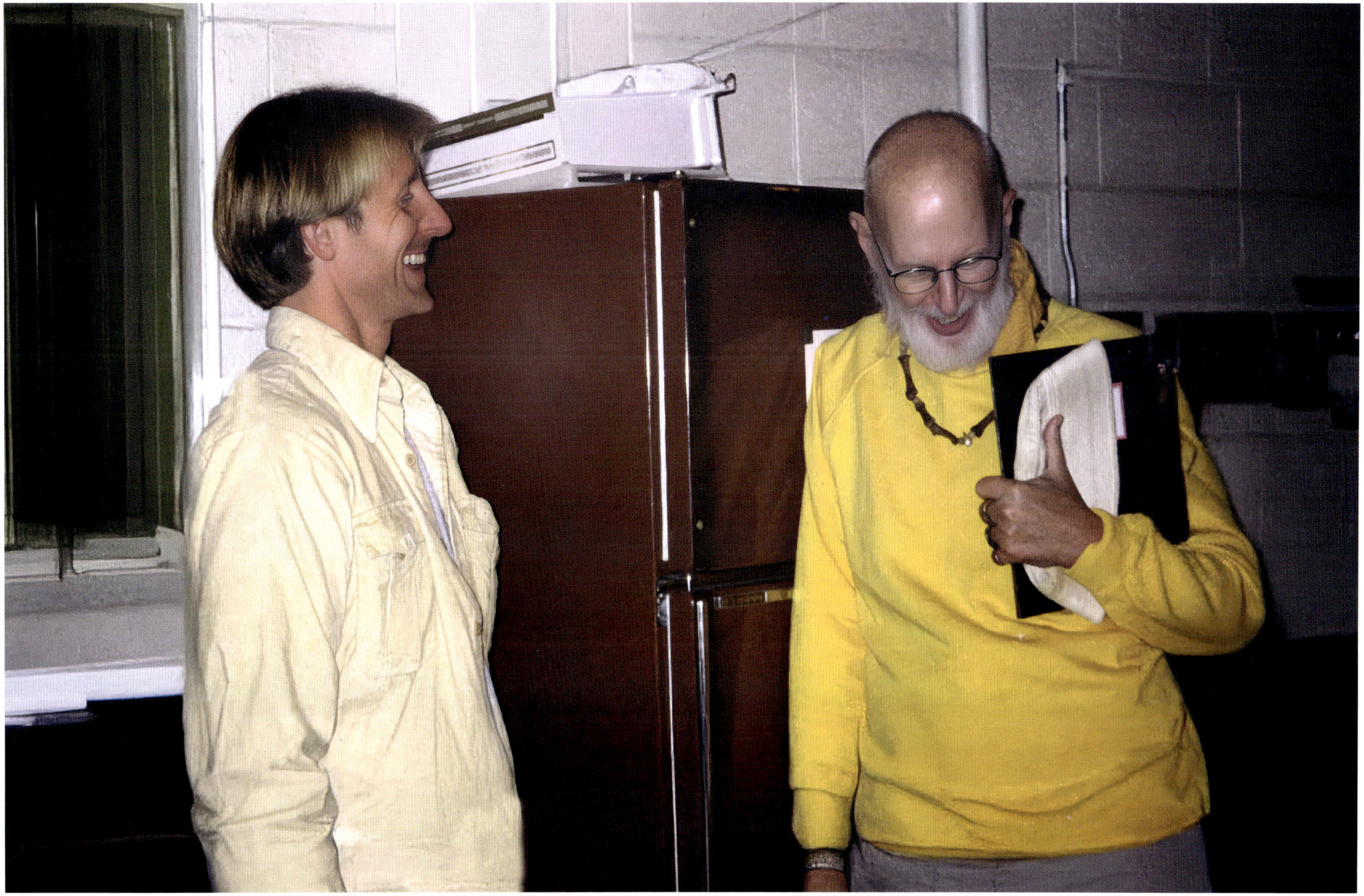

Photo courtesy of Joyce Kenney

EG: No, I've had a very dull and dreary life.

JK: Oh, come on. What about your life in New York now? It was so glamorous, I imagine, compared to being on the Cape, with the opera and ballet . . .

EG: Well, I went the New York City Ballet, every performance they did in New York for about twenty-five years. My life used to revolve around it, it's true. I mean, all the time I was in New York, I don't think I was ever home one night. I think I've figured I had never been home one evening that I was always out at something or other, but I'm not sure that that qualifies being very glamorous.

JK: Well, the people that you drew for my favorite, *The Blue Aspic*, they're so glamorous. Are these people that you've met?

EG: No. It's very hard. I think it's very hard to figure out what you have based on real life—sometimes things are based on real things and sometimes not.

JK: Well, let's see. I wanted to ask you too about the theater groups, the Woods Hole and Provincetown productions—there was two places last year.

EG: Yeah, last summer, I did two sort of entertainments, as we usually call them, which are taken from both my published and nonpublished work. I did one three years ago in Woods Hole, and then last summer I was approached by both the Provincetown Theater Company and the Woods Hole Theater Company. I thought, "What the heck?" So I did two shows, which was fun and exhausting.

JK: Exhausting.

EG: They were completely different, and they didn't overlap, fortunately, too much. I mean, I think there was one week where both shows were on, but as far as rehearsal and everything, they were just separate.

JK: I'm trying to think of the other one, the Bug God is it? *The Insect God.*

EG: *The Insect God.*

JK: Well, that was sort of an interesting story. What was it based on?

EG: Actually, the inspiration for that was some medieval woodcuts of insects. I wrote some note papers for the Metropolitan Museum originally.

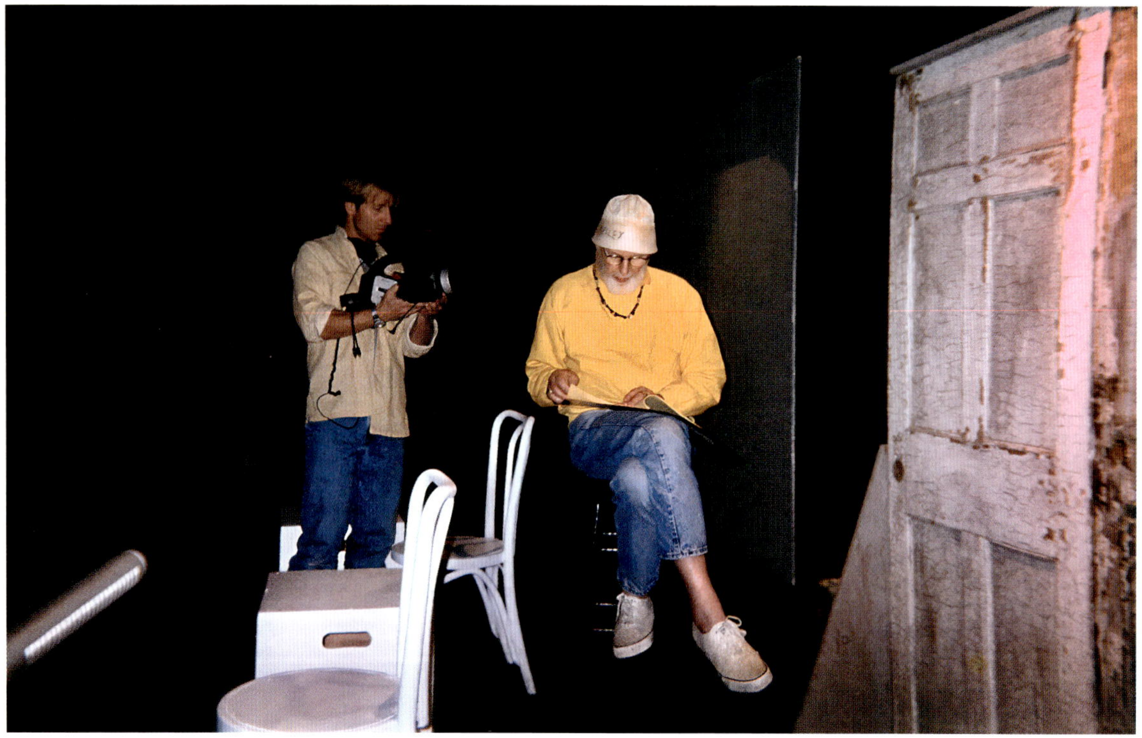

Photo courtesy of Joyce Kenney

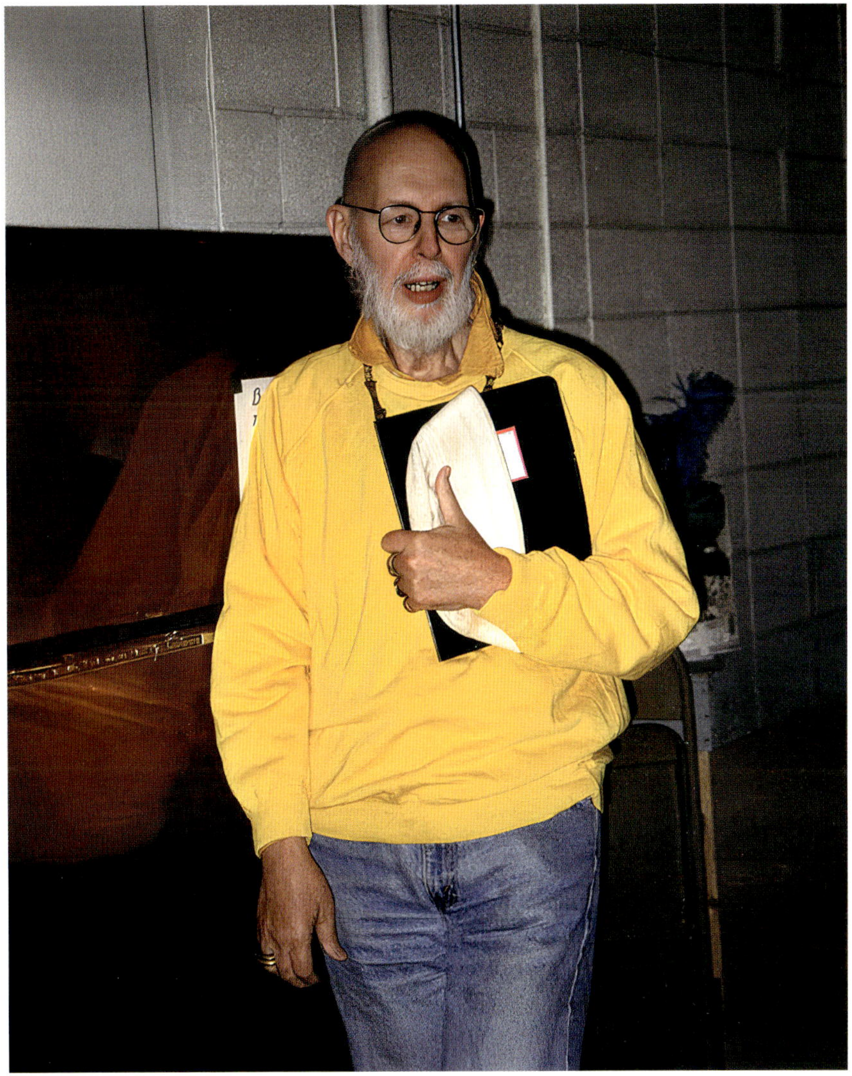

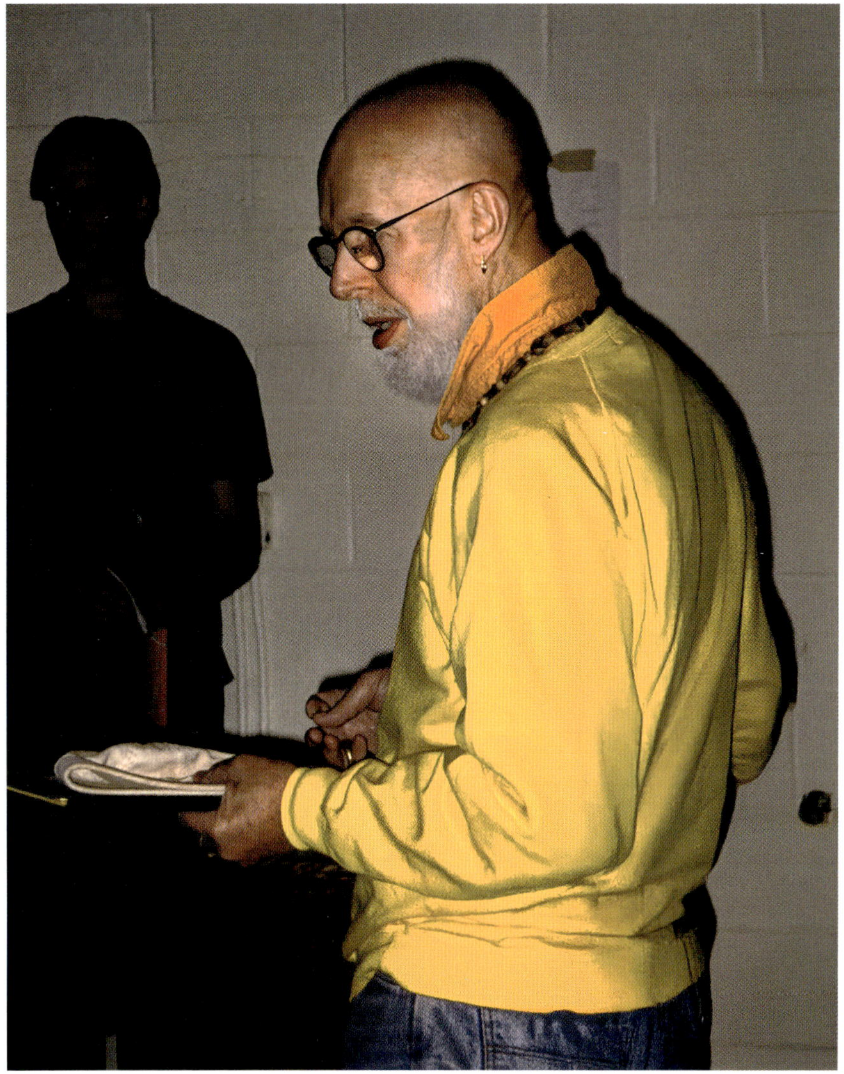

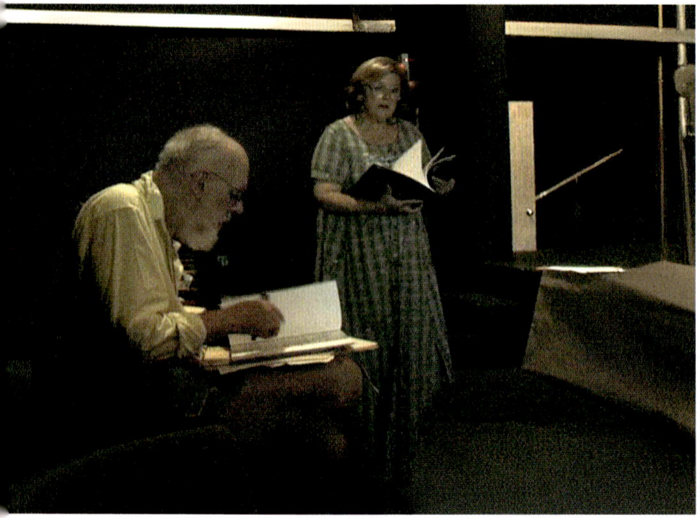

JK: So, your ideas come from older images?

EG: I never know where they're coming from. Sometimes I just read something in the paper.

JK: So, are you working on anything at the present, a lot of different things?

EG: Well, let's put it this way. I'm always working on a lot of different things. Actually, I'm toying with the idea at the moment of finishing up a book, which I've done a third of the drawings for, but I started writing it thirty-four years ago. So it's been sitting there, and I think I did the drawings about ten years ago, and for some reason or other I put it to the side and didn't have time to finish it.

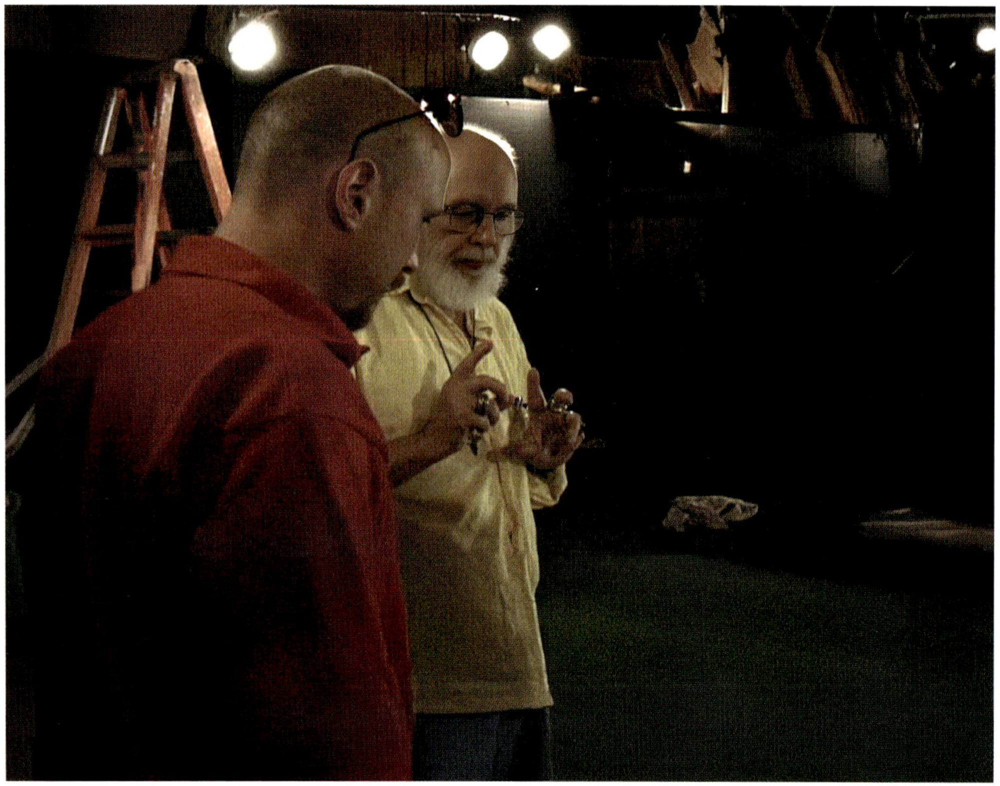

JK: So, on a rainy day you can pick it up?

EG: So, on a rainy day, I pick them up again, yeah. I'm just wondering whether I can get back to the same point, because they're quite complicated drawings and I'm just wondering whether I can get back into that and how long will it take me to get back to that complicated style I'd started.

JK: Now, do you have any plans to produce a television show here at C3TV [they met while taking a video production class together there]?

EG: Well, I have a couple of ideas. I've been doing some stuff with puppets in the last shows that I did at Woods Hole and on Provincetown. I've been toying with the idea of maybe trying to do some puppet things for television and also some live stories.

JK: Your live stories.

EG: Yeah. Some live stuff.

JK: Are you going to go into the big puppets for that?

EG: No. They're very small.

JK: Will you use actors?

EG: There are various people that I've used and who've done puppets with me before, yes. I think they are all wonderful.

JK: Now, I'll ask you about this book, is this your latest? [*Holds up* Amphigorey Also]

EG: Well, in a way, it's my latest. It's the last one that was commercially published, so to speak, that I didn't publish myself.

JK: Yeah, I thought this was fun. I'm still trying to get through it here, where I keep switching from page to page and story to story.

EG: Yeah, you have alternatives.

JK: Mm-hmm. Would there be any chance of asking you to read *The Blue Aspic*?

EG: I don't read well at all.

JK: You don't read?

EG: No, I don't read well at all.

JK: Okay.

EG: Thank you just the same.

JK: Maybe you'll just read it privately.

EG: No, I don't even read privately.

JK: Not even privately. Okay. Well, thank you for being here today.

EG: Well, thank you for having me.

JK: I hope that we can get together again, and when you have something new, let us know.

EG: Right. Thank you.

JK: Thank you.

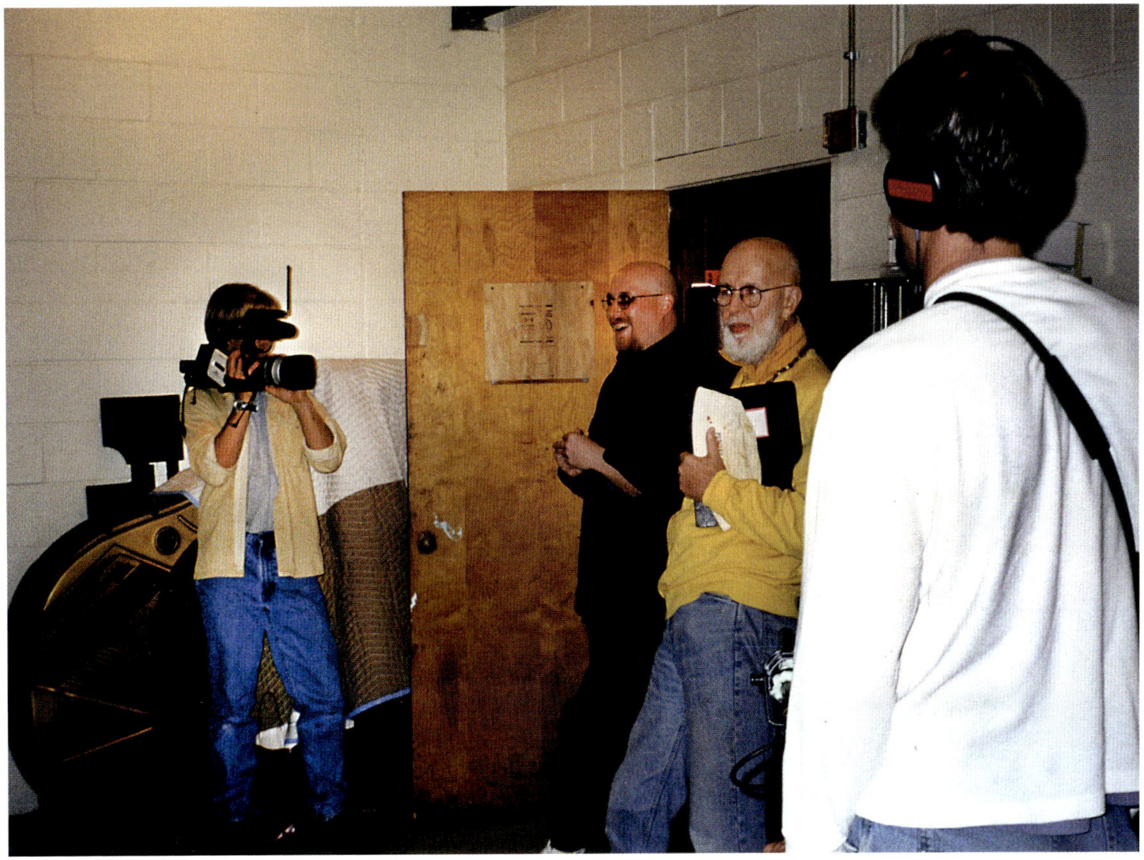

At rehearsal for *Hsst!*, October 1999

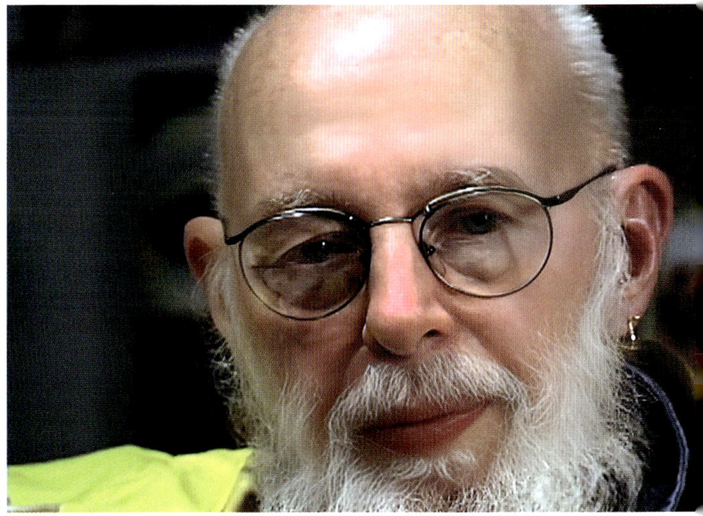

When Edward wasn't watching TV or drawing in his studio, he could often be found sitting at one of the tables set up with his three working typewriters to transcribe handwritten notes into book text and play scripts.

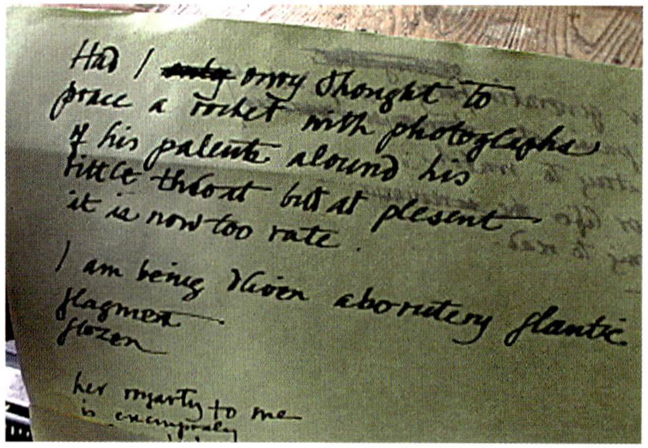

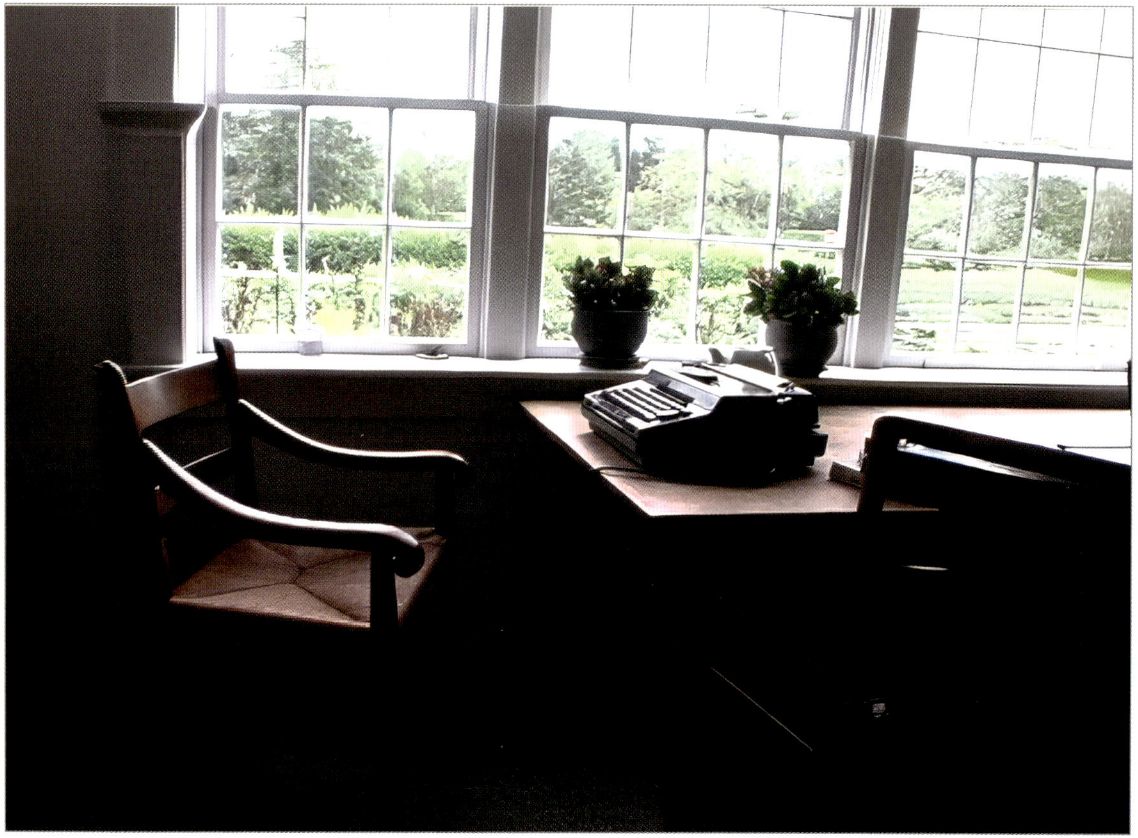

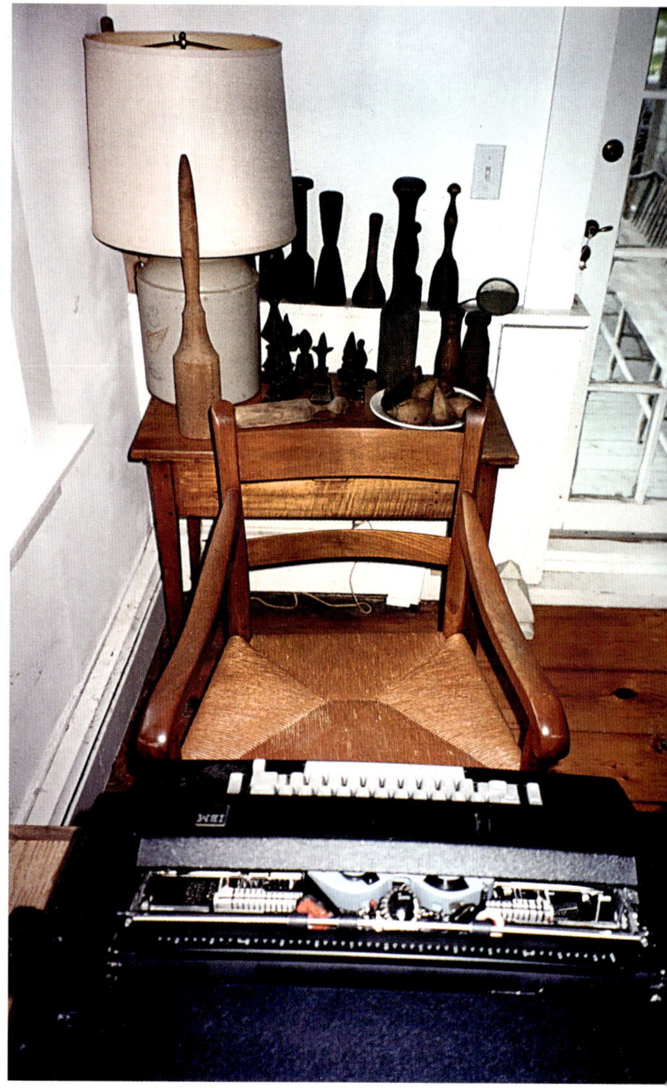

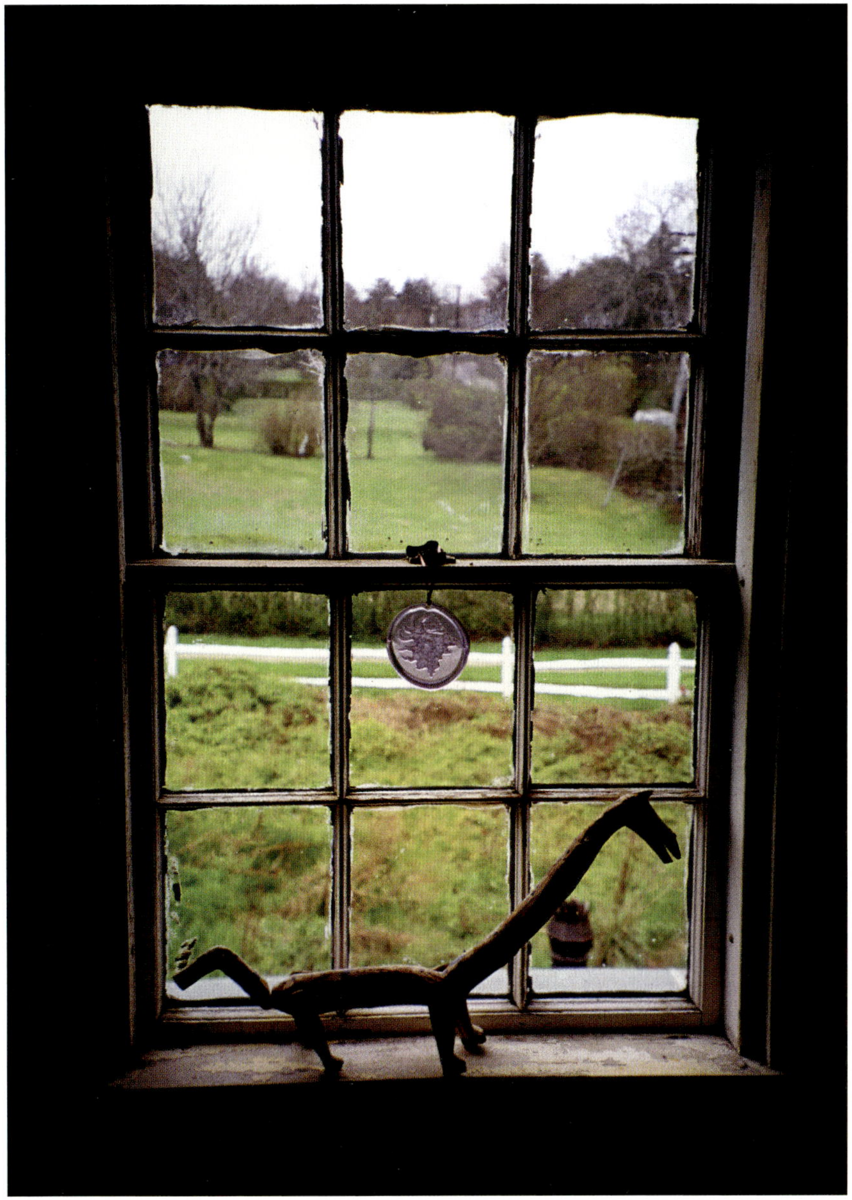

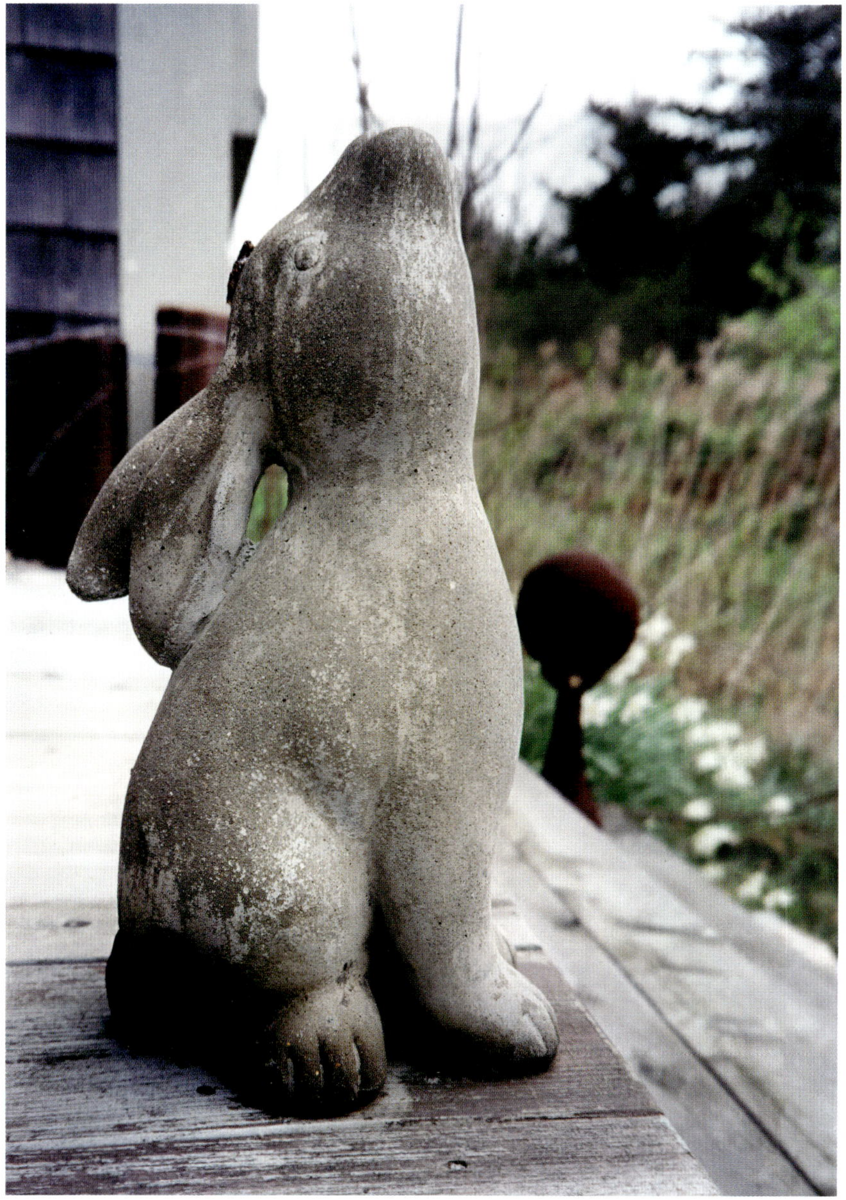

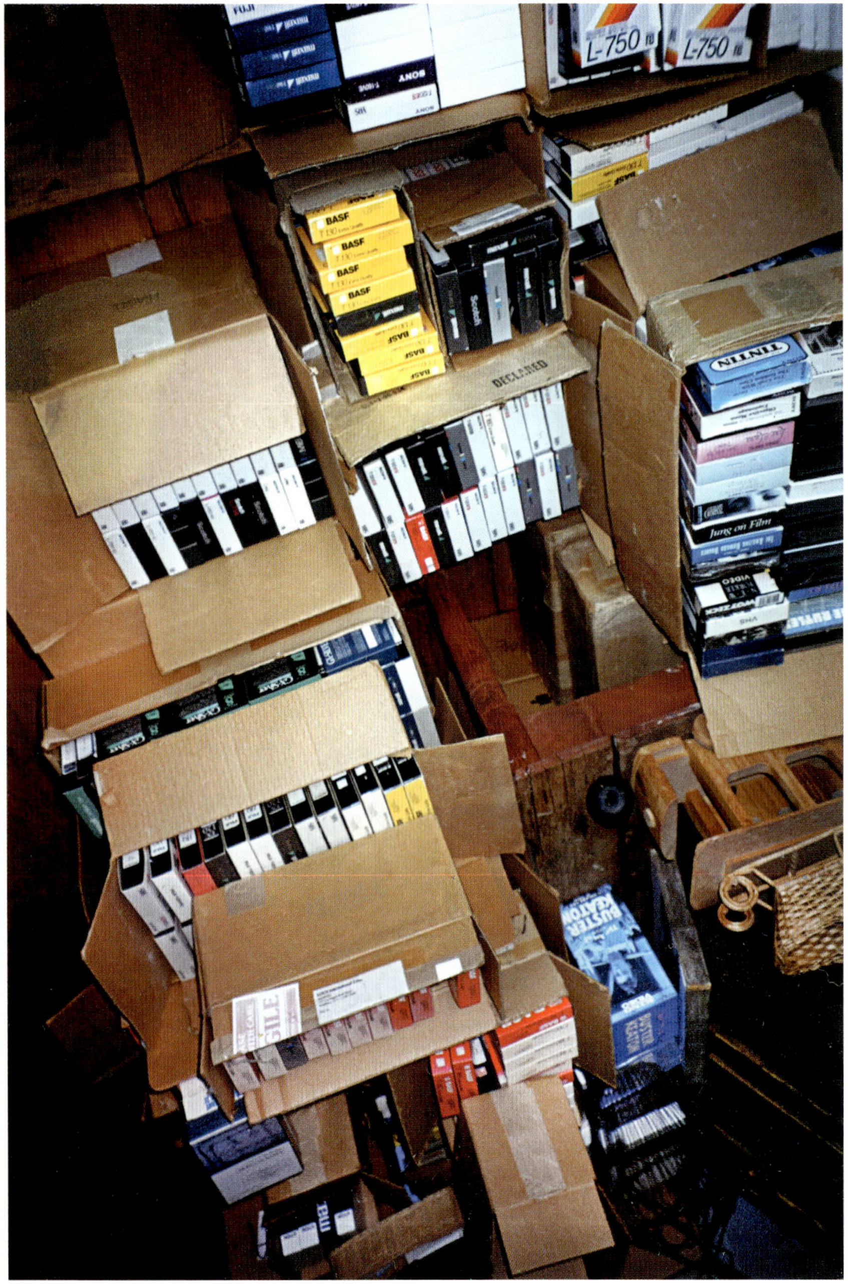
FUJI
SONY
L-750
L-750
BASF
DECLARED
TINTIN
Jung on Film

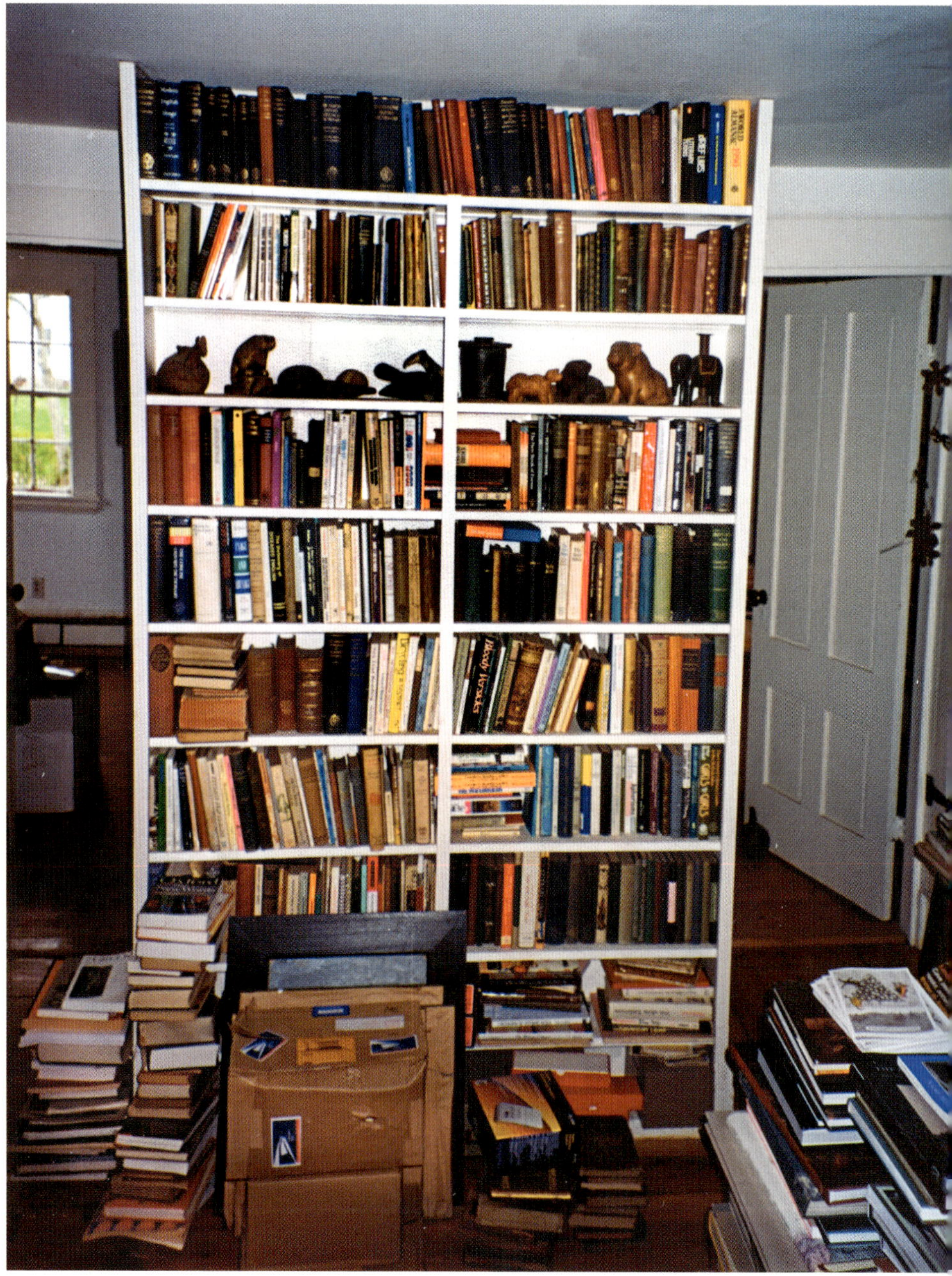

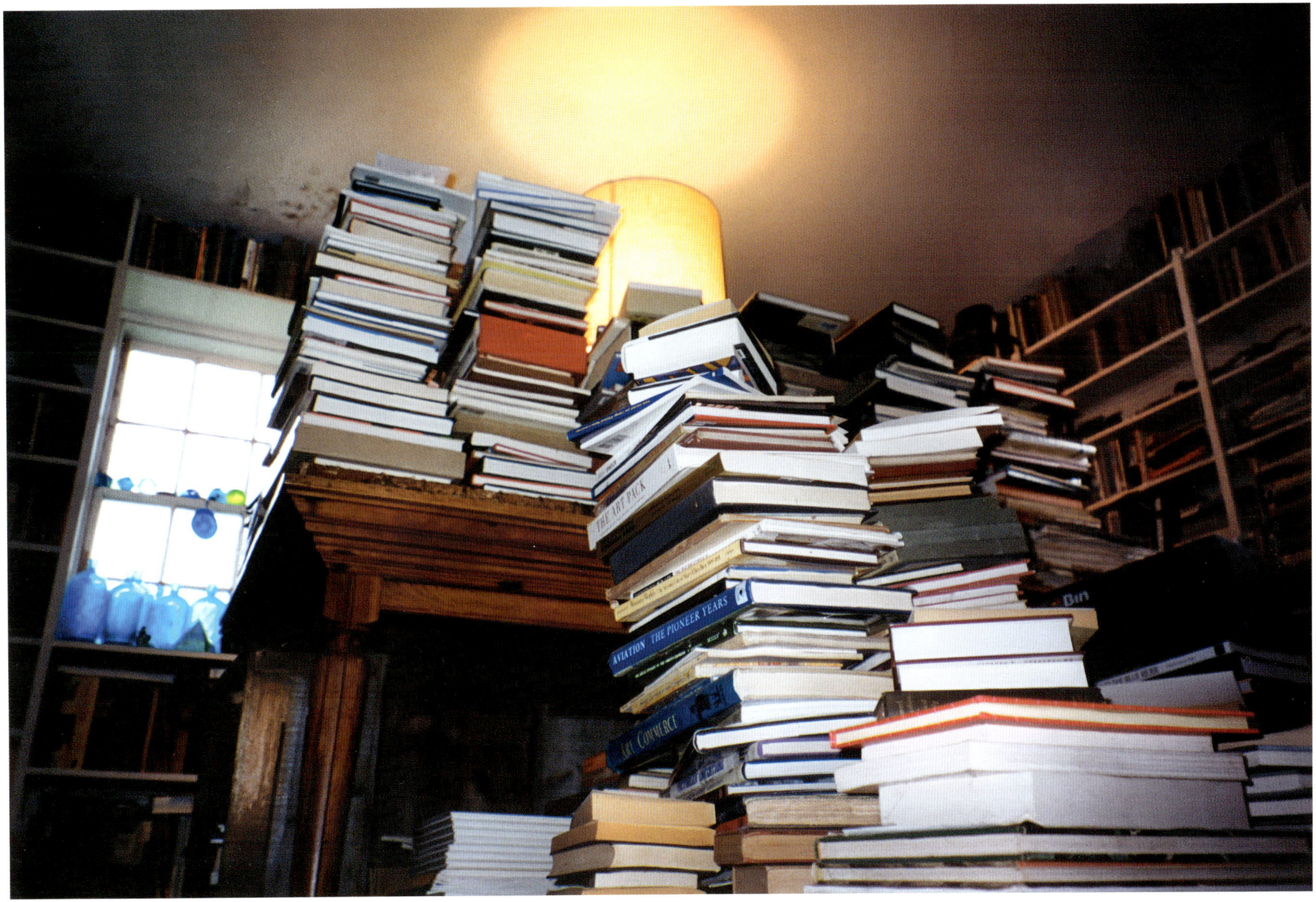
THE ART PACK
AVIATION THE PIONEER YEARS
ART COMMERCE

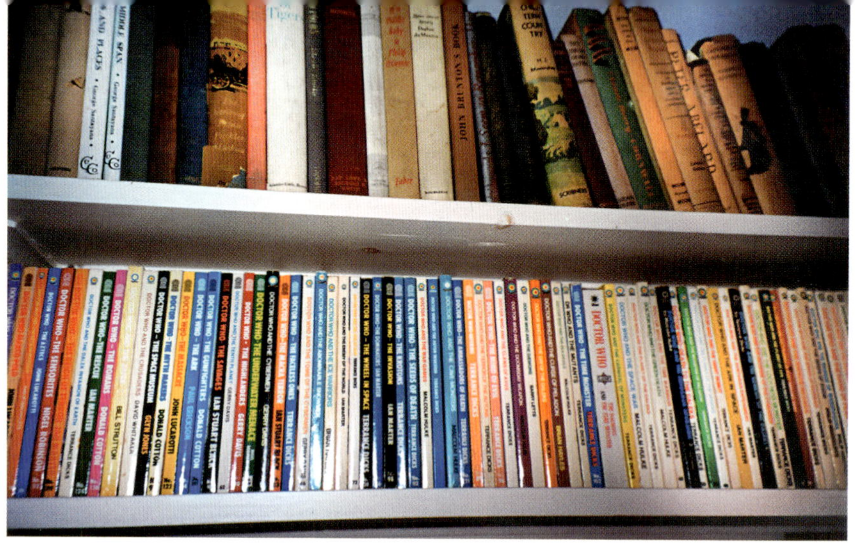

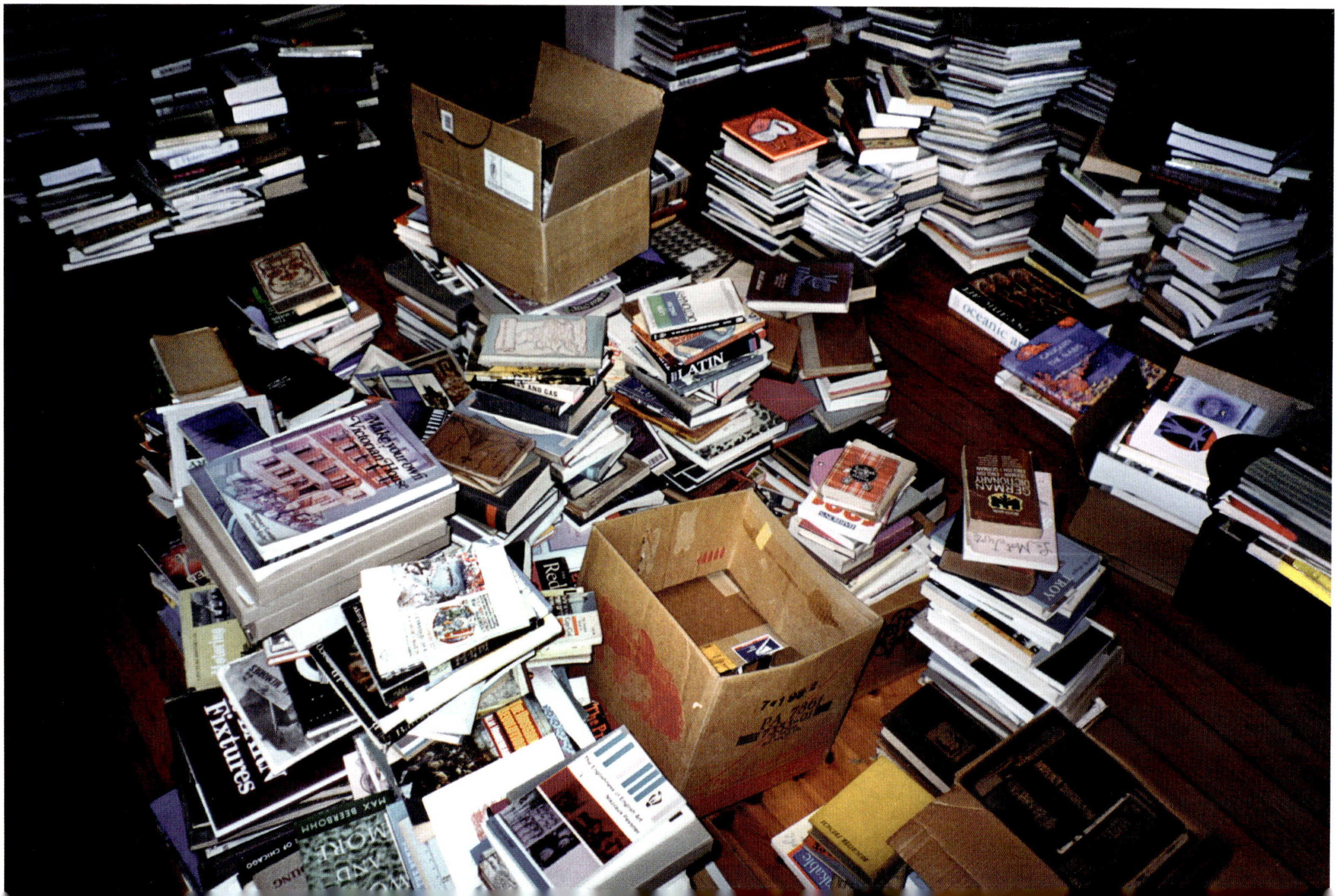

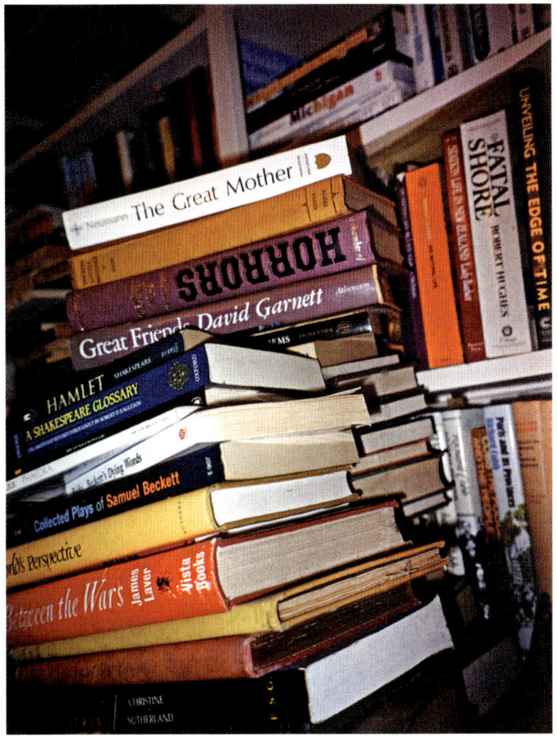

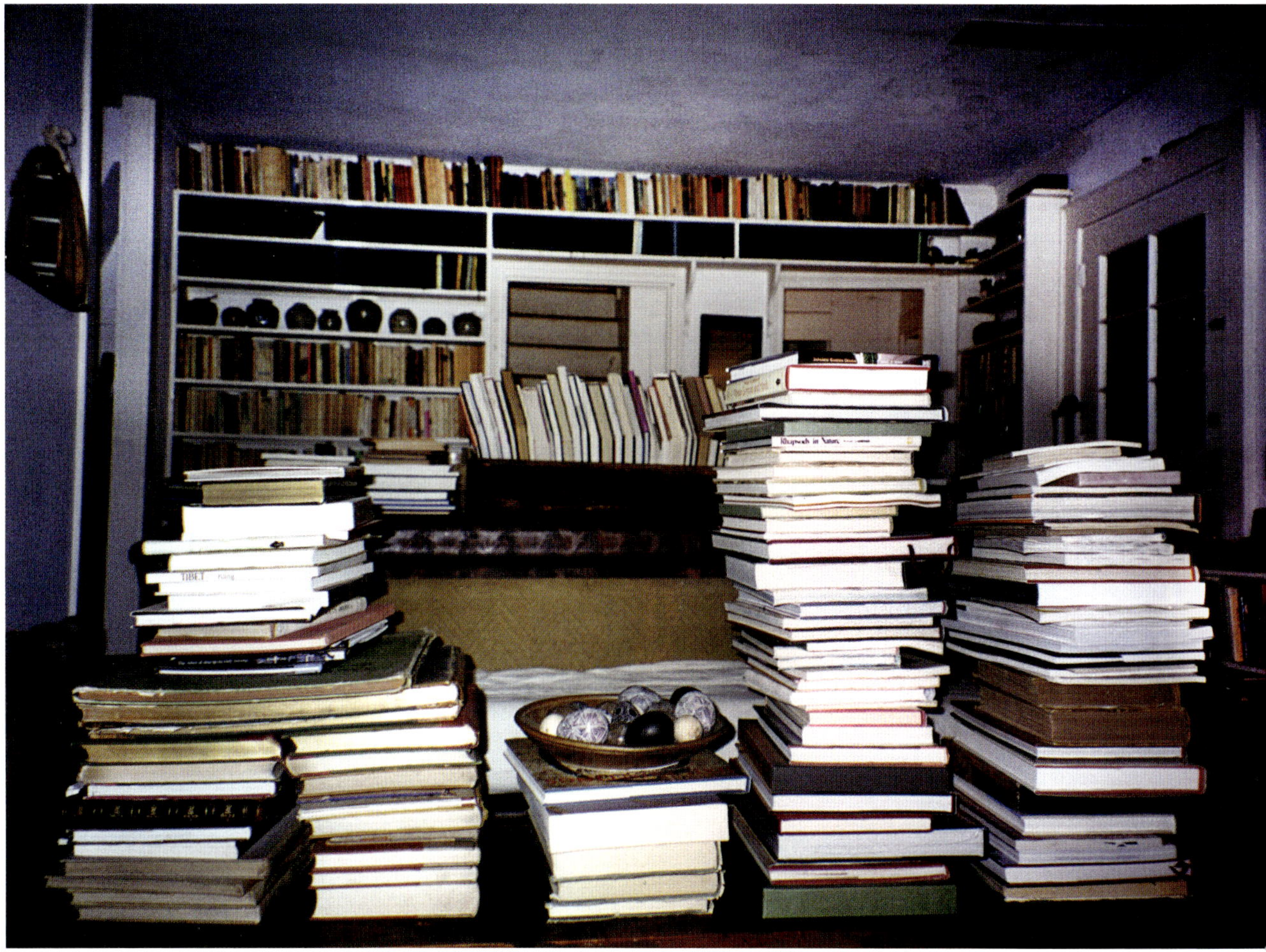

Throughout the house were various collections of books awaiting organization. Even the barn out back (see pages 134–135) had just been outfitted with custom shelves to allow overflow. Edward kept his front room and living room in a neater state of piles. He once said that it was always the plan upon moving into the large captain's house to keep it sparse and Zen-like. "We all know how that went!" he observed.

Many of his walls, however, if he didn't spend much time in that room (for example, his bedroom), were entirely devoid of decoration or artwork.

Julie Harris Interview

DECEMBER 8, 1998

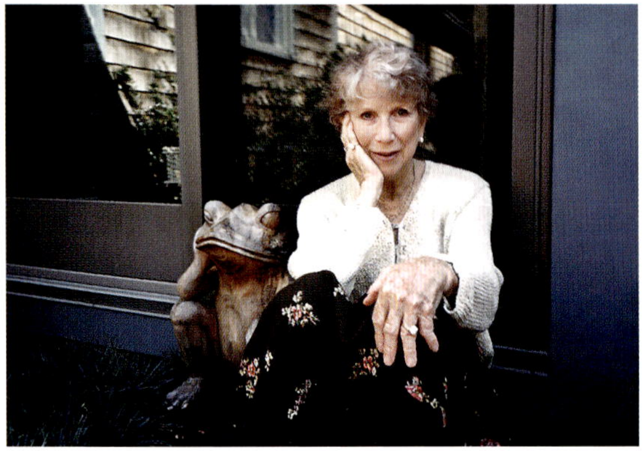

© Nancy Barr

Edward and actress Julie Harris were friends, and both were iconic figures in the Cape Cod theater community. Both were involved in the vibrant local theater community on Cape Cod. Gorey was a prolific contributor to community theaters in the area, designing sets and costumes, and Harris made her professional stage debut at the Cape Playhouse, a renowned summer theater in Dennis, Massachusetts. This shared involvement in the local theater scene meant their paths often crossed. At Gorey's memorial service in 2000, Harris read his story "The Osbick Bird."

Knowing both of them, Edward would often ask me, "How is dear Julie?" He commented to me when mentioning her work on TV in *Knots Landing* that that he wished she would do more "common man" productions here on the Cape and not always reserve herself for the classics.

Christopher Seufert: How did you come to know Edward Gorey; was it through his work?

Julie Harris: I don't remember my first Gorey book, honestly, but I do remember *The Beastly Baby*; it was such an odd little book. You know, he and I were born the same year, so I didn't grow up seeing his work. It wasn't until I was in my forties, I don't think, that I started to be aware of him.

CS: Oh, I'm so used to hearing about people's first children's book that I assumed it was further back. You know, he always wanted to get more into the children's category, but the publishers kept pushing back on it.

JH: Oh, I didn't realize. For me, I just kept running across his work, and of course, being so active in theater, you couldn't get away from *Dracula* when it was running on Broadway. The same thing that I enjoyed about his little chapbook was now onstage in this huge way. He won his Tony Award for that.

And when he moved to Cape Cod, we moved in the same circles, both in the theater and in the community at large.

CS: So you actually have a fair amount in common, both as theater pros and as Cape neighbors.

JH: We know many of the same people. He was such a sweet, sweet man. We also share the same birthday year, as I've said, so we were of the same generation coming out of the Midwest and braving the winters here on the Cape.

I just love hearing about his book signings, and we always have a little time to catch up then, and I usually get a pile of books and not only get one for myself, something I don't have yet, there's always something, but also give them out to friends.

CS: How do you keep in touch; do you connect socially?

JH: Whenever I hear that he's having a book signing, especially right in my backyard here in Chatham, Yellow Umbrella Books is one of [my] favorites, I get a pile of books to round out my collection and we have a little chat to catch up. He and I work in the same circles here on the Cape theater scene, and he's always got something on. He's such a sweet, sweet man, I enjoy him immensely. He wrote the sweetest note to me once when I was working on *Knots Landing*; I'll see if I can find it for you. I don't see him for a long time at times, but I do always enjoy knowing that he's out there doing his thing, which no one else can do.

CS: What of his other works do you connect with?

JH: Well, you could say that I began my professional career at the Playhouse in Dennis. One of my favorites is his Cape Playhouse poster from the '80s. There's nothing dark or macabre there, except it's all over a pure black background. It's such an unusual choice, with only the color yellow otherwise. The effect is spare and elegant, but there's a sense of humor that shines through. Always the sense of humor. And that's how I think of both him and his work.

CS: Me too.

JH: I also love *The Doubtful Guest*: "When they answered the bell on that wild winter night, there was no one expected—and no one in sight." Just as a piece of writing, it really sets the tone for a great story. His words are often overlooked, I think.

CS: Yes. Do you think he'll go on to have much of a legacy historically?

JH: I do. And when he's gone, I have no doubt that his work will go on to gain new appreciations. He's underappreciated now, I think. But for me, he's a friend and I like to think of him more as that than some formal macabre artist.

Carol Verburg Interview

SEPTEMBER 1, 2001

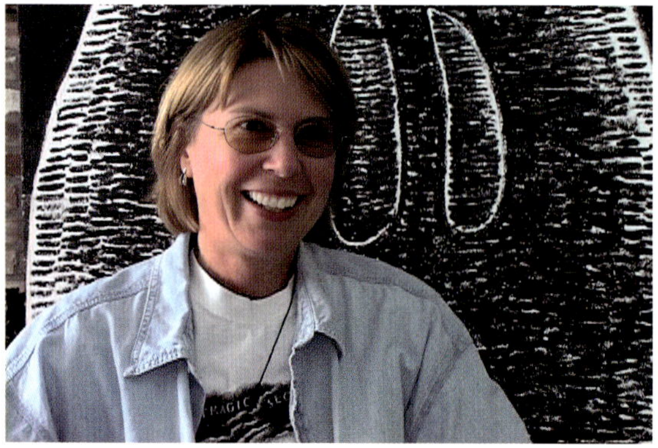

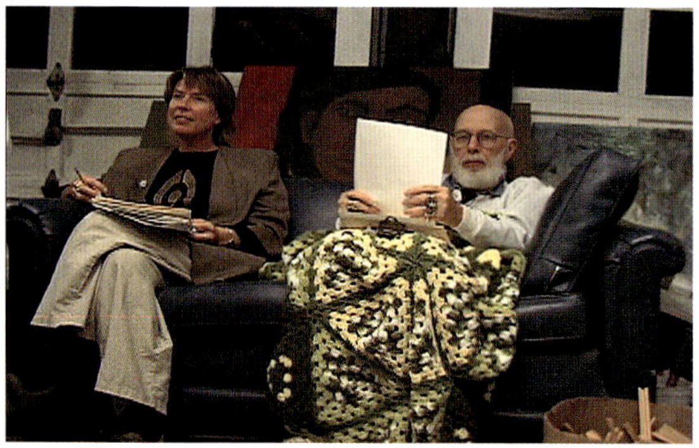

Carol Verburg was both a friend and collaborator with Edward from his first plays on Cape Cod in the 1980s through to his death in 2000. To call her merely a producer would be to minimize the amount of organizing, motivating, editing, and general fixing that she did for Edward in those years.

We sat down at her house in Yarmouth, Massachusetts, not too far from Edward's house, along with Theatricule Stoique actor Eric Edwards. He sat in with her interview, and she then sat in with his, in addition to doing solo interviews.

Christopher Seufert: Tell me about how you first became aware of Edward Gorey, his work or his person, or whichever one came first?

Carol Verburg: I don't remember how I first became aware of his work; it was just part of the cultural fabric. It was not anything I've noticed any more or less than anybody else's. I was always scared of scary things as a kid. The one time I read a Hardy Boys book, I had such nightmares and walking in my sleep that my parents never let me read another one. So I tended more toward the ship-that-flew kind of thing.

But when I moved here, my parents persuaded me to buy a house, and Yarmouth Port was represented to me as someplace where artists lived. And Edward and Helen and Herbert, I think, were the entire body of artists in the town, but I didn't know that. And I knew that this town where I bought a house was where Edward Gorey lived, and I saw his house. I didn't know that he had just moved there basically the same year that I moved to the Cape.

CS: What year was this?

CV: This was 1986. We both, Edward and I, each moved to the Cape, not being aware of each other in any way. And then in 1988 I staged an adapt[at]ion of Kurt Vonnegut's novel *Cat's Cradle* for the Barnstable Comedy Club, where he, Vonnegut, had used to work, and he had written it in Barnstable. And I had read it in Barnstable, and it was the twenty-fifth anniversary of the book. So it was a workshop production that they do every summer, something more experimental than their usual fare.

My sister wanted to come see it. She was working for Harcourt Brace Jovanovich in New York, and she was a children's book editor and had inherited an old contract with Edward, dating back about four years, that had just languished like so many of Edward's jobs have done over the course of time.

So she used that as her excuse to come to Cape Cod, that she was going to have dinner with him and talk about the book project and see if he wanted to proceed with it or cancel it. And in the course of that, she brought him to see my play, and we hit it off terrifically. And the three of us and my boyfriend at the time sat in the Barnstable Tavern across the street until it closed, just hanging out and talking, and I thought I really would like to do something with him sometime. I just really liked him.

So for me, it came definitely from the man rather than the work. The work wound up being an extremely illuminating aspect and manifestation of the man, but the man was extraordinary beyond anyone I've known or ever hope to know.

CS: What type of . . . what personal qualities did you . . . struck you when you first met him, I mean what about him personally?

CV: Well, he was very positive about my work, which was really nice because it was a very half-assed workshop production, but he saw through it to what I was getting at and liked the primitiveness of it. And we just talked about everything under the sun, which is always for me a great, great pleasure, and to find somebody else who took great pleasure in that right here on Cape Cod was a wonderful thing. I would not have dared to approach him, though, except that I heard from a mutual friend some years later that he was planning to do another show.

I hadn't known about *Lost Shoelaces* nor did I see it. Although coincidentally, my understanding was the way *Lost Shoelaces* came about was that Edward had made enough money from the designs for *Dracula* that had won that Tony in New York, that he was able to buy a house in Barnstable and eventually move here full time. And he and I each independently, not knowing each other at the time, went to see Jeannie Stevens's production of *Top Girls* by Carol Churchill, starring Kathy Smith.

And each of us independently found Jeannie afterwards and told her what a terrific production it was and how impressed we were with it. And Edward, I guess, then asked her if she would direct something of his, whereas I just thought, hurray, there's some good theater on Cape Cod. But Kathy, who was the lead in *Top Girls*, wound up being one of Edward's core troupe and worked with him for the next twelve or thirteen years.

CS: So after that, the first time that you met him, when did you have contact with Edward on a regular basis; did you see him around town?

CV: No, I didn't see him again until I was not living in Yarmouth Port yet. I was living all over the Cape in different places, and I got involved with the Provincetown Playwrights' Workshop, which was a new thing at that time or, rather, a revival of an old thing. I was one of the founding participants, and from it I became . . . I got drafted to be the president of the board of the Provincetown Theater Company and asked Edward if he would do a show with us.

When I heard that he was doing one in Woods Hole, I just called him, took my courage in hand and called him, and asked if he would bring it to Provincetown, and he said, "I would rather do a different show for Provincetown," so I said, "Fine" and set up a meeting. I had a director there from New York, a professional SSDC director, who was very, very interested in directing it, because at that time Edward had not ever directed anything, and it did not occur to me that he would.

But we had this meeting at my house, and Ray Martin-Wells, who is the founder of the Playwrights' Workshop and an ancient lady who had been part of the old Provincetown Theater Company back in the days of O'Neill and so forth, said at the end of the meeting, "Of course, you must direct it," and I'm sitting there with this New York director thinking, "Why did she have to say that?" But Edward said, "Yes, of course he would direct it," and that was the way events turned. Which meant that the production came out to be much more simple and primitive, which was always Edward's interest in productions rather than avant-garde, cutting-edge, highly choreographed, which was what the New York director would have done with it.

It would have been interesting to see in retrospect, of course; one can only be glad that Edward took on directing, because he got so involved in theater from that point, but which is why I was curious about Eric's memory of what or how *Stuffed Elephants* got started, because Edward must have been planning to direct that, but he didn't say, I don't think, at the time we were talking to him.

CS: What year was this that you put on this production in Provincetown?

CV: It was 1990, I believe. I'll have to check the notes, after, what did we do, something like twenty-three productions ultimately, so dates started slipping away after the first six years or so.

CS: What was the conversation like specifically when you called him? Did he answer the phone?

CV: Oh, he was very shy and so was I.

CS: Did he answer the phone though?

CV: Yeah. Oh, yeah, yeah. And he was very halting, but he said he would, as I say, he said he would be interested in doing the show, and we had this meeting at my house, which I had newly bought in Yarmouth Port.

CS: So how did that production go?

CV: It was great. It wound up . . . the Woods Hole production was scheduled for August, so we did ours in July. Edward wound up being way too busy. The two shows, the two tracks were somewhat different. In Woods Hole he always worked with Eric Edwards, Kathy Smith, Joe Richards, and Vincent Miave, and then whoever else of his original cast and whatever additions came down the pike.

But then in Provincetown, we had to hold auditions to get a cast, and we never . . . it's such a more transient place. I don't think we ever had more than maybe three holdovers from one year to the next, and there was never the kind of core troupe. I think there was only one, maybe two or three people who appeared in more than one of the three Provincetown shows.

CS: And so they performed; how many performances were there of that?

CV: I think we did three weekends, probably three or four shows a weekend: Thursday, Friday, Saturday, most likely, or else Friday, Saturday, Sunday. Once we saw how successful they were, I expanded the schedule, because from the very beginning I never knew what to call myself. I just was the person who made everything happen, who did everything that needed to be done, that Edward didn't want to do, that there was no other particular person to do.

So I was producer, on the one hand; I was assistant director, casting director, to some extent. Well, whatever needed to be done, I would do—sounding board, hand holder, I did the programs, I made sure that anything Edward wanted to design got designed in a timely way, I did the press.

CS: How did you do that? I mean, how do you . . . ?

CV: We just kept in touch.

CS: Did you ever have to badger him?

CV: Yeah, I guess so, I guess so, in a very gentle way. I don't badger . . . I think of Edward, the harshest thing he ever said to his actress, which I just love, was "Achtung, people!," and it was so effective. There's a line in *The Deranged Cousins*: "I cannot bear dissension." And that was something that Edward and I had in common. We both very much believed in resolving and handling things on the basis of good manners and reason, sweet reason, so we got along very well in that respect.

CS: So did you sort of develop a working relationship that you then continued, or when that ended, you just sort of . . . ?

CV: No. We did the show in Provincetown, it was great, and we went on to do two more, and by that time we had quite a tight working relationship. And we both were really tired of the long commute and never knowing whether we would be able to get enough actors or enough really interesting actors, so at that time I had been approached by Theater on the Bay in Bourne to direct a show there, which I had done, and then to become artistic director.

And since that was twenty to twenty-five minutes away, as opposed to an hour to sometimes two hours if the traffic was bad in Provincetown, we just shifted to working at Theater on the Bay, and I think that was really a very, very fertile period for Edward. He was really into theater by then. He had really . . . he had begun by taking pieces that he had written that he was curious about, pieces that he had published that he thought might transfer to theater.

But his original vision was still very two-dimensional, very book-derived, I think. And I think Jeannie and the Woods Hole crew helped him expand that, almost like the Popup Theater, into three dimensions, and my sense was that *Lost Shoelaces*, the show that Jeannie directed, was much [more] highly choreographed than anything that Edward ever did. But he began to see the possibilities for writing for theater, and there again, as I got to know him better over the subsequent years and learned more about his experience with the Poets' Theater in Cambridge, I realized that in a way after half a century, he was going back to what he had done in college; this position that he was no longer in as a writer and artist of having nothing expected of him and nobody particularly paying attention, judging, reviewing in any high-stakes way the work that he was doing.

So he was completely free to experiment, to bounce things off people; some pieces would work, something brilliantly and unexpectedly, some pieces that you would think were going to be brilliant would just somehow stay flat. Some pieces he would do three times over in different ways; once with puppets, once with live actors, once with a combination of puppets and live actors, to just see what would happen, and he found a freedom to do that, to experiment and create in theater. Whereas by this time, his position as a New York artist involved things like "Will you please sign 10,000 book plates," which were mind-crushingly boring for him.

So he really blossomed all over again, which I think is the story of Edward's life—he was perpetually blossoming all over again because of his ceaseless curiosity and boundless intellect and imagination.

CS: Tell me a little bit more about your working relationship as far as how you complemented each other, what your styles were. He was director, you were producer; I mean, how did your personalities fit together professionally?

CV: Well, he did not like to come to decisions, and that pressed me to come to decisions. He didn't like to be specific; he liked to invent everything as it went along and invent it all over again the next day, if time permitted. But the fact that I was also at this point sort of running the theater company meant that I had to be sure that the show came in on schedule.

So I started being stage manager and writing down all the stage directions that he and the actors would work out. Because if I didn't, the chances were he would not get to the piece again for another week; he would come back and then nobody would remember what they had done, and it would all start all over again, which was very interesting for Edward, but would have meant that it could have taken us years to get a show onto the stage. And I was also focusing on things like, to me his work is very dense, and it seemed to go best with an audience if you limited the number of pieces in each act and in the overall show.

Of the three shows we did in Provincetown, the one that was the most successful was the shortest, and I really felt it was because people really had to participate in his work with him, which was part of what he wanted. As an artist and a writer he had been very solitary and very independent. His vision was unique.

Nobody could keep pace with him in any way, I don't think, so collaboration was really new and strange to him, and he would dip a toe into it and then back off, like a maiden at a beach, and then plunge in and then dash back out again.

But his pieces were very dense and required the audience to focus really closely, which is something that audiences are not so used to doing anymore, especially because there isn't a through line and there isn't the kind of repetition that you get in Shakespeare, for instance, where the writer knows that the audience is going to be going off and buying food or throwing things or wandering around and greeting their friends. But for Edward's shows, you really had to be right there or you would lose something and not be able to pick it up again, and then in three to five minutes, the piece would be over.

So I was perpetually trying to get him to keep each act well under an hour, because that seemed to be about the limit that an audience could digest at a sitting. And that was really hard because he was always thinking of more things that he was curious about, and his shows came out well over two hours. So that was . . . I would say that was probably the biggest thing that we argued about, and I always lost, but I just felt that I needed to remind him of this. And as I say, the one time that he did make a relatively shorter show somewhat grudgingly, it was very successful and it got bigger audiences and better reviews than the other two.

CS: Tell me how the arguing happened as far as the actual language that you would use.

CV: Well, sometimes I would just get really impatient and say something to him during the rehearsal, but I usually tried to do most of the talking about that either in a bar afterwards or in the car on the way home. And he usually didn't want to hear it and would only let me go on for about a minute and a half before he would change the subject, and then I would understand that he had taken in whatever of what I was saying he wanted to take in, and we would talk about something else.

I had enormous respect for him, and I did feel sometimes that he was so much on his own track that it was almost necessary for me to be a little bit more nagging almost than I was inclined to be in order for him to really listen to what I was saying, and usually it was completely about practical matters, like "We really need to rehearse this piece again; the actors don't know their lines. They're asking what they're supposed to be doing" or "This act is running really long; is there anything we can tighten up?," that kind of practical questions.

But on the other hand, things like doing the designs, ordering mugs, having T-shirts made, he did that himself and donated everything to the theater company. Whatever company he was working for, he did enormous amounts of design and manufacturing labor and contributed everything without even a murmur, without even letting us know how much it cost or making any avenue where he could be paid back. He was extremely generous in his support of all the companies and people that he worked with.

CS: Were the actors generally paid?

CV: No, not at all.

CS: So everyone was donating their time?

CV: Yeah.

CS: How did the casting happen? I mean, what was sort of the process?

CV: In Provincetown, we would just put up an audition notice, send it to the papers, and then go and see who showed up. Usually you would have two nights of auditions for maybe two hours apiece. Although I think in Provincetown sometimes it was such a long trip that we would only have one, and then all kinds of people would show up and Edward would just pick who he thought was interesting. Sometimes it would be the people who were really gifted and capable, but very often it would be people who would just sort of stand there like sticks and not do anything, and that interested him, and he liked it. He really had really unpredictable, to me, taste. He saw things I didn't see. It was his work, of course; he was staging it, and that, of course, was what kept me interested was that I never could anticipate where Edward's mind was going to jump.

CS: How would he come to that decision? Was it a consultation, was it a very verbal "Yes, you. No, you're done, go away"?

CV: No, no.

CS: Was it a private consultation or did they find out later, did the people before they walked out the door?

CV: No. I would make up audition forms, and they would fill them out and we would write comments and then we would confer afterwards and Edward would say, "I really liked that boy." He always called them boys and girls. "I liked that girl," and I might say, "Oh, yeah, he was really good, perceptive about your stuff" or "But she didn't move, she just stood there and read the lines," and then Edward would just make his choices.

He liked to bounce things off me, but I didn't feel that he ever, at that stage he didn't lean on me particularly. He was really experimenting and he was very used to working by himself, so that was, at that point, that was where we were. Bourne was where Provincetown and Woods Hole came together, and I think that was, as Eric was just saying, that was why Edward really flourished there. He had . . . every time we did a show in Provincetown, it was walking out on a long limb because you never knew who you were going to get or what was going to happen, who was going to show up; whereas in Woods Hole, he had this core group that he had clicked with right off the bat.

So when we moved to Bourne, which we had discovered because of going to see his old friend and actor Eric Edwards's production of *Antigone*. That was a place where the actors from Woods Hole could commute to, which they couldn't to Provincetown except for one of them for one show and then . . . but meanwhile he could bring all the things that he had discovered working in Provincetown, which was an incredibly creative, no-holds-barred, cast-caution-to-the-winds kind of atmosphere in comparison with the rest of Cape Cod. So working in Bourne was terrific from that standpoint.

It was a little tricky at first because I was used to being Edward's right hand and 50% of his left hand as far as getting the shows done, whereas the Woods Hole cast that he was now working with was used to doing everything themselves. There hadn't been a person like me in those shows. So we were perpetually running into each other a little bit at the beginning because I would assume something was my job, and they would assume that they were going to work it out on their own. They were really startled, I remember, by the idea that stage directions were being written down by somebody else who would then, when Edward would say, "What did we do last time?," I would tell him what we did last time, rather than just sort of the actors being responsible for remembering it.

But that easily worked out and we wound up doing some really amazing stuff. That was also where the first winter that I went to California was the first . . . Edward was on such a roll. He did three shows within that year. I urged him to do something that he hadn't written while I was away, because by then we had enough design people and cast people and everything else, that I was pretty sure it would go on fine, and he picked *Salome*.

I said, "How about an Oscar Wilde?," thinking that if you let Edward loose on something like *The Importance of Being Earnest*, it would just be phenomenal. But he chose *Salome* and did the absolutely weirdest production of *Salome*, which is already very prone to weird productions, that perhaps anyone has ever seen, along with the puppet play *Six Who Pass While the Lentils Boil*.

CS: When did that one go out?

CV: I don't know, I would guess around 1995. I can't tell anymore without looking them up on the chronology, because there are just too many of them.

CS: Do you want to ask something else, Eric?

Eric Edwards: I'm enjoying this so much. It's unbelievable.

CS: Before we move into the mid-chronology?

EE: *Salome* was February of 1995.

CV: Yeah, 1995.

EE: Then it was *Stumbling Christmas* in 1996.

CV: Yeah, that was the first Christmas show in Bourne. He did two of what was meant to be a trilogy, the *Stumbling Christmas* and the *Blithering Christmas*, not in that order.

CS: I was always curious about why you all would do two productions at the same time. I mean, it was a two-part show with *Wallpaper* and *Heads Will Roll*. Was there some sort of a grand scheme for doing it like that? Why have two entirely different productions in the same performance?

CV: *Heads Will Roll* and *Wallpaper* came about because *Tragic Secrets* aborted at the last minute when one of the actors was injured, and we could not replace him. We could not do the show that we had envisioned, so we did *Heads Will Roll*, which we'd already developed independently for another venue, I believe.

Yeah, we had done it at a couple of different places, I don't think we'd done it at Theater on the Bay in Bourne at all, so I said, "Well, obviously we can't do *Tragic Secrets*, why don't we do the biggest piece from *Tragic Secrets*?," which was *Wallpaper*, one single long narrative piece, the most narrative thing Edward had done, and then just couple it with this piece that's already rehearsed that we have enough cast members left to perform. So that was how that came about.

And he had already done the postcard, and we just pasted over *Tragic Secrets* on the postcard with *Heads Will Roll* and *Wallpaper*. We redid the poster, and then the original *Tragic Secrets* actually reemerged years later as most of *English Soup*. But Edward was also forced to take the role of the telegraph boy in *Wallpaper* to replace the actor who was injured.

CS: Did he enjoy that, do you think?

CV: Oh, yes. He loved it and he was terrified. He forgot his lines even though he had written them and he knew them backwards and forwards. As soon as he stepped on a stage, they would drop out of his head. So fortunately, being a telegraph boy, he could be carrying a telegram and he would just look down at the telegram at strategic moments and read his lines. Of course, Vincent, who was acting opposite him in many scenes, made a point of trying to throw Edward off, which he succeeded in doing a number of times. It was very funny to all of us, but I wondered how it was for Edward and how it was for the audience.

CS: What was it that Vincent did, and how did Edward react?

CV: What did he do? He had a bit with a rose. He carried a single rose, and he would put it in his teeth or behind his ear or he would hit Edward with it or kiss Edward, or just physical contact with something that was not in Edward's repertoire. Those of us who got to know him well occasionally would transgress, but Vincent just really pushed the limits in *Wallpaper*. I remember him kissing Edward and Edward being flustered beyond endurance not knowing what to do about that. I got to where in later years when he would take me to the bus when I was flying to San Francisco and I knew I wouldn't see him for a few months, I would always give him a hug and a kiss on the cheek.

CS: Did he hug back or was he like, no no?

CV: He was kind of rigid, but he got to where he knew it was coming, and he was willing to admit that this was okay. It's like with a cat; his level of physical contact was cat level. He lived with cats all the time, and that was what he was used to.

CS: So you can pet them or not pet them?

CV: Yeah. And you don't really engage emotionally with them on a deep level.

CS: Tell me about Edward's relationship with . . . do you think he did these plays thinking about the public, and not necessarily whether they could digest it, but did he ever think about attendance and . . . ?

CV: No. He liked it. Woods Hole was a sophisticated enough audience that he always packed the house, whereas Bourne it was theatrically—how to put this—it was not a place where anyone would expect to find innovative theater. Even the people who ran the theater company were quite intimidated and disconcerted by Edward's work. The audiences were not always as good, and that was also true in Cotuit.

He minded that people, that more people didn't make the effort, didn't get it, didn't get what he was doing, but at the same time what he was doing was finding things out. That was always his first focus, was to try something and see what would happen, which was why each rehearsal was like a performance. He came to every rehearsal as he came to every performance, to see what would happen.

Usually in a rehearsal period you're trying to get the show to some level of quality where it can then [be] turned over to an audience like a gift. But for Edward, I always felt that the actors were making the gift to him and he was making the gift to them, and I really did learn over the course of my theater experience that that is really what theater boils down to, that you can amuse, startle, delight, terrify an audience.

But they go home to their own houses afterwards, and by the next day it's just a memory. Whereas the people who are working on the show, it really does change your life. It really affects . . . it absorbs such a huge amount of your time and energy, and it is probably the next most intimate relationship after the relationship you have with your closest significant others.

The people that you do theater with are very much your significant others, as if you were a team of trapeze artists leaping off into space, trusting that someone is going to catch your ankles and swing you to the next place. So that was what it was about for Edward. He had worked so long, so independently.

When you're a writer and an artist as he was making books, you're sending messages in bottles, you're just putting them in the bottle and throwing them into the ocean, and maybe two years later, after the book is published and has gone out to the bookstores, then you hear messages back. But with theater, it's immediate. You make it and something happens right there, and you depend on other people to make it with you. And I remember him saying in an interview that was published, "I never collaborate."

And then someone years later in another interview asked him about this, said, "Well, you've been doing theater," [and] he said, "Oh, well, that was then. Now I collaborate like a mad thing."

CS: Yeah, I think that was Dick Cook. Wasn't it the Dick Cook interview?

CV: I don't remember.

CS: Yeah. I think it was from Dick Cook, I actually got the rights from Dick Cook to use his interview for that.

CV: Good. That was a good interview, I do remember, but I don't remember what . . .

CS: Yeah. It was a good half hour of stuff, so . . .

CV: Andy Brown said that the interview book that's coming out has something like seventy-eight interviews and draws on it, so I never remember; I've read probably about half of them, and I don't remember what information was in which one anymore. Also, Edward himself told me so many things too.

CS: I found . . . did you find that he said, sometimes it seems like he would say one thing one time and the next and then he would say its exact opposite at another time? Do you think he was someone that kind of changed the way he perceived things, or would he sort of do that as an experiment with interviewers or with people that he'd say things for effect or . . . ?

CV: He had an enormous mind and he was able to see things from more angles than most people. And I think depending on the context of the question, a different answer might be appropriate. I don't think it was that he changed his mind so much as that he could just see a different angle being the appropriate one to answer from, from one time to another, or a different aspect of the situation being the one that applied in a particular context what somebody was asking.

CS: Tell me about the way he used language. I don't mean necessarily in his books, I mean that's kind of a . . . he obviously has a love of names and language and experiments with that, but I mean also the point where I think there's a thing in *Heads Will Roll* where it was a whole different language that he created.

CV: Yeah. Well, he didn't create it; someone else did, but yes.

CS: Oh, okay. But I mean the way he, you know, "I'd rather be hung by my thumbs." Tell me a little bit about the way he expressed himself verbally?

CV: Well, he loved old clichés as he loved transcended vegetables and fruits like the eggplant and the kumquat and objects like library paste. He also liked phrases. He liked clichés like "I'd rather be hung by my thumbs," or there were . . . his speech was peppered with expressions that my grandmother in Baltimore might have used. So a lot of them were familiar to me, and one that interested me was that he always said, "Oh, for the God's sake."

He never said, "For God's sake," and I wondered if it was that old shibboleth about taking the Lord's name in vain or if it was just something that he got up to at Harvard that he never changed afterwards or what? But Noelle said that she went to hear John Ashbury read and that John Ashbury talks very much like Edward, and apparently everybody who was part of that Poets' Theater circle developed this particular mannered way of speaking that Edward . . . he was the only representative of that group that we knew, so to us he seemed unique, but apparently it was partly just a thing that they did.

CS: Do you think he had a tendency to sort of exaggerate, I mean, he did sort of seem to have that, you know, if he didn't like a movie, it was the worse movie ever. I mean did he exaggerate for effect?

CV: Well, he didn't excoriate so much as he just didn't want to . . . he just wanted to be really clear that this was just not even worth discussing. He wouldn't go on and on and on usually about something that he didn't like. He might be extreme to just get rid of it. He might be extreme a little bit at lengths to be sure that it was gotten rid of. He never took the kind of pleasure in being negative that so many people take. He found so many aspects of the world, however grim they might be, absolutely fascinating and intriguing, that he wound up having a really positive outlook in that sense that he was always moving forward out of curiosity.

CS: When did your relationship sort of become, you know, when did you develop sort of a personal component to the relationship, and what form did that take?

CV: 1995, '96 after *Chinese Gossip*. I had . . . I don't think I really want to talk about this. It had to do with a relationship that, in my life, that was kind of triangular involving Edward, and when that became a horror and a nightmare, Edward kind of made me realize that the things that I had been drawn to were things that Edward himself could perfectly well offer me.

And I wound up just suddenly sort of discovering what had been right there in front of me all along, that this was a really sustaining person in my life. I was at that point, young and active and envisioning, finding the ideal mate and riding-off-into-the-sunset kind of thing.

But Edward kind of made me see that my destiny was not that, and that instead it was to have this incredibly intense, creatively based, intellectually based, imaginative, being giddy, being silly, being delighted by things, but always with a certain level of reserve, which was not for me, up until then was very foreign in my close relationships.

CS: How did he . . . I mean, did you guys have a conversation one day or was it something that . . . I mean, how did he get all this across to you sort of; I mean, how did that communication happen, I mean?

CV: The fact that we were able to realize all this was what made it possible for us to have as close of a relationship as we did, and it was really never explicit in any way. It was the things that he did, the choices that he made, the fact that he never spoke to this third person again without ever saying anything about it made it clear what was happening.

It's really not . . . Edward didn't talk about things. He came from an era when you didn't talk about your feelings. Much of what I learned about him came out indirectly, and because working together is such a close and intimate and trusting kind of relationship, I felt that we really got the best of each other.

We really, the whole group, got to see each other at our most radiant and creative and energetic, and I'm really thankful to have had that context to get to know Edward and also the other people that we worked with.

CS: Does the group still maintain itself today, or do you find you're sort of spinning without a center now that Edward's not here?

CV: Well, I felt that we were still together and spinning without a center when we did *The White Canoe*, that it was really hard to do that, that he had left us this beautiful gift, this script that he had written for us and we had to do it. But to do it without Edward was just devastating. It was not that it was difficult; it was just that it was missing the most important piece, which was this wonderful collaboration which he was always the center of.

Even with the shows that I directed, the straight shows that we did in between his shows, like *Hamlet* and *Gift of the Gorgon*, he was always involved. We had lunch constantly and talked about everything that we were doing, and his ideas went into everything I did and his ideas went into everything he did, but I feel like I'm wandering way off the subject.

CS: Back up and tell me a little bit more from the start about *The White Canoe*.

EE: Just why don't you explain that he paid a great deal of attention to what you did, because this was very much at least in terms of theater his closest relationship, and which he's not mentioning is that things would appear in his plays or lives that he would take from *Hamlet* as a result of having done *Hamlet* with her, been involved with Carol and the things that Carol did.

And he would comment elliptically in his plays on Carol's work, the same way he would comment on actors' lives, and he was always terribly aware of putting those elements into his own life because they were part of his life.

CV: Yeah, I felt that we had a great responsibility in being the context of Edward's creative life at that point. And it was so bizarre to run into people from New York who would come down to see the shows and realize that they thought this was just what he did on the side. That to somebody in New York, Edward's real work was signing 10,000 book plates. Whereas to us, it was making theater.

He was doing work so avant-garde, so completely original, but it wasn't happening in New York and it wasn't with the goal of getting onto Broadway, and so to the rank and file of people in New York, it was of no significance, it was just a casual amusement. Whereas I imagine that as people look back at the Poets' Theater now and say, "Well this was a great seminal, theatrical movement," they're probably going to realize that likewise what he was doing here on Cape Cod was really extraordinary.

Some people did. A lot of people would come from wherever they were. I had some friends who came every year from New Jersey, and my friend Betty Ann, who would come from Pasadena if she could, she had a house here, but she always tried to see Edward's show.

CS: I was just thinking, could you just angle your chair a little bit more this way now, just a few inches. Yeah, okay.

CV: My body or my chair?

CS: Yeah, either one, that's fine. I just wanted to keep that angle because I think you were already talking to Eric, and it looks funny in the camera. But anyway, we have a lot of stuff to talk about, but can you back up on *The White Canoe* and tell me a little bit of the story about what is *The White Canoe* and how it started?

CV: The last three years or so of Edward's life, I was spending longer and longer periods in the winter in San Francisco. So our creative discussions were fewer. We talked to each other on the phone at some length at least once a week, but when I was here during the summers, we would have lunch every day and we would go to movies, we would go to dinner, we were constantly talking about stuff, and so I didn't hear as much about what he was thinking and what he was working on as I did when I was here.

So he told me that he had had a request from a composer in Germany, someone had written and said he'd seen some puppet excerpts on the internet and had Edward ever thought of writing a musical piece, an opera for puppets, and Edward said, "As a matter of fact, I do have an idea for that," and he wrote the libretto and sent it off to Germany. And he told me about this.

I was very excited about it because I thought it was a natural. Edward's comprehensive interest in music plus his interest in movement, poetry, ballet, and opera; it just seemed like it would be a really wonderful next step, but he didn't hear from the composer for a long time, and then he would get back a letter and he didn't know really where the thing was. And then suddenly he died at a time when the English banned the Tiger Lillies, who had just done *Shock Headed Peter*, which was sort of a puppet opera.

Were just on their way to work to meet him and work with him, so *The White Canoe* had not been uppermost in our conversations. Also, the Cotuit Center for the Arts had just burned to the ground, which was very much uppermost in our conversation, our last conversation. It happened just before he died. So I moved into his house after he died, at the request of the executors, and in keeping with my promise to Edward some years back that if anything ever happened to him, I would make sure that the cats were okay and I would see that they were taken care of.

So I moved into his house and took care of the cats. He died on a Saturday, and on the Monday, the phone rang and it was the composer calling from Germany saying, "This is Daniel Wolfe, the score is finished, *The White Canoe* is finished." And we talked for quite a while, and I told him that Edward's group of actors was still together and we really should do it and could he send it, and he of course wanted it done.

We were both just devastated that Edward hadn't gotten to hear it, see it, but we also felt that it was something he really wanted to do, and there was absolutely no doubt in my mind that he would be extremely frustrated, even in death, if it just sat and languished.

CS: So did he ever hear any of the music?

CV: No.

CS: It was completely done . . . I was really struck by it because it really did seem right up at Edward's alley.

CV: Yes. Dan had sent him some sheet music for it, and Dan said, "Do you want me to send you the whole score?," and according to him, Edward said, "No voice, no piano, no point."

CS: What does that mean?

CV: That he couldn't sing it, he couldn't play it, there was no way that he would be able to translate the written score into anything that would be of any use to him. So I think Dan just sent him a tape to listen to. I'm not sure of that, but if Edward listened to it, he didn't tell me or Dan anything about his reaction, and I don't think he did in fact listen to it after all.

CS: So when did you actually decide to put it on, and how did you get the ball rolling with the actors and everything?

CV: Well, we were all in touch because of Edward's death [April 2000]. It was a huge event. It completely changed all of our lives because a very important piece of our lives professionally and personally had been this annual collaboration on some kind of a theater piece or other.

I had called the actors, the core people in particular, when Edward was in the hospital in a coma, and Eric and Joe and Kathy came over to see him, fortunately all at the same time. We happened, the four of us, to be there when the cardiologist came in and told us how lucky we were to have had this last ten years, that in fact Edward had—as he and I put it—had a dickey ticker for a lot longer than he had told all of us.

And it was far from losing the additional ten to twenty years I had always hoped we would have with Edward. According to the cardiologist, we had had in effect already gotten an extra ten years, so that was an easier way to look at it at the time. Nevertheless, I don't think there was any doubt in anybody's mind that we still wanted to do a show in the summer as we always did, and we still wanted to do that especially once the art center had burned down [Cotuit Center for the Arts]. We had to resuscitate it and find a new location; who else was going to do it?

The Cotuit Center for the Arts organization was a sanctuary for artists, which what Edward and all of us had liked so much about it. So we did *The White Canoe* just as sort of a resurrection or a testimony, a tribute. Edward's friends Helen Pond and Herbert Send made a little set to go around the smaller set that Edward had made of three doors that we used for some of his other puppet pieces. So, Herbert and Edward created it together with the help of Rick Jones.

I rounded up the usual suspects. I have a page in my address book under F for "friends of Edward" that has the names and phone numbers of all the actors, and I called everybody and said, "This is what's going on," and everybody who was available participated.

CS: Did it feel like Edward was still present during rehearsal, or did it feel like he was not?

CV: To me it felt like he was not there; I felt bereft. I felt acutely how much I missed those unpredictable leaps he would make. And in the papers that his executors were finding in the house, you would see some of these leaps, like Spirits of the Swamp, Louie Fuller Sleeves. I knew that to Edward that meant something concrete and very specific that he would have made for the Spirits of the Swamp as a costume, and I had no idea how to go about implementing that.

He sewed all the puppet costumes and he frequently, if not always, made new puppet costumes for each puppet show, depending on what was needed. There were certain costumes that recurred, like the dogs or a dark-blue costume or a black costume that you could use more than once, but, for instance, when he did *Omelet*, his puppet version of *Hamlet*, he made velvet costumes like the velvet costumes that he had essentially designed for my production of *Hamlet* and a little velvet Rosencrantz and Guildenstern with two heads.

So we didn't have him to do any of that, and I knew that the libretto must . . . he must have had very specific ideas about how the libretto would translate visually, and we had no access to that because I hadn't even had a chance to talk to him about it in any detail. It hadn't been something that was on the verge of production; he didn't even know it was finished.

So to me, his absence was palpable and devastating. But two close friends of mine who knew Edward who came to see the show, both hard-headed, science-oriented women, approached me afterwards and said, "I felt Edward there," and neither of these was a new-agey kind of person who you would expect to be looking for spirits hovering about, but they both just really had very powerful experiences of his presence.

I yearned for an experience of his presence. I just missed him intensely twenty-four hours a day, seven days a week, while we were doing this just in general.

CS: How do you feel, I mean how did it come off for you, do you think? Was it satisfying or was it a disappointment?

CV: Yes, it was satisfying; I felt it was really important for us to do it. I felt that it was a beautiful piece. I think I felt that it was the best thing he had written for theater. I felt that he had really gotten it right and had really pulled together everything that he had been doing over the last dozen years. His experimental bents, all the different kinds of influences from kabuki to opera. The great breadth of his interests was so enormous.

I felt that he had combined all that with enough dramatic structure to make the piece really successful, and the dance music had by and large carried out just what Edward wanted from the songs and from the lyrics that he wrote. And I just, I hated it that he couldn't be there for it, because I thought it was just a wonderful piece. But I was really, really glad that we did it.

CS: Well, when you say you missed him seven days a week, what are the things that you miss about him professionally during that week. For example, how did you work together and how did you get the logistics things done? Tell me about the lunch meetings and the things you would accomplish there at Jack's Outback.

CV: Well, one of my very favorite things in my life was having lunch with Edward, because over the course of any single lunch, as much as I . . . I'm sorry, Jack, but I really never liked the food at Jack's at all. I would go for Edward. In fact, there was one year, the year before Edward died, that we were eating at the Mercantile every day because Edward discovered he could get a really good meal and also have enough left over for dinner. The food really was good, and Jack wasn't well that year, so it wasn't like Edward was missing seeing Jack every day. He was still going for breakfast to Jack's and seeing him.

But generally lunch meetings were at Jack's andwe would just sit there and throw ideas around. An epistolary play began when we were just looking around at *Irma Vep* [Louis Feuillade's *Les Vampires*, 1915] and *Love Letters* [A. R. Gurney, 1989]. Edward despised *Love Letters*. I have directed it under duress at the request of some actors, and I forget how I wound up with this idea of *The Love Letters of Irma Vep*, and Edward just took off on it and that become an epistolary play.

So for both of us, he would come in to lunch every day with this handful of yellow papers with his black calligraphic handwriting all over them and tell me what he had been thinking of. One day he came in with this drawing of the bong bug and I didn't understand what he was saying, and it turned out it was the bah humbug, which was this insect he had created for *The Haunted Tea Cozy*, which was his rendition of *A Christmas Carol*, which went on to fame and glory.

And which we had hoped to adopt also as a puppet play, but it hadn't quite . . . he hadn't been satisfied with where he got with it, and he hadn't wanted to . . . another year and I think we would have done it as a puppet play. But we would go through *Buffy the Vampire Slayer*, *The X Files*, whatever movie he had recently seen, whoever I had recently talked to from the group.

I tended to keep more in touch with them than he did. He never . . . he rarely called people. He called his oldest friends, but he didn't call the actors much. He usually just called me and asked me to call the actors, which I was happy to do, as much as I don't like making phone calls. So we would just cover a zillion things over lunch, and we'd be right in the middle of some incredibly intense creative back and forth and someone would walk up and say, "Oh, I saw your car outside, would you mind signing these four books for my niece? She's just four and she's already such a big fan of yours."

And I would be, of course, ready to leap up and strangle this person, wrestle with them to the floor, and stuff coffee Jell-O down their objectionable throat, but Edward was just pure graciousness and would change gears instantly, and then we would have a hard time getting back on to whatever extremely satisfying track we had been on before this diversion.

CS: Were the lunches, for you, a place more to do business or to socialize? Was it more "All right, we've got to get this done, we've got to get the costumes, you know, we've got scheduling logistics" or was it more like "Oh, I've got a great idea" that you would accomplish?

CV: Well, nobody ever said, "I've got a great idea." Edward would just come in with whatever idea he had, and I would always have my idea du jour, which was some totally cockeyed scheme that I thought one or both of us should undertake. But then the logistics had to be done, and I would always bring that up or he would bring it up: "Well, when do I need to do the T-shirt design?," that kind of thing. But that was just the price we paid for the creative part.

CS: What types of things did you guys do on a personal level? I mean, when you went out, when you hung out just as friends, what types of things did you guys do?

CV: Mostly we'd go to movies, sometimes dinner. I didn't like a lot of the things that he did with a lot of his other friends. I mean not that I disliked them, but they were things that I didn't want to go along with. He had, every weekend he went yard sale-ing with his cousins, and when his friends Mel and Alex were in town, they might go to antique shops or go up to art galleries or very often they would go to a late dinner and a late movie, and I always preferred to go out early and then come home and read before I go to bed.

And also, Edward's relationship with each of his friends was different, so that his friends have not wound up all becoming one big bereft group other than the actors, who are one big group already, because he had different things in common with each person that he knew and had a really close friendship on a completely different basis with each person.

CS: What are the things that you miss most about him now when you wake up?

CV: Being able to talk to somebody about absolutely anything and knowing that he'll understand, knowing that he will always appreciate what I have to say and be critical in a constructive way, if at all, and will encourage me by example and precept to my best work. That's just so miraculous. There's so few people who you ever get that from, and I couldn't believe he could die.

He was just too essential to the world as I know it. And that was my first reaction when I got the phone call that Rick called to say that he had had a heart attack and was in the hospital. I said, "I can't bear it," and I meant that absolutely literally. I just didn't know what . . . how the world could go on without Edward, and it still seems to me amazing that it's still here.

CS: Question, Eric?

EE: No, she did a nice job.

CS: Tell me about the house and what you know about what might be happening there with the museum.

CV: This will be history by the time this gets to air.

CS: Will it ever air, who knows?

CV: To err is human.

EE: Divine.

CS: What do you think Edward's legacy is, I mean professionally; how do you think history will treat him?

CV: I think different people over the course of time will discover different facets of his remarkable multifaceted intellect and personality. I think that the things that he's known for now, the intricate cross-hatching and highly controlled drawings that he did, are so different from the free-form, multifaceted, multicultural influences that showed up in his theater. So I think people are bound to become more curious about the theater over the course of time.

It was much more avant-garde and not at all what people expected, so they just didn't know quite how to categorize it, how to think about it. But I think as people get less concerned about that and more concerned about the substance of the work, that they will be finding a lot of interest in Edward's theatrical work.

CS: Wow, it's still going. It's amazing. All right, we're still rolling.

CV: He must have more things he needs to get into the record.

Eric Edwards Interview

SEPTEMBER 1, 2001

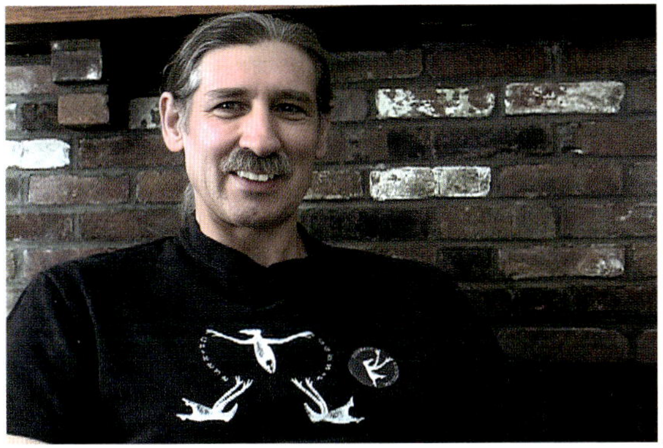

Eric Edwards was a core actor in Edward's theater troupe Le Theatricule Stoique and is also a teacher, poet, and spider expert living in Falmouth, Massachusetts. Carol Verburg also sat in on the interview.

Christopher Seufert: Okay, so let's go ahead, Eric. We're just basically having a conversation. You don't have to worry about the camera.

Eric Edwards: It's just a conversation.

CS: And act like the questions are very advanced and like you're having trouble understanding them, because my intellect is so capacious.

EE: Really, yeah. [*Laughing*]

CS: And witty and urbane and all this stuff. Act like I have a tremendous poise, very gracious and refined.

EE: Somebody that should be explained so to, yeah, someone with status, like tremendous amount of stuff, such an honor.

CS: Okay. So what's your first memory of Edward Gorey or your first—not necessarily when you met him, but when did you become aware of Edward Gorey?

EE: Yeah, I became aware of his work in the '60s, when little books started to appear. And I thought not much of it in particular, except that I liked it because it was surreal and absurd and that was something that appealed to me, especially artistically; the paintings, surreal paintings and some surreal theater.

But I never really understood surreal theater, so I really didn't care for it. And a lot of the European absurdist theater has a subtext that's political or cultural, and I never got that, so I kind of liked the surface. I was like the most shallow theatergoer for absurdist or surreal European stuff, because what I liked was just the images. I think it was more like a Dali-type surrealist, just into those shocking images.

But Edward had this really very American perspective on absurdity, and that was original in my opinion. I've been brought up in New England as pretty relentless, American-style, pragmatic stuff, which I really despised for no good reason, just temperament. And all of a sudden here was an artist that seemed to feel the same way; that all this pragmatic stuff was completely irrelevant.

So I liked his stuff, but I didn't focus on him at all.

CS: That's a word I don't really—I've always acted like I understood it, but I don't really.

EE: Well, I think pragmatic in the typical sense would be something that's practical, that has a purpose or is useful, gets things done, makes sense in the world of mechanics or plumbing or wiring something or painting.

CS: So it's like with a, like Shaker stuff or the Pennsylvania Dutch. Like their style is based on function.

EE: Yes. So the beauty comes out of a different aspect of their life, but the end product is supposed to be completely functional. Yeah, Shakers are a good example, because people rarely perceive the pragmatic side. What they see is, so this is very useful, but what they like about it is the elegant simplicity of the function.

CS: Yeah, hold that thought. Can I close this door?

EE: Yeah, the creaking door. Another unpublished work.

CS: It is absolutely astounding, actually, when you think of that. I mean, everything you read about Edward is so English. Tell me more about this American—I mean, I've never heard anyone say that Edward had an American feel to him. So—

EE: What I saw was that he used this kind of English, what would you call it, this English front, this English—this sort of Anglophilia, this love of English stuff, this kind of pseudo-class attitude in America. So for me, I knew he was American and I knew that he was using this as a kind of trope—that's not quite the right word either—but it was I think in the lowest form, you would say it's like a gimmick.

But for him, it wasn't a gimmick. It was a gateway into this absurdity of value. And in order to represent it right, he had to put it in a place that looked not like the United States.

CS: I see what you're saying. So the Americanism comes from the fact that he was poking fun. It was English.

EE: He was using it, he was using the English picture, the English style.

Carol Verburg: And the setting.

EE: It wasn't until I met him personally, when we did a play together, the first play in 1987, that the rest of Edward Gorey came into focus for me, so it was really interesting.

CS: How did you meet him and how did you become involved in this play? Did you seek him out?

EE: Well, I don't know how. He somehow got interested in doing a play of his own devices. Somehow he got involved with Jeannie Stevens, and I had done some theater work with her so that was the initial connection. I was one of those sort of actors that Jeannie knew about, and she thought I might be appropriate to work with Edward's stuff.

CS: Why do you think she felt that way? Did she see some things in common?

EE: Yeah, I don't know. I mean, at times you think, "Well, Eric has this—the right sort of stage face or the right kind of artificial distance, that sort of pose." You never know what a director thinks of an actor since half of the director's perspective is "This person is technically competent enough, that kind of thing, deep enough," and the other half is "This person's enough of a whore that they'll do what I say. That they won't require their own means, their own image."

They'll just do what you want them to do. So you have to have both things, and so I think that Jeannie just saw that sort of thing.

CS: Tell me about when you first met him; was it at a rehearsal or was there a formal "Eric, this is Edward; Edward, this is Eric"?

EE: It was a rehearsal of a bunch of us getting together with Jeannie and Edward in Woods Hole. I have to say one other thing, that I think that for a lot of people, they assumed—because this is a very weird thing—that I for some reason—maybe it's my personality or my temperament—they assumed that I already knew Edward, that I was like up on Edward, that we were somehow running in this parallel track, but we didn't know each other at all.

I just knew he lived on the Cape, that was about it. This vague sort of few facts and interesting guy and that was it. I didn't pay any attention at all to him. So people would assume that I—after this play, for example—they'd say, "You must have known Edward for a long time." And I said, "Well, not really. I just met him like two months ago." But there was that kind of, for me, very flattering sense, that in some intellectual way we were not far apart.

Our personal relationship was more than just professional. He was interested in everybody that he worked with, and anybody who became his friend, he became personally interested in whatever was going on with them. I found that surprising sometimes because I'm fairly reticent about personal stuff. I don't like to bring it to other people, especially in the theater, but that's not true of everybody. And Edward was—once he was your friend, he was rather generous personally.

CS: Tell me about how you actually met him when you walked into the rehearsal.

EE: We had a rehearsal and he was introduced by Jeannie to all of us. And I don't remember precisely what was said, but she talked about the play. He talked about the play and got scripts and we started dealing with it. Talked to him after. And during rehearsal, of course. He would show up at every rehearsal, which is one of these typical things he would do for the next thirteen years.

So we just started to treat, actors in general and me as well, just started to treat him as one of the crowd. It took awhile maybe, a couple of weeks. I remember very clearly one of the first conversations I had with him was about a book he was reading, which was a book about spirit photographs that he had found, long out of print, completely ludicrous book, but with these gorgeous old—it was an old book too.

I mean, just something left over somewhere in some used bookstore like Parnassus. And he was spending a lot of time with this particular book. And that surprised me and amused me. And so we talked about that a lot, and I never forgot that. I actually used that in some of my own artwork later on, because I knew, for example, that he would understand this business about spirit photographs, you know.

CS: You mean the fact that a lot of them were probably faked and sort of tongue in cheek?

EE: Yeah. He was always fascinated with people that believed in this and how these things—he would not make a judgment about the people. I'm sure he felt the whole business was ludicrous, but that's what interested him; how is this ludicrous situation so beautifully worked out by people? How are these fake photographs handled with such sincerity, such rigid belief.

And it was quite charming to get this perspective from him, because normally most people would look at something like that, if they weren't supernaturalists to begin with, and they would just say, "Oh, what a bunch of crap."

But for Edward, this was something that happened in the world and it happened on the fringes of legitimacy, and he loved that. He was willing to stare down every detail and use it.

CS: So this first play, what struck you about it? You said he came to every rehearsal. Was he directing or producing?

EE: He did not direct it but he did write it. It was based on his stories. Some had been published, some had not. And so some of the things that we were doing, you could actually refer to pictures in books, and other things were just text that we then had to completely develop on our own.

However, the interesting thing is that if something had appeared in a book, this text that we were using, he was not interested in replicating what the book had done at all. There were certain essential ingredients that he wanted to maintain, but he didn't want to see onstage the picture that he had illustrated. He wanted to see something else onstage.

I think that for this production, *Lost Shoelaces* [premiered on August 13, 1987, at the Magic Oyster Theatre in Woods Hole, Cape Cod], he was principally interested in seeing what theater was like for his stuff. How do these puppets look? How do these actors work? And Jeannie [Stevens], the director, was very interested in ensemble work for actors. And Edward, I think, enjoyed that, because you could see how pliable acting could be visually if you knew what to say or if you let your actors go a certain distance.

A lot of interviews, some of the—as you know, he would talk about the actors or the puppets running amuck. And this is something that we figured out very early, especially with puppets, that there is a kind of anarchy underlying this thin veneer, a very rigid storyline, this text, which was immovable, but this sort of energy that was invested into this story was always on the edge of anarchy.

Because when you do it right, it gives a very uneasy picture to a rather banal and kind of trashy storyline or ridiculous storyline, and he loved that. He loved that.

CS: So he cultivated that?

EE: Yeah, oh, yeah. He'd pull it in when he didn't like it and then he'd sort of prod you when he wanted more.

CS: When he was actually directing, when it was more him putting on the play—

EE: That was after that first production, he said, "That's it. Nobody else directs." And he would take suggestions, and Carol might have more insight into that, but it was very clear. I think he said it to me directly at one point, he said, "After Jeannie," whom—he appreciated her and he learned a tremendous amount, but he had this incredible ability to learn at incredible speed.

So, this high level of ability to absorb at a great rate. And after one time—and this was true throughout my experience with him—if something was done by other people, he could praise it, but generally speaking, he wanted to keep his distance from it, because he really, with the plays that we did with him, he wanted to have complete control or at least complete artistic control, over how it looked and what his actors did.

CS: What was his style like as far as a director goes?

EE: The best way I think I can describe it, not being professional, would be he would give us the text or what part of the text was ready and—especially as time went on with the actors, he'd work with us, the same people over and over again, and he could show up with some text and the rest not there, but he knew that we would pick it up as he got it to us.

He was confident that things would go his way. What he would do is give a text and we would assign parts, sometimes that would change, but often he had some idea of who he wanted to do what. And then he would let us play. And as soon as he saw something as we were working it out or he would have a general picture and he'd say, "Will you go over here and you do that, you do this," and then we would do that and a lot of other things. And he would start to pick and choose or he'd start to say, "Why are you doing," you know, he'd say, "Why are you doing that; that's completely wrong."

And then he would explain something to us. A lot of times, we had to wait quite awhile in rehearsal to get an explanation for something that we did not have a clue about how he wanted it done or why he wanted something done.

CS: So maybe what you're suggesting is that maybe he didn't know and he was looking for you guys to come up with various possibilities and he would kind of stop: "That's what I want."

EE: Yes. Yeah, he'd do that—

CS: Or "Definitely don't do that."

EE: Yeah. Sometimes I'm sure he was just looking; he didn't know. In other times, I think it was he didn't know how to let us know. I'm sure of that. He knew what he wanted, but it was—he didn't see it even close or he thought maybe it was there, but then after a while it was clear that we didn't have any idea and he'd have to tell us.

I think he liked for us to stumble on things, number one, that surprised him, or number two, that it was the way he thought about it and we'd stumble on it ourselves. So he enjoyed both of those.

CS: Was that the early-on stages of rehearsals?

EE: Early on in—especially after a couple of shows, that's what he would do. He'd give you the text and he would kind of describe what he wanted, and we would start to do that or he'd just say, "See what happens." But he got to be better very—well, quickly, he would—as he did a couple of these productions, he got to know the basic outline of what he wanted his actors to do.

So as we picked up the text on a particular bit, he would say, "All right, now you do this, now you do that." And then you would fill in around this skeleton what happened. Sometimes he would say, "I'd really like a dance here or I'd like this to be sung." A little less as time went on, but in *English Soup*, all of a sudden this reappeared and he said, "Well, how do we do this?"

And Cathy Smith said, "Well, we could do it to a square dance." And he let Cathy Smith work the entire square dance out. And they would just determine—he would determine, "All right, this is where you say the line," and that sort of thing.

So it was really a mix. Sometimes it would be completely specific what he wanted or didn't want and then other times it would just be quite left up to the actor; you never could tell, never could tell.

CS: Was that sometimes a source of confusion or attention, because you didn't quite know necessarily what was expected at that particular time?

EE: Yes. Well, especially for actors, not so much for me temperamentally, but for other actors, they want to know where they're supposed to be, what they're supposed to do, how they're supposed to be like. And Edward would often have very little to say about that, wanting the actor to figure it out or decide for themselves or not having a clue. You never really knew or you often didn't know.

So, there were times when actors would get quite nervous or even upset about what was going on, on the stage, and then the rest of us were anarchists. We're just saying, "Well, we'll just do something else. We can make this even worse or even more strikingly strange." Then he would enjoy that.

I think he enjoyed—for him, every rehearsal. Once you get by the initial sort of reading with the script and fumbling around, every rehearsal for him was some kind of performance, and he got to see them all. And then night after night, we would try and do little things differently. We would try and do the play well, but we would also try to see what was in there that we could emphasize or add that might make him laugh, because we knew he was sitting in the audience. Alternatively we might also try something that we knew he would hate because it was so outrageous. He'd come back and he'd say, "Tut, tut, tut." But usually, he loved everything.

CS: That's very interesting, actually, because that's something that I picked up on in a sort of a subconscious way at the time, but I didn't ever really think of it that obviously. I did get the sense that rehearsals were almost a personal performance for Edward. He would let go of directing at times and it became a private performance for him. Then he would snap back into directing.

EE: I think rehearsal time for him often was letting him see his work be done in slightly odd or different ways; maybe mostly the same, but little differences every time. Or as he adjusted things and made decisions about things that he just enjoyed to the *n*th degree. I think for him, every night was a great evening. The work didn't always work out that way, but he certainly perceived it all as enjoyable, I think.

CS: How about those times when things would sort of get a lot of momentum with the side humor and antics and Edward would want to reel it in a bit, like, "Enough playing, get down to business." Was he fairly patient with those asides of the actors having fun, or did he ever just sort of get a little irked?

EE: Yes, oh, yes. There were times, especially with Vincent Myette, who was particularly energetic and inventive at the same time. Vincent and I would get into these little things where we would play. And Vincent, I think, felt particularly bound in sometimes and wanted to move the envelope forward, but then other people would do that occasionally too.

And if he really thought that people were just screwing around, he would get pretty annoyed, because then he knew that you weren't paying attention to the script and actually what was going on and finding something in it. You were just fooling around. So he would try to stomp that out pretty quick.

But then there's the whole business of that, what I was talking about earlier, the anarchy underlying this rather strict formal look on the surface. And he wanted that. He wanted actors to always be right on the edge and maybe something would happen that was within that structure that would pop up. And he loved that. So he wanted this very careful line, you know.

CS: At those times, was he sure to let you know, like, "Yes, do that again." Like, "That's part of the play now." Or were the things like some of you would do it different the next time and he'd say, "What happened to that thing that you did? I liked that."

EE: More likely the second. More likely, rather than say, "I like that, keep that," because I think he didn't want to frame anything too solidly. He didn't mind this kind of wavering, but if you did something good and then it didn't happen the next time, he would come up and he'd say, "Well, I really missed such and such." He would want something brought back to the way it was in an earlier rehearsal.

I do remember a couple of painful times. I always wanted him to praise my work, especially if I was doing something alone with the puppets, I really wanted him to enjoy that and if I did a lousy night with the dogs [dogs dancing sequences in between scenes], I could often tell.

CS: How? Would he joke?

EE: I just know that the timing was off and he'd be nice, but you didn't hear him laugh. He wouldn't talk about it very much, that's how you knew. You would then know that it just didn't work out that night. I would know that I just hadn't got that routine down or the timing down as it was all very much a living work from night to night. So the fact that he enjoyed that variation and aliveness created a kind of risk for everybody, a pleasant aesthetic risk that everybody wanted to take.

CS: Okay, let me just change tapes here. Where were we?

EE: Edward's theater in general. Most of the big things that we did were called entertainments, and they would be fifteen or so vignettes, either puppets or actors in front of the puppet stage or actors and puppets, some combination of that. You just go from one to the other. How they were tied in was only remotely logical at best.

So I have gorgeous memories and they are as fragmented as they are whole sometimes. Each piece is a whole piece, but the whole show, the unity of it, is based on some other factor, some sort of transcendent energy that comes out of the costuming and the flow, not from any logical direction. These were surreal pieces, remember.

Although you can never underestimate the power of the unconscious when he was forming these things, he had to come up with some sort of coherence, but that coherent element was just not always visible. My basic insight, I think, as an actor working with Edward's stuff and discovering how much I liked it, was that it was completely original in its perspective. It wasn't even the experimental theater that anybody has ever done before.

The stuff that he did was fairly unique anyway, the way he was interested in dealing with text and personalities or not dealing with them. So people tried to put it in some sort of category, or set of categories that would be acceptable as theater, and it really wasn't always even theater. It was Edward Gorey theater.

Other people could take Edward's stuff, like the musicals that were done. They were interesting and pleasant and they were fashioned into some kind of theater piece that people could understand as an evening of X or Y, but the stuff that Edward did with us was principally nothing anybody had ever seen before.

CS: I've read things that kind of refer to the theater that Edward did as kind of a throwaway diversion that kept him from his real work kind of thing. He once said himself that with every play we, his audience, were losing books. How do you feel about that? I mean, do you feel that his theater stuff was sort of disrespected in general or do you think that people just didn't get it on a fundamental level?

EE: Well, I think that his later theater did not fit any of the easy or acceptable categories. Of course, Edward lived in a much-bigger world than this little thirteen-year stint of theater that we did. So I think that people in that larger world had a very hard time accepting that he could spend this much time doing what they considered to be essentially—I don't know what the proper word is; I'll use diversion. And I think that that's what—probably when they were being kind, that's what they thought, taking a break from more serious stuff. That's a category problem, you know?

CS: How about when they weren't being kind? What would they say being completely upfront?

EE: They thought it was a waste of his time and they probably considered us to be sycophantic hangers-on. The reality was Edward Gorey was doing something that he wanted to do, and so we were ready and willing to be there to hang out with

Edward Gorey and essentially do his bidding. His friends and acquaintances from elsewhere might come in and see the play and have some kind of emotional problem with not being involved with Edward at that level. It was like a betrayal to them, perhaps.

Then there were other people who would come in and think it was marvelous and just wonder what this new thing of Edward's—or this other thing of Edward's—that they had never experienced was like, and they enjoyed it. The reaction to it from his larger audience could run the gamut.

CS: Tell me about the performances themselves. The two things I'm particularly interested in—you're welcome to expand on it, are his participation in the audience and also the general attendance and how successful the nights went off at various times, ticket-wise. Tell me a little bit about the performances and then the room itself at the plays, with Edward seated in one of the chairs himself.

EE: I would say—and Carol probably has a better perspective on this—as time went on, his shows were better and better attended consistently. It's just our experience as actors, as people on the stage, looking out at the audience or trying to appeal to an audience, our experience ran this huge range from everyone being completely engaged to half the audience departing at intermission.

You didn't know whether they were disgusted or just had put in their social graces and what all the variables might be. Then other times when the audience and the house was just packed everything you did was magical. As time went on, it was more like you would get a consistent audience every performance night, and we didn't worry about people leaving so much, or if some people left, that was something we all had already dealt with on more severe terms years before.

So the fact that six people—this whole group of one family would leave the front row all of a sudden and not be there, that wasn't so bothersome, but it did point out some of the difficulties of Edward's work and how different audiences can be one night to the next or one year to the next. It wasn't a measure of success for us and probably not for Edward either. In fact I know it was not.

But I do think that we developed an audience, an audience of people who had seen these entertainments before, knew what to expect and what not to expect. As a result, they came and enjoyed it and we had better attendance overall as time went on. The problem early on, we could have fabulously well-attended shows and the same show another night might be half a house or less. And there are several reasons for that. One of them was just that people weren't expecting or thinking about going to a Gorey show. It was a new medium for him.

And the ones in Woods Hole [Massachusetts], for example, were very typical Woods Hole productions. Most of the time, they were very well attended regardless of what people thought of them, but then towards the end if they were well-done shows, which I think they were in general, then people were struggling to get in at the end. They wouldn't come in the beginning and we'd have kind of half houses for a while, but then as the run got to the end, the last weekend or two, everybody was calling in to get to see this show. That's typical for Woods Hole. Really good audiences at the end, a couple of good ones at the beginning, and then people don't focus.

When we moved out of Woods Hole, where there were also lots of parking issues by the way, the consistent kind of audience stuff didn't happen. We had to rebuild an audience in Bourne and in every town it seemed. The Cape's like that. When we moved to Cotuit, I think we had crossed that barrier. Anything we did, people would come to and enough people were interested in coming to it. And maybe the fact that Cotuit is more mid-Cape had some logistical and convenience help.

You never know quite how to interpret what happened in terms of the play attendance itself. To put it this way, it's sometimes just plain misleading. You don't get exactly the answer that you should by looking at attendances.

CS: Tell me about his sort of participation in the audience as a member. I would expect the director to be in the back watching from sort of a distance or in back of the set and to be in a place that he can come up and talk to you as the play went along, saying, "You know what, the lighting really needs to be adjusted," or "You're really not hitting it—your pace is off." But he had this ability to watch. And I mean, I'm sure he was looking at that stuff too in a way, but he seemed to have been primarily concerned with enjoying it himself. Each performance he would laugh as if it were completely fresh to him.

EE: Yes, yeah.

CS: And some of it probably was, because you said, you've cultivated a certain freshness to it. I'm sure he saw things that you would do something you've never done in a rehearsal.

EE: That's right.

CS: But tell me about his sort of the way—I mean, he was there. Did you listen for his laugh to know when you've been successful, or just tell me about his—did you find it odd that he would enjoy it like that?

EE: I found it tremendously appealing. And I didn't initially listen for his laugh or key on it at all. I think for me, the appealing thing was this presence, a person who was doing—who had written this stuff or collected this stuff and seeing it all the way through, props. I mean, he did literally everything he could possibly do to put this show together and seemed to enjoy it. That's what he wanted; he wanted the Edward Gorey experience to be complete and completely his.

So the fact that he was there initially for years didn't make much of an impression on me. We were just happy and energetic and all shows were—every night was interesting. And so he played a role in that, in putting his presence in there. But then after a while, I started listening or keying more on what the other actors were saying. It was like, "Oh, I do X or Y and I heard Edward laugh," because they did something new.

And then it suddenly dawned on me that some of these actors were actually changing things each night to see if they could get a laugh out of Edward. And it wasn't big things. I mean, these were pretty good actors, so they're not just toying with stuff in a trashy way, but they would deliberately do that. So I started thinking about that. You know, I said, "Oh my God, that's maybe something I should do."

But it's very difficult for me, particularly, to do that, although I started to be more aware of when Edward was laughing or not. And I think in the last three or four shows, I think if Edward didn't laugh at times when I was working out on something, I took that as a sign that I had to work harder. Not necessarily alter anything dramatically, but it was something he enjoyed, but if this was a truly funny bit that I ought to be doing something a little different.

CS: What was your experience as a puppeteer before starting this?

EE: Zero.

CS: How did you go about training to be a puppeteer?

EE: Practice.

CV: Let me ask about that too. How do you know what the effect is of what you're doing when you can't see?

EE: Well, for a long time I didn't have any idea what the effect on the audience was of these puppets. Number one, the puppets are unique, although the actual style of the puppet, which is a hand glove puppet with a head that sticks on, is not unique. There are lots of kids who have done that kind of thing. Edward, immediately that he had decided he would use that kind of Punch and Judy–type puppet, developed his own aesthetic.

So even his puppets are completely unique. And then he would use other things. We did a whole show of puppets and puppets with people narrating, *Heads Will Roll*. And that show must have had the most incredible—we must have more than a hundred different gloves. It was this show about a material and then we had other things where the puppets were things like kitchen utensils and shoehorns and the oddest objects you could imagine that were puppets.

Early on, in the first couple of shows, we did clothespins were characters. Cathy Smith has a hilarious story about the—is it *The Second Mrs. Tanqueray*? Yes, where Edward was really quite annoyed, because we weren't putting enough emotion into these clothespins. Therefore—

CS: Which is the play within the play?

EE: Yes, yes. So Cathy Smith in exasperation at one point, here she's jiggling this clothespin for all its worth. There are red ones and blue ones and yellow ones and we'd use them off and on for various sorts of bits. And Edward would say, "Well, you know I want to see this clothespin emote," or "Do something meaningful," and Cathy Smith from behind the screen—I'm playing one character, I didn't know what to say except that "Oh, my God. This is like getting water from a stone."

And Cathy Smith goes, "Edward, they're only clothespins," which—and then suddenly things—we started working on very small nuances with inclining the clothespin or moving the clothespin a little back. Little tiny things. And that turned out to be more meaningful. What was happening was he didn't want it to just jiggle like some nervous needle on a gauge. And he didn't want it [to] be stuck still like just some blue stick.

But he wanted these very small nuances as if you were moving. He could see this character in the clothespin moving around the furniture in the apartment on this little stage. And that's what he wanted to see. So we started doing that a little bit, and that was very good. But I don't think he knew himself exactly how to do it. He expected us to figure out how to put more emotion into the clothespin.

And those things you learned by dint of just hard labor. The other things we did, we would get—he would have an idea, like I want dogs to dance to this music. And some of us like to do that. I like to do it. Other people did not want to handle this type of things at all. And you would just work away at it. And after a while you got to the point where if you did dogs in another show doing something slightly different, you would still know that the dog had a personality. And he wanted the dog to dance and be joyous or moping or something. And then you just acquired this kind of aesthetic approach that was an Edward Gorey approach.

CV: Can I interject and ask one thing about this—my recollection is that all of Edward's shows were both live actors and puppets, except for *Epistolary Play*, unless—if you count the narrators. Is that right, my recollection?

EE: Well, if you count the narrators, yes. Some shows, I mean, just had narrators for puppets, like *Heads Will Roll*.

CV: There was no pure puppet show with no human voice, no narration?

EE: No.

CV: And there was never a show that was just actors and no puppets except for *Epistolary Play*?

EE: Correct. *Epistolary Play* was only the actors. The things like *Six Who Pass While the Lentils Boil*, without its companion piece, would have been strictly a puppet show, because everything is narrated from the actors doing the puppets. And that's interesting.

CV: I'd like to go back to *Lost Shoelaces*. Edward had Jeannie Stevens direct and then three years went by until the next show. Can you tell me how *Stuffed Elephants* [1990] came about with Edward now directing?

EE: I don't really remember that. I know that when I met in Edward in 1987 to do *Lost Shoelaces*, that this was one of the profoundly fundamental theater acts that I wanted to perform. I like normal theater. You and I have done lots of normal theater or what we would consider more-standard kinds of theater, some of it gorgeous, gorgeous stuff, but Edward's theater was completely unique and one of the endless satisfactions for me, as I'm sure for the rest of people involved, was that you entered the Gorey world from the books now in the theater. That's what it was so I think it was natural that he came to direct it himself.

People think a Gorey world is represented by his brooding English pictures, the Victorian settings, and all that, but that's not the entirety of it. The Gorey world was a complicated, vastly ingenious, tremendously interested-in-detail world, that ranged from the completely abstract to the completely bathetic.

CV: And it drew on the entire history of art.

EE: That's right, yes. The entire history of literature and theater, shadow plays, everything. He liked it all.

CS: You say it's a vast world; yet, there are things that are particularly Goreyesque, very particularly and minutely part of his world, that I can also see. Can you describe a little bit what the overall aesthetic is?

EE: Yeah. Well, I think that in the theater he was able to combine both the abstract images and elements that he liked, that he came back to over and over again for whatever reason. It's the same way any artist might use a motif again and again, as a part of their personality. With Gorey there were both the abstract and the physical in the theater world, so that the eggplant as a prop, or the aubergine, would come back over and over again from play to play, sometimes.

For example, the dogs would come back over and over again. And there's probably a whole list if you want to be technical, but, for example, the eggplant as a recurring motif. What he liked to do was to have it appear in two ways. The first way was just its own brutal "thereness," the sort of strange milky opaque quality of eggplant, which I think he thought was an otherworldly fruit.

So that was one thing. It was just the reappearance of the eggplant was always mysterious in one sense, because it was just itself and alone. But the other thing was that having these things recur, he could do different things with them. So the eggplant recurs in both ways, as itself, as mysterious, and kind of unapproachable, but then the way these characters suddenly encounter it is this sort of—the infinite possibilities, as sort of anarchic possibilities, of having these supposedly stable objects recur in strange, surreal, or ordinary guises. He loved doing that.

CS: It had a certain quality, kind of a 2001 quality to it, with the obelisk. You know how you see these themes with people approaching the obelisk. It's almost like a tongue-in-cheek eggplant.

EE: Well, I think there was that. There's always this potential of this—until you see the show, you never know quite how this eggplant is going to be dealt with, but if you went to more than one of these shows, you didn't know quite which ones might appear and might not appear. Most of the ones you had seen before and expect, like the eggplant, we would try and get them in. If Edward didn't have them in, the actors would try and get them in by the time the show went up.

CS: What were the types of things Edward was attracted to? I'm always struck by like there's a certain quality to turnip sandwiches and artificial grape soda. I mean, he found these things—it's funny. Artificial grape soda, it's such a basic—I don't know. Can you describe a little bit more the things that Edward was drawn to? I mean, there's a definite difference, like I think one thing that you're struck by when you see the theater, and also

Edward in person, is his love of color compared to his artwork. I did hear him say once in an interview that "I've loved color, but it was always easier printing-wise to do black and white." There's kind of a practical limitation that he felt early on.

EE: Yes.

CS: Did he have this love of black and white?

EE: Not particularly in the theater, yeah. In the theater, I think he allowed his color sense to just play into the way he wanted the piece to look. However, if there was ever a question, it would be black and white, that would be the choice, but I think there are a couple of reasons. You pointed out one good one, which is his training, his background, this business of printing. And he was in publishing and he was in a black-and-white world for a long, long time. Although not in the ballet world, but you know the stuff he dealt with, the way you could communicate all sorts of emotions in grades of light and dark. You can do it all just with your pen.

So there wasn't any need to particularly be obsessed with any other color. And I think that it also played into a lot of the moods that he worked with. But this idea of the objects that he liked, like ink blotters and library paste, as Carol mentioned, and the—I can't even think of them right now. You'd have to run by them and say, "Oh, yeah, that again and again and again."

CV: The antimacassars.

EE: Antimacassars; that's a good one. But one of the things about a lot of those objects is that they are often quite banal, but they're often very close to the edge of uselessness. They're marginal objects that people sometimes invest a tremendous amount of emotion with because this is my antimacassar from my grandmother, but what in the world is this good for? It hangs on the arm of the chair that people never put their oily—maybe at some point there was—when people used pomade, there was a point of putting it on the back of the chair, like stuff like that.

But that's long gone, so these things persist in time and become ever more useless as time goes on. But they're still there, you know, that sort of object, indefinable in terms of what energy it might possess still, but also undeniably there, unaccountably there.

So fruitcake has to be sort of archetypal object that he loved to deal with. And we dealt with fruitcake in show after show, always to its devaluation you hoped, but never quite. I think that represented for him some kind of archetypal food object which you could not define in its weight, in its density, in its kind of odd conglomerate look, just had a peculiar force about it, inexplicable force that he loved to mess with.

The other thing that he would do with these objectifications is he'd picked out elements from his actors since he liked to use the same actors over and over again. He would pick traits or things that they would do and he would use them. He would write them right in. And we would have little—you know, actors would have little rituals. And if he figured those out that you were using them or that there was an actor who did that, he would often write that in. And there are a couple of personal ones of mine that he like—man, once he really got on to it, he would use it.

CS: Like what?

EE: Well, one of the problems with the shows that we would do in August is that I would have to go away to this annual Quaker meeting for a week, so he would adjust the schedule of these plays accordingly. That's how much he was dedicated to his troupe of actors [Le Theatricule Stoique]. If they had a problem, he would change things and the same with me as an individual.

So if I had to be away for a week, he would alter the whole production schedule just to account for my absence or try and make it work but then he would also refer to me as being a prisoner of the Quakers [*laughs*]. That was not a dig really, I thought it was funny, he thought it was funny, and little comments about the Quakers and how oppressive they could be were always made in a very gentle offhanded way. I think really the idea appealed to him a great deal but he would tease and I thought it was hilarious because he actually had a humorous perspective, rather than feeling inconvenienced.

In that regard, we used to—and we still do—have a funny tradition among some of our actors to tease Edward back. We developed this tradition of saying the word "kumquat" at the end of each performance; somehow getting it in, this way or that. One of us would try to get it in so it's not noticeable, with other scripted fruit references or something, in some other appropriate way.

But he did catch on after a while that we were putting kumquats in there into every play. After that, he took up the joke to make kumquats appear, either physically or verbally, in all the other plays. We would do anything to undercut these little things or to incorporate them into his work to push his buttons a bit; he loved that.

CS: So how do you account for that?

EE: I think for him it was a bit more than a joke in that it's part of how ideas and objects work in space and time for Gorey's world. The emotional and intellectual fabric of his art in theater was permeable. He used it all.

CS: I saw an interview where you said, "He had to watch himself sometimes because he could have a tendency to get cute." He was asked, "Define for me what's anti-cute and what's cute." And his example was actually the way teddy bears have evolved, because they used to be long and sinewy—and then now, they had become plump, fluffy, and cute. They have these eyes and they're pudgy, and I thought it was quite a good example to use to define what's cute and what's not cute. I was struck watching the plays that there are moments that are certainly quite cute, but there's also moments that have a certain unabashedly sublime, beautiful, elegant quality.

EE: I think the term is bashedly. [*Laughs*]

CS: Yeah. It's almost like the whole play, all the tongue-in-cheek jokes had been a way of getting you off balance so he could have in this one moment of just sheer beauty. Like there are times, I think, maybe it was *Heads Will Roll* with the moon and the music. And there's certain moments, they're just really beautiful and you think, "God, these are puppets, but this is really a beautiful human moment, a very profound kind of twenty seconds here." And it's almost like the whole play you wonder if he's been trying, as an excuse, to get to this—I don't know. What do you think about it?

EE: I'm glad that they happened, those moments, because I think that that meant we were working with good material intensely, but I don't think there was any intention ever to get to those places. And I think those are just for good enough situations, those things occur in some lives, for artist's lives, and you get them. And especially in the theater, there's sort of an ephemeral thing, where if the writing is good enough, actors might run into those moments more frequently, more than once in a decade or something. But how good does the writing have to be?

CV: I don't think it was all the writing. I think he was gravitating toward beauty like Chris says. He would throw some piece of music, like that duet from *Lakmé*, that was so excruciatingly beautiful that there's no way around it. Something beautiful had to come from that, but he would never deliberately write something in the text.

EE: No, that's right.

CS: It's almost like he, from what you were saying, it's almost like he didn't see the beautiful as necessarily more important than the humorous part of life, generally. They just happen, and each is just as valid as the other.

EE: That's right. Yeah, I think Carol's point is he had picked up this piece of music, a couple of pieces of music in *Heads Will Roll*, and they're gorgeous. There what he wanted was not to undercut the kind of exalted energy that was represented. I mean, it's short and ephemeral, but what he wanted to get to allow the puppets to do was in the puppet world to become this exemplary transcendental moment that the music expresses, even in the form of very simple puppets.

He sort of allowed it all to happen. He wasn't always going after the absurd nature or the anarchistic energy. He wanted to let flourish all of the anarchic energy, but also including the beautiful, and including the haunting sense of yearning that people might have in the moment.

That moment I think happens in various ways for audiences. It happens for actors and for directors, all in different perspectives during a play. This sublime sort of moment happened to me a lot in his plays. Maybe that's the drug that drove me as an actor with him.

Here Edward had picked up a bunch of fragments of Newton's Latin exercise book, and for an unknown reason I just grabbed that for myself. I just said, "I want to do this on my own." And I worked out this little routine, this totally surreal routine, that we occasionally obliterated by having a stuffed animal thrown over the side or something. Various antics always happened on the side, depending on what was going on, but this had a pretty strict routine that I followed. I think there were nights when I went out and did that alone and I had that audience so tightly involved in this completely invisible story within a story that was built around a rather arbitrary set of fragments of Newton's Latin exercise book for children. That's ecstasy. It was just so terrific to have that moment within the play itself.

It becomes a moment in and of itself that kind of lifts you out of time, and once you've had it, it's not like you need the thing to survive because you've experienced it. This is true both for the actor and the audience hopefully.

CS: What was your relationship like with Edward aside from the plays?

CV: Do you mean their intense sexual relationship? [*Laughs*]

EE: Yeah. You mean our love affair? I am not sure I can go into that in great detail even at this late hour.

CS: I mean, like phone calls, lunches, were there letters?

EE: Flowers, iron frogs passing back and forth. No, I would call him often and I preferred to visit him, go to Jack's, occasionally to his house, not often. Most of the time—

CS: Can we hold on? Tremendously aggressive raven.

EE: Yeah, the crow.

CV: I think that's Edward not wanting Eric to reveal so much.

EE: Right, yeah, exactly. The black bird has approached and said, "No, no, no."

CS: Silence!

EE: Yeah.

CV: What is it that the crow says? Beware of this and that.

CS: That's in one of his books, actually.

EE: Beware of this and that. That's like the hippopotamus from the plays. It's like this absolutely perfect element, this box with the thing in it, which to us, this little inside group, knew what it meant. I think personally with Edward, you have to understand that most of the time, I preferred to leave Edward alone. I figured—when I felt I needed to see him when he did some artwork, that kind of thing, I'd go see him, or Carol was doing something and she said, "Come along," that was good.

Occasionally, just went and visited him because I wanted to visit him, but most of the time I felt that if he was working, that was the best thing that I could hope for, that he would show up with another play soon. And there was a time there when it was pretty routine. We knew we'd be in touch or Carol would be in touch or we'd have a birthday party for him or something.

But I tried not to be too individually taking up his time, but I did on occasion. That's what I would say. But the thing for me was, and I suppose this is understandable as a completely subjective feeling, but that's fine with me, because that's—see, that's all I have—is that whenever Edward and I were together, there was like no distance between us.

Partly, it's like Carol said, that he was just so widely read and widely interested and if he knew you and liked you, then the shy barriers fell down. But we would spend some time, some hours together driving in the car or something, and we were just happy to be in each other's company.

We once sat in a car for about twenty minutes listening to this symphony, trying to figure out—neither of us could figure out what this symphony was. And it turned out to be just one of these unedited versions of Beethoven, one of the most obvious seven or eight or something like that. And we're both sitting there for twenty minutes listening to every note, every detail, at the Silver Lounge.

It was a gorgeous night and everybody else was indoors partying, and we're just sitting there trying to get this thing down. It was amazing how we were both sort of led astray from this simple analytical answer, but if you just listen to the music a little more offhandedly. We were so into this piece of music. And it did go on, because it was doing all the repeats and that sort of thing.

I think that I just felt comfortable with him, so when we were together we talked about this and that and a lot of times didn't talk at all. I didn't try to promote my personal relationship with him. I thought the best thing I could do for him was to do what he needed for the theater. And I think he liked me, so that was great. I just adored it. I wish he was still here today, because I would just do theater forever. That was one of the things I think he could count on me. If he said he's going to do his theater, Carol would call up and say, "We've got a project, are you interested" or "We need you," and I'd say, "That's it."

Other people would sort of say, "I'm tired of Edward's stuff. I want to do some other theater." That to me was irrelevant. That wasn't the point; doing this kind of theater, that kind of theater as far as I was concerned, as long as he was doing theater, that was the first priority.

CS: What are the things that you miss most about him now, a year and a half later? It's a long enough span of time when you can feel sort of the hole that he's left. I'm sure there're lots of things that you personally miss? Everyone had a different relationship with him I'm sure.

EE: Yeah, I think so. I think the thing that I miss the most is the next piece. This tremendous—the loss that the world for me, the world per se, is not a poorer place, but for me the world is a poorer place, because I locked onto this genius who lived close by and liked the person that I was, liked the stuff I did. He gave me profound compliments on work that I did.

And I felt like I understood him pretty well, at least from anything that I was interested in, where our interests intersected, let's say. So not being able to have the next piece of theater, even if we do theater, and there's a fair amount that we could do, stuff that Edward was interested in doing or possibly interested that never have seen the light of day.

But that's his work. And I think having someone like Edward as a friend is one of these ineluctable times in your life. You got them when you got them and that's it. Everything else is secondary.

And as long as he was alive, clearly, doing theater was how he most wanted to interact with me and other people. We had other sorts of interest like this art and poetry and things like that, but they were generally played out mostly in the context of when we were doing theater, because otherwise I would be taking up his time when he was doing something else.

You figure, if he's not doing the theater, then he's busy catching up on his commission work or other work that he wanted to do, so why would I bother him with that. But when we were doing theater, then these other things were—his time was more available. And it was a lot of time. I guess that's what I miss the most is spending a lot of time with all of those people.

CS: Was the Theatricule Stoique a family of sorts?

EE: I suppose some people would say that. It was a dysfunctional family that created this very functional original theater. It had to be, it had to be. For one, Edward's nature did not easily accommodate people that he didn't know, although if he likes somebody, if he had an audition and he liked somebody, then he could open himself up very quickly to them, but it's amazing how the thing is self-selective. He would open himself up and take somebody into the cast.

But if they didn't like Gorey stuff, they'd do the show and then they were out of there. The rest of us not only like doing the stuff, but he could depend on having us there to do this, to work on it, to go to the next thing.

The Epistolary Play, which was probably one of the smaller casts that I was in with him, it was only three of us onstage, only two any one night, and tremendously complicated, tremendously quiet piece, no puppets at all, but it was a unique event. It was something Edward wanted to work out and he wanted to work it out in his way. And the fact that I could do that—I mean, it was clear that I was going to be one of the people there if I lived, because that was my commitment, and to see how we worked out this little particular problem or diversion this time, I lived for that.

CS: That play, *Wallpaper*, it was one of the few plays that I saw where it wasn't a puppet show; it was real people. How was the decision made and why was the decision made to use real people. Tell me a little bit about Edward's involvement as an actor in that.

EE: I think part of Edward's involvement as an actor in *Wallpaper* was accidental because it was put together with *Heads Will Roll*.

CV: Well, basically we were starting to do *Tragic Secrets*, and it was knocked out and so we had to put together something else and we—

EE: Yeah, that was pasted together. There were some hard times with the actors and how the ensemble worked together. It wasn't always smooth. So I think *Wallpaper* was times where we had these beautiful moments, intensely clear moments of acting, and then also some of the worst acting moments.

I think that people who saw Edward onstage understood how things could be done by him and they understood some of the logic. I mean, he's playing an eleven-year-old telegraph boy trying to deliver a message, twelve, if he lives, that kind of thing, "If I live." But he didn't try to look like that or anything, so that all of the absurdity and the logic was intensely present when Edward was onstage.

And the reason for that was then other people could accept because they were not willing to criticize the author, the creator, as much as, say, we'd criticize actors. They'd say, "Actors aren't getting to the point" or something, and all we were doing was feeding off Edward. He would say, "Don't try to make this realistic. Don't try to make this logical. Just, you're in this particular bit of costuming, I just want you to go out and do this, say these lines, and move over here or move whatever way you like but get this side of the stage and interact with this person somehow."

Wallpaper was a good example of where I ran amuck somewhat, putting pipe cleaners in my hair and then on my fingers, and I started transforming my character into this as the *Wallpaper* went on into this Nosferatu-like vampire busily collecting his girlfriend as getting closer and closer to her, but I think probably one of the best nights of *Wallpaper* was when we did it very straight.

There was a little trope that he had for ghost stories and for ballet movements. There was a certain movement that we all did with regards to *Wallpaper*, and that was a ballet move. And he loved commenting on that, just see how we all did it and how all these descriptions of *Wallpaper*, which we—you know, a little discussion about color and pattern always played into that sort of thing, always.

CS: Did you see when you look at his, like the bulk of his work, like the books that he's gotten out, the type of books that everyone is familiar with, do you see a discrepancy between that kind of—the artwork, the black-and-white cross-hatching about kids being oft every which way and the person that you knew? Do you see a discrepancy there or is that just one aspect or—I mean, tell me about the relationship between the actual person and the artwork.

EE: Well, I think he changed through time and I think the business, his reputation, was formed more on the line of *The Gashlycrumb Tinies* or some of those limericks that he wrote which were particularly horrifying, wonderfully horrifying, or some of those other book stories.

But as time went on, he grew less and less interested in that sort of in your face. And he certainly didn't want to be known as an artist that did that particular kind of thing. And so, although that kind of story appears in the theater stuff, it's probably, as time goes on, less and less of interest to him. And what he became interested in was applying his peculiar perspective to all different kinds of stories and scenarios, possible elements.

And he, I think also, one of the changes through time that worked for Edward was that his interest in imaginative theater grew. He became more interested both in narrative or pseudo-narrative theater, theater that appeared to be storylike, and at the same time, he constantly undercut it. And then things like *Heads Will Roll,* where there was a fantastic profusion of purely imaginative, of what you would call abstract in some more technical world, moments that are just pure beauty.

CS: Did Edward have a lot of people that approached him after his performances, fans asking to sign things?

EE: Yes. Yes.

CS: How did he deal with that?

EE: He was usually pretty good as long as they—he would talk with them, but he was shy and he usually had something on his mind. That's usually what that kind of standoffishness meant. It would come up in productions, and he'd be wanting to go backstage or he'd be waiting to talk to somebody like Carol about how things were and what was going on. He's very practical in that sense, keeping things going the right way.

And people would come up with books or with a program or whatever and tell him about how they were a fan and tell them who they were. And sometimes there would be an occasion where he would meet somebody truly interesting. But in general, I think he treated it very well, including children and all that. He actually had a kind of an interesting take on children and their presence. He was kind of sweet toward them. He treated them kind of like hairless cats or something.

But he was never ungracious or ungenerous, quite remarkably the opposite. Very shy though. Again, he liked to be with the people he knew and felt comfortable with. And everybody else was just kind of there, passing through. He could have good nights and bad nights. Some nights, he was quite gracious and outgoing, and other times he just was terribly impatient, just like anybody.

CS: Did you ever—I mean, were you ever surprised, the things that you read sometimes? After you knew him personally through thirteen years and every once in a while, these interviews would come up? Did you read things there? Were you like, "I didn't know that?" Or "God, you know, he's never mentioned anything about that."

EE: I mean, for the most part when I said, "Oh, I didn't know that," in those interviews, what it would be would be facts about his life, because I really didn't key on his biography; it was always the art. The art meant everything, and if there was something that was actually important to him biographically or something that suddenly made sense to me doing the theater because I heard this biographical fact, that would be interesting.

But the way he responded to interviews, for the most part, I was not surprised at all. Not surprised at all, because I felt that he had the work and he wanted to be well known and all that, but he really didn't want to—like a lot of people in that level—I think didn't really have much of a clue as to what people wanted from him when they would interview him. And a lot of people wanted something very specific.

They wanted the glory of the old books or the pictures at the beginning of a mystery, the really nasty, dark Gorey, and this was not who he was. It's like people coming to visit a poet because he wrote a certain kind of poem and the person showing up expected to have a certain kind of "You wrote this poem; therefore, you understand me," and usually the artist is saying, "Who's this nut on my doorstep?" or "What do they want from me?"

So interviews, for the most part, that I read, were generally not surprising. Sometimes they were funny. I think they were inadvertently funny, not because the interviewer wanted them to be, but because we understood how Edward was responding.

I remember one interview that I thought was particularly quite charming in one of the Cape Cod newspapers, where he said, "What do you do most of the day?" And he said, "Dither." "So what do you worry about?" He was worried about getting work done. He said he was worrying about the fact that he could dither around all day and not get anything at all done. And then he somehow had to figure out a way not to dither, because actually dithering about was the most fun thing you could do; not be stuck to a schedule, have to get something done.

I generally lived it in a way that every time we did a play or we were going to do a play was very happy time for me, you know, that kind of thing. So the way things—sometimes working out the rehearsal period could be really tough, trying to get to a place that was—

Edward liked that we were good at and that everybody in the cast was handling well and all that. Sometimes we had some wacky additions to our cast. And so the rest of us, who would just be cruising along, no problem, and then the new people would be going, "Oh my God, this doesn't make any sense" or "This is so freaky" or "Why am I here?" And you'd say, "Oh, Jesus. Why did we hire—this person could be really good, twice as good as I ever could be onstage, and yet they're sitting there worrying about what this means or how to do this."

And you say, "You have nothing to worry about. You just go out and do the thing." But they were worried more about do they look good wrapped up in all these weird coils of some bizarre thing that Edward wanted them to wear. And I said, "Just act." Or "This story is stupid. Why do I do this stupid story? I have to act the part of a woman who falls off a cliff, and she's not even interesting to begin with."

And you say, "Well, that's the point. The point is to make this entertaining, interesting."

CS: Was it in the back of your mind, knowing that he was sick and that this might be the last play that you might do? I mean, did you feel a certain consciousness like that, like, "I better enjoy this"?

EE: Well, not really. There were times when he was sick, physically ill with one thing or another, when we might have a longer period of time where we didn't do anything or you didn't hear from him. I'd call him up and leave a message, but he wouldn't respond or I'd go to Jack's and he wouldn't be there, stuff like that. And I really didn't want to pursue that if he was really busy or not feeling that well. I'd say, "Well, he's just not going to want me pressing him as to when the next play is," that kind of thing, or showing up wanting his approval.

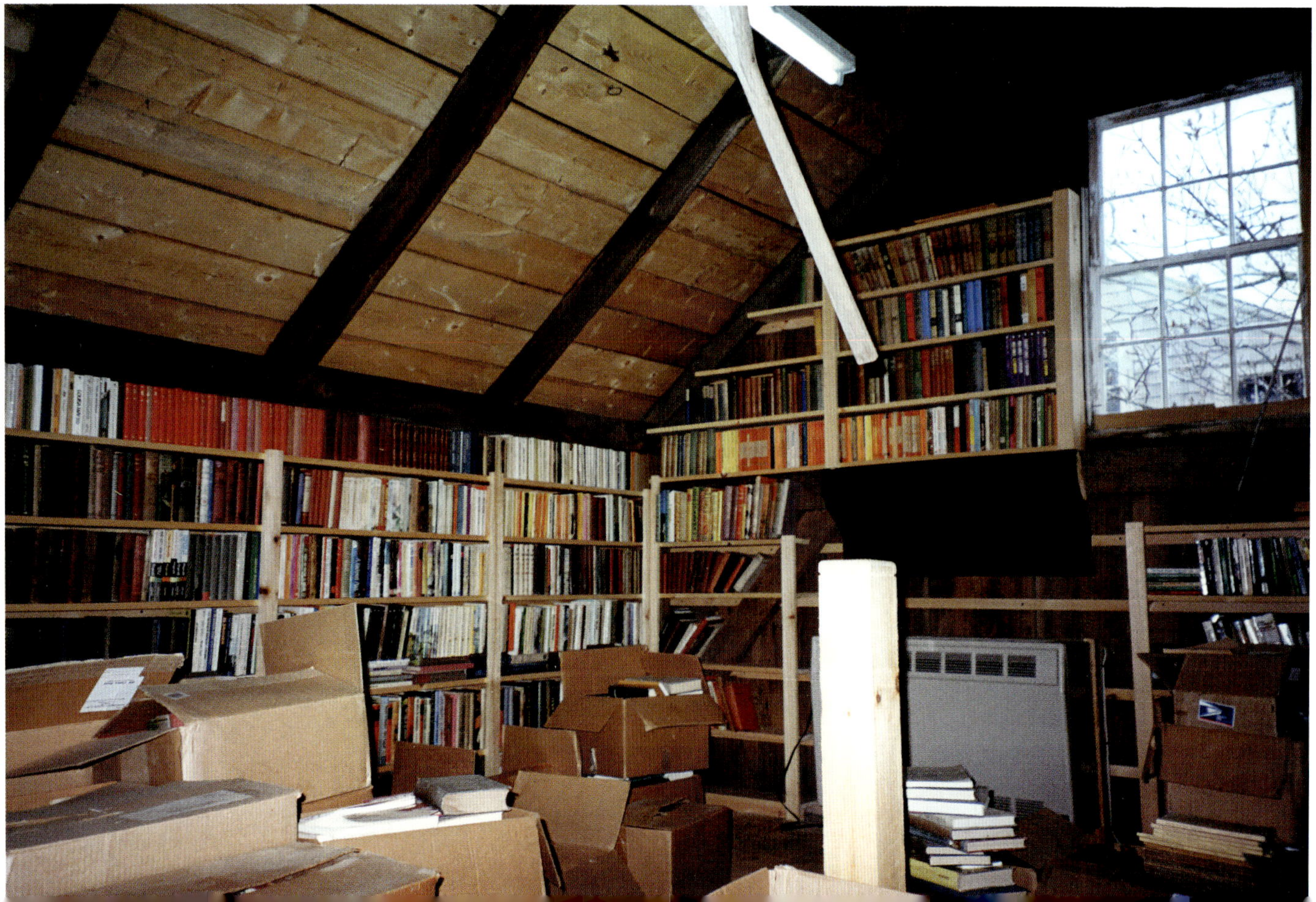

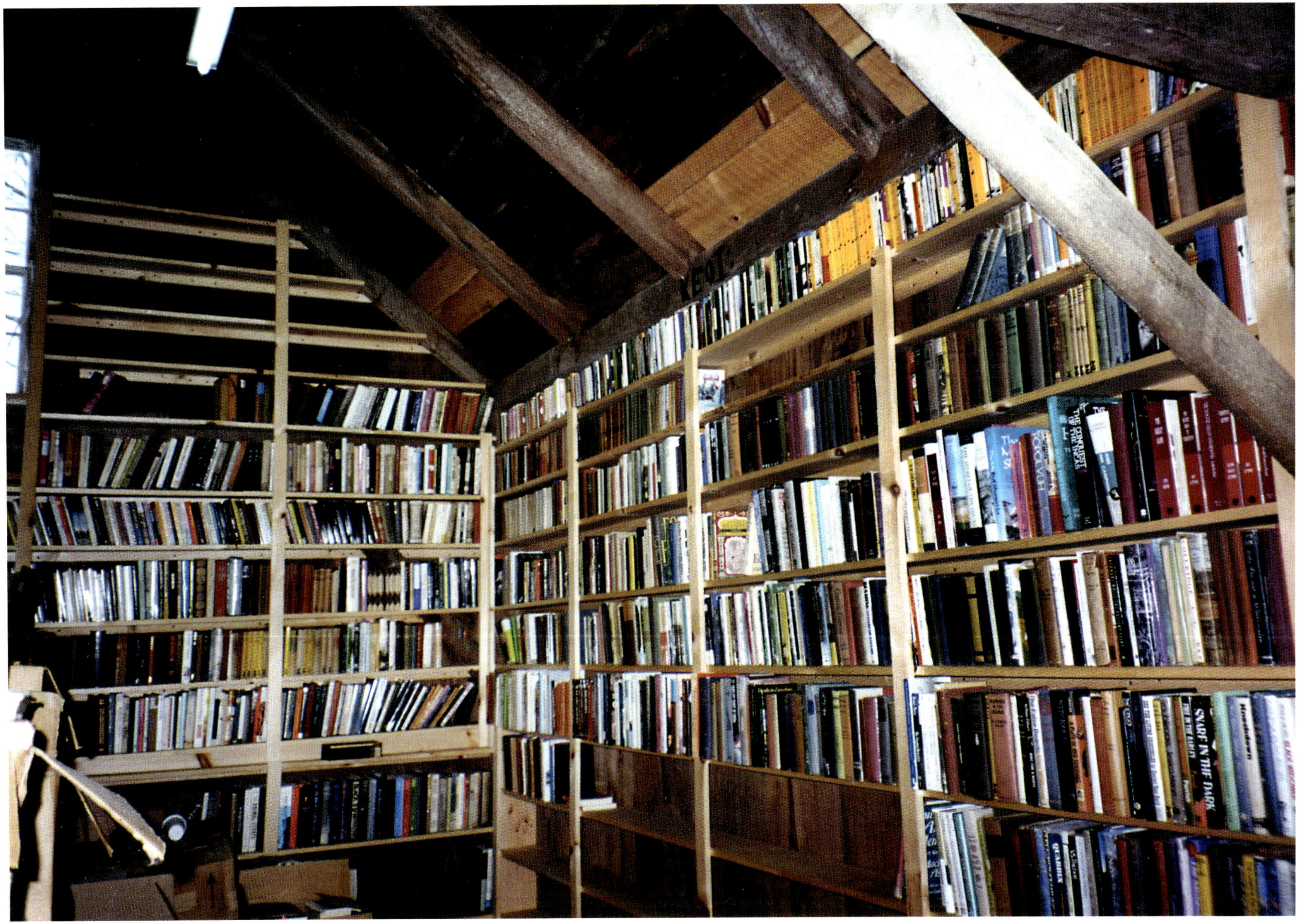

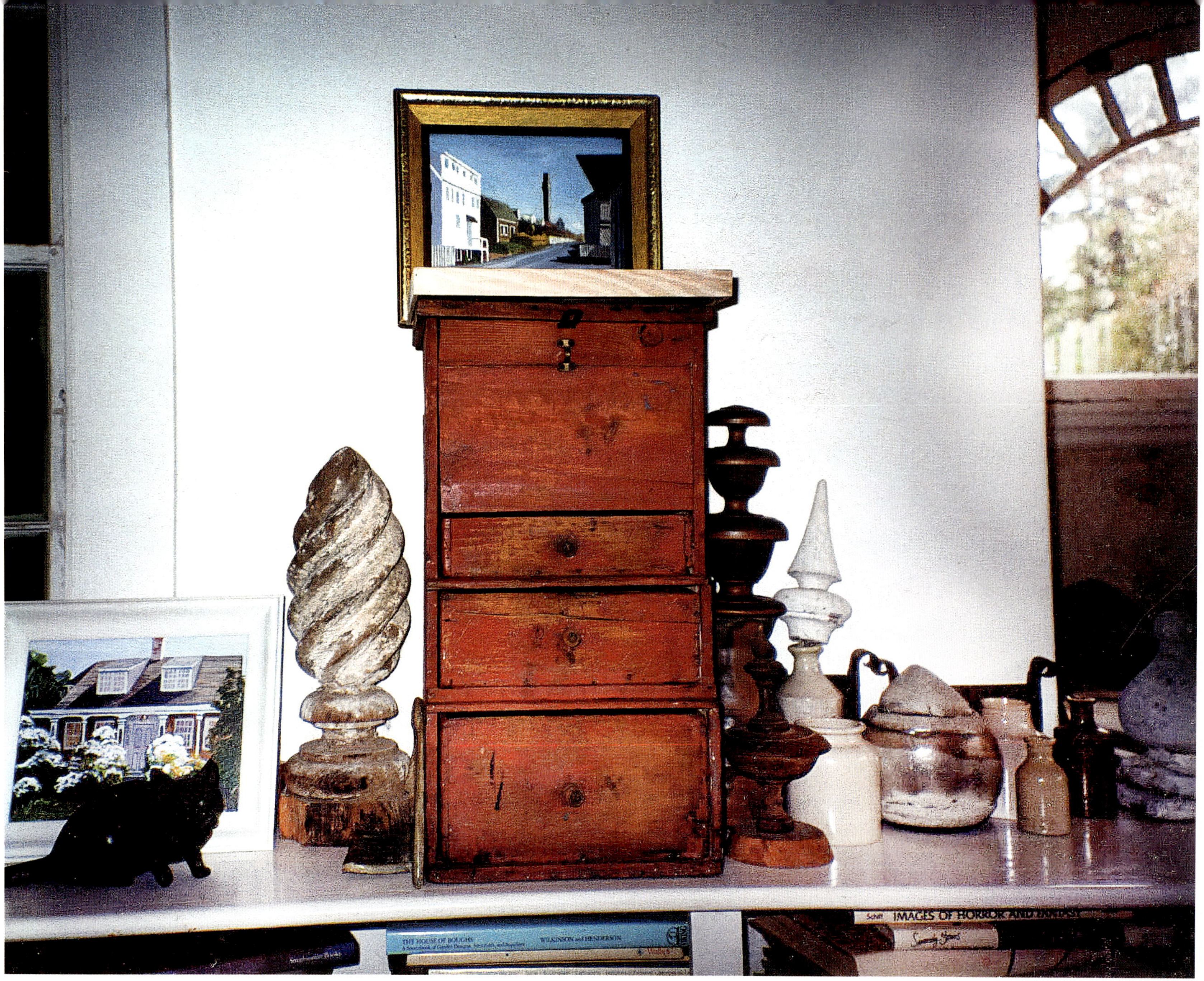

Exploring chests like this shows the extent of his collecting and the nature of the common aesthetic according to Edward.

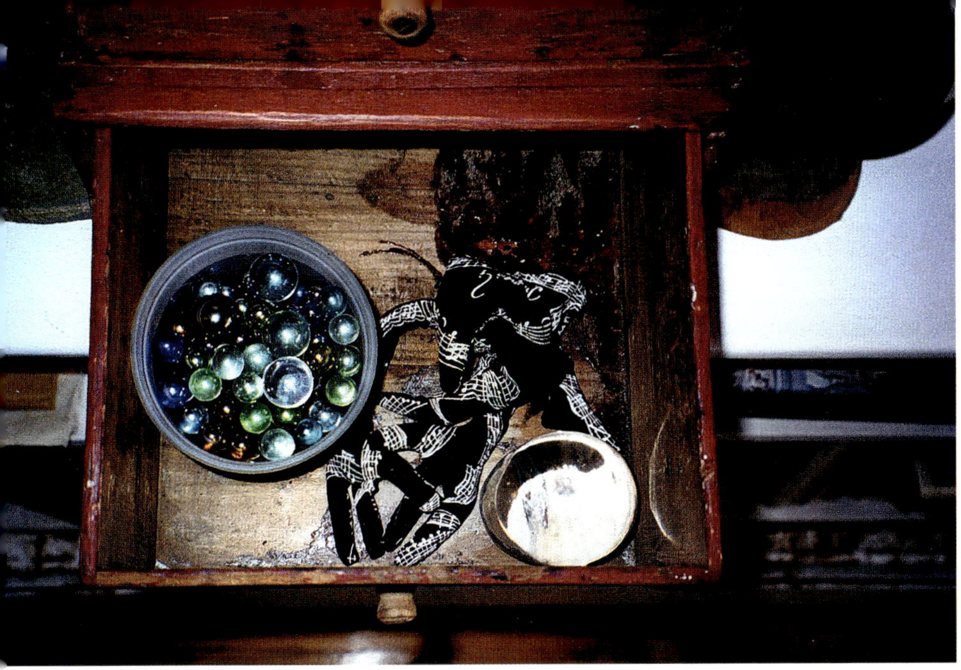

Drawer #1

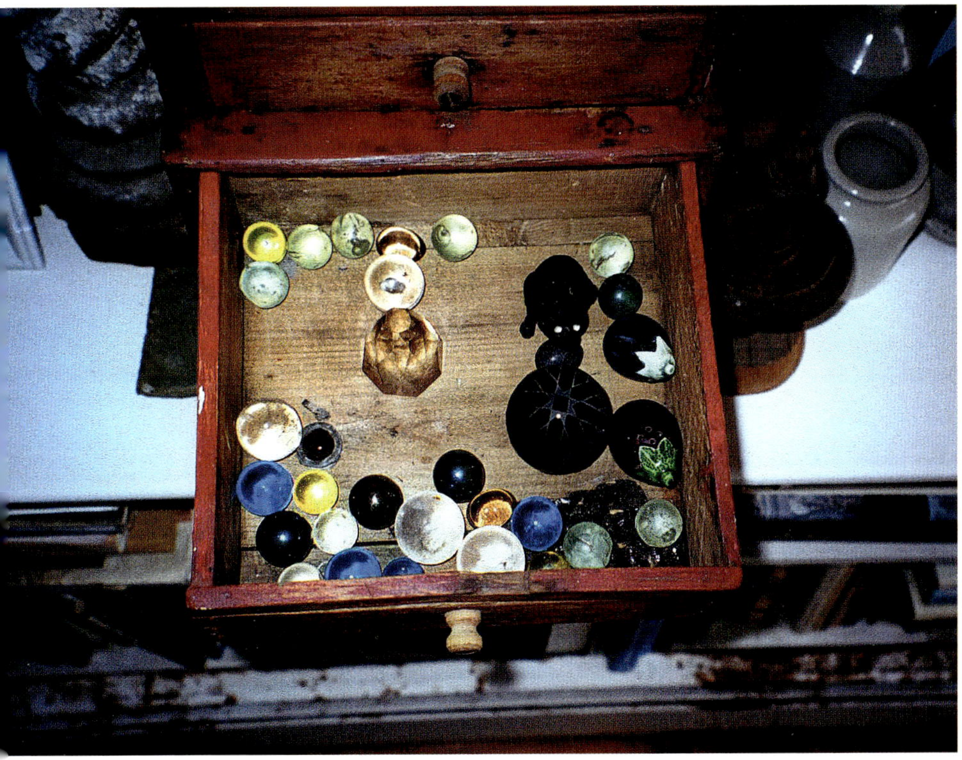

Drawer #2

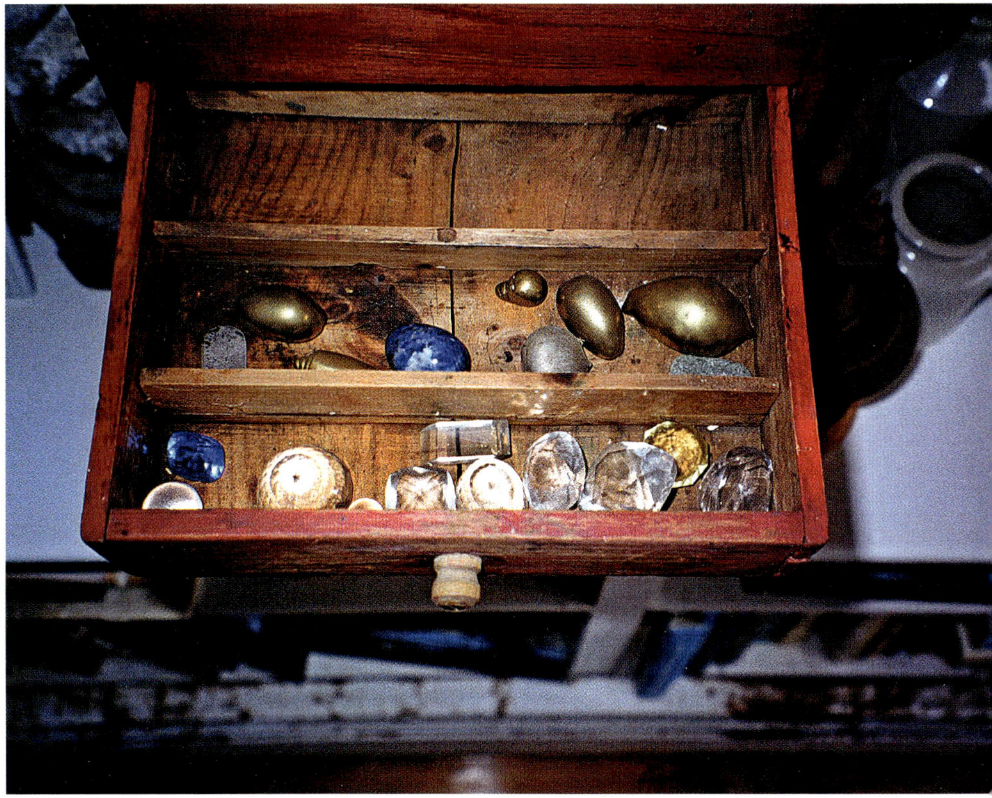

Drawer #3

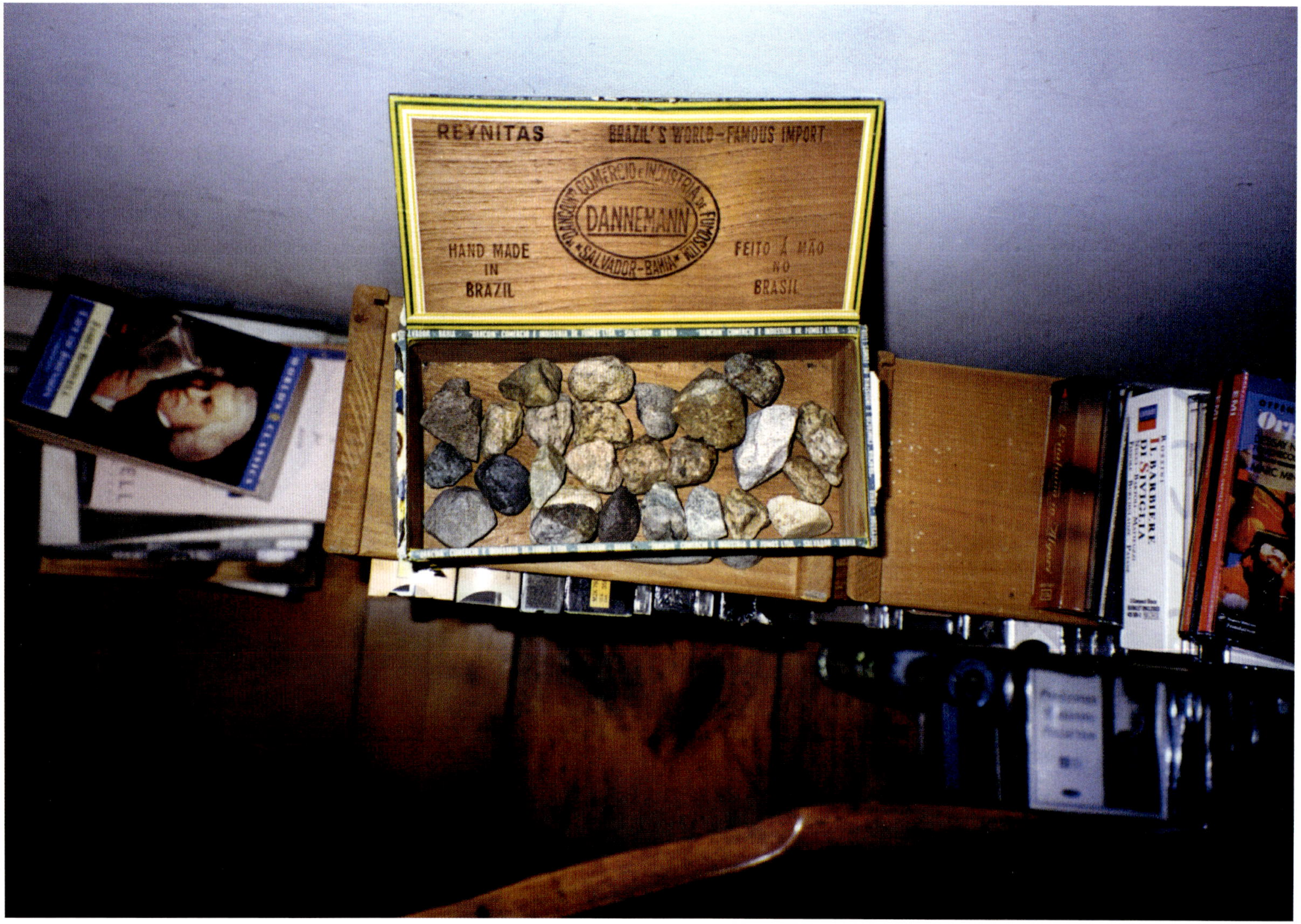

Just what similarities bound these small rocks in Edward's mind is uncertain.

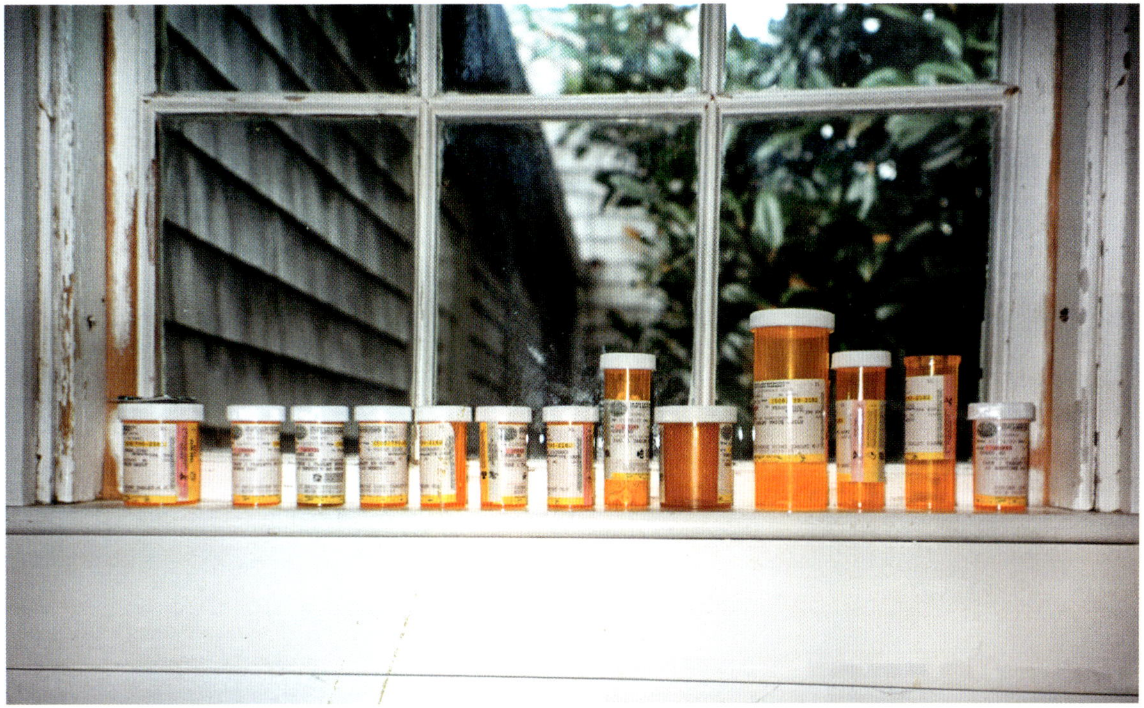

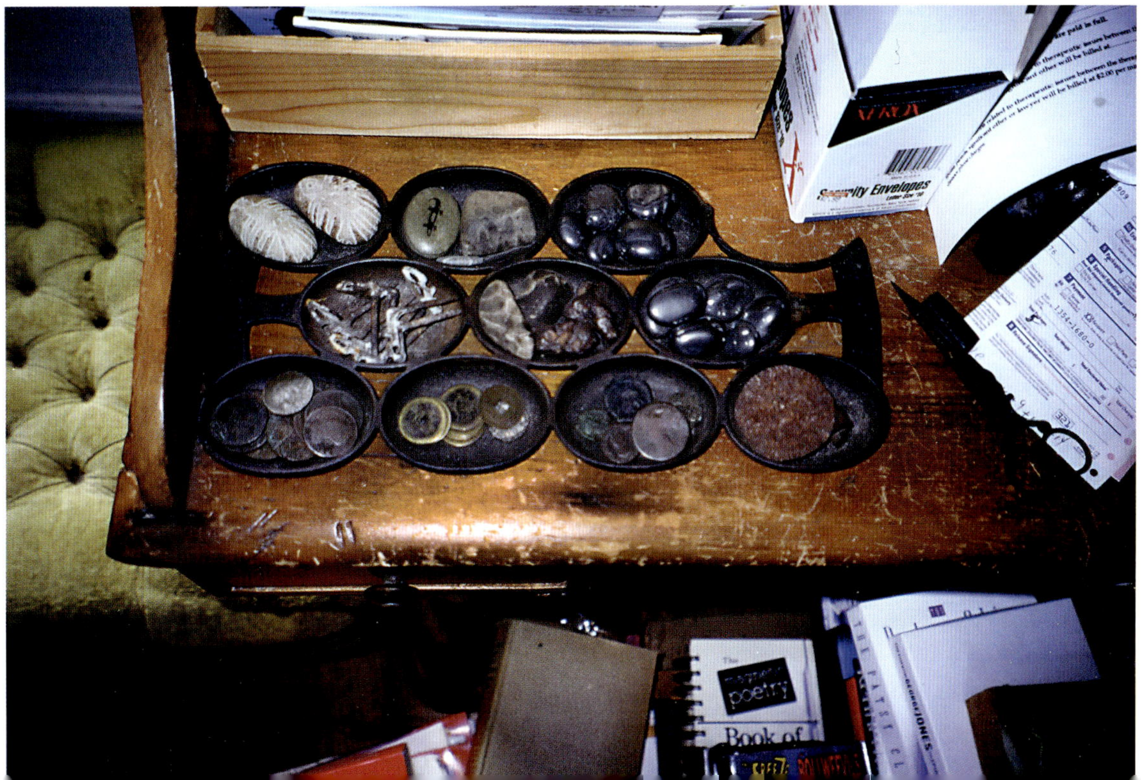

It was my hope that Edward and I would be shooting until 2005 or so, allowing me to get the 200 hours or so needed for one of the classic Maysles brothers verité-style documentaries, such as *Salesmen* and *Grey Gardens*. Rather than shoot in a short, intense period, however, my plan was to have a softer touch with Edward, shooting more as I got to know him more. Our relationship as friends, in this case, was crucial to the outcome, as I saw it. This is one of the things I think he liked about my approach and why he was overall so energetic in his support of the project. Over time he became a bit of a grandfather to me, as a byproduct of this approach as part of the production.

Many times he would find a way out of shooting what I had in mind, such as long stretches of him working, only to give me something entirely different, such as long conversations about *The Mary Tyler Moore Show* or about his life with five cats. So my shooting scripts and pointed interview questions were generally replaced by Edward taking over the directing role by default, himself, and I was happy to lean into that approach. If we had more time, it would've yielded so much more material and so much more about Edward himself, the person behind the artwork.

Unfortunately, he was more sick at the onset of the project than I fully appreciated. He suffered from heart problems, prostate cancer, and diabetes. The extent of the health problems he was coping with became clear when I went into his master bathroom, with the window ledge full of medications, after his death.

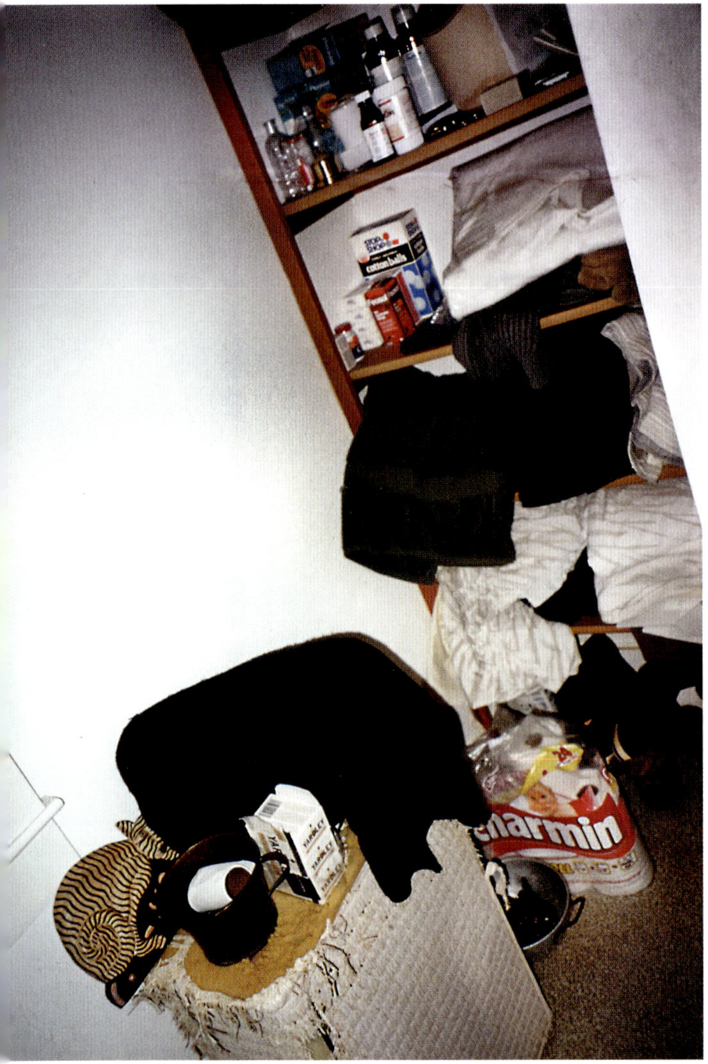

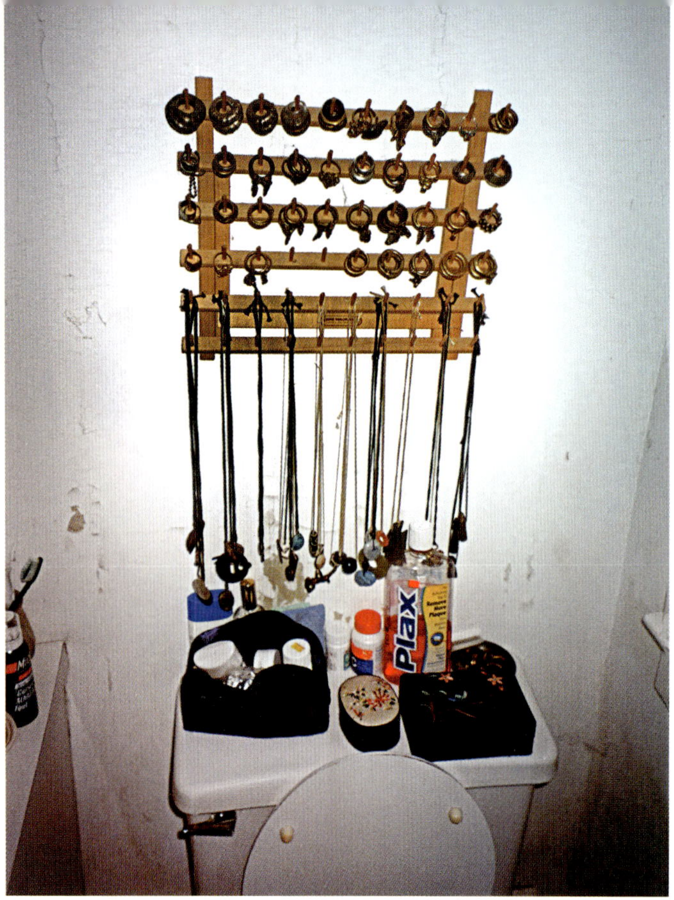

One problem with the sound in the documentary is that the wireless lavalier microphone was competing with the clank of Edward's multiple heavy, often-African-in-design necklaces. Typically I would put some gaff tape around the necklaces at the bottom when he wore three or four.

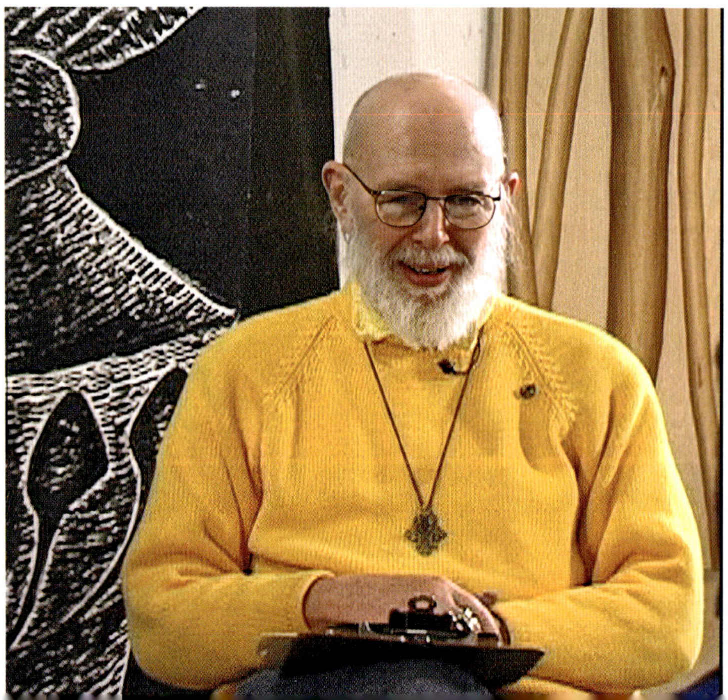

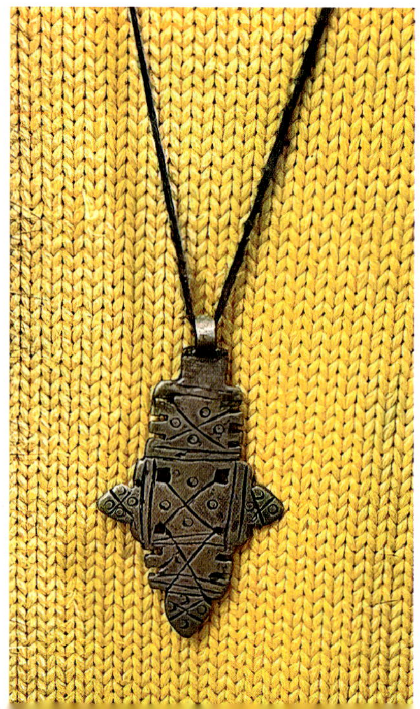

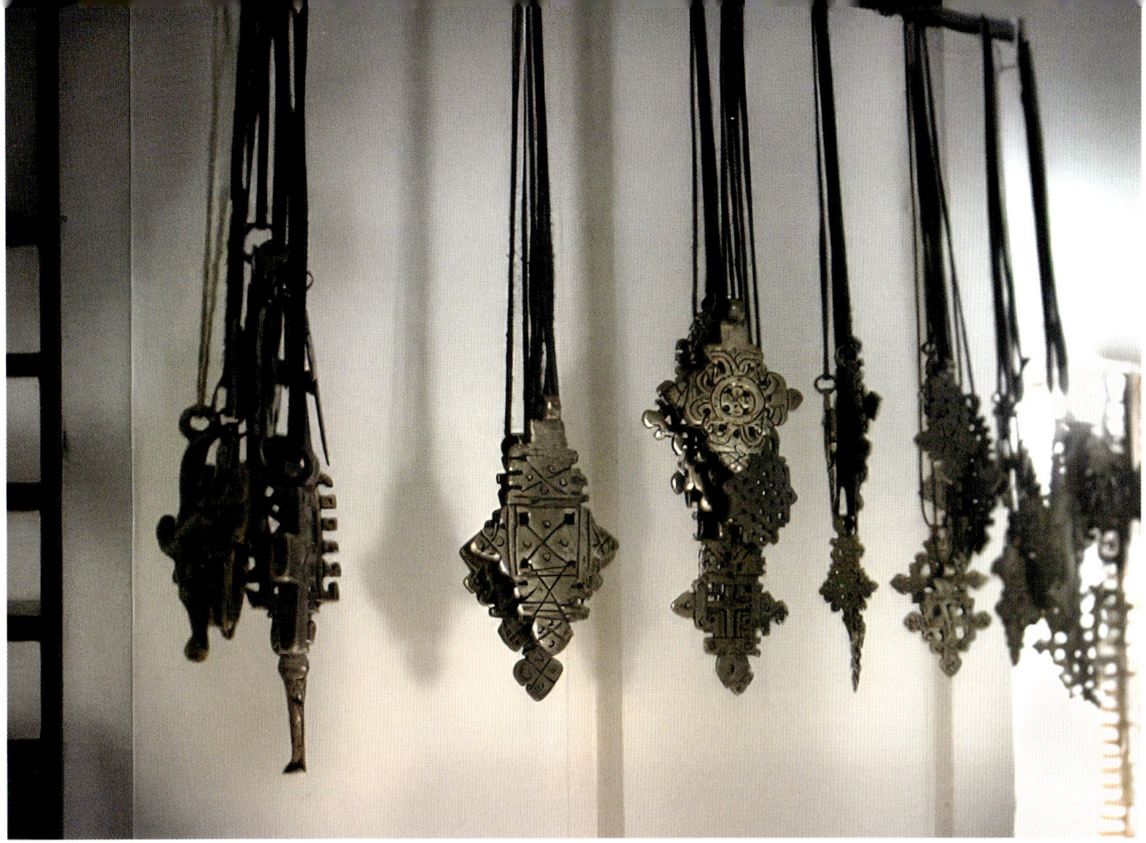

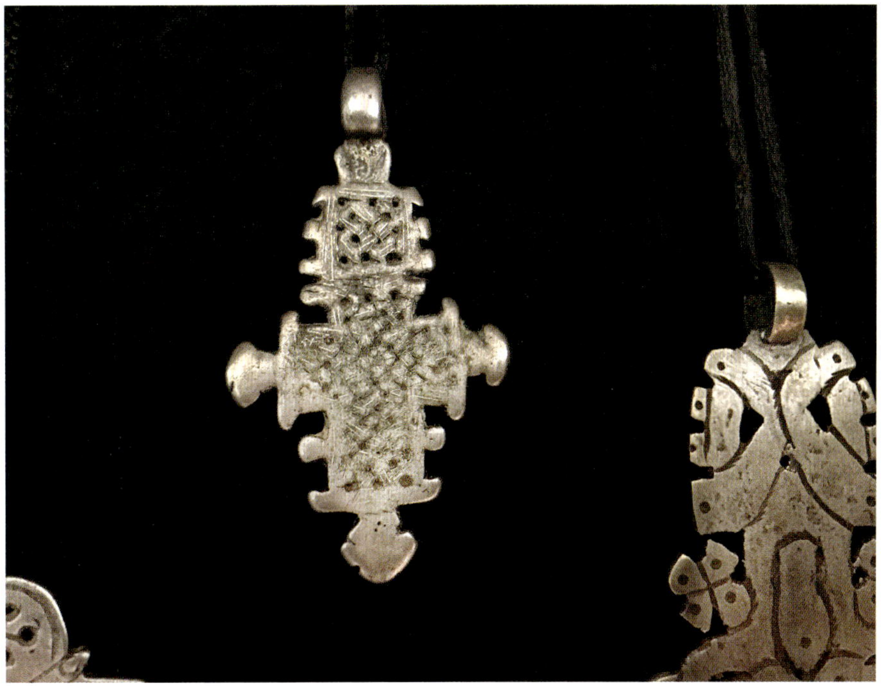

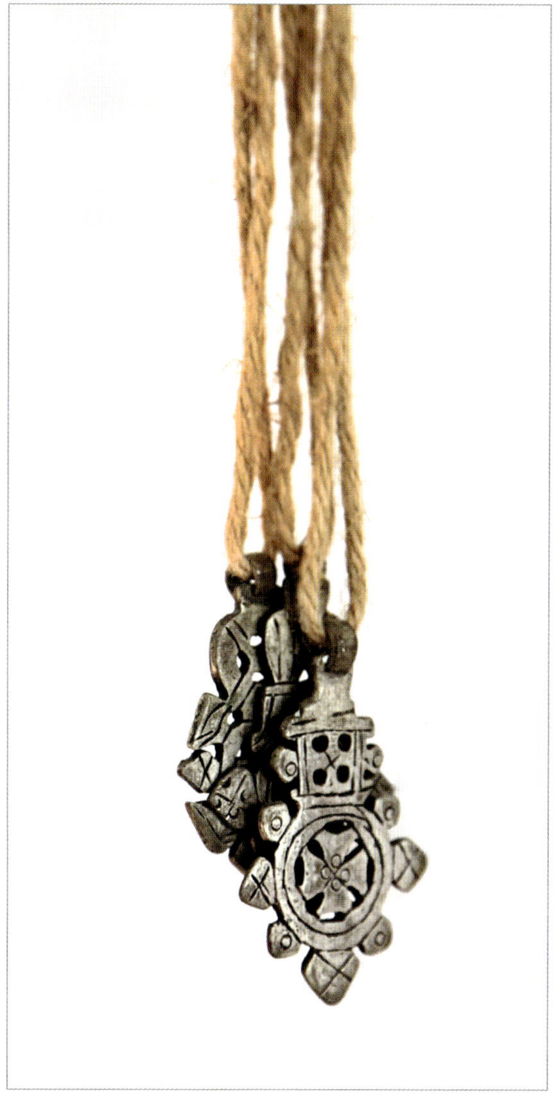

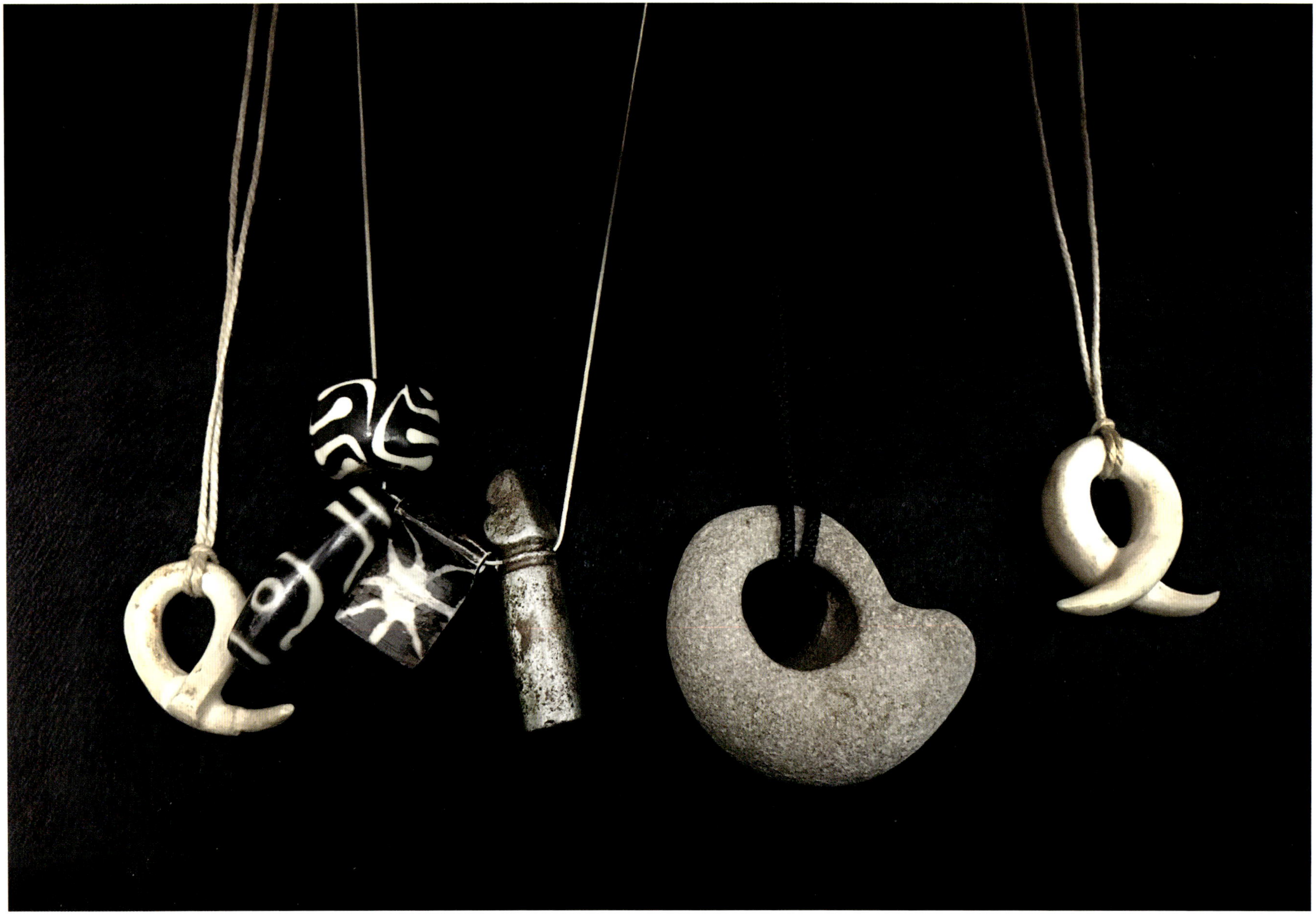

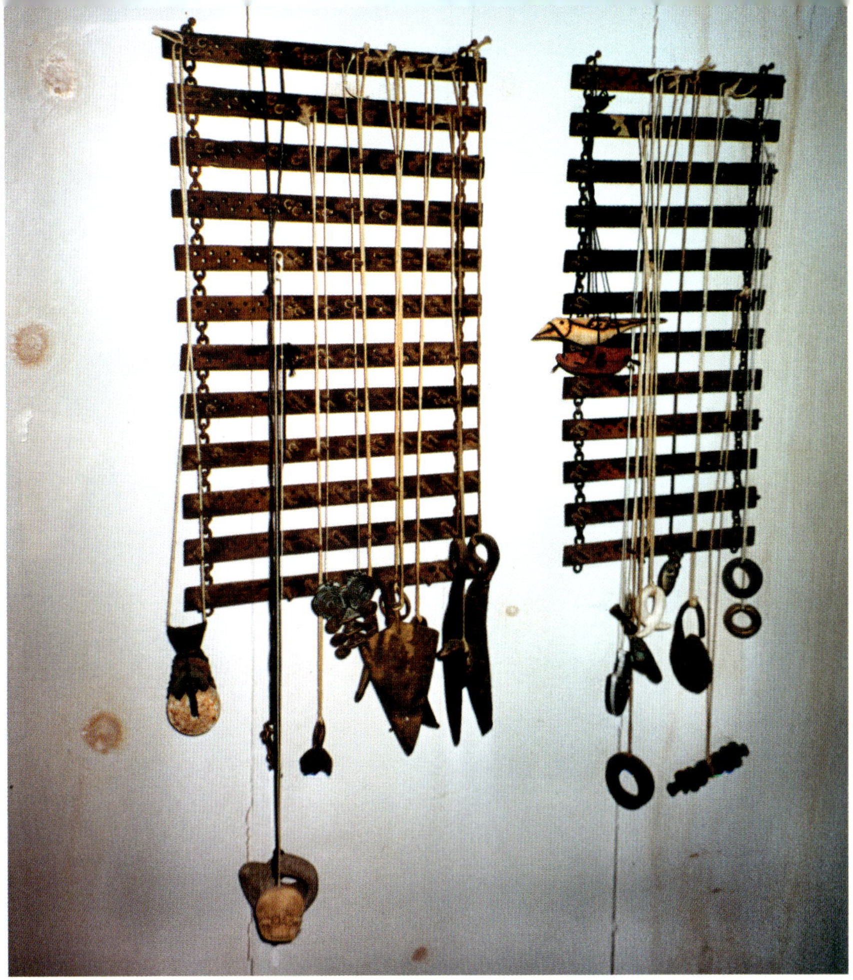

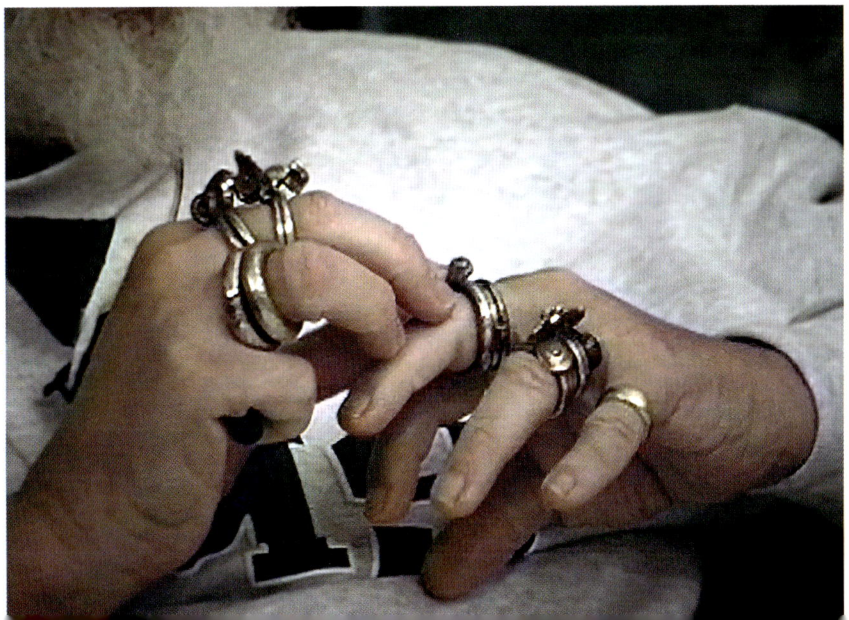

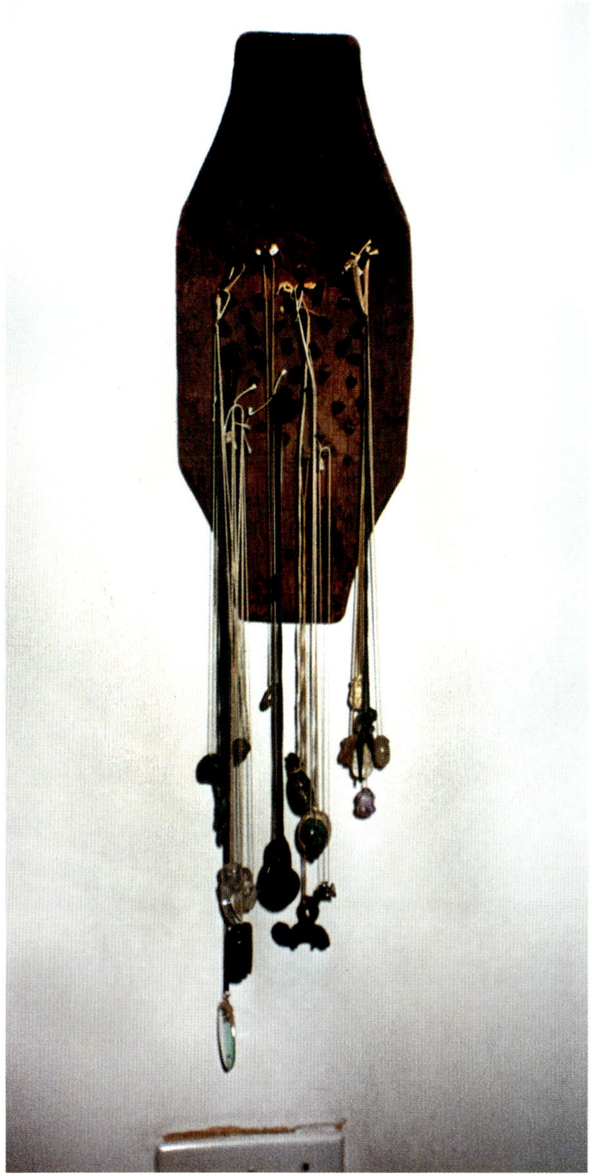

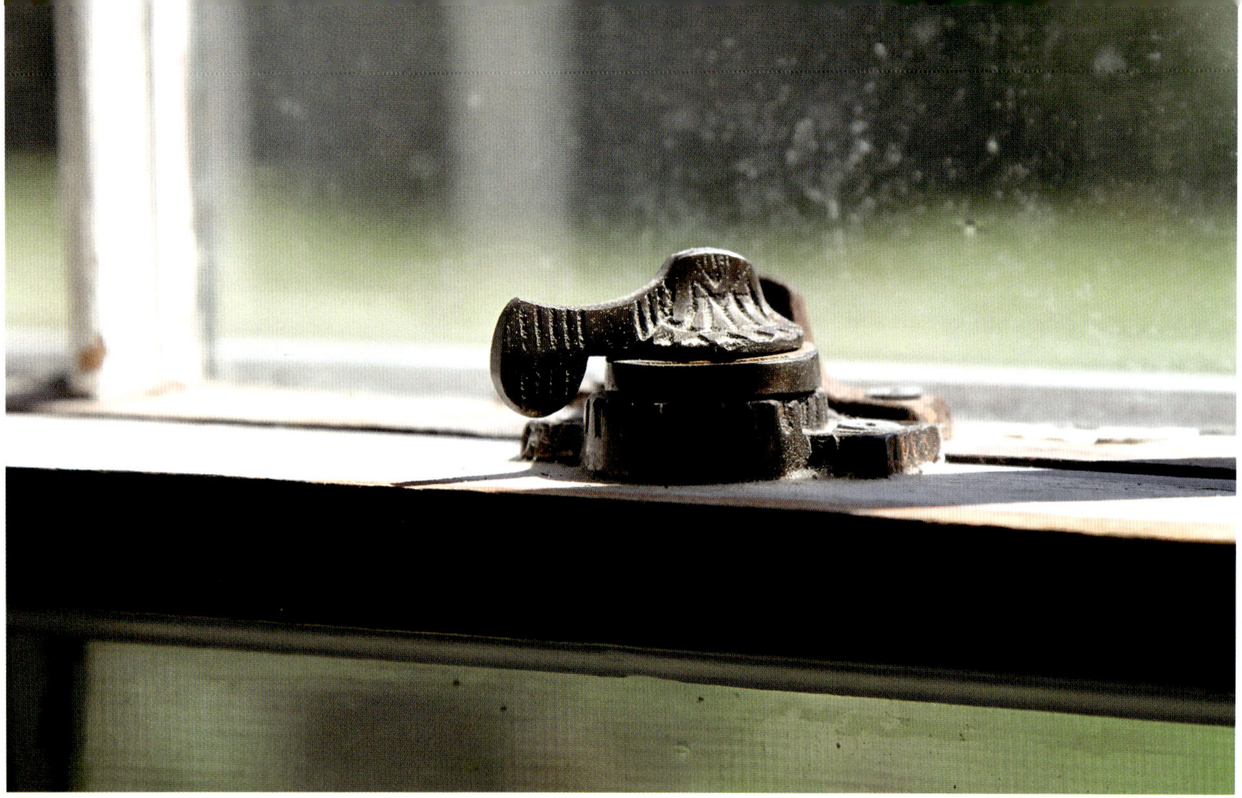

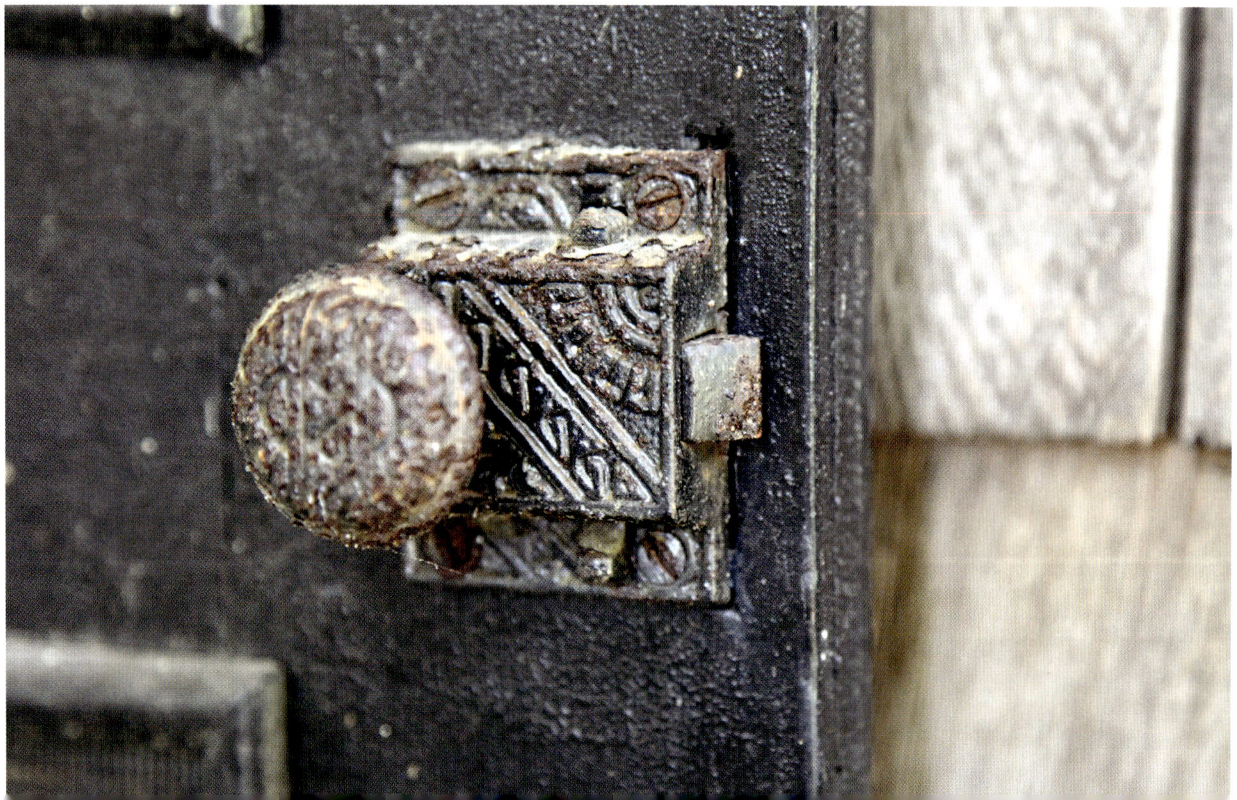

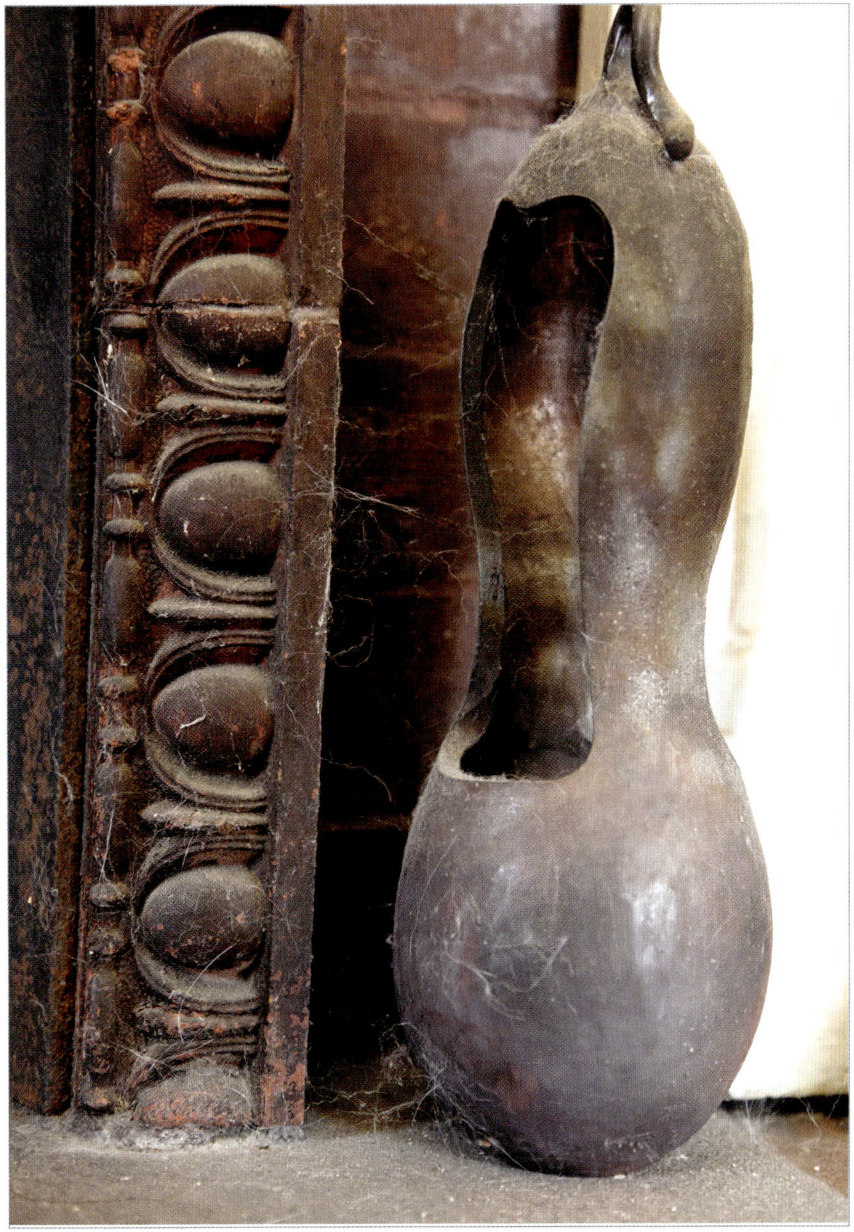

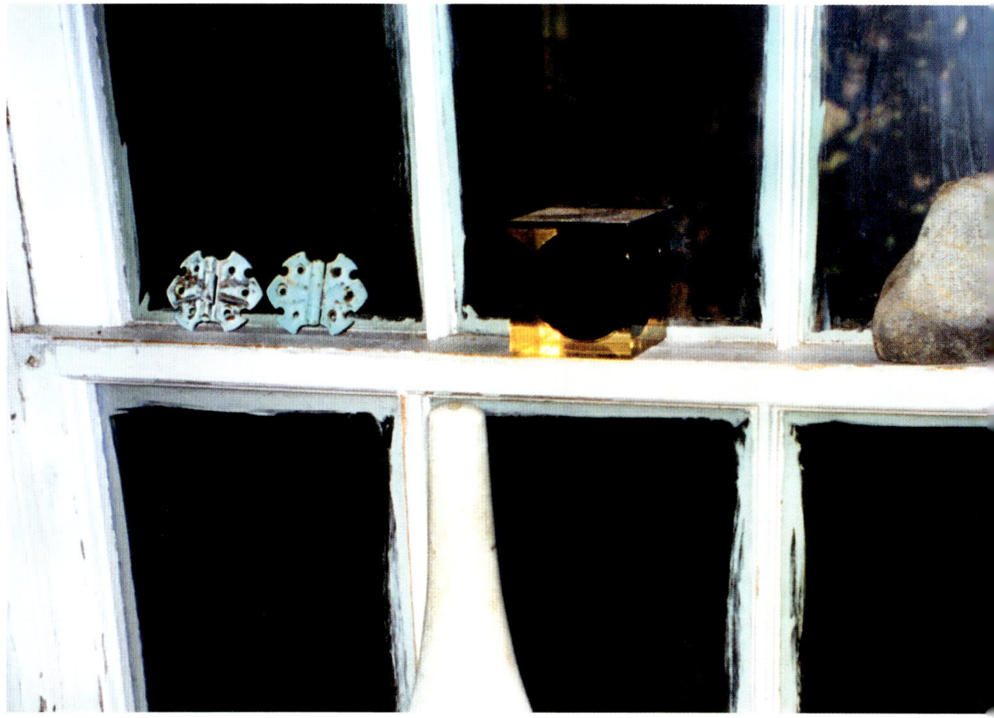

Edward found his overall aesthetic in the smallest of places, even in the antique architectural details of his house. Once when I was shooting a rehearsal at the Cape Cod Museum of Art, Edward looked down and picked up two large oblong pieces of bark mulch. We all then received a spontaneous window into his singular imagination at work.

One piece he shook with his left hand: "I love you, I love you, I love you," he exclaimed to the right piece, with which answered, "I hate you, I hate you, I hate you!" The left one cowered while the other continued, "Ooh, I'm going to hit you, I'm going to hit you!" Edward gave us this dark mini play delivered comically with a smile and then pocketed the mulch pieces to take home.

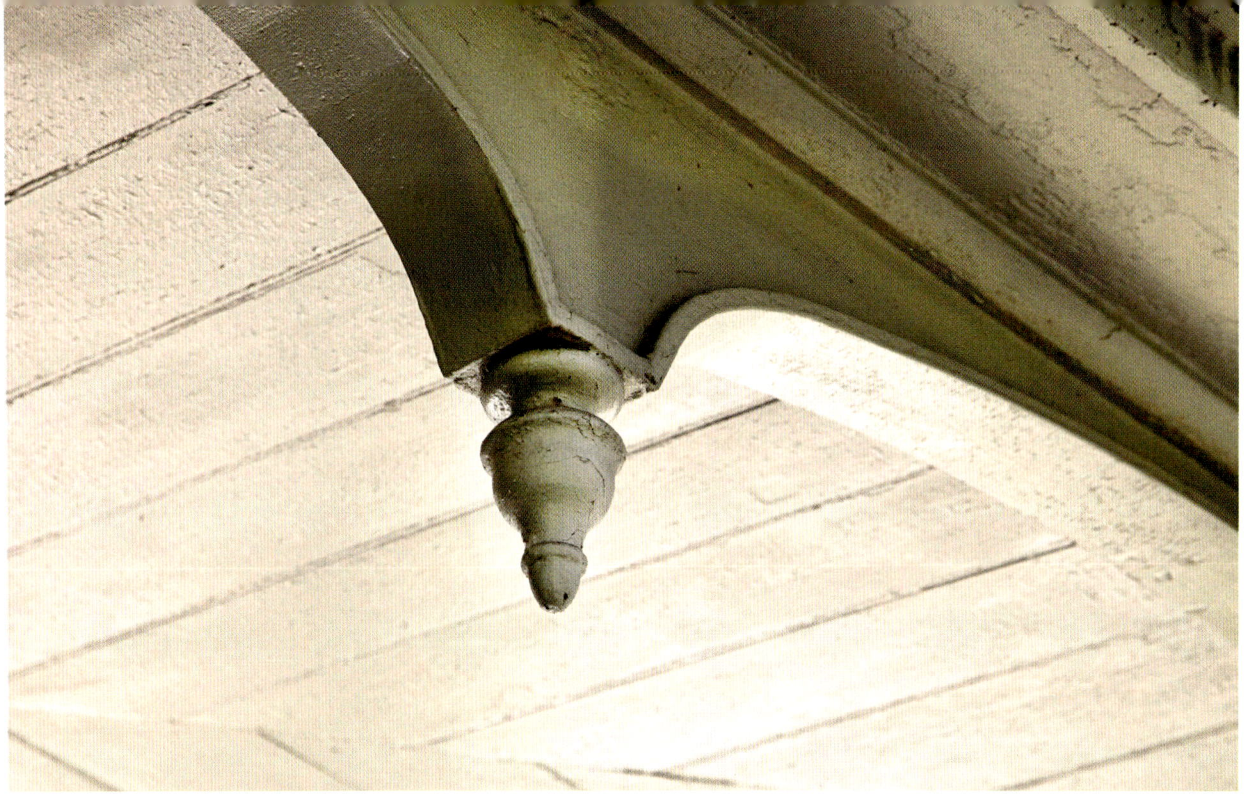

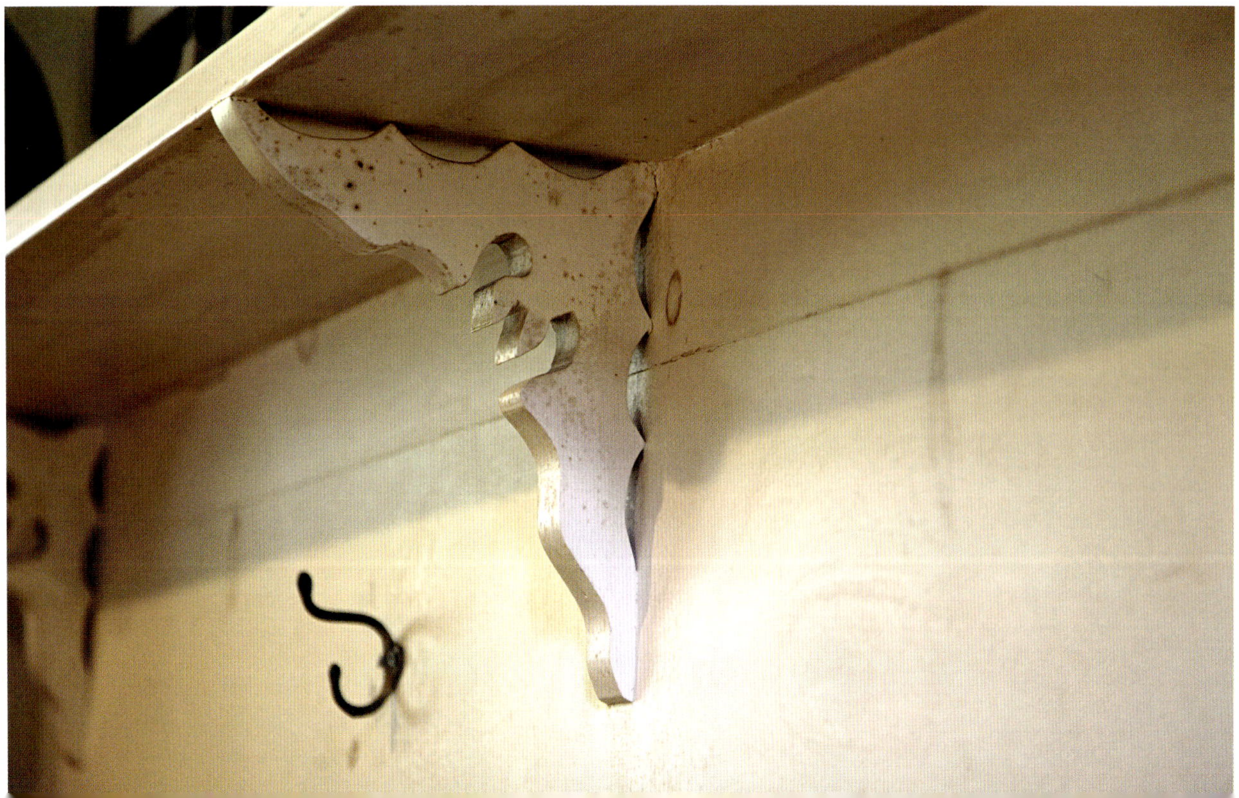

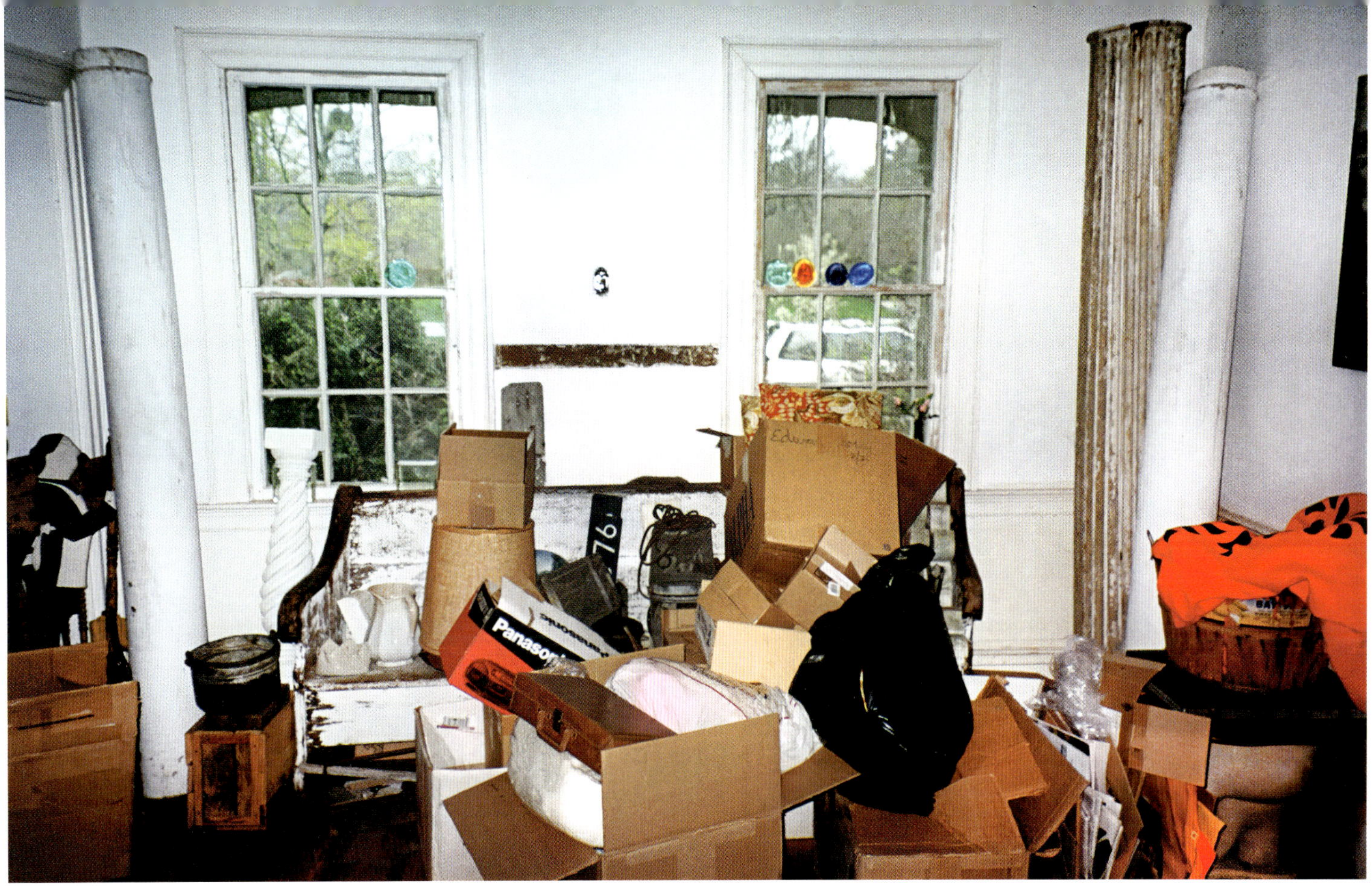

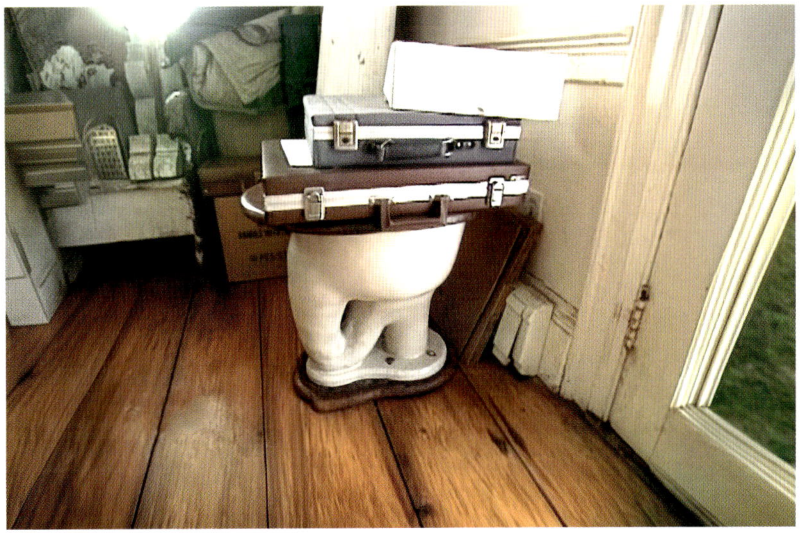

Even a toilet became art for Edward. He had this one turned into a table for his foyer.

Edward's bed as he left it, glass of water and watch by the bed side.

Looking at his bed, I was struck by how utilitarian that part of the house was. For someone so steeped in artwork, his own and others, I found it remarkable how blank his walls were—no paintings, etchings, or scriptures, as if sleep to him was much more of a blank canvas where he recharged and recalibrated a mind that otherwise had so much input.

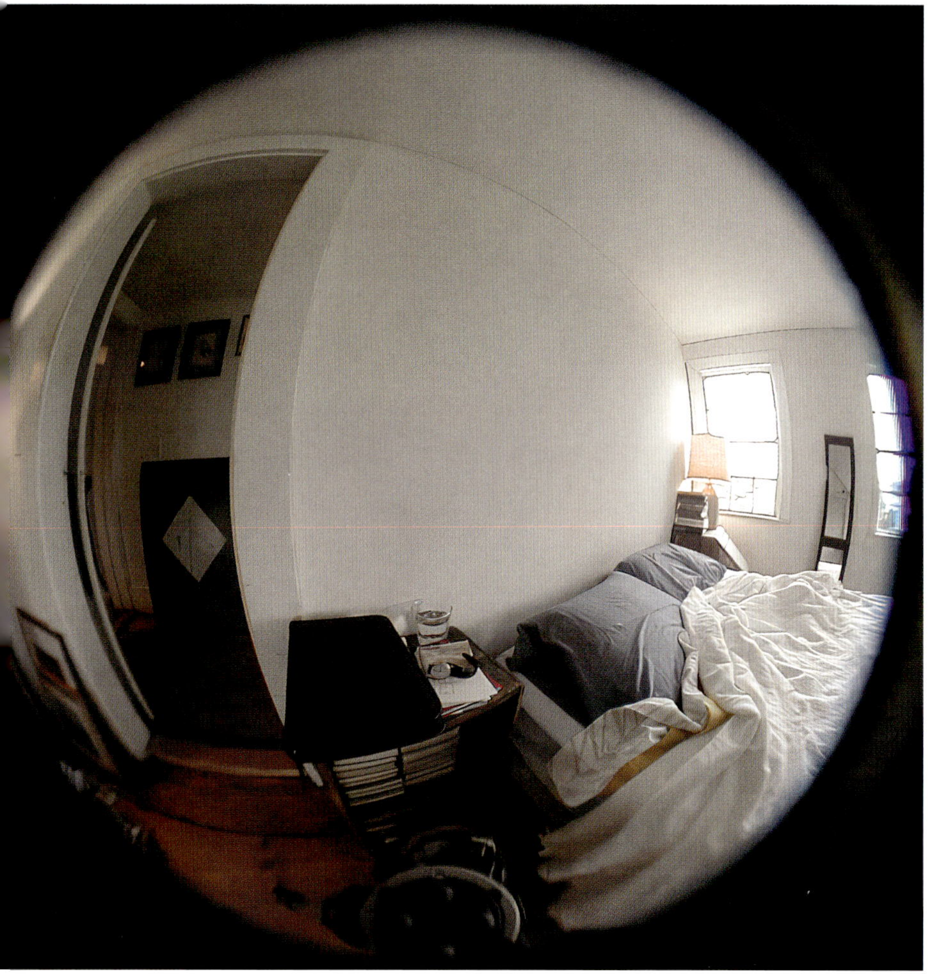

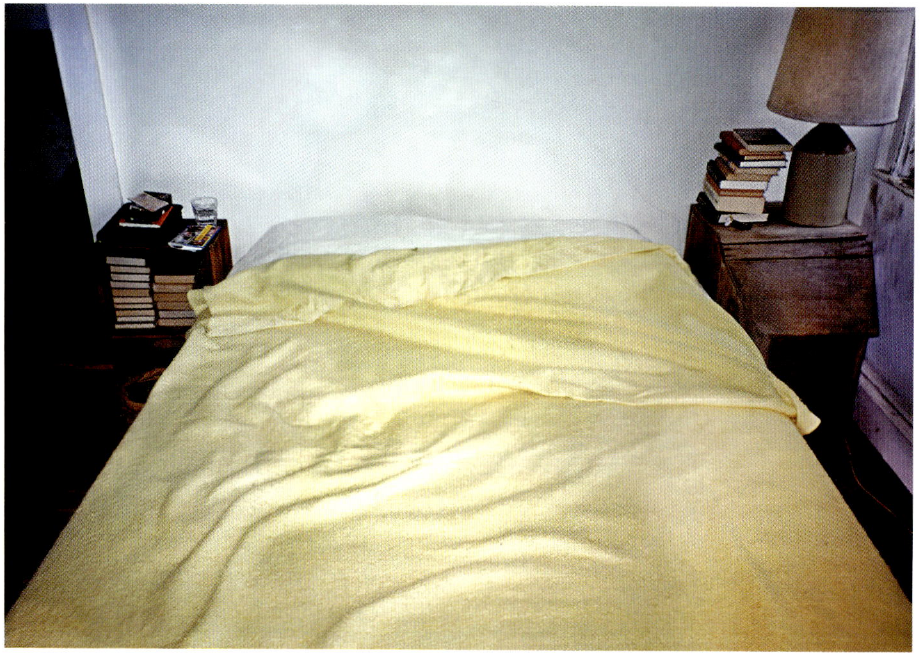

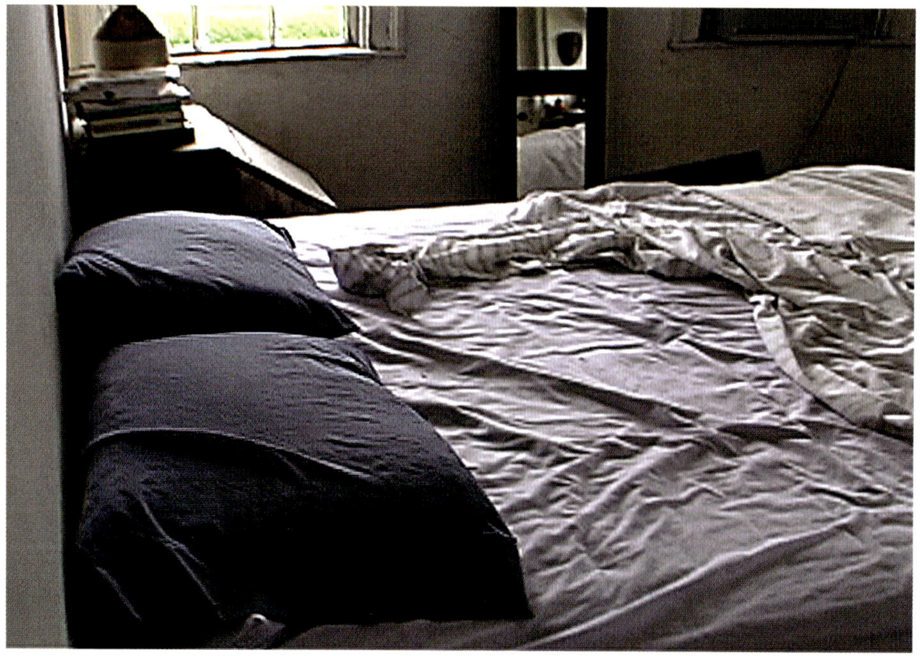

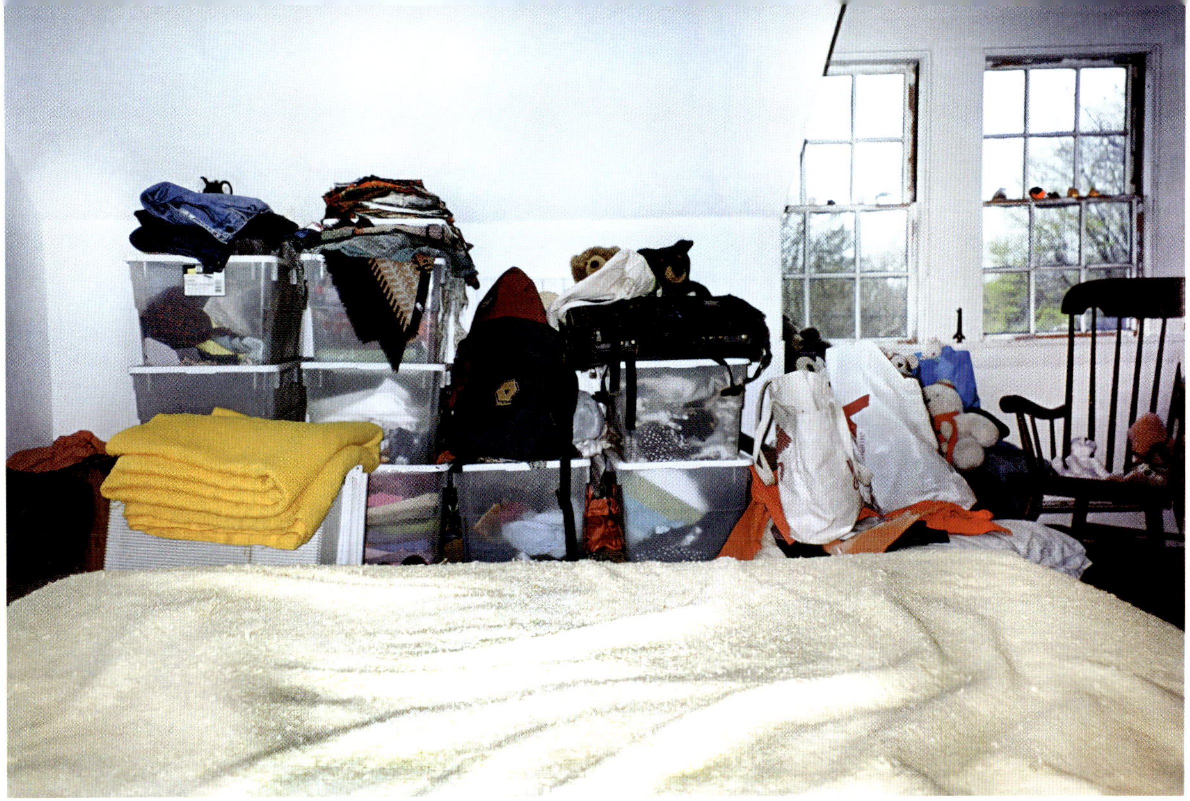

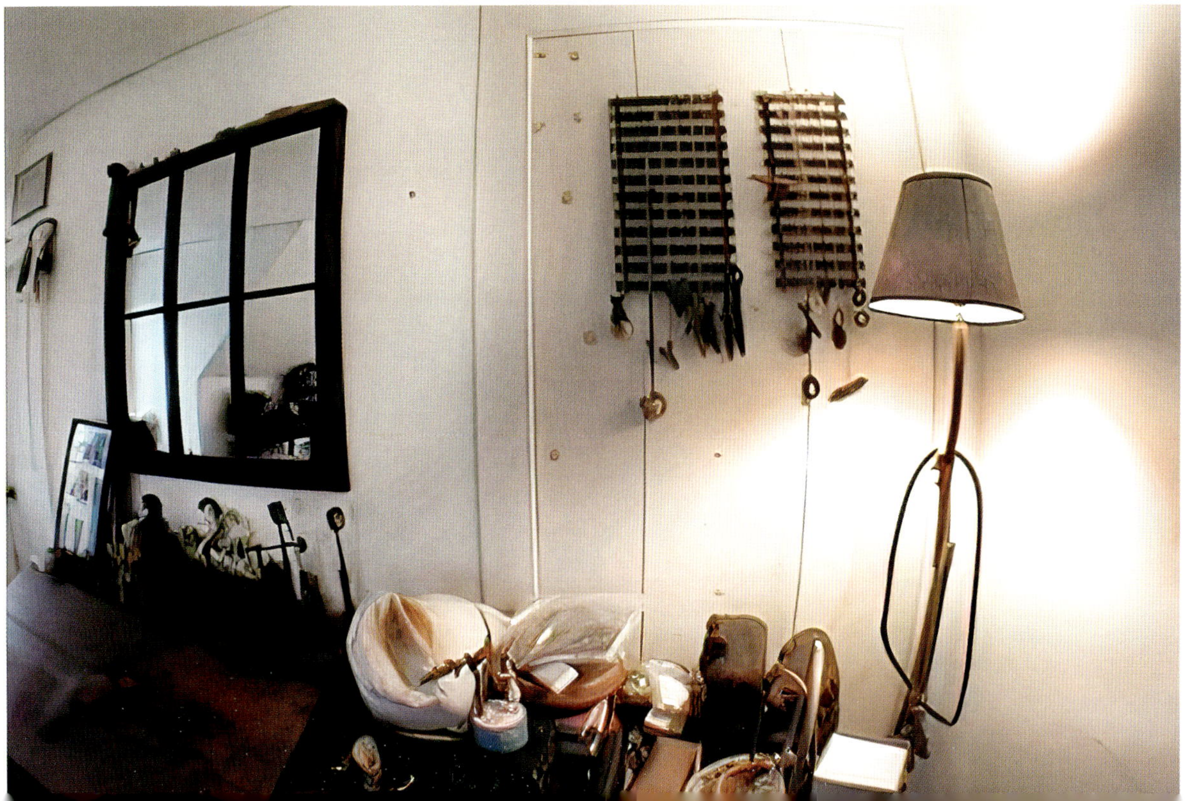

Edward allowed me to tour his house several times, and his bedroom was one of the tidier rooms, though he did not normally make his bed, as in the above photo. At the foot of the bed were his theater supplies, puppets, and smaller set elements, such as tapestry backgrounds. Like most people, he had a glass of water and wristwatch on one nightstand and a few current books in various stages of reading/rereading on the other.

Like with a lot of older people, I don't think he needed much sleep. He seemed to stay up late and be at Jack's Outback down the street for breakfast like clockwork with whatever sleep he was getting in between. In one of our first conversations over beers (he liked Heineken) at the Kettle Ho in Cotuit, he admitted to having trouble falling asleep and would sometimes lie awake until the birds chirped and then finally nod off. I don't know if he napped.

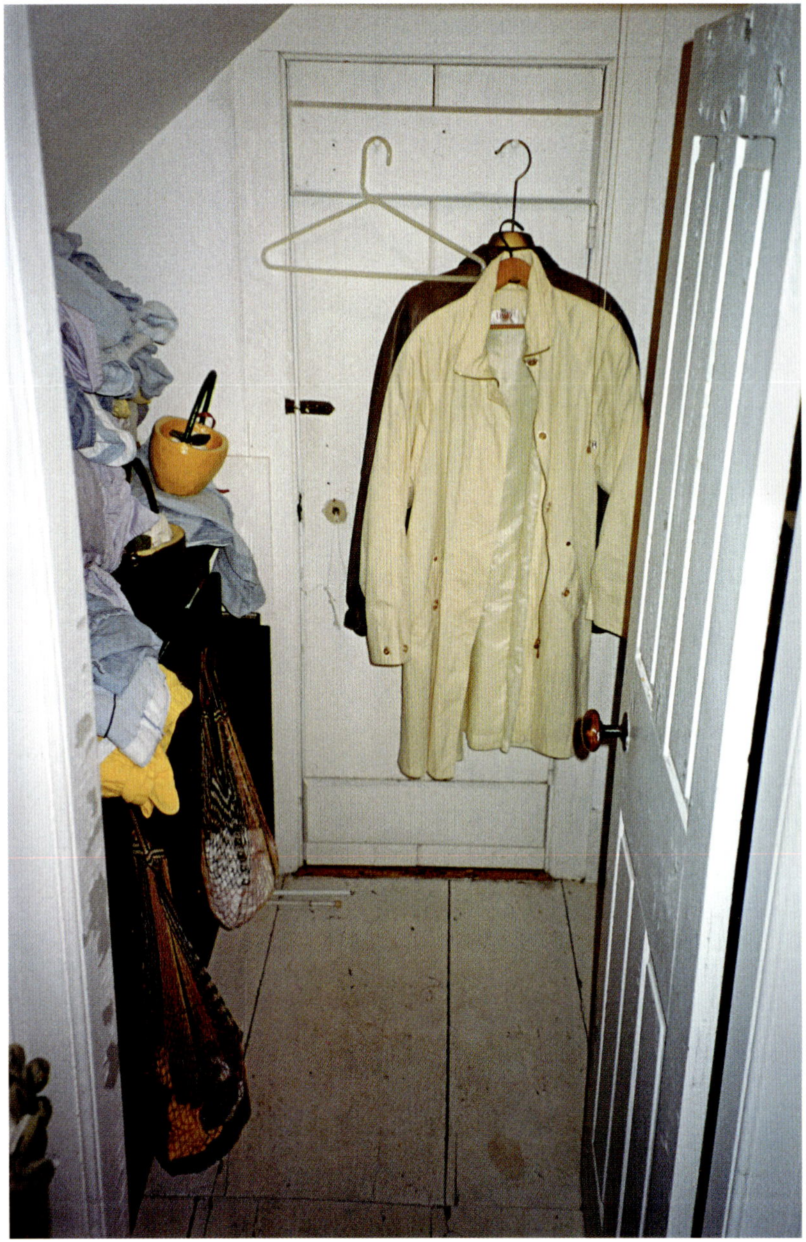

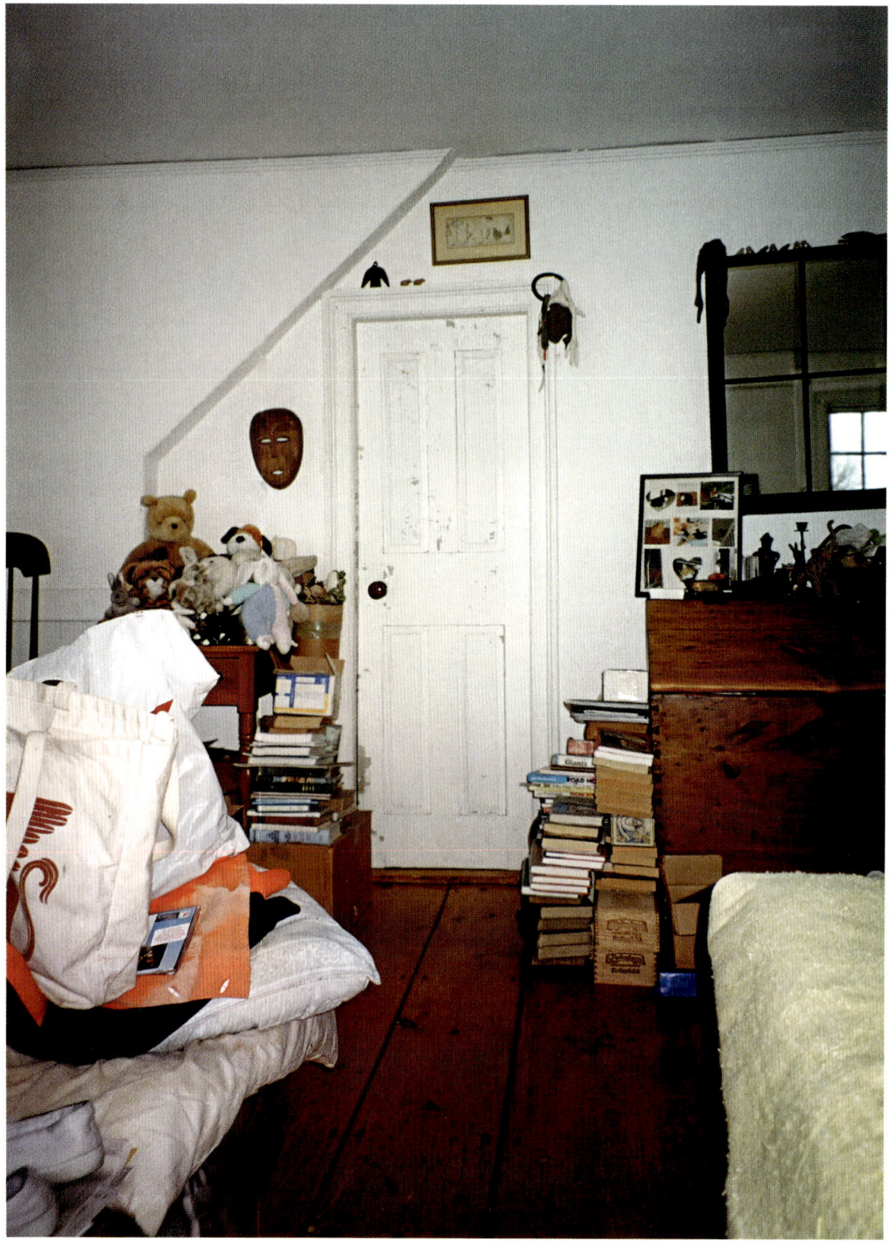

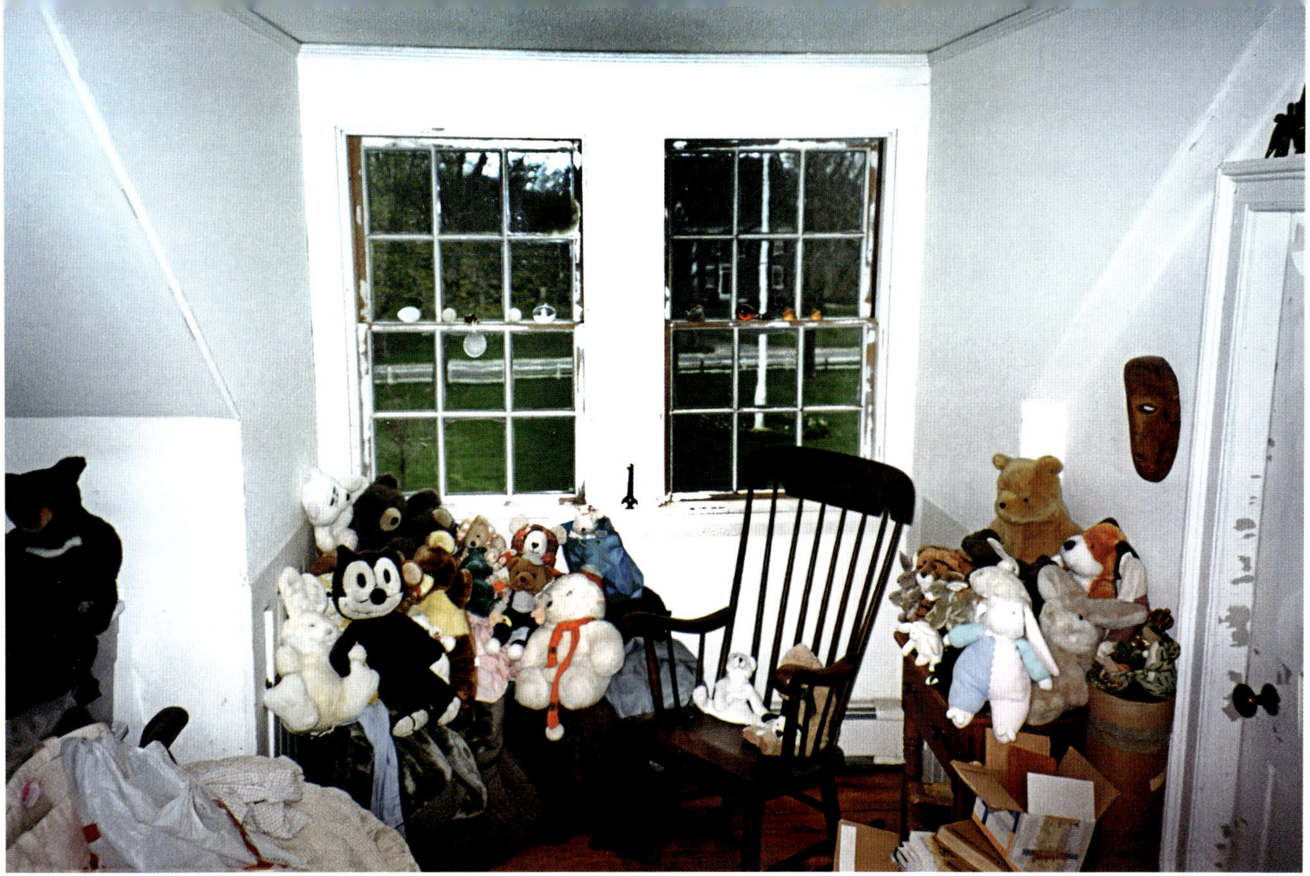

Although Edward could be extravagant with his jewelry and coats, his core clothing, usually blue jeans and yellow shirt, had a uniform-like quality similar to Steve Jobs's mock turtleneck.

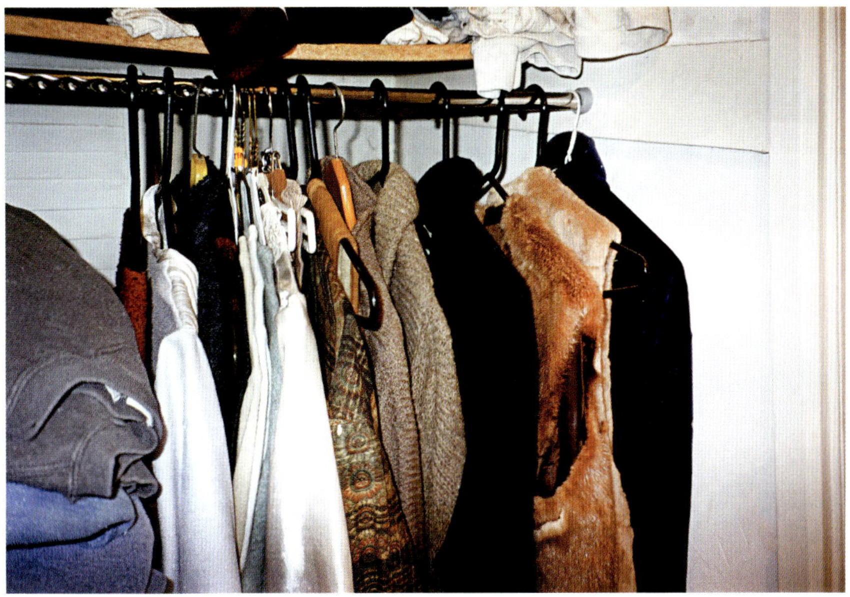

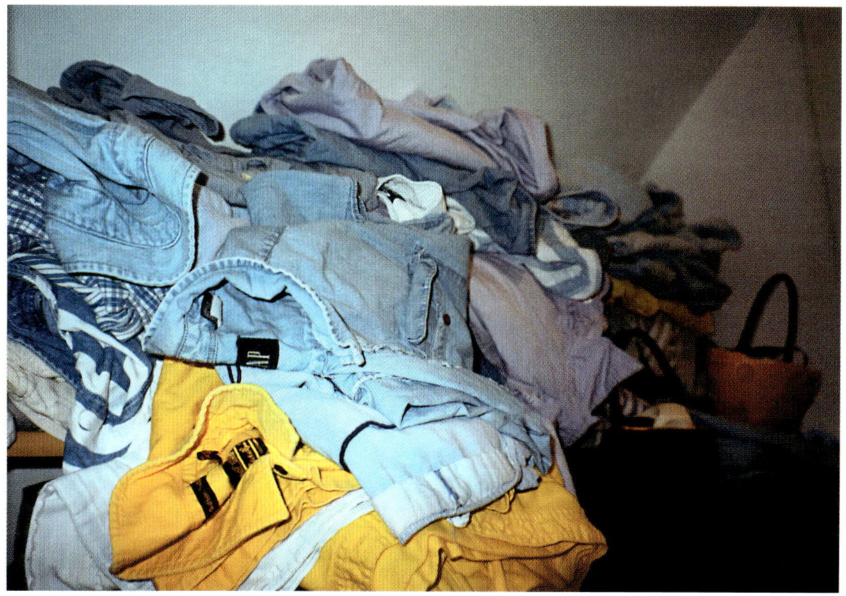

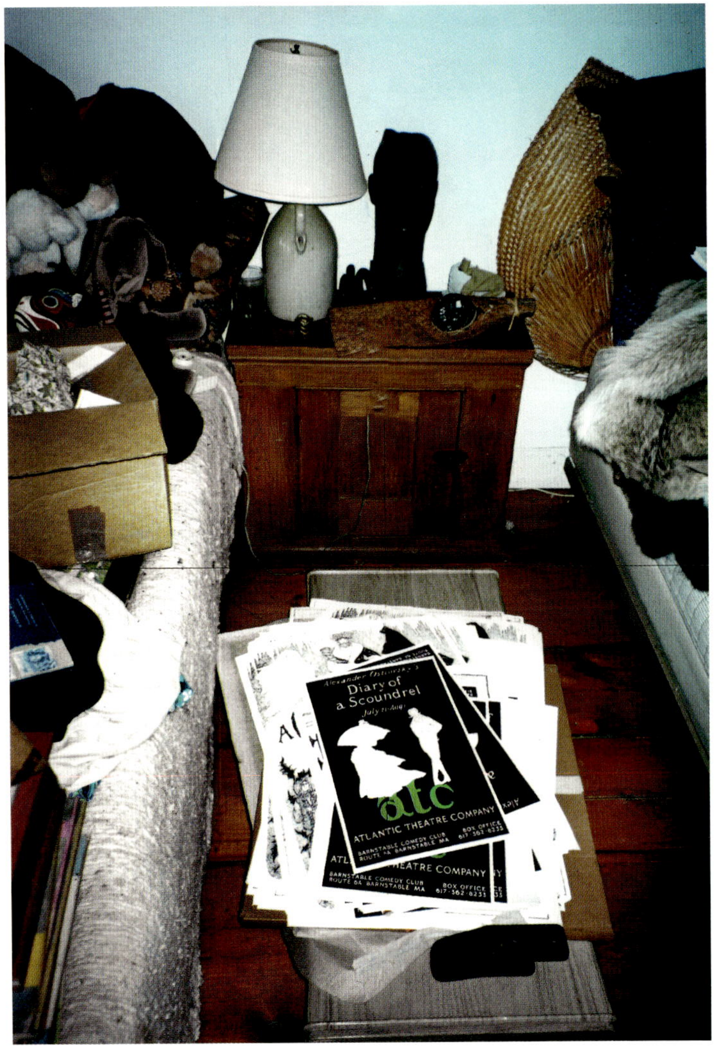

Edward's guest bedroom

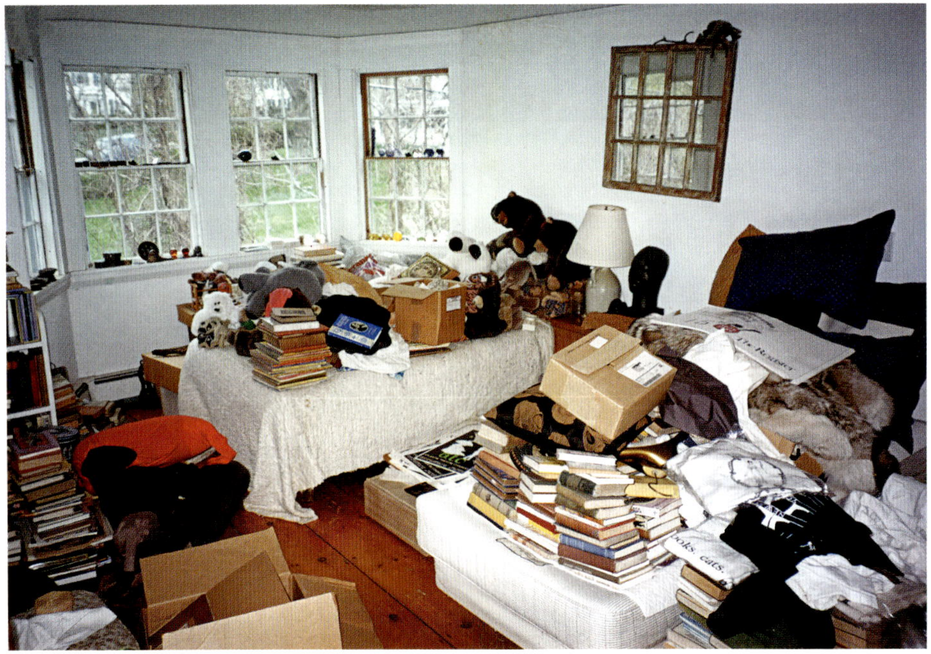

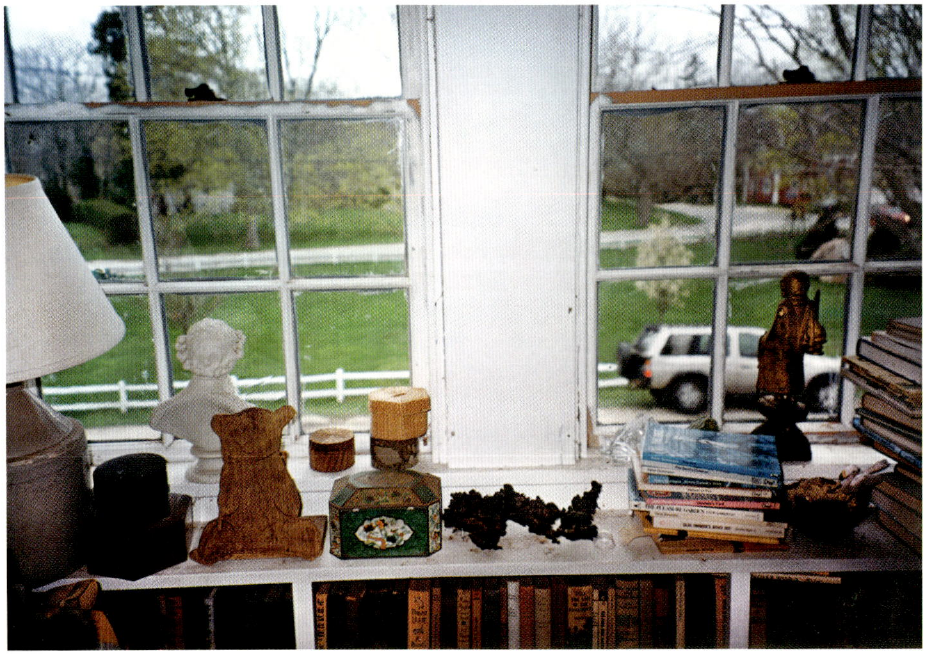

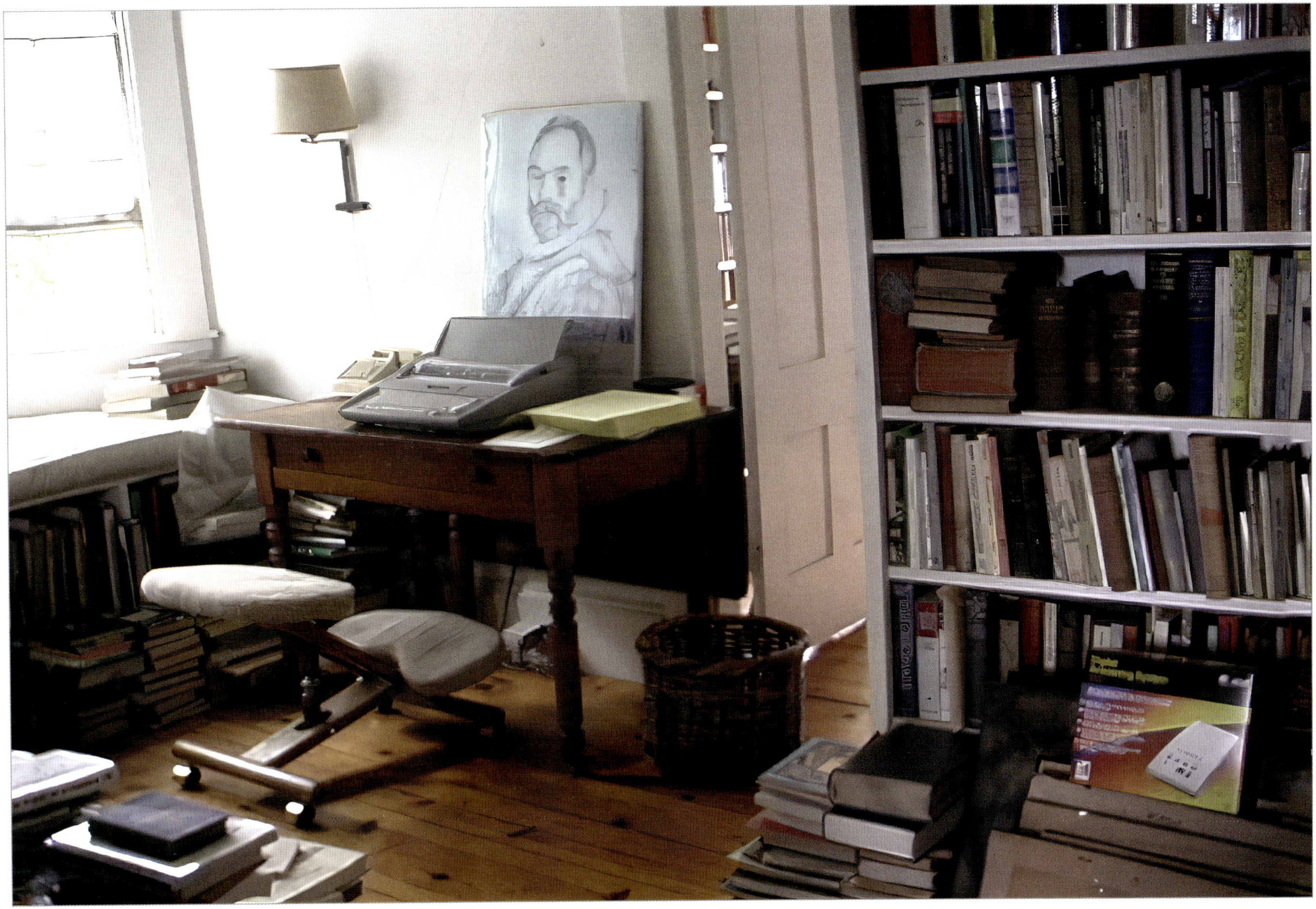

Edward's work desk with word processor in August 1998

Edward's work desk with new Bondi Blue iMac.

Edward was always learning new ways to approach his art. As a case in point, he regularly took classes at Cape Cod Community College, including, literally, basket weaving. He was known for exploring animation techniques at the Cape Cod Community TV station, where I was on staff in Yarmouth, Massachusetts, when we met. He used D-Paint and Lightwave on an Amiga Toaster setup, initially, and those unfinished and probably abandoned animations will be featured in the documentary, per Edward's direct request. In 2000 he had also just purchased the groundbreaking Apple Bondi Blue iMac and a carful of software/hardware to bring his art into the digital world.

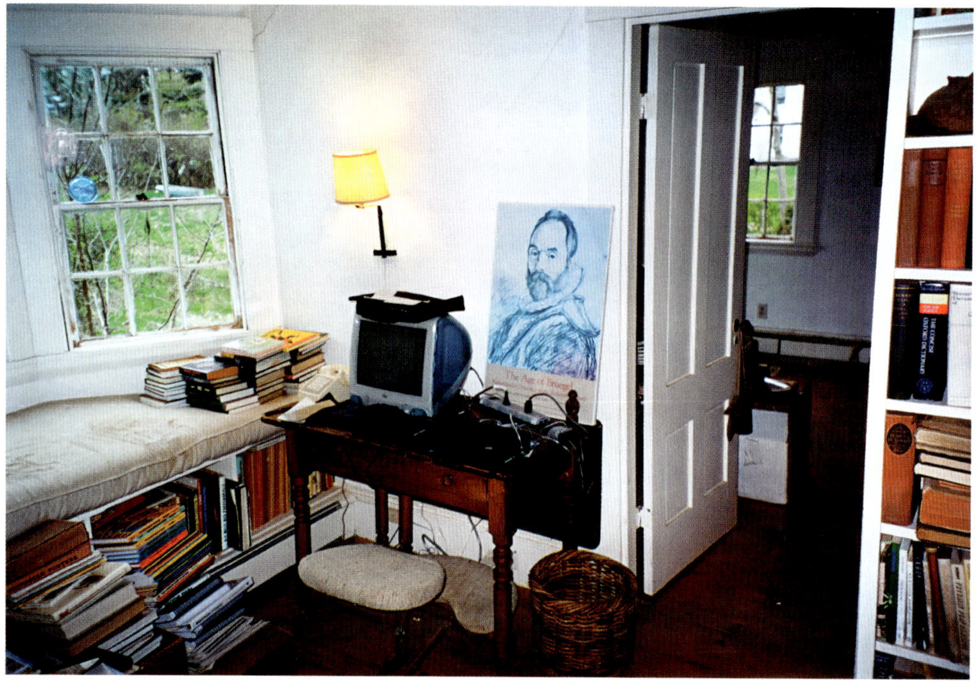

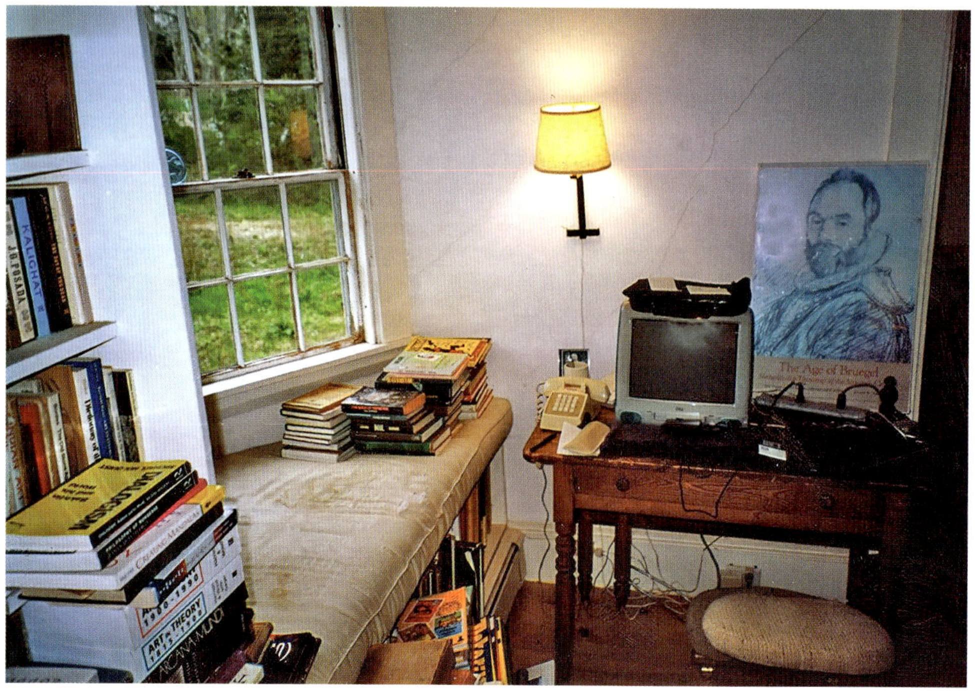

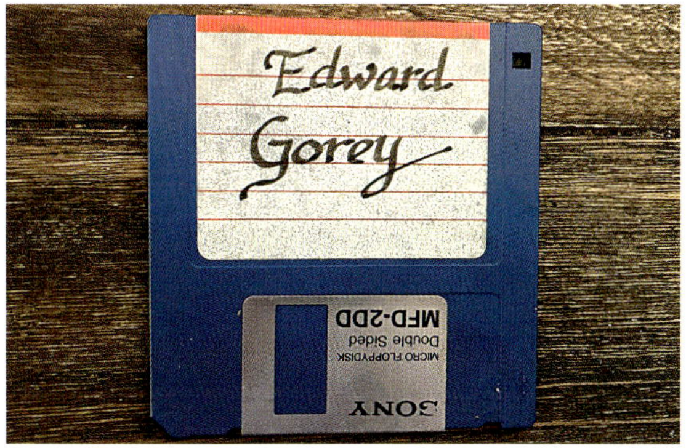

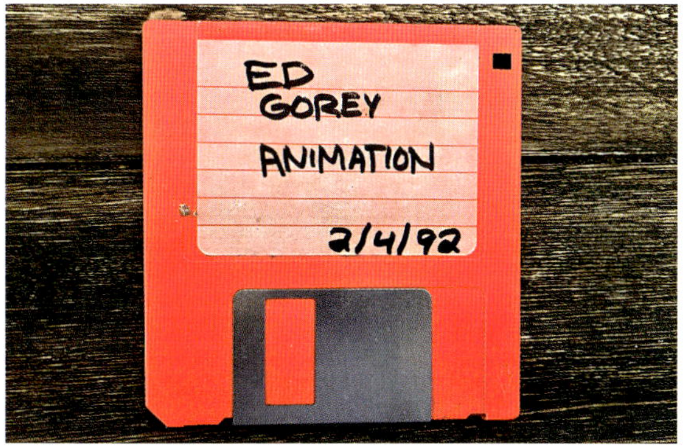

In my opinion, Edward was exploring the idea of doing animated movies himself and also finding a digital way to compensate for his self-professed declining ability to do the intricate cross-hatching, for which he was most known.

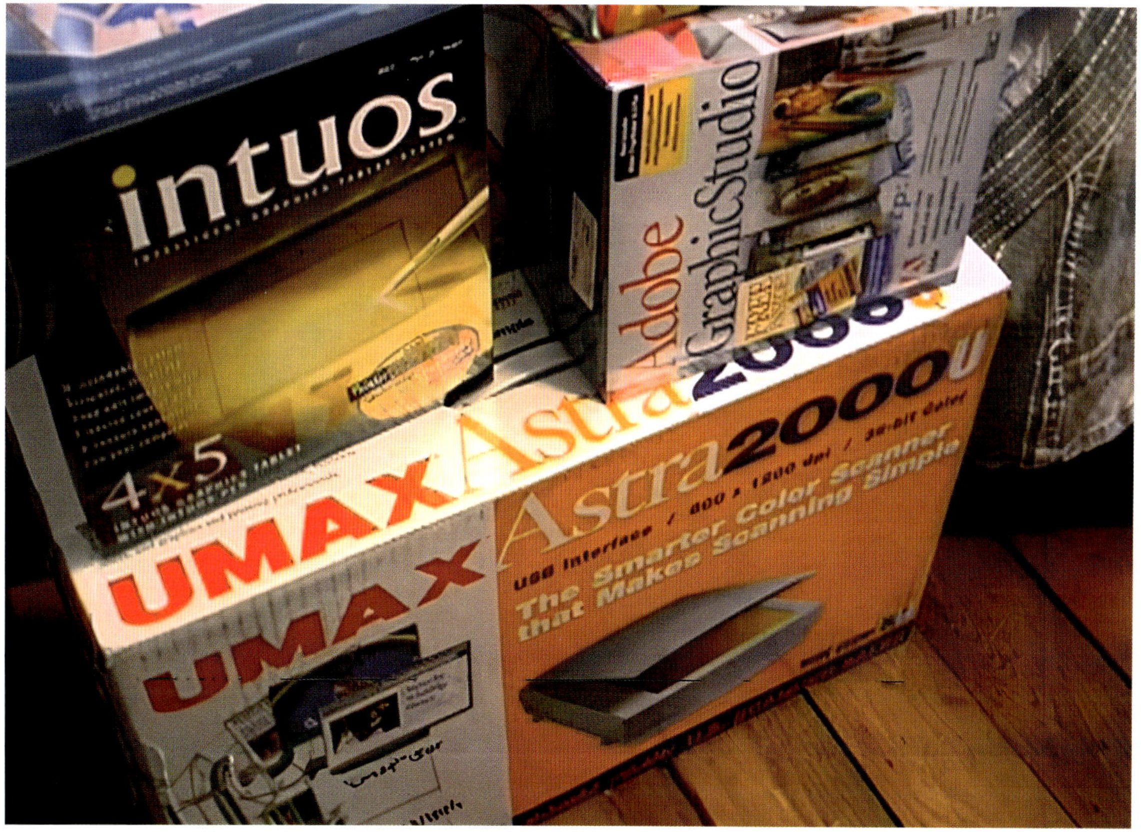

A color scanner, a drawing tablet, and the complete Adobe Graphic Studio hints at his seriousness to take things from analog to digital. Unfortunately, he passed on, leaving this new gear still shrink-wrapped.

After he passed away, the hospital sent his belongings home in a plastic bag, his jeans and white Sperrys, of course, along with some books that I believe his producer and friend Carol Verburg brought to the hospital to read to him while he languished for that short time in a coma. His passing was quick and sudden, and my last act of production during that time was to record his answering machine, which I mastered out for the Gorey House for their use in exhibits. It was such a documentary of who he was that it's the best place to start if you're looking to find out about the person behind the artwork. "You've reached Edward Gorey's answering machine, wait for the beep." Delivered deadpan of course.

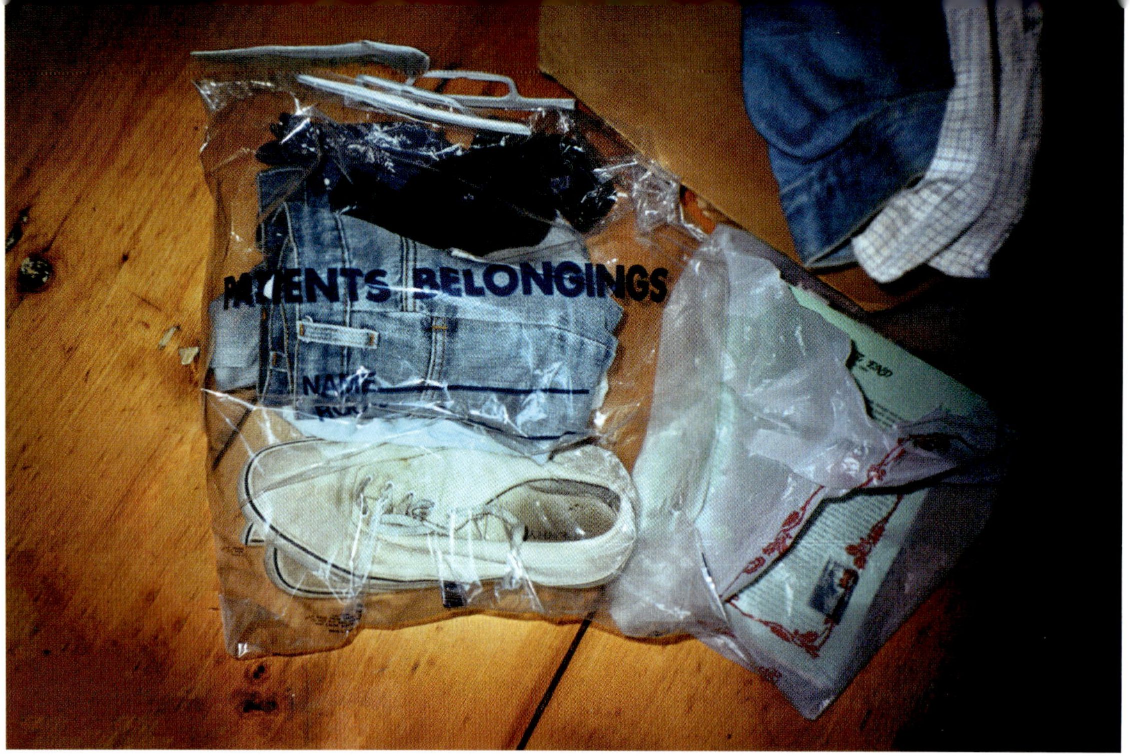

Actor Eric Edwards offers Edward his favorite, a tin of Altoids.

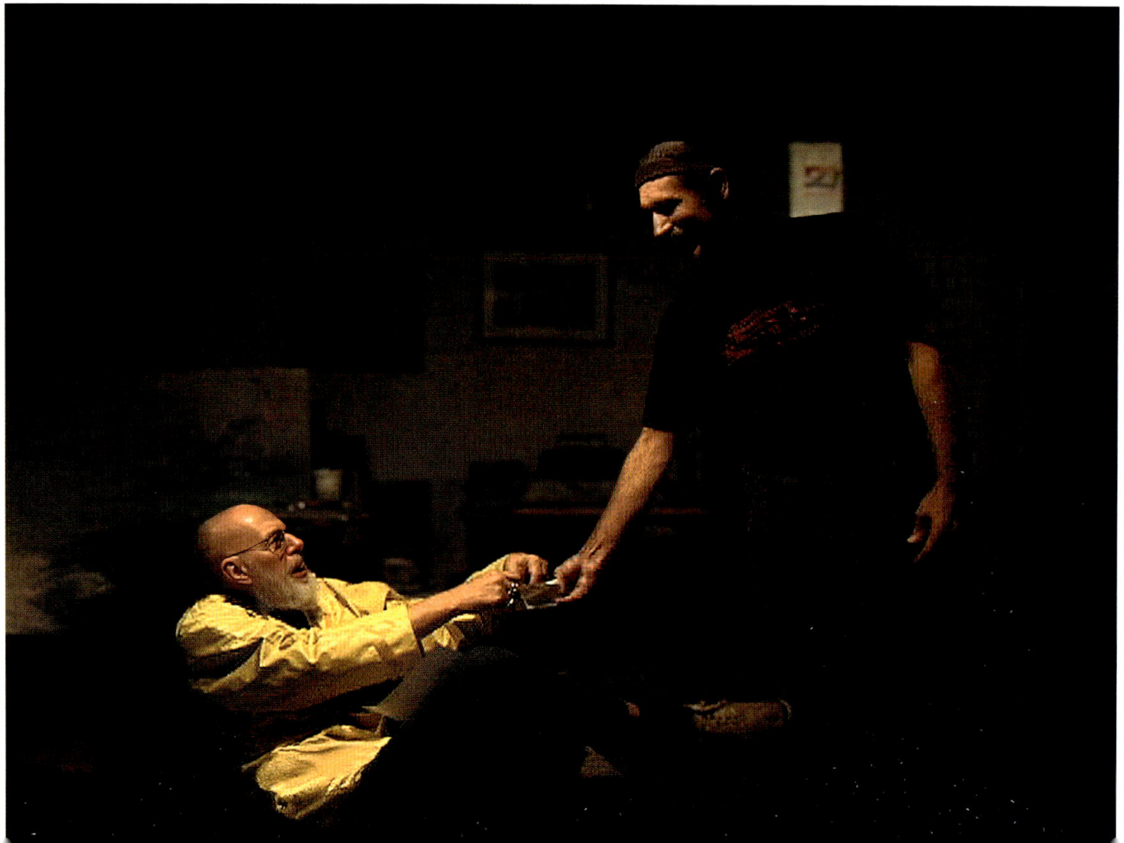

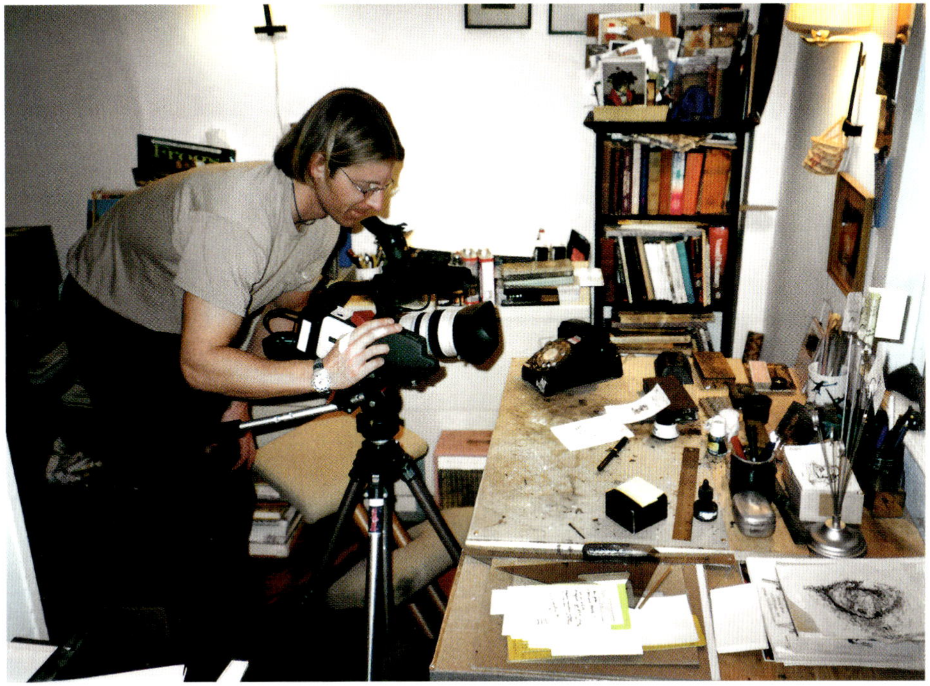

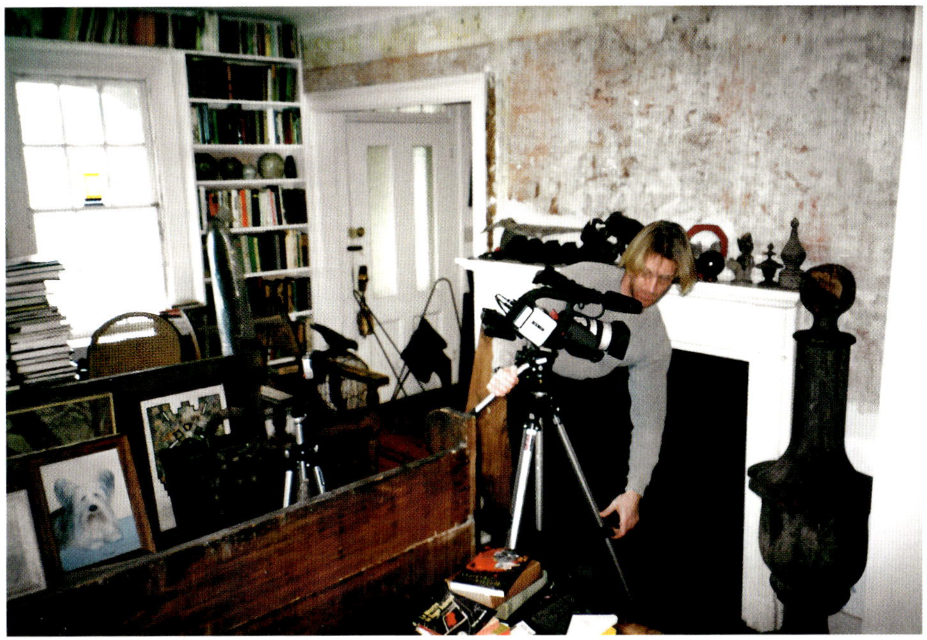

The author shooting video and photos in Edward's house

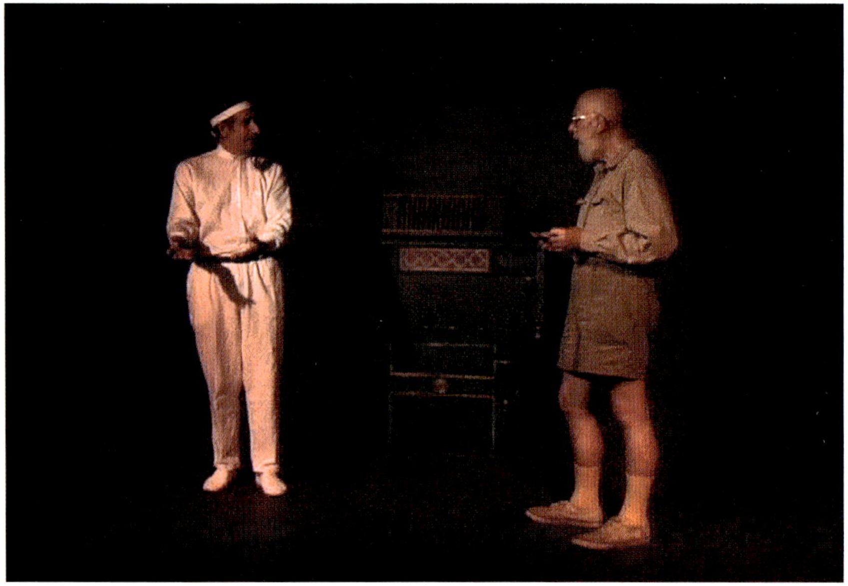

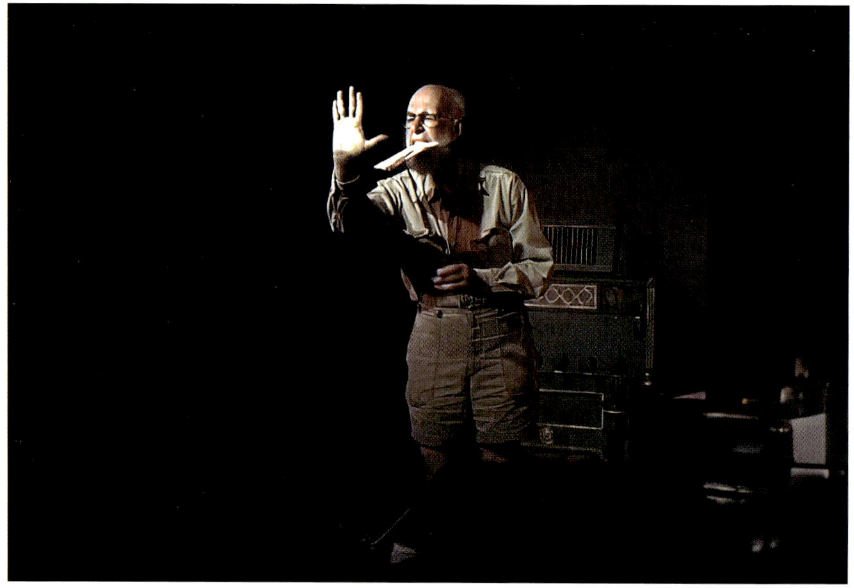

Edward acting in his play *Wallpaper* with actor Eric Edwards at Theatre on the Bay, Woods Hole, Massachusetts, in August 1996

Edward directing a rehearsal for *Cautionary Tales for Children* in Cotuit, Massachusetts, in October 1996

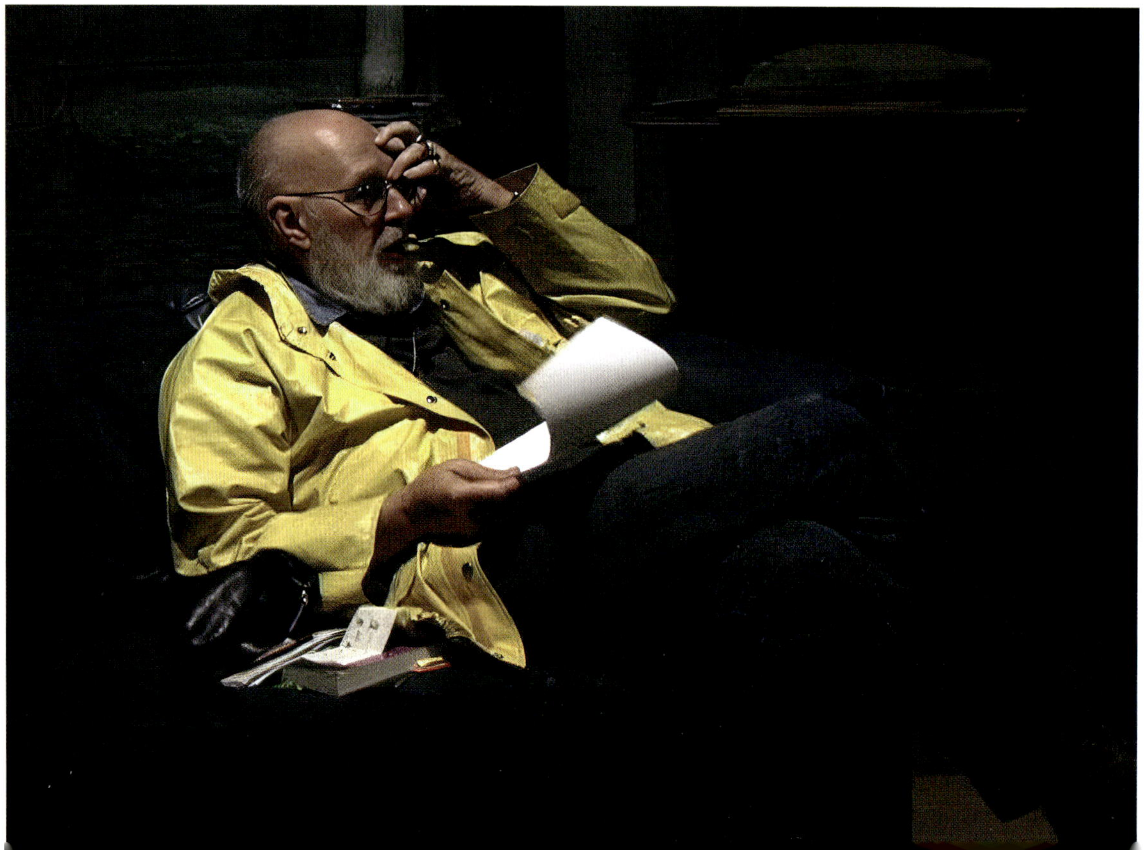

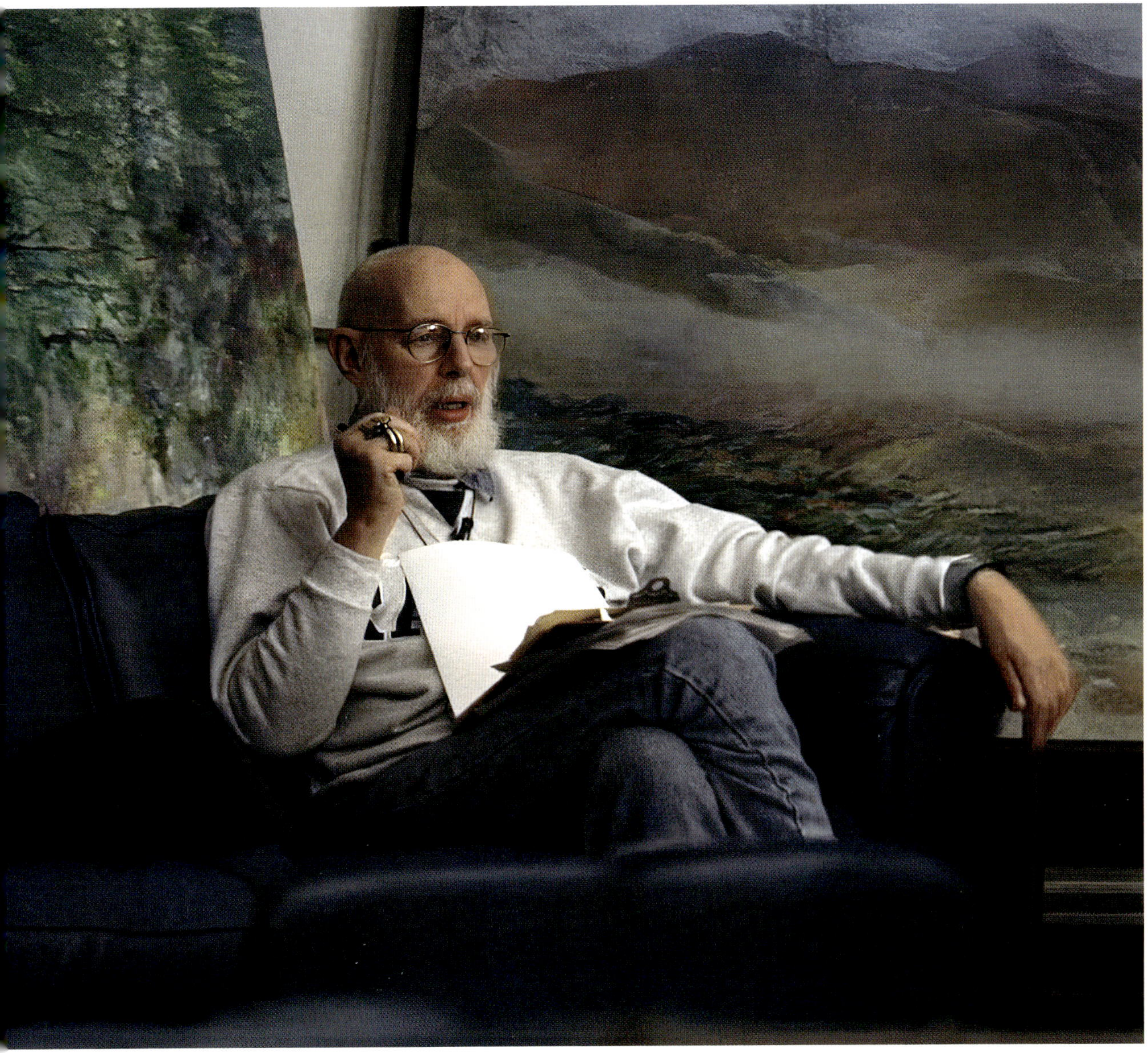

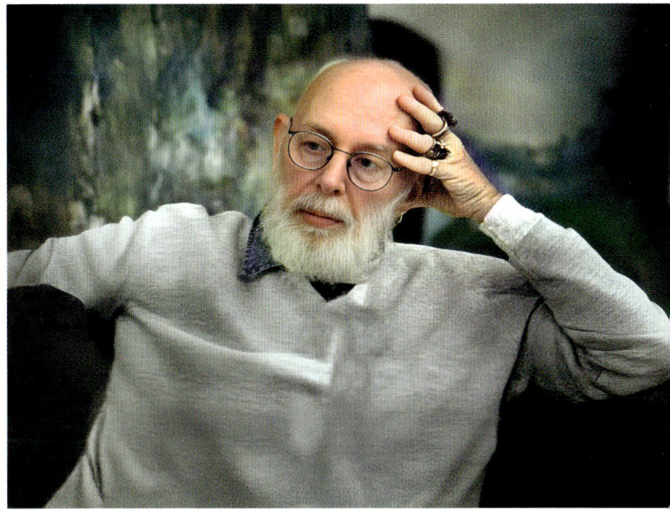

Edward in rehearsal at the Cape Rep Theater, October 1999, with the author and sound man Richard Robbins

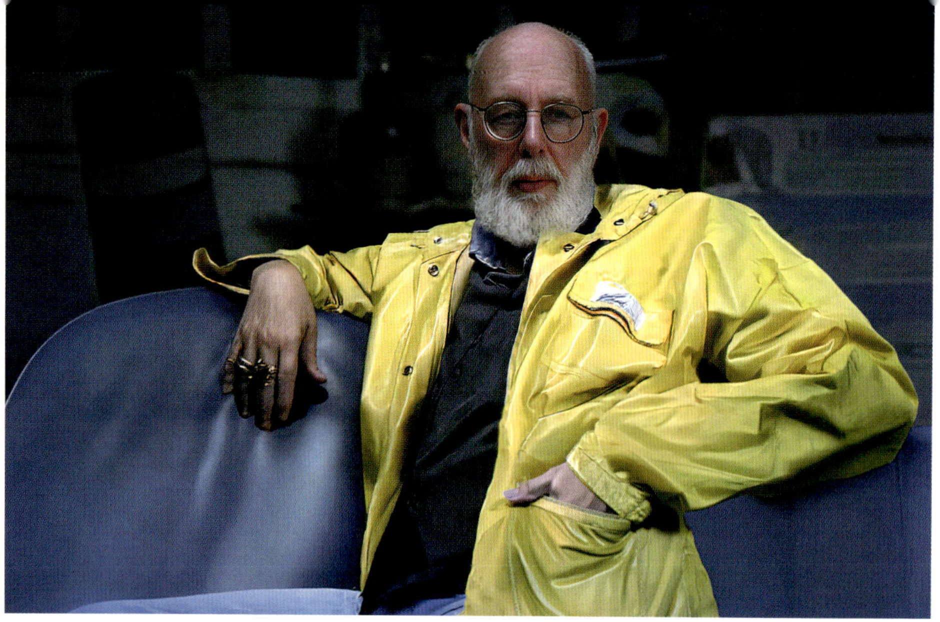

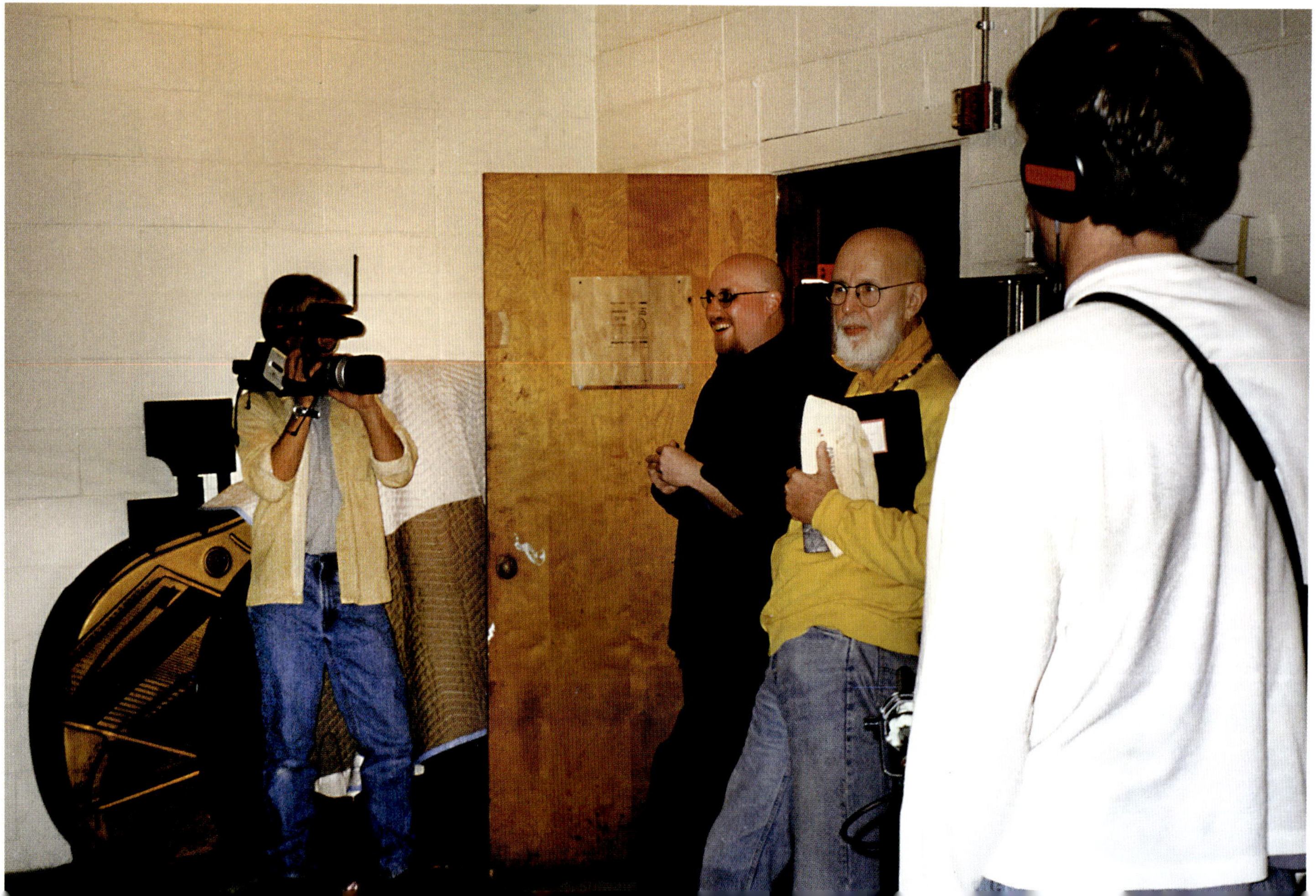

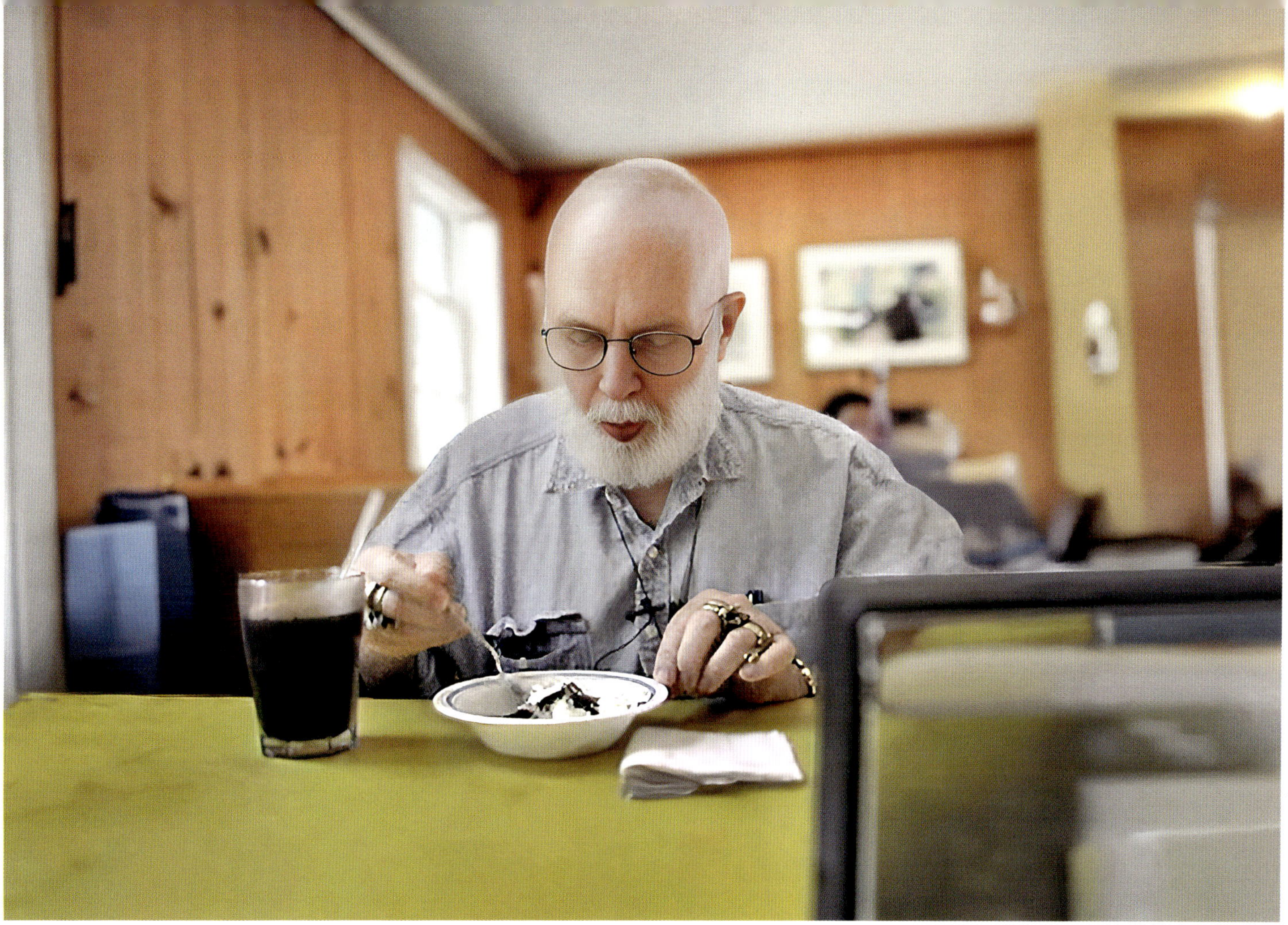

Having lunch at Jack's Outback in Yarmouth, Massachusetts, August 1998

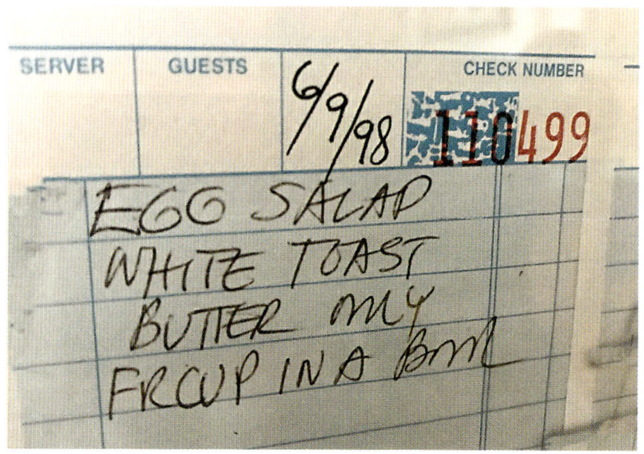

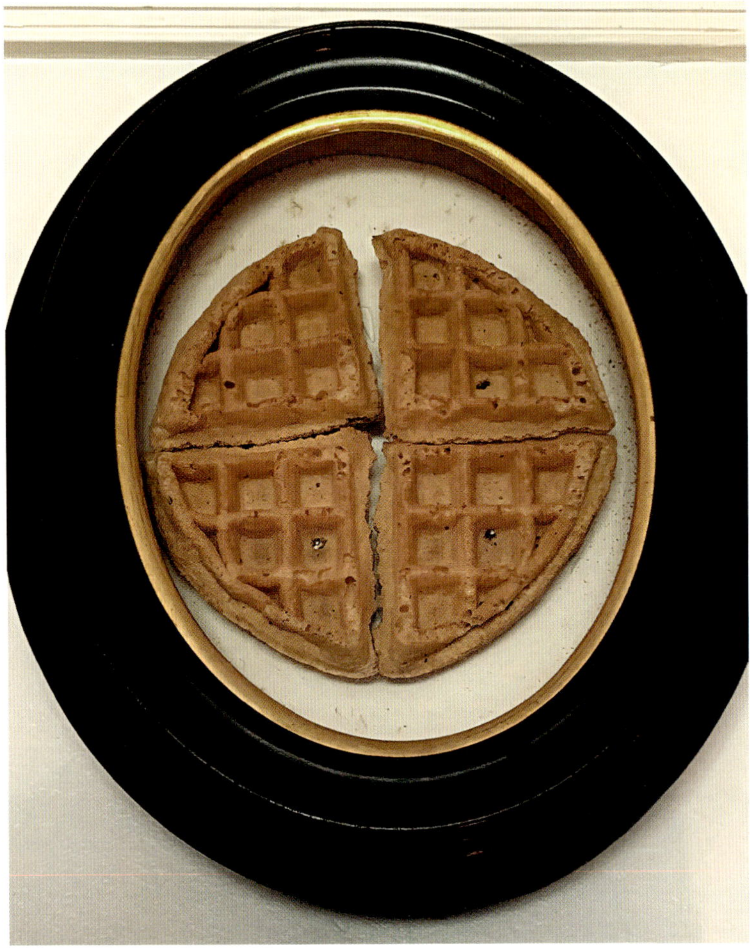

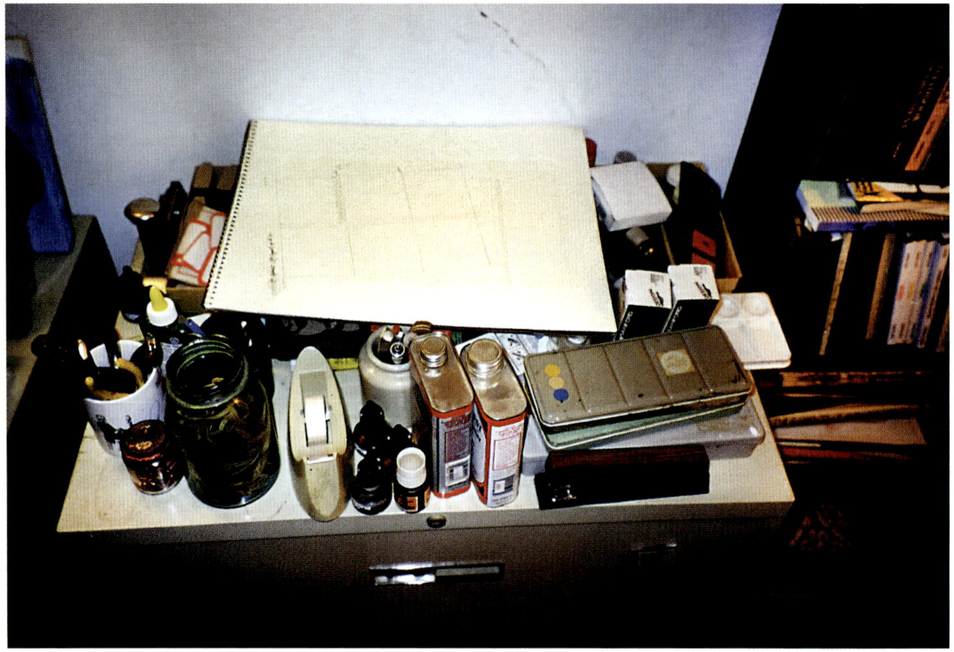

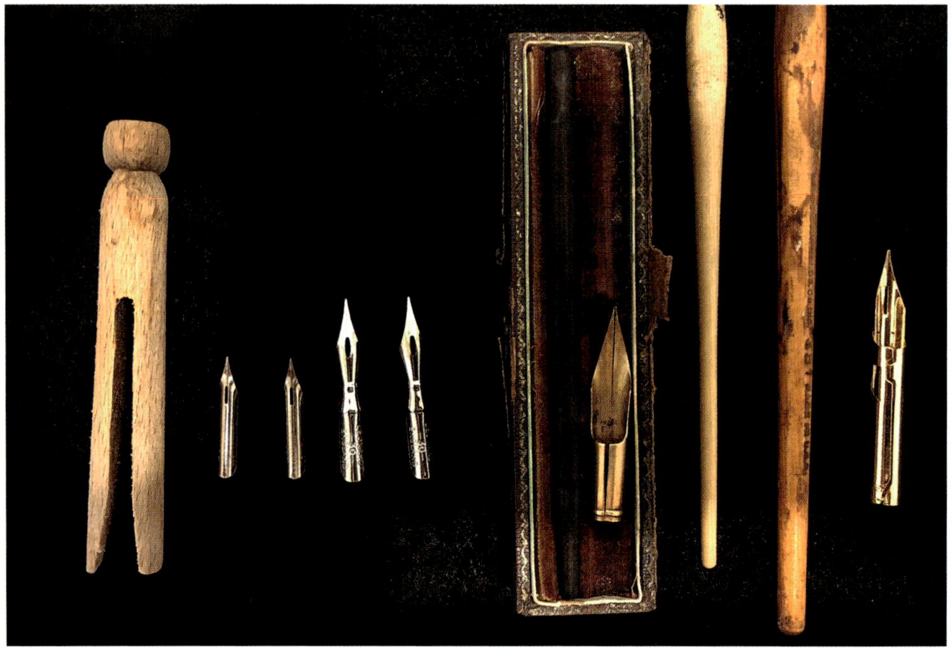

Edward's favorite pen tips were discontinued years ago. He was able to secure enough remaining supply for himself "for many lifetimes."

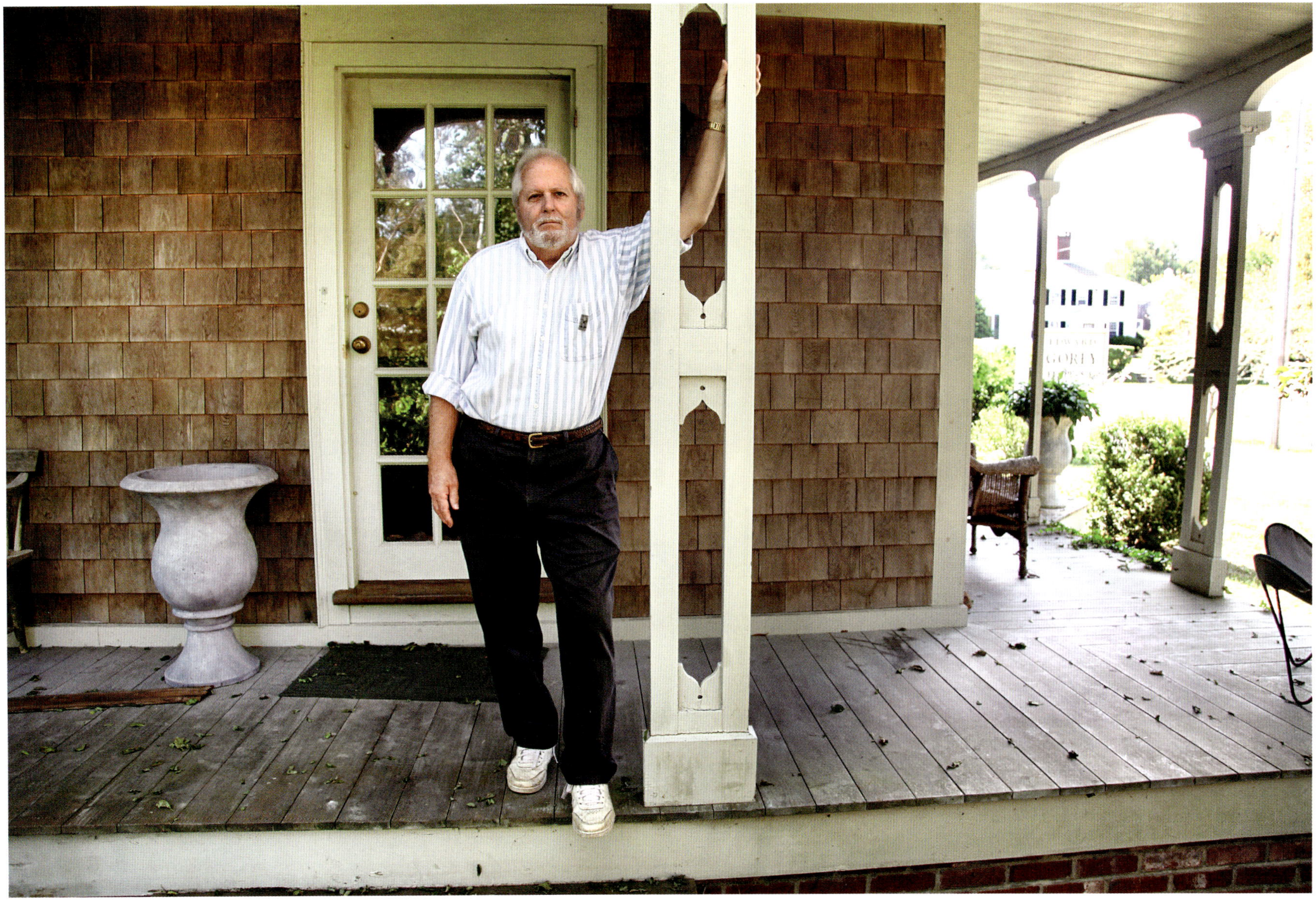

Museum curator (and Edward's friend) Rick Jones stands at the side door used by Gorey during his life.
Today the outdoor spaces are cleaned of the types of sculptures and displays that populated its entryway then.

Some of these objects outside Gorey's side door disappeared in the weeks after his death, such as this welder's mask (*far right*).

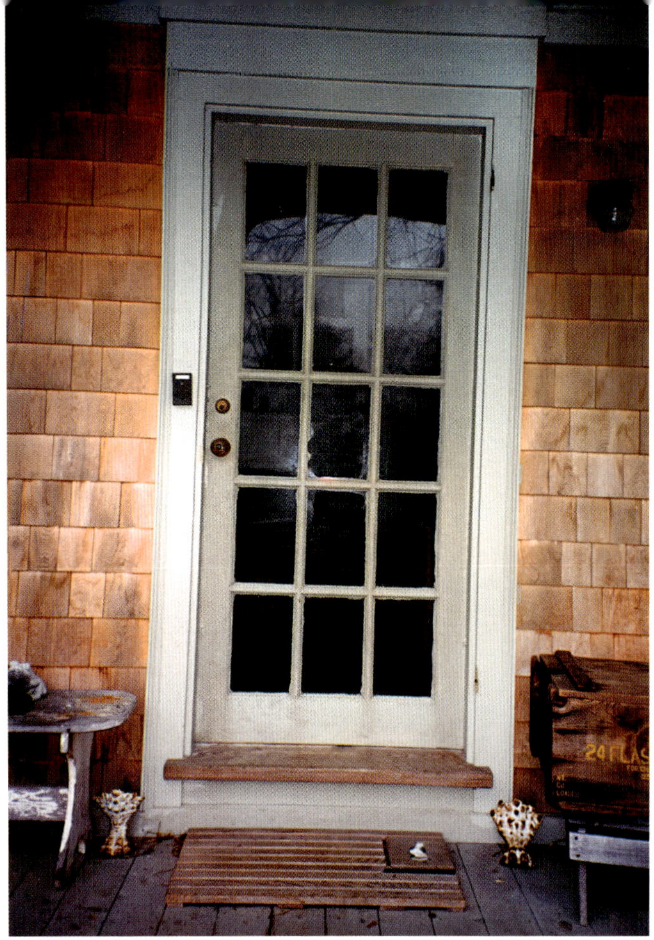

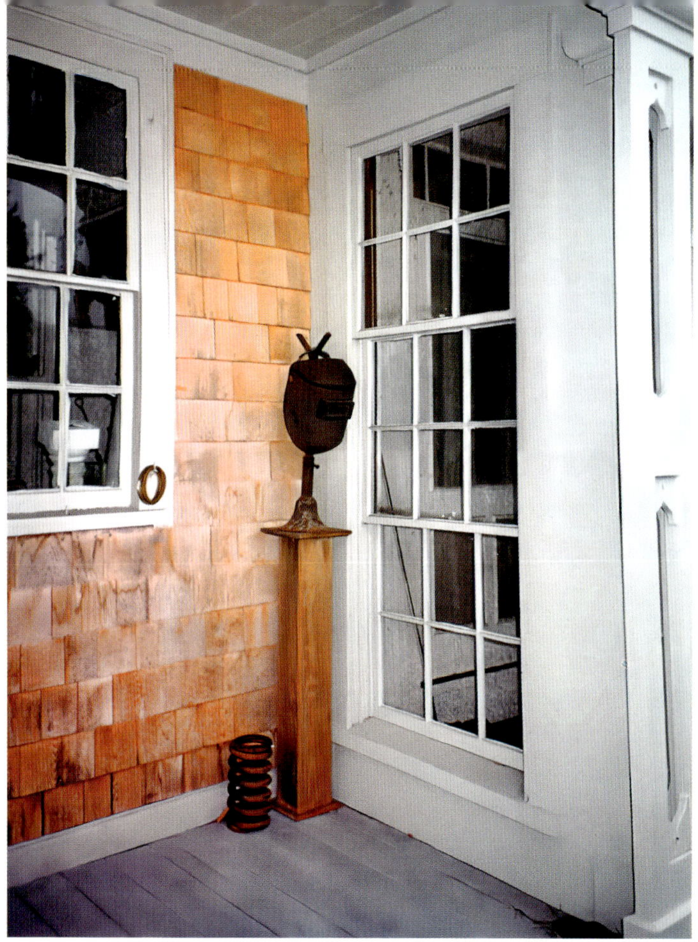

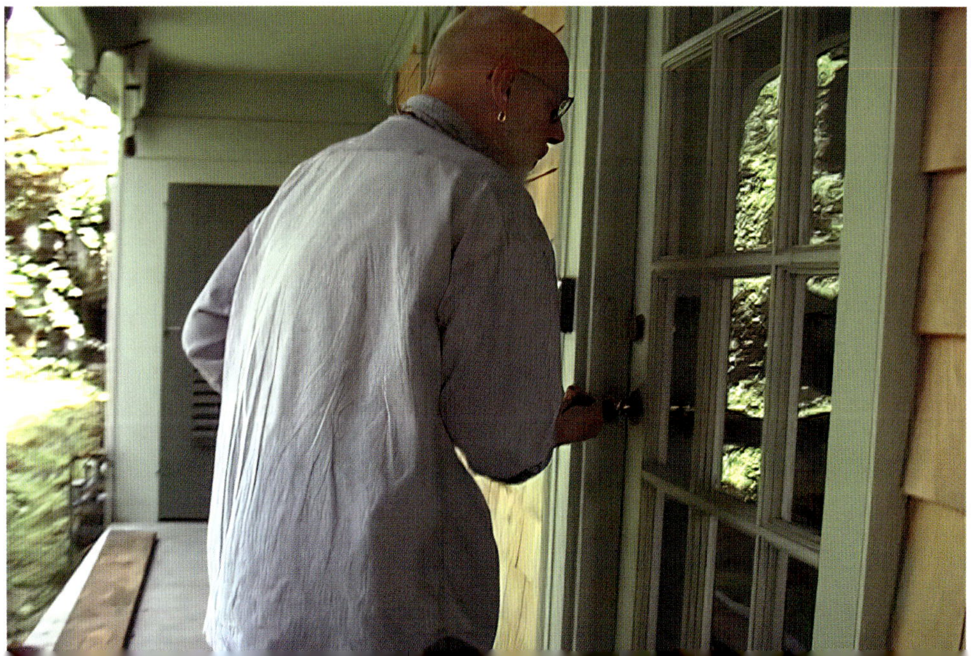

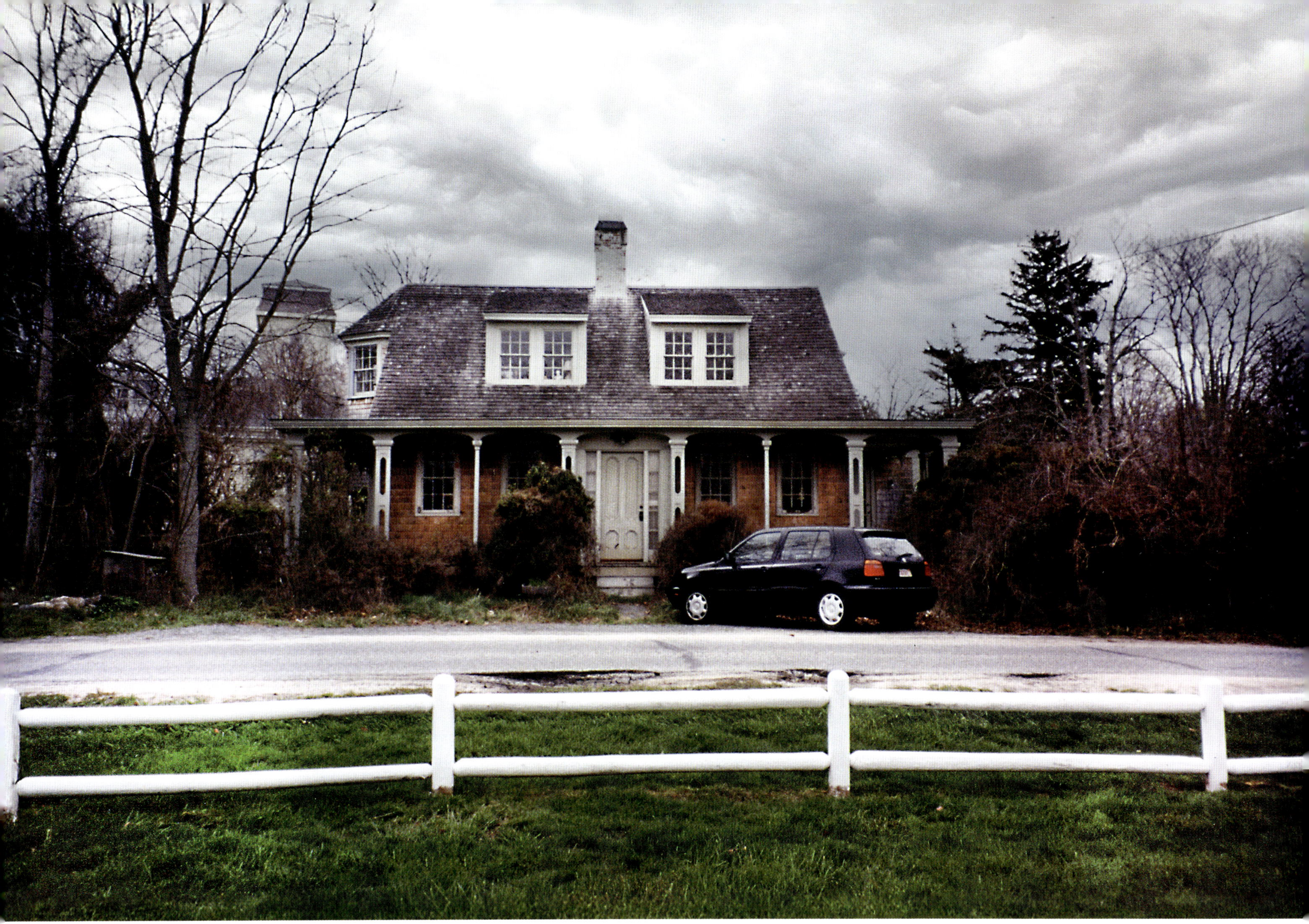

The original state of Edward's house is overgrown and unmowed, a quality not seen today in the more manicured museum grounds.

The overgrown south side of Edward's house, complete with his satellite dish, is now the museum parking lot.

As a favor, Edward had an antique car, owned by his friend Rick Jones, in his smaller barn, along with his bicycle.

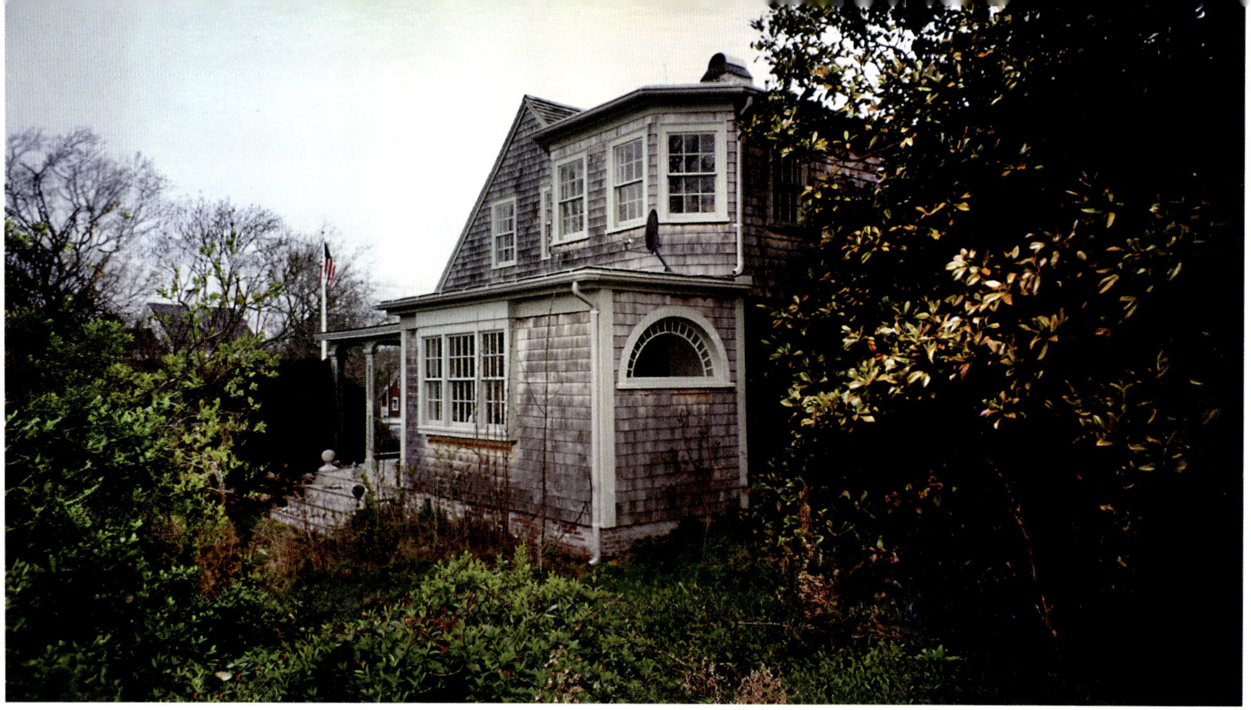

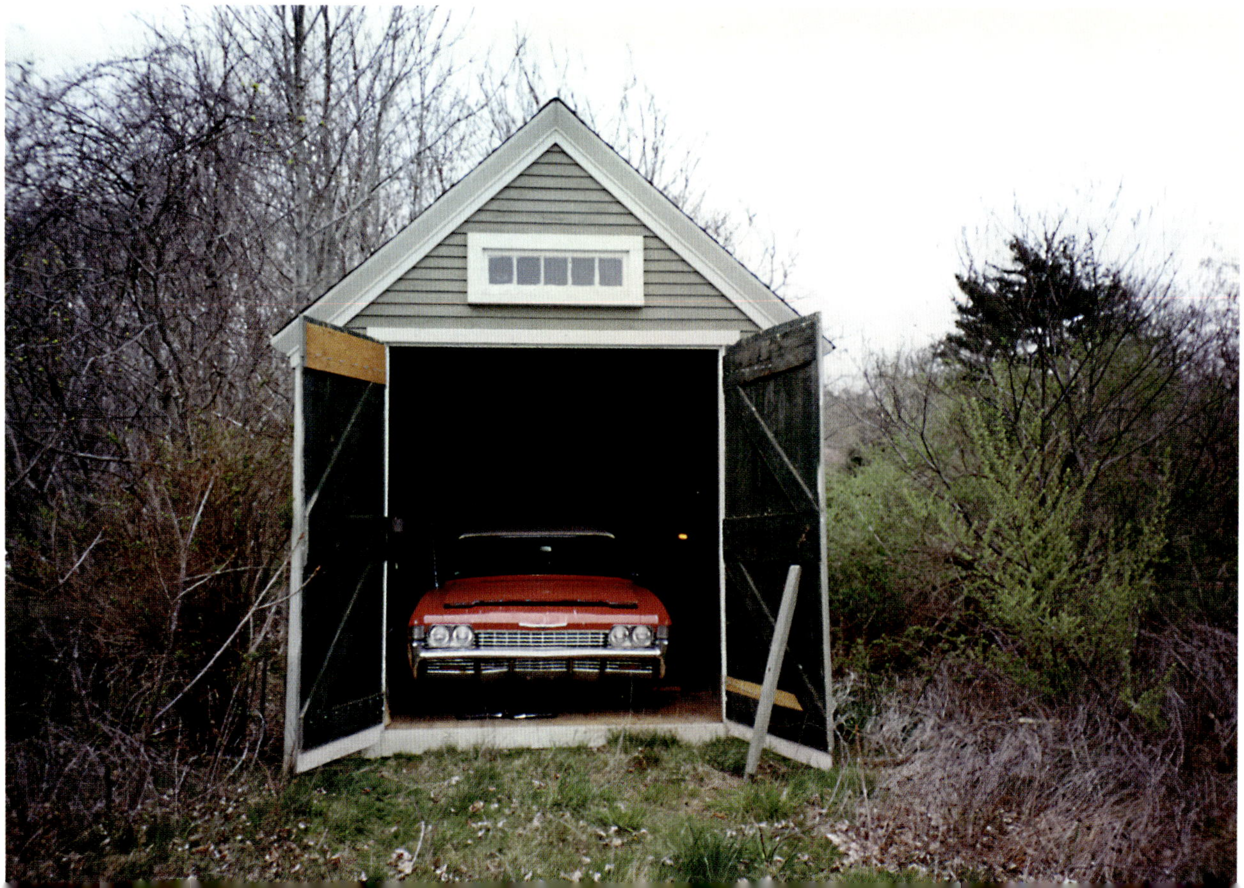

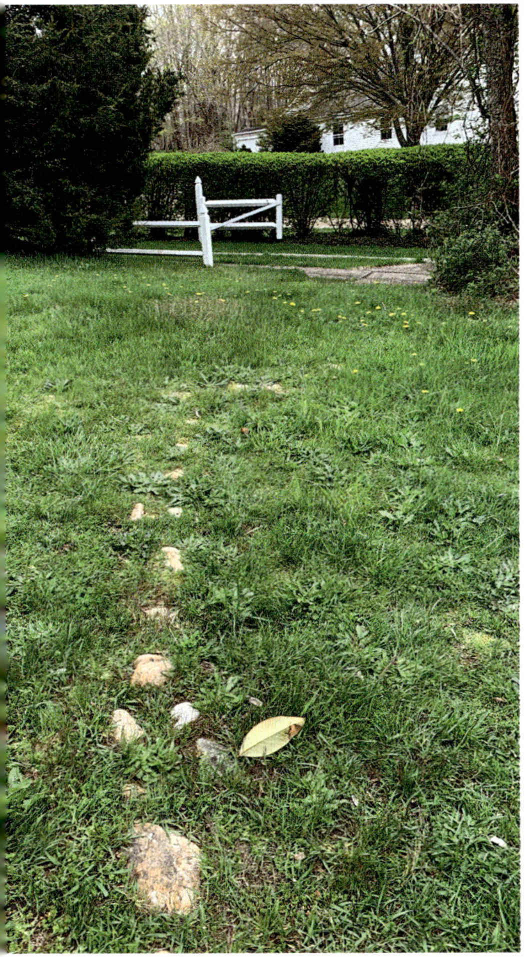

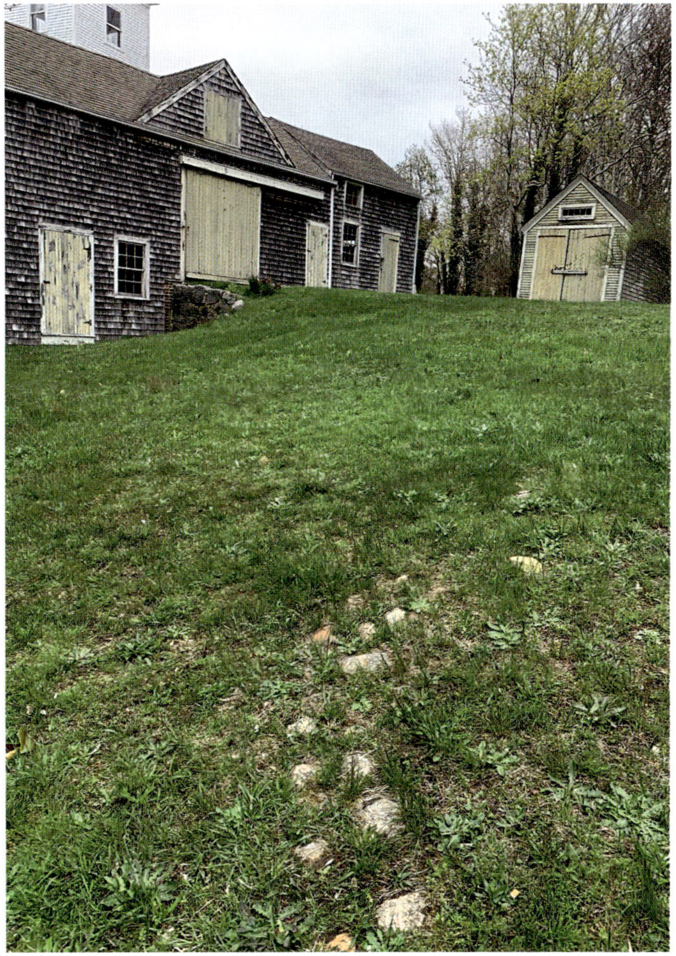

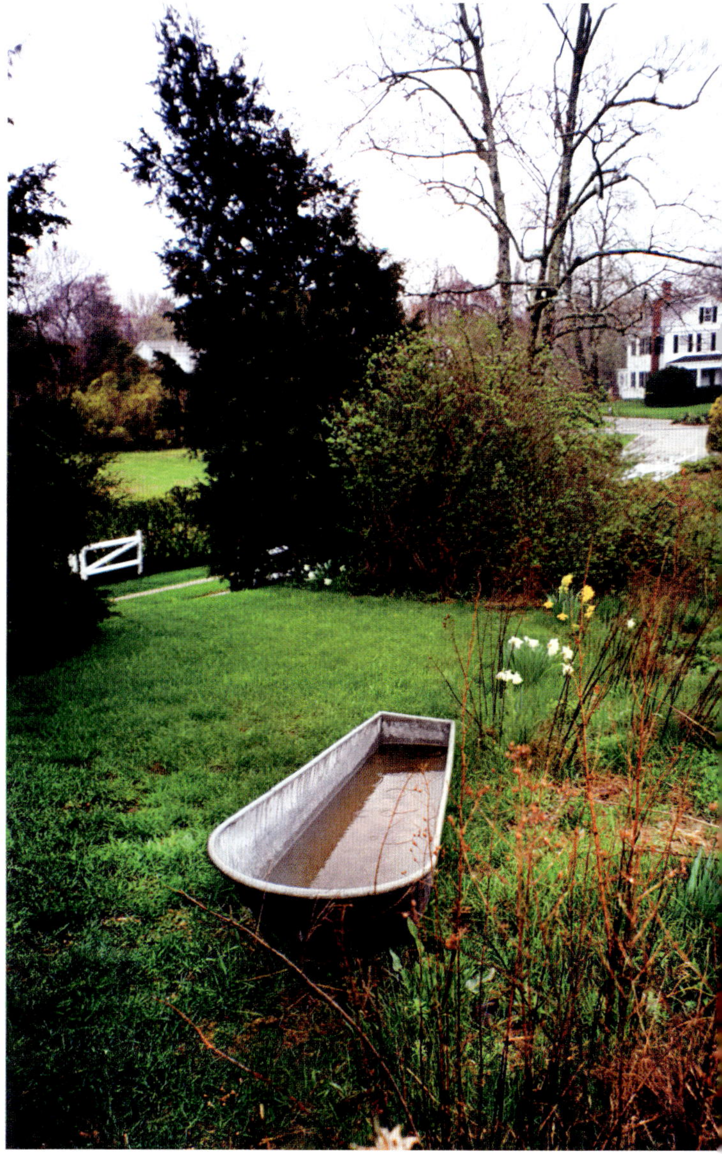

After his death it was found that Edward had left a surprise installation of rocks in a serpentine pattern under his overgrown grass. In many ways his work is continuing to be discovered in just this way.

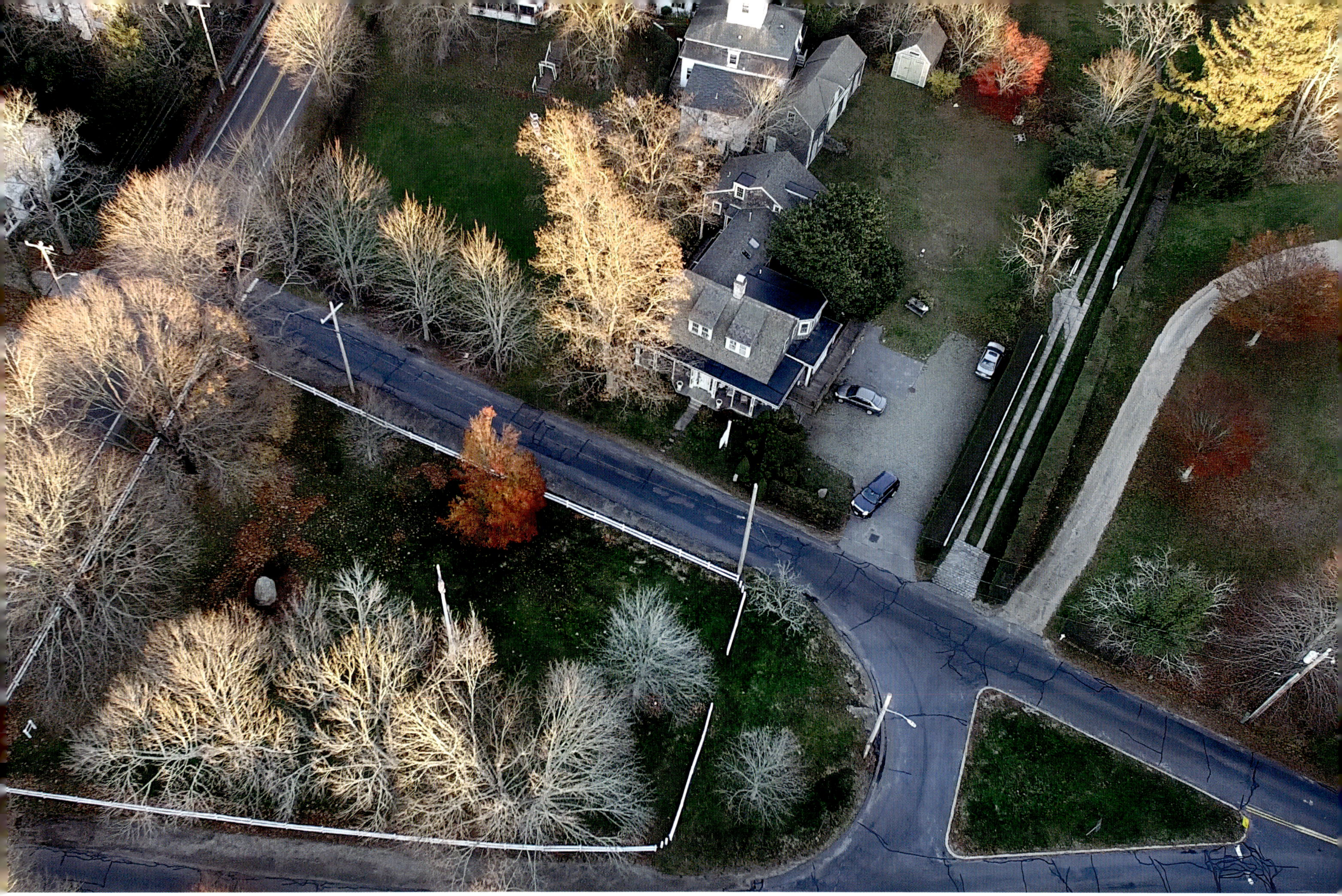

Aerial of Edward's house and property, where the rock serpent can be seen

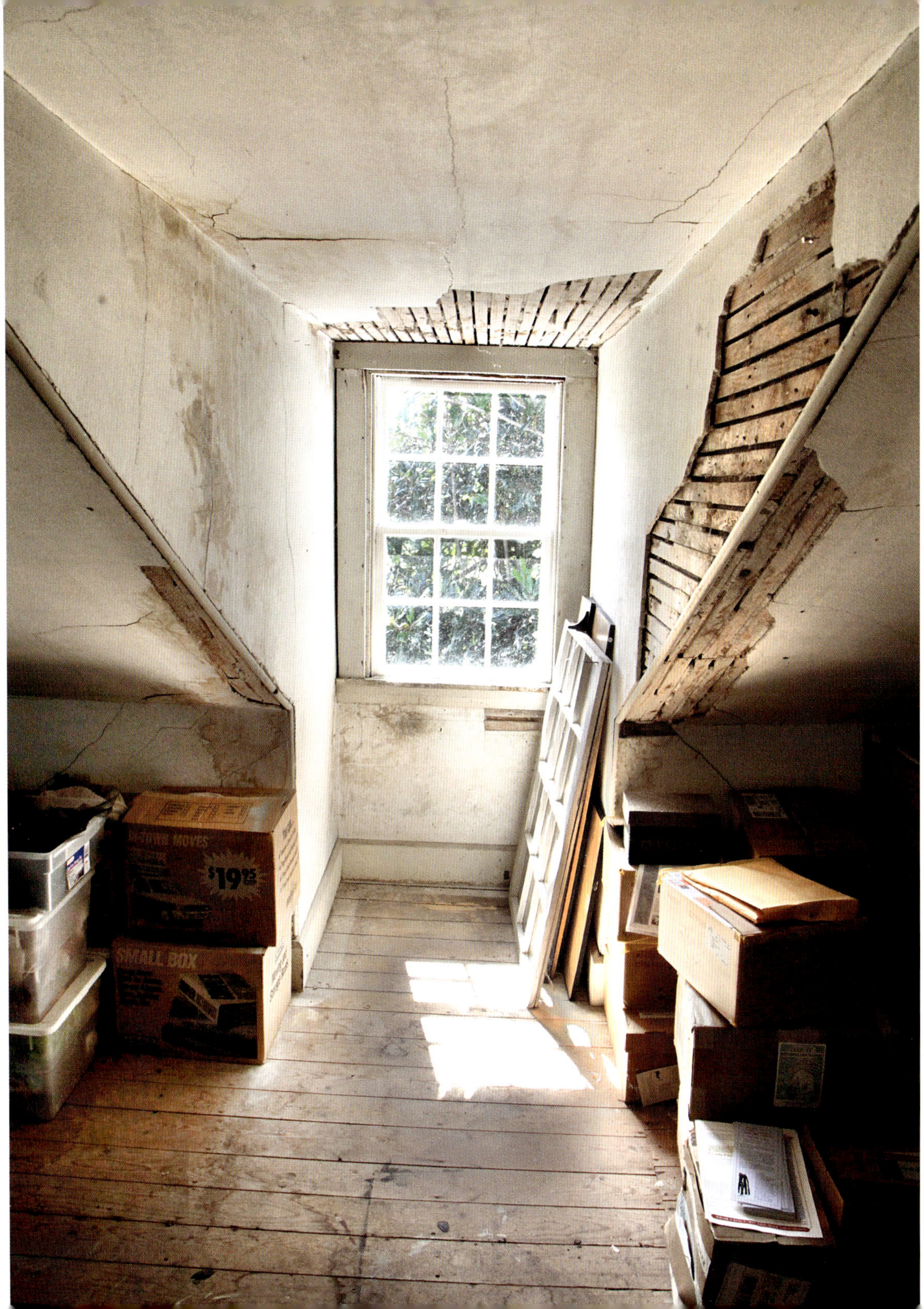

Edward's attic today is maintained in much the same way as it was during his life, including little nooks of figures (*following page*).

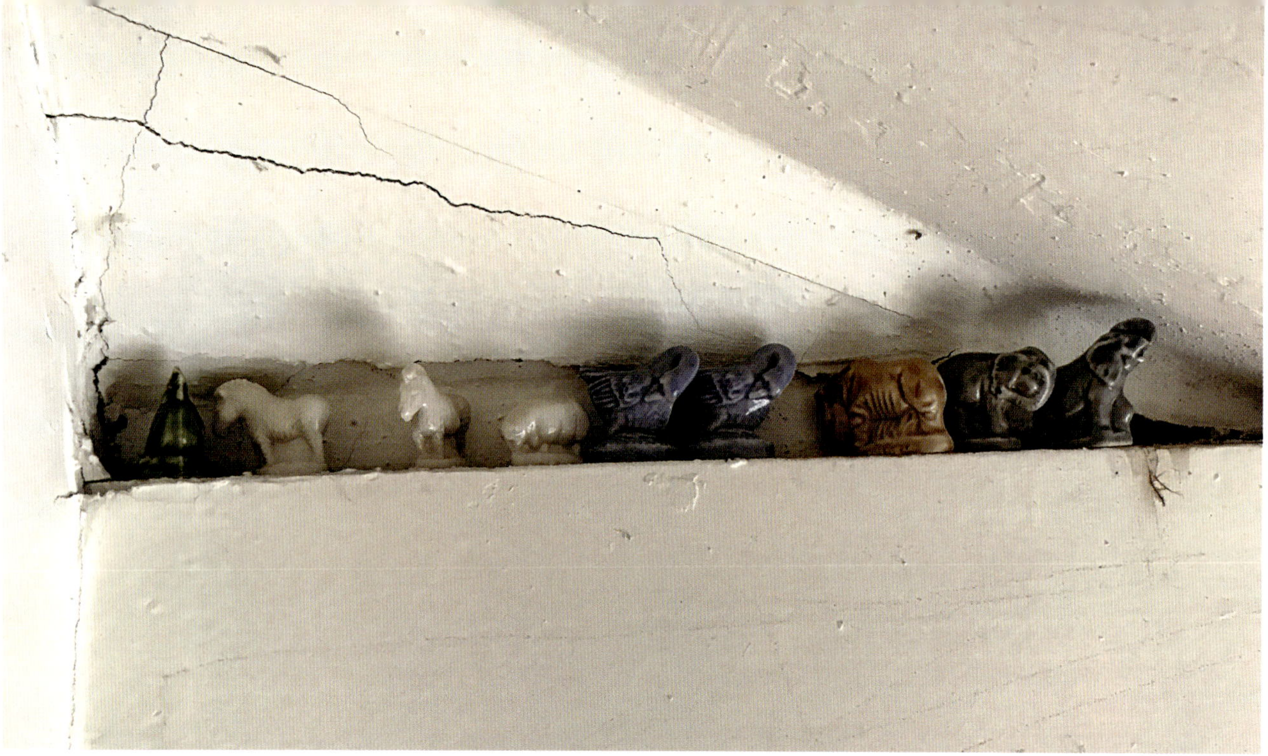

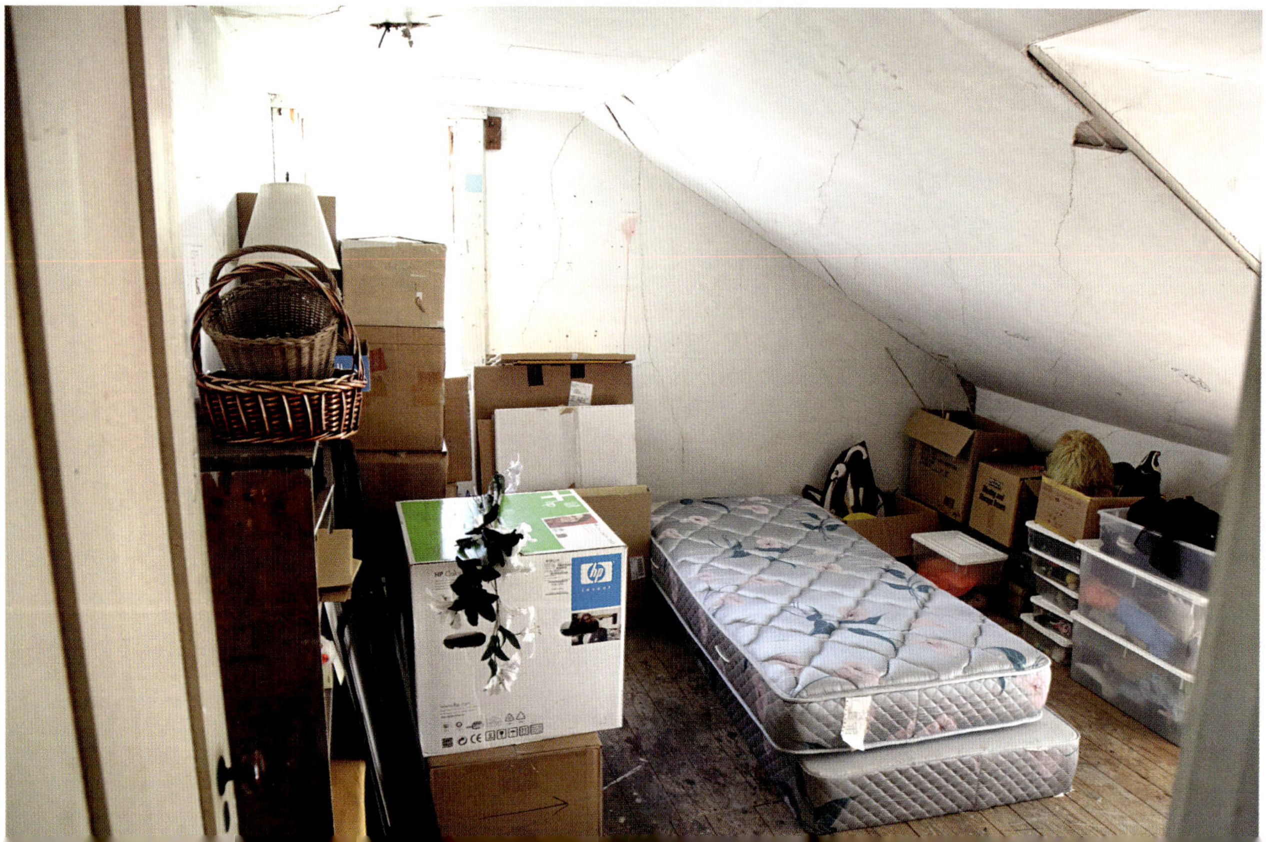

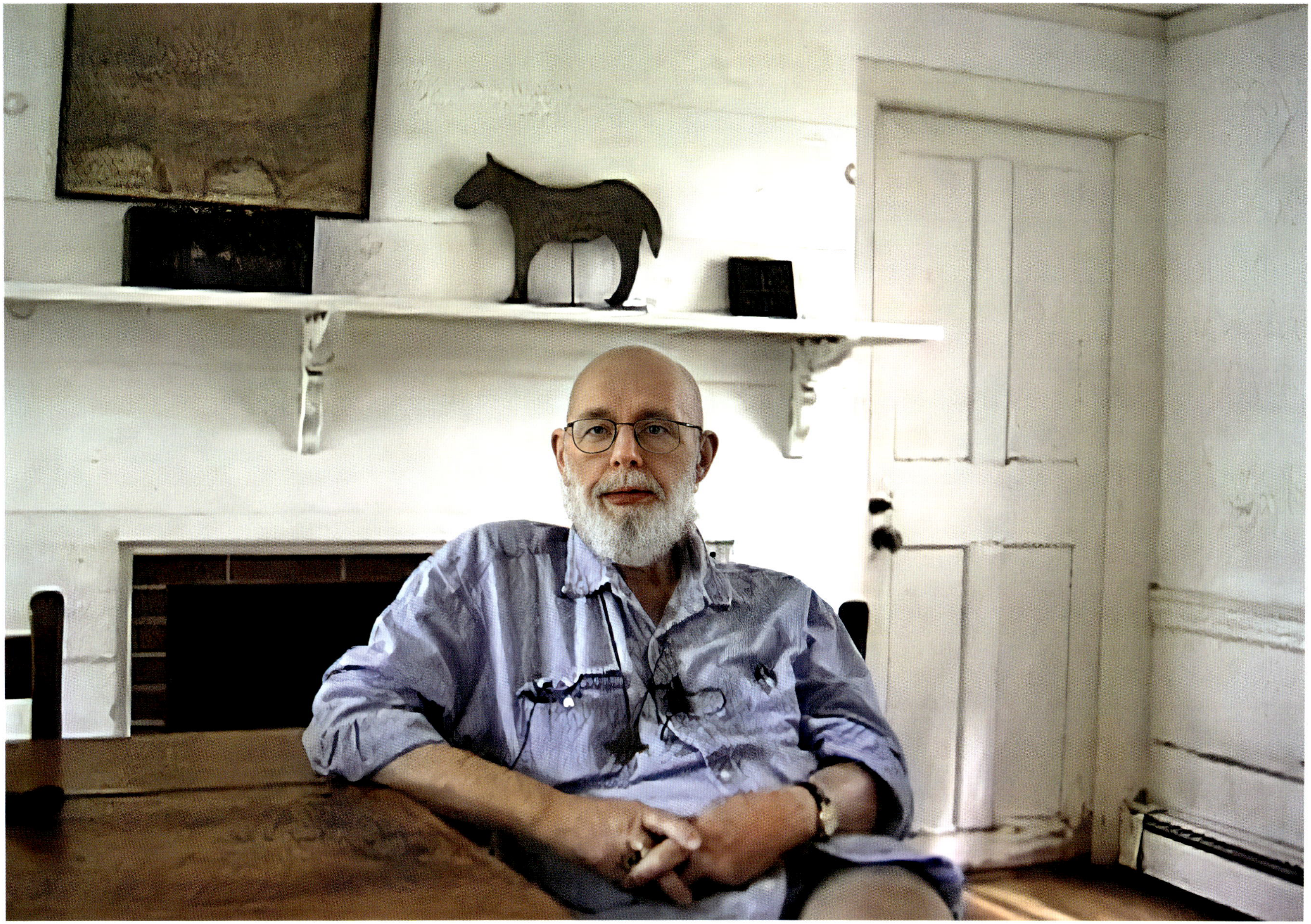

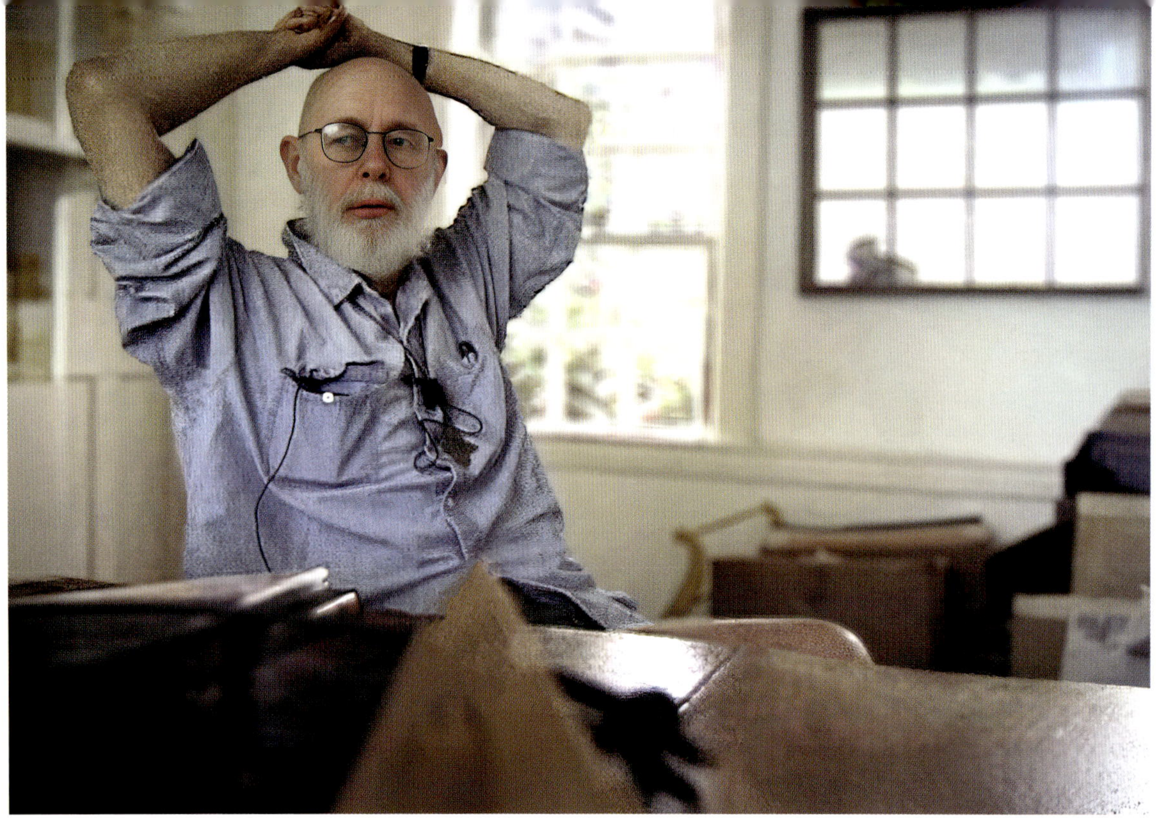

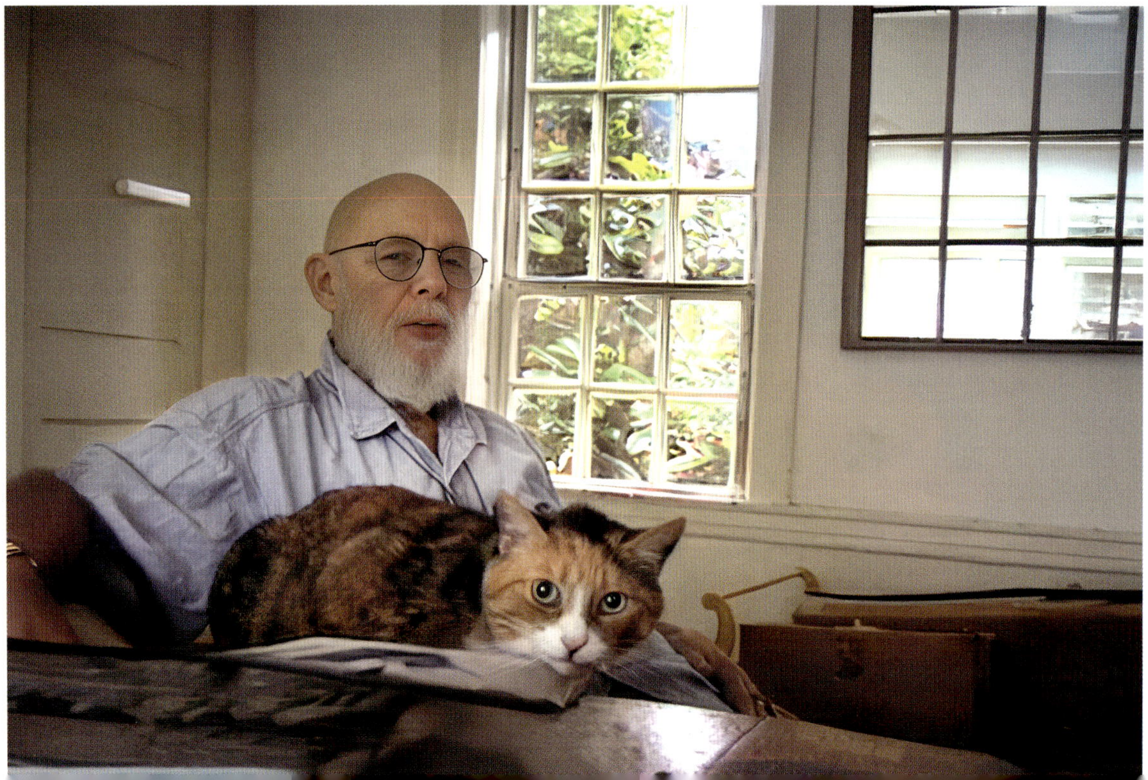

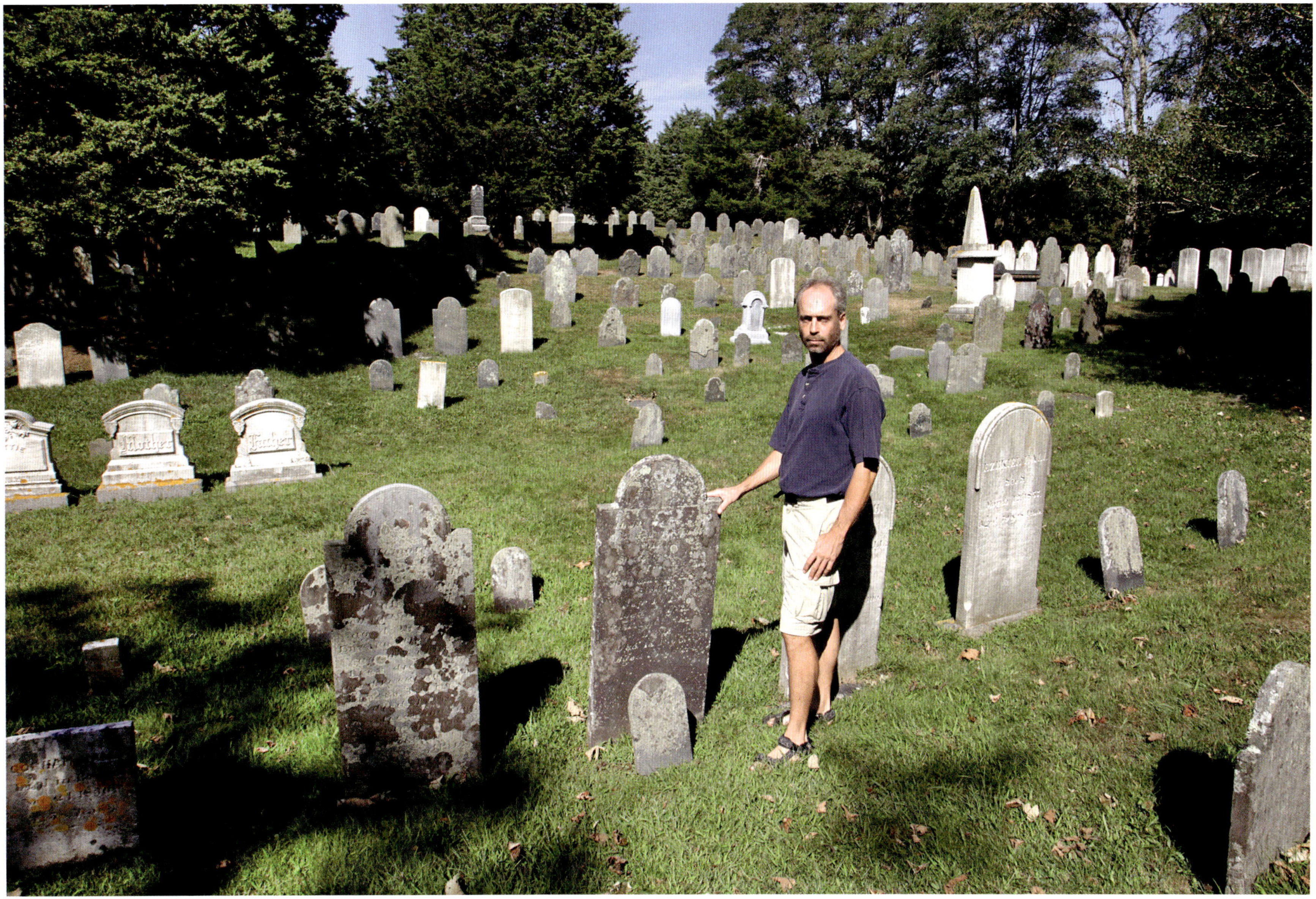

Edward's cousin Ken Morton stands at a Barnstable cemetery visited frequently by Edward. Its colonial mortuary artwork inspired some of his.

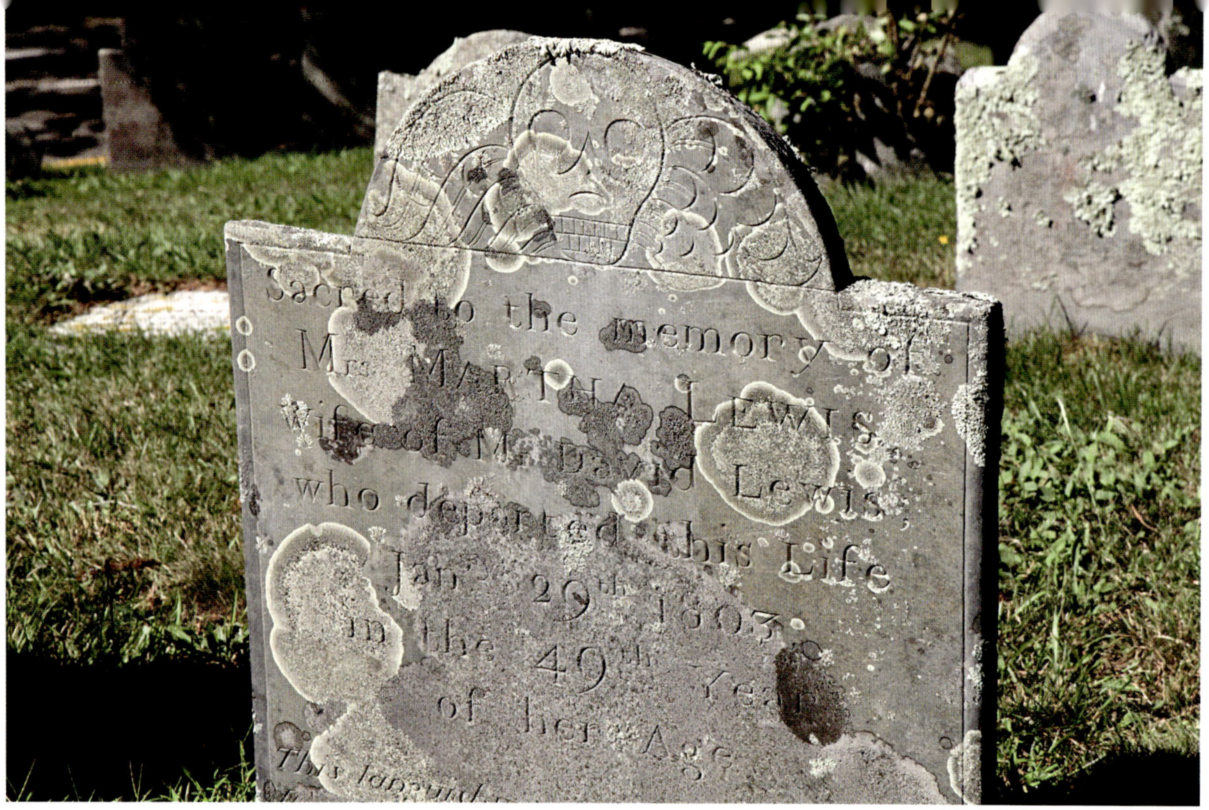
Sacred to the memory of
who departed this Life
Jan 29th 1803
in the 49th Year
of her Age

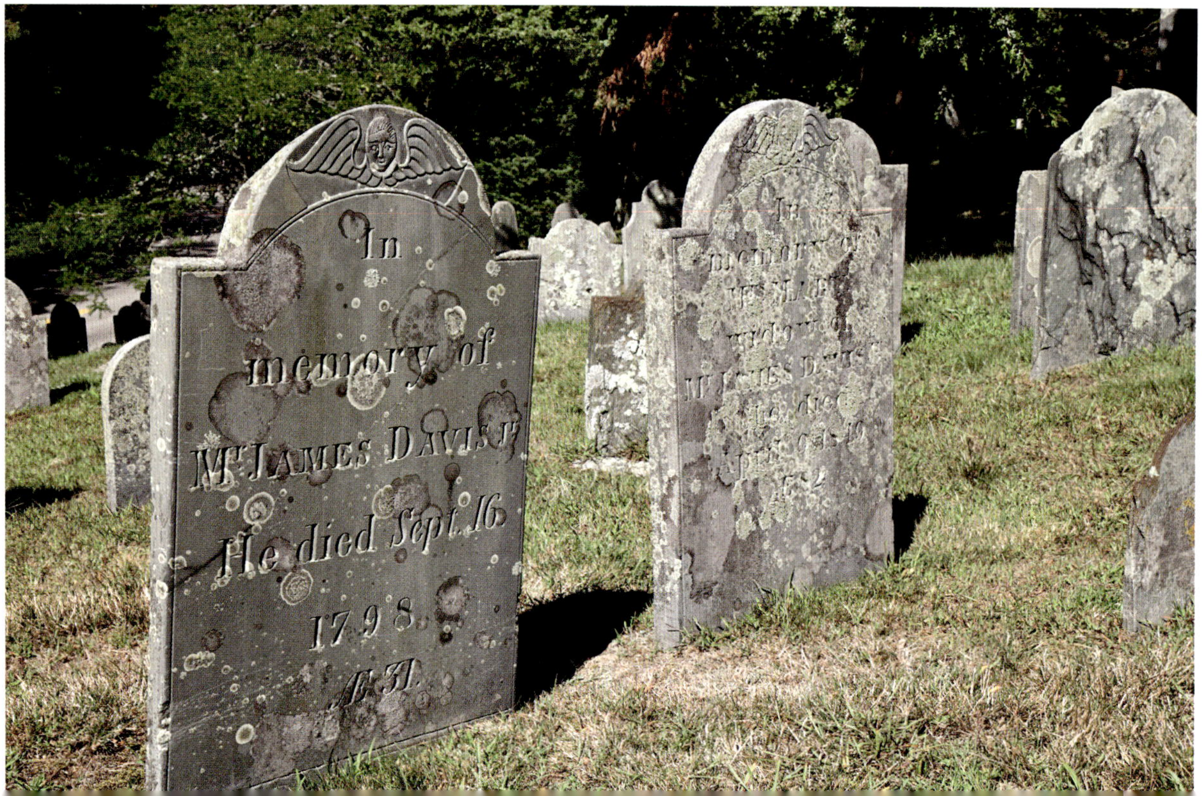
In
memory of
Mr JAMES DAVIS
He died Sept 16
1798

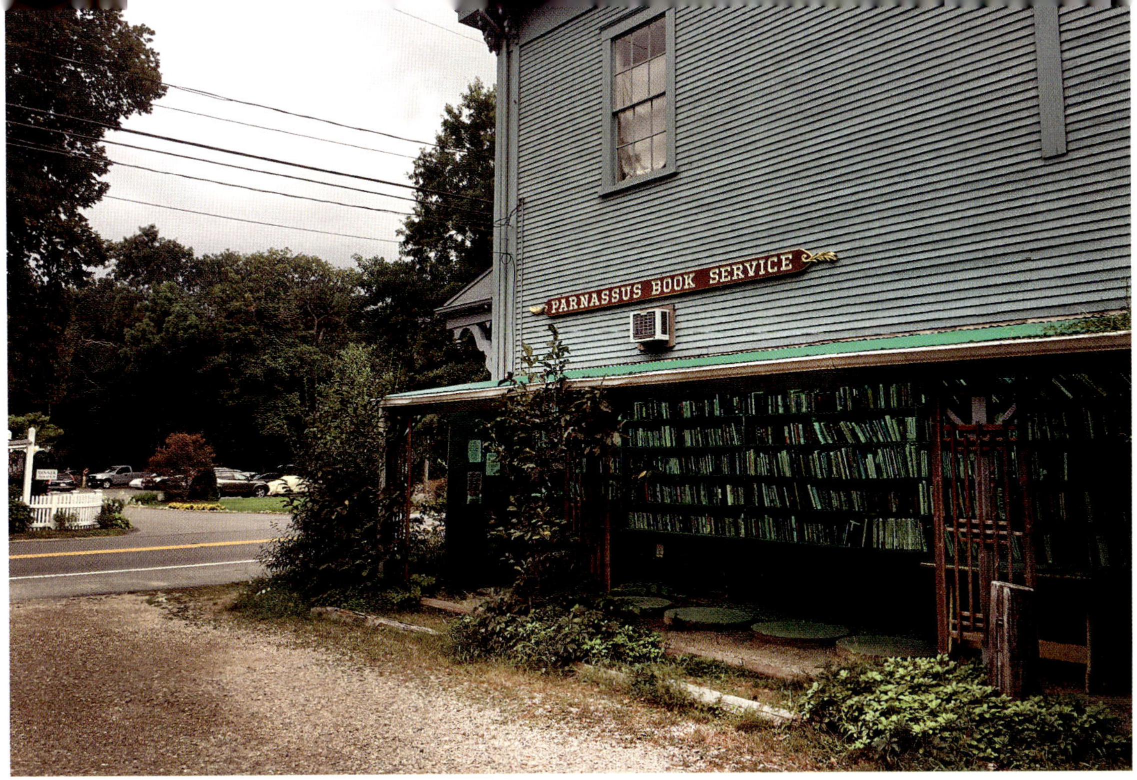

Edward's favorite bookstore, just down the street from him, Parnassus Books. The high stacks and cluttered aisles of used books were quite up his alley. They continue to carry a nice collection of signed works by him.

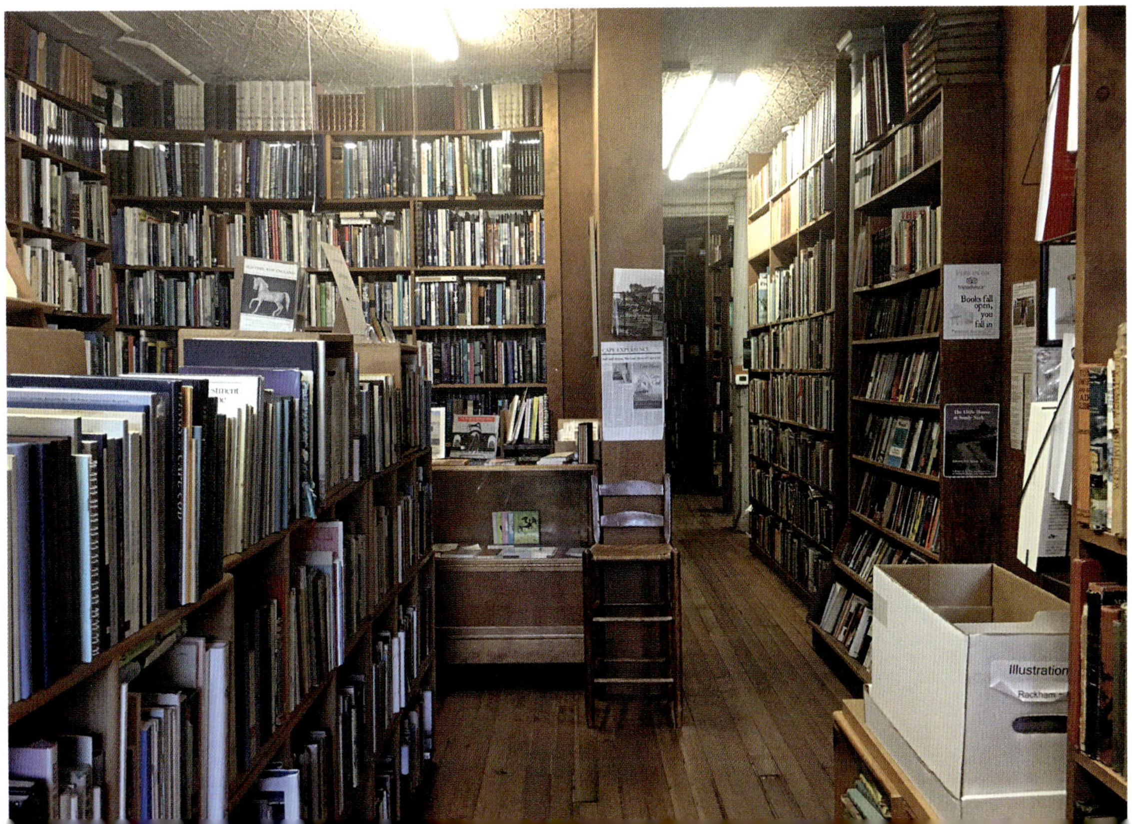

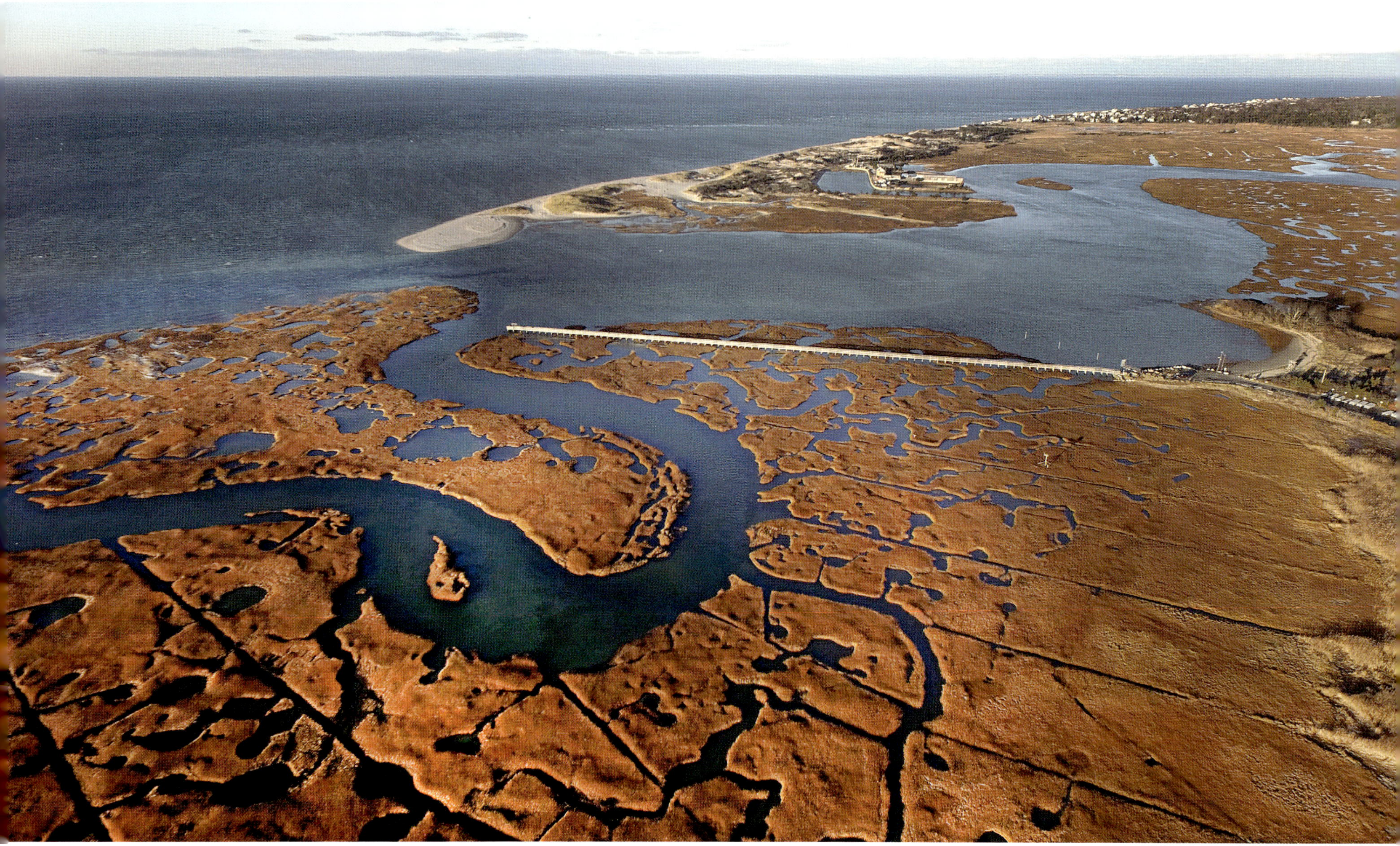

The Bass Hole Boardwalk in Yarmouth (also near his house) was one of Edward's favorite walks. He appreciated the deep orange of the marshes more than the autumn trees.

Edward often wore a World War II US Navy "Dixie Cup" hat stenciled with P. Parsley's name.

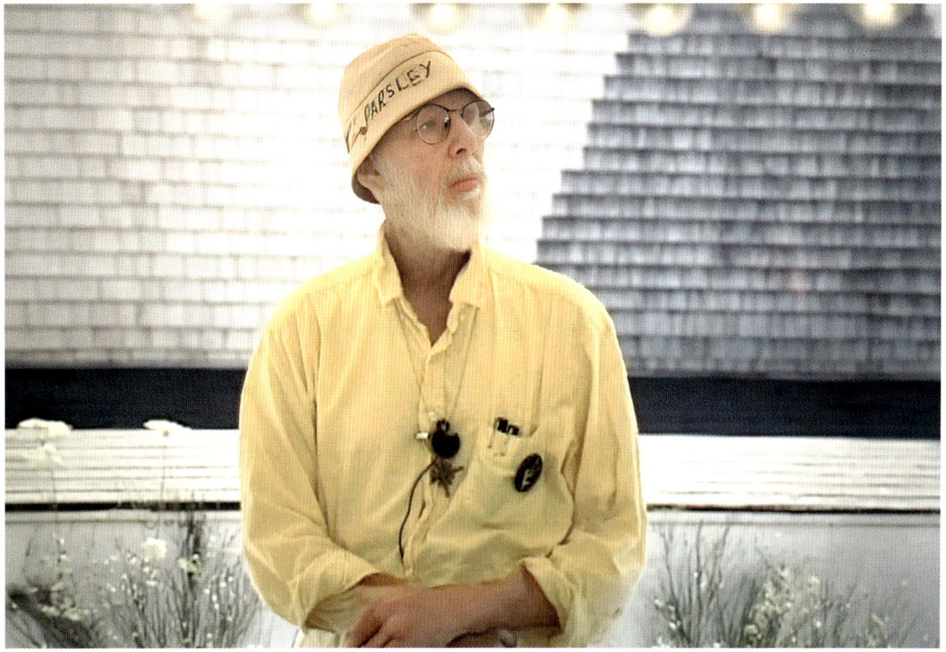

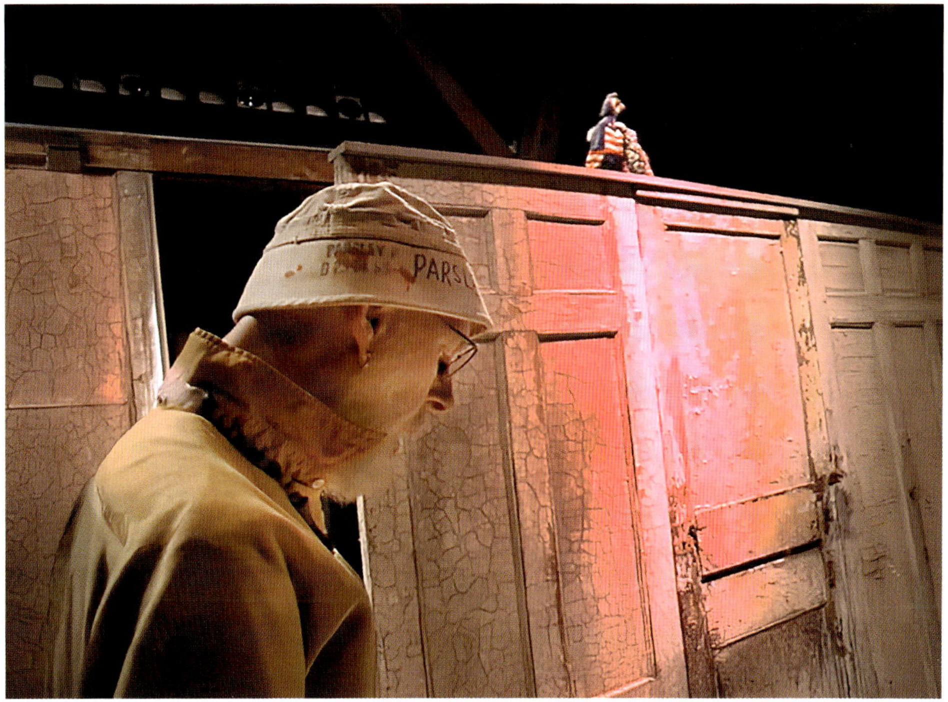

Edward enjoyed participating in his plays as narrator and actor and also hand-creating the props. This "play within a play" was a script in its own right, featuring colored clothespins for actors.

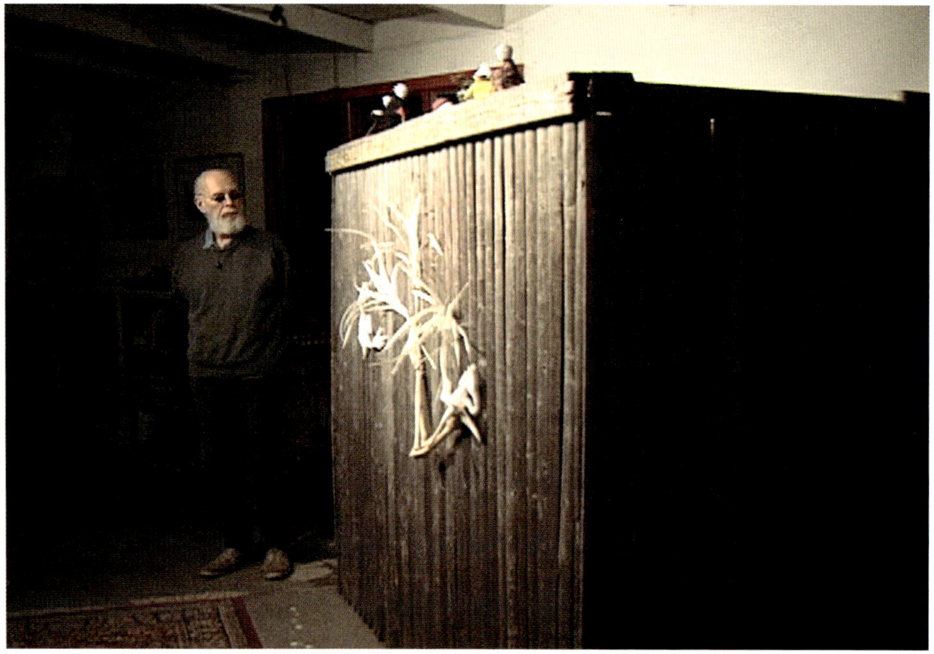

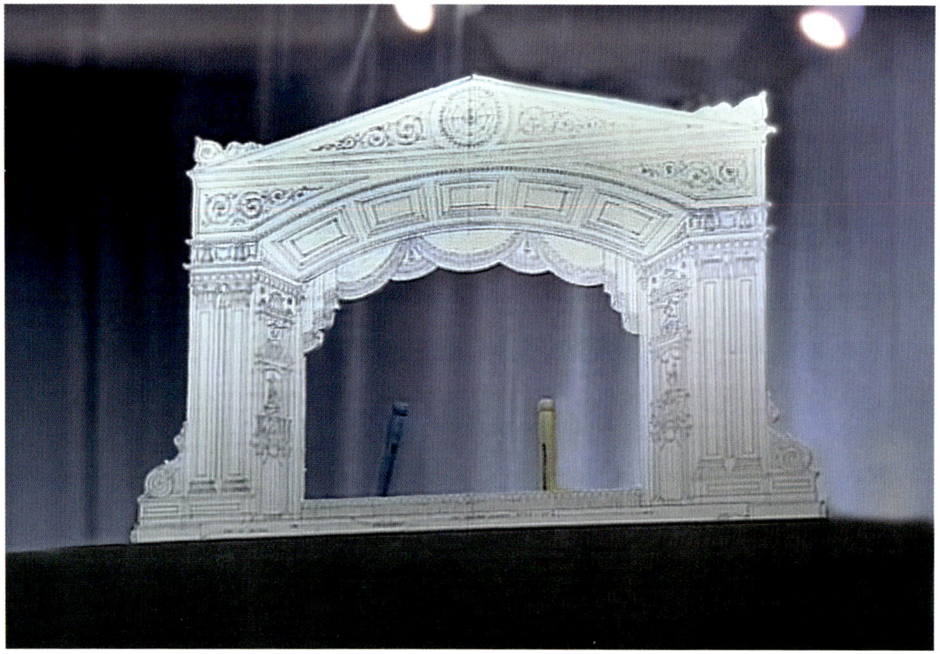

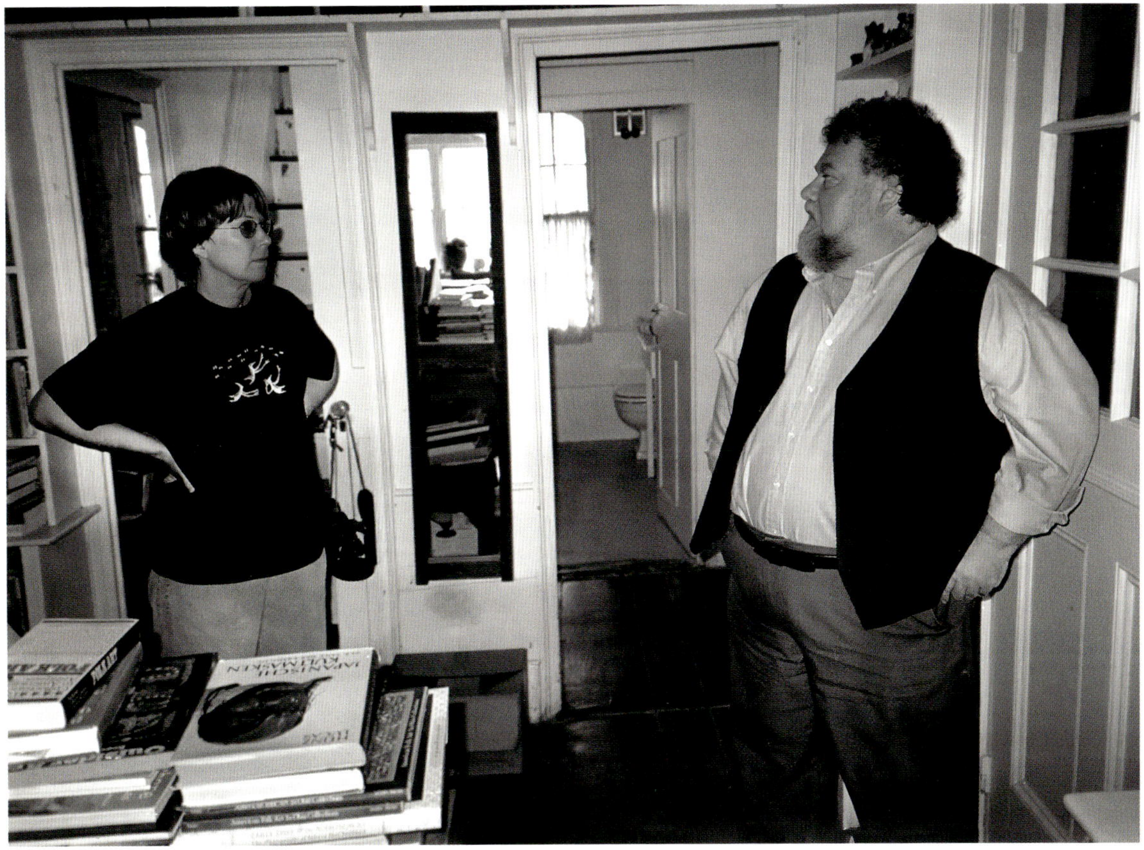

Edward created new works not only with his local theater but with a social network. He often spent time with his actors and cocreators outside the plays. One of his favorite hangouts for a beer was the Kettle Ho in Cotuit.

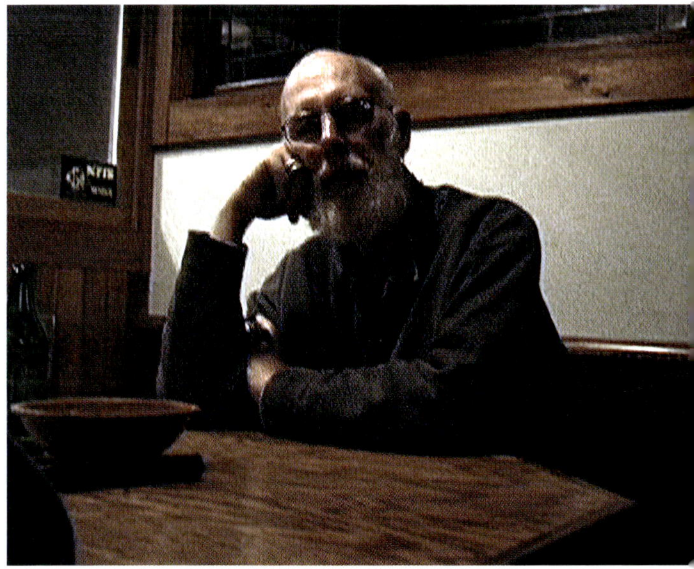

Edward's "Elephant House" on 8 Strawberry Lane was built by Captain Edmond Hawes in 1820. His children improved and remodeled the house. These photos taken in 1860 show the patterned wood supports that are so characteristic today. *Courtesy of Historical Society of Old Yarmouth*

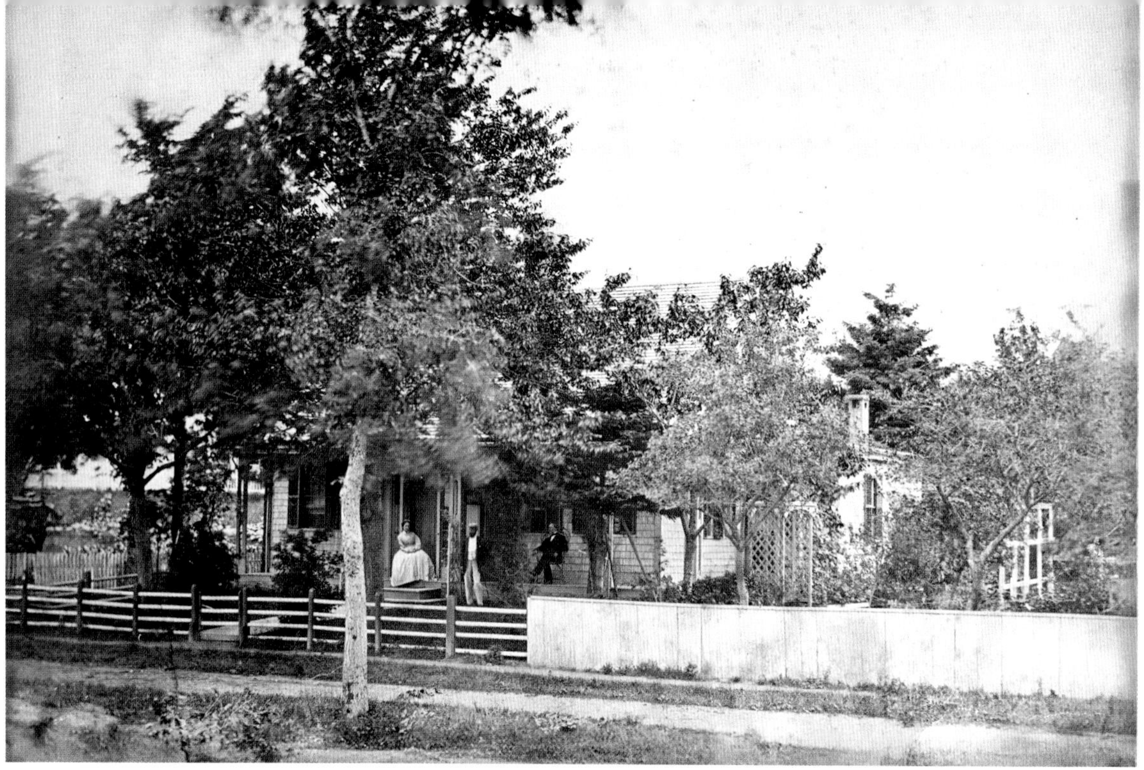

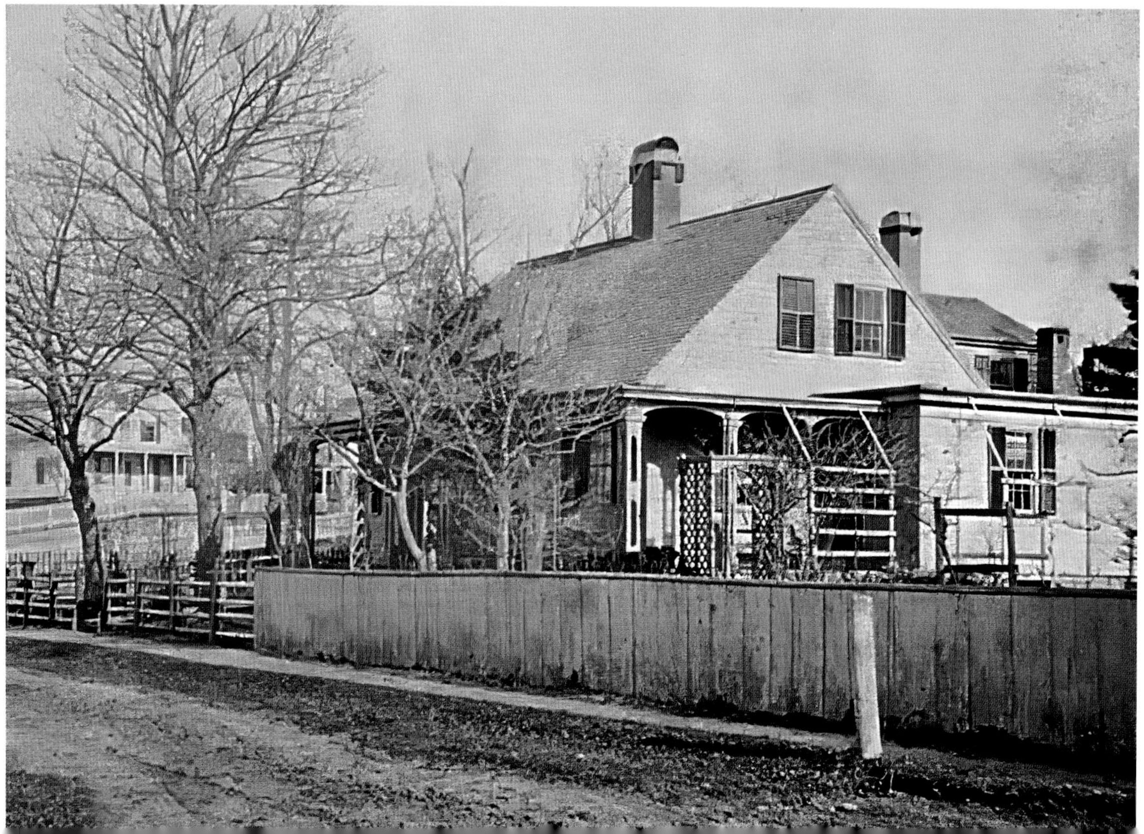

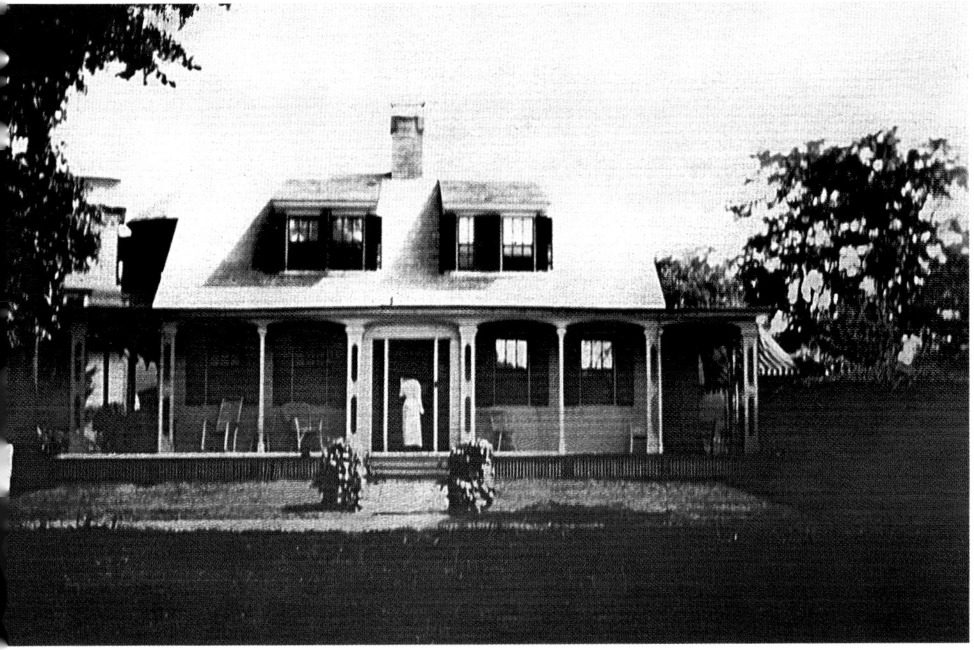

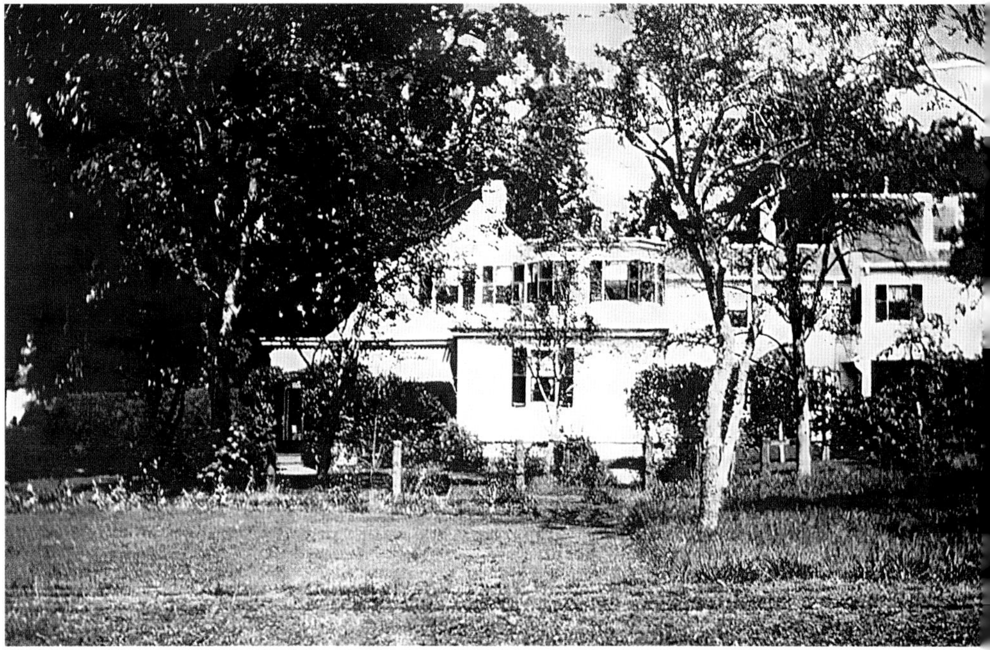

Edward's house in 1912

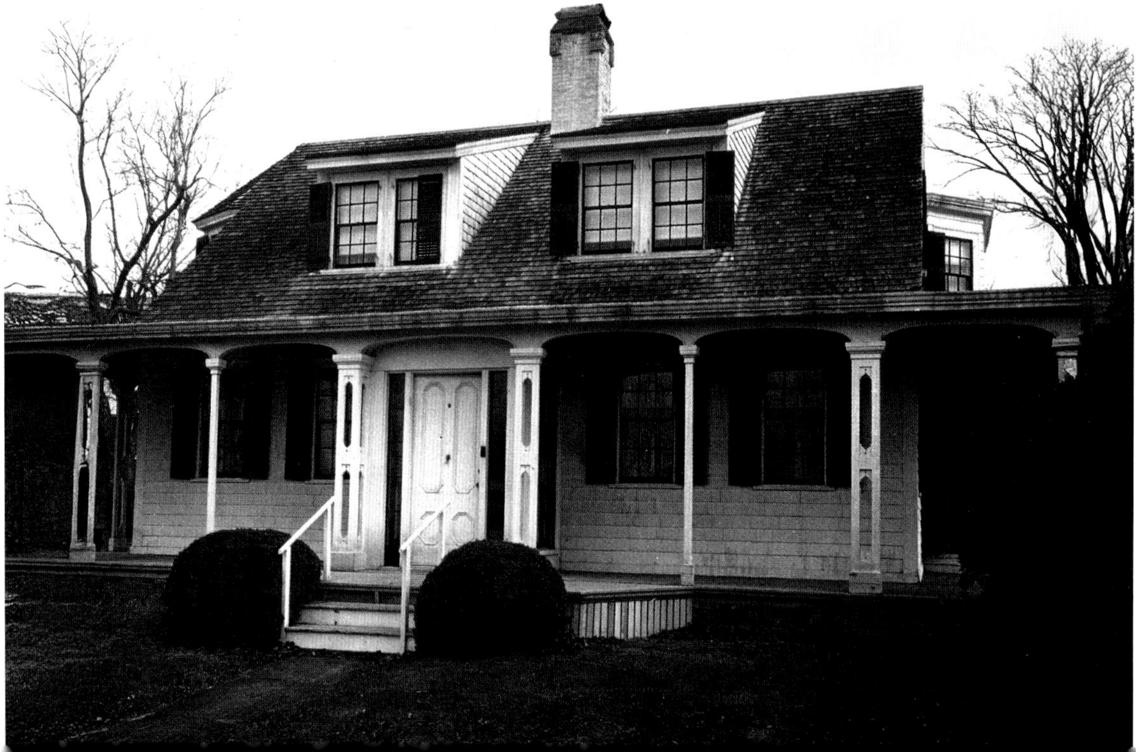

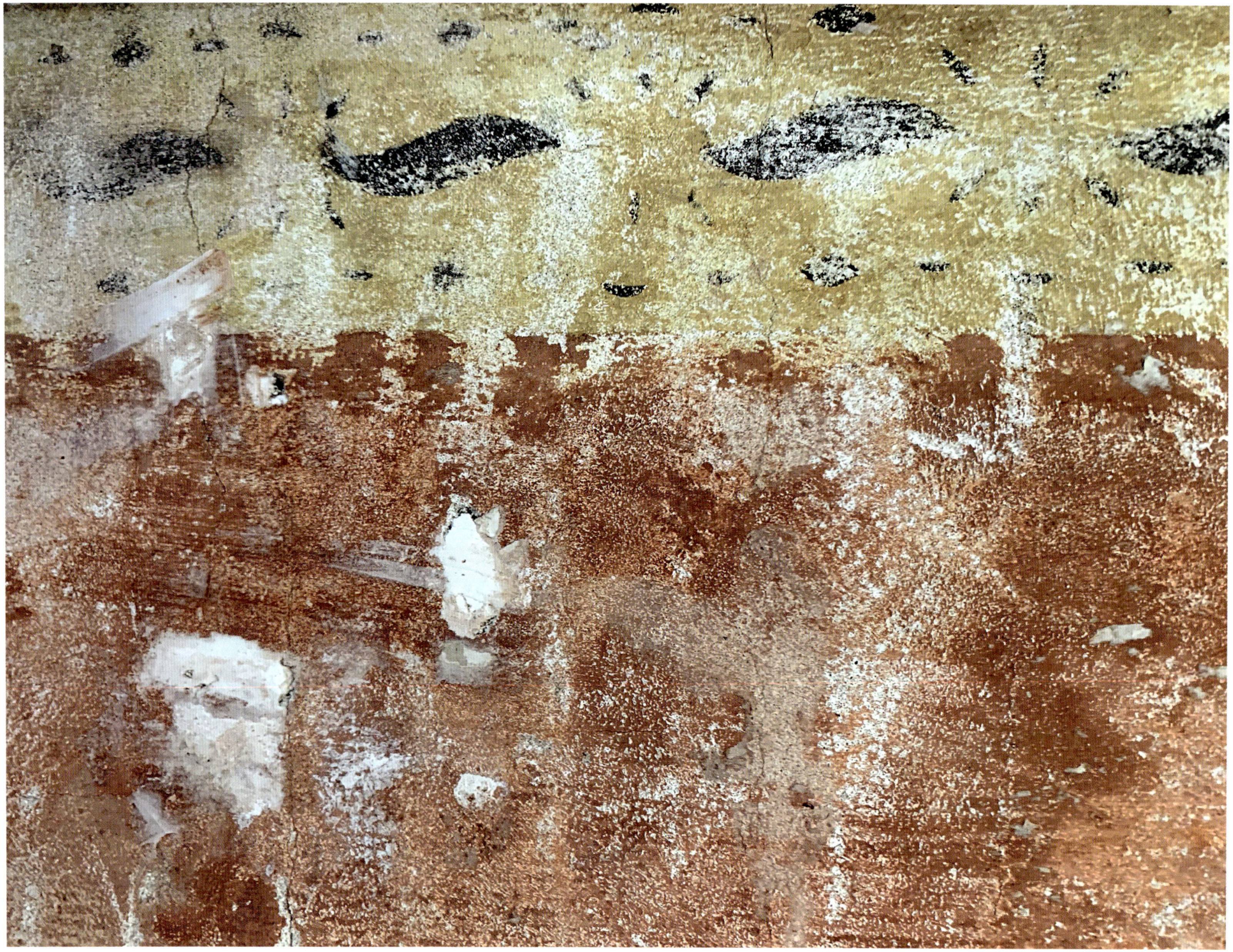

When Edward pulled wallpaper down in his main living room, he discovered the original stenciling from 1820 underneath.

Edward's house at 8 Strawberry Lane, Yarmouth, at night

Mark Romanek Interview

DECEMBER 6, 2002

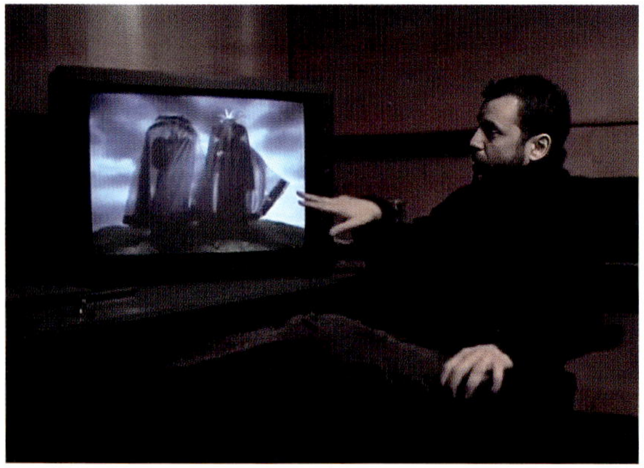

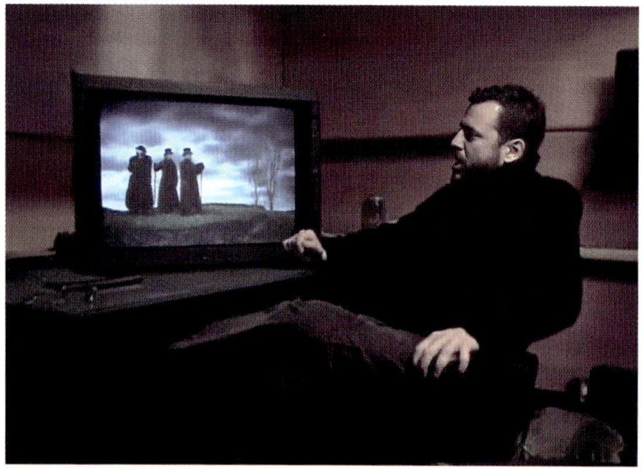

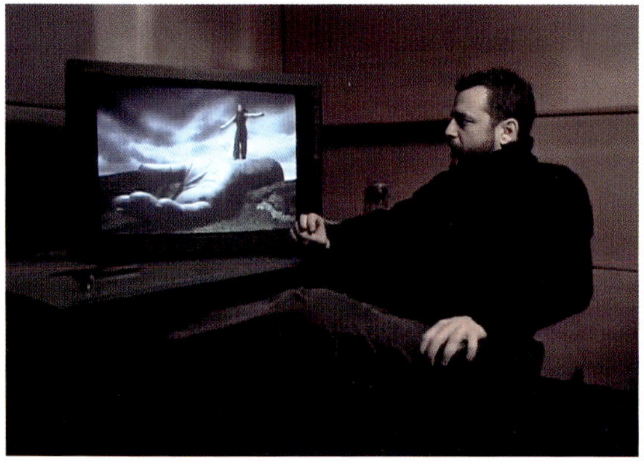

Mark Romanek is most known for directing music videos for Madonna, Johnny Cash, and Michael Jackson and for the feature film *One Hour Photo* with Robin Williams. He was inspired by Edward Gorey's work for the music video of the Nine Inch Nails' song "The Perfect Drug." Released in 1997, the music video incorporates familiar Gorey elements like pale, glum characters in Edwardian costumes and oversized urns.

Jenn Pitman and Helen Chough: Hi, Mark, thanks so much for meeting with us. We'll just play the tape and maybe you can go through it in real time for us. [*The Nine Inch Nails music video for "The Perfect Drug" begins to play on a monitor.*]

Mark Romanek: Some of this is Gorey and some of it is just Goreyesque. That urn is strictly Gorey; it's actually his urn. Generally this is all shot sort of in Gorey's world. That other urn is right out of a Gorey image. The fact that a little girl's legs were sort of cut off but there's no upper torsos, completely Gorey idea in terms of framing, although it's not exactly from a specific image.

This landscape with those type of clouds and those costumes are lifted straight from Gorey. Also this obelisk, we broke the obelisk because it's a square format, it just seemed like it would fit in better. Those veils and those hats again were just taken from a Gorey image and made real.

We found this giant hand as a prop in a prop house. There's a giant hand, I think, pointing down in one of Gorey's images, but this particular prop worked better just lying on the ground.

The image of the vulture is taken from an old daguerreotype, so there are also a mix of Victorian images. This giant kind of abstract painting here is a Gorey image with the little bench in front of it. I love the way the light catches the guilt frame there.

This kind of contraption behind Trent is again taken from an old Victorian photograph. This topiary here is obviously lifted straight out of a Gorey book image.

In the video overall there's a certain influence of Stanley Kubrick's *The Shining*. I always wanted to have someone singing with condensation coming out of their mouth, just because it's a way to see the singing and it seemed to suit this project. There is sort of a narrative to this, but it's completely fractured, not unlike a Gorey story. It doesn't all have to really make sense and I don't know all the details, but you don't know whether he killed this little girl or he loved this little girl, or whether the girl is a relation of some kind, so, there's an innocence to it or it could be something more perverse.

This idea of the absinthe is the connecting piece between the Old World and the New World. He's singing about a perfect drug, and I think he is really in fact singing about love. Making that drug absinthe is the thing that allows me to connect to that Gorey sort of late-nineteenth-century or early twentieth-century Victorian kind of universe. This is sort of the absinthe nightmare, during the percussion solo. I thought it really lent itself to lightning flashes, so we made it green lightning like it's a bad absinthe trip. In each setup, we did kind of a lightning thing.

This sort of rooftop thing, though, I think came from being really influenced by *Mary Poppins* when I was a kid. I just like *Mary Poppins* as it's the first movie I remember seeing and so there's a lot of *Mary Poppins* in a lot of my videos. [Laughing]

These costumes are straight from Gorey, and one thing I had a problem with in transposing Gorey into cinema was that Gorey has no camera close-ups. Gorey is all master-shots framing, so, like this shot for instance, which is a close-up of a wider image, I just couldn't think how to frame it, because when you look in Gorey, there are no close-ups. He just creates a series of master tableau shots, and I was really having a hard time figuring out how to do proper camera coverage if you're truly trying to re-create a Gorey image.

I like the idea of this little girl as sort of androgynous. Some people thought that it was a little boy, but it's a beautiful little girl named Martha who I haven't seen since. She's probably a grown-up now, of course. That androgyne is also Goreyesque.

So, the thing to get from this video is that some of this is straight Gorey and some of this is just more generally sort of Goreyesque. I love that his world is just this hermetically sealed universe that I could draw from. It's so beautifully designed, and that's part of the appeal as well. It's just so hermetic; nothing exists outside this bubble that he's created, this antique, wise, funny, universe. It's just got everything for me.

JP: That's so great. I love *Mary Poppins* too.

MR: Oh my god, I love that film; except of course for Dick Van Dyke's terrible cockney accent, it's just a perfect movie. When it comes to Gorey and the Nine Inch Nails video, I would hope that it's clear that this was a blatant *homage* to Gorey done by me as a true fan. I wasn't just "ripping Gorey off" or passing off these images as my own. I'm such a big fan, and it was done with that kind of full respect. In fact, I collect his work as a superfan and am always on the lookout for his one-of-a-kind prints and artworks.

Helen Pond Interview

SEPTEMBER 2, 2011

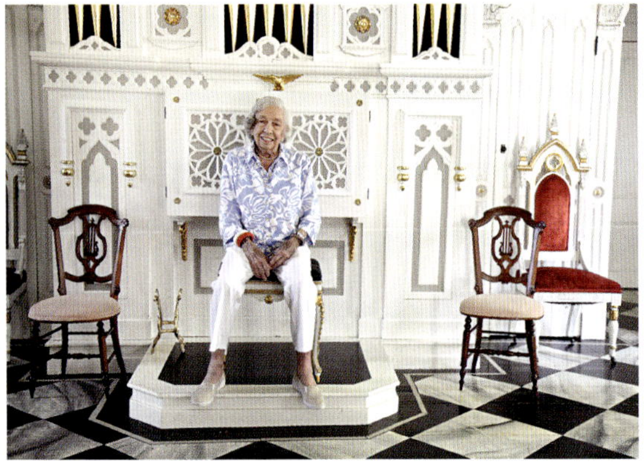

Helen Pond was a friend and associate of Edward. Along with her husband, Herbert Senn, Pond was a renowned theatrical set designer with whom Gorey had close ties through their shared community in Cape Cod. After his death she worked as a docent at the Gorey House museum. When Herbert was alive, the couple declined to be formally interviewed together for the documentary; however, Helen agreed to a very brief interview while I shot her portrait on assignment with her at her home one summer day. I took what I could get, asking her Gorey questions as I shot her portrait around the church that had become her home. She passed away in 2017.

Christopher Seufert: This is an amazing space. How did you come to own an old church?

Helen Pond: It was an 1800s Universalist Church, but we were able to purchase it as a private residence and make it our own. The pipe organ from that time still works, if you can believe it

CS: Amazing, and you've fixed it up yourself?

HP: Well, that was Herb's project, but we're set designers by trade, of course, so knew exactly what to do.

CS: I won't get too personal about your relationship with Edward; I know you don't like to be too public with it. I do appreciate just talking about it this way. Was your relationship with Edward more professional or personal?

HP: Well, I could go on and on professionally about him; he was a great man of many talents but he was a gentle person and a true friend to me. We often ate together at Jack's Outback or the Yarmouth Inn. The Cape Playhouse was something we both had in common, along with friends like the great actress Julie Harris. We would often have him over on Christmas mornings, and he would have us also to his house.

He was a brilliant and creative spirit, and I miss him every day. Herb was also just as heartbroken as I was. Losing him was a real loss for the world, not just here on the Cape. We held his memorial here, and you should've seen the turnout.

CS: I shot his play *The White Canoe*, which was put on after his death, and saw that you did the sets, which were fantastic. Would you say that he was what you'd imagine upon viewing his work?

HP: Oh, heck no. Not at all. He was a big teddy bear. I didn't know every last thing about him, but he was a great friend and we collected all of his work, but I don't think anyone really knew him completely.

CS: That's what I keep hearing. What sort of person was he to you?

HP: He was a brilliant and creative spirit, as everyone knows, and a great friend to me personally.

Andreas Brown Interview

JUNE 9, 2014

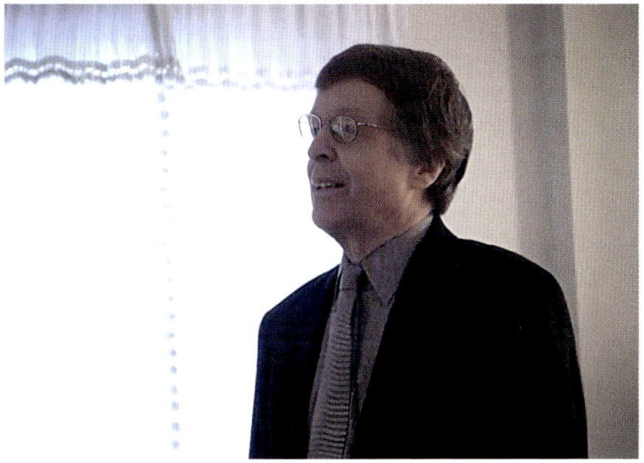

Andreas Brown, then coexecutor of the Edward Gorey Charitable Trust, was a friend of Edward's since taking over the Gotham Book Mart in 1967. Andreas declined to appear in a video interview but agreed to do an audio-only telephone interview. I met with him in person that June at the Gorey museum to do more followup interviewing, but he declined to elaborate on recording so unfortunately that additional conversation goes undocumented, my last with him before he passed.

I do remember, however, that he had heard of me stating that my perspective on Edward, coming from an anthropology background academically, was that he seemed like the last of a dying race, completely singular. Andreas reiterated to me to turn that around and think of him perhaps as the first of a new race.

Andreas Brown: Hello, Christopher, just a moment here . . . Now, I'm all set on this end. Just making a tea. I'm still on Cape Cod, staying at the Edward Gorey House.

Christopher Seufert: Thank you, Andreas; let's jump right in. What personally did you admire about Edward Gorey's work?

AB: What I personally admire about Gorey's work is his perfect highly detailed cross-hatching technique. You could even say that his traditional pen-and-ink drawings have the quality of a steel engraving because of this. The detail is just endlessly rewarding.

CS: What about the content of his work struck you?

AB: Well, that's not a question that's easy to be concise in answering. In short, for me, his work was not derivative of anything that I'd seen before; it was just so astoundingly unique in terms of the stories as a combination of his text and drawings, as whole works of art. However, as I know now, he had influences reaching back like tentacles into the works of many, many historic and significant artists. The nonsense work of Lewis Carroll was one of his greatest influences, certainly, to keep it brief. And then Edward has thrown those tentacles, if you will, into a whole host of present-day artists, such as Tim Burton, as the most well-known example of the mainstreaming of the Gorey aesthetic.

I also very much admired his discipline. He turned out all of his books and drawings while tucking his tall frame into what was quite a small studio desk space, both in New York and on Cape Cod. If he had his pen points, inks, and paper, I don't think he cared too much where he was physically, he was focused in that way. Now, if he could not get one of these things, it would certainly throw him off, but once he got going he really was a very focused and disciplined artist, contrary to what one might hear about his TV habits and long lunches.

CS: Yeah, I've seen his space here and it certainly was cramped, especially with the type of chair he had, which was one of those therapeutic chairs where you lean forward on your knees. Have you actually seen him at work?

AB: No, no, I can't say that I have. I've visited quite a bit, but he likes his privacy and focus when it comes to that. I certainly do see him scribbling and drawing away on his small paper notebooks. He's always producing some small scrap of paper or reporter's notebook even from his jacket or shirt pocket, in the way of many other writers, and writing down something he's thought of or he wants to remember for later. I see that quite a bit, and he might do this when we're talking or otherwise engaged.

CS: Yes, he has a writer's way about him, doesn't he, in that way?

AB: Well, if you've read *Mr. Earbrass,* that says it all really, the way he sees himself. It's one book at least that comes straight from the way he sees himself creatively, and certainly it's well established that he wrote the words before he ever did the drawings. He was an author first and foremost and an illustrator second; that is, in the way he saw himself.

CS: How do you see his movement into plays and theater in the last fifteen years or so of his career? He seemed to really enjoy them and all the hours with the crew and rehearsals on top of that.

AB: (*Laughing*) Well, remember, plays were not necessarily a new thing for him. He was quite active at Harvard and of course he won a Tony for his work on *Dracula* in the late 1970s. So, I'm not convinced that the plays he put on here on the Cape were something new. To my mind they were less of a move forward than a return to something comfortable. Of course, the plots were often lacking in complete logic, which might lose the audience for a while, but in the end they were a good time, certainly for Edward, who enjoyed being in complete control with the music and the outlandish narratives. He perhaps enjoyed the social aspect of it, rather than being in his studio illustrating a book with the light on on a Cape Cod winter night and nothing but the TV going.

He really was a lot more social than people give him credit for. A reclusive hermit he was not, though he did not suffer fools gladly in particular. He was not above creating a convenient circle of friends for himself when it came to the plays and all the hours of rehearsals he spent with those with whom he collaborated.

Edward was certainly no stranger to dark subject matter; however, I wouldn't classify him as macabre and I don't believe he would as well. Though of course, works like *The Gashlycrumb Tinies* do fall into that category; it's too much of a simplification to apply that term to his work in general. He invented creatures, loved language, absurd phrases and names, Victorian and Edwardian characters and settings, nonsensical narratives, but let's not forget his very, very keen sense of wit, which was substantial throughout.

CS: When I first started I was quite idealistic, just coming out of a graduate anthropology program. I had never met anyone quite like Edward, and he struck me as so unique to the point that he seemed like the last member of a dying race or tribe. Like the last Yahi in California. Or perhaps an alien crashed to Earth. Now, years later, I don't know that I'd express it quite so extremely, but I do still feel that he was a complete one of a kind. What's your take on that?

AB: Well, I do think you've hit it; however, I'd perhaps take the opposite approach. I think of him as a tribe of one, but perhaps more from the idea that he's the first of a new race, as in an artist way ahead of his time of whom people are just now coming to appreciate. Every year now, more people are attempting to understand his art and who he was as a person.

CS: That's an interesting take. Is there anything I've missed when it comes to Edward, anything that you think absolutely should be in the documentary?

AB: Well, let's see. The person behind this voluminous mountain of artwork that he's left us, and we at the Charitable Trust are still going through it all, was quite different than the gruff, English, Victorian, gloomy gentleman as whom he was often portrayed. He was a kind man; there was not a mean or cruel bone in his body, I don't think, and that's why I think he left his worldly possessions to the sole benefit of animal charities, and not just the cute animals, but the underrepresented ones, like spiders and bats. This is where he wanted whatever commercial success he had postmortem to go. And I don't see his artwork doing anything but gaining more and more admirers. So, Mr. Gorey will [be] getting known by more and more people as the years go by. He's not going anywhere even though he's passed away.

If you can do that, without getting too bogged down in the macabre caricature, then it'll be good for his legacy.

CS: Thank you, Andy.

AB: You're quite welcome; thank you.

Daniel Handler Interview

SEPTEMBER 16, 2014

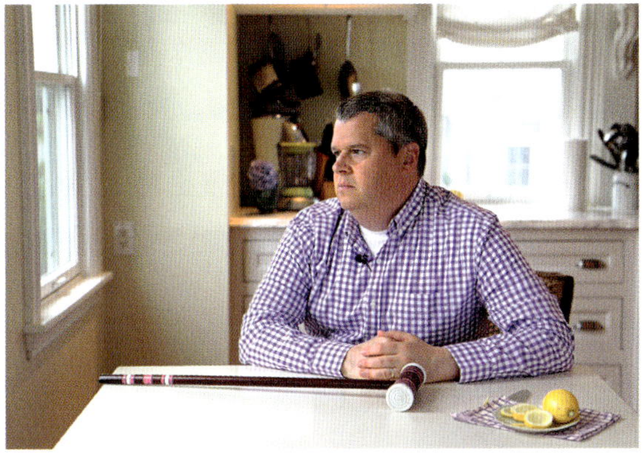

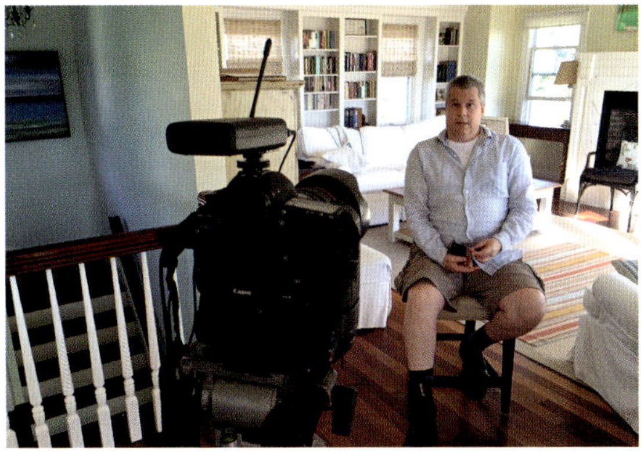

Daniel Handler, a.k.a. Lemony Snicket, is heavily influenced by Edward Gorey, who served as a major inspiration for Handler's *A Series of Unfortunate Events*. Handler was a voracious reader as a child, and his first Gorey book was *The Blue Aspic*. We interviewed Handler in the living room of his summer home in Chatham, Cape Cod, just a few miles from today's Gorey museum.

Christopher Seufert: So, why don't you just say your name and who you are, and we'll tag it in the front?

Daniel Handler: Sir, my name is Daniel Handler, a.k.a. Lemony Snicket. I write books mostly about terrible things happening to children.

CS: Tell me about the first Edward Gorey book that really struck a chord with you.

DH: Well, *The Blue Aspic* was the first book I spent my own money on. I think I was about ten, and I had seen Edward Gorey books here and there in people's houses. My parents didn't own any.

My parents had a ton of books. *The Blue Aspic* was the first book I bought with my own money, and I had seen Edward Gorey's work here and there. There are a few people who had a couple of books there, and it was an experience growing up where I would be in someone's living room and I would take down what looks like a kid's book, and I would open it and it was this dark, strange world. That was so hypnotizing to me.

I didn't know what they were. It was like the first book I saw that was a complete mystery to me. They were shaped like a kid's book, they were little, they had an illustration and a caption on the other side, or they had the language of a picture book, but the narrative to a child was incomprehensible, except when it was terrifying.

So, I thought about those books all the time, and I remember I thinking that it seemed almost like pornography to me to ask for it or to try to get my parents to buy me one, because they were so weird and I knew they were so weird. And so, I bought one at this bookstore in San Francisco with my own hard-saved allowance, and it was *The Blue Aspic*, which was about murder and opera. My parents were big opera fans and I was a boy soprano. I sang in the opera when I was a kid, and so that world was somewhat familiar to me, and I just love the narrative. I mean, it's a crazy, crazy story, and then on from there, I started to buy a lot of Edward Gorey.

My eighth-grade girlfriend, Elizabeth, had *Amphigorey*, and it never occurred to be that there would be such an anthology. She said, "Oh, I have a bunch of them. They're in this anthology," and that kind of blew my mind.

CS: Yeah, it's like, you think it's a new band and that you're just getting your hands on something that hasn't quite made it out into world, and someone says, "Oh, I have their greatest hits."

DH: Yeah, or that somehow the fact that they were anthologized made it seem like there was something more to get a grip on, when before, they were just mysterious, mysterious objects to me.

I think that because Edward Gorey and his various pseudonyms, which are always kind of obvious anagrams or super wacky, were part of the mystery. Somehow Edward Gorey seemed like he was in those books himself or that he lived in a world that was like that of his books. It just never occurred to me that he was an actual guy sitting someplace drawing and writing. That just seemed wrong at that time.

And that became something that was just a huge influence on the world of Lemony Snicket. When I started to write these books for children, I wanted to present a world in which the mystery was still intact. The adaptation of the Lemony Snicket persona and publishing the books under the name of the narrator, Lemony Snicket, and then to have these photographs of me with my face obscured and all that, and to never admit that I was Lemony Snicket to my readership seemed as important to me as the text of the books themselves.

I think when you meet other people who read Edward Gorey when they were kids, everybody made up something about him. Everybody said, "Oh, obviously, I knew these were old British books," or "These were books that were really written by some famous author. They're really by Virginia Woolf," or "They're really by this person."

Oddly, I always felt I was almost ashamed the more I learned about him. I would just get some scrap of information of "Oh yeah, he was involved in a Broadway show." And I would think like, "The Edward Gorey I'm thinking of couldn't be involved in a Broadway show unless it was a murder backstage in 1910." And I think the mystery of that kind of elusive but very tangible mystery of Edward Gorey is to me what survives.

You feel like you're in a world of Victorian literature, but then when you read actual Victorian literature, they don't have that same quality. There's a hint of kind of orientalism and foreign and exotic work in there, but you can't quite pin down either. It seems very romantic, very cynical. It seems ironic but it's not campy. It just has this world of its own.

The first time the Lemony Snicket's books were reviewed in the *New York Times*, they called Snicket "the love child of Edward Gorey and Dorothy Parker," and I thought, "My life is now complete. I'm exactly where I wanted to be my entire life."

I think he moved into the mainstream kind of unexpectedly, and when the first Snicket books were written, I would walk around and say, "I am a rip-off of Edward Gorey," and everyone would say, "Who is Edward Gorey?" And the best that I could come up with was that he had done the credits for *Mystery!* or that he'd illustrated the John Bellairs books. Even then people said, "How can you be a rip-off of somebody while only vaguely recalling?" It was about five or six years later when people said to me, "You know, you're kind of a rip-off of Edward Gorey." And I would say, "Yes, yes, finally! Finally, he's gotten popular now that everyone knows what I'm saying."

CS: That's interesting; when it comes to the documentary, I'm still explaining him to most persons I meet.

DH: Well, I mean, in many ways, he inhabits this strange diagram. I mean, he's not quite a fine artist; nobody is going to say, "Oh, this is one of the most remarkable visual artists of our time," even though I think he is, but no one will say that. He's not really in the world of children's books, even though he did a ton of that. Nobody really puts [him] in with Maurice Sendak, even though maybe they should. He partly lives in this world of the mainstream where Goths want him and steampunk wants him in this English Victorian world. Yet, he's a contemporary American. So he slipstreams all that, which is admirable to me. All my favorite artists are hard to pin down what it is that they're doing. I think that's interesting.

CS: Yeah. When I meet people now, if we get into kind of deep conversation, I'm looking in their eyes when I say the words "Edward Gorey." It's like a secret society password. And I'm looking to see if it authentically hits anything with them, because usually it's totally recognizable within a second.

DH: Yeah.

CS: If there's no hint of recognition, then I just move on. It's like a password that I just slip into conversation just to see who the person is, and then I act accordingly.

DH: Yeah, if you mention Edward Gorey to someone, you either get "Who?" or you get "Oh, of course!" Either he's such a genius that everybody wants to talk about, or they don't know who he is, which I like too. I like both of those things.

CS: For me, it's different because I did a documentary with him and I was sort of with him. So for me it's like, "You knew Edward Gorey?" And more along the lines of fanaticism.

DH: Yeah. Well, it's fun to visit his house, but it's strange too, because in my mind I don't think of Edward Gorey as someone you could know. I just think of him as part of this magical world. I mean, there are other artists that I think of that way, and they're often from a bygone era. Do you know what I mean? It's like I kind of want to close a bar with Raymond Chandler, but also maybe it's good that I didn't because maybe on the way to the bar, he would say like, "Oh, I actually need razors; we've got to go CVS." Then you'd be like, "Now, I'm at CVS with Raymond Chandler. This isn't going the way I wanted."

CS: [*Laughing*] A letdown. Yeah. It's definitely those people that are bigger, people like Jack Kerouac, where there's an American myth around him that's so much bigger than his actual work that's very far removed from his actual personality and stuff.

DH: I think I disappoint people that way too. People come and visit—or not come and visit, because they will meet me and they'll say, "Oh, he's not always in the trench coat brooding or something." And, I mean, I remember when I read that big piece that came out of the *New Yorker* about Edward Gorey which talked about him watching *Golden Girls* reruns, and I was like, "You somehow wanted to think that all he did was watch Japanese puppet shows or something."

When the first two Snicket books were published, I sent them to Edward Gorey with a note saying how much I admired his work and how I hope that he forgave me for all that I stole from him. Then a short while later he was dead, and s o I always had this fantasy that I killed him, that he opened the letter up and thought, "Oh my God, this is such a rip-off. Send forth my lawyer and then, boom."

It's probably not true. Probably my package was part of a mountain of packages unopened in his house, but I mean, I think all the children's books that he illustrated have a touch of magic about them. Even the most-ordinary ones can't help but to be weird and dark when Edward Gorey illustrates them. He did work with some really good writers with picture books, but even then his illustrations were on the mark in that way.

DH: My wife and I just bought a copy of *Freaky Friday*, this edition of *Freaky Friday* that Edward Gorey does the cover of, and just looking at it, it makes you realize what a weird book that is and what a strange journey *Freaky Friday* is. Previously, I just thought of his goofy Disney light, light, light thing, and it was amazing just looking at the book. I suddenly thought, "That's a really weird book, *Freaky Friday*." That's a really weird idea, and I think it's partly due to Gorey putting that dark magic on everything he touches.

CS: Yeah, he worried about cuteness; he felt that sometimes he had a tendency to get cute, especially when it came to his cat drawings. His definition of cute was teddy bears.

DH: Right. Well, with that cat stuff, some of that cat stuff is indeed cute. Well, I mean, I think that [my] own books benefit from this kind of ghetto that happened with children's literature for a long time, which is that no one was paying much attention to it. It's where the wild things came from. It's where Roald Dahl got to be such a big figure of making very strange books that people were just thinking, "Oh, that's for children; just print it and hope for the best."

You don't find that in picture books now. The artists who are making their own weird, wondrous work are not being published by Harcourt for children, because children's literature has so much attention now. There's so much money attached to it, so the weirder stuff is happening further up there. That's what I think is so marvelous to see, how he was ranked in the middle of that. He's being published by bona fide publishing houses, and yet, the books feel like they're hopelessly out of print and they're passed from person to person. It feels like some lost item, but really, he was right there publishing them, and that's so fascinating to me.

CS: He also was really one of the first self-publishing authors. When he couldn't get a publisher, he said, "Well, waste not, want not," and he didn't like to let it go unpublished, so he would pay for it on his own press and put it on whatever the size of the drawing was.

DH: Right, whatever he wanted, yeah.

CS: He'd always try to get them to publish them as children's books, and they rarely ever did because they felt the subject matter was too dark for them. Go to a store and say you want to find Edward Gorey books, and he always seems to be in a different category than you'd expect. The bookstores don't seem to know what to do with him.

DH: Yeah, if you're going to a bookstore and look for Edward Gorey, he's not in children's books at all. He's in maybe the graphic novel section or he's in maybe the art book section. No one knows where to put [it] in, but it's pretty marvelous to think of a body of work that just slits all genres and definitions that people try to put on it. That's interesting to me.

CS: What are some of the things that you've seen the last, say, ten or twenty years, in the world of film, music, and otherwise that you would say are influenced by Edward Gorey? Is there something that you've said to yourself, "Oh, there's some Gorey in that."

DH: Gosh, what isn't? I think you can just see Edward Gorey nowadays in art and illustration, and in film and in music, videos, gothic subculture, comic subculture, steampunk, and all kinds of Victorian, Edwardian, the kind of magical culture.

It's like a band that will develop on the grounds that it didn't sell a lot of records, but everybody who bought one went off and formed a band themselves. Similarly, I think then anyone who looked at Edward Gorey went off and did things. So the imaginary cocktail party in which Lemony Snicket is standing around with Neil Gaiman, Tim Burton, Guy Maddin, Amanda Palmer, Trent Reznor, and Michel Gondry . . . all these people—we all owe everything to Edward Gorey.

CS: Yeah, that totally rings a bell with me. What's the most mainstream thing specifically that you've seen where you can say there's some Gorey influence? Was it something like Batman?

DH: God, I don't know. I'm the wrong guy to ask about mainstream. I do think that Tim Burton probably took the torch from Edward Gorey and ran the farthest with it. I think the work that he and Henry Selleck did with *The Nightmare Before Christmas* would have a hard time existing without Edward Gorey.

Of course, I'm a pretty powerful rip-off of him too. I don't want to call myself innocent by calling other people guilty.

CS: Tell me specifically what the source is for what you do; for those who aren't familiar with Gorey, could you just spell it out?

DH: Well, my favorite Edward Gorey books were these books that had children in danger and had a large looming mystery like *The Hapless Child*, *The Insect God*, *The Gashlycrumb Tinies*, and *The Blue Aspic*. These books that had terrible things going on but dared you to laugh at them, dared you to think it was funny, never winked at you about them, and only said, "This is awful," and let you laugh at it. That.

I took all of that. I read *The Hapless Child* to tatters when I was a kid, and it is about an orphan that goes through a series of unfortunate events. Then the idea that there's a mystery, that idea that there's more to what you're looking at than what you're looking at is really powerful in his work. Of course, he's not the only artist who did that, but he really brought it to a lot of people. This idea that beyond the card catalog and beyond googling, there's some mystery about something.

I think when you're a kid, you look at your favorite images, you want to know what's outside the frame, and Edward Gorey really built that a lot. He made up characters and he pretended that you knew what they did. He would make reference to fictional works of art and fictional composers. And when I was young, before the internet, I'd made lists of those things because I thought, "Maybe one of them is real." And even when I was old enough to know better, I thought, "Maybe if there's just one of them—maybe he's going to lead me some place."

I still remember, right before he died at the turn of millennium, some website asked a bunch of people about neglected books of the twentieth century. I was scrolling through it and I remember that all the questions that people asked seemed super obvious to me. Then Edward Gorey just listed two or three books that I had never heard of in my life, and I thought, "Are these real or not? Is he messing with me one more time?" So now [as] an adult I went and found them, and they were hopelessly obscure and hopelessly magical, but it was almost that I couldn't read them for their own thing because as I was reading and I was thinking, "Edward Gorey also read this and loved it. Edward Gorey also had this strange thing at his disposal." And it was quite marvelous.

CS: That was beautifully said. Yeah. I think he was absolutely totally serious when he said, "There's no difference between *Golden Girls* and Feuillade's *Les Vampires*."

DH: Yeah.

CS: I don't think that for him, the high and the low arts, no difference. They're both equally to be respected. He was honest to God really into *Buffy the Vampire Slayer*, and when he said *The Mary Tyler Moore Show* was the greatest show ever made, he was completely serious. It wasn't a tongue-in-cheek thing. Some don't agree, but that's my thought.

DH: Yeah. I think all the artists that I genuinely admire have that kind of broad taste. There's no musician I really admire who when you see them being interviewed or you talk to them personally won't say, "Oh, I love this piece of tinker toy pop and I love this high-art thing. I love all this stuff." Certainly it's the same with writers. A writer might say, "I read all of this." I never stopped reading the Hardy Boys even though I'm also translating finished poetry. There's all that out there, and when you see how wide Edward Gorey's proclivities were, he also gave back very wide. He was at home looking at weird, old Japanese arts and junk TV at the same time. He pushed it all out, and you see traces of it in high-art stuff, really, really lowbrow things in animated entertainment that's been seen by gazillion people, and then weird kinds of installations that haven't [been] seen by nobody. I think it's great that it came from a guy who is watching *Golden Girls* reruns and also reading some of the most obscure literature known to man.

CS: Why should people care about Edward Gorey? I've been trying to think of a better way to ask that, and it made me sort of throw away, but I'm trying to think of the first frame of this documentary, when you see him walking down the street and you just see this eccentric guy in a fur coat. What is it about this person who lived and died and created that people should care about now that he's gone?

There's obviously a percentage of people that will go see his work, [but] it doesn't ring any sort of bell for them, and they won't care about it. They don't need to worry about Edward Gorey. On the other side, there's a whole fan base out there, but then there's a whole third group of people that would just love Edward Gorey if they knew of him. However, through the various tricks of the world these days, it's really hard to get any direct exposure with Edward Gorey, and I'm hoping this documentary reaches those people.

What is it that's completely fresh and unique about Edward Gorey that's not going to show up in your work or Tim Burton's or anyone else's? Or what is it about Edward Gorey that people need in their lives?

DH: I think when you read Edward Gorey, it's an exploration of a hidden world underneath or beyond the one that you can see. If you open up one of his picture books, you think, "What is this? There's something I'm not quite grasping?" It's like there's somebody leaving the room and just the trail of their cloak is visible. You think, "I'm missing something." There's something ultimately ungraspable about it, and I think that that's so marvelous. I love to show him to children because it's not something where we say, "Look, it's the whole world and we've made it for you." There's something beyond it. There's something that lurks underneath it. And I think that's the reason why it's so appealing to children when you're looking around and there's all these motivations and agendas and ghostly things that are above and around you that you're not quite grasping.

You're a child and you walk into a room, and something is going on but you're not understanding it. I think that when you walk into a room where something terrible has happened in an Edward Gorey book, you have that same experience. That's what's magical about him to me is that otherworldly touch.

I never did get to meet him, but it's my understanding from people who hang out with him that he was both a collector and a reader, and he was interested in a great many things. But there is still something beyond this basic eccentricity, something beyond his work habits and his aesthetic. There's something there that is a mystery. This mystery—that's childhood, that's life, that's art, and that's Edward Gorey.

CS: He was a man of contrasts; he was gregarious in the way that a cat is. He'd be perfectly happy out socially, and then he would just simply walk away when he was done, without a lot of fancy explanation. He was friendly, he was unpretentious, he was not mean to people, and he wasn't really looking to lord his knowledge over you. He could talk but he had no interests in sports or in political conversations.

DH: Whenever I imagine meeting Edward Gorey, it's like the first twenty minutes of a classic horror movie, where I would be in a carriage. Then the carriage driver would say something like, "I will go no further," so I'd have to take my own suitcase up to Gorey's house. There's ivy growing all over the gate, and I would go in. The front door creaks open and some servant would say, "You have to wait here." So I would wait in this sumptuous room on the side that would have a mysterious brandy or some other liquid in it. Finally, Edward Gorey would come down and say, "I'm so sorry I kept you waiting" and "Won't you join me in a sip of this mysterious liquid," that's what I envisioned.

Then the first time I actually went to his house [on Cape Cod], the docent is like, "Yeah, that's where he had his fridge." And I was like, "He didn't have a fridge. He must have had an icebox and some absinthe, and that's it." So, he's turned out in many ways to be actually quite ordinary even though what he did was make the extraordinary ordinary. He drew and wrote a world in which catastrophic things were happening with utter regularity, and so it makes sense to me that he had a strange brain inside an average head.

CS: I'm always interested in the difference between someone and their artwork. Do you think there's some dynamic tension or creative juice that happens between the type of work someone creates and the type of person they are?

Edward had a certain intensity, like the obsessiveness of this cross-hatching technique; he was just completely compulsive and exacting, and yet he could be quite freewheeling at the same time. He loved to do local theater in his last years because it would change every night, and every night was a new thing. He was not a very hard director with the actors; he gave them a lot of free range by saying, "Just do it" and wouldn't give them very specific direction. He didn't really want to control them in that way; if they didn't get it, then he didn't really want to explain it. Can you speak in any way about that dichotomy and how something like that exists in one person?

DH: In my experience you never know what an artist is going to be like, and I'm mostly hesitant to meet artists I admire because I want to like them. If I don't want to like them, then I don't want to meet them. There are a few artists I've in fact passed up the opportunity to meet because I was afraid that it's not going to be a good hang, it's going to wreck it for me.

I really think with Edward Gorey, it just kind of depends on how you look at him. Was he a guy who would hang out with you for a while and tell a few cheap jokes and move on? Yes. But he was also someone who could carry on intelligently about hopelessly obscure material. So, I don't know what to make of it.

To me what is most interesting about him is how he's brought such strange and fringy ideas really, really close to the mainstream, and that he took really weird things and brought them into more or less the mainstream of American culture, which is pretty remarkable. That's always been interesting to me in terms of my own work. I always thought, "I'm going to bring the name 'Baudelaire' to Wal-Mart." I'm excited about that, and I think that Edward Gorey brought a certain sensibility that could have been in a hopelessly New York or otherwise insular hierarchy and instead that sensibility really went everywhere, and that to me is what's remarkable about it.

For example, I'm really into the *Purple Rain* by Prince, which is like a mess but it's a massive record. It was made over just a few days. It kind of breaks all these rules, and yet it was the number one pop hit record for a long time. There are a lot of records that are weirder and there are a lot of records that are more popular, but there are not so many records that are that weird that were also that popular.

Edward Gorey had some of that same kind of thing. There's a lot weirder art you can find than Edward Gorey, but there's also not a lot of weirder art that you can find than Edward Gorey that is in the credits of a television show that everyone has seen. You don't see that a lot, and I think that's pretty magical. Those are the artists that I put him with, those who have taken their own strange thing really, really far.

CS: That's something I've never quite heard articulated in that way. There're indeed a lot weirder artists than Edward Gorey. He's not the most eccentric person.

DH: Yeah, he's not Henry Darger, also a weird dude who lived in a world of his own making on paper. But Henry Darger was utterly ignored, to put it mildly, in his lifetime as an artist. Edward Gorey, on the other hand, was doing the covers of the *New Yorker*. He made it out there. I wish he was still doing Broadway plays because Broadway would be something I'd want to go to then.

He wasn't a snob, either; he never got too big to do small stuff, like local posters, and also really mainstream stuff. I admire him. There goes a wonderful man.

CS: What has the world lost when they lost Edward Gorey? What are your last thoughts about him?

DH: Well, I didn't know him personally. When it comes to his work, for me, why his work is still so alive and so present is that it's still so slippery. He hasn't been relegated to a museum. He isn't kind of stuck forever in a gift shop or relegated to a few picture books. You still see his work everywhere. Literally, you see his work everywhere, and then you see his influence everywhere, and it's just part of the slippery mystery that he always was.

I think the mystery of him endures. It endures in his work and it endures in him, and you can make a million documentaries about him but I don't think you're ever going to grasp what it is about him that made him such a great artist; that's what makes him so interesting.

CS: Great. Thank you so much.

DH: Sure.

Paul Theroux Interview

AUGUST 11, 2017

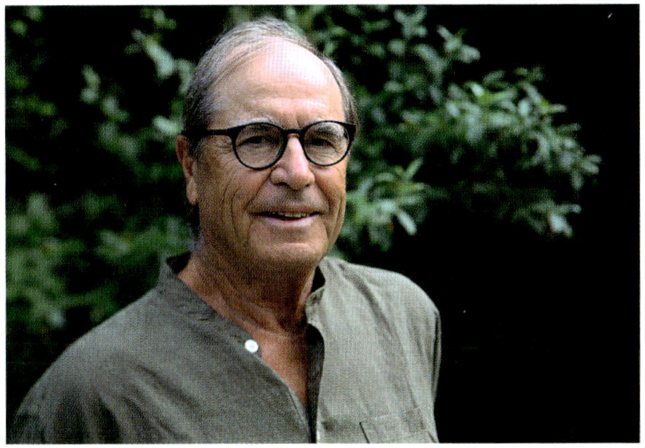

Paul Theroux was a summertime Sandwich, Massachusetts, resident and neighbor of Edward Gorey on Cape Cod, where they occasionally socialized and dined together. They also collaborated on an illustrated story for the *New York Times Book Review* in the fall of 1990. The resulting story, titled "The Return of Bingo Humpage," was published in the newspaper and later as a limited-edition booklet signed by both authors.

Christopher Seufert: Let's talk about Edward Gorey's writing style. As an author, how would you describe his style? In a way it's kind of primitive, don't you think?

Paul Theroux: The Edward Gorey style, the Gorey story, is a very curious thing because I don't know anything in literature or drawing that resembles it. It's an amalgamation of a lot of things. English, sort of quaint English country house. And then visually, strange-looking people wearing un-English-looking clothes. I mean they're wearing raccoon coats and sneakers just like Gorey himself, so there's people who look like Gorey in it.

Or they have a top hat or there's a strange bicycle or a weird car. And then there's some unnamable wicked thing that seems to be happening at the same time. So there are these three elements, as I see it.

And Gorey is a minimalist, actually, in narrative terms a minimalist. But in drawing terms it's very suggestible because there's an urn, there's a lizard, there's a crocodile, there's a dagger. There's a woman with mascara eyes, funny hat.

What is interesting speculation to me is what period is Gorey generally writing about? Is he writing about the turn of the [twentieth] century? They all seem to be taking place before the First World War for sure.

I mean, one assumes. And the setting is always in England. Gorey is from Chicago, lives on the Cape, and we're in England now. So it's all in his head. And he's kind of invented Goreylandia, which is a place where there are orphans, there are waifs, there are beggars, there are high-society ladies, there're weird murders.

There're people with dangerous proclivities and beastly babies and whatever. And all that's in his head. And I don't know anyone else who does it.

CS: No? Anyone similar?

PT: Well, in a way he resembles somewhat Jorge Luis Borges, the Argentine magical realist or, you could say, writer of parables. Very, very short stories. And you think Borges's stories are only a page or two.

And I see that Gorey is someone who never wrote at length. It's always small passages. But what Gorey does, the technique and effort in his stories, is first imagining an image, putting an image down, and then shading with the cross-hatching.

CS: What do you think of his drawing technique?

PT: If you look at the Gorey picture, it's full of small brushstrokes. And those small brushstrokes in a way represent for me the effect for what another writer would be pages and pages of text. And I know because he's said to me, "I just sit here all day, just shading."

I mean, I knew him reasonably well. He knew my brother [Alexander Theroux] much better. But I also spent quite a bit of time with him, and I never got anywhere in terms of figuring him out.

I'd say, "What's this all about? I don't know what it's about." And it was always "I don't know."

But I do think he knew. He knew very well what things were about. I've never known anyone like him. He was full of paradoxes, too, which is the way he dressed. Some people just say he's a very private person, that he wants to be inconspicuous. Well, I say, if you have rings all over your fingers, you have a beard down to your sternum, you're wearing a raccoon coat and earrings and funny plimsolls, as they call them in England, these weird sneakers . . . I think, what the hell? You want to be inconspicuous? I don't think so.

It was all one big paradox. I know that he had passions. The ballet was certainly one, but then when George Balanchine left the ballet, he dropped it, came to the Cape, and he never went back to New York. So, man of paradoxes.

CS: What do you imagine his attraction to the Cape was? Do you think that's perhaps something that you have in common? What's your attraction to the Cape?

PT: I think that what my attraction to the Cape is—solitude, nice weather in the summer, seclusion in the winter. He was Gorey. He could have all his habits on the Cape. His habits were work, cats, eating lunch at the same restaurant every day. Usually, you know, he always ate the same things, like Jell-O, a cheese sandwich, or whatever it was. It was nothing, you know. Simplicity. It wasn't like going to a gourmet restaurant in New York.

He was a man of very, very solid habits and plain tastes. But he could keep to his habits regularly here. And I think he stayed on the Cape, and liked the Cape, because he could work here without interruption. Oh, he hated interruptions and he did have a wide circle of friends, you know, people who lived on the Cape.

We tend to live in this bubble, really. People think, oh, it's so social, the Kennedys, Hyannis Port, Barack Obama, Clinton comes here, you know. Well, that's bull, really. It's not like that. I mean, people live on the Cape to be left alone. In New England, people don't even say hello at the local post office.

You know, you see people there. I've lived here virtually in every summer of my adult life. I've had a house here in Sandwich since about 1975, so that's a long time. And I know a lot of people here, but I don't have a lot of close friends here. And I don't think that Gorey necessarily did either, I think Gorey loved his privacy.

That's not to say he couldn't be social, at the same time, you know, when he went out, raccoon coat or hairy coat, earrings, you know. And he had a ring on every finger. They were silver rings or bangles. I remember he came to my house here one time and it was a chilly day in September. We had been visiting a neighbor and it was kind of chilly, and he came into my library there in the house and he said, "Oh, it's toasty warm here!"

Have you ever heard anyone say with such enthusiasm, "Oh, it's toasty warm"? No, I don't, at least not a fully grown adult Chicagoan author.

"Oh, it's toasty warm!" So. And it was his manner. He was always kind of putting it on.

He was a very, very likable person, of course, but I think someone that was ultimately very hard to know.

CS: Yes, he was somewhat like a cat in the way he could come and go with people.

PT: But he was always game. Game for a movie. Game for a meal. Oh, yeah. I mean, I'd say, "What are you doing tomorrow?" "Nothing" was always the answer. You know, "How about tomorrow evening?"

"Working all day." And then he had his cats, and I think he had some aunts or some close female relations who lived with him or near him [Eleanore Garvey and "Skee" Morton]. I think that was his life and social circle.

CS: Yeah. When you think of Gorey historically, how do you think his work will be regarded, you know, as time goes on?

PT: I think that Gorey's work will be always held in high regard.

CS: Do you see him as someone who just distilled other things down or was he totally unique?

PT: No, I think that Gorey's importance is that he created his own world. It's the Gorey world. And he populated it with particular people, certain events, diabolical events, and all the paraphernalia. He ultimately created this world by drawing upon a lot of different sources, but so many other sources that he ultimately made it his own. He'll last because he was unique in the end. Someone unique, just so unique that there's no one like him.

It's sui generis, as they say. So he's himself. The other thing, matter of factly, is that Gorey is very easy to translate into other languages, publishing-wise. And I know he's translated into a lot of different languages, German, French, Italian, for one. I have the books here in my library, some of them. And a man or a writer that can be translated easily into other languages, particularly one so visual, is one that will last and last.

Also, you know, the nature of his work is one big marketing opportunity. There're Gorey postcards, Gorey greeting cards, Gorey pillows, shawls, all the things that he sort of made in his lifetime. He made those stuffed rice dolls, little frogs, little things. My kids have some that he gave to them, because my kids knew him reasonably well too. He was very nice to them, by the way.

So, in the end, he'll last. But there'll never be an absolute Gorey boom. There'll never be everyone in the general population collecting Gorey.

He'll persist in the way that very good writers persist, that, you know, Sherlock Holmes or, I don't know, Felix the Cat. They're always there. They're just features of the literary landscape with their own markets.

In his lifetime, I don't know that he made that much money, but he always had an audience. There were people who collected his books, and they were always sold through the Gotham Book Mart. So he always had an outlet and made it work. Later on, he always had ideas for plays, and they had amazing titles. One was called *Tinned Lettuce*, I remember. I never saw them myself. He had a little group of amateur actors.

CS: Yeah, it's interesting. I never thought about that idea, tinned lettuce, which doesn't exist, right? But it could. You could see where that would be possible.

PT: Yeah.

CS: But why would you want a tin of lettuce? Because it has no value, very little value.

PT: No, but he knew what he wanted to do. So he had these amateur dramatics on the Cape. It was obviously a little grassroots group. A theater troupe is always fun, a group of like-minded people. They like each other. "We're putting on a play! Let's put on a play!," and they put on the play.

And they would put on the play, but it never went to Boston or New York. It was always local, Woods Hole, Yarmouth, just somewhere right here. And he put it on in the way that it's like an amateur theatrical. This was the way the Provincetown Playhouse [with Eugene O'Neill] first existed up the Cape here. But I have this very strong feeling that he knew what interested him. He knew what he wanted to do, and so he always got the results that he wanted, and it worked.

No one else could know what he wanted, so he just was plowing this furrow. He never went left or right. He never wrote an autobiography. He never wrote a short story. He never wrote a novel. He just did what he did, and he knew exactly what to do. And so his work is all of a piece. There's the ABC book and all the little stories with his pictures, and they're always the same length. I mean, a Gorey life's work is on a shelf, and with those size [of] stories it's not even a big shelf.

It's just a shelf like that, but that's it. He was taken very seriously by Edmund Wilson. Edmund Wilson wrote an essay about him, and he knew some significant literary people.

CS: Tell me about his influences as you knew them?

PT: I thought of Gorey with admiration because he was such a reader, and he read everything. He read very seriously, and you don't meet people who read widely. People think they read, but they don't. They don't read. They don't read. And here he is reading Henry James. He read B. S. Pritchett. He read English writers. He read American writers, and he had strong opinions about them as well. He watched movies and had the same strong opinions about movies too.

CS: That's a real reader, right? He read people that he knowingly didn't like, and then he'd go and read them several times.

PT: Yeah.

CS: Did you talk about books and movies with him?

PT: He asked me once. He said, "What are you doing?" I said, "I'm writing a script for Nicholas Roeg."

He said, "Oh, he sounds a bit familiar. Who is he?" I said, "Well, he made this movie called *Don't Look Now*."

"Oh, I hated that movie," he said. "That's the one with the little dwarf. The little dwarf stabs the other one. Oh, God. That was awful."

He's awful; because I'm working for eight months for this guy [*laughing*]. He's telling me, "Oh, he's awful. I hated that." But then, on the other hand, he'd say, "Oh, did you see *No, No, Nanette*?" or some other movie.

Barbara Bel Geddes. He was watching *Dallas*. He said, "Have you seen *Dallas*?," which was a soap opera of the 1970s.

I said, "I've seen some." He says, "Isn't Barbara Bel Geddes someone to die for?" I said, "Well, you know, I can take her or leave her."

"Oh, I think she's fantastic." Uh, okay. He really seemed to work in the extremes that way, right?

CS: Everything is the best and the worst. Yeah, yeah, yeah.

PT: But I really liked seeing him. He was just so committed to his work; he was such a worker it was hard to see him. He was so dedicated that he kept out of sight and he valued this solitude.

You know, the people who are like that care about their work. I'm that way myself. I don't like interruptions. I don't like people dropping in. I don't like commitments. I don't like making plans. I like being here and not being disturbed, and that's sort of my life on the Cape. I'm not here to be social. There're no interruptions for me.

But if you saw Gorey, you'd say, "Well, tomorrow night, do you want to come over and have a meal?" He'd say, "Yeah."

"What are you doing tomorrow night?" I'd ask. "Nothing," he'd say. "Okay, let's do it," I'd say. So we'd make it work. And then I remember one time he said, "What do we have?" I said, "Well, we're going to have haddock, and I got haddock and some mashed potato."

And he'd say, "And beans, I'll bake beans." Beans!

So we'd kind of mock the meal and then eat it and then have a nice time and then go off again to our own worlds. But he really is to be admired for his work, all the work that he did and the effort that he put into it, for creating this world that hadn't existed before but will go on now forever.

CS: You collaborated with him also, correct?

PT: One day around, I think it was the fall of 1990, I got a message from the *New York Times* saying, "Would you be willing to write a story based on either of these two Edward Gorey pictures?" One of the pictures was of a crocodile holding a Christmas ornament. At the time, I was traveling in New Guinea and I was writing a book called *The Happy Isles of Oceania*, doing the preparation for it, paddling a kayak along these islands. I saw crocodiles all the time at a distance, estuarine crocodiles. So, I was also in places where there were people who were highly superstitious and believed that you could be body-snatched by a crocodile. They believed that you could turn into a crocodile and that crocodiles were sacred. Furthermore, the canoes in New Guinea were in the shape of crocodiles.

So, I said, "I'll do the crocodile picture." And I wrote the story, which came quite easily because of my experience in New Guinea and my love for Gorey's work, which was full of visual suggestions.

So, he has his family, the crocodile, a Christmas tree, and the sort of English country house that he was fond of. And I was very happy with the story. In fact, I published it on its own in a book called *The Return of Bingo Humpage*. Bingo Humpage is a guy on an island who somehow turns into a crocodile. A very Gorey thought, I would venture. I never did find out what Gorey thought of it. We never discussed it, actually. There were other writers who also wrote stories based upon those images, but I like mine, though. I think mine's funny.

CS: Perfect. Thank you. I have one more question, a bit more general. It's probably an insufferable question.

What is the key to writing for you? And I don't mean good writing, any writing. What's the key to just getting words on the page, would you say?

PT: The key to getting words on a page is pretty simple. It's having something to say. When you hear about someone like this MacArthur Genius Grant awardee who was talking about how difficult it was for him to write. He had written a successful book and was having trouble with his second book. He's a writer in residence at a big university, making a lot of money, and he was talking about how difficult it is to write.

I say, "It is difficult to write, but it's impossible to write if you have nothing to say. If you have something to say, then you just need to find a way of saying it. Either a short story, an essay, a poem, a play, or something. But let's say you have an idea and there's something there, there's a person, there's an idea, there's a bit of dialogue. That's how it all happens.

People who don't write much really don't have much to lament. I mean, there's a writer called Ralph Ellison who wrote a book called *Invisible Man*. His tragedy, people say, was he wrote *Invisible Man* about the Black experience in New York. He was from Oklahoma, actually, and then the tragedy of his life was that he never wrote a second novel. He wrote a version of it.

CS: Did he never write a second novel, really? Huh.

PT: Yeah, no, he never wrote that. He never wrote another book. But, you know, this other writer that I'm talking about is called [name omitted].

CS: Oh, yeah. I know.

PT: So, [name omitted] gave a talk about it all, how difficult it was. Oh, really? You know? Won the National Book Award, MacArthur Genius Grant, got a job at MIT. What the fuck. You know? Oh, if it's so hard to write, then I say you've got nothing to say, man. You wrote your life story. Now you're teaching and you've got students adoring you and you've got money and you've got the MacArthur money and a Guggenheim and everything. Have a beer, you know?

CS: Yeah, I guess some people have one thing to say, other people have lots, and most have nothing. I can see where if you really have something to say, the actual writing of it shouldn't be the problem. You're not writing? Do you really need to say it?

PT: Okay, so we were talking about . . . So Ralph Ellison wrote *Invisible Man* about the Black experience. It's a great book, and then his tragedy was that he couldn't come up with another book. He started a novel called *Juneteenth* but was published posthumously.

There are biographies of him, but he wrote one book. Well, you know, Emily Brontë wrote one book, *Wuthering Heights*. She was happy with that. It's a good book. J. D. Salinger wrote one full-sized novel. That's it except for the short stories. Fine. You know, there's no more there.

Some people write one and they're happy with it. I've written more than one, but I would say that if you want to write something, it helps to really have something to say, to have an idea, an actual idea, any idea, a bit of dialogue, a character, the arc of a narrative, a beginning.

That's not to say that writing is easy. Writing is, in fact, very difficult, but if you have an idea you're off.

CS: Do you think you agree that writer's block is a thing? Or would you say that you just don't really know what you want to say yet if you've got writer's block?

PT: I think there's such a thing as writer's block. Knock on wood, I've never had it. I've just been stuck for ideas. I've never had an idea that remained unexpressed. But I've had long periods of nothing. I split up with my wife, and I felt that someone had hit me on the head and also made me sick and miserable, and I couldn't write anything except about how miserable I was. No one wants to read that, so you take a trip.

It's happened to me many times. And you get sick. I've never written about being sick on a trip. I've had stomach upsets. I've had malaria, but who wants to hear about that? So I didn't write about it. After my divorce, just very difficult. Then I got back on the beam.

I'm quite interested in writers who write one book. I'm interested in writers who write in old age. I'm also interested in prolific writers. The most prolific writers I know . . . I mean, Georges Simenon wrote seventy-five Maigret mysteries. But he also wrote about 200 real novels.

They're short novels, but they're very good novels, and many of them have been made into movies. So, Simenon is one of my heroes in a way because he's just such a wonderful writer. He's full of ideas, full of plots. Graham Greene was quite prolific. Ambrose Bierce, very prolific, given his short life.

Same with Jack London, who died at forty. Look at Jack London's output. He was writing every day and always had something to say, so there are plenty of people doing it. Jack London was not a hack writer. He was young when he wrote his autobiography or at least a book based on his life, *Martin Eden*. He wrote a great book about drinking.

CS: I've read them all. I love them.

PT: *John Barleycorn*.

CS: I like that one on the ocean.

PT: *The Voyage of the Snark*, *The Sea Wolf*?

CS: Yeah, *Seawolf*.

PT: *The Seawolf*. Okay, so there are a lot of secrets to writing. I don't have any secrets to share, but I do know the obvious thing is it helps to have something to say. Then if you've got something to say, you're good. I will also say that based on my most of a lifetime of experience that it doesn't help to cater to a writer's vanity.

CS: Such as . . .

PT: Giving him or her lots of money. Elevating them. Giving them a medal. Putting them on a postage stamp. Making them important. These sorts of things. What helps a writer is work. The key to writing a lot is just writing a lot. It's excess. The more you write, the better able you are to write. It's not "Oh, I'm going to sit down and write now." You just sit down every day and do it, and if you sit down every day like a job and do that, it comes.

Neil Gaiman Interview

OCTOBER 28, 2018

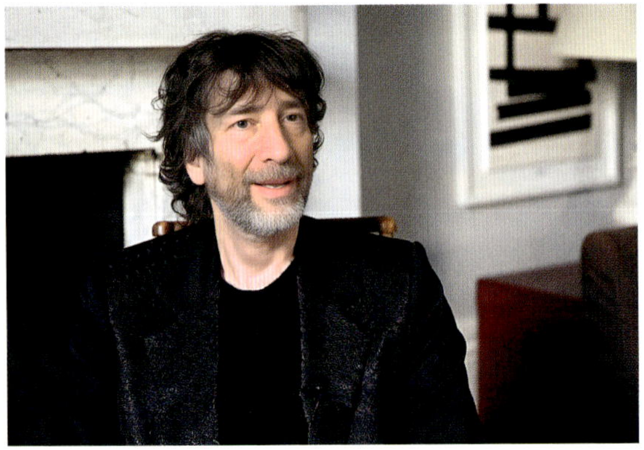

Edward Gorey had a notable influence on Gaiman's most well-known novel, *Coraline*. Gaiman in fact had hoped that Gorey would illustrate *Coraline*, but Gorey died the same week that he finished the book. They both share a sensibility that blurs the lines between dark and whimsical, charming and macabre, and often incorporate elements of loneliness and absurdity.

I traveled to his rental home near Camden in London, England, and he took time out of his Sunday for this interview.

Christopher Seufert: Let's start with your name and occupation.

Neil Gaiman: My name's Neil Gaiman and I'm a writer.

CS: When did you first become aware of Edward Gorey?

NG: I first became aware of Gorey without knowing who he was. I was about ten or eleven and got a copy of *The Shrinking of Treehorn* for my youngest sister. I was given an allowance to buy her books if I read the books to her, so I would go out and buy children's books because I was a precocious little creature and I was reading the *Pan Book of Horror Stories* at that point. I would go and buy children's books for my sister Lizzie, and I remember buying *The Shrinking of Treehorn* and just loving it, loving the illustrations and staring at them.

I remember loving the awkward Victorian delicacy of this very odd book. So that was when I encountered his work first. The first I remember knowing who he was would have been an anthology of dark fantasy book stories, edited by Kirby McCauley. I think it was called *Dark Forces*, but I have so many books on my bookshelf, it would be hard to go back and check.

That would have been early 1980s, and there was a Gorey story in there. That was when the penny dropped that this was somebody whose work I had already encountered in *Treehorn*. I now became excited and fascinated and went out and bought myself the first two of the *Amphigorey* series. Over the years that followed, I would buy those lovely little small books of his, which always seemed to be noun-and-adjective books.

Then I made sure that my children grew up with that gloriously disturbing alphabet of children on the wall of the room [*Gashlycrumb Tinies*]. I started buying signed Gorey prints for a while and finally ended up buying an original piece of Gorey art for myself, which I'm very proud of. I don't know what books it's from. It's definitely from something that I don't have, but it's children gathered around a sickbed and it's a glorious little piece that hangs in my bedroom to this day.

CS: So when you started your creative life . . . started writing. I don't know what age that was . . . how did Gorey's work start to influence that?

NG: There are things of mine that I can point at very obviously and say, "This is Gorey's influence."

I did a book called *The Dangerous Alphabet*. There is a story told, but it was writing a poem in which you would never [be] quite sure what had happened. It was dark and it was dangerous and it was strange, and there were pirates and murders, and dirty deeds done in the darkness, and that for me . . . that's obviously Goreyesque. Abecedaries, people just don't do them anymore.

I'd seen a few of these ancient ones, but for me, Gorey was the attitude. When I started *Coraline* I thought, "Now this is a Gorey story." It felt Goreyish in my head. Gorey was always going to illustrate *Coraline*, and it felt really strange and peculiar. We had just started reaching out as I finished the book, because I wanted to have a finished book that I could send out to him. The book took me ten years to write, but I remember at the end of 2000 finishing the book and three days later learning that Gorey was dead.

There was something very strange and odd about that, the idea that I had been going to give him my book. Finally I had that first thing I was looking forward to sending him. My initial feelers had been put out with the information that it would be received encouragingly, and then all that went away.

CS: That would have been good for both of you. Of course, he had good success with *Dracula* in theater, but *Coraline* was a big hit both as a book and in the movies.

NG: *Coraline* would have been great for him and it would have been great for me. It would have told people what kind of thing that it was straight out of the gate, which would have been wonderful.

I didn't see the PBS *Mystery!* opening until I came to the US later in life.

CS: That was my first exposure to him, but I didn't know who he was and I never met him again in an art sort of way until I was in my twenties. I remember feeling like it was such a cruel bait and switch, ya know, eight or nine years old. And seeing this animation mini story in the opening that sucked you in and then the rest of the show was something else entirely.

So the next time your parents watch it, you run in, just watch the opening, and then leave when it starts. So I watched it for the opening.

As a person, Edward Gorey had a personal continuity to his personality throughout his life. In other words, as he became more well known there seemed to be no real effect on him. There's an unchanging quality to him and his aesthetic, I think, from his early days at Harvard all the way into his later years.

NG: If you achieve a certain celebrity and financial success at the age of fifty, you are the same person you were when you were struggling at age twenty-three. I got the feeling with Gorey that he never did do that one thing. I don't know that he reached a level that threw him into the popular world, that giving him a sudden amazing success, with the effect being that he carried on being himself from the beginning all the way through. There was a glorious consistency to who he was.

He started off living the life he wanted to live, and he just maintained it despite whatever success he did have. On the other hand, he had enough success to continue doing what he wanted throughout his life.

CS: Was there anything about the man that inspired you? When it comes to Gorey, are you interested in the artist behind the work or was it primarily the work itself?

NG: I would have loved to have met him and talked to the man, but I started out my life as a young journalist interviewing authors, artists, and celebrities. I've met most of the living artists and authors whose work I admire already, and somewhere in there I learned that the art is the art and the artist is a talented human being who gets to both make the art and then have to carry the talent around with them and still have to deal with the everyday world.

I've become friends with many artists I admire, such as Ramsey Campbell and Peter Straub, and that's huge and delightful. I do love that I know Stephen King and that Joe Hill is a friend of mine, but still, the horrific, scary, disquieting world in a Peter Straub is still as noble and distant as if I didn't know the gentleman who wrote it. The same goes for the strange art and worldview of Ramsey Campbell. Knowing Stephen King gives me no insight into the dead body in the bathtub in *The Shining* and gives me no insight into the tapping on the window in *Salem's Lot*.

I am no closer to the art through knowing the people, though I do wish I'd met Gorey.

I'm really looking forward to seeing your film because I'm looking forward to seeing more footage of him, the man behind the artwork. I do wish that we'd been able to collaborate, as I say. *Coraline* was written for him, but I don't feel like I missed something by not having interacted with the human while he was alive and drawing. The person is not the art and the artist isn't the art. We must never ever confuse the storyteller with the story that's told.

There's not always a real connection. Sometimes there is; I did a reading of *Coraline* in San Francisco, and it was a three-and-a-half-hour event. I practically had no voice left. I got to the end of this thing and as I finished, author Daniel Handler leapt to his feet, clapping and shouting, "Again! Again! Read it again from the beginning!," and I was just like, "Of course you just did that and nobody else." It was pure him. That's who he actually is.

CS: The same sense of humor that's in his work.

NG: There's a real difference between somebody reading one of my stories and me reading it to them myself. I know what things are meant to sound like. I know if a line is meant to be funny.

CS: What are some words and phrases about Edward's work that you feel embody the nature of it?

NG: Edward Gorey's art is Edwardian, and yet, somehow timeless while always being not of this time. So Gorey would create art that felt like it had been drawn one hundred years ago with the sensibility of now and with people from now.

There was something balletic about it, something Jazz Age about it, with an embrace and love of the monstrous. He was like an English writer named Harry Graham, who wrote what were called ruthless rhymes. Reading Gorey, it feels like you have a wise and mordant observer from a distant time who is sitting in a corner somewhere, drawing impossible things happening to unfortunate people.

Even the effort of describing Gorey means you have to start rummaging into those places in your vocabulary that you don't normally get to go, because you are going to have to find words that have not really been in common use for seventy years.

Gorey is so absolutely unique; yet, his influence is now everywhere. Gorey's influence is obvious on me and those like Tim Burton and Lemony Snicket.

I think Gorey's influence now is in its second and third generation; people like Henry Selick, as well. He actually made the film of *Coraline* and *The Nightmare before Christmas*. Again, Gorey influenced people.

When I found his books, buying the actual small Gorey books, I found a tiny bookshop in San Francisco that had lots of them, and every time I went to San Francisco, I would buy a few more and bring them back. I wind up giving them to people because I would encounter people and go, "You need this more than I do," and these books would just go as gifts. I was never sure if they like them or not, but they always made the right noises.

I always feel that if somebody likes Gorey that they were the right kind of person. You know there's a basis for a potential friendship, just as you know that if Gorey meant nothing to somebody, you probably aren't actually going to hit it off.

CS: Do you think he's gonna be known, as years go by, in the history books as a great artist?

NG: Actually, no, I don't think that Gorey is ever gonna be in the history books as a great artist, 'cause I don't think that's what he was. I think great artists are something else, entirely. I think what Gorey was, was a work of art himself, and I think he may well go down in the history books as a glorious and unique work of art.

CS: Favorite Gorey book?

NG: Favorite Gorey book? My mind just starts breaking. I have enormous fondness for *The Curious Sofa* because it is a work of pornography with nothing rude in it.

CS: Well, if this was *The Newlywed* Game, you won, 'cause your wife [Amanda Palmer] picked the same thing.

NG: Really?

CS: Yes, so you win the hundred dollars.

NG: I love that. Did she pick it for the same reason or for different reasons? I do love the fact that it's pornography in its attitude and not in its content. There is just something glorious about that, but *The Doubtful Guest* is also wonderful. Basically anything; they all qualify.

The *Amphigorey* series is probably my favorite Gorey work because everything's in there.

CS: Seeing the works in relation to each other, being able to turn the pages, rather than jump from book to book, makes a compilation make more sense for him.

NG: Yeah.

CS: I love those compilations with all the bite-sized stories one after the other.

NG: I do love the compilations. What frustrated me is what you lose in the tiny books. It's just that sense of opening the page and getting one image, one image here and the text over here. Then it's one image here and the text over [here] again, and then you need to turn the page. There is always that sense of continuing surprise and curiosity that pulls you through. You also get to see the images in the size that he drew them, so there's that as a case for seeing the stories in their original form.

CS: Do you know why they are all different shapes?

NG: No.

CS: He self-published so many books in between his regular books, so he had a lot of freedom. He didn't have the patience to always publish them or, that is, to wait to get a publisher.

NG: Yeah, I can relate.

CS: He never wanted to publish in any other size than how he drew it. So, whatever size he drew the drawings, that's the way it was published and just another way that he had a great impact upon the literary machine.

NG: I know bookstores where he would sign Edward Gorey books; they would sell and do very well. They always loved the fact that Edward Gorey came in and blessed them, and then he would also sidle off with a stack of books that struck his own fancy. I never cared whether the story is true or not. It is just so perfectly

Goreyesque of a story that I would love it to be true. Childlike.

CS: Yeah, there was a childlike quality to him.

NG: I think you need to encounter Gorey at the right time in your life and in the right place in your head, whether that's childhood or not. You need eyes good enough to be able to see all the fine little, little cross-hatchings and scratchings and a childlike sense about you.

CS: Would you say that you really consider Gorey to be the source for you, or do you tend also to go to, like, Tim Burton and Lemony Snicket as well? Do you feel that they're all drawing directly from the source? Are you drawing from each other?

NG: I definitely don't think that I draw anything from Lemony Snicket or from Tim, because they all came much too late in my creative life. I was already me and I'd been already writing and stuff, so I was formed by that point. Gorey was in there while I was being formed, and I think he and Gahan Wilson, probably together, had a lot to do with forming my attitudes. Gahan was much more flat cartooning and jokes that had dark and hellish punch lines, while with Gorey, the punch line was never quite there. It was always that ambiguity that appealed to me.

We just resonate on the same level. It's like you hit a G and another G vibrates. I was the kind of person, just as Daniel Handler was the kind of person, just as I'm sure Tim Burton was the kind of person, who . . . when you see Gorey's stuff, you recognize it and you feel at home. You feel like you are part of a group, part of the gathering.

You feel in some way that Edward Gorey is speaking directly to you. The shared influences that I would point to on my work would be to point to the grand gothics. I'd point to all of the country house mysteries, E. F. Benson as a horror writer, and Robert Aickman.

It feels to me like every Aickman story should be illustrated by Edward Gorey, because they were both doing the same thing. It's all in the implications and the overtones and it's not in what's been overtly given to you. It's what's happening in the darkness, what's happening in the shadows, what's happening where your eyes don't go.

In Gorey, there is an attractiveness about his people and there's an attractiveness about his world. It all seems to take place in England, in a country house, in somewhere between 1919 and 1931 from the styles, but you can never be quite certain.

It is a country house created by P. G. Wodehouse. It's a country house created by Wilkie Collins. That country house has those servants and it has all the people who are there. It's going to have a lord of the manor and it's gonna have a chauffeur. Inside will be all these young people and old people, and yet, it is going to be timeless and strange. There could be bear attacks and there is a sort of a weird homeliness to it. These enormous, palatial, nightmarish, museum-decorated mansions also somehow feel like small suburban houses.

I don't know how he does that, but you feel at home there. You don't feel alienated, you just go, "I love this." There is all of the Victorian influences that were around in my childhood.

You see, in the 1960s and 1970s, every home wasn't actually a 1960s or 1970s home. Lots of them were in fact 1930s or earlier homes, because time leaves little eddies and bits behind. People do not always redecorate. So I'd be passing by houses built in the 1890s or in the 1800s. We lived in one, so it felt very familiar, in a very strange way. You'd update the bathroom, but that was about it. The rest, Victorian.

CS: What is it about the two of you as artists? Is it the same audience for you?

NG: I don't know if it's the same, I don't know if Gorey's audience and mine are the same audience. I do think they have a huge overlap.

Both of us have the same phenomenon, which is, in my case, "Neil Gaiman, who's he?" or "Neil Gaiman, oh my God! He's my favorite writer!" and not a lot of distance between the two.

I think the same thing goes with Gorey. There's, it's either "Edward Gorey, never heard of him . . . who's he? . . . what did he do? Oh really?" Or it's "Oh my God, Edward Gorey! I love him!" Then people will start telling you about *The Curious Sofas* and such. So for me, I think the weird joy of Gorey was that he didn't ever change who he was or what he did to suit the marketplace. What he did was what he was, and what he was was what he did. This isn't to say that he wouldn't design you a poster for your cat show. But he'd go off and do a fantastic, beautiful commercial poster for a cat show.

It wasn't that he only did one thing and did not do anything but that one thing. I think he did lots of things, but all of those things, you could see they were coming from a unique point of view. They were coming from a point of view where everything was absolutely and utterly personal. So, you can tell at a glance that the person doing them didn't mind if you liked them or not.

CS: He could get a call from a fan and say, "Yes, let's go out to lunch," would go out to lunch with some unknown fan, and at the same time, his editor couldn't get ahold of him for three weeks. He did what he wanted; he still wanted to have a relationship with people and be a human being and be able to choose.

I don't think the level of success he had changed any of that. He didn't have any problem with saying "Yes" too much either.

When it comes to *Coraline*, was there anything that you knowingly drew from? Do you think it was more in the background?

NG: You see, for *Coraline*, there is attitude, and the attitude is more who I'm telling the story to and are they willing to listen to the story?

That, for me, was quintessentially a Gorey approach. It was this idea that you are just telling the story that you want to tell. Ninety-nine out of a hundred people are going to just not be on your wavelength, and that you're fine with that as a writer. They're gonna look at a story like *Coraline* and just go, "It's too weird." Then one person is gonna go, "This. This is the most beautiful thing I've ever seen." There's a willingness on the part of the audience to be that in a world that is somewhat disquieting. So, the biggest thing I felt that I gained from Gorey was just the willingness to go, "Okay, I'm gonna do a story for five-, six-, seven-, eight-, nine-, ten-year-olds, and it's gonna be scary."

Knowing as I wrote it that one day I wanted to send it to Gorey, that I wanted him to draw it, meant certain things about the character. Coraline in my head was a tiny little Gorey figure. Just the imagining of her . . . if Gorey is doing a drawing it, Coraline is never going to fill the drawing. She's always gonna be a small, white-faced, blank figure with terrifying things around her, even if the terrifying things are just shadows in the shape of the world. She's going to be this little thing. That Gorey idea kept me going in a weird kind of way, that idea, the taste of the story.

CS: It reminds me of *The Hapless Child*.

NG: Gorey's children all tend to end up dead, whether they're devoured by bears, carried off by illness, or simply drowned underneath the ice. So, when I think of Gorey, I also think about things that are there at the corner of your eye.

My wife was reading my book *Anansi Boys* the other night for the first time, and she said, "What is it with you and flapping things that might or might not be birds, but a sort of raggedy seen-from-the corner-of-your-eye in trees and things." I'm like, "I, I, um . . ." Thinking about that question now, though, the answer is they're very Goreyesque. You can't quite tell what it is either way. It's Gorey's use of ambiguity.

He has a willingness to never spell anything out. It's perhaps more than a willingness, but a refusal ever to spell anything out. He will give you the pieces. It's almost as if he'll give you a crossword and you have to fill it out yourself. He's filled out a lot of it for you, but then you're also not quite sure if you filled it out correctly because he might have given you only half a clue. Then there's something that contradicts it. So Gorey's way of constructing stories was deeply, gloriously ambiguous. He would give with one hand and take with the other, and you just had to enjoy that.

CS: Yeah. Any other Gorey stories or observations that you'd like to make?

NG: I do wish Gorey had been more popular. I wish you could talk to people about him and everybody would recognize him. I wish that his style, his uniqueness, the vision that he had, was understood and delighted in by everybody.

At the same time, I'm also accepting of the fact that it isn't. Maybe thirty years from now there will be Gorey shops that will sell nothing but tiny Edward Gorey books, Edward Gorey prints, and Edward Gorey posters, and you will go there and it will be the world of Gorey, but probably that will never happen.

NG: [*The sound of his son returning from the playground*] And I think we're done.

CS: That was a beautiful ending with your son entering.

NG: Well, this came out pretty good . . .

CS: Thank you so much, more than generous.

NG: You're so welcome, Chris.

CS: This was a beautiful interview. I'm so glad I gave you that space at the end.

NG: [*To his son*] Hi, Sausage! Hello, Ash, did you have a good time with mama?

Danny Elfman Interview

MARCH 11, 2019

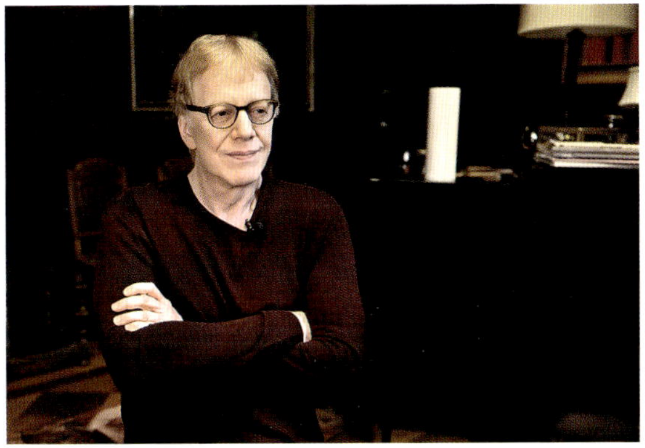

Danny Elfman is a soundtrack composer and musician. His and Edward Gorey's creative outputs are often compared for their similar blend of dark whimsy and horror. Elfman is known for his scores for films by Tim Burton such as *The Nightmare Before Christmas* and his eighties band Oingo Boingo.

The crew (Doug Lloyd and Elsa Munroe) and I were informed by Mr. Elfman's assistant that he would not be able to meet us at his studio that day. Having flown out to LA from Cape Cod for the interview, my heart sank. When we called back, we were asked instead if we wouldn't mind meeting at his house that he shared with his wife (actress Bridget Fonda) and son. Even better.

Danny Elfman: Uh oh, that chair is broken. Better get another chair. Two sides are already disconnected. That's going to go. Grab a safe one there.

Christopher Seufert: Well, it's like the old interview tactic where you have the person who's being interviewed, you know, use the uncomfortable seat and you have all the power.

DE: Well, or the tactic that puts the interviewer in the very chair that's about to go down.

CS: [*Laughs*] Yeah, see, now I'm lower than you. I'm not sure this is actually a good idea because we should be the same at least for the camera angle.

DE: You want me to just look at you? Not the camera?

CS: Exactly, yeah, just look at me; we're going to ignore this.

DE: Okay, so I'll just aim to the top of your head.

CS: Well, everyone, we're off to a great start here. Places, everyone. So if we could just start with the traditional, say your name and your occupation, just so when I die, this footage has that in there.

DE: To the camera?

CS: No, just say it.

DE: Okay.

CS: And now we know how you want to be referred to for the lower third.

DE: My name is Danny Elfman. And what was the other information?

CS: Occupation.

DE: I am a composer or a decomposer. [*Laughs*]

CS: Okay, I'll try to get serious, so maybe we can start with how you first came in contact with Edward Gorey's work.

DE: Let's see, I could barely have been a teenager. I don't know how it started, but it was the alphabet [*Gashlycrumb Tinies*], of course, that I just knew about forever. I probably couldn't have been fifteen or sixteen at the most.

CS: Where was this book? Did you have it or was it your parents'?

DE: No, they wouldn't have, and that's why I don't know, because we didn't have the internet back then, but I remember very little of my childhood. So, the fact that I don't recall that is normal for me.

CS: Well, what Lemony Snicket told us was that he almost considered it like pornography, and then he would sneak out to these bookstores and walk back to his house with a couple tucked carefully under his arms.

DE: Yeah. Yeah. And then it was really more like high school age.

CS: What was your reaction to it as well?

DE: Well, of course the humor immediately appealed to me. The dark humor at that age was like seeing something totally on the nose for me, but the drawings were really the thing. I remember seeing cartoons, you know, that were Edward Gorey or Edward Gorey–inspired and kind of knowing who he was. But I still don't exactly remember the initial source.

CS: Maybe the *Mystery!* series PBS opening?

DE: This was, I think, before that. I'm trying to think of what magazines might have had some pictures when I started to become a little bit aware of his work.

CS: He was on Dick Cavett in the mid-'70s. I don't think he was on TV much. Of course, *Dracula* on Broadway was kind of where he entered the mainstream for a lot of people.

DE: Right. When was that?

CS: 1977 to 1979 or so.

DE: So when did he write the *Tinies*?

CS: In the '60s, like late 1960s.

DE: Yeah. So that would have been like middle school, high school age, somewhere in there. The artwork appealed to me. There was a certain point in my twenties when I realized, or came to the conclusion, that I was born out of my time. There were two time periods I felt I belonged in, and one of them was late Victorian and one of them was Harlem, 1933, and I kind of gravitated between these two. There was no doubt that I did not feel like the '60s or the '70s. I maintained a fascination with late Victorian and collecting late Victorian scientific and anatomical scientific instruments. At my studio I've got a pretty decent collection of late 1800 scientific material going back to the early 1800s, a number of microscopes and optical devices. I love the fact that everything from that period looked beautiful. Everything was made of brass, and I kept that fascination because I got more successful and I was able to start looking for and obtaining a lot of really beautiful objects from that period.

CS: Would you say that your interest in this aesthetic comes from a shared inspiration with Edward Gorey, or were you more in parallel?

DE: Both. I felt like I was in parallel, but I think it started with his drawings, really. The look and feel of his drawings got me interested in that era, and then the interest in the era then kind of moved into both science and art, the feel of it, the architecture for sure. My first exposure to this aesthetic would have been to Gorey.

CS: You've got my brain spinning because you're the first person, and I mean I've been enmeshed in this twenty-five years, the first person to mention science in this way.

DE: It never stopped, you know. If you look at the books by the side of my bed, you have every Arctic and Antarctic expedition done from the middle to the late 1800s. I'm just really intensely obsessed with these late Victorian Arctic expeditions. The search for the Arctic Sea was like a big one. The reasoning and the science behind it was that they thought the earth was like a living organism with a circulatory system in the ocean currents that went from the bottom to the top and then back around again. They were sure that there was a warm sea in the middle of the Arctic that no one had found, and the amount of lives that went to finding that was remarkable. If you saw *The Terror* on TV recently, that was what that was all about.

CS: I loved that.

DE: They took this real expedition, of course, and took it off into a bit of fantasy, but the real story of that expedition is truly amazing.

CS: Now that I think about it, that whole world that he created is evocative of all the very early stages in transportation and the technology of film cameras. It was almost like even the houses in Gorey's world are the houses of, like, retired explorers because they're loaded with things like taxidermy and trees brought back from distant voyages. Exotic carpets and statues.

DE: Well, those are all the Goreyesque things that I now collect. I have quite a bit of taxidermy, even here in this room. My wife [Bridget Fonda] had a Hollywood family, and there're a few pieces that have legends associated with them, having been shot by people like John Huston, but my own things are definitely Victorian-era taxidermy and big carpets like you'd see in Gorey's drawings.

CS: He would get so focused onto creating every possible detail on those carpets, wall tapestries, and wallpaper.

DE: Which clearly I could tell. So that became my model of looking for a home. I wanted to live in a big old house with giant carpets and didn't quite find it. I mean, in Los Angeles it's like what are you going to do? However, I got as close as I could.

CS: So, here's the crux of it for me. How do you take those aesthetics and apply it to music?

DE: Well, it's not so much the music as the aesthetic, because I can't say any of my music is necessarily Victorian inspired, which I don't find inspiring. My musical influences all bounced around, starting in the big-band era and progressing forward into Russian influences. Then there are the words in my lyrics. So you know "M is for Mara, who washed out to sea." I'm not quoting correctly. "N is for Neville, who died of ennui." That type of lyric definitely entered my subconscious even when I was writing lyrics for *Nightmare Before Christmas*.

CS: Do you think music like new wave has certain elements like a pop punk quality to it, or, say, could connections be made from punk music to Edward's art? Are there shared aesthetics in the offhand quality of it? Do you think there's anything in there?

DE: Yeah, that part I wouldn't agree with because the punk aesthetic was so spartan, it was all minimalism, you know. You sleep in a room with nothing but an old rug and a sleeping bag on a floor, whereas the Victorian era was plush. Rooms were big, carpets were plush, beds were overstuffed, walls had fabric on them. I love that aesthetic. You know when I first saw this room that you're sitting in? If I were filthy rich, there would be tapestry on the walls just like that, but the person who did this rare work of putting up an entire 25-foot wall of fabric retired, and we never found anybody to really do it and then finally just forgot it. This was like a custom print that we were getting from Italy. It was super expensive anyhow.

CS: So when you see an object like you're talking about, in your mind are you thinking that's kind of Goreyesque?

DE: No, I just think of that as something I want in my home, or that's a room I'd like to live in, and it all ties together. So, I don't think specifically, "Am I thinking of Gorey" or something

Gothic. He's part of what's always there for me and what I recognized in these dark images in his books that I just came to love.

CS: If you were to look at your entire body of work, is there one thing that stands out as particularly Goreyesque?

DE: You know, I would have loved to do music for a Gorey-inspired play, but it just never happened. I keep wishing for something that I would design that would have that look and that feel to the music that I could do and would be good at in that way.

CS: What are some of the qualities of it or phrases of the individual work?

DE: Well, I think it's something that I applied in my work, but not frequently and specifically in a Victorian way. It's dark but it's also whimsical and lyrical, but there's also kind of a little bit of a twist to the lyricism. That's how I think of kind of the core of me, so how that applies to my music I don't really know, but this is what people tell me. It's kind of dark but also whimsical, and these are the things that would make me think back to those early influences and Gorey.

CS: That's exactly what I was after. So if you think about when you began working with Tim Burton, would you say that it was a similar type of recognition when you saw Tim's visuals?

DE: Yeah. I mean, it's that parallel thing. Definitely. We had the same influences when we met, and we realized we were two kids that grew up on monsters. We both loved Edward Gorey, and I could see it very clearly in the drawings that he was doing. If you look at Vincent, for example, one of his early shorts that was the first thing I saw of his, there's clearly a strong Gorey influence in the characters and how they look. And when you see his really well-rendered drawings . . . the backgrounds, and the textures are obviously inspired by Gorey as well. It would be hard to see that the inspiration didn't come from there. So, we were alike in that way. The Edward Gorey books, the monster-movie growing-up his, his idol was Vincent Price, mine was Peter Lorre. So we had a lot of parallel kind of influences. That he didn't seem strange to me.

CS: Yeah. Someone said that *The Melancholy Death of Oyster Boy* was like a tribute to Edward Gorey. Would you say that's fair?

DE: Yes, well, I can't speak for Tim, but I would say it's fair to assume that.

CS: So if you both have this parallel aesthetic that you recognize in each, what's a typical directorial instruction from Mr. Burton when you're working on one of his films? Is it specific or is it more inspirational?

DE: It's definitely, definitely not specific. There is not a lot of instruction from Tim. Tim responds to hearing music. He doesn't give instruction about what should or shouldn't be a starting place. We really don't talk about the movie very much before I start. That was true for *Beetlejuice*, *Nightmare Before Christmas*, *Corpse Bride* . . .

CS: Macabre and whimsical would be sort of a general starting point, it seems like.

DE: We wouldn't even discuss that. We know each other's tastes well enough and this is just how we both see things, so there's zero discussion about that. I'd see the images from *Corpse Bride*, from *Nightmare*, and go, "Yeah. Makes perfect sense to me," and he would go, "What do I have to explain about this?"

So there was this one Victorian-inspired piece of music in *Corpse Bride* where I was turning the clock, because, you know, my biggest inspirations musically when I'm doing a musical like that for Tim would be both Gilbert and Sullivan and then Kurt Pyle, who was later in the early part of the twentieth century. So there was one piece I wrote for the wedding in *Corpse Bride* that I got to touch on Gilbert and Sullivan, and they're like absolute favorites of mine, where I got to have choruses of men going, "Huzzah!" And I've always wanted to do that, many men going, "Huzzah!"

CS: It sounds like the two of you are fairly steeped in the same influences. Can you tell me more about all of your other influences? I mean, just who you're influenced by? I have a feeling that it's a family that's somewhat interconnected.

DE: Well, if I'm writing a song, it's gonna be Kurt Vile. You know the Brecht in Vile influences is huge on me, and Gilbert and Sullivan are going to be huge on me. I don't know who else. There're very few influences from contemporary songs written after the '30s or '40s. Definitely Cole Porter. And I do love *Sweeney Todd*. Probably the most contemporary piece that I really love musically would be Sondheim. For me to love a piece of music for a musical written as late as the '80s is really rare and unique.

But then orchestrally it's Russian straight through, starting with Stravinsky, then to Shostakovich and Prokofiev. To a certain degree you'll find some Eric Satie and Tchaikovsky would be probably the earliest of the influences of mine, but you know the big three: Prokofiev, Shostakovich, and Stravinsky are really where my world turns around musically.

CS: Music was huge for Edward. He was literally just putting music straight into his filter, and it would come out on the page. One can't stress how big an influence music was for him. A big part of his collecting was CDs and music, and if he couldn't find something he owned, he'd just go get it again.

DE: He would have loved the days of ripping music and creating playlists that are there forever.

CS: Yeah, he would have, absolutely, and he jammed his plays on the Cape, these little small plays, full of the music that he loved. He did a lot of Beethoven bagatelles, much of the music that you're mentioning like Satie. I'm in awe of how the disciplines are crossing over and speaking to each other, but let's sidetrack for a second and talk about the influences of your most mainstream work like Oingo Boingo and Weird Science. Are these influences still finding a way to seep in?

DE: No, I don't think so. I think you know when I do different things, I just go all the way over from one side to the other. So when I started a rock band, I'd heard ska music from England, you know, and I said, "Okay, I'm done with everything." It was the same thing I did when I heard Stravinsky and threw out all my records in the late '70s. When I heard ska, I just said, "I want to do that now," and I just dropped everything and started a rock band, and the influences were completely different again.

Likewise when I started scoring, it was very important for me to drop every influence of rock and roll that I had ever picked up to that point and start without any of that in my mind at all. After many years I did do some scores where at least I brought in a little bit of electric guitar and drums and had fun with that, but other than that small bit of crossover they're just different things. I don't like it when I hear pop songs in orchestral music. On the other hand, I don't like rock music that feels like Beethoven chords put to a rock beat. That bores me, so I actually try to keep everything as separate as I can. That's the way my mind works anyhow.

CS: So would you say that you were doing something with Oingo Boingo at that time period that did fully flower once you got into the soundtracks of the movies into the '90s and everything?

DE: No, it's the same thing that's just dropping suddenly into Oingo Boingo out of the blue. It was less than a year between me doing this very elaborate cabaret theater show to, like, just scrapping it all and starting rock onstage with no theatrics. Then when I started film music, it's like, "Now, forget Oingo Boingo." I'm now thinking of Bernard Herrmann and Nino Rota and the film composers I loved growing up and how they would approach this kind of music. I don't think Oingo Boingo came to any full flowering. Many people would tell you Oingo Boingo's best days were its earliest, and that's why I wanted to get out of the band so badly, because I had no interest in any of the early material anymore. However, I do understand what it's like to be a fan of a band. You go to a concert and you want to hear their early material, the stuff that you grew up on that you really love. You can't ignore it as a musician, but on the other hand, I was only interested in the later stuff and eventually reached a point where I never want to perform these songs again. You know, whether I ever do or not now is another story, but back in those days I was never interested in anything I had done before whatever I was doing. I never listened to an Oingo Boingo album once it was done, and I never listened to a soundtrack album once it was finished.

When I did the Tim Burton twenty-five-year-anniversary set, it was the first time I'd listened to any of the scores of these except for *Alice [in Wonderland]*, which I had just recently finished that the year before. Listening to the early ones was like, "Really? That's what *Batman* sounded like?" Oh my God. *Peewee*, that was super primitive, you know; it was interesting because it's like I hadn't remembered that's how I wrote. I just, I don't keep my older stuff too. It drives people that work with me crazy.

They would like to archive things, but I don't keep them. When we tried to put those things together, I didn't keep any old stuff. I didn't keep old tapes, I didn't keep notes, I didn't keep music. Like once I'm done with it, I don't care. Throw it out. I can give a shit, so I'm the worst archivist in the world. My assistants had to spend like three months combing through storage rooms looking for unmarked boxes with demo tapes of early Tim Burton film scores, because nothing was labeled or marked. For all I knew, it was all in the trash bin.

CS: Would you say that your films are primarily geared for children? I'm pushing a hot button there on purpose with you, but here's my motivation. What do you think the connection is between the dark macabre places and how children respond to that so positively?

DE: Well, I always knew that, but you know others really didn't. When *Nightmare Before Christmas* came out, every song I wrote went through my daughter first, who was about ten. She loved and would approve everything. When we did the press junket, Tim and I would come out at the end of the movie and it was just miserable. Every single journalist would lead with "So this isn't for kids." I go, "What do you mean? "Well, this is too scary for kids." I go, "Why?"

CS: That's what I'm talking about. It would drive Edward crazy.

DE: They'd all say, "Well, ya know, stuff like it's too scary for kids, isn't it?" I would always have the same answer, and I'd have to say it over a hundred times in one week. I'd say, "Are your kids afraid of Halloween?" "No, they love Halloween." So we'd say, "Then it's not too scary for kids." Then I would get feedback like "They torture Santa Claus, don't they?" And I'd respond, "No, Santa Claus gets hung up and it doesn't seem to irritate him very much. It makes him a little grumpy and everything's fine. It was not torture. He's not even very angry about it, and he seems mildly annoyed at most by an inconvenience. No, he wasn't tortured." But you know that was the perception, and that's why it's so gratifying when the movie had its resurgence fifteen years later and the following had all been kids. So-and-so is five years old and he knows all the lyrics to this song, or I get videos sent to me all the time and some little kids singing a song from *Nightmare Before Christmas*.

I always knew it. Tim knew it, but Disney didn't at that time, nor did anybody else. To their credit they figured it out after the fact, and I'll always feel grateful for that. Most studios would not have rereleased a film from fifteen years ago. They'd say, "That ship has sailed." Disney was clever enough to get beyond when an animated feature meant *Aladdin* and *Beauty and the Beast* and *The Little Mermaid*. So even when they did a test screening for little kids, which was ridiculous, with an unfinished animation where there're still pencil sketches on the screen and these little kids going to see a Disney animated musical. They're expecting *The Little Mermaid* and they get a *Nightmare Before Christmas.* They're like, "What?" So that was a rough time.

Tim put it best once when he was getting hammered on one of the *Batman* movies by the censorship bureau that was going to give it a restricted rating for nothing specific. It was *Batman Returns*, and there's no violence and there's no sex. The only violence is just bang bang you're dead. People fall down. No gore and nothing graphic. It just set the expectation that it was all just too dark.

Tim said to me, "This isn't scary for kids, this isn't dark for kids. You know what's scary for kids? The sound of Dad walking in the house drunk. That's scary for kids. This shit isn't scary for kids!" And he's absolutely right. You know what's scary for kids is things that are real and scary. Not scary for kids is imaginary dark things that are clearly done in an imaginary way. Granted, when something gets too graphic I could understand a lot of kids really don't want to go there, and there's a good argument why they shouldn't. My son does, he likes horror films, and I go, "Well, that was me growing up." All I ever saw as a kid was horror films. My parents had no idea what I was seeing. So stuff like what you're talking about, I feel, is misunderstood.

You know, the early Burton films were the kind of stuff I would've loved as a kid, but what are you gonna do? It's like people have to figure that out for themselves.

CS: Yeah. Thanks, that was beautifully said. If Edward were alive today and his people got in touch with yours about some collaboration, what do you imagine that collaboration would be like? How would you do music to a Gorey animation? Would it be the same as the stuff you do for Burton, or do you think slightly different?

DE: It's hard to say. I approach everything with a different sensibility because each director is going to be slightly different.

CS: What do you imagine it might be if it was just Gorey?

DE: It just totally depends on what it was. Dr. Seuss, or Theodore Geisel, approached me about doing a musical with him, and I thought that would've been great fun, but he died before we did it. Similarly, I'd love to have had a chance to meet Gorey, or to collaborate on a piece; of course that would be wonderful. I think I'd be just perfect for it, but what it would be I have no idea, I couldn't tell ya.

CS: What do you imagine the relationship is between Gorey and his artwork? You yourself probably get approached by people who expect you to be a certain way, considering what they know about your music, and yet, you're different in a lot of ways. Most artists are different from their artwork.

DE: Well. That's true. Unfortunately, most people who come into my home and my studio and look around, they go, "Yeah, that's exactly what we expected." [*Laughs*] I hate to be right on the money, but it's, it's hard to get away with it because it's what I'm into. So in that sense, my environment does reflect my perception, which is pretty much my personality, but I would have no idea about Gorey. I mean, I know people that are into very dark art; yet, they live in very clean environments that don't feel how I would have expected.

On the other hand, that doesn't surprise me. Everybody needs something different to inspire them, and I understand when somebody needs absolute order in their life, especially if they've got a disorderly mind. You want a real clean, orderly space with clean lines.

I'm the opposite. I turn everything into a museum, but I'm also somebody who's been a collector since they were eighteen years old collecting objects and oddities. So my space always starts out clean and then give it a year or two and it looks like a Gothic museum. When I worked with Tim in New York on *Sleepy Hollow* and I lived there for like two months working with them from my hotel room . . . it was like the joke of the hotel. I just started buying stuff at flea markets every Sunday, and by the time I left my hotel room it was like a little crazy Gothic museum. I ended up getting Indian fabrics, darker fabrics, and putting them over the windows to make filtered light. I didn't like the white light and I like filtered light, and so anywhere I go, the clutter follows.

That's just what I like in order to function. I've also got a very cluttered mind, and you think I'd want a really opposite space, but it works for me just to see all the things that scared me as a child, looking back at me as an adult, because most everything I collect are things that terrified me when I was little.

CS: Edward would have probably said the exact same thing that you just said; you guys are similar in that way. I have an interview with him talking about when he moved from New York to the Cape, to Cape Cod, and how he intended on moving in there and making it sort of feng shui-ed, very Zen, spare place. Within months the house was just creaking with books, to his own frustration, because he's like, "I just can't stop myself."

DE: Yeah.

CS: So, to approach that from a slightly different angle. I've just heard so many people talk about how they were sort of equally interested in Gorey as a person and not just his artwork. I was wondering if you share that or if your interest in Gorey is really all about the artwork?

DE: I was always really curious about Gorey, but I'm a lazy researcher so, you know, I was into his art. I wondered what he was like. But it's crazy, I also wondered what Stravinsky was like, and I've got four books on him and haven't read any of them yet, so I'm just bad that way. It's like I want to just know the person, but I don't want to read the four books because I'm just lazy that way, for lack of a better word.

All of my energy focuses into the music that I'm working on all the time, and very little's left when it comes down to reading about something. I end up reading about an Arctic expedition done in 1875 because that's the kind of story that I could hold on to, and when I read I start and stop, start and stop. I go through many long periods where I just can't read anything except when I'm going to sleep, and it's hard to read two pages at a time and then your eyes give out. I hardly ever get the breaks I need to read these books when I'm reading myself on a daily basis; it tends to be nonfiction, easy-to-follow fantastic stories. For me, reading Shackleton's adventure, I could do that over and over again. It'll just hold me, but a biography, I just never finish even one of them. I've had this biography about Einstein sitting on my bedside for at least six years. I'm intensely interested in it, so shame on me.

I have the imagined character of Edward Gorey, and I guess I've been satisfied with the imaginary Gorey that I have constructed via his art. He may in fact be nothing like that. By the way, sometimes it's better not to know your heroes. Alfred Hitchcock's a hero, and then more and more stuff comes out about what he was like, and I'm not sure that I want to know this. He's still going to be my hero; it's just going to make it harder to deal with this part of him. Nothing will make him not my hero.

It's the same with both John Huston and Stanley Kubrick. There's a certain part where I'm fine with just who I imagine that person to be. I love their art, and their art is part of the DNA of what made me, so learning about their shortcomings and flaws and what bad people they might have been in various ways, it's almost something I just don't want to know. You know the people who grew up with and loved Michael Jackson their whole lives are feeling this right now. That's got to be hard.

CS: Music is so personal.

DE: It was an influence on them. If his music influenced the core fabric of their DNA as they learn that that person did terrible things is hard. So sometimes I want to be careful about scratching too deep because if Edward Gorey was a horrible person, I don't want to know that he beat people or tortured animals. I don't want to know that stuff. I just want to hold on to this Gothic, eccentric character that I imagine in my mind's eye is clever, strange, and has this twisted humor. I imagine him as an eccentric but kindly fellow, and I'm happy with that imagined version. Now if it turns out that that's what he was, all the better, but I think that's one of the reasons that ever keeps me from getting too deep into my heroes' lives.

CS: Yeah, I love that, thanks. Let's go to the big picture in sort of an academic way. Do you think he'll be seen as a significant artist in the art history world of nineteenth- or twentieth-century artists? Will he go down as someone who lasts?

DE: I think his work will sustain because in the same way that I also collect the art of Louis Wain, a schizophrenic Victorian artist who drew cats . . . at any time I can get a Louis Wain piece, and I can get books on him and that's over one hundred years old. I think Edward Gorey will be the same. His stuff is so unique. I think it will appeal to generations for a long time, and no one's going to come along that's just going to wipe that out. I think he'll go through a number of rediscoveries. People will suddenly go, "Oh my God, I never heard of this. Look how amazing it is. Who would put that much detail into essentially an illustrated cartoon. It's incredible. And look at these stories and rhymes. Look at all the things that he came up with." I think it will endure. He may go through periods of being forgotten momentarily and then back again. That's just how culture works.

CS: In the artwork you collect, what is most like Gorey's aesthetic?

DE: I have a skull hanging over that table. That's one of my favorite pieces. I do collect a lot of old bones. It's a very old specimen of a spider monkey. My favorite specimens really came from universities somewhere in between seventy-five and one hundred and fifty years ago. For example, I have five shrunken heads, and I've got skulls from Egypt and mummified hands. I have skulls from Peru that have been purposely misshapen. These things fascinate me.

CS: Is there anything that I've missed that you feel like it would be good to talk about in terms of your own work and connection to Edward? I don't always get it right.

DE: Oh, I don't think so. By the way, speaking of books, if you want to check out the ultimate nonfiction story, you should read *In the Heart of the Sea*. These guys spent many months in a whaleboat after being sunk by a whale, and they're stuck in this little lifeboat crossing the entire Pacific Ocean. They had to resort to cannibalism. If it were fiction, you'd go, "Yeah, right, there's no way this happened the way this happened." But of course, it did.

CS: Are you off to work?

DE: I'm off to the studio beneath us. My studio, which happens to be a basement, is all concrete. Floors, walls, and ceiling, with a 12-foot ceiling . . . We don't know what it was previously or why the room was built that way. You don't put in a torture chamber or a kill room without a drain. [*Laughs*]

Doug Lloyd [Camera]: No, of course not, everybody knows that.

Elsa Munroe [Camera]: Everybody knows that.

DE: Everyone knows that; here, let me turn on the lights.

Clifford Ross Interview

JULY 24, 2019

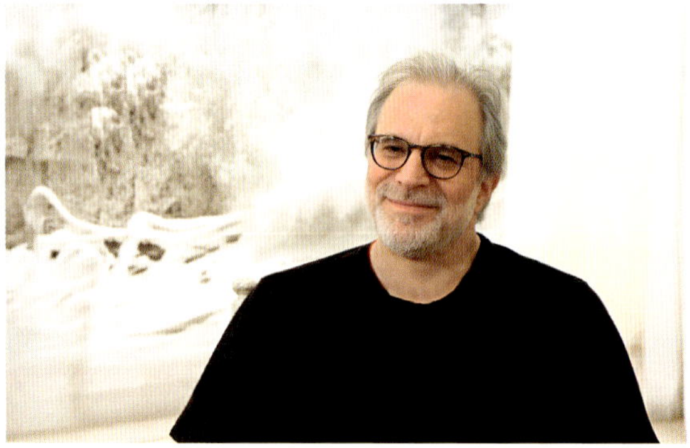

Clifford Ross was a friend of Edward's for over thirty years. He curated the first major survey of Edward Gorey's work for his senior thesis at Yale University in 1974. The accompanying exhibition catalog was titled *Phantasmagorey: The Work of Edward Gorey* and was published by Yale University Press. He also wrote 1996's *The World of Edward Gorey*. We met for an interview at his studio in New York City.

Clifford Ross: I'm Clifford Ross, and I'm an artist and a longtime friend of Ted's.

Christopher Seufert: Did you call him Ted?

CR: Yeah, I think I called him Ted most of the time. I have no idea where I picked that up, but it seemed like a number of people really close to him called him Ted, and it just felt natural.

CS: Yeah. Yeah, I was just with a group of people that always called him Edward. And I think it was just that one level removed.

You know, I think with his inner circle it was always Ted, but with everyone I heard it was Edward. For me there was a large age difference, so I was practically at Mr. Gorey even though we became friends, you know?

CR: Mr. Gorey. That's funny.

CS: So you first contacted him professionally? Was it about his work?

CR: Yeah. The first contact I had, I'd never heard of Edward. I was seventeen years old and I tended to haunt old bookstores below 14th Street. I would buy things that were peculiar and interesting with no particular rhyme or reason.

One day I found a tiny little paperback that was, if I recall, largely a black-and-white cover with some pink, and it was such a strange-looking thing. It was called *The Willowdale Handcar*. I bought it for fifteen cents, maybe a quarter, and stuck it in my pocket. I remember looking at it on the way home and I was sort of fascinated with it. I was a senior in high school and I really didn't think much more about it. It was just sitting there, somewhat haunting me, and about six months later, I think it might have even been during the summer, I was walking on 47th Street between 5th and 6th.

It's a block I had never walked on that I could recall, and I was looking around because there were all these diamond merchants and things. It was so peculiar.

CS: "Peculiar." That word keeps coming back every time I talk about Edward or his work.

CR: So there was a sort of a magnetic pull to my right, and my head swiveled and there it was: the Gotham Book Mart. At this time the Gotham Book Mart was so famous. I had never heard of it, though, so I just looked at this incredible window of books and funny objects and I realized that it was a place I had to go into. It looked like a cave of magical things. So I walked in and wandered around, and it was indeed filled with magical things.

I found one bookshelf, maybe two, that were filled with books with similar spines. The style looked as if I'd seen it before, and, in fact, it was one or two shelves of books by Edward Gorey, so I sort of reached in and began pulling them out. I was riveted that there were so many books of this general type by him. It was like I'd fallen into some macabre and yet sweet version of Disneyland. I'd never seen anything like it.

It was a total world. This was before I had decided to become an artist, not that one decides, but before I became an artist, let's say. While I was flipping through the books, somebody tapped me on the shoulder and it was Andreas Brown, who owned the Gotham Book Mart at that point. He said, "Oh, are you a fan of Mr. Gorey?"

I said something like, "I think I might be, but I'm not sure." He said something like, "Good answer. When you're done looking, come on to the back and see me."

So I probably stuck around that bookshelf for half an hour, maybe more, and I wandered back through piles of books and all that into this incredible inner office, the inner sanctum, and Andreas was there sitting at a desk.

As I crossed through the doorway, there was one of those vibrations, and on the left was Edward Gorey himself. He was sitting there, then looked up, somewhat flustered, bewildered, slightly embarrassed, and vaguely curious. He didn't say a word, but he had on one of his big sweaters, all the various rings, the necklaces, the great beard. And I think he had on those little eyeglasses of his, because he was busy reading or hanging out with Andreas. So that was my introduction.

CS: Wow, what year was this, about?

CR: Probably around 1970.

CS: I had never heard that story before. I'd never made it to the Gotham Book Mark myself before it went bankrupt. So, did you have any conversation with him at that point?

CR: Yeah, we were introduced. As I recall, even though it was summer, there was a big raccoon coat lying nearby, and clearly that was his raccoon coat. I thought, probably not in this phrasing, but what a cool cat. I mean, the beard, the rings, the whole thing. In 1970, that was the edge of things in a cool way.

And he was sort of shy, but sort of intrigued because maybe Andreas said, hey, there's some kid up in the front who's attached to your books, and, knowing Edward, he probably would have said, "Oh dear, that's just terrible," but there I was.

We had a really nice talk, and even though I grew up around a lot of artists, there was something so focused about Edward. He was so much sort of a magical world unto himself. I was quite drawn to him.

CS: So it was sort of a one-two punch meeting his work and then meeting him in the flesh pretty close to each other. It's kind of a heady brew.

CR: Yeah, I don't think I experienced it initially that way as a seventeen-year-old. It wasn't so much that I would have thought of it as something major, having met artists before, but the world of Edward Gorey, as I had already begun to understand it from buying that first book, was a very intense and particular essence, something that I thought probably didn't exist except in another century.

Yet, here was this guy who was clearly living out his fantasy, his vision in a complete way, whether it was how he was dressed or the books he was creating, and I found that very compelling, someone who knew his identity in that way.

CS: So that piqued your interest enough that when it came to school, you did your master's thesis about him?

CR: No, not at all. I think as a seventeen-year-old in search of an identity for myself, perhaps just running into Edward, I was intrigued because there's an identity somebody can have and live a life. I found it rather stunning coming from a fairly straight background.

I don't mean straight sexually, but just more straight as in a tight background. I was so enchanted with him and the work that I think over the next year, I picked up a few more books for $3 or $5 from Gotham Book Mart, and I also began going, whether it was in New Haven or elsewhere, to a lot of old bookstores to buy them on the cheap. Over the course of the next several years, I probably must have purchased twenty or thirty books and became a real aficionado.

CS: Most of them, a lot of them, were probably first editions, I would imagine.

CR: Yeah, I think a lot of them were, and I would sort of trade upward if I found one that was less dog-eared than another, and I'd sell the more dog-eared one back to Gotham Book Mart and I sort of inadvertently became a collector. While I was at school [Yale University], that's when I really became interested in and eventually addicted to art, both as an artist and interested in art history.

When it came time to do my thesis as a senior for the art history department, I decided rather than write yet another essay on Van Gogh, and there have been so many, I thought, why don't I try and do a retrospective and write an essay with a catalog on the work of Edward Gorey? It was such an outrageous idea. There was no one at Yale who knew anything about Edward Gorey, so I picked the art historian who was a specialist in northern sun landscape painting, and somehow or other he actually did know of Edward Gorey, and he thought, wow, you know, here's a crazy student with a crazy idea. Let's support his effort.

So I did the first retrospective of Edward's work as a senior at Yale and wrote a catalog and became a great friend and passionate fan of Edward Gorey.

CS: So you contacted him a bit throughout the process while you were at Yale. Did you see him in person in New York or on the Cape?

CR: Yeah, during those years, he wasn't living on the Cape full-time. He was still in New York, and I would see him mainly in the first year or two at Gotham Book Mart.

If I came in, he was there a lot of the time. As a junior, I was getting more and more interested in him, and I was faced with the knowledge that I'd need to do a thesis about him. I asked him about it and he said, you know, that classic constant refrain of "Oh dear, why me?" or something like that, but he acquiesced and was very helpful, and Andreas Brown was an enormous help.

By the time I was a senior I was really spending weekends in New York looking at art, and not just Edward's. Edward and I would often go to see exhibitions together, whether it was contemporary art, or we'd go to the Met and look at the old guys.

So we got to know each other pretty well, and I got to know a good bit about his taste and what he hated as much as what he loved, and we developed a real friendship.

Andreas had predicted that he would never come up to see the show of his work, which was in the Sterling Library. But in fact, Edward came up to Yale to be there. He wouldn't come to the opening of the show, but he slipped in a couple of hours before and we did a little walkabout, and then he jumped back on the train and went home.

CS: Yeah, he didn't travel much at the time that I knew him, and he wouldn't even go to Boston, really, but I think it just got less and less over time.

What else do you remember about him during that period? When you went to the art exhibits and to the openings, it was, knowing Edward, it was usually tied into sort of some activities of going to get some Chinese food or whatever. I mean, he was pretty gregarious, and I imagine it wasn't just going to see the artwork. He'd have an evening around it. I mean, what else did you learn about him?

CR: You know, our art visits in New York during that period and after really were like this. I'd meet him at his apartment and off we'd go. We might go to a Joan Washburn or Anne Ryan show. It wasn't always super-well-known artists.

He was incredibly informed. He had very strong opinions. He was erudite. He knew so much about art that it was part of my own art education. We could look at a Goya print together, or we could look at Anne Ryan.

He had zero interest in Pollock. And so, of course, I would put him in front of a Pollock just to get his reaction. So over a period of time, I would say Edward was a real source of knowledge for me, not just in terms of what he knew about, but watching him react to things.

I think he would watch me react. Sometimes the reactions were not about the art. In fact, the day we went to see, I don't know why the Anne Ryan thing is always on my mind, I didn't meet Edward at his apartment that day. I met him downstairs in whatever that building was, I think in Midtown, and as I approached the building, there was a strange yellow glow. In fact, he was dressed in his yellow hand-knit hat that he had made, leopard-skin gloves that went up to his elbows, and a yellow raccoon coat, blue jeans, and white sneakers.

Over those particular few hours we were together, I remember he was always expiring over the fact that anybody might stare at him. He would do so much to get noticed and then always be near expiration over the fact that anybody looked at him. That sort of incredible, crazy conflict of "Look at me, don't look at me!," it was amazing.

It was quite fabulous because people either noticed him as a character, I suppose he became a character out of his own books, but the other thing is he had a renown, celebrity. Occasionally over these times together, people would come up to him and say, "Mr. Gorey, I'm a big fan." No one needed to ask him, "Are you Mr. Gorey?" People would know by one look that he was Mr. Gorey.

CS: Yeah, I can imagine. How did it come that you did the book [*The World of Edward Gorey*]? Were there steps in between or was the book sort of a natural outcome of curating the show?

CR: Well, the book came many years later, in 1996, so twenty years after my graduation from Yale in 1974.

CS: Were you developing a friendship in that time?

CR: Yeah, over that period of time we stayed in touch. I would visit him up at the Cape at a certain point, and there were all sorts of memorable moments over that twenty years. The reason I think I ended up putting that book together, and I had this idea to do the book for a while, was that I had sort of another life besides making my own art.

I was very interested in animation and popular culture, and I felt that Edward's work would be a fantastic basis for a television series, for theater, or for even a feature film. So I had optioned the rights to all of his work in 1985 with his blessing, and we made an arrangement.

I went off to Hollywood at one point to introduce Edward Gorey to Hollywood and vice versa. As it turned out, all the people that I wanted to meet, of course, already knew of Edward Gorey. So, oddly, Edward was generally thought of as sort of effete, part of a very specialized market.

However, those special people that both knew and loved his work were extraordinary. So when I went out there I had quite a range of meetings. Lisa Henson, Jim Henson's daughter, immediately said, "You've got to meet my father," so I found myself actually back in New York meeting with Jim Henson about Edward. Jim Henson was a huge fan.

At one point, I was in a room with fifteen of the Disney Imagineers. Those are the people that cook up the theme parks and the theme rides at Disney, and they had put together a presentation to show me. Edward, of course, would never go to LA, but they were keen on the possibility of an Edward Gorey world, say, within one of the parks. What was awkward was that they wanted me to sign a ridiculous Disney OK contract. It was the opposite of an NDA.

It was you disclose everything, we disclose nothing, and we own it all. And so I couldn't actually have the full meeting, and Edward refused to go to LA, refused to let the Disney Imagineers in.

So what happened over time is that it became clear over about six, seven years that Edward was going to confound every effort I had to bring his work to a wider audience. He wanted that sort of, I don't know if it was secrecy, but a relative anonymity to the wider world. And at a certain point I just thought, I don't want to disturb his balance, "Let him have his peace and quiet."

However, I did want to do something about him, and that was how *The World of Edward Gorey* book came about. I had the idea to do the book, and at that moment I knew that besides putting the shape of the book together, what I really wanted to do was interview him. I invited a friend of mine to come in and write an essay for the book, and it was truly a work of love. It was really an antidote to my failure to bring Edward's work to a wider audience through television and film.

CS: Yeah, I can see that being a perfectly reasonable pivot. And then perhaps the book can help to catalyze something else that's in another media or something. So it seems like a perfectly sound thing to move to something that Edward's used to.

CR: Yeah, I mean, basically, it was not some strategic vision on my part to do the book and follow by more interest and so on. It was literally an act of creative frustration. The guy is not going to let me make a TV series. He wouldn't come in to meet with Jim Henson. Jim, I think, offered to go up to the Cape. Ted said, "No, not really, thank you." He refused Jim's interest. I think he was flattered, but he really wanted to keep to his own quiet rhythm.

So that's the story of that book. During that twenty years I got the phone call one day from Andreas Brown that we had a problem, and the problem was that Edward had moved up to the Cape, had emptied out his apartment, and the landlord had gone to his apartment and found a real human skull in the closet.

The police wanted Edward Gorey. I mean, it's not legal to have a real skull in your closet, and it was just so typical of him. There were many things like that that happened over the decades I knew Edward. Things Goreyesque always happened to Edward Gorey.

In relating that story I remember that he seemed so absolutely gobsmacked that he just had forgotten about the mummy head. It was the furthest thing from his mind, and that's so him; as far as I could tell, anyone else would be quite aware that they had a mummy's head. To him it was just "Oh, yeah, a head." Like he'd simply forgotten about it.

Well, the apartment in New York and the home up on the Cape were both filled with staggering quantities of beautiful, nonsensical, slightly threatening, and lyrical objects. It was insane but it was everything about Edward.

This is a man who could recite Proust, who also knew all the words that were uttered by Adam West as Batman in the television series. The scope of what interested him was so wide that at any given moment he could not possibly be in touch with everything.

You know, Edward was not a man of his time. Edward lived in his own head, and I also think he lived in history. Other than that, I would say he lived with his books, he lived with his cats, and he had an incredibly existential existence.

He went to Jack's Outback for two or maybe three meals a day. He was a creature of habit, and the habits were all wildly eccentric, but he lived in a bubble of his own choosing and manufacturing.

CS: Yeah, which was remarkable. I was struck by that too, as a young man looking at that. It hit me, I think, the same way it hit you; it was just like, "Oh, you can do that, exactly what you want." And I've gotten inspiration from that since then. It's like, I can create whatever life I want and I always think about Edward when it comes to that.

It's like, "God, that guy really did it. He created the type of world he wanted for himself."

CR: I think Edward is a true north, in a way, a north star for me, in the sense that he was committed to a life that he fashioned himself, and I don't think he had a real drive for success, although I think he cared that the work he did was good or the best he could do. I think he wanted to spin a web, a web of his own dreams, and it just came out of him. He worked all the time at that little desk with that little pen and sometimes a brush.

But you realize this is a guy dedicated to a vision, and it's fantastic, it's inspiring. I think, certainly for artists, a young artist like me, when I was in my late teens, early twenties, discovering art making, and although most of the art and the artists that I was looking at were mainstream of a sort, Edward really was the iconic figure, in many ways for me, of what it meant to be a dedicated artist.

CS: Do you think money and his relative success financially helped that? It seemed to me that just about the time he moved, and I know he moved from New York not totally willingly. I mean, he was essentially kicked out by his landlord; from what I've heard, it was rent-controlled. He found out that Edward was living on the Cape, probably just enough to disqualify him from that rent-controlled apartment. And that he put the kibosh on any further leases and Edward had no choice but to basically be full-time up on the Cape.

CR: Well, I actually don't think some of that is entirely true. There may have been a circumstance where Edward moved up to the Cape in part because of this problem with the landlord, rent control, and so forth, but he was done with New York, totally. He'd gone to every single practice of the New York City Ballet for decades, and then I think he really wanted to retreat more into his own world, instead of participating so much in the world of New York. I actually think it was his own choice to retreat.

And I also think that his economic situation, his financial situation, was indeed part of it.

CS: Which coincided with the *Dracula* royalties.

CR: Yeah, the *Dracula* royalties on a scale of things were not that great. It enabled him to make the transition and get that wonderful house together. But that wonderful house, in quotes, was always falling apart. Edward did not live or work for money, quite the contrary. He, I think, made enough so he and his cats could survive.

He could also buy an occasional quirky piece of art. He had a very interesting art collection but he was not wealthy. He did not pursue money. He pursued his arts and lived for his cats.

CS: Yeah, that matches with who I knew. I had no idea there was anything in the way of any extra money at all. So tell me, let's backtrack a little bit to what you were talking about with the house. How he moved into this place and created this almost exhibit for himself within the house, the energy and vitality he found in everyday objects.

Tell me a little bit about the world that he created, since you wrote the book about the world. I mean, he did create this world. You realize that there's something going on that's more thoughtful than someone just hoarding when you go in there.

I would find, first of all, if you go back to his house from week to week, you realize he's changing the exhibit. This moves over here, that moves there. He would move things around; the objects didn't just collect dust. You see things that are facing inwards rather than out, they're at his height level, not lower, and you can see that he's entertaining himself with this house.

For example, he had that statue in the window of the hidden room, I think it's a bust of Mark Twain or Charles Dickens looking outwards, and one can see that there's something different going on than just the average person furnishing their house. He's creating a world, curating an art exhibit for himself.

I was also struck by how he delighted in his own artwork. He would put his posters up drawn from his work; he drank only out of his own coffee mugs. He enjoyed his artwork, not that he wanted to talk about it.

CR: Well, I don't know if I'm interviewing you or you're interviewing me.

CS: [*Laughs*] I'm getting lost in trying to prompt.

CR: Well, you don't need to that much because I actually, I'm not sure I agree with some of the things you're saying. I saw it differently, and it may be that there are two realities.

I don't think I own the only vision of Edward Gorey. I think Edward, extraordinary character and artist that he was, could be many things. I think he was one thing for himself, and that was in the business of putting outside of his skull the things that he had inside. So whether it's the books or you were just referring to his house up o n the Cape, the insides of that house were essentially the insides of his brain. It was his world, his real world that he believed in and that existed.

He wanted to make real out there, not just the world he thought existed or should exist, he wanted to make it exist. I think it was very comforting for him. I wouldn't say he was really a full recluse, because he went out of the house to go to breakfast or lunch or occasionally he would do these productions in a storefront theater. I was involved with those, but the thing that was amazing is that the house was the fulfillment of his own fantasy and visions. It was filled with stuffed animals, some of which he made. I don't think he had a lot of his work around. I actually, other than a little nod of amusement at drinking coffee out of a cup that had a Figbash on it, there really wasn't a lot of his work around.

He didn't tend to have framed drawings. To him, that would have been pretentious. If there was a poster lying around, it was sort of vague pride in something he had done with some director or something, but it is not that usual. It is true, though, that if you breathe in the air in Edward's home you're breathing in Edward Gorey as much as any artist I've ever seen. It was so intense.

I've made it a habit to visit artist studios, and it's very touching and powerful to, say, go into Pollock's studio and to see the drips on the floor where he was working. With Edward it wasn't just the studio, which was a simple desk; no, that was just a part of his creative universe, a collection of hundreds of thousands of things, books, jewelry, architectural elements like finials, toilet bowls even, and somehow everything that got inside that house became an Edward Gorey object. That's the power of an artist.

He would take an inanimate object and give it life. He was a Taoist, he studied Zen, so that the idea that an inanimate object would have a life was consistent with his beliefs. He really believed that a chair or a grain of sand or a needle and thread had a life. It's sort of amazing. The world is filled with animation and activity that's far beyond what the eye normally sees.

Edward came down to my loft one day on Broadway in the mid-'80s. I was using papier mâché at the time to make very lofty and very romantic artwork, to build up surfaces with texture and to paint on them. Edward was rooting around my studio as if there was something for him to find there. There are no two artists less alike than Edward Gorey and me, but we have this strange symbiotic friendship in some way. I watched him as he's poking at this and poking at that, and finally he says, "What's that?" What he'd seen was a wet lump of papier mâché. I said, "Pick it up and help yourself." And I brought him over to a 20-gallon drum of half-worked papier mâché, and he blankly stares into it. Edward was not a man of large gesture like I am, and I think he was appalled at the large scale I was working at. I said, "Why don't I leave you alone for a while; I'll see you in a bit," and I left for probably forty-five minutes or so.

When I came back in, he was seated in a chair and there were about three or four tiny little papier mâché heads, the most peculiar heads I've ever seen in my life, sitting right next to him. He had already begun to fashion things, and those became the papier mâché heads of his puppet theater, and I had the joy of giving him a new material to use. He was quite dexterous and could use almost any material that he wanted to: needle and thread, fabric, sequins, buttons, pen and ink, paper, into something that he could work with.

CS: Yeah. And it seemed to me, seeing him in the last few years, he was still doing that all the way through. You know, he was doing a lot of plays at the time, and I think some people saw that as a retirement, but from what I saw, it seemed really like he was someone that was constantly, really, truly, honestly looking for the next thing that he wanted to do.

He was taking basket making at the community college, he had started to do animations on the computers at the local public-access station, and he was just continuing to be an artist, despite growing older. Let's talk about how prolific he was.

CR: As far as I knew, Edward worked every day of his life. Although he probably would have denied it, he did do masses of work. A lot of the work, of course, has never been seen. There are manuscripts that I've seen of operas, lyrics, book ideas, just copious amounts of prodigious output. Edward actually created and published an enormous amount of material: his own books, book covers, collaborations, *Dracula*. This is a guy who did *The Mikado* for Baryshnikov at the Kennedy Center. I may be conflating it, but he worked across a lot of media and at the same time was doing all the other side things like the animation that was famously done for *Mystery!* He handed them off and gave them [Derek Lamb and his team] a blessing, told them what he liked or didn't like, but it was sort of a remote bit of creativity. He produced so much work on top of the collaborations, and I think it eventually will all come out. I've been privy to a fair amount of it as a past executor of the estate, and I saw some of that material. There was a manuscript this thick [*gestures*] that surfaced about one year ago. So obviously, years and years after Edward's death, he had sent it to somebody to see if that might be explored. And it was the material for a full-length opera, a lot of it's visual.

As a person, he was more than just his work. I remember Edward walking in his yellow raccoon coat, he was always shy, but I always loved how he felt when I hugged him. He really was the classic teddy bear, Santa Claus character. And he was so shy and so flamboyant at the same time. So Edward is a character himself and he put himself into his books, I think, for a reason.

He was fiercely, fiercely educated. He was ravenous about culture, literature. That's well documented. He had to be one of the most well-read people that I knew, and far past anything I could keep up with. But, you know, he would make some throwaway line about the *Iliad* and you realize that he knew the *Iliad* backwards and forwards. Nineteenth-century French literature. The number of sources he could draw on was one of the most fascinating parts of Edward Gorey. You know, Adam West in the *Batman* television show was one of his favorite things. So were flapjacks with maple syrup at Jack's. The number of things he was passionate about are just a staggering array of things. Yet, if you pressed Edward, asked him what he really cared about, he would say, "Oh, not really anything." And so there was this constant set of conflicts. Edward was one big basket of conflicts. Flamboyant and very shy.

CS: And I can hear you trying to root that out a bit in your book interview [*The World of Edward Gorey*, 1995]. You're saying, "Well, are you into *The Honeymooners*? Is it *The Mary Tyler Moore Show*?" And he said, "Oh, I don't like *The Honeymooners*, but I love *Mary Tyler Moore*."

CR: I can't really say what the best clue is to synthesize what Edward's about. The best answer is his books or his theater productions. Edward was such a mass of inconsistencies and brilliant sparks that it's impossible to wrap your hands fully around him without looking at the work. You know, he was so shy. That graciousness was hard for him and yet he was a very gracious guy.

He never wanted to make people uncomfortable, even if he did, by his sheer presence. You know, somebody that's uncomfortable around a flamboyant guy with a white beard wearing a raccoon coat, he's not going to care about that person. He's still going to wear the raccoon coat, the sneakers, and everything else. So he was sort of fiercely loyal to himself, but he never really wanted to impose himself on others.

It was incredible, he was filled with dichotomies, and of all the characters in Edward's books that I think came closest to who Edward was, it's *The Doubtful Guest*. *The Doubtful Guest* is Edward Gorey. He was capable of that shyness. He would put his nose potentially to the wall and not move. You know, would he ever actually do that? I think he thought about it every day of his life and maybe did it in secret. He never did it in front of me. But I can see the Doubtful Guest, who, by the way, if you recall, came and never left. And I think Edward came into our lives as a creative person. He and his work came into our lives and he'll never leave.

CS: Yeah, I think you're absolutely right about that. It's a great way to look at him. I know he was somewhat inspired by silent films, you know, D. W. Griffith, Buster Keaton, Feuillade . . . Can you tell me a little bit about how silent films influenced his work?

CR: You know, I'm not a scholar so I only know pieces of the puzzle. That's Edward Gorey, and there are so many bits and pieces. You mentioned Feuillade and silent films. He was fascinated, I think, with any artist who could communicate with minimal means. Although he did do color, I think his greatest devotion was to black and white, devoid of color. And I think that his passion for Buster Keaton, which, you know, he would speak to me about, the era of silent film fascinated him.

If you think about an Edward Gorey book, it's black and white and it doesn't talk. In black-and-white films there are often the title boards that are intercut between shots. Well, Edward's texts are laid below the images, so I think there was a natural affinity for minimal means to try to express oneself. So it's natural that silent films would be a favorite of Edward's, but he did not, to my knowledge, keep up with all the Hollywood blockbusters. For example, I don't think he saw movies like *Terms of Endearment*. He would have been exasperated with all the emotion, but he was a great devotee of film.

He loved John Ford westerns, which is something I never would have guessed. I mean, you know, shoot-'em-up violence is just not Edward. The blade between the ribs and, you know, the plunging dagger might have been him. Of course he loved things like *Dracula*, *The Hunchback of Notre Dame*, the great black-and-white horror stories, and of course Mary Shelley original books. The things you would expect Edward to discover he discovered and then made them his own. What's amazing is all the things that you never would have expected Edward to care about, which he also inhaled and stitched into his life's work.

CS: What would he have gotten from something like *The Mary Tyler Moore Show* in particular? That show has come up several times, and I know he was also into *Buffy the Vampire Slayer* and *Golden Girls*. But what is it about something like *The Mary Tyler Moore Show*? Is it just a personal entertainment?

CR: Whether it's *Mary Tyler Moore* or *The Golden Girls*, he loved stories and characters who were complete in and of themselves. He liked worlds, and if you think of *The Mary Tyler Moore Show* there is a very specific character. He would not opine about how important Mary Tyler Moore was to that moment in time. Culturally, in America, he didn't give a shit about that. What he cared about was probably somebody who had a way about herself that was forceful and upright, and the world could not really impact on her for very long. She moved forward like a force. I think Edward would have responded to that, and he loved humor.

Edward was a terribly funny guy and he loved to laugh. It may sound a little pedestrian, but why did he like *The Golden Girls*? It made him laugh. There may not always be in Edward some big, deep, lurking thing behind a piece of his work or behind something that he loved. Freud made that great comment, "Sometimes a cigar is just a cigar." Sometimes *The Golden Girls* is just a funny TV show, and Edward loved to laugh.

CS: Yeah. Tell me about his love of the nonchalant. Like he preferred some beautiful old tool as opposed to some work of art that was agonized over. He liked things that were offhand or nonchalant, and didn't want anything too sincere.

CR: There's an irony in that Edward liked the simple, deft act when he himself labored over his work. If you look at the distance between the first handwritten words that might have generated a book and then the various levels of typescript that he would create, looking for the storyline or narrative line or even the poetic bon mot. He was a restless perfectionist. He would sketch it out as a pencil sketch and then carefully do an ink drawing over it so the finished work can look simple or easy.

There's a simplicity to all the cross-hatching, as well. There's a consistent passion with Edward for the simple thing. We were talking earlier about the objects in his house . . . the stuffed animals he loved were simple stuffed animals. They were not very fancy ones. The objects that he often picked up were extremely simple, very rarely complex, but they were objects which allowed one to fantasize about something else. Life is a bank shot for Edward.

Here's the thing and here's where the thing sends you. That's what he was as a person. That's what he created as an artist. There's this simplicity to understanding and appreciating Edward's work. One laughs, sometimes one just simply smiles, and sometimes one recoils. Other than those three things, I'm not sure what Edward would like you to do with his work. If you got fancy about it, if you got into references to art history, I really don't think he was going for a sophisticated response. He wanted a visceral response. A bit of a smile, a bit of a laugh, a little bit of horror, a little bit of understanding, but keep it simple.

I do think part of the joy of Edward is there's this lurking complexity. You can ponder if you want, but the choice is yours. Take it the way he meant it, take the gift of a simple line, whether it's drawn or written.

CS: That's beautifully said. Can you tell me how it came about that you shot portraits of him? How he would have indulged the posing and stuff like that?

CR: Yeah. Listen, I loved Edward. I certainly had so much respect for him as an artist, but I loved him as a person. I loved who he was and I loved who he was to me. He would never have wanted to think of himself as a mentor. I'm not even sure that he would have acknowledged a friendship. He was diffident by nature, but when I was around Edward I found myself unencumbered. As I got interested in photography, and I don't photograph people, it was very natural for me to say, "Hey, Ted, let me take a few shots." He'd object and sort of go, "Oh, I don't really want to. Do I have to?" But the way he expressed it was clear that he'd let me do it, and with the pleasure of two friends having fun.

There's a sequence I shot at one point when we got to that long wooden walkway out into the cranberry bog [Bass Hole Boardwalk]. It was a cold day, we had on coats and gloves and all this, and one naturally thinks of the most-absurd things possible around Edward, because absurdity was one of his hallmarks. I don't know what possessed me, it was preposterous, but I said, "Ted, what are all those ballet poses in those Degas sculptures, a grand jeté?" So Edward just took flight and suddenly I had photos of Edward Gorey dancing like a prima ballerina.

You know, people just don't think about Edward cavorting, but if you look in the books, the creatures cavort, and so did Edward that day. I was blessed because Edward would cavort with me and we had fun.

Everything was not about his art. Everything was not about my art. It was about two people who had a lot in common. And it's probably one of the biggest presumptions of my life to think that Edward Gorey may have loved me as I loved him, but that's something I'm just going to keep on thinking. I loved being around him. He was fantastically open. Anytime I wanted to visit him on the Cape, I was welcome. He knew that I was allergic to cats, so it was safe that I wouldn't stay at his house or even ask to, but he made every effort to make me feel at home and wanted in his world. To feel wanted and to feel then temporarily at home in the world of Edward Gorey would be anybody's dream.

CS: That was really well said. Thank you for commenting on your friendship in that way. I really appreciate it.

CR: Can I just say something that's on my mind? Because you're really good in terms of knowing so much about Edward, and there is something I sort of, I'd love to just mention.

Edward had a lot of people who were dedicated to him, old friends from the past, young friends, older friends, artists of different types. Even though he didn't seem to make a lot of effort, the way most people might, to keep a circle of friends around him, Edward kept friends for a very long time, and I think that he saw those of us that were his world as actually part of his family.

He was never married, didn't really carry on any long-term, deep romantic relationships. You know, people that are looking for some big revelation about Edward and his romantic life and things like that are missing the point. I don't remember exactly what Ted's comment was, but Ted was not going to be defined by his relationships. At the end of the day, I love him, someone else loves him, and we respect him.

At the end of the day, Edward Gorey was the consummate artist. The fact that we might respect him as a person, be interested in him, it was about the work. At the end of the day, that work sits there as this incredible, mysterious thing which he has landed in our world, and we're going to be pondering it forever. And as much as we want to dig into what Edward was about, really, we should all be satisfied with that work. Pick up one of those small books, leaf through it, find yourself enchanted with a world you never knew existed. That's Edward Gorey.

CS: What did you think about when you heard that he died? What were your thoughts? Was it a surprise?

CR: Edward dying was a blow. Edward certainly never took care of himself. I mean, he didn't exercise, he wouldn't go to the doctor. I knew that there were some health issues at one point. Edward's, the sort of bigger-than-life figure that I probably felt would never die because I didn't want him to, but it was when I heard how he died that surprised me. He just expired, but it was consistent with what I think Edward would have wanted as an adios.

CS: How do you think he'll be remembered as an artist?

CR: Edward himself didn't really think that much about how he would be remembered or how the work would be. This was the work he was capable of. I think Edward is a much more profound artist than people understand, even up to now. An artist like Charles Burchfield actually made a living making wallpaper and doing commercial art, which was what Edward would do as well. I think Edward belongs in that line of American eccentricity in the arts. And there's a little-known artist named Louis Eilshemius who, for a period of time, did these very simplistic little paintings of floating women. They are preposterous, but Louis Eilshemius was true to himself, and the best paintings by him are still floating around.

I think Edward certainly has already achieved a level of fame beyond someone like Eilshemius, and his work is going to become more and more appreciated in terms of its lyricism, its darkness, its very particular quality. And, you know, obviously I'm a big fan, but let's let time sort it out and not guess how good he is. Let's enjoy the work.

CS: Thank you. Anything else you think should be said?

CR: I know exactly what should be said. If you asked Edward today, from beyond the grave, if he wanted to have this documentary made, what do you think he'd say? "Oh, do I have to?" And yet, some part of him wanted it. He let you do the work.

CS: Yes, well, he realized that I was actually letting him direct it by default. I didn't push him where he didn't want to be pushed.

CR: Well, let me say this for you, I'm just going to say it for you. Edward might have hated the fact that you were making this movie, and then he would have done everything he could to help you make it.

CS: I love that. That's great. Thank you.

CR: You're terrific, Chris. I'm really happy for Edward that you're making this documentary, because the spirit with which you're doing this is so Edward. It's like, "Bullshit, let's make a movie. Let's try to make a movie, and let's see what comes out." That was the spirit, and let's do it over thirty years. That's the spirit of Edward when he would do these theatrical performances.

Terry Gilliam Interview

OCTOBER 23, 2015

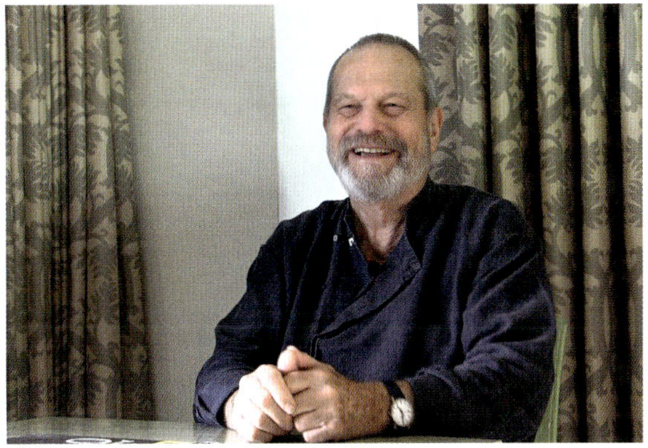

In the fall of 2015 father and son team Ben and Jim Wickey led a crew for a Mooncusser Films interview of Monty Python's Terry Gilliam (*Time Bandits, Brazil, 12 Monkeys*), intercepting him while he was in the United States for a talk in Glendale, California. Fans and critics often compare Gorey and Gilliam, with some noting that Gorey's work feels "Python-esque." Both are known for a nineteenth-century Victorian/Edwardian Gothic aesthetic. Gilliam generously hosted us in his hotel room. Like many of our interviews about Gorey, it was a brief window resulting from the good graces of many people and collaborating forces.

Terry Gilliam: Are we rolling. Test one, test two?

Mooncusser Films Crew: Are we rolling? We are. We'd like to start this with anything that you'd like to talk about first, then we've got a couple of questions to throw at you.

TG: All right. About seventeen years ago, the band the Tiger Lillies had done a show called *Shockheaded Peter* and I got to know these guys. Then there's a group called Artangel in London and they got the rights to a lot of Gorey writing that had never been published. Edward had agreed to let the stuff be used for potential projects.

There were a variety of stories there. There's a splotch on a windscreen, it looked like Jesus and all sorts of wonderful things, strange stories about rooms and wallpapers. We were talking about working with this material as a musical, involving me and these two groups. So, the Tiger Lillies had written and recorded these songs with a group called the Kronos Quartet, all based on Gorey's writings, words and everything.

And, I thought, "Oh, how do we tie all of this together?" I thought, "Let's do a play that starts with a dance of death in reverse," where you see people coming out of the graves and then death takes them all dancing backward toward an old people's home. And then, the whole thing is about old people dying because then we go back the other way. But they would do these songs before they died and then they would die happily.

There was one about a girl, a ballerina, the girls who didn't like her put glass in her slippers. There's another one about a chandler who hangs himself. So I began producing it by arranging to get these old actors, 80-year-old people, to sing and dance, and they would be in the home and then a story would be told, and they'd sit down. And as they were telling it, they would kind of revive and become young and beautiful, ballet dancing and all this, and then die.

Each one was going to be like this. We never got it all together. It still floats around in my head as a possible thing because the songs were so good, so creepy, and Gorey's words were wonderful.

MF: Now, you said that it never happened. What happened to that project and the Kronos Quartet?

TG: I eventually moved on, as we do. It's the nature of things with projects, you get distracted. Something else comes on that grabs your attention, while some other project is still incubating and you leave the baby to die there, and move on. I put on the big heavy fur coat and I go off in black and white. I exit out into the snow-covered bleak landscape like Gorey would have done.

MF: And so now, you just mentioned his specific style. Do you find him to be a singular artist with his style, fur coat, and aesthetic as you mentioned, and if so, where do you find he has a place in history among twentieth century artists? Someone like Max Ernst.

TG: Oh, is he a fine artist then? I don't know how to judge art and clearly the art market doesn't know how to judge art either, but Gorey has always intrigued me. I mean, his *Amphigorey* with his wordplay just like the late nineteenth century, early twentieth century, tragic tales. His black and white drawings are so beautiful because they're all simple and clean and precise. He's created all these loose characters, particularly the evil ones that float through . . . I just loved it. He's created a world that just doesn't exist anymore and he just did the nonstop humor of death and tragedy better than anybody else.

What fits in the history of twentieth century art, I have no idea. He'll probably get stuck in the book of illustrators as opposed to the book of fine artists. Fine artists are basically—the modern ones are calm and they're very fine at their art of conning people out of big chunks of money.

But somebody like Max Ernst you mentioned, again, it's the same slightly strange world because Gorey's stuff is neater and a little bit more understandable than a Max Ernst. Max Ernst and his collages put things together in a way that you can't quite explain. So, I would say Ernst is much more surreal than Gorey. Gorey is just basically late nineteenth century. It's strange actually.

Max Klinger is someone that I would think Gorey reminds me of a bit more. Max Klinger was a Viennese symbolist and he did a series of beautiful black and white etchings, the story of a glove, and he involved the same kind of things and the same kind of romantic world, of tragic love and wistfulness, something being lost all the time, and never attainable. Gorey just did it more humorously, that's what he did.

MF: How did he impact your work and, if he did, do you also see the impact on other artists?

TG: I don't know. What specifically I've taken from Gorey is being inspired by his black humor, I suppose, his wit and his joy of tragedy. There's something wonderful about that, which always made me laugh and smile but I certainly don't think I stole anything specifically as Tim Burton did. [*Turns to camera*] "Oh, hi Tim, I didn't know you'd be watching this. I take it all back. You didn't steal a thing, you're an absolute original." Now let's get back to the interview.

MF: Would like to expand on that?

TG: No. I think I said too much already.

MF: So, you mentioned his style and his gore; were you ever truly shocked at the content and did you find that shocking and liberating in any way?

TG: No, he never shocked me. He just made me smile that you could be that grisly, gruesome, and humorous all at the same time. Again, his style is such because it's simple and stylized. It's never actually gory. It's very tasteful. The sad, tragic, consumptive deaths or being eaten by bears, whatever it took, it was always —the entirety, quite precise.

MF: So would you say there's less subtlety to it and is subtlety and shock that important?

TG: Subtlety and shock and awe. Subtlety, shock and awe, now, there's no subtlety and shock at all but I suppose other people would be disturbed by Gorey. He never disturbed me. It was liberating because one could be that dark and still have an audience. And especially, it's good stuff for children to read because children, rather being coddled all the time, must be encouraged to understand there is darkness afoot out there in the world.

MF: Do you feel that the macabre is important to art in general? And do you think he pushed the envelope in that way?

TG: Yeah, he made the macabre really successful. He also made it acceptable. Due to him it can now be found in smart bookshops with well-dressed people reading it. He was never a horror man and it was never gratuitous. It was tasteful and witty, and upper-class. I've always felt that way and I really felt he's a classy guy who's got a weird and wonderful dark sense of humor.

MF: Would you have used the word "absurd" and if so, what is absurdity to you?

TG: It's like children should be obscene and not absurd or is it the other way around? [*Laughs*] Children should be absurd and not obscene. I don't know. I do like the term. Absurdity is Gorey's kind of play. His play with words was always smart. He could rhyme. How about that? I rhyme quite badly.

I don't know. I don't know what else. See, I don't analyze things. I never do. I just like things and then wallow in the fact that somebody has got parts of my brain ticking in a way that nobody else does.

And, there's something in that Edwardian sense, Edwardian is a period that people don't talk much about. They said we go from Victorian and then suddenly, the next thing you know you're in the Second World War, but Edwardian is a very specific time where drinks had to be just right. The tailoring had to be precise, everything was there and yet, there was tragedy all the time. All those people dying of misbegotten love. Then, these dark men that would wander in, breaking the hearts of young girls who are vulnerable beyond their wildest belief.

MF: Fools! We have to get some more, this is interesting. Well, can we hit you with another question? Did you ever meet him and were you surprised that he was an American?

TG: I think I met Edward Gorey but it may be a complete lie. I feel if I haven't met him, though, I should have met him. And if I didn't meet him, it's his fault for leaving me brokenhearted. So, no.

MF: That's simple. Thank you so much for all you do.

TG: Well, I think because I read all of his stuff. It's partly because I read all of his own unpublished material that we were going to use in his possible play that I felt I really got to know him, if not necessarily in person. And there were letters that were being written while this was going on.

So, in a sense, I really felt I knew the man but deep down, I probably never did. It always happens and the great thing about getting old, you can invent your history. [*Winks*]

MF: Why do you think his work was never translated to the screen?

TG: Because Tim Burton didn't get the money. Sorry, and I didn't either. No, I mean, his stylization, the very stylized way of telling the story is very important and the film would have to be very stylized.

I think when I look at it, I think about the hotel, the Hungarian one, Wes Anderson just did last year, what was that?

MF: *Grand Budapest*?

TG: *Grand Budapest Hotel*. I think Wes Anderson could do Edward Gorey quite well because of that precision. Wes is so precise and formal in the way that he moves the camera, there's a formality that is required to do that and I think *Grand Budapest Hotel* has elements that were very Goreyesque in the characters and what they realize.

MF: In the small sets that moved into animation illustration when they meet.

TG: I don't know. Do they ever?

MF: We're actually creating animation for the documentary.

TG: Go on and just cut his stuff out, that's what I would do. I would. [His style in Monty Python.] Michael Palin and I are always talking about this stuff and he was—see, he could have done Gorey, he could have played those characters, he had the correct voice and the bearing exactly. He could have done any of those characters. Gorey's not with us anymore though, the bastard.

MF: Yeah.

TG: You go off and then you die.

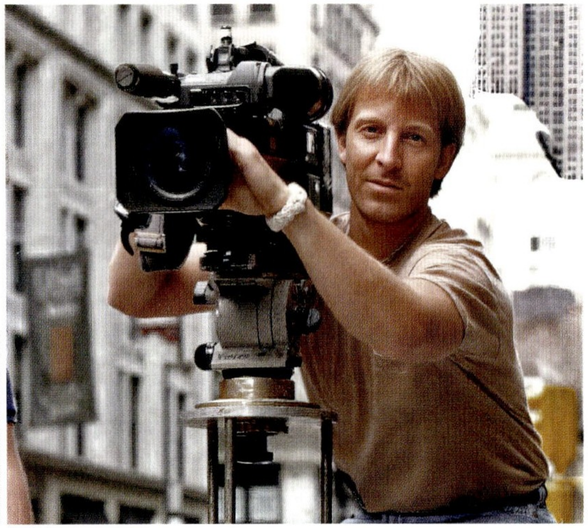

Christopher Seufert is the producer of the only documentary film to be shot with and agreed to by writer, illustrator, and artist Edward Gorey before his death in 2000. Seufert spent the final four years of Gorey's life working with him.

Seufert has produced award-winning films with journalist Walter Cronkite, musician Suzanne Vega, filmmaker Albert Maysles, and others.

He is also the author of six photography books, including *Cape Cod & Islands Reflections*, *The Cape Cod National Seashore: A Photographic Adventure & Guide*, and *Cape Cod: A Drone's Eye View*. He lives with his children, Ethan and Stella, on the coast of Cape Cod.

www.EdwardGoreyFilm.com

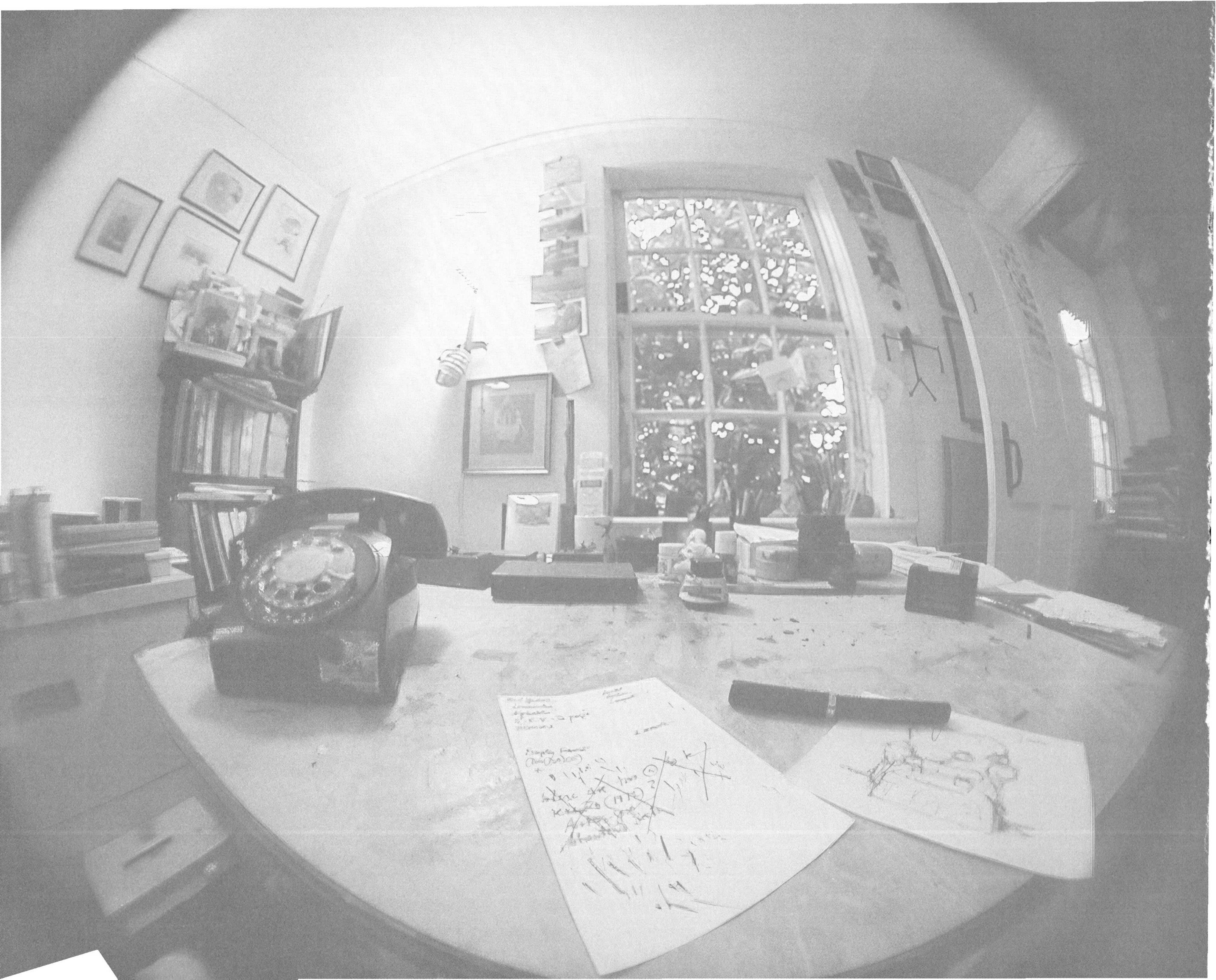